PAPER FAN

THE HUNT FOR TRIAD GANGSTER STEVEN WONG

TERRY GOULD

THUNDER'S MOUTH PRESS
NEW YORK

PAPER FAN

THE HUNT FOR TRIAD GANGSTER STEVEN WONG

Published by
Thunder's Mouth Press
An Imprint of Avalon Publishing Group Incorporated
245 W. 17th St., 11th Floor
New York, NY 10011

AVALON
publishing group incorporated

First published in U.S. by Thunder's Mouth Press 2004

Originally published in Canada in 2004 by Random House Canada, a division
of Random House of Canada Limited, Toronto.

Library of Congress Cataloging-in-Publication Data is available.

Some sections of this book appeared in different form in *Saturday Night* and
Vancouver magazines.

Except where noted, all photos courtesy of Terry Gould.

ISBN 1-56025-622-2

9 8 7 6 5 4 3 2 1

Designed by Carla Kean
Printed in the United States of America
Distributed by Publishers Group West

To my grandfather
the king of empty heroism,
and to my father
who overcame the legacy

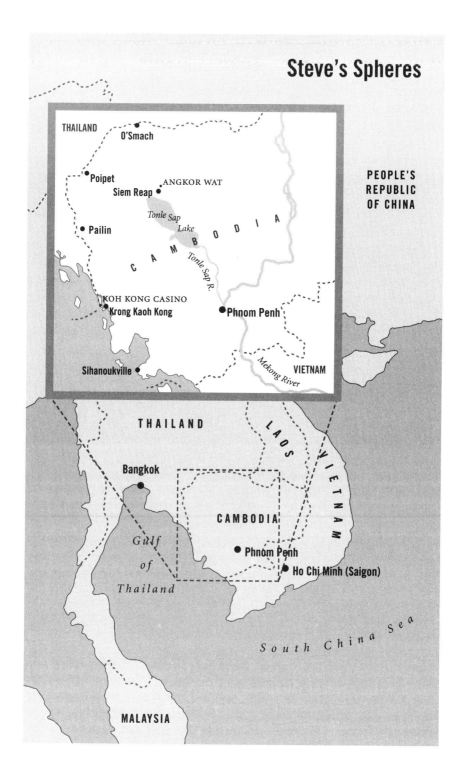

Steve's Spheres

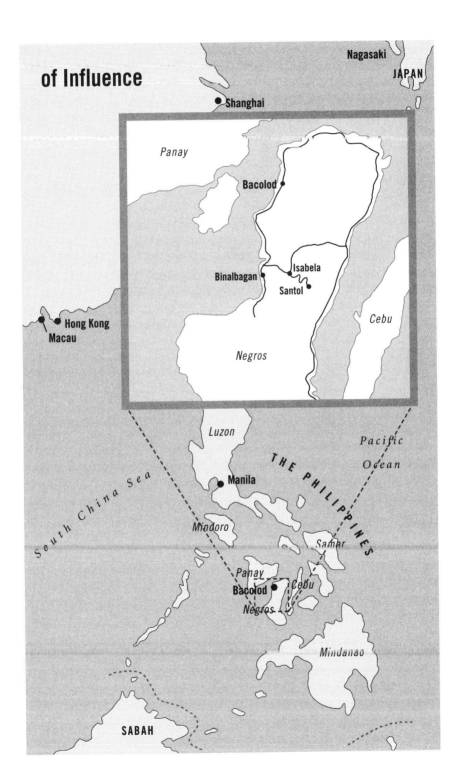

But if you refuse to fight this righteous war,
you will be turning aside from your duty.

—BHAGAVAD GITA

This could be REALLY dangerous . . . ! Just have a look at the size
of those teeth . . . ! I'll have to be SUPER careful! No room for even
one mistake . . . ! Oops! Watch it! Yow! Didn't I tell ya?
Okay, one more try. Watch me!!

—STEVE IRWIN, *CROCODILE HUNTER*

CONTENTS

PART III

PART I

CHAPTER 1

THE GARDEN OF REFLECTION

This sealed urn contains nothing but the mortal ashes
of the late Mr. Steven Wong.
—ROGER CERDEÑA, FUNERAL SERVICE DIRECTOR,
PASAY CITY, METRO MANILA

There is no marker where the Paper Fan's ashes are buried. The Schlipfs, Kosakas, and Holts are remembered with bronze plaques, but the Triad official has only an empty square of fescue to show for his life. "You're sure this is his plot?" I ask Kein Battistone, the Forest Lawn Cemetery's family service counselor.

Kein takes a step forward from where he stands discreetly behind me. Hands behind his back he bows slightly as he says, "Absolutely, Mr. Gould, that's his plot, I'm positive." He pulls from his breast pocket a photocopied map, shielding it from the rain with his palm. "Wong, Steven Lik Man. 1992. The Garden of Reflection. Row 2–C, Plot 582." He kneels and pats the forlorn-looking bare spot. "Steve's urn is right under here, I can assure you."

I consult my own map and scan the terrain. Everything is as Chuck "the Chink" Gough drew it after Steve's death. I'm eight paces east of a pretty copse with a pond in the middle. Orange carp are nuzzling the surface of the black pool and starlings squeal among the maples. Chuck the Chink, who is actually a white man, was part of Steve's crew at the height of its ride. "I know Steve's happy in that Garden of Reflection, Terry," he told me. "He liked the birds and the fish, ya know. Also, the family's got a great fucking view when they pay respects."

I orient Chuck's scrawled word "mountains" against the checkerboard of plaques marching up the hillside to the view, but white clouds hide the Coast Range. It has been warm and sunny for several days leading up to this ninth anniversary of Steve's death; then, last night, an Aleutian wind blew in, laying down a sad gray shroud over Vancouver.

Kein has turned his eyes to the hidden mountains too, and appears to be thinking of something pleasant. He's a young goateed fellow, his khaki shirt good-naturedly adorned with a Bugs Bunny tie. He seems like the kind of person I can talk to. "Key-in and Bat-a-stone," he told me in his office, explaining how to pronounce his name. He's done me a big favor, leading me through the thousands of graves in the rain to find Steve.

"Is it common when the family buries ashes that they don't put a marker down?" I ask.

"Is it common?" Kein replies. He massages his goatee in thought. "Well, the marker takes two or three months to make, and then the family usually assesses their financial situation. Sometimes a family says they can't afford it, and it just gets left there without a marker. There's lots of different reasons. May I ask how you know Steve?"

I hesitate—a Chinese man in a trench coat has wandered up and is standing 30 feet away, looking down, a bouquet of flowers hanging from his hand. He leans forward and places the flowers on the grass, cups his hands and brings them to his forehead in a pronam. I'd thought about flowers myself, but when it came to paying for them at my local supermarket I broke into laughter. I gave them to my wife instead.

"I'm a journalist," I tell Kein, when the man has strolled away. "I used to write about Steve—I'm writing about him now. But I've never been to his grave site."

Kein looks at me curiously. "What did he do that you're writing about him?"

"Oh, he had an interesting life," I say. "And an interesting death."

"Ohhh-*kay!*" Kein nods and narrows his eyes, surveying my pad, camera, and shoulder pack with new understanding. "So I guess he was murdered then, or—"

"There were things that went on."

"Well, it must be drug-related. We get them *allll* the time. For us it's like a common occurrence. That's a reason there wouldn't be a marker here. If he did something wrong, or if his death in some way involved criminals, then the family's leaving it unmarked, because they don't want the people to know where he is."

"To tell the truth, Kein," I say, "he was on the run."

"There you go! That tells me a lot right there. The family doesn't want anybody to know where he is."

I ponder Steve's blank patch, thinking of his parents, brothers, and nephews, not to mention his half a dozen mistresses, one of them married to a billion-dollar gambling racket. "It's already been nine years," I say.

"Well then, he must have had some heavyweight people after him. Maybe the family's waiting a nice round ten years. Enough time for the people who were after him to forget. But then, you obviously haven't forgotten him," Kein laughs.

"No, not me," I say, and snap a picture of the grass, stomped flat by the family of the Schlipfs. "I'll never forget Steve."

As we walk back towards the paved path I stop, dig my wallet out and give Kein my card. "Maybe you can let me know if Steve has any visitors."

Kein *tsks* his tongue in regret. "I don't know if I can do that for you. But some inside information I *can* give you is that we have only three spaces left here. Three hundred and ninety dollars."

"Is that a good deal?"

"A deal!? Are you kidding? Whispering Pine is two thousand." He points across the lawn. "Heartland is five thousand. So for this location, yes, you've got a real bargain. In fact, in *fact*—" he says, checking his map, "you can have one right here if you want it."

"Ten steps from Steve," I say, looking down between my feet. If I could collar him that way, I'd do it in a second.

Steve's funeral was held on a hot, mid-August afternoon in 1992, two weeks before he was to have gone on trial for masterminding a heroin conspiracy, and not long after a judge had returned his passport so he could travel to Hong Kong to meet his fiancée's parents. A dozen Vancouver gangsters, gang tarts, lawyers, and a couple of undercover cops from the Coordinated Law Enforcement Unit filed into Mount Pleasant Funeral Home to pay their respects to the two-foot urn about to be buried beneath the Garden of Reflection. Some of the attendees, like Steve's mother, Yue Kim Wong, were distraught with grief. Others, like Chuck the Chink, were steely-jawed and stoic. Still others—the cops come to mind—could hardly suppress their smirks. Steve, they'd learned, had hastily purchased a million dollars in life insurance just before flying to the romantic East to meet the parents of his future wife, a woman whom Steve had named in an affidavit as Patsy Chan. Yet four days ago Steve's mom had told investigators from the RCMP that she'd never heard of Patsy Chan, and that, while her 28-year-old son had a slew of girlfriends, she knew of none he wanted to marry.

I had first met Steve in early 1990, just after he'd beaten to death a rival mobster on a crowded Chinatown street. At the time, Steve was the manager of a Vancouver bodyguard firm called Kouzins Security, staffed by his murderous, 30-man Gum Wah gang. Owned by a convicted heroin trafficker named Ray Chau—the son of a senior partner in the gambling empire of

Macau's famous billionaire, Stanley Ho—the chief function of Kouzins was to protect heroin barons as they got off the plane from Hong Kong and Macau. Patsy Chan, one of Steve's many mistresses, was Ray Chau's wife.

Despite his rarefied connections and busy sex life, Steven Wong was not very impressive-looking. He was five foot four inches tall and weighed 150 pounds—a seemingly amiable pudgeball with thick glasses, a high, almost childlike voice, and a habit of punctuating his sentences with a schoolboy's nervous giggle. With only an eighth-grade education and a hood's sense of fashion, he struck most people—including the judge who gave him back his passport—as the antithesis of a sophisticated Asian mobster. Nevertheless, for the Mounties and the Vancouver city police who had been chasing Wong for years, he typified Asian criminal success. Locally he was the boss of Vancouver's most powerful street gang, whose top rankers referred to him by the delicate nickname Paper Fan—*Tzs Sin*. Internationally he was a fighting official in the 14K Triad—among the largest of the Chinese mafia groups and the one that dominated Macau. Outrageously wealthy for an unemployed 26-year-old, Steve retained a prominent Vancouver city councilman as his lawyer and had no adult criminal convictions, notwithstanding his numerous arrests on suspicion of murder, manslaughter, extortion, drug running, and credit card fraud. "He really is the big gangster in town," the Asian Crime Squad's Martin Turner once told me.

Born in Hong Kong, raised in New York's Chinatown, a criminal since the age of 11, Wong had set up a masterful organization for the recruitment of Vancouver's most vulnerable teens into a life of war. He portrayed himself to judges as doing nothing more than running a service organization for underprivileged immigrant youngsters, and spoke of his lieutenants as social workers initiating the dispossessed into his self-help society. But Wong used his charges mercilessly, molded them into monsters of themselves and then put them in the literal line of fire for his own benefit, until, one after another, their lives were as good as lost.

Between the time I first walked into his home and his death two and a half years later, I had betrayed Steve twice. Nevertheless, before and between betrayals, I had become his friend, and as much as anyone in his gang, I regretted his passing. Indeed, I felt partly responsible for the Mountie investigation, Project Bugs, which had led to his arrest and then to his extensive transformation and uniting with heaven.

I still regret not being there for his emotional send-off at Mount Pleasant. The morning of August 14, 1992, I received a cryptic call from the police advising me to stay away from what my contact described as the latest Steve caper, and because I'd lived under a Mountie protection program for half a year because of him, I thought that was a good idea. The police were certain Steve was still alive. He'd flown to Hong Kong in the company of a girlfriend and, after a hop to Macau and a meeting with some important colleagues, flown on alone to the island of Negros in the Philippines, where he was met by a Vancouver heroin dealer engaged to the daughter of the wealthiest and most influential lawyer on the island. A few days later, on July 19, 1992, Steve took a motorcycle-taxi excursion into remote mountains. Tragically, the taxi tipped over and Steve bumped his head on a rock and died. A senior inspector with the Philippine National Police, who was a friend of the lawyer's, retrieved the body and turned it over to the heroin dealer, who ordered it cremated. The lawyer then put together a stack of affidavits and shipped the package to the Canadian embassy in Manila. Two weeks later a Canadian death certificate was issued and Steve's sack of ashes was delivered to his parents.

This was a scam if the cops had ever seen one, although in the weeks following the funeral, the knowing smirks of the police turned to grimaces. The theoretically dead Steve could not be compelled to appear at his trial, and the judge soon severed his case from his coconspirators without issuing an arrest warrant for his failure to appear in court. With no warrant to justify an investment of resources, the Mounties were forced to terminate their investigation. By the spring of 1993 it looked like Steve had succeeded in making a mockery of the Mountie motto.

At that point, Steve became my life's work, my life's study, my obsession. The insurance companies had by then learned of a two-part TV exposé I'd done on the Paper Fan—the one that had put me under police protection—plus a subsequent article I'd written about his ruses and capers. Looking at forking over a million dollars to Steve's parents, they put an ex-CIA agent on the case and called me. I jumped on the story and began phoning my police contacts. A month before Steve's demise, the RCMP's Drug Intelligence Unit had published one of my investigative articles in their eyes-only bulletin, distributed to drug agents across the continent. The intelligence officer who edited the bulletin had appended my phone number to the article, along with an invitation to readers to get in touch with me. I received calls from U.S. and Canadian undercover officers, members of strike forces, and federal customs officials. To all my cop sources I now related the most recent revelations concerning the Paper Fan's disappearance. The insurance companies then put me in touch with agents in the Philippine National Bureau of Investigation, who asked me to become their back-channel to the RCMP until Canada launched an official investigation. By the first anniversary of Steve's death my home office had turned into command central of the hunt for Steven Wong.

Today, Steve is no longer officially dead. Interpol has a Red Alert/Dangerous Person arrest warrant out for the Paper Fan, and his updated résumé reads like a Hollywood script—a postmortem panorama of organized criminal adventure that circles the Pacific Rim, from Macau to Japan, from Cambodia to the Philippines. All the years Steve's urn has been interred in the Garden of Reflection he's been thriving on the corruption of six state governments and their law enforcement agencies, so well protected by officials that even when the cops know where he is they can't nab him. I've been around the world three times trying to arrange that nab, and one thing I've learned hunting Steve is that in his world it is often impossible to tell the fox from the hounds, or, for that matter, from the elect gentlemen who supposedly control the hunt. Living by a code of convenience that is far more natural to men than the rule of law, politicians, police, businessmen, and criminals often sprint along in one big pack, sometimes nipping each other's heels, sometimes licking each other's faces, and sometimes inviting one another back home for all-night mah-jongg parties. Forced to work according to their right-side-up rules, Canadian cops don't have a chance of arresting Steve in his upside-down world.

On the other hand, I am unencumbered by international agreements and law enforcement protocols that are followed by good cops but not by bad cops. These days, the Paper Fan is back in the Philippines, well ensconced with police buddies and smack in the center of the astounding corruption that in early 2001 brought down President Joseph Estrada. But I've got a friend on the inside there, a senator who is the ex-chief of the Philippine National Police—currently being investigated by his senatorial colleagues for drug trafficking, murder, kidnapping, money laundering, and illegal wiretapping. The perfect cop to arrange the extraordinary rendition of the perfect gangster.

As I say goodbye to Kein Battistone and leave the Garden of Reflection, I admit to myself that I just can't give up the chase. My next play in this game with no rules will be to book another ticket to Manila. Call it a journalist's penchant for throwing good money after bad, or the desire to smash Steve as an icon to the underside of man, or just my own Steve-like urge to fight: all of it makes me helpless in the face of my strange hobby. I know I'm not alone in my pursuit, of course, but as a civilian and not a cop I do sometimes get lonely. More often than not, I'm just scared.

CHAPTER 2

THE GOLDSTONE

———

We don't hurt anybody unless we have to.
—STEVEN WONG

It was dusk on December 28, 1989, shoot-out time in Chinatown. On Keefer Street, in the heart of Vancouver's Chinatown, the Goldstone Restaurant and Bakery was doing a brisk business. A huge fluorescent-lit eateria and pastry shop, the Goldstone was thick with cigarette smoke and deafening talk from hundreds of college and high school students on Christmas break. The sidewalk in front of the restaurant was crowded as well. Working-class people on their way home were stopping off to shop at the neighborhood's fruit and vegetable stands, its curbside pushcarts, and herbal pharmacies. The smells of frying spices, pork and chicken, and the songlike calls of Cantonese street hawkers filled the air. Just blocks from Vancouver's banking towers and underground malls, Chinatown's narrow lanes always reminded tourists of a bygone era, when city stores were all open to the street and neighbors walked the sidewalk from shop to shop, chatting, arguing, and bargaining uninhibitedly with proprietors they had known for most of their lives.

If the old ways were preserved in these streets it wasn't because the city had designated Chinatown a theme park for tourists; it was because Chinatown was a living ghetto, continuously inhabited by a single ethnic group since Vancouver's incorporation in 1886. Around the corner from the Goldstone was the headquarters of the Wang Sang Company. Founded by Yip Sang in 1888, the company had served some of the 15,000 laborers who had emigrated from the Pearl River Delta to build the Canadian Pacific Railway and then had remained in B.C. after the job was completed. There were those still living in Chinatown who could trace their heritage back to the men who'd patronized the 32 Chinese laundries, general stores, and import firms that were up and running at the time the first steam engine pulled in from Toronto. As in many ethnic ghettos, however, insularity was both a chosen way of life and one imposed from without. The descendants of the men who had worked the gold fields up north and built the CPR also had a family connection to the night of February 24, 1887, when a mob of several hundred workers belonging to the Anti-Chinese League held a meeting at City Hall to protest the hiring of cheap Chinese labor, then descended on the district. The mob broke windows, set fire to businesses, and forcibly loaded the inhabitants onto wagons, driving them from Vancouver. Out of the hundreds of violent ruffians who participated in what came to be called "the expulsion of the Chinese," the Vancouver police arrested only three.

The Anti-Chinese League's effort at ethnic cleansing ultimately failed; by spring the immigrants had stubbornly returned to their ghetto. Nevertheless, 20 years later hundreds of thugs organized by a group called the Asiatic Exclusion League tried again. This time the ghetto's residents boarded themselves up in the backs of their buildings and refused to leave. Not until just about every store window in the ghetto had been shattered and many buildings had been burned did the police finally move in. One rioter received a short jail sentence, a handful of others got slapped with small fines. When the Chinese complained bitterly to the federal government, Vancouver's member of Parliament, R. G. MacPherson, blamed the victims for their misfortune, which he claimed was the natural outcome of their unchecked immigration into the province. "B.C. is white man's country," MacPherson declared. Robert Borden, a future prime minister of Canada, concurred: British Columbia had to be kept "a British and Canadian province, inhabited and dominated by men in whose veins runs the blood of those great pioneering races which built up and developed not only Western but Eastern Canada."

Parliament responded to the racist rhetoric with a succession of "head-tax" laws that attempted to stem the Chinese influx, charging each immigrant up to $500 to enter Canada, then it cut off immigration entirely with the Chinese Immigration Act of 1923. Local restrictive covenants already prevented the Chinese from buying property outside their ghetto, and, denied the vote until 1947, all the residents could do was fecklessly protest each new insult and then turn inward. In their homeland the Chinese called Canada *Gum Shan*, "Gold Mountain," but after settling in Chinatown they quickly learned it was a mountain that white Canadians did not want them to climb, nor was its gold something white Canadians wanted to share.

The fact that the Chinese had survived and prospered within this sea of hostility was largely due to their self-help societies. Most of Vancouver's

Chinese immigrants came from the Sam-yap and Sze-yap districts that surrounded the city of Guangzhou (then known as Canton) in Guangdong Province. These districts were home to hundreds of self-help societies, and when the Cantonese-speaking Chinese came to North America their societies came with them. Based on clans, districts, and professions, the societies were originally formed in response to the anarchy that had plagued the region for centuries. Fifteen hundred miles from a weak central authority in Beijing, the whole of southern coastal China was an orderless realm at the mercy of foreign invaders, pillaging bandits, and the rapaciousness of local warlords and civil servants. As a result, the societies assumed many of the responsibilities of a regular government. They offered schooling for the young, care of the sick, upkeep of temples, the running of workers' guilds, and the maintenance of civil law through extralegal courts. Because they existed outside the political realm established by the latest predatory governor, conquering general, or imperial appointee, they were considered a threat by the "authorities," and were therefore run in secret. So efficient were these "secret societies" that they gave rise to two telling Chinese sayings: "Armies protect the emperor, secret societies protect the people" and "The officials draw their power from the Law, the people from the secret societies."

At the time of the passage of the Chinese Immigration Act, there were 54 societies in Vancouver's Chinatown, including 26 based on clan, 12 on home district, and five on trades. Some were run in secret, such as the offshoots of the Hung Shan Tang, founded by Chinese gold miners in the northern town of Barkerville in 1863; others, like the Chun Wah Commercial Association, were run quite openly as legally constituted organizations. Most of the societies were meant to serve the needs of common people, and to this day Chinese-Canadians broadly refer to them as "benevolent associations," as in the umbrella organization called the Chinese Benevolent Association. In the United States, where the Chinese faced violence and harassment even more egregious than in Canada, the tradition of self-help societies was carried on in the form of societies that came to be called tongs, the Cantonese word for "town hall," the place where the newly formed associations met to plan ways to help recent arrivals with food, rent, and medical care.

Unfortunately, in China a number of secret societies also served as a cover for organized crime, and when the benevolent associations came to North America, so too did these groups. Known for centuries in China as the Hung Mun societies—of which the Hung Shan Tang was one—they would eventually be labeled "Triads" by Western police, after the three-cornered ritual flags found hanging in their ceremonial initiation lodges. In their early days the Triads were, like the original Italian Mafia, a patriotic movement whose members were sworn to overthrow foreign invaders and unite the country, but, like the Mafia, they had evolved in the early 20th century into a loose federation of over a hundred strictly criminal syndicates. In southern China—particularly Guangdong and Fujian Provinces—and in Hong Kong and Macau, almost all criminals beyond the level of street thief belonged to one or another of these often warring Triad societies, and they were famous for ruthlessly settling differences among themselves, collecting extortionate "dues" from Triad members and nonmembers alike, and supplying underworld services that included gambling, opium, and prostitution. Almost as soon as the Triads arrived in North America they established a licensing system that assigned these same activities to their members in Chinatowns across the continent. To the dismay of the legitimate citizens of the Chinese communities, the Triad gangsters were sometimes the very leaders of the benevolent associations and tongs meant to help the community.

The Vancouver police, who were slow to stop the riots in Chinatown in 1887 and 1907, were not aware of the finer points of these criminal secret societies, but they knew gangs were organizing and promoting prostitution and gambling in Chinatown, at least insofar as their own investigation revealed that Chinatown's beat cops took payoffs from criminals in return for looking the other way. They also knew that Chinatown's dens of iniquity had some clientele from outside the Chinese community—a fact that did not please Vancouver's upholders of morality. Especially after opium was outlawed in Canada in 1908, Chinatown found itself constantly decried in the press as "depraved" because of its various corrupting vices. The pioneer city certainly had other underground haunts that catered to inebriation, sex for money, and jackpot gambling, and which were run by affiliations of shady white men who also preferred to act in secret, but the means to those same enjoyments in Chinatown seemed more nefarious to the white population. Instead of raucous bootleg drinking barns there were dark, utterly quiet, and weirdly odiferous opium dens. There were sing-song houses with mincing, bound-foot women in thin silk *cheongsams* instead of brothels with the more familiarly corseted white women. And there were gambling parlors that featured not poker but *fan tan* and *pai gow* high stakes bead and domino games at which a worker might win or lose a week's wages in half an hour. Perhaps most frightening of all, while white criminals enforced the rules in their underworld haunts with bruisers who brandished guns and clubs, the Chinese used gangs of black-garbed professionals, in the U.S. sometimes called "hatchetmen" because they wielded meat cleavers.

On this December eve in 1989, the storied opium dens were gone from Chinatown, replaced at the edges of the 10-square-block neighborhood by the heroin-shooting galleries of the welfare hotels. The sing-song joints too were a thing of the past, having evolved through the decades into massage parlors. But Chinatown's legendary pai gow parlors and the secretive organizations that ran them remained. Two of the parlors were a couple of blocks from the Goldstone, one floor above the street in decrepit buildings erected not long after Yip Sang's day. Legally registered "social clubs" requiring a membership fee to enter, the Hoi Ming Gwok and Duk Yee Entertainment Societies were crowded round the clock with patrons, many still in their teens. Although these kids won and lost thousands of dollars at a draw, the management of both establishments maintained to the police that the great mounds of $100 chips tossed into and pulled out of the pots every few seconds were "for entertainment value only"—as the large signs above the chip cages clearly announced.

In one corner of the Goldstone sat a group of about two dozen young people ranging in age from their late teens to middle 20s. The males of this bunch were known to the police as patrons of the pai gow parlors, their notoriety arising less from their penchant for gambling than from their habit of forcing big losers to accept instant loans at usurious rates secured by life and limb. Many of these young men were dressed as if in uniform—in zoot-suit jackets and baggy trousers worn under long black coats, with their hair greased to a patent-leather sheen and coiffed with a duck's ass in the back and a rooster tail in the front. Wearing gold rings embossed with flowers, they were all members of a criminal Chinese street gang called the Lotus, and the Goldstone was their unchallenged turf, as were its surrounding blocks and the neighboring schools that served as their reservoir of recruits.

At 4:23 P.M. a black Mercedes and a jalopy pulled up in front of the Goldstone's glass doors and half a dozen men got out, led by a short fat Chinese fellow wearing a leather jacket and chrome-tipped boots sharpened to spear points. The new arrivals had barely taken seats by the doors when three Lotus gangsters reached into their girlfriends' purses, pocketed the pistols they found there, and approached the intruders. One of the Lotus members, a 19-year-old named Tony Yeung, ordered the new arrivals to leave. Steven Lik Man Wong, the pudgy leader of the party crashers, sang a disparaging reply in Cantonese and looked away from Yeung in disgust, at which point a metal chair crashed across his shoulders. His five compatriots leaped to his defense and the group spilled out the doorway, soon joined by the rest of the Lotus. At some point during the melee—no one can remember exactly when, or even why, since Steve and his boys were out-numbered three to one—Tony Yeung pulled his 9mm automatic and started firing. A 41-year-old passerby went down screaming. One of Steve's boys also went down. At which point Steve, who'd been chopped by Lotus cleavers, shot by Lotus bullets, and was a master of street combat, bravely grabbed Yeung's shooting arm, wrestled him to the ground, and in his high-pitched voice screamed an order to one of his soldiers. The boy ran over to the nearby Mercedes, seized a tire iron and brought it down upon the thrashing Yeung's forehead until blood began to spread across the pavement. Steve then calmly stood up, confident that he had successfully challenged the Lotus on their own turf. He took out his cell phone and dialed 911.

The night's violence led the news on all Vancouver's TV stations and the next morning the spectacular torment of the wounded passerby dominated the front page of the *Vancouver Sun*. In a picture below the fold, lying flat on the ground with their hands behind their backs, were five Lotus gangsters, uniformed cops stepping over them like they were Vietcong prisoners.

I clipped the *Sun* story and filed it in one of the half-dozen boxes of folders that lined the walls of my home office. At the time, I had been writing about underworld groups for two and a half years and was particularly intrigued by the international scope of the Chinese gangs. Asian crime squads from Vancouver to Los Angeles had told me the same story: local Chinese gang leaders like Steven Wong were often not acting on their own, but were commuting to Hong Kong for instructions. They were serving a larger purpose, the cops said, frequently dictated by their Asian-based dragon heads.

When Tony Yeung died a few days after New Year's I anticipated that the *Sun*'s headline—"Gang-fight charges expected"—would be fulfilled. But the Vancouver police informed me that Steven Wong was still cruising Chinatown like a king. The manslaughter charge against him had been withdrawn. "We couldn't prove it wasn't self-defense," said Constable Bill Chu, one of the frustrated officers in the Asian Crime Squad.

Steve's technique in intimidating the Lotus while avoiding a manslaughter charge increased my interest in the young gangster, whose name had been cropping up more and more in my interviews with the police about other violent gang incidents. Although I'd never met Steve, I had been trying to arrange an interview for months. In the summer I'd spo-ken with Steve's lawyer, a distinguished city councilman and former may-oralty candidate named Harry Rankin, and asked him to pass on to Steve a warning message I'd received from one of Steve's enemies in California's Wah Ching gang, Leo Ng, to whom I'd been introduced by the head of San

Francisco's Gang Task Force. The message was, "Oh Steve, he too crazy for San Francisco—maybe better tell him no good for him if he come here." I thought Ng's veiled threat would at least earn me a return phone call from Steve, but he never responded to the message, nor to any of the pages I left on his cell phone. I'd visited his Gum Wah gang's hangout at Fraser Billiards a couple of times, but Steve was over in Hong Kong on both occasions. I went down to the car shop he was listed on court documents as managing, but the owner informed me that Steve managed Green Auto Body from a distance. I'd talked to a clutch of kids I knew in the Lotus gang and showed up where they said Steve would be on a Friday or Saturday night, but I always wound up just missing him.

One option I hadn't tried was the most obvious, and also the most dicey: going right up to his house and knocking on his door at an hour when I was sure he would be home—that is, anytime before 2 P.M., since he was a late cruiser and a late riser. Finally I phoned the CBC-TV newsroom in Vancouver and made a proposal. Why not wire me up, I asked CBC senior producer Sue Rideout, park a van a block from Steve's house, and film me as I conveyed the warning from the Wah Ching gang? If Wong invited me into his house to get the details—and I managed to keep him talking—we could get Steve on tape personally narrating a documentary on the ins and outs of the West Coast's Asian gang scene.

Rideout and the other higher-ups at the newsroom held a meeting to weigh the unorthodox venture. It turned out there was a clause in CBC's ethics manual that allowed for such a tactic—provided the interview served the public interest. Still, it was risky. Steve was freshly blood spattered, known to be hot-tempered, and not likely to react kindly if, in the midst of our chat, he discovered that I was secretly taping every word he said, and that there was a telephoto lens glued to his living room window. Of utmost importance would be how I handled myself once inside the door. Aside from reading some of my work, Sue Rideout didn't know me at all. Maybe I was a suicidal cowboy—a concern I countered by explaining that I was 40, had been married for almost 20 years, and had a 16-year-old-daughter I wanted to see grow up.

Sue went for the proposal, putting me under the wing of David Paperny, a producer who would go on to receive an Academy Award nomination for a documentary on AIDS. In late January 1990, I went down to the CBC newsroom and Paperny took me outside for a screen test. Having been a part-time television and magazine model as a child in my hometown of New York, I found talking to the camera a piece of cake, and Paperny assessed me as a passable stand-up for the piece. He then took me into the line-up office to get my wish list of objectives for the project. I told him that, as a journalist, I wanted to expose Steve for his alleged links to Hong Kong, but in addition, as a one-time English as a Second Language teacher, I wanted to put a stop to what Steve and the other gang leaders were doing to the kids in their charge. Ambitious goals, I admitted, but they had become important to mc in these last few years.

CHAPTER 3

BRITANNIA

———

Terry's particular strengths are his warm and caring personality,
and his ability to make each student feel important.
—BRITANNIA HIGH SCHOOL TEACHING REPORT, 1987

If eighth-grade dropouts could claim an alma mater, then Britannia Secondary School in East Vancouver was Steven Wong's. In the spring semester of 1987, 10 years after Steve had abandoned his academic lessons there, I showed up as a student teacher and got a firsthand taste of his criminal underworld.

Britannia is a huge brick edifice with the cornices, pediments, and pillars typical of the high schools built in the British empire at the turn of the century. It dominates a strategic hill overlooking Vancouver's inner city—called the school's "catchment area" by education bureaucrats. Back in the 1980s that area included the welfare hotels around the container port down on Burrard Inlet, most of Chinatown, the heroin-addled alleys and hooker strolls of the Downtown Eastside, and a square mile of working-class houses and apartment blocks that were home to hundreds of newly arrived and very bewildered teens—among them Cambodians, Vietnamese, and ethnic Chinese who had been shaken out of Southeast Asia in the wake of the Vietnam War and Pol Pot's Khmer Rouge genocide.

I'd only just moved to Vancouver in the fall, at the end of a 15-year stint in northern B.C., but I'd read the city papers up north and was aware that some kind of exotic gang activity was emerging in the immigrant sections of the city. I say exotic because it bore no relation to the hoodlum hijinks on the more prosperous west side of town, where delinquent teens stole cars and broke into stores, and was closer to the organized viciousness I had grown up with in faraway Brooklyn.

For instance, I knew that a couple of years ago a clean-cut young couple from Taiwan named Jimmy and Lily Ming, owners of a chic downtown restaurant, had been kidnapped coming home from a wedding. A ransom of $700,000 was demanded and when it wasn't paid the Mings were cut into pieces and dumped beside a rural highway in garbage bags. The police questioned members of a gang called the Viet Ching—ethnic Chinese from Vietnam who hung out in Britannia's catchment area—but the mostly white officers hit a wall of silence and made no arrests. Three months after the Ming kidnapping, Ricky Choi, the middle-aged manager of a posh Chinatown restaurant called the New Diamond, was shot to death on the street. Choi turned out to be the second in command of a Hong Kong Chinese gang called the Red Eagles, rivals to the Viet Ching and the Lotus gangs for control of the criminal pie around Britannia. There were witnesses—four of Choi's "gang associates"—but they refused to cooperate, saying "they'd look after the situation themselves," and again there were no arrests. Chinese community leaders, fearful of the gang cells growing in their midst, lobbied the Vancouver police department to hire more Asian officers, and the department responded by setting up a specialized Asian Crime Squad, modeled on those in Seattle, San Francisco, and New York, which had all recently experienced gruesome Chinatown gang massacres.

Like most of the residents of Westside Vancouver, my ESL professors at the University of British Columbia seemed oblivious to all of this—at least judging from their course content. While I was trained to recognize signs of student "culture shock," no professor even hinted that schools like Britannia might be standing squarely in the middle of an active Asian street-gang scene—or that the kids I would teach faced the daily temptation of what would later become known as "recruitment."

On the other hand, a couple of my younger fellow student teachers, who had been raised on the east side of town and had graduated from schools like Britannia just a few years earlier, seemed as savvy as cops on the beat. When one young Britannia graduate learned I would be doing my practicum at his old school, he offered up some information that he said was widely known to the kids in the neighborhood—even if our country-club campus hadn't heard the news. The Chinese businesses near the school were paying protection to the students, he said, and those that refused the squeeze were being punished. Indeed, on January 19, the weekend after he told me this, three businesses were hit in back-to-back armed holdups, among them Vancouver's largest Chinese movie theater, the Golden Princess, which was just a few blocks from Britannia.

And so, a week later, as I drove through Chinatown and up onto the hill Britannia crowns like a redoubt, I found myself making some mental adjustments. I was preparing to enter a subculture I had been away from for a decade and a half, but which had never really left my mind. I hadn't encountered an Asian gangster in my life, hadn't even heard that mysterious word "Triad" yet, but I had a good idea of what to expect. Whether the bad guys spoke Cantonese or Vietnamese or, for that matter, Italian or Yiddish, a gangster was a gangster in my view. And I knew how gangs worked—I had a mobster pedigree that went back to the turn of the century.

"What a colorful youth Al Gould must have had!" was the way Rabbi Paul Plotkin nostalgically phrased it at my father's funeral in Fort Lauderdale's Beth Am Synagogue. "Al, I understand, grew up in proximity to Bugsy Siegel and Meyer Lansky. Al's father was acquainted with various associates of Mr. Arnold Rothstein. The vivid sense of life that must have given Al—one can only imagine!"

In the pews of the synagogue, 50 frail men and women, all in their 80s, shifted eyes at one another, as if to say, "What's this young rabbi doing—trying to get us killed?" Like my dad, these old New Yorkers had all led (mostly) honest lives; yet, like my dad, quite a few of them had known a gangster or two in their day. Someone like my grandfather, Nathan "The Castilian" Gould, whose straight-razor sobriquet derived partly from the name he bore when he got off the boat that had taken him from Odessa to New York in 1910, and partly from his conniving, dark-eyed wickedness.

From the beginning, in the old country, Nathan Castaline had been tied up with the precursors of the modern Russian mob—those *belle époque* Jewish extortionists, murderers, and smugglers made famous in Isaac Babel's *Odessa Stories*. As my father would tell me, Nat lived by the self-justifying ethos of all gangsters born into excluded minorities—Irish, Chinese, Italian, or black. The way Nat saw it, the czarist government was corrupt, oppressive, and rabidly anti-Semitic: its leaders were criminals and its police were members of gangs themselves. Blocked from making his way in the world legitimately, Nat came around from the other direction. "Al, you got a right to everything the *goyim* got," my father remembered Nat telling him on Manhattan's Hester Street. "You ask once nice and then you take." Nat also offered my dad another bit of Lower East Side advice—one shared by ethnic gangsters everywhere, including in Chinatown, a block west of where they lived: "Keep it in the community. The *Yiddishkeit* are more afraid of the Cossacks than they are of us."

The criminal Jews who lived by these sayings were just getting established in North America when The Castilian arrived. Once ensconced among them, Nat said goodbye to my grandmother, leaving her to a lifetime of sweatshop toil raising the three kids he'd abandoned. His ultimate boss in the Jewish crime hierarchy was Arnold Rothstein, credited with inventing the modern system of organized crime—a corporate structure that embraced legitimate and illegitimate enterprises, that employed accountants as well as assassins, and that offered high-profile donations to charities and secret payoffs to politicians. When Prohibition became law in 1920, Rothstein used his influence to considerably boost Sam Bronfman's liquid exports from Canada, as well as my grandfather's career in cross-border transport. After Rothstein was murdered in 1928, Nat's younger accomplices went on to become legends. The accounting genius Meyer Lansky set up the corporate alliance between the Sicilian and Jewish mobs in the '30s. In the '40s the glamorous Ben "Bugsy" Siegel built Las Vegas's famed Flamingo Hotel—the casino that got the whole town rolling—murdering up to 12 men on the way to achieving his dream.

My grandfather never made a big name for himself. A wheel man, a hapless enforcer, and probably an informant, he was in and out of jails and ambulances for 40 years, until he took a five-story fall from a rooftop—possibly thrown by *untervelt menshen,* no one knows.

I do know that we were the last ones he turned to for help. Out of jail in 1953, he was desperate for refuge from old enemies and for a place to rest his cancer-racked body. He tried approaching my grandmother Rose on her way home from work, but she beat him with her purse and pushed him down into the gutter. Anticipating that he would attempt to persuade my father to take him in, Rose raced to our house ahead of Nat. I was four, playing with a mechanical roller coaster on the living room floor when he showed up. At the door, in front of my weeping dad, Rose spit in Nat's face and cursed him in Yiddish—opened up with a lifetime of wailing history—the lament of most gangster wives (repeated for us once a week until her death at 101): "You bastard, may a beet grow in your belly! You caused us so much pain in our lives! What you left us to live on you could hold between two fingers! Go back to your crazy dog friends, rot with them in filth! I hope they kill you slow! You should shrivel with a dark disease!"

My mother intervened, asking Nat to leave until everyone had calmed down. When Nat pleaded men were after him, my grandmother bellowed to my father, "*If you let him in, you throw me out!! Let him call the police!!*" But the police (the Cossacks) were never an option. Two weeks later my grandfather was dead on the sidewalk.

Nat's world left a Jovian impression on my father, and on me. Al was deeply ashamed of his own days on Hester Street, where he ran for a time with Lansky's and Siegel's young enforcers. He only told me about them and the cause of his associations—The Castilian—just before I moved out, and then only in the most deflating terms.

"What's to tell? They shot him in the groin, the belly, he was in the Tombs half the time," he said, referring to my grandfather's wounds and to his incarceration in the Detention Complex in Chinatown. "When he got out he took me to the *bordel*—a whorehouse—introduced me to the worst *gonifs* in the city. What the hell did I know."

"Yeah, but Lansky and Siegel—they're like Hollywood heroes!" I marveled.

"Terry, heroes they weren't, I got away from them as soon as I could. Some kid working for Ben Siegel once handed me a gun. I was 16! 'You stand here and wait for us.' They were maniacs, Terry. Most of them were dreck."

But they were dreck we never wholly escaped. The year my grandfather hit the ground we moved to an ostensibly middle-class section of Brooklyn that stood at the volatile convergence of three neighborhoods: Brownsville, Bedford-Stuyvesant, and East New York. The corner I lived on, Carroll Street and Rochester Avenue, overlooked Lincoln Terrace Park, a no-man's-land between the black, Puerto Rican, and Italian gangs that dominated their three respective turfs. At least once a year they met in the cement park and carved each other up with broken beer bottles below our window—I can still hear the bloodcurdling screams of boys as they were tortured. Their violence washed over all of us. When I was eight I was beat up and robbed crossing through the park to P.S. 189. My uncle was shot in the stomach and lungs when I was nine. My mom's best friend was raped. My father was robbed with a switchblade held to his neck, then beat up.

That was the low end of gangsterism—kids working their way up. On the high end we had the more sinister but publicly polite Italian Mafia, big fat guys or sallow skinny ones who visited the neighborhood once a month. They ran their operations out of two businesses that adjoined our apartment house. Hymie's, where I bought my daily dose of ice cream, was a Jewish-owned candy store whose south wall was lined by wooden phone booths and a bookie board to record the standings for the chain-smoking crowd of men in fedoras. Next door, where I had to go to buy my father's after-hours packs of Camels, stood a nameless dark saloon always filled with red-lipsticked black women who lounged at the bar in tight shiny dresses, looking totally bored.

When the young hoods who watched the streets outside of both joints began taunting me for fun, I decided it was best to make friends with their bosses inside. I was in the heyday of my modeling career then, and so I hit upon the idea of regaling the Jewish and Italian operators with tales of the 20-year-old *shiksas* I posed with for the *New York Times*. At the age of 10 I was discovering a couple of things about gangsters, and myself, that would allow me to communicate with bad guys for my whole life. The first of these was that they liked to laugh, but only at the expense of others. Trained to project what others wanted, I knew how to make them laugh. Dressing room space was at a premium between shoots, and the women I modeled with changed clothes in front of me while I did my homework.

"And they were talking," I'd say. "About boyfriends."

"Ha! Ha! I'm dyin'! These women got no shame! They fucking stand there naked in front of a 10-year-old talkin' dirty!"

"Yeah, one said her boyfriend put her feet on the wall!" I recollected, not quite knowing what she had meant by that.

"*Gevalt!*" a Jewish rounder exclaimed in dire envy. "This kid's the luckiest in the fucking world!"

The second discovery I made was that I had the kind of clean-cut Jimmy Olsen face these mobsters trusted, and more—felt affection for—something my father, then kicking a Dexedrine habit, was too indisposed to offer me at that time in his life.

Since they dressed and looked like my dad, there was probably something more going on in the back of my mind, but this dalliance was a very temporary relationship of convenience. When one wise guy was nearly kicked to death outside the candy store, and I leaned out my bedroom window and saw him staining the concrete, I instantly outgrew the magic dragons at Hymie's. But not its legacy of unbounded deviousness.

I came to think it ordinary that every corner of life was rife with bribes, tribute, and amateur extortionists. In order to ensure mail delivery, we gave the postman an envelope every Christmas. To my teachers who didn't report the weeks of school I missed because of my modeling, we gave a bottle of Sam Bronfman's best (plus an envelope) at Chanukah. On cold days the steam heat in our building would conk out unless the super got his. Once, the apartment of an eccentric widow who lived downstairs from us was broken into. The thieves turned the place upside down looking for her cash box. She called the police, who took down all the details, including where she hid her cash box. She should have offered them more than tea and biscuits, because the next time she was broken into the only item she found missing was her cash box.

When I was 17 my father put some money together from his sandwich-maker's job and we moved to Brighton Beach, just as the newest wave of Russian-Jewish gangsters began moving in, and in such numbers that it later became known as Little Odessa. Soon the shop owners had new banks to borrow from to cover new debts incurred in places just like Hymie's. Mobsters like Evsei Agron and Marat Balagula eventually arrived and founded a criminal network that would stretch from Moscow to Toronto to Vancouver's own misnamed British Properties—extorting, defrauding, and killing—part of the same continuum, immigrant gangsters asking once and then taking.

The ubiquitous corruption infected all of us. The gangster dreck were of good use to respectable families like ours when we needed them. When I got my girlfriend pregnant in 1966, and procuring an abortion meant making a pact with the devil, my dad knew the devil to phone. When I went shopping for my first car, and I only had $600 scholarship money to spend, my dad told me, "Lemme call Johnny." Two days later I was driving a Rambler Classic with only 10,000 miles on the odometer. When I crashed it and needed a cheap radiator, I called Johnny myself. And when I got drunk at 18 and put my fist through the display window of Bergdorf Goodman on Fifth Avenue, my dad made another call. Things got fixed at the police station.

Full disclosure: I also learned how to chisel like a petty gangster. To put myself through Brooklyn College I drove a cab. My father's best friend also drove a cab. After my first couple of weekends on the job, my dad's friend sat me down in our living room. "Do you steal?" he asked.

"No," I said.

"You gotta steal, Terry."

"Suppose I get caught?"

He shrugged. "You're not talking about robbing. Take it off the meter. Charge 'em ten bucks from LaGuardia. Saves the passenger two. You'll never get one who says no."

He was right. I stole a hundred times in two years—grand larceny—and no one ever said no.

I met my wife, Leslie, driving cab. She was actually the only female New York cabdriver at the time—and may have been the first. An idealistic flower child and artist, she'd attended Woodstock, but she stole too, like me, to help put herself through Brooklyn College. And like me, she was encouraged by example. Her father fixed TV sets, and sometimes fixed them when they didn't need fixing. Her father's best friend was a mafioso who hung around the nightclubs along Rockaway Boulevard, later featured in the film *Goodfellas*. WASP society seemed so corrupt—why should the military-industrial complex get it all? After all, Leslie and I thought, they wanted to send me to Vietnam and kill me as soon as I got out of school. For what? To make them richer? To hell with them. We had a right to everything they had.

In the weeks before Christmas 1970, I took a job as a temp sorting the heavy volume of packages at the downtown Brooklyn Post Office. My supervisor had X-ray eyes. His corner of the basement quickly became known as "the store," where his friends could buy presents at a markdown. He also ran a bookmaking operation. We students—those who saw nothing wrong with it—spent our days cruising the immense building taking bets on basketball, hockey, horses, dogs. The day before Christmas, my last day of work, the police showed up in trench coats and took my supervisor for a walk. I spent Christmas week barely able to breathe, waiting for a knock on the door. I called Johnny, and he said to forget about it, they weren't interested in Brooklyn College kids. "Just get rid of all your swag," he cracked. And if I had any problems I should drop by—he knew someone. I should drop by anyway, he hadn't heard from me since the radiator, and here I was asking for advice again. "That's not nice, Terry."

The laughing innuendo in his voice was so clear it frightened me as much as the police. It was like an idiot face had just popped out of a jack-in-the-box in front of me: Surprise! Have you heard the news? There's good and there's bad!

That summer Leslie and I drove out west—the first time for both of us. We camped and backpacked in national parks for three months. In Jasper we stayed put by the Snake River for a week, reading Thoreau, Emerson, and Alan Watts. We asked the same question at the same time: "What are we doing?" Like my dad on Hester Street, I realized we had to get away as soon as we were able. *Completely* away.

Richard Nixon, that paradigm of honesty, instituted the draft lottery that fall, based on birth dates. My number—212—was well above the announced call-up maximum of 170. We went to Canada anyway; perhaps I was one of the few men of draft age who emigrated at that time purely because he wanted to, rather than because he had to. My wife and I crossed the border at Osoyoos, B.C.: we had a dream of an honest paradise that would be out of reach of a corruption so profound that it left no one untouched. We drove and drove—or ran and ran—until we felt safe from Brooklyn. For $7,000 we bought 160 acres of wilderness 700 miles north of the border. We built a big log home in the middle of a green field on a forested mountain slope that overlooked a river valley quilted with farm fields and towered over by snowy peaks. Honest Canada was so honestly good to us that after René Lévesque was elected premier of a separatist Quebec we entered the Smithers courthouse and became dual citizens. Canada just seemed like a country worth fighting to keep together. Even in town no one locked their doors, and you never heard of break-ins.

Not that we had a hell of a lot to steal. In 1983 I got a letter from the Canadian Pension Plan informing me that if I continued earning the same amount as I had over the last 12 years, I'd do very well in retirement on $30 a month. The next year the well went dry. We needed a new roof. The pack rats and bats found a way into the attic and we couldn't get rid of them. When our daughter went away to the Royal Winnipeg Ballet for the summer of 1985, and was assessed as having talent that should be cultivated, Leslie and I again had the same thought at the same time.

Maybe it was time to go back into the world and put some of what we had learned to work (and get paid for it). I had just published a book of short stories and I had no thought then of becoming a journalist. Rather, I had an idea I'd like to teach kids, perhaps about the lesson I'd learned at 21—that there was good and there was bad—the moral inherent in a lot of literature. Jobs for English teachers were scarce, but having English as a Second Language on your résumé was a ticket. And so at 37, I went back to school—in Vancouver, Odessa's sister city—where the karmic merry-go-round brought me right back to where I'd started from. Only this time I swore I'd never steal again.

I parked my car opposite Britannia's back entrance on Cotton Drive, where the street bordered a quiet little park fittingly called Grandview, then held my breath as I descended a stairway to the wide asphalt school yard. Right across Burrard Inlet were the snowy North Shore Mountains, their shoulders carpeted in green forest and crowned by those majestic outcrops that look so much like the stone lions in front of the 42nd Street Library. Off to the left of the school was Vancouver's skyline, its clean glass office towers silhouetted against a clear winter sky, and beyond that the gleaming Tantalus Mountains lining Howe Sound. You could see the blue water where the inlet made its entry into Georgia Strait and feel the endless Pacific Ocean beyond. I'd always believed that a city you could see out of made people less desperate. It didn't seem logical that bad things were happening here. At any rate, there were no obvious gangster signs in the school yard, like thugs in black leather jackets dealing little packages.

My ESL adviser, Jackie Freer, had told me her beginner classes were held in two shack-roof trailers outside the main building. These "temporaries" had been installed when the Asian immigrant wave had begun rolling in during the late '70s, although the trailers had since grown permanent foundations when the wave hadn't rolled out. Walking into the school to ask for directions, I bumped into a uniformed policeman standing by a stairway, the butt of his big revolver prominent as a baseball bat. I asked if there was any trouble, and he said he was the school's liaison officer—it was just his job to hang around. That was my first clue that something was wrong at Britannia. Even where I'd gone to high school we didn't have uniformed cops in the halls, at least not cops who were stationed there for more than a day or two after 911 calls.

The policeman pointed me to an exit, and I wound up at the front entrance of the school, beneath a big sign that warned against trespassing. Just this side of a hurricane fence that walled the school from the city were the two temporaries, their walls painted tan, with cheery orange doors. When I walked into Jackie Freer's class, 30 Asian teens with coal-black hair turned around as one and looked at me. They ranged in age from 13 to 18, and not one of them smiled. Indeed, they turned right back to the front of the room, as if more frightened by the interruption than entertained.

Jackie introduced me and then returned to her lesson. She was surrounded by objects that served as learning hooks: a telephone book, enlarged bus transfers, and a poster showing the correct way to hold a pencil.

"You have to teach them how to hold a pencil?" I asked her after class.

"You really can't take a lot for granted," she replied, meaning some of her students had spent ages three to six in a war zone, six to eight wandering the countryside, and eight to 13 behind barbed wire in a refugee camp. "You give them a pencil, and they use it like a chisel."

She gave me a resource book and we spent a couple of hours going over ways to bring the classroom to life. As I was leaving, I asked about the policeman in the hall. Jackie said he was there because they'd recently had some problems with "outsiders" coming into the school. As a student teacher I should report any suspicious activity, but I should leave the handling of what I saw to the staff.

It was dark when I got back to my car, Friday night, and I was tense. My wife was still up north trying to rent the property, and the last thing I felt like doing was heading back to my dreary kitchenette. So I walked up to Commercial Drive, which some of my fellow students at UBC had told me had the best coffee shops and restaurants in the city. It was a cosmopolitan strip, making it evident that in the not-too-distant past the neighborhood had been a melting pot for immigrant Italians, Portuguese, and Greeks, and that Latin Americans as well as Asians were now in the melting pot with them. I toured north towards the docks and found the neighborhood rapidly deteriorating, until by the bottom of the hill at Hastings, the Drive was merely seedy and dirty, peopled with staggering drunks and hookers and choked with snarling traffic. I turned around and walked back until I got almost to Broadway, where I stepped into a cheap Asian restaurant.

I can sit and read over a meal till closing time, and it was getting close to that hour when the street outside was torn in two by sirens. The whole of Commercial Drive seemed to be headed on foot up to Broadway and I joined the human stream. Half a block west of the corner was the glaringly illuminated Golden Princess movie theater, and something was terribly wrong. Perhaps a hundred Chinese people were directly in front of it, blocking the street, some women were crying, and there were more police cars with swirling bubble-gum lights than I'd seen since I'd left Brooklyn.

It was the night of January 23, 1987—and I was witness to a watershed event in the life of Vancouver, at least in terms of the public's awareness of Asian gangs. A Vietnamese ethnic Chinese by the name of William Yeung, a member of the Viet Ching gang, had walked into the Golden Princess, pulled a five-shot Rossi revolver from his black trench coat, and in front of the entire theater shot a Lotus gang member named Tony Hong in the eye. By Monday morning the words "Asian gangs" would be on everyone's lips, and would stay there for three years, the Golden Princess hit marking the beginning of a barbarian struggle between Vancouver's five big gangs.

CHAPTER 4

GANG WARS

We provide for these guys.
—STEVEN WONG

The gunsmoke from the Golden Princess hung in the streets around Britannia for the entire month of my practicum. Every week there were clashes between groups whose alliances and borders were as convoluted and shifting as those in Europe during the Thirty Years War. The struggle was so chaotic it resembled disorganized crime rather than organized crime, and the police were worried it might end in a massacre. Four years ago, just across the border in Seattle, a Chinese gang had executed 13 men in the Wah Mee gambling club, the worst such incident in American history; a few months before that, three were shot dead and eight wounded in New York's Golden Star bar; in 1977, Chinese gunfire killed five and severely wounded 11 in San Francisco's Golden Dragon Restaurant. Each of these Chinatown bloodbaths had been preceded by feudal struggles between young princes out to extend their reach over a few blocks, using the slaughterous tactics of 17th-century warlords.

The Asian Crime Squad saw ominous signs that Vancouver could be building to the same climax. The three most established Asian street gangs—the Lotus, the Red Eagles, and the Viet Ching—were all becoming destabilized, having suffered decapitating arrests and assassinations, leaving their leadership to younger, more volatile, and less businesslike little brothers. At the same time, the era of flux was opening the field to aggressive competition. A multiethnic gang called Los Diablos was emerging in the southeast corner of the city, founded under the guidance of a young Iranian martial arts master named Babbak "Bob" Moieni, who strangely held membership in both the Chinese Lotus and the everything-but-Chinese Los Diablos. The Lotus's strategic move in inducting Moieni into their exclusive club was aimed at outflanking a venerable Red Eagles gangster who had recently formed the Gum Wah, or "Golden Chinese." In that winter of discontent Steven Wong, who held a street doctorate in seduction, was actively recruiting the best prospects right out from under all the other Chinese gangs. The Asian squad were beginning to notice Steve coming up the middle, and, given his success at raising troops, he was the one they *least* wanted to cause them migraines as he went to war with the rest of the city.

The first time I heard Steven Wong's name was on February 13, 1987. I remember because the next day was Valentine's Day and I was giving four high-beginner students a lesson in the school yard on how to make time with a white girl. They were ethnic Chinese from Cambodia and Vietnam, and by every definition of the word they were outsiders, even at Britannia. They had bad teeth, bad vision, bad nerves, and wore oversize sweatshirts and baggy pants, not because they were emulating the gang fashion in L.A., but because their clothes were from the Salvation Army—the real origin of American-style gang wear. Every day after lunch they would head to a remote corner at the sunny end of the playground to have a smoke, squatting like paddy farmers with their elbows on their knees. Since our goal at Britannia was to get the high beginners to speak English outside the classroom, and two of the boys were in my classes, I got in the habit of following them across the yard to their private corner, sharing my Camels and my student teacher good cheer.

After I'd learned to squat like a pro I began to encourage small talk about their lives, taking the path of least resistance with one of my students, a teen who spoke the best English of the crew and who seemed the most on the ball. His buddies affectionately called him San Yeung T'ou, or "Goathead," probably because he was blessed with a receding forehead, although I used the nickname too because of his stubbornness and capricious sense of humor. He was from around Kontum, where my wife's brother had been a radio repairman during the Vietnam War, and so I felt a connection to the history that had landed him in Vancouver. When Goathead was three the Vietnamese Communists had won their two-decade war against the U.S. and then promptly launched a war against the Chinese businessmen who had backed the Americans, of which San's father was one. The whole family was moved out of their home to a re-education camp, which San's father did not survive. In 1981 San, his mother, her brother, and his children joined the hundreds of thousands of others who fled Vietnam by boat, winding up penned in a refugee camp in Malaysia where they waited years until they were finally accepted by Canada. San's mother didn't come over with the kids, however, and the boy's explanation was that she was too sick to travel. Was she still alive? I asked him. Was she coming to join him in Canada? He didn't know, and his offhand dismissal of the subject showed me it was just one more trauma moving through his system.

All four of the boys—or "my guys," as I would ever after refer to them—lived in noisy Hastings-area apartments, with a relative if they were lucky; or, if they weren't lucky, with a friend of a relative. The kids' guardians worked long hours, and so the dwellings were empty when they left for school and empty when they returned, making them literally in need of someone to wipe their noses. That February they each endured at least one seven-day cold and didn't hesitate to use their sweatshirt sleeves as hankies, causing the white girls they ogled to regard them with unfeigned disgust. With cut-out hearts pasted all over the school, I decided this was definitely "a teachable moment." I assigned Goathead the part of a disinterested girl, and one of his little buddies the role of an interested guy. They played the game something like this:

"I want date with you. You want date with me?"

"I no want date with you. Teacher say you wipe nose on shirt, shit in yard, I no want date with you."

"Oh, you have nice titties. I want to kiss titties. *Tsk-tsk-tsk.*"

"First you pay me money. Then I give you fucky-fucky. No before. Ha ha ha!"

At that, my guys shoved each other and hee-hawed and broke into Khmer and Vietnamese and Chinese for especially graphic cursing. I stopped the vaudeville vulgarity and insisted that now was the time for them to get serious and maybe they would get lucky tomorrow. It was their assignment: they had to come up with fascinating opening lines, learn how to be polite and persuasive. God knows, they'd all had very interesting lives.

"Okay," I told one of the Chinese-Cambodian kids. "I'm Marla." I batted my eyes and put my hand behind my head. "Oh hello," I breathed. "Will you be my Valentine?"

"Marla, yes, be Valentine."

I waited.

"Yeah, *and?*" I asked.

"Say where you come," advised Goathead, the teacher's pet.

"I come Cambodia. Small city. Very nice place. By lake."

"Oh how interesting," I said. "Which lake?"

"Big, big lake. Many, many fish. We catch many fish there."

"You fisherman there?" Goathead asked.

"No. I work on farm. Fish after."

"When you go from there?" Goathead pursued the lesson.

"Long time now. We go first Thailand. Mother, sister step on bomb. Then father no come with us. Have stay with them. Then I come here—"

That was about as far as we got in that disturbing Level 2 session on Valentine's Day greetings. For just then a metallic gold Trans Am came rumbling towards us on the street above, with its 400 horses vibrating the air so concussively I could feel it in my sternum. My guys stood up. I stood up. The Trans Am stopped, idling with the force of a steel mill. An older teen in the passenger seat gazed down at us, wraparound sunglasses across his eyes, one arm out the window, a cigarette loosely pinched in his gold-ringed fingers. I could see a gum-chewing Asian girl of about 16 in the rear window. Goathead brushed past me, hopped the fence, and ran over to the car. "Who's that?" I asked the other kids.

"Friend."

"They look like fucking gangsters," I said. "Whaddaya mean *friend?*"

Goathead looked back at us, whistled through his upper teeth and fanned air towards the ground with his palm, Asian style. The other boys instantly snapped themselves over the fence. The girl in the back and a twin friend—both in high boots and microminis—got out and crammed into the front seat. My guys crammed in the back.

I took note of the license plate, but I hesitated to call the liaison officer. Where I came from—Brooklyn *and* up north—the ruling ethic was that you might let air out of someone's tires or pour sugar in their gas tank, you might even shoot them for good cause, but you never turned them in.

"Hey!" I called, deciding to handle it on my own.

I jumped the fence and ran over to the car. "Are they coming back soon?" I asked the driver, trying to be as friendly a white Joe as possible while still making my identification of him official. I smiled ear to ear and then looked at my watch. "We only got fifteen minutes left till the bell."

The driver looked at me through mummy-slit eyes. The girls' perfume was thick as gas in the car.

"I see you don't need my help," I told my guys.

"You want kiss pretty titties?" cackled Goathead, slapping the back of the front seat. "Ha ha ha! Oh Mr. Good, no look sad, I just make joke."

The driver twisted slowly around at Goathead, and it was then I noticed the lotus-embossed ring on his left hand. Goathead said something in Chinese, then told me, "I say, 'No worry, very good teacher.'"

"They come back few minutes," the driver shrugged.

Walking back to the school I tried to come up with a plan to deal with this. These days, as in most big cities, the ESL Department of the Vancouver School Board has a special component of its course content dealing with gangs like the Lotus. The subject is handled head-on, like drinking and driving, with graphic instructional videos and frequent lecturers from the Attorney General's Department. But back then, ad hoc reactions by the administration were the norm: gang-affiliated troublemakers were given a couple of chances, then transferred to another school, then bounced from the system if they persisted in breaking the rules. Aware of these responses, I put myself in the shoes of my guys. On the one hand I knew I would be drawn to gang kids because they gave me what I urgently needed—girls, money, kinship, entertainment—and expelling me from school would drive me right into their criminal arms. On the other hand, as a former troubled high school kid myself, I remembered the teachers who *could* have ruined my life by reporting me to the administration but didn't.* And so I decided to give my guys some slack, find out what they were up to, and offer the kind of big brother–type companionship in the school yard I'd once benefited from. When I think about it now—and I think about it—I realize that when it came to Asian gangs, I didn't know what I was doing. But then, neither did the city.

My guys came back for the last 15 minutes of the day. Back in our favorite corner at three, Goathead told me where he'd been, and that it involved nothing illegal. Someone named Ricky Tang was about to get out of jail and then be deported to Hong Kong. But before he left the Lower Mainland Regional Correctional Center, a rival gang leader named Steven Wong was going to have him ritually harmed. The deed was to be done with "Hong Kong choppers" (that is, meat cleavers) and weird chains with points on them. One of my Cambodian guys had been paid a few bucks to phone this warning message to Ricky via a Khmer-speaking inmate—it being assumed by the Lotus that none of the eavesdropping prison guards spoke the language.

Although the details were not conveyed very smoothly at the time, I now know the origin of the Ricky Tang–Steven Wong affair. It dated back

---

*At the end of my last teacher practicum *New York Newsday* ran a retrospective on my high school graduating class and made my troubles a matter of record: "Terry Gould was different from most of his Wingate classmates. He went to school drunk some days, smoked marijuana and had an active sex life. A former child model who appeared as the kid behind Colgate's invisible Gardol shield, he fashioned himself a writer in high school and published a poem about his drunken thoughts in the student literary magazine. One teacher remembers him as brilliant but troubled." "Wingate High School Class of 1967—20 Years Later," *New York Newsday,* June 10, 1987.

four years, and was over recruitment. In November 1983, Ricky Tang, then an 18-year-old Britannia student in charge of recruitment at the school for the Lotus gang, had spotted Steve, then an up-and-coming Red Eagles officer, breaking up a one-sided fight between two Eagles and an immigrant youngster in Grandview Park. To an outsider it would have looked as if Steve were saving the skin of the kid, a 13-year-old who was being badly pummeled. But Tang instantly recognized what Steve was up to. Steve's standard technique was to have a couple of his boys target a newly arrived Asian immigrant, let them torment and terrorize the boy over the course of a week, then one day drive up in a fancy Beemer and put a stop to the scene with a wave of his hand. Then he'd invite the kid into his car and take him to Fraser Billiards, his hangout, introduce him to compliant gang girls and gang members, all dripping with the accoutrements of wealth and privilege accrued by members of the clan. The victims almost always fell for the good cop–bad cop routine, seeing Steve as their savior. The next step for Steve was to richly reward the kid for some easy crime—maybe picking up an extortion check or making a dope delivery. After the kid experienced a month of blow jobs, coke, and shared lucky money, getting him to drop out of school and assigning him to regular work was no problem.

And so, when Steve drove away with the grateful youngster, Tang and two other Lotus jumped in their own car and followed. It was not the sneaky technique but the public violation of a treaty that pissed the Lotus off—it seemed directly designed to make the Lotus suffer a public loss of face, an all-important commodity in the highly competitive recruitment racket. The Eagles and the Lotus had just come to an understanding regarding recruitment capitals on the east side of town: Britannia in the north belonged to the Lotus; John Oliver Secondary in the south belonged to the Eagles. To Ricky, Steve's blatant violation of that treaty could not go unanswered.

Steve dropped his young charge at Fraser Billiards, then drove west with a couple of Eagles to Churchill Secondary—crucial territory to both gangs because it was a foothold on the west side of town that held a burgeoning population of wealthy Hong Kong immigrant kids ripe for extortion. When Steve and his companions strolled into the suburban-looking yard, Ricky pulled a chopper from his glove compartment and the other two Lotus pulled out wooden fish clubs. As if they were conversant with the military tactics of Sun-Tzu or the hunting pattern of wolves, they separated and came running at Steve from three directions. Steve's left and right flanks dissolved, but brave Steve stood his ground. By the time the Lotus were through with the then-skinny hood, he was tenderized and in need of 25 stitches in the hospital.

Four years later Steve's desire to take vengeance on Ricky before he was deported seemed understandable, but Ricky, who'd been convicted of assaulting Steve and had spent the ensuing years in jail, had more of a right to bear a grudge. "I got Steve to testify in that case," the Asian Crime Squad's Bill Chu would later tell me, referring to a concession that was almost never granted to the squad by members of the Chinese underworld. "By the end of the trial, I think the jury and the judge hated Steve more than the accused, because he was just a bragging asshole. Total arrogant son of a bitch. With Steve everything is built on ego."

That Steve was still alive and still a working gangster so many years after grandly testifying said something either about his genius for dominating the street or for the flabbiness of the gang world's enforcement of the code of silence. Probably both. The fact was, my being in on the discussion with Goathead and crew introduced me to a modus operandi of the gangs that police around the world make good use of when handling informants. Under the right circumstances, the archly secretive world of Asian gangs collapses. Gang members may not talk about themselves, but they gossip about the enemies they want to sewer. Chinatown, the restaurants, the drugs, and the schools all form golden squares of criminal opportunity that the gangs battle over. And the more they eliminate their enemies through backbiting and informing, the fewer foes they have to fight.

I mark the moment that Goathead told me the rumor about Steve's planned vengeance as my first experience of a journalistic thrill—the feeling of being on the inside of "a story," one that most people, unless they are cops handling informants, hear about only from the outside. And I have to admit that in a part of my mind I reassessed Goathead as a bankable asset, even as I lobbied discreetly about the dangers the gold-ringed hoodlums posed to him.

For the remainder of my practicum my guys showed no overt signs they were going bad. They weren't conscienceless kids; they weren't even tough guys who challenged school authority. They remained easygoing and deferential, even sweet—except they had this "affiliation" that every so often sucked them out of school for an afternoon.

February 28, the Saturday night after I finished my practicum, the Viet Ching and the Red Eagles shot it out at the Akasaka nightclub on trendy downtown Richards Street. On Sunday the TV stations and papers were full of speculation about which gangs were behind this latest act of mayhem in a crowd of innocent civilians. When I went back to Britannia to pick up Jackie Freer's teaching report at lunchtime on Monday, there was Goathead in our corner, eager to tell me who the shooters were (Hy Hang and Khai Truong of the Viet Ching had started it, he said) and who took bullets (a fellow by the name of King Nang "Kim" Tam, Steve's right-hand juvenile).

Over the next six months, as I gradually began to moonlight writing magazine articles, Goathead and another of my guys began spending weekends in the Lotus's safe house three blocks from the school. They saw less of their relatives, almost certainly got up to things they wouldn't want me to know about, and finally donned the Lotus rings. (The other two never made that formal jump, but kept up a gofer affiliation with the Britannia pair and their flower-ringed friends.) In the fall I began a teaching job across Burrard Inlet, theoretically a world away in the posh neighborhood of West Vancouver's British Properties. I say theoretically because my new school, Sentinel Secondary, had an ESL program filled with millionaire Hong Kong students, and within a week I discovered that when they took their Beemers downtown they were almost always hit up by the gangs.

Then, two weeks into my tenure, Bob Moieni, the Iranian Lotus member who ran the Los Diablos gang that fought Steve, was hog-tied in his home and executed with a shot in the forehead.

In the midst of the mayhem, Bill Chu, a movie star–handsome Chinese-Canadian who was the only Asian on the Asian Crime Squad, explained the big picture of Vancouver's gang scene to me. Despite their headline-making violence, Asian street gangs bore only superficial resemblance to the color gangs then blasting away at each other down in Los Angeles. The Crips and the Bloods might terrorize East L.A. and deal street-level drugs, but their influence began and ended in their neighborhoods. The Asians, on the other hand, were "highly mobile" and sometimes "well connected in North America and overseas through their top leaders." In a way, they were the lowest tier of a larger eminence, a junior form of organized crime, with a clearly defined hierarchy, headed by a *dai lo,* or "Big Brother," and with wartime alliances, ententes, and secret treaties that divided the city's rackets of gambling, loan-sharking, extortion, prostitution, recruitment, and, of course, drugs, since they were always available for hire by overseas interests to run heroin. Or worse. It was the Asian Crime Squad's suspicion that the murder of Jim and Lily Ming back in 1985 involved more than the $700,000 ransom their abductors demanded. Ping Ching Ming, the father of Jimmy Ming, had been an opponent of the Triad-seamed Taiwan government. The year before the killings, another opponent of the government, a California journalist named Henry Liu, had been shot dead by assassins dispatched from Taiwan by the United Bamboo syndicate. Rumors in the Asian underworld were prevalent that the United Bamboo had hired the Viet Ching to do the deed in Vancouver, and the VC members had merely tried to reap an extra windfall on the revenge-inspired murders.

By 1987 the Viet Ching were actually in the process of being overwhelmed by arrests, defections and violent retaliation for the Golden Princess—part of a long-running eclipse in power that explained why my guys, natural Viet Ching material, had been scooped up by the Lotus and not the VC. Targeted by the Asian squad and a specially appointed gang prosecutor, Jim McBride, who put together B.C.'s first anti-gang strike force, the VC's decline spurred the other gangs to move in on their territory and take out strays, either in battle or by feeding the police bits of information, which led to more arrests. The gang had a brilliant young lawyer on their side named Ian Donaldson, a member of one of Vancouver's most respected law firms, Oliver & Co., but despite Donaldson's best efforts, the VC's *dai lo* Allan ("Little White Dragon") Keung Law went down on an extortion charge, followed by William Yeung for the Golden Princess. By the time of Moieni's murder, the VC were just a rump force fighting to hold on to their few remaining extortion and pai gow rackets.

Goathead refused to speak to me about his own gang, but Martin Turner, Chu's British colleague on the Asian squad, filled me in on the Lotus's colorful history as well as its "domestic and foreign interplay." Founded in 1976, the Lotus were near the top of the heap for many years, although by 1987 they too were becoming more diffuse. The gang was headed by two Chinese-Canadian toughs named Park Lo and Albert Kong. Park was a short, violent muscleman who had recently begun to use "his own products" (that is, drugs) and now hung around grungy Eastside pool halls, but he was one of the pioneers of the modern Chinese-gang scene, getting his criminal start in the late 1960s and early 1970s in what was euphemistically called the Vancouver Soccer Club, a Chinatown sports association that grew into the Jung Ching gang. Back in those days Park was a graceful persuader with a subtle mind, and in 1978 he'd helped to engineer a merger between the Jung Ching and the emerging Lotus and took control of both, and then of the Asian entertainment business in Vancouver. At the time I did my teaching practicum at Britannia, many of the movies, videos, and live acts coming into town from Hong Kong were still being booked through agents of the Lotus.

In this capacity the reach of the Lotus stretched down through Seattle to San Francisco, where they were allied with the Wah Ching gang, headed by a glamorous young Chinese-American by the name of Vincent Jew, who was himself allied with the bosses from various Triads in Hong Kong and Toronto, as well as tongs across the U.S. It was an alliance confirmed by the Hong Kong police in January 1983 when they monitored and then busted a meeting of dragon heads at the Miramar Hotel in Kowloon, Hong Kong. Law enforcement got a glimpse at how organized organized crime could be. Along with the cosmopolitan Vincent Jew, the gathering included Hong Kong's Lau Wing-kui who, 15 years before, had founded Toronto's powerful Kung Lok Triad and now headed security at gambling king Stanley Ho's Lisboa casino in Macau, and who was also part owner of Ho's floating Jumbo restaurant in Aberdeen Harbor (see source notes). Also in attendance were Danny Mo, the Kung Lok's current dragon head in Toronto, and several wealthy Chinese businessmen from Southern California connected by the police to organized crime. The object of the meeting was to formalize cooperation between the Hong Kong Triads, the North American tongs, and the emerging Chinese gangs, ostensibly with Vincent Jew negotiating on behalf of the West Coast of North America, Danny Mo for the East, and Lau Wing-kui for Hong Kong. It was, of course, the height of arrogance for each of these mobsters to assume they could speak for anybody but their own organizations, for in their respective hometowns they each faced a patchwork quilt of competition.

One of the arch-rivals to the Wah Ching–affiliated Lotus—deadly enemies to the Lotus for most of its existence—was the 100-member Hong Kong–Chinese gang called the Red Eagles, or Hung Ying. The Red Eagles were affiliated with Hong Kong's 14K Triad, which many Triad hands considered to be the overseer of Toronto's Kung Lok Triad. The Eagles' specialties were heroin, which made them rich, and recruitment, which made them potentially the biggest street threat to all the other gangs. They were headed by a computer-store owner named Wayne Shi ("Chicken Wings") Mah. A few years before, the Canadian Chiefs of Police had identified the Eagles as the most dominant gang in Vancouver, but by 1987 Mah was having problems with his own membership—or rather, with one member, Steven Wong, who at the time, his head swollen with becoming a fully initiated 14K member in Hong Kong, was forming the Gum Wah out of ex–Red Eagles and new recruits. His temerity inside and outside the gang world was soon to become legendary. In July 1988 Wong went so far as to appeal a decision by the police to refuse him a permit for a handgun, opening himself up to a catalog of testimony attesting to why the police were aghast that he even had the balls to make such a request. The Asian Crime Squad's Martin Turner testified that Steve was the current leader of the Gum Wah, and a leader of the Red Eagles as far back as 1978; that he was attacked by the

Lotus gang at Churchill Secondary in 1983; that Wong was at a friend's house on October 6, 1984, when his friend was shot in the back; that the next day Wong was in Denny's restaurant when another person was shot; that Wong was shot at by a suspected Lotus member the next month; that an Uzi machine pistol had been seized from his house during a police raid in 1985; and that a switchblade was then seized from his vehicle as he cruised Britannia. Last but not least, the police believed that Wong was a heroin trafficker. Indeed, by the time the judge handed down his decision on the gun permit at the end of November 1988, Wong had been indicted for conspiring to traffic heroin. (The charges were later stayed when his lawyer successfully challenged the admissibility of a wiretap. In Canada, a "stay" suspends charges, which are dismissed if not reactivated within a year. Steve's charges where dismissed.) In his reasons for denying the gun permit, Judge Keith Libby archly remarked that, despite Wong's contention he was an upright citizen whose favorite hobby was target practice, it was "almost too coincidental" that he'd been found in the vicinity of so many shootings, gun seizures, and gang rumbles. "There was even more we could have said," Chu would later tell me. "He was a good suspect in a rip-off a few years back, that son of a bitch. We're convinced he shot a Triad guy in a heroin deal in front of the Blue Boy Hotel." Steve, in fact, had been right there in the parking lot at the time of the shooting, and, as was his habit, just after the shooting he had phoned the police on his cell phone, claiming a car had pulled up and someone inside had blasted the fellow before squealing away. "It's ruthlessness like that allows him to push the Eagles aside and maneuver in his Gum Wah," Chu said.

Ruthlessness was the watchword of another of the Asian squad's targets, the Dai Huen Jai, or Big Circle Boys. Occasionally working in cooperation with other gangs like the Gum Wah and Lotus, but always staying apart from their internecine wars, the Big Circle Boys got their start in 1967 as a tight corps of People's Republic of China soldiers stationed around Guangzhou on bases that were identified on army maps by big circles—hence their English name. Involved in Sgt. Bilko–type corruption scams, they were purged from the army and handed over to the fanatical cadres of the Cultural Revolution. Like millions of others with "capitalist tendencies" during that era, they were thrown into re-education prisons where they were put to punishing hard labor. A group of them escaped to Hong Kong, semi-legitimately claiming refugee status, and quickly got back in the rackets, with some joining the wave of Asian refugees that came to North America after 1975. These were the vanguard of many Big Circle Boys to follow, a fair proportion of whom had never endured the Cultural Revolution at all and were flat-out bogus refugees who would form a loose affiliation of businesslike cells around the world. Like the Red Eagles, like Steve, they spoke Cantonese, and fit right into Chinatown's crime scene—extortion, smuggling, murder, and the armed robbery of new immigrants.

Certain extremely violent Vietnamese "no-name gangs" were also on the rise—along Kingsway, the wide thoroughfare that slices diagonally through working-class Vancouver from near Chinatown to the city's border with Burnaby. A section of this commercial avenue, a few miles southeast of Britannia, had been dubbed Little Saigon, and the no-name gangs—of pure Vietnamese extraction—were generally referred to by the police by the first names of their bosses, as in "Lee's boys" or "Danny's boys." The Chinese gangs had a near-racist contempt for these Vietnamese kids, whom they considered to be the lowest of the low because of their total disregard of innocent (usually Chinese) people's lives. It was the war-hardened Vietnamese who invented and made famous the "home-invasion" robbery technique, in which a crew would pile through the door of a Chinese mansion and at gunpoint put the whole family up against a wall, torturing one or more occupants until someone revealed where the cash was hidden and usually raping the women in the house before leaving. Quite often the gangs doing the robbing and raping were on exchange programs from other cities across the continent. Marcus Franks, Bill Chu's counterpart in Westminster, California, an L.A. suburb with a population that was 50 percent Vietnamese, told me Vancouver's teens would take morning flights to Los Angeles and drop in on a Vietnamese café. There they would learn from their compatriots the location of a likely Chinese candidate for a home invasion. They would pull a job that night and the next morning be back in Vancouver sipping sweet coffee on Kingsway, open to a reciprocal arrangement when Vietnamese gangsters from L.A. or Houston flew in. Fearing murder by the local Vietnamese gangs, the victims would rarely report the home invasions. Indeed, one of the greatest ironies of the late-'80s gang scene in Vancouver was that the Chinese gangs saw themselves as the only force that stood between their own community and the anarchic Vietnamese.

Oddly enough, it was not the Oriental gangs that caused the Vancouver School Board to finally set to work developing a gang-awareness component in its curriculum. It was the aforementioned Los Diablos, the least organized and least Oriental of all the competing groups. Possessing the extroverted panache of an L.A. color gang, the LD was the one on the lips of my upper-class students in Sentinel Secondary School when I started teaching there in September. The equal-opportunity gang's members—

Hindu Indians, Muslim Middle Easterners, Catholic Filipinos and Hispanics, with the odd white Protestant thrown in for good measure—lived along the southernmost stretch of Kingsway where it cut through Red Eagles–Gum Wah territory. Boldly announcing themselves with red-and-black Puma tracksuits, they began to clash with Steve's boys. The big turning point in the evolution of Los Diablos came when the Lotus saw an opportunity to bring them under their sway as gofers and enforcers in their battles with the Red Eagles–Gum Wah. The Lotus needed a liaison, somebody to keep the crazy Los Diablos onside, and they found a likely candidate in a six-foot-two-inch 16-year-old with an expertise in martial arts. That was Bob Moieni, and of all the headline violence in 1987, Bob's murder was the most disturbing to the educational system, lending some weight to a general feeling in the Chinese and Vietnamese communities that victimizing a young man not strictly considered Asian was somehow worse than victimizing an Asian.

Bob Moieni was initiated into the Lotus in March 1987, in a sloppy approximation of the ancient Triad ceremony, with a few ornate oaths and the drinking of blood-mixed wine. He was made an enforcer, which meant collecting extortion payments from Chinese restaurants and gambling parlors, and beating up rivals in other gangs. Wearing both his Lotus ring and Los Diablos tracksuit, Moieni skirmished with the Red Eagles–Gum Wah, the Viet Ching, and the Vietnamese gangs almost weekly. However, Moieni came from an aristocratic Tehran family and had been running with the gangs only since his expulsion from school a year ago. Apparently, the solidly criminal life he was leading began to take its toll on his conscience, for in late August he admitted to his older sister, Mattie, that he was now committing "very evil deeds." She assumed he had then asked to leave the Lotus, because a couple of days later he told his family that if any Lotus gang members phoned, they should say he was not around.

A week into the fall school term, plainclothes police began visiting Moieni at home, spending a couple of hours at a time in his room on each visit, talking quietly. His mother, Robabeh, became convinced her son was informing on the Lotus as a way to get the police to lobby the schools to allow him back in. She was likely correct: the police were very worried about the Lotus's explosive alliance with the Los Diablos against Steven Wong's new gang.

Behind Steve's recruitment capital of John Oliver Secondary School was a McDonald's restaurant in whose parking lot the younger members of the Red Eagles–Gum Wah congregated with new recruits. While Moieni had ostensibly backed away from the Lotus, his Los Diablos gang friends were still in tight with a Lotus plan to outmaneuver the Gum Wah by sending the LD boys in strength into the area. It was both an invitation to combat and an attempt to make Steve's gang lose face in front of prospective recruits.

On the night of September 17, 1987, a coleader of the Los Diablos named Yawer Khan led about a dozen LD to the parking lot. On the way, Khan phoned Bob to join the fun. Bob's sister Mattie told me she was certain Bob refused, because after the call he began pacing the house nervously. The phone rang again, "and the way he was talking I knew it was one of the Lotus. They must have been persuading him or ordering him to do something." Bob, who had been conspicuously absent from activities for a couple of weeks, his days interrupted only by occasional visits from the plainclothes police, agreed to go down to the rendezvous.

The fighting was brutal. Moieni showed up at the tail end of the battle to see that Yawer Khan had got the worst of it, beaten to the ground with a pool cue by Steven Wong's young enforcer, Kim Tam, a onetime friend of Moieni's until the day the two had joined warring gangs and become deadly enemies. The police arrived and began arresting the combatants. Khan was streaming blood and the police saw Bob point his fingers like a gun at Tam, as if to say, "You're dead for this."

Moieni was let out of custody a couple of hours later. Close to midnight, two plainclothes officers paid him another visit. Robabeh was furious. "They [the Lotus] must be watching the house!" Robabeh told me. "Because he was telling them [the Lotus], 'No more, I am finished with you guys.'"

The next morning Moieni slept in while his mother and two sisters left home for work and school. Mattie was the last to leave. "I always, *always* locked the door. And I can picture it now—I locked the door. But the door wasn't locked when Mom came in later."

Later was just after 4 P.M. Moieni lay by the couch in the living room, bound and gagged, a bullet hole in the middle of his forehead. Beside his body was a turnip, used as a silencer for the gun, with a bullet track through it.

The family and most of my students were certain it was the Lotus who'd killed one of their own. Rumors that Bob had been trying to get out of the gang were so blatant among the Los Diablos members I talked to that I became certain it was the Lotus, too. Meanwhile, Kim Tam was not a suspect because he'd been arrested after the fight and was still in jail at the time of the murder—sometime between noon and 3 P.M., according to the coroner. As for Steven Wong, he had a solid alibi placing him at Fraser

Billiards when Bob was shot. Goathead offered me what I took to be an overly excessive protestation in defense of his gang: "I never hear nobody say anything bad about him. That is the truth. You should look the fellows he fight with."

The police naturally said nothing at the time, but two years later, when I began to look more closely at Steven Wong, Bill Chu shared the following about Moieni's cold case. "I don't think it was his own group that murdered him," Chu told me. "We have [other] suspects in mind." A year later, Martin Turner, who by then had transferred to the Transit Police, was slightly more specific in his speculations. "I still believe it was the Gum Wah. It's the most logical; and that's the one I would like to go with if I were putting money on it." Turner, who had been monitoring the affiliation between the Lotus and Los Diablos at the time of Moieni's murder, put himself in Steve's boots: "It was building up to where it was tit-for-tat fighting. We won today, we lost tomorrow. And that's no good, you gotta keep winning and put the other guy down." His hypothosis about the killing pointed to the Gum Wah: "This is becoming a pain in the ass for Steven. It's drawing a lot of attention to his group. It's hard to move around. You've got fights going on which no one is really winning. So now it's time to show who's tough guy on the block. 'Let's go kill him then.'"

For two years after Moieni's murder, open war raged between the Gum Wah and the Lotus and Los Diablos, with each gang doing independent battle with the Vietnamese and the remnants of the Viet Ching. In October 1987, Wayne Shi Mah was shot and wounded in front of a downtown nightclub. A few months after that, a spectacular running gun battle took place on a Woodland Drive overpass between two dozen members of Los Diablos and the Gum Wah (still called the Red Eagles in the press). The Wild West shoot-out peppered the surrounding houses with bullet holes and badly wounded one of Steve's up-and-coming lieutenants. In the opening three weeks of the 1988 school year, the police broke up 14 battles between the Eagles–Gum Wah and Los Diablos, prompting the department to set up a special Southside Gang Squad.

By the winter of 1989, with Wayne Shi Mah out of the picture and the Eagles almost completely absorbed by the Gum Wah, the Lotus gang, now claiming Chinatown as its own, tried a final push against Steve, making a direct power play in Gum Wah territory by sending their own troops to recruit around John Oliver, with orders to murder any Gum Wah who might interfere. They lost that battle: Kim Tam ambushed their raid with a platoon of Gum Wah. The next evening, the Lotus attempted to burn down Kim Tam's house. Steven Wong tracked down the driver of the getaway car,

Jimmy Wu, and terrorized him until he gave up the Lotus arsonists. Tam then hunted the perpetrators until he found them extorting a hairdresser's in Gum Wah territory, and pounded their heads into a table. The Lotus retaliated by pressing charges for assault, followed by a series of drive-by shootings at the home of Steve's boys. Finally, Steve had had enough. In late December 1989, strategizing like a 19th-century general, he decided it was time to carry the war into the heart of the enemy's territory. That was when he targeted the Goldstone.

CHAPTER 5

LAUGHING MAN

———

Hey, Phu . . . you wanna hear something funny? I got a reporter here. . . .
He seems like an okay guy. . . . The thing is, like this guy, he's not gonna
screw you around. All he wants to hear is the other side.
All he's been hearing is the Lotus crying.
—STEVEN WONG

From within the screen of the snow-covered van we watched Steven Wong's house. It was February 15, past 4 P.M., yet we saw no footprints from Steve's door to the street, no tire tracks from his garage to the road. The snow had kept him home.

John Collins, the cameraman, leaned over and tucked the radio mike behind the inside of my lapel. David Paperny put the headphones on for a sound check. "Give me your code sentence if you get in trouble."

"Okay, if you hear me say 'Life begins at forty,' you'll know I'm in immediate danger."

John lowered the window six inches, hoisted the camera and zeroed on Wong's front door, then swung the lens to the living room's picture window. The shades were drawn.

"I'll come up with an excuse to open the blinds," I said.

"Just keep him talking and we'll be happy," said David, straightening my lapel.

I jumped out and began staggering through the wet snow, up the block to 5018 Clarendon Drive. It was a catalog-order big house, aspiring to mansionhood and typical of the tile-roofed "Vancouver specials" being built by nouveau riche Asians on the east side of town. It had tacky brick-facing on the first level and a glaring white second story with wide bay windows and balconies. The house filled the corner's double-wide lot and went all the way back to the fire lane—room enough for parents, brothers, aunts, cousins, and a platoon of Gum Wah bodyguards.

Halfway up the block I began rehearsing the strategy I would be taking with Steve. I would open with the stock-in-trade of grifters around the world: compliment the target for possessing the opposite of his most embarrassing deficit. In the case of the eighth-grade dropout Steve, I would mention I knew people who were in awe of his intelligence. Second—and it would be important to braid this around the first—I'd casually let Steve know I was buddy-buddy with his enemies on both sides of the law, hinting I could be a help or a threat. A third maneuver would tie a bow around the other two: I would take advantage of what one of my educational-psychology professors once called "relational imbalances." Steve was 26, I was 40. He was Chinese, I was white. He was an outsider, I appeared to be an insider. My guess was that as a Canadianized gangster and a braggart, he was not averse to recognition from the dominant culture. I suspected he would therefore respond to a white-establishment father figure who offered him respect for his underworld attainments as well as a humanist's concern for his safety. On the face of it, I would be the street-talking schoolteacher Steve never had. In reality, for the sake of all the Bob Moienis of the world, I would be scheming gangster-style to betray him.

I crossed the street, pushed open the wrought-iron gate between brick stanchions and walked up the path to the gilded doors. I knocked on the frosted glass. I waited.

A boy of about 13 cracked open the door. That was Gerald, Steve's nephew.

"Is Steven Wong in?" I asked, my heart thumping.

"Who?" he said, as if he'd never heard of his uncle.

"Steven," I repeated. "Is Steven Wong in?"

He looked me up and down. In my blue trench coat, blue shirt, and blue tie, I didn't look like a killer. I looked like a cop. That, of course, was deliberate on my part. Steve always talked to cops. Still, I wondered, what kind of gangster lets his little nephew answer the door when there'd been gunfire all over the city for months?

"Uh, yeah—hold on," Gerald said.

At that I almost turned around and gave a thumbs-up, then remembered John and David were right there beside my heart, listening, and right up against my back with the lens.

Finally, there was Steven, just a little taller than Gerald but 50 pounds heavier. He wore a white silk shirt, black jeans, and cowboy boots with silver toes that came to spear points. He had a broad face, and terrible vision. He squinted at me through thick aviator glasses.

"Steven?"

"Yeah."

"Hi, I'm Terry Gould and I've been trying to talk to you for the longest time," I announced, with unfeigned relief that I was finally in front of him. "I've been trying to pass a message to you through Harry Rankin—your lawyer?"

He turned that over in his mind for a moment, looking at a spot in front of my shoes and leaving me to study the unruly cowlick pointing at me from his thick head of hair.

"Yeah, yeah," he said.

"I'm friends with your lawyer?" I went on, not entirely a lie, since I'd kidded around with Rankin after city council meetings. "And I was down in San Francisco over the summer?"

That did it. He looked up at me with the recollection in his gaze, his bulbous nose literally lifting to sniff this reporter who'd been leaving messages about the Wah Ching for months. *You're the guy,* his magnified eyes seemed to say. He scanned the street behind me, a half-second search that took in a thousand threats. Then he made the worst mistake of his life.

"Why don't you jump in, man, come in, man."

"Thanks a lot, man."

The house was purest white, quite cold, very bare, and spookily lacking the scent of a home. The foyer ceiling was 20 feet high, and from it hung a crystal chandelier dotted with little yellow bulbs. At the top of a flight of stairs at the end of the hall I saw an elderly Chinese couple eyeing me from an opened door. That was Cheung Ing and Yue Kim Wong, Steve's father and mother. Yue wore a black quilted vest and Cheung a thin brown sports jacket. I raised my hand and smiled and they moved wordlessly back and closed the door.

Steve led me down the spartan hall and pushed open a door on the left that was flush with the wall, with no molding around it and no knob, just a brass circle for a key. He held the door for me to enter and, as he bolted us in, I found myself staring across the vaultlike living room at something I instantly recognized. Above a stone fireplace was an unfurled red paper fan, and hanging across the fan were a pair of wooden-sheathed ninja swords with lacquered hilts. I'd seen this display in a photo the police had confiscated in a house raid after Steve had returned from being initiated into the 14K in Hong Kong. In that photo a considerably skinnier, 21-year-old Steve had been posed bare-chested before the fan and swords, his finger on the trigger of a huge machine pistol, with another machine pistol holstered beneath his armpit, the twin shoulder straps nicely framing, on his pectorals, two winged-dragon Triad tattoos, and an eagle on his right bicep. Now, atop the fireplace mantel, I saw a statuette of the red-faced Triad god of war and plunder, Kwan Kung. A cluster of incense sticks burned before the god's altar and on its back wall were the Chinese characters that stood for Hung Mun—the universal Triad order.

As I took a step towards this striking ceremonial arrangement, a white Pekingese leapt from the couch and cut me off, growling at my feet. The growling prompted a pair of canaries to begin frantically whistling in their bamboo cage in the kitchen. Adding to the hubbub was a loudly bubbling 20-gallon aquarium. Not only was the place noisy as a menagerie, but in front of the drawn blinds was the additional layer of a polished silk curtain decorated with shiny gold dragons. Now, how would I get those layers open?

Steve sat down at a black lacquered dining room table in an alcove between the kitchen and living room. Slouching back, he asked me if I was a journalist or a reporter—a distinction I found amusing.

"Uh, both," I replied, sitting across the table and rushing to finish my opening line. "For the longest time I wanted to meet you," I said. "Because you're the smartest guy in the group. In Gum Wah, anyway—and I've had a lot to do with your cousin."

"You mean Bill?" he asked, referring to Bill Chu, for whom the family relation was a perpetual embarrassment—one that Steve always mentioned on the witness stand.

"Yeah," I said. "He's giving you a raw deal."

"Yeah, I know that," he said, raising his arms and clasping his hands atop his cowlick.

"Now why the fuck is the guy downing on you so much. I can't figure that out."

"I don't know. We're not from the same side of the family, anyway. His brother married my cousin."

"All I know is, of all the guys I met in the works, everyone says you're the brightest of all of them. Thing is, you should have been able to get that gun permit you applied for two years ago. And Ditchfield got on the stand there—"

He waved his hand above his head at the mention of Chu's colleague Peter Ditchfield, then corrected me: it was Martin Turner who had taken the stand. "He lied like shit," Steve said.

"I know he lied like shit. But it's on the fucking record. I mean, the papers covered it. And the way they dealt with you was unforgivable. I mean, you ran a legit business. Green Auto Body. And they so did a job on your name. What I wanna know is, why aren't you suing them?"

"Why am I not suing them?" Steve asked. He seemed to ponder my question for a moment, then leaned down and picked up his rat dog. He scratched it between the ears. "I never got around to it I guess."

"Because they're putting it like Gum Wah guys are bad guys. I don't figure that. Gum Wah guys, you help them, I figure. You got 'em jobs to begin with."

"Oh yeah," he said, absently lifting his dog's paws and inspecting the nails. "They were doing pretty good until the police came into the shop and harassed them. And they got fired. Laid off."

I shook my head in sympathy. "So they're all gone now from Green's Auto Body. Did they get jobs again?"

"No, because everywhere they go, they get hounded by the police."

"Yeah, I was talking about that with Harry. And with Phil. You know Phil Rankin?" I asked, as if I didn't know the answer. Harry's son was a lawyer who often acted on behalf of Asian mobsters and who had been cocounsel with Ian Donaldson in the extortion trial of the Viet Ching leader Allan Keung Law. The police tended to lump the Rankins and Donaldson in the same boat: left-wing bleeding hearts who roundly attacked the credibility of meathead cops, both in court and in the press.*

"Yeah, Phil's doing a couple of cases for me now," Steven said. "Immigration. Not for me, for my sister. I'm Canadian. She moved to the States, she's trying to come back now."

"So, you take guys like Phil and Harry Rankin on the one side, and they know what's going on," I said, "and on the other side, you take the Asian Crime Squad."

"They don't know dick," he replied, startling me by thumping the table with a stubby forefinger. "That's what this is all about, they don't know dick. They assume!"

"They're assuming a lot!" I said, trying to sound just as volatile as Steve. "And one of the things that this is all about is racism. There's an exposé here I could do on what's going on."

Steve mussed his already unkempt hair. "Ah, I have enough publicity already—"

---

*That previous May, the vocal Phil Rankin had told me, "The gang thing has been blown out of proportion and sensationalized to aid the careers of prosecutors and cops. It's in the interest of the police to make the problem bigger than it is, because they get budget and prestige from the gangs. But my experience and gut instinct tells me they're full of shit. They don't know anything about Chinese culture, and don't admit that most gang members are unemployed, unskilled, uneducated kids drifting around without serious criminal involvements."

"Yeah, but it's all bad publicity."

"Yeah," he agreed.

"And I think it's time for some good publicity. One of the worst things is this stuff you're getting from Park Lo and the Lotus."

That surprised him. "Oh, you know them too, eh?"

I kept my eyes on his, telegraphing a maximum amount of confusing innuendo as I said, "Yeah, and they started it, right?"

"Yeah."

"And the last thing that happened at the Goldstone bakery, that's their fault."

"Well, the police were there, there's witnesses there *saw* it happen," he replied, drawing on what was obviously a considerable reserve of indignation. "We weren't armed then. We went down there to eat, and we saw the guns being fired, and we stopped them from looting the place. We held them down for the police. We phoned the police, and that's what happened."

"You phoned the police, right!" I said. "But they're not saying that now. The police aren't saying you phoned the police."

"You know how many fucking witnesses?" he dismissed the cops, disgusted at their perpetual misrepresentation of the facts. "This is four o'clock in the afternoon, Chinatown central. What are you gonna do, kill the guy? You can't, there's laws."

"So you phoned the police—so why didn't the papers phone you up and get the right story?"

Steve dropped his rat dog flat on the carpet and leaned towards me. "Okay—I'll tell you the right story," he said, wagging his thumb and forefinger at me. "The Lotus guys are putting a couple of my guys in jail where they don't belong. They're saying that our guys are taking out their guys, assaulting them. Our guys are getting all these raw deals with the police. They're being charged and going through the court system now. I got a guy I just hung up with. He's inside the remand center, he's been there for the last three months. No bail. For assault. The Lotus tried to burn his house down, and he came out and caught the guy. And the guy ran away."

"Which Lotus guy was that?"

"Ah, what's his name," Steve said. He bent over and placed his palm on his rejected mutt's head, then lifted the dog to his lap again. "See, the Lotus guy admitted to us that he was the driver." Steve hesitated, then appeared to make a decision. "Jimmy Wu is his name. His house was shot at a while back. He's been at all the drive-by shootings."

"Jimmy Wu. And yet he's the guy getting away with it."

"Yeah. They're charging our guys because Jimmy keeps crying wolf, because the police are hard up against our guys anyway."

"How you gonna dispel that image?"

His eyes narrowed as he appeared to weigh the options for a public relations makeover, one of which was sitting before him. "Ah, I guess it comes with the territory, eh?"

"Yeah, I guess." I laughed. "I mean you're doing pretty well here." Maybe he didn't need to dispel the image, since the territory was obviously paying dividends. "Anyway, it's a gorgeous place," I added, looking around at the lacquered sideboards with their gold filigree and the expensive bamboo screens on either side of them. He'd bought the place for his parents for half a million a couple of years ago.

"Ah, it keeps me alive," Steve said to the middle of the room.

"You're still running a business?"

He shrugged one shoulder, still looking at empty space.

"No, huh. You can't get work?"

He swung his gaze back my way. "Ah, every time I try the police come around and tell the owners I'm using the place for a firing range," he complained, "or it's a headquarters for the gangs, I'm trying to siphon the gangs through there."

I *tsked* in disgust, offering the opinion that Vancouver must certainly be a tough place to do business. Different from Brooklyn, where I grew up, or Hong Kong, where they left you alone.

"Yeah," Steve concurred, "I was born in Hong Kong. I grew up in Vancouver and I grew up in New York. I just came back from there two weeks ago. We were in the Jamaica, Queens area."

Now that was something worth knowing, I thought. In recent years pockets of middle class neighborhoods in Queens had become New York's second Chinatown, dominated by two gangs called the White Tigers and the Green Dragons. Over the summer they'd been involved in a number of anarchic shootings, one of which had taken the life of a white bystander in a restaurant. I pocketed that jagged-edged tidbit and returned to the subject of the Asian squad's respect for his intelligence, which Steve seemed to misinterpret as a sign of their affection for him.

"I know, there's some police out there do like me, because I stand up to the Vietnamese," he said. "We started against them a couple of years ago, and that's why they're not that rough anymore."

"Did you flatten them?" I asked, because I knew the Vietnamese tended to arrive at the homes of enemies in force, and with propane torches.

"Well, when I was younger. I'm not worried about it any longer." He put his arms on the table and looked me in the eyes. "Look, I don't need this kid stuff, this drive-by shooting stuff anymore. This is my parents' house, eh? And I don't want—" He paused, sighed, looking at the door, suddenly touchingly exhausted by the battles on his threshold. "The thing is, we're Orientals, we got problems, we take them out on the streets, we don't want to bring them home," he went on, as if he was excluding the Vietnamese from the realm of Orientals. "And I don't mind talking to you, it's not gonna hurt me. I can even get you a couple of guys you think is hard-core members, they're pussycats—but they been pushed to the limit."

"You can get them to talk to me?"

"Sure," he said, sitting back like a gangster don. "I tell them to open up, they'll open up."

"Well, why don't we do that then? Tell the real story."

He took off his Coke-bottle aviators and cleaned them with the front placket of his silk shirt as he thought about the possibility. "You know, we're not keen on journalists." He looked through the lenses at the ceiling, as if trying to see into the future, then put them back on. "I mean, you seen what happened at the pool hall, the cameraman and everything?" he asked, alluding to an incident a few weeks before, when a crew from CKVU-TV boldly entered Fraser Billiards and sandbagged Steve and half a dozen of his boys. His enforcers upended the camera and then closed in tight around the intruders. "We told them, 'You leave quietly, or else,'" Steve said, recollecting the terror of the news crew. At that he broke into a smile, his first of the interview, and giggled. "Hee, hee, hee. They left."

"I can't figure why they did that," I said. "Because you don't harass innocent citizens."

He giggled again. "You ever see us beat up on some innocent guy?"

"No, because I think you're above that kind of thing. You're a respectable businessman. There's an organization, and the organization is fed up with being pushed around. It's Gum Wah. By the way, why did the Gum Wah and Red Eagles split?"

"The Gum Wah's not part of Red Eagles," he instructed me sternly.

"But you were once part of Red Eagles."

"Yeah, but I was a lot younger then."

"And then you outgrew them?"

"Yeah. Gum Wah and Red Eagles are local. And most of my friends are from the Orient."

I glanced at my watch. Nineteen minutes.

"Would you ever go on camera for us and talk about this?" I asked.

"I don't think I would," Steve said, "but I know a couple of guys who would. Who do you work for now again?"

"Well, right now I'm with CBC," I said.

I stood up, trying to kill time while John changed tapes and also to draw Steve over to the window. "Hey, those are *gorgeous* fish!" I crossed to the aquarium by the living room curtains, knelt down and peered at a strange species of goldfish that looked like it had tumors behind its eyes. "Where can I get fish like these?"

"Those? You get 'em in Richmond," Steve said, mentioning a suburb that is Vancouver's version of Queens, chockablock with the international airport and serving as the city's second Chinatown. "You gotta watch how you feed 'em or they don't breed," he advised. He came up beside me at the tank. "Chinese goldfish. Anything gold in Chinese means good luck, for money."

"I don't think you got anything to worry about when it comes to luck." I slapped his shoulder, still examining the mutant monsters.

"I got nothing to worry about, period. What should I worry about?" He sat down on the couch and I lowered myself onto the next cushion. He suddenly seemed very much at ease. I reached up and pulled the curtain back to better admire the polished dragons.

"I mean, they're saying you never been in jail more than a couple of days."

"Days?" He laughed. "Hours, they mean. Hee, hee, hee, you know that song 'I Never Picked Cotton'? Well my song's 'I Never Did Time.'"

"So you never been convicted of a crime—well then, why does the Asian Crime Squad cause you so much trouble?"

"I guess they have this thing about Orientals," he cracked. "I think it's all in their heads. We don't hurt people. You ever read in the newspaper that I ever hurt somebody? Why should I hurt somebody? Hee, hee, hee. I could go to jail, the way the cops work."

"That's it, never, and I think it's important that's told. So you think you could get some guys in here to talk about it?"

"I just have to make a phone call and you can have all the guys in here you want. Where's this story gonna go, on TV?"

"I'd like it to," I said.

"Well, like I said, we get a lot of negative responses from the press, but all I can tell you is that if it wasn't for us, this city would be a lot worse from the Asian gangs then it is right now."

"The Gum Wah keeps the Asian gang activity down?"

"Well, who else is gonna fight them?"

"You mean the Vietnamese?"

"Well, you heard about it." He put his arm up on a bolster and stretched his leg out on the cushion, settling in. "You know about us, Ditchfield told you about us. What did he say about us and the Vietnamese?"

"He fears the Vietnamese a lot more than he fears you."

"Well, of course—I'm harmless to them. What am I gonna do? I'm not gonna fight the police. But the Vietnamese—they're just like a little boy, he kills once and gets away with it, he'll kill again. If you let them push the Oriental people around they'll take over this city. It's like the Goldstone bakery, the guy shot off the gun, if we didn't do our best, who knows how many people woulda got killed? You know, I don't want to see that happen. I cry when I see Orientals hurt, you seen them on TV. They're my own people. They can't protect themselves. And the press—" He paused, made his fingers into a gun above the bolster and casually, disconcertingly, pointed his forefinger between my eyes. "If I was a gang member and you weren't, and we were walking down in Chinatown and I didn't like the look of you, and I pulled a gun and blew your head off—" He shot me and then placed his hand into an imaginary shoulder holster. "There's nothing you could do about it."

"Nope," I said.

"See? I don't like that kind of shit. But that gives the gangs more power and face. You don't fucking see Oriental gangs advertising in the papers for members," he said, as if murder was the best advertisement for recruitment. "Ah, if you want the real low story of what goes on, I can get you guys to talk to you. I can even show you where we hang out. Fuck, we're harmless."

"Instead of that bullshit that CKVU did," I said. "See, that's the kind of stuff that gives all the bad press."

"I'll tell you one thing, okay?" he said, pushing his glasses up on his nose and pulling his leg off the cushion to lean forward. "CKVU comes in there with cameras—now the Lotus knows how we set up the pool hall." He raised his hands in front of his chest, then opened them at 90 degrees, replicating Fraser Billiards's double set of doors. The second pair, at right angles to the first, were locked in the evenings to prevent an unencumbered invasion during high-occupancy hours. Unfortunately, CKVU had filmed the elaborate entry procedure. "So next time the Lotus comes in there," Steve said, "they're gonna start shooting away. You know why? The Lotus are declining right now because of what happened down in Chinatown. Who's gonna join them? That's why they have to get face, that's why they have to hit us. . . . Now the camera opened the doors for them. See, I don't think I'm smart or anything, but logically the press is fueling this fire, which they shouldn't be. Sure there's a lot of drive-by shootings going on. You got on record there how many drive-by shootings there are, how many of our houses got hit. One Lotus guy's house gets hit, the press is all over everybody. But our house gets hit, there's no press. There's two or three of our guys that got shot at—nothing, not even a word in the newspaper."

"Why are they prejudiced against you then!"

"It's not that they're prejudiced against me—there's a Southside Gang Squad in our area—"

"Who go after Los Diablos and those guys—"

"Yeah, right. So everybody knows what's around the area. And the press gets word of it, they just go crazy over it. Something's ten feet long, they say it's twenty. I got a guy for you who's accused of assaulting a Lotus guy—he wasn't even there. He'll tell you the story."

"You're great to me." I slapped his knee.

He returned the slap and winked. "Hey, you got a job to do. I understand that. Just like a policeman, they got a job to do. But some people take their job too seriously. You understand what I'm saying?" he asked, smiling.

"Absolutely," I smiled back.

"Ah, everybody's trying to make a living," he went on philosophically. "Fuck, we're all on this earth to make a living. But the cops, they get too personal. The thing is, fuck, I don't like the way Bill approaches me. You know, he comes up and sucks up to me and then he tells all the guys, 'Fucking Steve,' this and this. And then he comes up to me and says, 'You should help me, Steve—I'm your blood. We're cousins.' But you know, if he approached me in a different manner—I'd help him. I tell you, there's a lot of policemen out there that I did help in a couple of cases. I mean, fuck, I talk to 'em. A couple go out with me. But some people, they treat you like pricks, you're gonna treat 'em like pricks, too."

That was nice, I thought. Got him admitting to being an informant.

"I have to ask your advice on something for my own personal safety," I said, pursuing a related subject on my mind. "I'm gonna go over to Park Lo's place—"

"In Burnaby, yeah. He's living in Burnaby for a while, on Hastings Street. We keep tabs on each other. But—" He held up a warning finger, and then turned it back on himself. "He don't know where I live."

"Uh sure. Now, I know the guy, just two months ago, he knocked two guys' heads together in a restaurant."

"A male and a female."

"And there was a cop there?" I asked. I'd heard from Goathead that Steve was keeping tabs on Park through a cop he was awfully friendly with.

"Yeah, that cop's my friend," Steve said.

"Which cop was it?"

"I don't wanna say."

Suddenly Steve dropped his eyes to my jacket as if he'd noticed something revealed by the angle of my lapel. His expression changed, and the blood began to beat in my temples. His smile dissolved completely and he leaned all the way forward. "The thing that worries people here is that thing there." He smiled coldly, lifted his finger and moved it towards the radio mike. I was about to say, *Well, I guess life begins at forty,* when he placed his finger against my heart, an inch from the mike, and scratched my shirt with his long silvery nail.

I looked down. "I'm wearing blue?" I asked.

"Well, it looks like a cop uniform. I mean it may be Calvin Klein, but still, you know. You just gotta be careful."

Fuck, *jeez,* I thought, trying to force the terror to drain from my system.

"I'm safe to say that Park Lo would blow my head off if he got mad at me," I casually said, because getting my head blown off was all I could think of at the moment.

"You're safe to say that he don't live alone. He's got a couple of guys working for him most of the time."

Still flustered, I cracked that maybe I should get a couple of unemployed Red Eagles for bodyguards. "Danny Win—is he an Eagle?" I asked. "Or, no, he's a Vietnamese. I don't know. Bill Chu mentioned him."

"Ah, I don't like a lot of Red Eagles. They're scumbags, eh? They're a bunch of lowlifes. Just a minute, I'll find out." He lifted his cell phone from the coffee table and punched a couple of digits.

As he stood up and paced into the middle of the room, I turned around, grabbed the cord and yanked the blinds up all the way, then looked through the window as if I was trying to better survey the falling snow in the twilight.

"Hey Phu," Steve asked into the phone, "who's Danny Win that's a Red Eagle . . . ? You don't know him, eh . . . ? Hey, you wanna hear something funny? I got a reporter here, and I told him about your situation, about you getting charged for a fight that you weren't there. . . . Yeah, he says if you wanna talk to him, he'll talk to you. He says that you guys are treated unfairly—so he says. . . . He seems like an okay guy—you wanna talk to him, or what . . . ? The thing is, like this guy, he's not gonna screw you around. All he wants to hear is the other side. All he's been hearing is the Lotus crying. . . . Do *I* think you should talk to him? You got nothing to lose. You might get a girlfriend with all the publicity. . . . Okay, stay in touch."

"Is he coming over?" I asked as Steve came back in my direction.

"Ah, I can get ahold of him anytime—" He stopped himself, his eyes going wide at the sight of the open blinds. "See, for your own personal safety, I'll tell you, you have to leave this like this," he told me, reaching behind the couch and dropping the shades with a hurried flick of the cord. "Los Diablos lives around the street—"

"I guess I shouldn't write that, though."

"You're a journalist," he said magnanimously, "you can write whatever you want—just not my address. I don't need no drive-bys. Same with you—you write something, you don't want some asshole know where you live, eh?"

"Sure, okay, well," I said, in response to that. "The most important thing is that I tell what you want to be told. And if it's Lotus that's causing the fight, then that's important that gets told."

Steve sat down on the couch again and pursed his lips. "Okay, this is for your own personal reference, between you and me. The police know it already anyway. Lotus was recruiting around J.O., you know, John Oliver High School? So a couple of our guys went up to them and says, 'Fuck off, get outta here, don't recruit in this area.' Because they were recruiting. So they lost face, they took off, right? That night, they went to burn this guy's house down, which was the guy who told them to fuck off. You know who Kim Tam is?"

"Yeah, I know Kim Tam."

"So they went to burn Kim's house. So Kim came out and saw the car, Kim knows who they are. So the owner of the car is one of our guy's girl-friend's cousins. So we caught up to him the next night. So we said, 'Look, you fuck—' Because they poured gasoline all over Kim's house, they were just gonna light it. So he told us who did it, who he drove, and whose idea it was. So we figured, he's a small kid, there's no use beating the shit out of him. So we let him go. His name's Jimmy Wu. So we let him go, and the next day they caught up to the guys who tried to burn his house down in a hair-dressing place. And Kim went in there, with no weapons or nothing—and Kim put the guy's head into the counter while the guy was extorting the place. So a couple of days later, this Lotus guy went and phoned the police and he started laying charges. He named all our guys that were there, plus a couple of guys that weren't there. Okay? Now my guys are in jail, charged. And we're down a couple. So then they move on another of our guys. Now *that* guy has been shot."

"So it's a matter of life and death now."

"You got it. After the Lotus guys got kicked out of J.O. they started shooting at our places. So one day, we went down to the Goldstone to have coffee. That's their hangout, right? And the guy pulled a gun, he started firing a gun. And that's when we caught up to him and nailed him on the ground. We didn't nail him on the ground," Steve corrected himself, "we got him on the ground. And we called the police and the police arrived, but the guy didn't make it. He died. He died a little after New Year's. But whatever the case is, *he* pulled the gun."

"He deserved it."

"Yeah. The thing is, our guys were shot at, they didn't go after him until an innocent bystander was shot. There was no weapons on our side. I got the police report. I'll show it to you later. I get the police reports too. Hee, hee, hee."

"Oh you do, eh?"

"Hee, hee, hee—yeah. So anyways, we had maybe six guys all together at the Goldstone, and there was maybe twenty Lotus guys. And I cut him off— he was with a friend with a gun, and I got him on the ground, and we just called the police from there. Someone said we hit him with a pipe. I got hit too. I don't know who was doing the hitting. There was a lot of people there."

"Where'd they get you?"

"Oh, on the side here. But I'm a big boy, I'm not gonna cry. Anyway, we went to the police, we cooperated, we went up to the police station, right away [the police] change their story, they say, 'Look, you guys are gonna be charged with manslaughter.' Right away we had our lawyers down there, we got out of jail that day. If the police gave us a chance to talk—we woulda told them everything, but they didn't. But anyways, like what's happening, these Lotus guys lost face now. So now they put Kim in jail, Kim Tam, eh?"

"So what are you gonna do?"

"There's nothing you can do. These are new recruits, so the police don't acknowledge they're Lotus when things go to trial. So now you know what's happening. Our guys are really upset. We're the ones getting put in jail, when we're not the ones doing shit. After Kim went to jail, there was a drive-by shooting at his house, they shot his window, and then a drive-by shooting at his parents' house, twice. Nothing happened to a Lotus yet. Nothing! Because we stayed low. Because there's gonna be charges pending down in the Chinatown thing. We don't need any more problems than we can handle, so we stayed low. Finally one of our guys got pissed off. They shot at his house and they missed his parents, I guess they went for him. So he went to shoot at their house to see how he liked it. So right away the press picked up on it, the cameras went to the pool hall and everything."

"Steve, this sounds like kid stuff to me," I said. "And it could get you killed, too. Really. Where's that gonna get you? You get it in the spine, you're in a wheelchair the rest of your life."

"Yeah," he agreed, "the street's at the real low level. Nothing I can do about it, 'cause they are just kids. New recruits, eh?"

"But you're their leader," I offered. "You just said, 'I tell 'em what to do, they'll do it—'"

"Well when you start out, you gotta work up to make a name. I was like that. Fuck, I been in the situation since I'm like ten, eleven. Everybody that comes through the ranks starts out somewhere."

"And then what, they move into Triad? What's the big one around here, by the way?"

"14K."

"Yeah, so when you get old you become 14K Triad? You ever get over to Hong Kong and talk with 14Ks?"

"Doesn't your intelligence tell you that?"

"I figured that."

"They think that I'm a drug smuggler, that's what the police probably told you," he sneered. "They think that our group smuggles drugs because our group's back in the Orient so much."

"The police think that about the older guys," I told him, "even in the Lotus, which is more affiliated with Sun Yee On Triad. And Danny Mo— You must know Danny, back in Toronto? What's Danny's Triad?"

"Kung Lok."

"Yeah, Kung Lok Triad," I said. "The cops know that the young kids are the street kids. But they're the ones they worry about, 'cause they're the ones doing drive-by shootings. 'Cause the older ones get mature, they become businessmen. Like you."

"I'll tell you right now," Steve replied, hitching his thumb over his shoulder, "no drive-by shootings happened until the spics and the Hindus came out and formed the Los Diablos gang. Before them there was no drive-by shootings. Before that, they didn't like you they came up to you and they tried to blow you away, but they didn't do a drive-by. The thing is, a drive-by shooting, we don't agree with that. Because what happens if you hit someone's brother or sister or something like that? The press is all over it and then you're fucked. That's bad publicity. See, say someone came by here and did a drive-by shooting, they don't know who the fuck you are. They try and shoot me and they hit you. That's what I mean. I don't agree with that kind of shit. You don't like someone, you go find him and you fucking take him out to the island."

Meaning Richmond, I supposed, although I felt as if we were sitting in Hymie's back in Brooklyn and he was talking about Long Island.

"You ever been initiated in 14K?" I asked, figuring it was time to ask.

"I don't want to say it," he laughed congenially, "but you know, you already know."

I looked at the scarlet spread fan on the wall, and the swords, and the implacable stare of Kwan Kung. "I know you have," I said. "Those initiations are beautiful ceremonies. They go back hundreds of years."

Steve followed my gaze to the altar. "They go back longer than that," he said, lowering his voice in reverence. "They go back since time began."

"I mean their Paper Fan guy—you've seen his outfit."

"Mmmhmm. *Rashu. Pak tsz sin.* Different ways to say it."

I didn't know if he meant those were the names for the outfit or the rank. "Four-twenty-six is it I think they call him?"

He shook his head. "That's another."

"Oh yeah, that's right," I corrected myself, as if I knew all about it, although I was still a little confused by the ranks and mystic numerology of the Triads. The number 426, Steve would explain to me a few days later, designated a Red Pole enforcer.

"I mean you start out as a 49," I went on, referring to a numbered rank I was sure of, which stood for a lowly soldier. "But you're way above a 49 now. What do they call you now, what's your rank now?"

"I'm the only one in Canada," he said flatly.

"You're the only one in Canada?" I asked. "You're the only one in Canada who's a *rashu* or—"

"I won't tell you, because if you print it, then they'll know who it is," he interjected, referring to the police. "That's why I'm not worried about other people. See, someone's gonna knock you off for that," he pointed at me. "That's why they ain't gonna say something like that."

I wasn't sure if he meant he would knock *me* off if I revealed his Triad status, or someone would knock *him* off. I pursued the original premise for my calling him instead. The Wah Ching.

"Yeah, Wah Ching came up here," Steve replied, "you know how fast they went back down?"

"You sent them down, huh?" I said, venturing that that was why they wouldn't welcome him in San Francisco. "Wah Ching's pretty powerful though. You know Vincent Jew. You can't tell me you're gonna handle Vincent Jew."

"I'm not scared of anybody," he giggled, "except my girlfriend." That would be Laura, I thought, a gorgeous woman I'd heard about on the street who was in the real estate business.

"You gotta be scared of Vincent Jew though," I said. "I mean, maybe in New York there's somebody higher than him, but—"

"Well, I come from the ghettos of New York too. I've seen it all. Put it this way. You let someone push you, they're gonna keep pushing."

I agreed on that point: certainly nobody was pushing him from the Eagles now, although at one time they'd had quite the reputation for taking care of dissidents and competitors.

"See, that's why I'm talking to you," he told me, his aggression rising at the thought of the gang he'd successfully usurped. "Red Eagles are scumbags, I'll tell you that much right now. All they know is ten-on-one. A real man would take you out to the alley and he'd just fucking whip your ass."

His stupid dog jumped to the couch and Steve held a finger to its nose, making it go cross-eyed. "Okay," I said, swinging the subject back to the Triads, "so at twenty-six you've gone just about higher than anybody else in the town?"

"There might be someone higher than me," he casually replied, "but not that I know of."

"Certainly not Triad-connected," I said. "I mean, your guys go back to Hong Kong and then they come here, and they go with respect."

"Yeah," he affirmed. "See, Vincent Jew and all those guys, they go back to Hong Kong, that's where the battlegrounds are. That's where everything gets hammered out in the gang."

"When was the last summit that you had with Triad guys?"

"We don't have 'last' summits." He shook his head, patient with my ignorance. "We always talk to them."

"You're always talking?" I asked. "Like long distance on the phone to Hong Kong?"

"Yeah."

"Aren't you afraid they got your phone tapped?"

"They already got it tapped," he nodded downward to his cell phone on the table. "That's understood."

"So you don't talk about important business on the phone."

"There is no business to talk. What's there to talk about? They're the police. My friends are the police, you know that. They give me all the police reports. My friends in Hong Kong are the police too."

"In the Hong Kong Triad Society Bureau?" I asked.

"Look, half the Hong Kong police *are* Triads," he stated unequivocally. "That's why no one talks to 'em. Maybe there's always gonna be some honest cops, but fuck, they got problems. See, I'm brought up in the Old World. I came here when I was like four. I been back to the Orient at least seven, eight times. So I know both sides of the world. I speak both languages fluently. Why are people gonna trust cops when half the cops in Hong Kong are Triads?"

"They got this anti-corruption bureau, what's it called?" I asked.

"ICAC," he replied, using the acronym for the Independent Commission Against Corruption, set up in 1974 to combat the rampant Triad corruption and infiltration of the Royal Hong Kong Police.

"Half of them are corrupt, too?"

Steve looked at me as if I were an ignoramus. "What do you know about Triads?" he asked. "The Triads were first formed in the 1600s to overthrow a government. They did that, right? After that they was perfectly organized, there was no reason to disband it. So they went criminal. Okay, the police are already Triad members. You know who ICAC gets? The ones they throw to the wolves. Just to get them off their backs. How many retired Hong Kong policemen still live in Vancouver? I know a couple of Hong Kong police are retired here. How do they get the money to come over here?"

"Ah, they're fuckin' millionaires," I said, aware he was probably referring to policemen connected to a scandal in the '70s when a cabal of RHKP veterans, known as the Five Dragons, left the Crown Colony with their bags filled with millions they could not have accumulated on their lowly salaries.

"They're fucking more than millionaires," Steve said. "You just don't know. Give you an example." He mentioned the name of a prominent billionaire in Hong Kong, and then contrasted him to one in North America. "You guys might think, Donald Trump, he's a rich guy. But whenever you're that rich in the Oriental community, you're connected."

I asked whether that created some golden extortion opportunities when their relatives traveled here.

"Okay, I'll tell you how the system works," Steve said. "You're in Hong Kong. I'm the police anyway, so I'm corrupt. You fly to New York? Great. I'll make a phone call. It's gonna take you thirteen hours to get over there anyways. I'll make a phone call to all my friends, tell 'em whoever it is is flying over now. I'll fax you a picture of him. When he comes over you pick him up. So they pick him up, they bring him to a hotel. Then they phone his parents up and say, 'Look, we got your son, you don't pay us the money, he's gonna float back in a bag.' That's the way it works. Who they gonna turn to—the police? How the fuck they know this guy is on the plane to begin with? Because the police informed them. Immigration, everything. Everybody's connected."

I said there had to be *some* honest cops over there.

"There is clean cops," Steve concurred resignedly. "There's always gonna be. But you go watch a Chinese movie. The cops never win. They always get killed. Why do they always depict the police as corrupt? Very seldom do they depict the police as law-abiding."

"Well look, you pay three taxes in Hong Kong. You pay to the government, you pay to the police, and you pay to the Triads. Right?"

"Well, the police is the Triads."

"Okay, same thing," I said.

"Yeah, one section of the city is run by all policemen, instead of Triads," he explained. "Because they *are* the Triads. When the gang members go out they pray to a god for protection. When the cops go out, they pray to the same god. What does that show you? They belong to the same organization, that's all there is to it. People will tell you otherwise, but they're fucking lying to you."

"You're talking about Kwan Kung?" I asked, looking to the statuette over the mantel.

"Yeah. Gwang Gong is what we call him," he said, smiling at his god.

I knew the allegiance of various sectors of society to Kwan Kung wasn't as cut-and-dried as Steve was making out. In fact, Kwan Kung was also the sunny god of luck and of small businessmen, honored by legitimate proprietors in Chinatowns the world over. I'd also seen Kwan Kung in his green-and-gold regalia looking down on the tables in Vancouver's gambling parlors. The memory reminded me to ask Steve about something else. When I'd gone looking for him in Chinatown a couple of weeks ago I'd found one of his favored haunts padlocked.

"What happened to the Duk Yee Gambling Club, that pai gow place?" I asked.

"Well, they closed it," he told me, "because of the Red Eagles causing too much commotion"—a euphemism, I gathered, for extortion.

"I heard some of those pai gow places, a guy drops three or four hundred grand, they tell him, 'You gotta pay it back or we get the house—you just visit some relatives in Hong Kong and bring back a shipment of paintings.'"

"Yeah, that happens," Steve frankly admitted. "It happens quite often. I'll tell you. Everything's run by the gangs: the gambling casinos, everything. So they know. They know when you're doing bad. They know when you're doing good. The people in the community. They know, Oh, Freddy 'n' the boys, they went around to the casinos, they been to the whorehouses. 'Cause they run all the places. So they know, they been doing good lately. Then one day you find out, they're really in the shits, they haven't been around for a long time. And I seen him, he wants to borrow money. So they get him on the next plane. Then you know. He's not shipping no paintings. He's shipping heroin."

"That heroin that's coming through, it's going to New York, Detroit, and Boston?" I asked, turning the wheel on the conversaton so we drifted further in the white powder.

"Yeah, it's coming through here," Steve said. "See, most of the 14K protect the heroin trade. The big drug dealers, they come over here and we provide escort service for them. We don't care what they do, we don't know what they do. We're just asked to look after them. So they don't fucking get hauled off into a hotel room and get extorted."

"So you just provide protection for those 14K couriers?" I casually asked, though I was floored by his admission.

"No, not the carriers," he hedged. "The bosses. We don't protect the carriers. We got problems with that if we do."

"So they must have people on this side moving that heroin stuff," I went on.

"They're well connected all over," Steve replied, staying in the third person. "14K is big. They have so many affiliated gangs, and so many of their own people. You understand, eh?" He pushed his glasses up on his nose again, as if debating whether to go on—and then did. "They got so many throughout the U.S. and Canada. They wouldn't wanna know me telling you this but we probably even have twelve-, thirteen-year-olds. The thing is, we're not proud of it. These things are going on. But life goes on. We can't help it. We're just like a grain in the fucking sand."

"Yeah, I guess when you're talking about a $300-billion trade, human life doesn't mean too much."

"That's why most of our guys don't have the insights of these guys," he replied, referring to his new recruits, versus the veterans coming over from Hong Kong. "That's where the insights come in. That's what we provide for these guys, so at least they know what they're up against. See, they look down the block, they see, 'The guy's got a fucking nice car, and I got dick. What are they doing that I ain't doing?' They join the gang, well, they're making money here and there. Then they get caught up in the gang situation. It's not fair but that's life. We're just here to struggle," he went on. "We're just here to survive. We're not the majority here, we're the minority. Everybody's against us. The public, the press. So we're fighting a losing battle. So we're not gonna fight the press, we're not gonna fight the police. But if some scumbag's gonna get in our way, we're gonna fight them. 'Cause why should we step aside? The minute we step aside, that's when you're gonna see this city go chaotic. Fuck, you remember when no one fought the

Vietnamese? A couple of years back they blew a guy's fucking eye out right in the theater."

"Yeah, Tony Hong," I said. "He was fourteen—"

"You know what, lemme call Phu again," Steve said, the talk of violence perhaps reminding him of his 21-year-old Chinese-Vietnamese enforcer, who'd been shot in the chest during the Woodland Drive overpass battle, and was now facing assault charges in another matter. "He'll talk to you so long as I tell him to. I'll get him over here with a couple'a guys. It's just that I'd kinda like to take these guys aside first, because they get kinda tough." He giggled. "They won't touch you—if I say so, they won't touch you," he repeated, punching in Phu's code. When Phu answered, he gave him a one-sentence order, then nodded confidentially to me to indicate Phu was persuaded.

By the time Steve got off the phone, he had warmed even further to the news angle. "Maybe me, you, and Park should get together, eh? I'll head down there with you sometime. I'm not scared to talk with him. He told me, if his guys cause any problems, he'll blow their heads off. That's what he says," he shrugged, knowing that Park was losing control of his gang. "The only thing you have to be careful of is that sometimes with him, the light's on but nobody's home. He's not gonna wanna see me, I'll know that. We're on different streets."

"So suppose I go down to the pool hall on my own—" I began, but he interrupted me with a royal wave.

"You're free to go wherever you want. You go to the areas where we frequent, nothing's gonna happen to you. Just tell 'em you're a friend'a mine and they'll leave you alone." He grandly put his hand out and I shook it.

"Steve, what made you hit the street to begin with, when you were a kid?" I asked.

"Oh, I guess friends," he sighed. "Friends go out, they wanna get in trouble, you know." He paused, and there was something about his demeanor, his suddenly shrinking physique as he addressed this question, that made me like him. For the first time in our conversation I admitted to myself that I was feeling guilty—what I was doing to Steve could get him murdered. "I been in lotsa trouble," he said, looking 10 years younger than his 26 years. "*Lotsa* trouble," he told the rug. Steve, too, was once a recruit, in New York's gang-ridden, tong-run Chinatown. He just got started earlier than most—his first arrest came at 11.

"You ever think of going back to school?" I really meant the question—I honestly hoped there was a way out for him, some miraculous escape from what was going to come down on his head very, very soon.

"I do think about it, but I haven't got the qualifications," Steve said. "I'll tell you, I wouldn't mind going back to school, but I wouldn't wanna cause the school problems. It attracts the police, and, you know, they're gonna be calling their other guys, the Squad."

I couldn't resist the segue. "I don't think there's any guys on the take on the Asian squad, do you?"

"No, I don't think there is. Put it this way, I respect the police more than I respect any gang," he said, surprising me. "That's all I can say. But they're going about things wrong. They know the theory of gangs—they have some successes breaking down some other gangs—but you know the smart groups, they ain't touching them. I'll tell you why," he said, leaning forward. "The young guys start shooting at each other. That's why you're here, right? 'Cause of all these shootings, right? What do you think the older guys are doing?"

"They're moving heroin."

"That's right. They're moving some kind of drugs or whatever. And they're laughing. Because you guys are all over the little guys battling it out on the streets. But that's not where it's at."

"You mean, because Vancouver is always concentrating on the little guys, the guys that are busting heads on the street, we're missing the big stuff?"

"That's *right*," he nodded vigorously. "We told the cops that day at the Goldstone who had the guns. We told them! They didn't have the fucking brains to search the people. And after the cops saw our struggle with them they didn't give us a chance to talk, they hauled us off. We woulda told them it was the girls had the guns."

"It was the girls?"

"See, there were three guns involved in the whole thing. All three of them were brought by Lotus guys. One guy had the balls to shoot. Two of the other guys went back into the restaurant and put the guns in the girls' purses, and the girls walked out with them through the policemen. We woulda *told* them that. So Bill Chu came in and told me I was being charged with manslaughter and being held for that. What evidence do they have?"

"Okay, Steve," I said, "if you were to see me tell this story then, should I say, 'That stuff that happens in front of Goldstone is kid stuff, the big stuff is heroin. You're wasting your time going after kids'?"

"It's *not* a waste of time, that's what the public's more concerned about," he said, surprising me again with his bizarre civic-mindedness. "It's these drive-by shootings and murders. But the thing is, everything starts from something. Somebody older's giving these little guys the guns. The problem lies with the younger guys *and* the older guys. They need each other."

At which I thought, You're the older guy, Steve. You're giving them the guns to cause the police to be distracted from your heroin trade. What I said was: "But you never hear about the older guys. I mean, the big guys, I think they're businessmen."

"Well, I don't know," he said, heavy on the irony.

"You do know, you're just not telling me! You could be famous, Steve. You could take the whole town now if you wanted to. The cops would—"

"If they knew the way Orientals think," he interrupted, "and they stopped and *asked,* they would know already. Orientals are brought up differently, with more respect. It's all face. That's why there's the battles."

"You're a brave man, Steve. You're a marked man."

"Yeah, but who's marking me? The Lotus!" he said, contemptuously.

"Steve, our lives are in the hands of fourteen-year-olds."

"Yeah, but see, the thing is, the fourteen-year-old will know what will happen when he came in to do us. Either he'd blow us all away, or he won't walk out the pool hall. Which way would you go?"

"If they pay me enough, I might try it."

"Yeah, but the thing is, you might have a semiautomatic, thirteen shots, fifteen at the most, maybe sixteen if there's one in the pipe. Well, there's twenty of us—what're you gonna do? Last two guys are the ones who are gonna fuck you up. You may blow everybody else away—if you don't, you're nailed."

"Do your guys carry at all?" I asked, reflecting on the fifteen-shot machine pistols I'd seen him packing in the photo the police had seized. Sixteen with one in the pipe.

"No," he declared. "That's our stronghold and we don't have to carry. If you consider someplace your stronghold, then why do you have to carry weapons?"

The cell phone tweeted again, and I looked at my watch. I'd been here almost two hours, getting into the beginning of the work night for Steve. This time the call was from Kim Tam, locked in the maximum-security remand jail. Steve told Kim they finally got the *Province* newspaper to retract an article that stated Phu was at the Goldstone killing, which had brought unneeded heat down on his head. Steve then told Kim he had a reporter here who could help his case, and handed me the phone.

I was tempted to tell Kim I used to teach a couple guys connected with the enemies in his worst nightmares, but thought better of it. Instead, I shot the breeze with the poor caged kid, asking about the sleeping arrangements, and his innocence. "Yeah, I'll be outta here soon, no worries," he said, putting on a brave front. "So how you gonna help my case?"

"Just tell the truth," I said. Then I added, jokingly, "Not you, me."

It went right over his head. He asked for Steve, and I sat down and listened to their conversation range from the Goldstone to the hairdresser shop to the drive-bys and arson attempt. It had all happened in the space of a couple of days. This was their workaday routine—the kind of life they had led for years. It was only remarkable if you forgot that Al Capone was at the height of his violent reign at 26 years old.

"In the long run you never know what might evolve from this," Steve told me when he got off the phone. "Because the Lotus is trying to get their face back. We're not on the offensive now. We're on the defensive. But we're not worried. You know, Harry Rankin represents a couple of the guys that are charged."

"All of you guys got white-collar counsel," I said.

"Nah look, I'm just a common man," Steve replied. "I just don't like being pushed. Hong Kong, here, anywhere. I think Bill probably told you that. I don't care if it's the police, anybody fucks around with me, one way or another, I'll catch up. We're movin' now. Look, these Lotus guys put this innocent guy in jail—" he bent a pinkie down. "Los Diablos fingered Tam for attempted murder—" he counted another digit. "But it wasn't Kim. There was a gun drawn, but it wasn't him who drew it. There was twenty Los Diablos guys. So he'll win his cases. They've offered him a plea bargain for common assault. You already know the *Province* printed that Phu was at the Goldstone bakery—" he pulled a third finger down. "That's why his house was shot at. He wasn't there, so we got the *Province* to retract the story. We had our lawyers on it. All my guys are doing is trying to struggle through life without getting picked on."

I stood up, feeling exhausted, but night owl Steve was just getting going: "I'm just telling you how it all started. Lotus are a bunch of babies. They tried to recruit where they shouldn't have and so now they got their ass kicked in. So first they try and burn Kim's house down, and now they put him in jail. What kind of justice is that?"

"Okay," I said, "so can you arrange for a meeting with you, me, and Park?"

"Sure, I know people know him. I'll set something up for you. Monday sounds pretty good to get together for me. You're welcome back here anytime."

I excused myself and went into the bathroom, where I flushed the toilet and said into the mike: "Okay, I think I might as well get you guys in here. This guy Phu'll be here any minute."

When I came out, Steve was over at his altar, dusting incense ashes into a pile, notelessly whistling. "Hey Steve," I said, not believing I was going to just come out with it so casually. "I got some CBC-TV guys coming to pick me up here now." I looked at my watch. "They're probably in the van outside now. You mind if I go out and get 'em and bring 'em in here to meet your guys?"

"Sure, fuck! I got nothin' to hide," Steve said. "Bring 'em in!"

John, David, and I entered the house through Steve's private entrance on the side street, John carrying his camera, his pockets loaded with gear. It was bizarre, but Steve didn't bat an eyelash, so completely had I gained his trust. I was the emcee to this unusual gathering, and Steve was the only one who seemed relaxed. I made the introductions all around, as if my crew hadn't been listening to every otherworldly word of our conversation. On the last handshake, a lean sullen fellow walked in through the open door, shaking off the snow. His hands were jammed in his coat pockets and a cigarette slanted from his lips across his chin. Steve turned to feeding his fish. "Phu, these are the guys who are gonna make you a movie star," he said with his back to us. Phu looked me in the eye, crushing me between his narrowed lashes. Then he flipped his rooster tail back off his forehead with a jerk of contempt. He looked at Paperny.

I was familiar with that look, but there was no reason Paperny would have been. During their apprenticeship, gangsters spend hours in the mirror practicing ways to add maximum menace to the glare. Bad guys use the look all the time in a standoff or during an extortion attempt because it announces: "I am an out-of-control evil psychopath, capable of anything, and right now I want to make you watch as I pull your intestines out." Those who are good at the look are usually prepared to deliver on its threat.

"You wanna do it here or outside?" Steve asked Phu.

"I don't know," he said, running the look between me, David, and John.

"Why don't we do it right here?" I said.

"Yeah but nobody can know it's my house," Steve said.

"Oh they won't, we'll shoot it against the wall," I said. "Or sort of just anonymously on the street."

There were some other bodies at the door now, half looking in. Then they moved back into the snowy dark. With Steve's door to the house bolted behind us, the crowd definitely gave the impression we were boxed in. It was obvious Phu didn't want any part of this, and that he was coming to a boil. Paperny sensibly lowered the flame, and said it was getting late, we'd be in touch in the morning. My heart sank. I wanted to wrap the piece up that night, get the hell out of the story—Park or no Park—because I already knew the ending, and it wouldn't be pretty. But we needed another Gum Wah to back up Steve. We needed one of his main enforcers. Now I would have to hang around Steve in order to get him to persuade an uncooperative Phu to cooperate again.

To do so, I would have to become Steve's friend. Not *have* to. I *would* become his friend.

"I'll see you Monday," I told Steve. The short gangster shook my hand, patted it with his other hand.

Well, I thought, life begins at 40.

CHAPTER 6

HEAVEN, EARTH, AND MAN

———

*Only thing you can do for me is, you can find out if Bill and
them guys are up to anything new on me.*
—STEVEN WONG

Gangsters are good team players who generally exhibit a locker-room famil-
iarity with other men. Still, it surprised me when Steve answered the door
on Monday wearing only his polka-dot boxers, showing off his biceps and
his chest tattooed with the winged dragons and sharp-taloned eagle. He was
talking on the phone and barely interrupted himself as he turned back into
the house, whereupon I realized that the display was likely done on purpose.
Neck to waist his back was totally covered by a stylized tableau of a dragon
crawling against a background of tigers and flowers—a Triad montage no
one outside his syndicate world was supposed to see.

Steve moved to his altar by the fireplace and, still on the phone, fluttered his hand for me to have a seat on the couch. "*Pai jai*," he sang into the
receiver—drug dealer code for Canadian currency. He watched me with a
vacant stare, absently stroking the predatory creature on his soft right pec-
toral. Then he said, "Tripped and fell . . . Yeah, we phoned his people. . . . His
fucking book was all wrong. . . . Hee, hee, hee, I told that cop to take the
afternoon off 'cause now I was goin' home alone."

I laughed aloud at this remark, and Steve winked at me. Any cop listening in on the conversation would have instantly understood that Steve was
discussing the arrest of one of his clients at the airport, that the guy's passport was phony, and that a cash-stuffed suitcase had been seized. What
amused me was that Steve *knew* his phone could be bugged, yet he went on
tactically talking. In reality, on the street, on the phone, or to a cop's face, he
always let those on his tail know he was in the legal business of guarding
drug bosses, thus deflecting attempts to prove he was actually trafficking
himself. "Steve's cover is not having any cover," Martin Turner warned me.

"He *tells* you what he's doing. He shows you everything. He even tells you he just killed someone and says, 'Come get the body.'"

The see-through gangster punched off and put his cell phone on the sofa, then curled his fingers around my biceps. "Here," he said, "you know about this already, eh?"

He walked back to his altar and picked up a Bic lighter from the floor of the scarlet stage that was home to Kwan Kung. He lit two joss sticks, gave me one, pronammed, and held a prayerful position as he mouthed some whispered request. I put my stick in the three-legged incense burner and studied his god up close.

Ceramic statues of Kwan Kung can look fairly tacky at close quarters, but Steve's version was silky porcelain, artfully etched and painted with class. The god's right shoulder—the one from which his arm extended to grip the shaft of his halberd—was clothed in a battle uniform. His left side, however, was symbolically draped in the sweeping gown of a Confucian scholar. From the gown's horseshoe cuff Kwan Kung's other hand reached out with two fingers extended, signifying that he was the second of three generals who had sworn a blood oath of loyalty in a peach orchard 1,800 years ago. The gown was blue-green, the turban sparkling gold, the aged face blood-red with anger.

Steve lowered his hands and looked over at me. "So you know he started it all, eh? He keeps it all going."

"I know he started one of the first loyal brotherhoods," I said, a good student with the right answer. "It was during the revolt against the Han dynasty. His colors stand for Heaven, Earth, and Man."

Steve smiled approvingly, though his tilted head left a question hanging in the air. I told him I knew the details because back in 1983, as a guest of the Chinese Writers' Union in Beijing, I'd sat through six hours of the multi-night opera *The Romance of the Three Kingdoms*—the most popular Chinese opera of all time—whose protagonist was Kwan Kung. I was there for a climactic night, "The Oath in the Peach Orchard," the ceremony that for almost two millennia had confirmed Kwan Kung as the patron saint of all Chinese brotherhoods, in which loyalty is the most important virtue.

"Yeah, every Chinese kid has to learn that in Chinese school," Steven said. "Loyalty's what it's all about. 'Heaven and Earth witness our promise. Any of us is unfaithful, Heaven and Man take vengeance.'" He snapped his fingers and pointed towards the back of his suite: "I was gonna show you something." He turned and waddled out of the room in his baggy boxers.

Underlit by the candle, Kwan Kung's eyes squinted eerily into my own. I pronammed too, then placed a quarter in front of his upturned clogs. It couldn't hurt. Seven years back, when I'd returned from China, I'd actually bought a statue of the revolutionary general, and still had him in my office. Deified in the 1500s as the god of war by the Ming emperor Wan Li, Kwan Kung was reputed to be the only Chinese god who united the tactical advice of Sun-Tzu with the teachings of Buddhism, Taoism, and Confucianism. Buddhists called him "the Buddha Who Defends the Realm"; Taoists knew him as "the Emperor of the Eastern Peak"; martial arts masters saw him as the paradigm of *The Art of War;* and Confucian scholars said he epitomized *zhong*—the absolute loyalty that ideal citizens should show to one another. In China, where career advancement has always been orchestrated by a corrupt elite, and secret brotherhoods have helped ordinary people sidestep or overthrow their despots, loyalty and a warrior on your side counted for a lot. Kwan Kung fit the bill. Each morning, in modern Chinatowns around the globe, honest citizens honored him with candles and incense, just like Steve. I always pointed him out to friends—he was there in the back of the restaurant, in his scarlet house, god of both the restaurant owner and the gangsters who collected protection money.

Carrying a lawyer's folder atop a hardwood box that looked like it might contain dueling pistols, Steve came back into the room dressed in a white Donald Duck sweatshirt, jeans, and sneakers. "This is some of my reports that I was telling you," he crowed. He pried open the folder and took out a thick accordion document, whose sheets he let fan out to the floor with a flourish. "Anybody you wanna know about, just tell me."

"What's this—a rap sheet?" I laughed, thinking, *What are you up to?*

"You got it, hee, hee, hee. Anything they give to Hong Kong, I get." He threw another sheaf on the couch, then another. I looked over the life history of one David Lim, a 36-year-old Chinese-Canadian who'd been arrested a dozen times on charges of drug trafficking and possession of weapons. ("CONSIDERED DANGEROUS, PERSON IS A FORMER WRESTLING CHAMPION.") There were criminal bios of Park Lo, Albert Kong, and (of course) Steven Lik Man Wong, for whom there was a sheet entitled: "INFORMATION TO OBTAIN A SEARCH WARRANT. PURSUANT TO SECTION 11 OF THE *CONTROLLED DRUGS AND SUBSTANCES ACT.*"

"You know they had that Asia crime conference here last spring?" Steve asked me.

"Yeah, I was there for it."

"My friends went to it."

"Your Triad friends?"

"Well, what'd I tell you about the police?"

"Right. They're the Triads."

I took from my briefcase *Triad Societies in Hong Kong,* written in 1960 by Inspector W. P. Morgan, a Hong Kong cop with the Triad Societies Bureau. I turned to where Morgan showed a number of actors dressed in Triad ceremonial garb—the very photos I was including in the first of my two-part exposé on Steve, and which that morning I'd had filmed at the CBC building across town. The costumes were quite exotic-looking, featuring Buddhist robes, belts, sashes, grass sandals, and headbands, each unique to the rank of the wearer and usually donned only during initiations. "So do you ever get to wear this stuff?" I asked.

Steve gave me a high-chinned Mussolini look. "If I did, why would I tell you?" He flipped through the photographs. "Maybe if we did some business together first, eh?" he asked.

Here it comes, I thought.

"Anything that I won't get arrested for, Steve," I laughed.

"Who said anything about arrested? Fuck, I'll show you Lotus guys to write about, you won't believe what they're doing. Military weapons, Oriental girls they bring over—I'll take you right there to the massage parlors." He let that sink in a minute, with a lascivious grin. "Only thing you can do for me is, you can find out if Bill and them guys are up to anything new on me. You probably know already, eh? When was the last time you talked to him?"

"Well, Friday, actually," I said.

Beat.

"Yeah, so?"

"Nothing—just a formal interview on the gang scene."

"Mmmhmm. Nothin' about me?"

He said this so flatly, and with so thin a smile, I went cold, worrying whether some cop had revealed that I'd told the Asian squad that Steve would be the centerpiece of this project. The police had their own agenda, after all. Then again, Steve was perfectly capable of implying there'd been a dangerous divulgence when there'd been nothing of the kind. Bill had told me that Steve was famous for causing fights within the Asian squad by spreading malevolent gossip. He always attributed his knowledge to what other cops had told him.

"Yeah, we talked about you a little," I said. "Born in Hong Kong; grew up in New York—nothing most of the guys don't know. Why, were *you* talking to Bill?"

"I always talk to him. Well, not always, but when he comes around."

"So what's in the box?" I asked, not really changing the subject since I was sure he was going to haul out something to scare the shit out of me. Maybe a necklace of shrunken ears.

Steve opened his hardwood box and from the felt inner liner lifted a pair of objects that were strange enough, though not at all frightening. They were kidney-shaped blocks, made out of lacquered ceramic, painted scarlet, rounded on the top and flat beneath. Each was stamped with the Taoist *t'ai chi* symbol, the famous *yin* and *yang* circle. My face must have registered either relief or puzzlement.

"You don't know these?" he asked.

"Uh-uh."

"Fortune-telling. You ask him a question and you throw them." He handed me the blocks. "You have to ask it very simple."

I looked at Kwan Kung and thought: *Will Steve come for me after this goes to air?* Then I threw the blocks onto the fireplace tiles. The two kidneys bounced like plates on the outer hearth, wobbled, then came to rest flat side up.

"See, that means maybe," Steve said, leaning down and picking up the blocks. "'Maybe' means the question's too complicated. So you have to ask again."

I cut the second part of my question, then threw the blocks again. One fell flat side up, the other round side up.

"The answer's yes," Steve beamed. "So you're gonna score, hee, hee, hee!"

As he'd promised, Steve began phoning around to find out where Park Lo was lurking today. When he discovered the Lotus boss was shooting pool at Hastings Billiards, Steve set about organizing a platoon of highbinders to back us up when we walked into Park's lair. For Steve, the plan was exhilarating: he couldn't have asked for a better excuse to invade another Lotus sanctuary in order to dump on Lotus face. He was merely bringing his friend the CBC reporter over for a chat. Blame Terry Gould, not Steven Wong.

As I sat and watched him jovially arrange this invasion, I realized that Steve's life was war. From the moment he kicked into gear around 2 P.M. each day to the moment he retired near dawn, his every hour was filled with aggressive planning for battle. Pacing under the blazing gaze of Kwan Kung in front of the parallel swords, Steve suddenly seemed to me much more than a 26-year-old urban-gang leader. He seemed to be carrying forward the literal mantle of his inheritance. In his own way, Steve had introduced me to the deification of crime by the Triads, and to their metaphors and hero. The roots of their mystic associations were dear to Steve's heart. For almost his entire life he'd fed on the ancient roots, and now that he shared in their modern flowering he seemed to honestly believe in the theology that made sense of it all.

His assumptions about life were perfectly understood by almost every Chinese adult in the city. It wasn't just that Chinatown understood the Triads; it was that Chinatown fatalistically accepted their presence, since violent secret societies had existed in one form or another throughout Chinese history. Back in May 1983, three months after the gang massacre in Seattle's Wah Mee gambling parlor, Frank Chin, a young Chinese journalist, published an article in the *Seattle Weekly* that attempted to explain to the aghast white community that the catastrophe was just the latest battle in a 3,500-year-old conflict. "You have to know how Chinatown plays," Chin wrote. "You should know our life is war. . . . No matter when you were born in China or Hong Kong, and how long it was before you came to America . . . you are born in war. You will die in war. No one will win the war." That, Chin said, was the *way* of China, of Hong Kong, and of all the Chinatowns in the worldwide diaspora: "All arts are martial. All behavior tactical. All relations military. All friendships alliances. All form is strategy." When the god of Chinatown was the god of war, when he was worshiped by competing gangs, tongs, family associations, district associations, guilds, and unions, Chin wrote, peace was impossible. When the very concept of self was inextricably tied to martial conflict, wars were inevitable:

> Our first person pronoun, the Chinese "I," is made of two battleaxes crossed in contention. The battleaxes form the picture of a soldier drawing a long sword. In all its parts the Chinese "I" means "I am the law." "I am the law" is the substance of the Confucian ethic of private revenge. There is no God here. There is no "Revenge is mine sayeth the Lord." The ethic of private revenge is the heart of the Confucian Mandate of Heaven. That says power corrupts and the most benevolent and kindly government inevitably betrays the people, and private revenge empowers wronged individuals to band together to overthrow the emperor for unredressed grievances. Kingdoms rise and fall. Nations come and go. We hear it in the way you hear, "Once upon a time."

When the historical Kwan Kung was born around A.D. 150, this cyclical pattern was already accepted by Chinese philosophers as inevitable, like the rise and fall of a celestial tide. The pattern began with the Shang dynasty, around 1500 B.C., and has been repeated continuously to our own time. Political control over the heart of China, the Yellow and Yangtze river basins, expands under the rule of moral emperors, who have Heaven's Mandate to govern for the benefit of the people, which ushers in a Golden Era of great inventions and public works. The immoral successors of the moral emperors, by tolerating the gross corruption of appointed officials, engaging in murderous civil wars, and failing to keep up public works, always wind up forfeiting the mandate. The ensuing chaos gives rise to patriotic secret societies with mystical names—the Red Turbans, the White Lotus Society, the Yellow Turbans—who feel it their duty to rebel and restore Heaven's Mandate. At this point barbarians from the north and the west press in on the borders of the weakened nation and cause it to shrink back towards its heart. Finally the barbarians invade, conquer China and supplant the latest dynasty with their own. Eventually they too lose their vigor, and are expelled in a new patriotic uprising launched by new secret societies. For a generation anarchy reigns until a vigorous new dynasty arises, and the whole cycle starts over again.

The birth of the Hung Mun secret society was just one more wave in this eternal pattern.

The origins of the Triads are as convoluted as a fairy tale, with magic and history braided together. Steve knew the tale, but he was part of a vanishing minority of Triad acolytes. Most of his colleagues went through severely truncated initiations and got their knowledge of the Hung Mun from body-littered Hong Kong gangster movies, with hocus-pocus references to times past offered by a gray old man instructing a teenage devotee in the opening 60 seconds of the film.

The longer form of the Triad story begins in 1644, when Tartar tribesmen from Manchuria, the Manchus, swept over the Great Wall and ousted the teetering and corrupt Ming dynasty, founded by the righteous Emperor Hung Wu three centuries earlier. By 1674 the Manchu Qing dynasty had firm control over the northern two-thirds of China, but pockets of rebellion held out in the south. Battling these rebels, the paranoiac Qing court became suspicious of a band of 128 Buddhist monks living in a 1,200-year-old monastery called Shao Lin, in the mountains of Fujian Province. The holy monks of Shao Lin, worshipers of both Buddha and the righteous Kwan Kung, had developed a wondrous fighting art called kung fu, modeled on the leaping grace of fanged mammals and the swooping flight of birds of prey. The emperor became certain that the monks would one day turn against him, and ordered the governor of Fujian Province to wipe them out.

Two difficulties faced the Qing troops assigned the task: the kung fu skills of the monks made open battle with them unwise; and their mountaintop monastery, honeycombed with secret escape routes, excluded the option of simply setting fire to it while the monks slept. These dilemmas were solved when the Qing troops recruited a man whose name endures to this day as the Benedict Arnold of Triad history: a disgraced former monk named Ma Yee-fuk, who betrayed the layout of the monastery. Under cover of night, the Qing troops carried fuel to all of Shao Lin's secret exits, lit bonfires and then set fire to the monastery itself, trapping the innocent monks inside.

One hundred and ten monks burned to death but, through the miraculous intercession of Buddha, a huge yellow curtain fell from the ceiling of the main prayer hall and provided a firewall that saved the remaining 18 monks. Fleeing the destroyed monastery, the 18 monks were able to slip through enemy lines under the cover of drifting smoke and made it as far as Hebei Province, where lack of food and injuries killed 13 of their number. Starving, the five survivors stumbled to the shores of the Long River (Cheung Kong) and were saved when spirits came to them and told them to eat the sand. During their gritty repast, they uncovered a three-legged incense burner, on whose bottom was written: *fan Qing—fuk Ming.* "Overthrow the Qings, Restore the Mings." Within the burner they found a sheet of paper that prophesied that one day this mission would surely be accomplished. Grateful that their lives had been saved by the spirits, the monks held a sacred service, burning twigs as joss sticks and pledging themselves to fulfill the prophesy against the Qings.

Boarding a grass sandal that had magically turned into a boat, the monks crossed the Long River and eventually established a military headquarters in the city of Muk Yeung. There, in an ornate gazebo called the Red Flower Pavilion, they swore a blood-brother oath of loyalty and rededicated themselves to the overthrow of the Qings and the restoration of the Mings, which caused the eastern sky to become suffused in a red glow. This, they realized, was another sign from the gods, and they decided to give their secret society an official name. They chose Hung Mun (Hung Sect), after both the founding Ming emperor, Hung Wu, and the Cantonese homonym for the color red, *hung.* Their god of oaths would be Kwan Kung. Their fighting art, kung fu. Their motto, *fan Qing—fuk Ming.* Their sacred emblem would be a triangular pennant symbolizing the basic forces of the universe—Heaven, Earth, and Man—that divinely backed their mission. The secret society we know today as the Triad syndicate was born, and these five monks eventually became known as the First Five Ancestors.

Because of the brutality and corruption of the Qings, the revolutionary Hung Mun society spread rapidly across China. Five separate headquarters, or "lodges," were eventually established, from which the Hung Mun ran clandestine local governments just beneath the surface of Qing rule. Buddhism, Taoism, ancestor worship, and Sun-Tzu's patient, pliable military tactics became the religion and script of the Hung Mun. Since loyalty was of utmost importance to the society, the Hung Mun evolved ornate initiation ceremonies that replicated both Kwan Kung's blood-brother oath in the peach orchard and the story of the flight of the First Five Ancestors. New recruits were initiated before an altar that bore the words *Sham Tai Wong Fa*—"Extensive Transformation and Uniting with Heaven."

In all, 36 separate oaths were prescribed for initiates, with death by "a myriad of swords" and by "thunderbolts" the penalty for betrayal of the oaths. Hand signals for secret recognition of fellow travelers and their ranks within the organization were developed. Based on Taoist and Triad numerology, these ranks all began with the numeral four—symbolizing the four celestial seas that surrounded the earth—with the sum (or multiplication) of the numbers in each rank referring to historical dates or to lucky letters in Chinese calligraphy. The Shan Chu, or Dragon Head, was designated the 489 leader of a group. The Fu Shan Chu was the 438 Deputy Leader. The next three ranks, of equal importance and thus all bearing the number 438, were: Incense Master (responsible for initiation ceremonies); Vanguard (in charge of recruitment); and Sheung Fa Officials (a congress of advisers who had rendered great service to the society). Next came the 432 Cho Hai, who was the lodge's liaison officer with the other Triad groups and who also oversaw the collection of dues and protection money. A 415 officer, called the Pak Tsz Sin—or White Paper Fan—was a senior adviser noted for his business skills, knowledge of Triad history, and ability to strategize for the achievement of long-term goals. Within this hierarchy, and a coequal of the White Paper Fan, was the commander of a brigade of fighters in charge of enforcement of Triad rule in a district. A gang leader on the order of Steven Wong, he was ruthless in his use of force but also knew how to apply that force at a time and place where it would do the most good. He was the 426 official, or Hung Kwan—the Red Pole.

By 1800, the continuing misrule of the foreign Qing lords and their mandarin civil servants had made the Hung Mun the largest cohesive secret society in China. Millions of dispossessed citizens wandered the countryside, with no hope of bettering their lives, and these students, ex-soldiers, criminals, laborers, farmers, and political radicals swelled the ranks of the Hung Mun into a shadow nation within the nation-state. Yet whenever open rebellions broke out—some Triad-inspired, others led by secret societies independent of the Triads—the Manchus successfully suppressed them. In one campaign during the 1840s they beheaded, buried alive, strangled, and tortured to death more than a million people. In all, over 20 million people died in two decades of continuous civil war.

In 1841, following the age-old pattern of foreign invasion at the height of chaos, the British seized Hong Kong Island, and many Triads fled there, using the colony as a safe haven from the Qings. Six years later, British officials estimated that nearly three-quarters of the population were members of Triad groups, most hiding under the cover of artisan guilds, worker associations, and sports clubs. To raise funds to overthrow the Qings, the Triads in Hong Kong and on the mainland turned to extortion, piracy, and smuggling opium into China. By the late 1800s, illegal activities were the chief source of revenue, and topping the list of enterprises was their trade in opium. For this they could thank England.

To this day, Great Britain still retains the stain (and lives with the consequences) of being the largest opiate-trafficking outfit in history. Opium, smoked in India and the Middle East for thousands of years, was foreign to Chinese culture until the British rammed it down the country's throat during a century and a half of conscienceless imperial capitalism. The roots of this sordid enterprise stretch back to 1757, when the isolationist Qings, seeking to limit the influence of Europeans, decreed that trade with China could only be carried on through the remote port of Guangzhou, and that foreigners could only deal with a merchants' guild called the Co Hong. Trade flourished, with tea, silk, and porcelain being exported in far greater quantity than the European goods being imported. But a balance of trade that favored China was not what British imperialism was supposed to be about. To right the balance, in 1773 British merchants docked about 150,000 pounds of Bengal opium in Guangzhou Harbor and sold it to the Co Hong compradors, who began distributing it throughout the empire. China became intimately familiar with an economic law that governs the trade in addictive drugs, a law that defies the logic of supply and demand. Drugs are perhaps the only commodity where supply continually increases demand. Once introduced into the marketplace, there is always a shortage of drugs. The greater the supply of addictive drugs, the greater the demand. To this day, the theory and rationale of drug interdiction is based upon this counterintuitive law of ever-spiraling demand in the face of ever-increasing supply.

The Qings, obtuse in many other matters, recognized this horrifying principle when they saw the taxes they usually collected being diverted to pay for opium. The disease of drug addiction spread faster than a plague, with ever greater quantities of opium chasing ever greater demand. In 1796, Emperor Dao Gung issued an edict banning the drug trade. The British ignored the edict and kept on selling their Indian cargo to the Co Hong compradors, who passed on a slice of the profits to corrupt Chinese officials. Finally, in 1839 the Chinese tried to enforce their edict against the "foreign mud" by surrounding the British settlement in Guangzhou and cutting off the food supply. The British were forced to surrender almost three million pounds of opium, much of which the Chinese publicly dumped into the Pearl River.

This Oriental version of the Boston Tea Party was the beginning of what became known as the Opium Wars, a series of engagements that lasted off and on for 18 years, with the British fleet bombing Chinese ports at will, sailing up Chinese rivers firing upon towns, and seizing whole cities. In the end, Chinese junks were no match for the world's most powerful navy, and Queen Victoria claimed Hong Kong Island for Britain. With France, Russia and the USA joining the fray (and sharing in the spoils), the British achieved victory in 1859. The Kowloon Peninsula was added to the British colony and a prostrate China was on its way to becoming divided into "spheres of influence" by the Great Powers and, later, by Japan.

In the meantime, the opium trade followed the economic law of the drug trade, exponentially expanding. By 1880, 13 million pounds of opium were being landed annually at Chinese ports, supplying 100 million opium smokers and 15 million addicts. Opium (thanks to Britain) became the largest cash commodity traded in the world. Faced with a draining treasury, the Chinese began to tacitly allow its domestic cultivation in the hills of Yunnan Province, along the border of Laos and Burma. By 1900, domestic production reached 40 million pounds, although the demand was so great that China still continued to import the drug from burgeoning fields just across the Yunnan border in what would later become known as the Golden Triangle. The habit was also exported across the Pacific, carried to North America by the Chinese who emigrated first to the gold fields, then to the railway-construction camps of the Union Pacific and the CPR, and finally to every Chinatown from New York to San Francisco to London. Hong Kong itself became a city where opium was used as commonly as tobacco, and it remained a colony of addicts until the British rulers finally outlawed the drug in 1946.

For their part, the Triads, better organized than most trading companies and working in conjunction with a legion of corrupt officials and local warlords, took control of much of the trade, funneling at least part of the profit to a revolutionary movement that was destined to fulfill the prophecy of the Hung Mun. The movement was led by a distinguished Hung Mun member named Dr. Sun Yat-sen, head of the Kuomintang Party (KMT), who had dedicated his life to wrenching China free of its enslavement to superstition and despotism and establishing the nation as a modern democratic republic on an equal footing with all other nations. On October 10, 1911, the

KMT launched its revolution against the Qings and the 250-year-old dream of the Hung Mun became a reality when the last Qing emperor, Henry Aisin-Gioro Pu Yi, was toppled a few months later. In theory, the overthrow of the Qings and the founding of the Republic of China should have marked the end of Triad secret societies. But, in fact, 1912 marked a new beginning.

Because many KMT generals, officials, civil servants, and rank-and-file soldiers were Triad members, the Triads became an all but officially recognized brotherhood in Mainland China, with an estimated 35 million members. While Dr. Sun remained honest and idealistic until his death in 1925, not so his fellow Triad members. The KMT generalissimo who succeeded Dr. Sun, Chiang Kai-shek, has come to be regarded as one of the most corrupt and brutal national leaders of the 20th century—a gangster in charge of a nation whose everyday affairs were soon essentially run by gangsters. The Triads had helped put the KMT in power, the KMT was in large part ruled by Triad members, and, therefore, any Chinese citizen who wanted to rise in the military, in business, or in politics had to dispense favors to Triad officials. Chiang awarded these modern warlords exclusive control of neighborhoods, cities and sometimes whole provinces, where they were guaranteed immunity from prosecution as they plied their trades in extortion, drugs, and prostitution, sharing their profits with Chiang and his henchmen.

By 1927, the only feasible alternative to the Triad-dominated KMT were the Communists under Mao Tse-tung and Chou En-lai. Through the first two years of Chiang's rule, the KMT and the Communists maintained an uneasy alliance, Sun's Three Principles of "Democracy, Nationalism, and the People's Livelihood" being seen by Mao as stepping-stones to ultimate Marxist liberation. But when masses of people in China's cities began to turn to the Communist-dominated labor unions for redress against sweatshop owners and a KMT establishment that resembled Qing rule, Chiang decided to launch a surprise attack. On April 12, 1927, using the services of Shanghai's "Opium King," a killer named Tu Yueh Sheng who was the leader of a Triad group called the Green Gang, Chiang initiated a reign of terror that began with a massacre of Communists, union leaders, and left-wing sympathizers. So successful was the slaughterous Green Gang, that Tu was appointed a senior adviser to the KMT government, with his followers becoming the KMT's version of the Gestapo—arresting, torturing, and murdering Communists and anyone who criticized the KMT's astoundingly corrupt rule. Even in the face of Japan's invasion and conquest of Manchuria in 1931, Chiang still perceived the Communists as his greatest threat, declaring an all-out war against them in 1934. And, as in millennia past, endless civil war led to foreign invasion of the heart of China.

When Japan launched its attack on China proper in 1937, Chiang and his Kuomintang government reluctantly allied themselves with the hated Communists and halfheartedly fought the invaders. In the conquered districts, however, the last vestiges of Chinese patriotism were thrown to the winds by other Triad gang leaders, who openly collaborated with the Japanese administrators, assisting them in maintaining order and informing on partisans from Guangzhou to Shanghai. After the Japanese attack on Pearl Harbor, it was the Communists who bore the brunt of the fighting in Central China, while the KMT lived off the riches of American aid in Chongqing, their capital in the south, stockpiling weapons for the day when they would fight the Communists again. That day came after the Japanese surrender in 1945, when the Kuomintang and Communists picked up their civil war where they had left off eight years before.

In the south, Chiang assigned the task of fighting the Communists to a brilliant Kuomintang general named Kot Siu-wong, who began working to unite all the disparate Hung Mun gangs into an urban-guerrilla force. Establishing his headquarters in a house at 14 Po Wah Road in Guangzhou, Kot drew 44 separate Triad units under the aegis of what became known as the 14 Association, after the street address. In time, the word "association" was dropped and the letter "K" added, partly because of Kot's first initial and partly because of the letter's use as a designation for 14-karat gold.

The 14K, Steve's solid-gold Triad, was born.

Gangsters may have flocked to the 14K's Triad pennant, but the vast majority of peasant Chinese turned to the Communist red flag to liberate them from KMT criminality. In 1949 the Communists won their final battle against the KMT, and the Triads, their KMT generals, and several million followers fled for their lives, some to Taiwan with Chiang, others to the poppy-growing hills of Thailand, Burma, and Laos, and still others to Hong Kong, where they joined the already flourishing gangs. This influx into the royal colony caused an explosion of Triad activity, as well as serious friction between those mobsters who were already there and those who were just arriving. The British found themselves literally overrun with arch-criminals.

The British had been fighting the Triads almost from the day they had seized Hong Kong Island. The first anti-Triad laws in the colony had been enacted in 1844, but in the century that followed, the police had found it almost impossible to penetrate the guilds and associations that the Triads used for cover. Not only did the local Chinese population detest their racist British masters, but they were quite comfortable with the age-old practice of relying on secret societies to help them avoid the laws that restricted their lives.

By the outbreak of World War II, the Triads' membership and influence among the Chinese population was such that gangs had infiltrated the day-to-day activities of the whole colony, from the docks to the streets to the labor unions. The Japanese occupation actually solidified the Triads' position. In return for providing the Japanese with intelligence information and helping them to keep the population in line, the Triads were given free reign to openly run brothels (much in demand by soldiers) and carry on their other illegal enterprises without interference. More significant to the future of the Triads in Hong Kong, in return for cooperation the Japanese agreed to destroy Hong Kong's police records on the Triads. Investigation reports, lists of names, criminal records, addresses of meeting halls, and photo files went up in flames.

On their return to Hong Kong after the war, the British discovered that their colony had turned into a rat's nest of gang rule. At that point they made a crucial mistake. During the Japanese occupation the local police force had been severely weakened, and in an attempt to quickly rebuild it in the face of the explosion of Triad-run crime, the British launched an indiscriminate recruitment drive that swept into the service hundreds of Triad members, who promptly began corrupting the honest officers within the ranks. Soon the Royal Hong Kong Police became a virtual enforcement arm of the Triads themselves, with otherwise low-paid constables taking bribes and ranking officers running the rackets. The police conducted raids only to keep up appearances, shutting down Triad-run operations that the Triads themselves had decided were expendable.

Then the British made another mistake, as well intentioned as the first. In the aftermath of the Communist victory on the mainland, panicked Nationalists swarmed the borders of the New Territories. On humanitarian grounds, the British accepted 600,000 refugees into Hong Kong, most of whom took up residence in sprawling squatter neighborhoods on Hong Kong Island and in Kowloon. A vast underground economy of street peddling, small shops, restaurants, and factories emerged, virtually controlled by those Triads that had come across the border with the refugees. The Triad groups included thousands of paramilitary-trained 14K, the Green Gang, and Chiu Chow Chinese, an ethnic group from around the city of Shantou, which had been associated with criminal secret societies and smuggling for hundreds of years. Powerful local Triad gangs, including the Wo syndicate and the Sun Yee On, found themselves facing serious competition, and decided to take action. In addition to choppings and murders, the local Triads fought the competition with an interesting tactic: they hired the police to arrest their enemies.

The largest of these local Triads, the Wo group, reached a temporary truce with the 14K, and then targeted the Green Gang, hounding them out of their most lucrative ventures in the slums and eventually driving them out of existence. Meanwhile, as the Green Gang, the Wo group, and the Sun Yee On were at each other's throats, the 14K expanded with relative impunity. Oddly enough, under Kot Siu-wong's rule during this period, the 14K, though thoroughly criminal, remained dedicated to pursuing its war against the Communists in alliance with Chiang's Kuomintang in Taiwan. It retained this goal even after Kot's death in 1953, when its new leaders saw an opportunity to bring all of Hong Kong's criminals under one rule. Within a couple of years they had raised the 14K's membership to 80,000 and transformed it into one of the most aggressive and gratuitously violent criminal syndicates in the world, enforcing its rule through such an ungoverned use of maiming, torture, and murder that even other Triad bosses became fearful of a backlash. The 14K also dug its talons into a new field of enterprise that the Green Gang had brought with them from China: heroin.

This opium-based alkaloid had been discovered at the end of the 19th century and marketed by the German company Bayer as a "heroic" cure for morphine addiction. But heroin was in fact far more addictive than morphine, just as morphine, an opium derivative discovered in 1806, was far more addictive than opium smoking. Realizing the international market potential of the drug—millions of potential addicts living in dozens of countries who would pay billions for heroin—the 14K reached out to their KMT compatriots ensconced in the poppy-growing heaven of the Golden Triangle. The 14K then set up clandestine heroin laboratories in Hong Kong and established regular import runs of raw opium across the South China Sea.

By 1955, with vast profits at stake, the violence between the 14K and its rivals, and against its civilian victims, had become so unrestrained that the chaotic situation in the colony was raised in the British Parliament, and the Hong Kong police were ordered to suppress the group. One raid netted 148 arrests, successful by European standards, but a drop in the bucket considering the city-state size of the 14K. A year later, on October 10, 1956, the 45th anniversary of Sun Yat-sen's revolution, the 14K attempted to take advantage of an anti-British riot in northern Kowloon, with the intent of ousting the colonial government and setting up a Triad state as an extension of the one in power in Taiwan. This was gangster revolution—wildly beyond the pale of daily choppings and murders that Great Britain had been putting up with since the 1840s. The British were outraged. They quickly passed emergency legislation and arrested over 10,000 14K members, deporting 600 of them to Taiwan (where Chiang immediately enrolled them in his new, quasi-official United Bamboo Triad). The British also formed the Triad Societies Bureau, a specialist force designed to root out corruption in the Royal Hong Kong Police as well as to investigate the rituals, history, and current activities of the estimated 300,000-strong Triad force in Hong Kong.

In the end, the crackdown was just a temporary setback for the 14K. By the time Steve was born in 1964, the gang was as powerful as ever, with secret-society lodges in many of the world's great cities.

They were also in control of Steve's future source of income: the Asian heroin trade.

CHAPTER 7

THE EMPEROR OF THE NORTH

———

A man's gonna fuck you over if he can. That's just the way it is.
—STEVEN WONG

As Steve and I drove through Chinatown with the top down in his scarlet upholstered Mercedes, it suddenly hit me that there were at least a dozen gangsters in the immediate vicinity who were trying to kill him. What if Park Lo had got wind of what was up and told his hatchetmen we were on the way to pay him a visit? Those long-coated boys on the corner could be Lotus-gang enforcers. They would be perfectly capable of leaning over and dropping a hand grenade in the front seat with us.

"Hey Steve," I said, "wouldn't it be healthier if you drove something that was less of a bull's-eye?"

Steve pondered my point for a moment, then wheeled into a junkie's alley and hit the brake. "How many license plates can you remember back there?" he asked. I said I hadn't noticed one. "Write these down," he ordered, and listed three plates from memory. Then he burned rubber around the block, came back onto Main Street and double-parked. The license plates he'd dictated were affixed to cars parked ahead of us. He giggled, then punched a code into his cell phone. "Just wait." He sang a few Cantonese words into the phone, then pointed to each of the cars and told me, one by one, who the owner was, his or her age and address, and whether or not they had any driving points.

"Nobody sneaks up on me. Nobody. Hee, hee, hee."

We hauled up on the north edge of Chinatown, a block east of Hastings Billiards and out of sight of its picture window. I remarked to Steve that Park was near the end of his days if he was spending his time in the middle of this 24-hour freak show—Main and Hastings being about as bad as it gets in Canada. "I guess he likes the company," Steve said, and chuckled, looking around at the strung-out junkies, twitching lunatics, and black-and-blue hookers who dominated the corner.

Ahead of us was a beat-up yellow Pinto from which emerged a young man with a punk haircut and bare ankles. He yanked at the crotch seam of his tight jeans, huffed up his big leather jacket and, looking left and right as if staring down the gods that had wrecked his life, embarked on a posturing journey of 20 feet towards us. Coming abreast of Steve's door he whined disgustedly in Cantonese, then spit into a pile of sodden cardboard in the gutter.

"Park took off," Steve translated for me. "They think he's over at the Hoi."

"The Lotus gambling joint?"

"It's not Lotus's, that's everybody's," Steve replied curtly. He got out of the car and raised his chin towards the corner of Gore. Under a jagged neon sign stood three young men, also dressed like hoods from the '50s. They left their posts and strolled over to us. Steve cracked a joke, apparently at my expense because they looked at me and laughed in my face, an unthinkable act if I had been Chinese. Their tubby boss flicked a hand at his Mercedes, whereupon the kid who'd told us about Park hoisted himself over the door, smooth as a gymnast, and swung down under the wheel without his loafers touching the upholstery. He popped the clutch and burned rubber around the corner, a maneuver which puzzled me until Steve strolled after the car, leading the way into the big-money heart of Chinatown.

This was to be a "face walk." If there's one thing that gives you big face in Chinatown, it's impunity: Steve had publicly killed a Lotus two blocks from here, gotten away with it, and now he was parading around with a ghost-person reporter to show he could get away with anything. Certainly everybody on Gore Avenue took notice of our advance, and went out of their way to make obeisances to Steve when his eyes fell upon them. Even as they haggled with customers at their clothing racks, old women in quilted jackets, baggy slacks, and embroidered Chinese slippers nodded beatifically at Steve. A cook in white, dumping a vat of grease into the street, shouted, "Hello Stevie!!" An elderly man in a T-shirt, pulling a cart through the paint-chipped portal to his grocery, raised his hand like he was hailing the mayor. To each of them Steve called a generous greeting in Cantonese. "Nehih ho ma!!" As soon as his gaze moved on, however, all smiles disappeared and eyes narrowed at his back.

"I guess you're the man now," I said.

"Nah, I just help 'em out," Steven offered modestly. "'Cause the cops, they don't even see when the Lotus and Vietnamese are doing their extorting."

Standing idle in a doorway to a seedy appliance shop, a gray-suited man of about 40 raised a hand that cupped a cigarette. Steve casually inspected the surrounding corners and walked up to him. They talked seriously for a minute, then both looked at me and laughed—again, motive for murder if I had been Chinese. I had to forcibly remind myself that all behavior is tactical, all form is strategy. I was winning, Steve had already lost.

He finished his conference with the man and came back to us, leading our formation onto bustling Pender, clearing the sidewalk like a v-plow. "You know, Park's kind've on my own time, my boss just wants me to find Phu," I confided to Steve as if he were my sympathetic coproducer. I looked at the members of Steve's crew and raised my eyebrows hopefully. "Any one of your guys would be okay, actually. He just wants a Gum Wah to explain things."

"Nah, they won't say nothin' for ya—I know that. But don't worry, I'll get together with your boss and tell him how we want it done. Then Phu'll know it's settled." Steve stopped beneath the orange awning to a herb shop, punched some numbers on his cell, waited, then left a stern message in Cantonese. "Okay, right now Phu's avoiding me," Steve confessed when he got off, sinking my heart. "But he'll do it. 'Cause once he said yes to you, he knows that's my face." He handed me the cell and told me to call Paperny and arrange a meeting next week at Tsunami Sushi on Robson Street. "We treat people right, then they treat us right. That's our deal."

"That's our deal," I said.

Five minutes into our zigzag march though the ghetto, a few doors south of the corner of Main and Pender, I heard the distinctive sound of big-stakes gambling, a furious clacking that resembles marbles raining on Formica—pai gow dominoes being dealt in the Hoi Ming Gwok one floor up. Steve and his boys turned into the black lacquered doorway and I followed them up the creaky steps to a ticket booth, above which was a sign that read, in Chinese and English, "Members Only." An old fellow in the booth waved us into the gambling parlor, a dingy room dominated by green felt tables and a big altar to Kwan Kung on the smoke cured wall. All four tables were in play, with 20 hands moving fast beneath the fluorescent lights. None of the hands belonged to Park. "Probably OD'd on the way here," Steve harrumphed, obviously embarrassed by the failure of his spy corps— a dangerous lapse in his business. Smiling obsequiously, the booth attendant padded by us in house slippers and knocked at an office door beside the cashier's pen. Meanwhile the gamblers either ignored Steve or acknowledged him with only slightly raised chins, their expressionless eyes impolitely studying my face. The house crowd ranged from rough-looking hoods in their teens to late-middle-aged burghers in suits. Three sportily attired couples in their late 20s sat at a table beneath Kwan Kung playing fan-tan. They looked like Hong Kong tourists, and probably were.

Finally, a genial fellow came out of the office smiling—Sloppy Jang. I recognized him from a previous visit I'd made here in the company of a New York cop during the Asian-crime conference. Sloppy lost his smile as our eyes met. Steve walked up to him, put his arm around the old fellow and turned him aside, probing, I assumed, for Park's whereabouts. While they talked I assessed the lighting in the room—it seemed adequate for the camera I'd booked to barge in next week. Not that I expected any dramatic raids to follow the exposé. Illegal gambling was so ubiquitous in Chinatown, and so much a part of its culture, that the police had all but given up busting the "entertainment societies" that ran the tables.

"You ever play?" Steve asked, coming to my side.

"I can't afford more than fifty," I told him, reaching for my wallet.

He shoved my arm aside. "Your money's no good here." He sat down on a stool between an old gent with bushy brows that hung over his eyes and a teen with a couple of vicious scars thick as fingers on his cheek. One of Steve's servants came back with a tray of 50- and 100-dollar chips. Steve set aside a few hundred for my nut. "I'll bet for you," Steve said. "You win, you win; you lose, I lose."

The dealer mixed the 32 dominoes flat on the table with crisscrossing hands, then stacked them quickly into a black brick of eight rows. Everybody anted up a hundred and was slid four of the laquered tiles. The players took a quick peek and threw in another hundred in chips. The old fellow with the grotesque brows then rattled around three dice in a tin cup and slammed it, open end down, on the table. Steve bumped the table a hundred, everybody flipped over their dominoes, and the guy with the brows scooped up $900. The hand had taken 30 seconds.

We were playing a sudden-death version of pai gow, with the dice determining wild-card value to certain pairs. There are dozens of versions of the game, with point and pairing combinations so complicated that unless you grew up playing it you could never become a master. I knew its rudiments, partly from watching it being played up and down the West Coast and partly from reading a report prepared by the Smithsonian Institute back in 1893, at the height of what was known as the Tong Wars. The U.S. government had funded the study so that law enforcement could understand what was taking place behind the locked doors of the gambling dens, the control of which was being bloodily fought over by armies of tong hatchetmen in New York and San Francisco.

Pai gow was reputedly invented by Kwan Kung or one of his two blood brothers to keep their soldiers awake during night watches, and many of its longer versions replicated the trio's waxing and waning fortunes in war. It was also a kind of game poem reflecting Chinese religious and political symbology. The number of spots on the dominoes and their red and white colors were divided into basic sets of pairs, the *man* or "civil" series, and the *mo* or "military" series, with the civil, in accordance with Confucian doctrine, valued higher than the military. The three highest-ranking pairs of the civil series were called, not surprisingly, Heaven, Earth, and Man—*t'in, ti,* and *yan.*

Pai gow was dominant in most Chinese gambling parlors, but the far simpler fan-tan was a close second, as it was in the Hoi Ming. It was played with a random amount of buttons poured into a bowl by the house and then withdrawn in batches of four. After each withdrawal players bet on the number of buttons they guessed would be left at the last draw—none, one, two, or three. The stakes were the same as pai gow and a player could win or lose a fortune in no time.

If only gangsters gambled at these games the drain on the community would have been less severe, but the Hoi Ming and places like it were patronized as much by the poor, the middle class, and the legitimately wealthy as by gang members. Vancouver's pai gow parlors ran 16 to 24 hours a day, seven days a week, and new haunts were now blooming in Chinatown's suburban annex, Richmond. People sometimes dropped $100,000 at the tables, loans were arranged by gang members at 70 percent a month, and poor men promised to pay off debts by working three jobs—or, as Steve and I had discussed, traveling to Asia and returning with paintings.*

I'd heard varied explanations offered as the cause of the Chinese passion for gambling. One, alluded to by Frank Chin in his explanation of the massacre at the Wah Mee gambling parlor, linked the national pastime to the unending wars the Chinese had endured over their 3,500-year history. In war, luck (or *joss*) counted almost as much as prowess, and the Chinese

---

*The illegal gambling in Chinatown was in addition to the legal wagering that took place in the government-run Gateway Casino, just half a block from the Hoi Ming. In 1990, receipts at the Gateway were higher than for any other casino in the city, even though Chinatown stood in the middle of Canada's poorest neighborhood. And what went on in Vancouver went on in most other Chinatowns. In 1992, journalist Gwen Kinkaid reported in *Chinatown: Portrait of a Closed Society* that New York City cops estimated some illegal Chinese casinos took in a million dollars a week each in profits, with hundreds of thousands of dollars on the tables at any one time. Meanwhile, the legal off-track betting outlet in Chatham Square, the heart of New York's Chinatown, was the top revenue producer of the city's 96 outlets—a position it had held for nine years running. "No matter where they go, Chinese gamble," Justin Yu, the onetime head of Chinatown's journalists' union, told Kinkaid.

came to worship *joss* as an immanent force in the universe, an intervening god who serendipitously meddled in life's affairs. Luck determined whether one lived or died in battle, whether one was born to a rich household or a poor one, whether a person lived under the thumb of a warlord who ignored the law, or a rare leader who administered it. Ultimately, the Chinese came to believe in luck as much as in hard work; ergo, their reverence for the god of luck, war, and gambling—the ubiquitous Kwan Kung. In a way, gambling was the invisible will of God made visible, and thus Chinatown's gambling parlors were like dark shrines where people prayed as fervently as they did in Buddhist temples.

Steve stood up from the table. He'd lost about three grand in five minutes, and it didn't faze him at all. "Ah, sometimes it goes like that," he said, and laughed.

"So who runs the Hoi Ming if not the Lotus?" I asked as we walked down the stairs.

"Nobody. Sloppy runs it."

"Yeah, but come on, Steve." I slapped his shoulder. "Some gang's gotta be in charge of helping out the losers."

"Well, the Lotus thought this was theirs until that stuff at the Goldstone. But we don't run anything. You go in, people know you, that's all. They get down in the dumps, they know who to talk to."

"So you give them loans?"

"Not me. I don't do nothing like that. But yeah, I know for sure some people take advantage of that. It's too bad," he said, walking to his waiting car on the curb. "If they were smart they'd never go into them places. Sometimes it's even worse for 'em if they win—then they get extorted by the Lotus. The guys that do that are scumbags. But the way they look at it, it's just statistics. Half the people's below average, okay? So if you can't take advantage of that you must be one of 'em. Hee, hee, hee."

Back in the car, Steve checked his pager. "Ah, I gotta take some guys to the airport," he said. "But you come around the pool hall anytime. Between friends, eh? No cameras there. You just tell this stuff about the Lotus and leave me out of it."

I toyed with the idea of placing a camera on a roof across Robson Street for the Tsunami Sushi summit, but David Paperny didn't seem to relish being filmed while Steve and I shucked and jived like gangster buddies. Indeed, in one of our conferences in the CBC line-up room he warned me about crossing a line that I would find it hard to recross when all this blew up in Steve's face—an ethical concern that irritated me. In theory, the only reason I was swerving all over that line was to fit the final piece into the project and put a stop to Steve's rising arc. This was war, and in war all arts are martial.

Of course, I was also having a thrill-seeker's ball on my tour of Lotus-run places the police hadn't yet learned about. There was a luxury massage parlor called the Coin Cache, which had just opened a mere two blocks from City Hall, employing women smuggled from Southeast Asia. They worked a week or so in Vancouver entertaining Chinese businessmen and then were shipped on to New York or Houston. There was a tony karaoke club called The Scene, down by the docks on Powell Street, with private rooms above the stage that rented for $1,000 a night; it was frequented by the Hong Kong entertainers brought over by the Lotus as well as by up-and-comers in gangs like the Big Circle Boys. Steve urged me to pass these locations on to the police—which I did without hesitation. In return I was rewarded with information about some parts of Steve's life that I hadn't remotely suspected.

He was atypical for a Chinese mobster in that he did business with select white heroin traffickers, who themselves were anomalous in that they hung around almost exclusively with Asian mobsters. There was Chuck Gough, a heavyset middle-aged heroin dealer who spoke fluent Cantonese, wrote Chinese flawlessly, and was a frequent flyer to Hong Kong, along with Chuck's compadre, a lean career criminal named James Patrick Newson— called "Sonny" by the Chinese, apparently because his temper (when he lost it) reminded them of the psycho killer Son of Sam. Sonny's reach extended to the Philippines, where a coup-plagued government, ubiquitous corruption, and guerrilla wars created abundant opportunities for drug traffickers.

And then there was Steve's amazingly busy sex life. His cell phone tweeted hourly with calls from the boudoirs of a legion of female admirers. Ignoring his physical package, women seemed to find his pheromones so irresistible that they gladly threw themselves into his crowded stable of mistresses. His number one girlfriend for years was the beautiful Laura, an operator in Vancouver's white-hot real estate market. Another, Patsy Chan, was married to the multimillionaire owner of Kouzins Security, the protector of 14K drug bosses on their visits to town. Lily Lee lived in Calgary and occasionally flew in to see Steve under the noses of the other two. A fourth, Suzie, also married and in her 40s, every so often made the trip to Vancouver from New York, although she was in the jade trade and perhaps had other business in town besides sex with Steve.

The pleasure I took in hanging out with Steve is hard to excuse, especially since I knew all along the suffering he was causing. A couple of days after my sojourn at the Hoi Ming, David Paperny and I interviewed a couple named Keith and Louisa Surges, whose adopted son, Joey, became thoroughly corrupted by the Gum Wah's machinations at 12 years old. They told their story sitting in front of a picture of Joey, whom they had brought over from Macau after Joey's father had murdered his mother. The couple enrolled Joey in an ESL program, hired a tutor, got him involved in soccer and basketball, and set him up with a paper route. The boy might have recovered from his trauma had not Steve's recruiters sniffed out his insecurity and begun to circle. Soon Joey was arrested for setting fire to a Lotus vehicle, then for shoplifting scams that also involved arson, and, as he turned 13, for street fights with Los Diablos. When his adopted parents tried to ground him, they received calls from little gangsters who threatened swords and lightning upon the household. When they begged Joey to tell his friends to stop calling, he gave them a gangster look that froze their blood. In 18 months Joey changed from a little boy to a hard-core teenage criminal. The couple became terrified for the safety of their two other children and in February 1989 they went to the Department of Immigration and filled out the papers to have him sent back to Macau.

And yet, cruising with Steve, I kept catching glimpses of a precriminal persona inside the Triad braggart who ripped off drug shipments, shot a partner in cold blood, corrupted scores of youths, and informed on compatriots. Steve was violent but not sadistic; calculating and brutal, but not gratuitously cruel. Hadn't he said that he let Jimmy Wu go because he was just "a small kid" and there was "no use beating the shit out of him"? The schoolteacher in me really believed that behind every young gangster—even one who ate up and spit out 13-year-olds—lay a history that made his criminal actions comprehensible, if not forgivable.

A psychoanalyst would no doubt tell me that I saw myself in Steve, that I was trying to kill him and love him at the same time. Or that the vicarious thrill I was getting from riding shotgun with the chief was a substitute for what I might have experienced if 25 percent of my genes had had their way. It's not inconceivable that I could have raced off down Steve's criminal road under other circumstances—if, say, I were not a smart white kid in a high school where minority fellows, pulling the kind of stunts I pulled, were regularly shunted off to criminal court and then jailed. I might have ended up there anyway. Perhaps my parents had their own *mishegoss*—Yiddish for individual craziness—but they were basically good people who were vastly relieved when I wound up merely being a misfit who took off for northern B.C. rather than a miscreant who joined the boys at Hymie's.

The turning point came for me at 18, when my folks sent me to a psychologist to talk things through. After a year of therapy, we worked out a plausible diagnosis: I was an active personality who became easily bored and then became depressed; in order to relieve the depression I became more active, taking risks whose consequences made me feel even worse. Once I recognized I was just trying to get away from depression, I consciously set about taking my mind off my feelings in an orderly way.

I have since learned that newsrooms and Formula One racetracks are full of type-A depressives who distract themselves from their unexplained blues in an orderly, if hyperactive, way. Prisons, on the other hand, are filled with type-A depressives who work things out in a very *dis*orderly way. Most of them have lived through episodes of traumatic abuse that so compounded their initial condition that by their mid-teens their ups and downs went off the chart, top and bottom. Usually they fell in with other type-A depressives and entered the reinforcing subculture of a gang. By the time they turned 18 their hyperactive criminal pattern was set.

Steve fit the pattern. Day in and day out he never rested because to rest meant, I surmised, to dive into the depression borne of the traumas he began telling me he'd experienced in New York's Chinatown.

Interpol lists Steve's place of birth as Hong Kong Island, but as a toddler he lived across the water in the heart of 14K territory—a rabbit-warren apartment block in Mongkok, at the north end of Kowloon Peninsula, near where the 1956 riots had occurred. Back in the mid-'60s, when Steve took his first steps, Mongkok was among the most densely populated areas of Hong Kong, its sun-starved, garbage-strewn streets walled in by shabby, mildew-stained concrete buildings. His mother and father, Yue Kim and Cheung Ing, ran a handbag stall on what was then colloquially known as "Women's Street," part of the cacophonous Tung Choi open-air market, which sold household wares and women's clothing. Steve lived above the market's noise and filth, just east of Nathan Road, in a two-room apartment with his parents and three older brothers. A couple of blocks west of Nathan Road was another kind of filth—the brothel capital of Hong Kong, run by the 14K, which enslaved young women to work its whorehouse cubicles.

Many poor Cantonese parents working 16-hour days send their children away to live with relatives. Years before Steve was born his parents had sent their eldest child, a daughter, to live in New York's Chinatown with godparents who had just emigrated there. When Yue and Cheung immigrated to Vancouver in 1968, they promptly sent their four boys to New York as well. By then Steve's older sister had married the owner of a bean sprout factory on Pell Street, and Steve, Donald, Robert, and Stanley were put to work in her husband's cellar. Except for brief stays in Jamaica, Queens, when his mother came to visit, the bean sprout sweatshop was where Steve worked from the time he was four until he was 11, living in appalling neglect in a roach and rat infested back room, working long hours before and after school, thinning and boxing sprouts and suffering harsh discipline at the hand of his overseeing brother-in-law.

As in Hong Kong, most businesses paid two sets of taxes: one to the government and one to the criminals. Around Pell Street, the collection of these taxes was the responsibility of the Hip Sing tong's army of enforcers, the Flying Dragons. Tax collection was done in the wide open. The smartly dressed young extortionists would visit the sweatshop once a week and were treated with fawning respect by Steve's brother-in-law. Regally they would drift in, take their red envelopes, and drift out, driving away in sleek cars with beautiful girls at their sides. To Steve in his Dickensian surroundings, the glamorous young men seemed to float above life, offering a promise of an easy existence that was as devoid of consequences as it was of loneliness and boredom.

When Steve was a child, the half-square-mile of Chinatown between Canal Street and Chatham Square was divided between three tongs. The Hip Sing ruled Pell, the On Leung and their Ghost Shadow gang ruled Mott Street, and the Tung On ruled Division Street, with soldiers composed mostly of Sun Yee On Triad members from Hong Kong. The modern gangs who enforced tong rule were not very different from the earlier gangs of hatchetmen who had made Chinatown into the murder capital of early-20th-century America. And the tongs were exactly as they had been 80 years ago, when they fought pitched battles in the streets over their block-sized empires of gambling, opium, and slave girls. Still xenophobic, feudal, and criminal beneath their old image of "benevolence," they initiated new members in a ceremony that included 36 oaths sworn before Kwan Kung, a bowing to the gods of hell, and a promise of death by a myriad of swords as the penalty for betrayal.

I used to drive my cab through Chinatown every shift in those days and, for all I know, I could have seen the little Stevie Wong in the seedy-looking, dangerous neighborhood. The open Tong Wars may have ended in the 1930s, but, unfortunately for Steve, and unbeknownst to me and most New Yorkers, Chinatown was then going through a transition that was ushering in a new era of violence. Liberal immigration laws, passed in 1965, had swollen Chinatown with a whole new generation of gamblers and entrepreneurs, and the tongs had started hiring and organizing the youth gangs flourishing in the alleys. By the early '70s the Hip Sing's Flying Dragons of Pell Street and the On Leung's Ghost Shadows of Mott Street were at war. God help one or another gang member caught alone on the enemy's street. Guns were everywhere, and reinforcements were always within earshot. A

Ghost Shadow shot down by a Flying Dragon on a disputed corner would cause friends of both victim and assailant to swarm to the spot and open up at each other from behind cars, with shop windows shattering and pedestrians running for cover.

The "godfather of Chinatown" during the last year Steve lived full-time in New York was Benny Ong, known as "Uncle Seven" because he was his parents' seventh child. Ong, who had spent 17 years in jail for second-degree murder, succeeded his brother as "adviser for life" of the Hip Sing in 1974. When Ong gave up his post by dying in 1995, at 86, the funeral went on for three days, supplying the FBI with an opportunity to take surveillance photos of the Chinese gangsters who had come to pay their respects, many of whom stood in a line during the service, their fingers held high in ritual poses that signified their rank in the tong.

The funeral-goers were among the wealthiest Chinese businessmen in the city, their incomes deriving from both legitimate and illegitimate ventures, including real estate and gambling, banking and extortion, import firms and prostitution, textiles and people smuggling, and of course, heroin. During Steve's years in New York, the heroin trade began to pass from the purview of the Italian Mafia to the Chinese mafia, the war in Southeast Asia being the catalyst. With CIA help, pro-American Vietnamese and Laotian warlords funded their armies (and their extravagant lifestyles) by establishing a network that started in the KMT-dominated poppy fields and laboratories of the Golden Triangle and ended in cities like Los Angeles, Chicago, and New York, with New York being the largest market for the drug. Between 1971 and 1974, Chinese heroin increased from 8 percent of the U.S. market to over 30 percent, with Vancouver one of North America's main ports of entry. By 1990, China white had risen to 50 percent of the total.

"I seen lots of gang stuff when I was in New York," Steve told me in Fraser Billiards while we rested between games over cups of gunpowder tea and mandarin oranges wrapped in red netting. "That was the first time I ever saw a bulletproof vest. They was wearing it right in the streets. They had every kind of gun."

Steve took a Swiss Army knife out of his pocket, gathered the discarded netting from our oranges and began cutting the diamonds up into little pieces. "You gotta do this," he informed me. "Otherwise the birds in the dump stick their heads in and get stuck and strangle. Or if it gets in the water, the fish get caught."

"I didn't know you were an environmentalist, Steve."

"Yeah, because I like birds and fish. I tell that to all my guys."

I laughed so hard orange spittle hit my knees. "This is great, Steve! Gum Wah's a green gang!"

He didn't crack a smile.

"What else they been telling you about me?" Steve asked, meaning the cops.

I was tempted to tell him that a word frequently used to describe him was "asshole"—cop slang for a violent criminal with no ethics, not even the criminal kind. "When they talk about you they use that expression 'Man of Honor,'" I lied. "But that's a Mafia term, not a Chinese term. What do the Chinese call it?"

"*Yo mien tzu.* Means big face. Same thing. Respect."

"So did you first get your face from joining the Flying Dragons?" I asked.

"Well, I got in trouble there, yeah. But I'm only eleven when I come back here, right? What am I gonna be doing joining a New York gang? But Chinatown's so small, eh? Everybody knows everything. But nobody *sees* anything. That's how the gangs operate."

"So what are you saying? You just ran errands for the Dragons?"

"Do you know Hip Sing headquarters?" Steve was addressing my question obliquely, referring to the old brick building on the corner of Doyers, with its bright green fire escape and the green and gold sign out front. I told him I had driven my taxi by that place every Saturday and hadn't a clue what was going on inside.

"Okay, well, the place my brother-in-law owned, Hip Sing was maybe a block away from it. You maybe didn't know what was going on inside, but everybody in Chinatown did."

"Including the heroin?"

"They wouldn't think nothing about it if they did, because Chinese people over here, they don't use heroin. How many Chinese heroin addicts you know? Very few. The junkies in New York is the spics, the coloreds, and the white people."

"So the big Chinese drug dealers don't worry about bringing the stuff over because their own people don't use it?"

"That could be one reason, eh? It's just something that the spics and the coloreds want to buy, so why not sell it to 'em? If their own kids were shooting up they wouldn't sell it, because Chinese is always big on families. But if they can make some money off what the whites wanna do and the spics and niggers— If they wanna do it, they're gonna do it anyway, so give it to them. You got your friends in the Lotus'll tell you that, too, eh?"

He smiled at me crookedly, pocketing his knife and the snipped-up netting. He raised his eyebrows, expecting a response.

"My friends? You mean Goathead and those guys?"

"Whoever you know that's Lotus that I heard," he said, inclining his head to the boys playing pool.

"I don't know about the Lotus being my friends, Steve, I advised him. "They're kids, I'm forty. Anyway, I don't play favorites with the gangs, if that's what you mean. Yeah, I listen to all sides, you, the cops, the Lotus—"

"The Lotus got no side," he insisted. "*They* started all this, they pulled the guns and set fire to my guy's house. If one of my guys is gonna talk to you, I don't wanna see one of their guys fucking lying on television. That's understood."

The memories of New York seemed to have excited his mean *mishegoss*. I decided to distract him with a couple of gossipy tidbits. The Triad bosses Steve protected often went dancing at a high-class nightclub on Pender Street called Ming's. The daughter of the owner was hooked up with a police officer we both knew. It meant nothing, but it was the kind of intelligence Steve relished. I also told him that the drug dealer David Lim had recently been roughed up by a couple of plainclothes officers during an arrest. Lim deserved it—there were witnesses who said he'd tried to pin one of the cop's heads in a wrestling hold—but I didn't tell Steve that part. After I gave him these morsels, I asked, *quid pro quo*, why he'd aligned himself with the 14K. When all he did was shrug and grunt, I said, "You can't let anybody know what I just told you. I'm trusting you on it."

Steve sipped his tea and then looked down at the swirling green liquid. "Where I'm from, it's 14K," he said softly. "I told you that, eh? Some groups is bigger, but they got the power."

"Because they run the heroin trade."

"Not just the heroin—everything. They got so many guys at the airports and this and this. Everybody'll tell you that. Anybody wants to do anything—I don't care if it's Wah Ching or whoever—they may tell you different, but they gotta deal with them. Who do you think they're gonna go to?"

"So do they come to you as a connection? Are you the guy who puts them in touch—the officer who makes the business arrangements?"

"You know what the cops don't understand?" he asked, avoiding a direct answer. "The cops got surveillance to see who's big-time in the gang—they think it's like the movies where everybody comes up and kisses his fucking ass. But you go to Ming's—the big man, he's the one goes around giving everybody a big hug. If I'm a nobody and I come up and give you a hug, you're gonna punch me down. But if I'm a big guy, I'll hug anybody I want. They gotta lose face and take it because I can do anything I want."

"Okay, so if you're the businessman," I said, addressing something that had been on my mind for a while, "if you're that guy who's giving everybody the hugs, how come you're the guy doing all the fighting? How come you street-fight like a 49, Steve, if you're this sophisticated businessman in town here?"

"See, that's what you think from reading the book or talking to cops," he replied, hitting his hand against my briefcase, which still held Morgan's *Triad Societies in Hong Kong*. "Every man stands up for himself!" he enunciated, startling me by thumping my sternum with his forefinger. "Whatever you are, unless you stand up for yourself nobody's gonna do business with you. The real fucking businessman, he's the one everybody's afraid of because they know him, okay? That's why I got to where I'm at."

"Which is what?" I asked quietly.

"It's not like what you think. Here I'm the head of our own group."

"Yeah, I know that, the *dai lo*."

"We don't use that—that's the word the cops use."

"So what do you use? Dragon Head?"

"Chinese, we say Shan Chu. Over here, that's what they call me because they know I'm over in Asia all the time. It's like, maybe you're one thing there, but when you're on your own boat, you're captain, eh? Hong Kong I'm something else, because so many guys is higher, eh? So when they come over, I'm here to protect them, make sure nobody interferes with what they want done. And if some scumbag gets in the way, too bad."

"You're their Red Pole enforcer."

He shied away from a direct reponse again. "You can do two things," he said. "You can be one thing when no one else is around to do it. You can tell 'em what's what, which group is which and this and this. You know who does that, don't you? The adviser."

"The White Paper Fan."

"What we say here is Rashu, or Pak Tzs Sin is what they say in Hong Kong. I told you that."

Those were the words he'd used during our first conversation in his house. I hadn't understood what he'd meant then, but I'd been doing my homework in Morgan. Pak Tzs Sin was Cantonese for White Paper Fan.

"Is that your rank, or just where you got your nickname?" I asked, because when we'd first walked in one of his oldest boys had called out through the window of a car: "Tzs Sin!" Steve had turned around, then gone back to the street to talk with him.

"That's what a few guys call me," Steve replied to my question. "All I'm gonna say is I got the rights to say, 'I don't care what you heard, that guy's a scumbag.' And I don't have to worry about the scumbag coming to blow my fucking head off, because I got the rights to say that, eh? That's what I'm supposed to do. That's why I come up through the ranks, to do that, so when they come over here, they're not blind. They don't care if him and me hate each other's face. If the guy's gonna help, they wanna know, and I gotta say so."

"You're their impartial adviser."

"I just do what keeps 'em from making any mistakes when they come over. Tell 'em what's what and protect them. That's what I do on this end. I don't even care if you tell the cops that. Fuck, they already know it."

At one of the tables somebody made the break with a particularly loud crack. I stood up, thinking, Whether you're a Red Pole or the youngest White Paper Fan in the 14K, or both, Steve, the cops know some of it, but not all of it.

CHAPTER 8

SHOWTIME

———

Inside Vancouver's Chinese organized crime! Tonight! An exclusive interview with one of the leaders of Vancouver's Asian gangs and his enforcer! Tomorrow! The link to the largest organized crime network in the world: the Chinese Triads!
—PROMO FOR *THE CBC EVENING NEWS,* MARCH 12, 1990

Tsunami Sushi was a kinky kind of place, known for its little Japanese fishing boats that circled the middle of the restaurant as a floating buffet. Patrons, mostly upscale Asian tourists and gang kids, hovered like herons on the shore, spearing their servings and then paying for their choices at the register. Of course, Steve and I weren't required to work for our salmon rolls, in any sense of the word. The fellow at the door greeted the Paper Fan with ecstatic servility—"Ah-so-nice-to-see-you-again-Mr.-Wong!"—and ushered us to a table overlooking fashionable Robson Street. Within seconds a carafe of sake and two boats of fish were set before us. The only element missing at our perfect repast was David Paperny.

"I wonder where he is," I said, 15 minutes later, scanning the street below. "Sorry about this, Steve."

"Ah, don't worry about it," Steve comforted me. "I bet he figures, he's late, you lose face with me." He gave me a strangely Yiddish shrug, raising one hand and pursing his lips. "Then he moves in where you're at, eh?"

He meant I had attained a position worth stealing, although in his mind my good fortune probably had less to do with journalistic access than with being on the verge of moving from gang-observer to gang-player, and then—who knows—heroin honcho. Surely Paperny would scheme to elbow me out of that lucrative spot.

"You figure that's what he's up to?" I asked. "I don't think he's that cold-blooded, Steve. He's a nice guy—"

Steve snickered and quoted a saying that had been used in Chinatown since gold-field days to describe white men: "Warm on the outside, cold on the inside. How long he's making you drag your ass to talk to Phu? Now we're gonna settle it, so where is he? Doesn't that tell you something?"

I reached for Steve's cell phone, but the gangster put his hand on it. "You don't wanna let him know this is costing you face. How much he's paying you anyway?"

I told him the pathetic amount—$1,200 for the project—although I was "in discussion" with the newsroom's *dai lo*, Sue Rideout, to double it.

"You're in the wrong racket," Steve advised. "I pay that to my guys for one trip to the fucking airport and back."

Five minutes later, in the midst of describing his latest first-class flight to Hong Kong, Steve focused his eyes past my head. "Don't turn around. Let the cheap prick know you don't give a fuck."

"Sorry I'm late, gentlemen," David said, pulling back a chair. "I got held up in the editing room. Nice place here, Steve, very nice. Interesting," he added, noticing the stream of floating sushi.

"Yeah, the boys like it," I said, cool as Steve.

David shot a glance at me, his perpetually inquiring eyes a bit more blue than usual. I casually surveyed the crowd. "Phu's a go," I added, to no one in particular. "We'll need a camera Wednesday at two."

"Phu at two," Dave rhymed dryly, noting the day and time.

"Long as you don't show who he is," Steve stipulated.

"Yeah, I want him in the shadows," I insisted to Dave.

"And Phu wants *me* there, that's the deal," Steve said. "Then he'll tell ya what the Lotus been up to with our guys. When's this thing gonna be on anyway?"

Paperny steepled his fingers. We hadn't worked out whether we were going to give Steve a heads-up or not. "Two weeks maybe?" he asked me, as if I knew. "Hard to say—could be three. We still have a couple of shoots."

This puzzled Steve. "Who else besides Phu?" he pointedly asked me.

I removed my eyes from Paperny's long face and put them on Steve's round one.

"Ah, you know, no Lotus are in it. Your side against Bill Chu's and them guys."

The Coordinated Law Enforcement Unit (CLEU) where Bill Chu worked was housed in a huge, utterly bland building, designed to be as anonymous as a tax department office. Even veteran waitresses at the Anza Club across the street didn't know they worked beside the nexus of the fight against organized crime.* So secret were the doings inside the block-long edifice that when we pulled up in a van and tried to film an establishing shot, two plainclothes Mounties came running out and told us to put the camera away or the interview was off. Ironically, while the public was forbidden to know the location of CLEU, a Polaroid picture of the concrete building was thumbtacked over the urinals in Fraser Billiards, with a Chiquita Banana sticker pasted to its corner and an arrow pointing to a mirrored window marked with a bull's-eye. "Banana" was an epithet that Hong Kong Chinese like Steve employed to refer to Canadian-born Chinese like Chu—who were supposedly yellow on the outside but white on the inside.

Chu obligingly gave us a mug shot of his detested cousin. We filmed it, then chitchatted in a conference room while John Collins arranged flattering blue lighting behind the gangbuster. John did such a good job that even my mother—whose tastes in men tended towards Humphrey Bogart—exclaimed when she saw the show: "Oh! what a handsome man that officer is! Whereas you—whatsamatta—you weren't sleeping then or what? Couldn't they use makeup? I could see every line in your face."

My opening question was simple. "Who is Steven Wong?"

"Steven Lik Man Wong is basically a typical gang member who has progressed into Asian organized crime," Chu told the town. "He was a Red Eagles member at thirteen years old and he worked his way up in violent confrontations with rival gangs. He went from street enforcer to the position where he is at now, leader of the Gum Wah.

"Now," Chu went on, tilting his talking head in a different direction, "Steven has another side to him, where he has connections to the Far East and is involved in various other crimes at a higher level. The heroin trade is a safe area to say he is involved in and he openly admits it. So I would say he's dealing on two levels. Internationally he has a longtime commitment to Asian organized crime groups to ply his trade of drug importation. Whereas on the street he is a violent gang leader, the one who has drawn our attention and is certainly a thorn in our side."

"Is it a mark of his intelligence that he hasn't been caught yet?" I asked.

"No," Chu replied curtly. "Steven's been lucky. He was indicted on a heroin conspiracy charge about a year and a half ago and, for one reason or another, his charges were stayed. But he may be here today and may be gone tomorrow. He himself knows he's treading on thin ice, and the violent

---

* In the late 1990s, CLEU was reorganized as the Organized Crime Agency.

confrontations between the Lotus and Gum Wah illustrate that he is not untouchable."

"When you say Steven may be gone tomorrow, do you mean dead tomorrow?" I asked.

"In a very basic way, yes."

He also had a swollen Achilles' heel—as I'd discovered—and Chu threw a stone of sarcasm at it. "If you or I were dealing with the heroin trade, we wouldn't want to bring attention to ourselves. Whereas Steven, he's a different piece of cake altogether. His ego grows as far as being recognized. Steven, with the profile of his personality, likes to be in the forefront and never forgotten. That's why he's chosen to be the Gum Wah leader, which in the opinion of our section is a violent Asian street gang that serves his wishes."

That night, across the pool table at Fraser Billiards, one of Steve's most violent gang servants contemplated me with mean eyes. Shooting a game with a Gum Wah gangster about Steve's age, Phu had a black zoot-suit coat slung across his arm like a bullfighter's cape, one pocket of which was heavier than the other. With every missed carom he glared at me as if it were my fault, then adjusted the coat.

I'd shown up to pre-interview Phu, although just now I wished I were doing it elsewhere and in the daylight. As I had walked in Steve my protector had walked out, hand in hand with his girlfriend Laura. That was when Phu had crossed the room in my direction and pointedly thrown his coat over his arm, as if he suspected I would snoop through it when his back was turned—a not entirely outlandish thought. A couple of years ago he'd been one of the main gunners in the Woodland Drive shoot-out. I wondered what caliber he was packing now.

"Laura's some chickie doll," I said to Phu, trying the colloquial approach. "You kinda wonder—"

"Fuckin' *what?*" he asked, and I thought, never mind the pocket, watch the cue.

His pool partner, resting his palms on his cue tip, regarded us without expression. At the surrounding tables, half a dozen other Gum Wah I'd never met also looked on with flat faces. One of them, chalking his tip, said something to Phu in a singsong dialect. Phu grunted.

"What's up?" I asked, smiling.

"He says you smile too much," Phu's partner said to me, in accentless English.

Now that it was pointed out to me, the muscles of my face suddenly felt awfully tired. Like most white people, since about the age of four I'd used my rubber smile to get what I wanted from strangers. The Chinese, who usually saved their smiles for friends, saw our outside warmth and inside coldness as our defining characteristic. *Gwailo* was their pejorative for us—"ghost person" or "foreign devil," take your pick. Both stood for more than our race.

"Relax, no one's gonna hurt you," said Phu's partner, who, I found out later, Steve had assigned to protect me. He laid his cue diagonally on the table, called Phu over, looked meaningfully at me and then at the line of club chairs against the wall. I took the hint and sat down on one of them. A moment later Phu put on his lopsided jacket and joined me there.

Over a pad I explained to Phu that it would be awkward and tense for him tomorrow, but he'd be wreathed in shadow. For now I just needed a few details of his life so I could ask him some pertinent questions that would encourage him to explain the plight of refugees and then the evil deeds of the Lotus.

Phu's halting English was peppered with so many angry expletives it obscured the tragic details of his life and made him simply scary—in other words, I realized, great for TV. Born in the Mekong Delta in 1969, he spent his first six years in a free-fire zone that went back and forth between the South Vietnamese Army and the Vietcong. His sister was killed by a mortar; at 10, he made the perilous voyage with his family across the South China Sea; they spent a year in a refugee camp in Hong Kong; and finally immigrated to Canada in 1980. That might have been the dawn of a new day for Phu were it not for Steve. The Paper Fan picked him up for the Eagles straight out of an ESL class and broke him into the glories of hooliganism. Twenty street battles and a 12-month stint in jail later, Phu left the Eagles and followed Steve into the Gum Wah. A year after that, defending Steve's territory in the Woodland Drive shoot-out, he'd taken a bullet in the chest.

In my opinion, Phu had zero to show for it. Despite Steve's claims that he paid his charges $1,200 for a single trip to the airport, I saw no evidence of wealth in Phu's life. He drove a rusted-out Datsun. His clothes were Cantopop fashionable, but frayed at the cuffs. Perhaps he was a killer, but I kept picturing him writhing on the street in agony after one of the senseless battles that served Steve's ends and no one else's, getting killed for nothing.

"Tell me honestly, Phu, what do you think of Steve?" I asked.

"What I think? He good friend. He help me." Then he said: "No more. I want play pool."

The next day, while Steve and I circled the CBC's headquarters looking for a parking spot, the Paper Fan noticed something I don't think any reporter inside ever had: the downtown building was difficult to assault. From the front the six-story structure gave the impression of see-through openness, but Steve-the-commando spotted the illusion. The ends of the building were solid concrete, the wall of windows on the broad back end didn't start until the second story, and while the main entrance may have been made of glass, it opened onto a plaza that was walled on three sides, making a flank attack impossible. "See, they give you a way in from Georgia, but look how narrow it is." Steve pointed to an alley through the concrete, then pretend-shot a couple of preppy CBC types emerging single file from it. I later discovered the corporation's Western headquarters had been designed in the wake of the 1970 October Crisis, when the Canadian government had been truly worried about revolutionary assaults. It took a warrior's eye to spot the real purpose of the architecture.*

We sat down on one of the benches in the plaza to wait for Phu, and five minutes later he came striding up, compensating for his fish-out-of-water feelings with glares at the overpowering building and curses in the direction of the privileged white folks enjoying their government-sponsored coffee breaks all around us. We paged Paperny, who came out with a Chinese-speaking cameraman, who led us to an atrium in the building and wired us up with the bright yellow sun behind us. Steve had a look in the eye cup to make sure Phu was in shadow and then courteously asked Paperny if he wanted to have a check. I took out my pad and asked Phu my first question. "You were in a refugee camp in Hong Kong. What was that like?"

"Bad. Got locked up."

I waited, but his bloodstained story wouldn't come.

"Locked up—like in a prison camp?" I asked.

"Yeah, like a prison camp."

"How did you get from Vietnam to Hong Kong?"

"Came in a little sailboat; twenty-six people in it. My whole family in there. A little boat."

"So that was dangerous?"

"Yeah."

Silence.

Oh well, I thought, on to gangster business. "So now you're an enforcer in the Gum Wah. Are the police giving you any problems for that?"

"Me, I'm not worried about going to jail," Phu said, waving a cell phone at me angrily. (Later, viewers watching us in silhouette went bug-eyed, thinking he was holding a gun.) "What for? I'm used to go in jail."

---

*The October Crisis was sparked by terrorist acts committed by a Quebec separatist organization. Prime Minister Pierre Trudeau declared a state of martial law.

"You're used to it? You've been in jail before?"

"I been in jail before! That's a couple of years ago, right?"

"What was that for?"

"No comment on that!"

"Were you innocent for that one?"

"No comment!!"

"I hear the Lotus are giving you problems, too."

"Me, I'm not scared, right? If they want to fucking look for me, come down the pool hall. Why shooting at innocent people, right?"

I asked him to explain the root cause of the conflict between the Lotus and the Gum Wah.

"Fuck their mother cunts! Lotus fucking shoot innocent fucking people all fucking time. Fuck!!"

"Maybe we should've rehearsed," Steve told Phu after we unwired him.

The first segment on Steve aired at 6:15 P.M., March 12. Nine hours later, about three in the morning, my wife shoved me in bed. "Oh shit Terry!" she hissed. "Someone's in the house!"

I sat up, moving my hand to the barrel of my old .303 farm rifle, which I'd propped by the bed before retiring. I listened but heard nothing. We lived in a block of run-down row houses on the University of British Columbia campus. Every floorboard in the living room downstairs and on the flight to our bedroom was a hair-triggered squeaker—a natural alarm system impossible to disarm. "What did you hear?" I whispered.

"Downstairs—I know I heard something!" she insisted.

"Shhh!" I did hear something. Someone was scratching the door, as if working a knife at the lock edge.

I dialed 911, gave the phone to my wife and, rifle in hand, moved sideways to the window. While she gave our address to the emergency operator, I flattened against the wall and hooked the curtain away with the .303's barrel. I felt like I was in a '40s film noir. There was Steve's Mercedes parked down below, with Phu and another Chinese kid leaning against it, the exhaust smoking in the cold night behind my own car. Then I heard soft tapping. I climbed on a chair so I could see straight down below. I was looking at the top of Steve's big head. His hand was stretched out against the front door, his head down, as if figuring out what to do next. If Steve were here to kill me, I thought, he wouldn't show up in his car and put his boys on display under the streetlights.

Tap tap tap. Scratch scratch scratch. Tap tap tap. It sounded like pleading, actually. Steve took a step back and looked right at our window. He turned around to his enforcers and pointed his finger at the parted curtain.

"Tell them he's not in the house, he's outside," I said to my wife.

"Oh God, it'll be five more minutes!" Leslie whispered from the phone in a panic. "She says they have to call a cop off another call!"

"I'm going to stall him. They'll see him outside."

"No!"

"He's gonna lose his cool and break in here. I don't want to shoot him."

I took the rifle and went down the stairs, flattened myself against the wall of the foyer by the entrance to the living room.

"Um yes, just a moment please," I said through the door. God, did that sound stupid. "Who's there?" Even worse.

"Lemme in, I wanna talk."

"Is that you Steve?"

"You fuck, you're a fuck, you know that?" Steve said. "You got your tape recorder running in there? You know you're a lousy fuck?"

"Why?" I said, trying to sound truly astonished. "Didn't I do what you wanted me to—I showed what shit holes the Lotus were. That's what you wanted so that's what I did."

"Shut up, you fuck! What's on this fucking part two? That's all I want to know."

"Oh, it's really light. It shows your sense of humor. I'll call you tomorrow morning, from CBC, okay? The police are on their way here."

"You call the cops on me, you fuck?" he said. "You think I'm here to rip your throat out? What am I gonna do, knock first?"

"Oh I know that. It's a nonthreatening visit, but I'm pretty sleepy. So I'll have to talk to you tomorrow."

"You cunt, you knocked, I let you in—you can't do the same for me?"

"Steve, you're overreacting. No one likes the way they look on TV."

There was no reply, just retreating boot steps, then the slamming of car doors and the squeal of Steve's tires. A couple of minutes later I heard the siren. From the time I phoned 911 to now, nine minutes had elapsed. But, in the end, I had judged Steve correctly. If I were Chinese I'd be dead now. But I was white and alive.

I spent most of the next morning in meetings at the CBC building, then on the phone with their Toronto head office, then on the phone with the Mounties and the Vancouver city police. CBC had received a call from one of Steve's lawyers and was trying to make a decision on whether to run part two, balancing the issues of the ethical treatment of gangsters versus the public's right to know about them. Meanwhile the Asian Crime Squad was trying to get Steve to calm down. I found out later from Martin Turner that, at the same time, they were toying with the idea of sending a video of the segment to Eddy Wong, Steve's Triad boss in Hong Kong, although having Eddy put a stop to Steve in the usual Triad way seemed rather crude. For their part, the Mounties were trying to decide on how best to keep Steve from putting a stop to me. In the midst of all these negotiations, the receptionist called me across the newsroom. "There's a Mr. Wong on line three."

"I wanna see what's in there and I want to see it now," Steve said.

"I have to ask the bosses," I told him.

"I don't like to make enemies for too long, you can ask my police friends, so I just want to see what's in there. All I know's what I been hearing."

"You mean you didn't *see* it?" I asked, astounded. "Well then, Steve, all this is over nothing! I'm not saying you'll love it—"

"Terry!" he said, and then fell silent for a moment. "Terry, shut up, okay?" His voice was low and even. "I just wanna see it. That's all. What I'm hearing, this could get me killed. Not just killed."

Well, I knew that was coming.

"Okay, Steve. Can I call you back?"

"It won't cost me anything to hold on," he said.

I went to David Paperny's desk and he went into Sue Rideout's office and she went into the office of the executive producer, Graham Ritchie. Graham told Sue to tell Dave to tell me to tell Steve that we decided it was best to allow him the courtesy of seeing both segments.

"Okay Steve," I said. "Why don't you come on down in half an hour."

"I'll wait out front—I'm a block away."

I strategized with David before the meeting, asking that it be made absolutely clear to Steve that I was affiliated with the organization—that it should be made even more clear that this was a group effort, with a lot of different players. Otherwise, Steve would see me as hanging out there on my own, easy enough to whack without then having to confront the CBC gangsters.

Steve showed up with Phu. Sue Rideout took a look at the corpulent hood as he waddled into the newsroom and I could tell from her expression that he did not meet her expectations. He was trying to keep his face businesslike, but a grin actually cracked through. In social situations, no matter what the stresses, he really was an irrepressibly friendly guy. Phu, meanwhile, tried to fry anyone who met his eyes.

What followed was one of the weirder meetings in CBC history. We sat in Graham Ritchie's office, with Ritchie playing the cultural-empathy card by repeatedly using the word *gwailo,* as in, "Now I know you think we're all *gwailos* here"—although, actually, I'd never heard Steve use that word. To describe white people he would use the ancient Chinese expression: *useless cunts.*

Steve wasn't listening anyway. He knew right away I was low man on the totem pole yet he kept looking at me as if I could fix things, set the clock back. Whatever was said, whoever was speaking, he kept his eyes on mine, his face showing total puzzlement as he searched for yesterday's friend. Here was a gangster who lived by manipulation and betrayal, who fully understood the Darwinian benefits of living a life based on lying, yet he had really believed he had met someone who understood why he shot people and ruined the lives of children and dealt heroin and spread rumors of police corruption; a *white* person who valued him despite, or even *because* of his evil deeds, and forgave him. He simply couldn't believe that I had used the trust he had in me to get past his radar for my own benefit.

Ritchie was explaining how I had come to CBC with a story that would "give shape and substance" to the violence in Chinatown, that would tell the real tale of the Goldstone to *gwailos.*

"Yeah, but you came in my house like you were my friend and you said this and this and this and you were *wired!*"

"Terry identified himself as a reporter and you talked with him," reasoned Rideout.

"Yeah, but I didn't fucking know he was going to *trick* me," Steve said, still looking me straight in the eye.

"You lead a very public life, Steve," Ritchie said. "Terry believed the public wanted to know about it and you said you wanted them to know."

"You told me this and this," Steve declared, his anger rising. "Harry Rankin, and Bill Chu and the Lotus gettin' their side. . . ."

This was developing into exactly what I was afraid of: Steve was putting all the blame on my deceitful wits—not illogically, but I felt somebody else should share the burden. I nudged David with my foot, who sprang to life: "Steven, all of us were interested in this story. It's a large issue in the city. And your side in it is large. It's a fascinating world you live in."

"You're on my side, right, Terry?" Steve said, raising his chin and leaning forward. "And you fucking call the *cops* on me!?"

"Okay," Ritchie said, taking charge and calling the increasingly hot meeting short. He graciously offered his office as a screening room and we foreign devils walked out and took a half-hour break.

"He's a punk," Rideout said contemptuously.

I felt like saying they're all punks—loudmouthed, violent, gross people—

stylish at times, yes, but there were no "men of honor" in that world. That was the story—all of them were like Steve. Still, at the moment I felt too short of breath to do anything more than agree.

"Well, it's *bad,* but not as bad as people were telling me," Steve said when we came back in, to my infinite relief. "There's things I want out of that second part. You got me threatening the cops in there and talking about my rank in the 14K."

Ritchie told him *we* didn't have him doing anything—that's what *he* said. Steve announced he would talk to his lawyer. As he left the newsroom I tagged along behind, sheepishly, with my hands in my pockets.

"Somebody said you work for the cops," he told me by the door.

"I don't work for the cops, Steve."

"I'm talking you wanna find stuff out, they wanna find stuff out—so that's working. So you're an informant."

"I'm a journalist, Steve."

"Okay, same thing."

And then he did the strangest thing he could have under the circumstances. He giggled and put out his hand for a shake.

After he left I called Bill Chu and asked what I could expect from Steve. "We had him in," he said. "He's got other things to worry about now besides you, Terry. He knows it's the stupidest thing he could do—if anything happened to you, who are we going to go looking for?"

This didn't reassure me, and the Mounties weren't so sanguine either—they had their own informants. The UBC detachment called me at the newsroom and said they were putting me under a protection program. I should leave the building by a different exit than I usually used and take a cab home instead of risking starting my car. They asked where my daughter went to school and where my wife worked.

An hour before airtime, Steve phoned again and this time he sounded wildly edgy. He asked me to read through the script and demanded that offending bits be cut. I heard him talking to Chinese voices in the background, then he shouted, "You *do* it, Terry!" There was some back-and-forth talk with the lawyers in Toronto, and at 5:30 I took the master to the editing room. "*I'm the only one in Canada. There might be someone higher than me but not that I know of*" fell to the floor, and the words "*I don't care if it's the police,*" got cut from in front of "*anybody fucks around with me, one way or another, I'll catch up.*" We snipped a few other phrases until I said, "That's it. It sounds too choppy now."

"Better it gets chopped than you do," said the editor, and laughed.

———

Two RCMP officers moved in with us that night and explained to Leslie and me what to do in case there was a ruckus.

"Don't come downstairs under any circumstances," Constable Mike Russell said. "Hide in a closet or under the bed. Remain quiet until one of us calls you."

"Otherwise sleep tight," my wife muttered to me as we squeaked up the stairs.

There happened to be a ruckus that night—although of the Keystone variety. The Vancouver police sent an unmarked patrol car onto the UBC grounds to check up on me, and the cops shone a flashlight at my living room window. That caused my two Mountie guardians to hit the rug and hunch-crawl to the door and the window in expectation of gunfire.

The cops stayed a few nights and then the RCMP technical crew came in and affixed a panic button beside my bed. "This'll send right to the station," a sergeant told me. "You press it, we'll treat it as a Code 3."

"So I don't have to dial 911?"

He seemed offended. "If you need to hold a hand for the minute it takes us to get here, then go right ahead."

My neighbors were very accommodating about all of this—even when the alarm went off by mistake. It was a warm afternoon in summer, my parents were visiting and Leslie and I were out with them on the town. All the mothers in the block of row houses were playing with their children in the backyard when the complex was suddenly surrounded by wailing police cars and officers in flak jackets holding high-powered rifles. Helmeted cops poured into the yard and told everyone to quick, grab the kids, go into their respective houses, get under the beds and to stay there until they got the all clear. Then they burst into our house and combed it for bodies.

When we got home and found out what had happened, my dad shook his head and said, "I wish I knew someone on the Coast here."

"Whaddaya talking about, Al!" my mother exploded. "Don't start with that 'know someone' business now. He knows the police. That's all he needs. *Know someone*," she said disdainfully.

"I'm just saying," he replied.

"Well don't say! Like they don't have enough trouble already? And Terry, promise me one thing. Don't you ever write about your own. Because *they* will kill you!"

"Your mother's right," Al said. "Brighton Beach you stay away from." He winked at me. "Even da rabbis don' say a void."

CHAPTER 9

PROJECT BUGS

Twice is too much!
—STEVEN WONG

Even with its excisions, "Inside Chinese Organized Crime" shot Steve up the chart of law enforcement priorities. At CLEU, transcripts of the programs were prepared and examined for incriminating quotes. Steve had skirted round the edges of a guilty admission, but hadn't gone over. Still, he was the first Canadian Triad to go on television and talk about his business. Gales of laughter at Steve's humiliation soon turned to serious discussions in the planning rooms. It was offensive to the Asian squad to hear Steve boast he had nothing to worry about because all he did was "protect" the 14K's heroin bosses. As city cops, however, they had neither the money nor manpower to launch the kind of long-term investigation required to prove Steve was a boss himself. That was a job for the RCMP, and the Coordinated Law Enforcement Unit was the place where city and federal forces meshed.

The Mountie Drug Section, based at RCMP headquarters south of CLEU, ran a squad called Unit One that targeted major heroin traffickers. At the time of Steve's leap to celebrity status, Unit One had been trying to discover the source of the steady stream of China white being dealt in grams and ounces on Vancouver's skid row. Watching Steve's rising arc, Unit One shared the Asian squad's belief that he could be the source of part of that heroin. In early April 1990, about three weeks after the CBC broadcast, Unit One accelerated its skid-row investigation, hoping to work its way up through street sales, distribution channels, and importation loads until its officers got to the top, where city and federal agencies suspected Steve resided.

On June 6, 1990, after nine weeks of undercover work, Unit One had a breakthrough. Constable Mike Littlejohn, posing as an outlaw biker, was closing a three-ounce heroin buy with a street dealer when out of the shadows stepped Steve's enforcer Kim Tam, who took the money directly from Littlejohn. "Equipped with recent information about Steven Wong," a Unit One investigator would later tell me, "we became confident we were targeted on a substantial Chinese organization, and that the higher-level supplier was Steven Wong. . . . Actually, our timing could not have been better."

The street dealer, Douglas Scott, was a busy man that night and mistakenly gave Littlejohn four ounces instead of three—an unexpected stroke of luck for the Mounties. Scott was now in the hole for 12 grand to Steve's gang, and when Littlejohn next met up with him he begged for his money, saying his suppliers were going to kill him. Littlejohn demurred and Scott, in a bad way to cover his loss, asked if the biker wanted to close a larger transaction, adding that "the leader of the organization" could sell him kilograms. Things were looking better all the time for the investigation. In anticipation of future wiretaps, Unit One code-named their operation Project Bugs, and declared Steve the main target.

As this high-stakes game got rolling on the east side of town, on the west side I signed a contract with CBC Television to write a two-hour docudrama called *Racing with Dragons: The Gang Life and Execution of Bob Moieni.* Boss of the project was a fierce newshound named Helen Slinger, Graham Ritchie's predecessor as executive producer of the newsroom. Slinger wanted the three-act drama of Moieni's life and assigned me a cast of dozens to interview or reinterview, including Moieni's family, his friends, gang friends (in jail and out), girlfriends, and my guys from Britannia. These conversations inevitably turned to the battle between the Gum Wah and Los Diablos on the night before Moieni was executed, and two names kept cropping up: Kim Tam, who I knew was in jail on the morning of the murder, and Steven Wong, who I knew had a rock-solid alibi at Fraser Billiards.

I'd been out of teaching for almost two years by then, having turned to full-time writing in the summer of 1988. For a couple of my crime stories about non-Lotus-related incidents I'd asked Goathead's advice on leads. In May I met him in the Lotus-run Coin Cache massage parlor, on the corner of Cambie and Broadway, two blocks from City Hall and five from CLEU headquarters. My former student was now the morning towel boy at the Coin Cache, not a bad place to have a job. The facilities were spotlessly clean, with weight-lifting equipment, a sauna, comfortable chairs, and potted palms in the lounge. Filipino, Chinese, and Thai girls dressed in short shorts and spiked heels practiced their art in five small rooms adjacent to the lounge, charging $55 for a back massage and $100 for the full treatment. Goathead was obviously making money from the Lotus—he now drove a company Trans Am—but he insisted that all he was involved in was keeping peace among the ever-changing roster of women and the big-tipping Chinatown boys they serviced. He did, however, hold some violently partisan views on the gang scene, and still hadn't completely forgiven me for writing an article in 1987 that blamed his gang for killing Moieni. Nevertheless, he'd *loved* the CBC piece on Steve, as did all of the young Lotus members, and told me I was suddenly a very popular man among Steve's sworn enemies, who had recently shot out the back window of his Mercedes, left dead chickens on his doorstep, and machine-gunned his cat.

"His *cat!?*" I snorted coffee through my nose onto the Naugahyde. "Sorry."

"Try shoot dog but only see Siamese," Goathead laughed, holding his arms like John Dillinger and spraying the fitness machines. "I think he be dead soon, Mr. Good. You know, so many-many people hate him."

"What about his bodyguard racket?" I asked, without even lowering my voice, since Goathead said his young *dai los* had urged him to pass on concrete details about Steve's life.

"Still he do," he said, and that fact didn't surprise me. As with many modern mobsters, being a 15-minute celebrity hadn't put a dent in Steve's business operations. At any rate, the stuff worth killing him for had been cut. "Nobody his side care he on TV. You write he tell his boys shoot Bob?" Goathead asked.

"We'll see on that," I hedged. "Right now it's still up in the air."

"So you tell cops he do Tsang," Goathead pressed, referring to Wan Chiu Tsang, the Triad heroin dealer Steve was supposed to have shot in the head in front of the airport's Blue Boy Hotel.

"They already know," I said.

"Why no arrest him then?"

"I'm doing the best I can. What else you got?"

"Okay, him and Kim work with Dai Huen Jai now—numba faw," he said. For that piece of news he did lower his voice. He was referring to the Big Circle Boys and to No. 4 heroin, the purest form of China white. "You tell cops, then they do something on Steve."

I wasted no time passing this tidbit along to an officer a few blocks away at CLEU. Calculating the weeks to the fall, when the panic button was to be removed, I was becoming more and more impatient for the cops to, in fact, "do something on Steve."

At the time, I knew nothing about Project Bugs. All I knew was that the fight against Asian crime had endured a setback. Fortuitously for Steve and all other Oriental gangsters, the Asian squad was just then undergoing some debilitating changes, thanks to a rotation policy that saw almost all its veteran officers transferred to other sections. The policy was supposed to foster well-rounded personnel and prevent corruption within the Vancouver Police Department, but instead it rotated inexperienced cops into the Asian squad who lacked the network of informants that were crucial to keeping tabs on the Chinese underworld. Of the old guard, only Bill Chu remained, and I was feeling increasingly vulnerable as I conducted interviews about Moieni's murder all over Steve's subterranean realms. As most of my interview subjects couldn't be relied on to keep a secret two minutes after we said goodbye, it wasn't very long before Steve jumped to conclusions. According to what Phu told so-and-so and so-and-so told Goathead—with several steps in between—Steve became certain that I was trying to get him before he got me—a not entirely wild theory.

Generally, when I'm working on a project that involves interviews with volatile people, I answer the phone not with a "Hello" but with a hassled "Yeah"—simply as a way of throwing antagonistic idiots off guard. The day after talking with a jailed Los Diablos named Teo Gill, I picked up the phone and before I could raise my grunt as a shield, the voice on the other end said, "Should've phoned me about Moieni, hee hee hee. You got your tape recorder on?"

"Shit! Steven?" I shouted—surprised as much by his voice as by the thrill I felt hearing it. Where was *that* coming from?

"I'm phoning you for one thing," he said, pleasantly enough. "Don't go calling the cops on me because they already know, okay? My police friends say you're doin' a movie about me. 'There's this murder, that murder, he's sayin'.' So my lawyer says that part's slander. So I told my police friends I'm gonna call you about it and I ain't gonna threaten you. So if you phone the police, like, '*Steve* called me!' fuck, they'll just laugh. 'Fuck, he's got no court order on you, do what you want.' That's what they told me."

"I don't believe that, Steve," I countered. "They would have told you not to phone me. I'm under protection now. From you. And you got me wrong on the movie," I went on. "I'm not writing about *you*. It's about Moieni, and you're not the bad guy in it—you're hardly in it at all, except as a minor character, completely overshadowed by the Lotus."

I let that insulting but true fact sink in a moment. *Racing with Dragons* was the story of Moieni's induction into the Lotus and his desperate bid to get out. In that context, Steve wasn't Moieni's dramatic antagonist—the Lotus recruiters were. Ultimately, it was the Lotus who had ruined Moieni's life, not Steve, whom Moieni hardly knew. "He was sixteen, Steve—a good kid, he got sucked in, and that was it."

"Yeah, it was too bad for him. You get in with the fucking Lotus, what else you expect? They're a crew'a shit-sacks. That's why—you ask around— I told my police friends, if he comes around the pool hall, I'll talk to him about it. I don't hold no fucking grudges. I'll tell him the right story."

"Whoa!" I said. "*I* don't wanna come around the pool hall and talk about *any*thing with you, Steve. No offense, but I didn't feel safe there even when you told everybody to lay off me."

"Hey, then come around the house. Am I gonna hurt ya there? Fuck, I'll even tell the cops you're on the way. You tell 'em too. Just no 911 shit and hidden camera. No tricks."

What was Steve was up to? I knew that Bill Chu would have told Steve that if he wanted to communicate with me he should get his lawyer to write a letter, and, in fact, a couple of days later I discovered Steve hadn't spoken with Chu about me since the night of the broadcast. On the other hand, Steve-the-informant had a mystery handler at CLEU whom he kept up to date on some aspects of his life, as well as on the activities of drug dealers he wanted to sewer. Normally, handlers cultivate what appears, from the informant's perspective, to be a helpful friendship, and it wasn't impossible that Steve's handler had told Steve he would let other officers know he was calling me—a casual favor that Steve would think mini- mized any chance of a backlash from the police. The problem with this spook relationship, of course, was that Steve excelled at manipulating his handlers. As the Asian squad's Martin Turner told me a few days before, "There've been so many investigations involving Steve, and it's like: Who's handling who?" Whether or not the handler had actually *wanted* to give Steve the green light to call me didn't matter, since, in Steve's crazy world, his gab sessions with "police friends" were often his best defense. If con- fronted, Steve would just construe the conversation to mean anything he wanted it to.

When I told Goathead that Steve had called, he saw it as a dire warning signal. "He gonna make a big deal with the cops about be friends with you, and when you turn up dead in six months they won't have no motive."

I thought Goathead was right. So, to keep the heat up on Steve after my protection came off, I walked into *Vancouver* magazine and proposed an article for the September issue, just about the time Steve would be thinking it safe to whack me. The article I outlined was to be a tour of gang hangouts, leading off with Steve's house. When I called the staff sergeant at my local Mountie detachment and told him what I was doing, he groaned, asked if I was nuts, and said he'd just pulled a car of auxiliary cops off baby-sitting my house at night.

"Gee, I'm sorry," I said. "I guess you never had much to do with journalists before this."

"Oh I have, but you're just a little different."

When I pulled up on Clarendon Drive I noticed that Steve's house was now almost as well protected as my own. A security company's sign stuck up from the lawn and four surveillance cameras on the eaves covered the streets and alleys. I waved to the camera in the front and went around to Steve's private entrance and knocked. My mouth was dry, but Steve did his best to set me at ease. He answered the door in his usual boxers and tattoos, holding a cell phone in one hand and his white rat dog in the other. "Hee, hee, hee, I just got off from my police friends," he told me. "We're talking about you."

"So that if I shoot you they'll come by and arrest me?" I asked.

"Yeah, I'm under protection too—from you guys," he said, meaning reporters. "Fuck I been getting lotsa calls from you guys. Pains in the asses."

He handed me Fifi—an intimacy that caught me unawares—and ambled into the back to get dressed. Creepy Fifi licked me with her cold little tongue and I let her down on the carpet. Steve had left his bedroom door open to keep an eye on me. "No one in the fucking closets here," he yelled. "You can check if you're scared."

"I'm not scared, Steve. I let the Mounties know I'm here."

While I waited I made an obeisance to Kwan Kung—"Let the Wisdom in your left eye and the Determination in your right eye be the source of my Cunning and Bravery"—and took out from my briefcase a present I'd brought Steve: the U.S. Justice Department's *Report on Asian Organized Crime*. It was the classified edition the San Francisco police had given me the summer before, with the appendix in the back that listed 58 hotshots and their Triad affiliations. In theory, gangsters were not supposed to be in possession of that edition.

"When did you get all the cameras?" I called.

"My insurance told me to. We live in a high-crime area." He was still giggling when he came out and, as if we were buddies again, headed straight for the couch to sit down beside me. "You know, the cops take forever to show up when you call 'em."

"And they're always here in a second when you don't."

"Naaa, naaa, naaa. Most of those guys in the Asian squad fucked off. They brought in a bunch of amateurs. They left Chu 'cause he's the only Chinese. Aside from Bill, I don't have much problem with the police anymore."

"What about the Mounties?" I inquired.

"What about 'em? Their main thing's drugs. Like I told you, we don't protect the carriers. We got problems with that if we do. We just provide escort service. . . ."

I let him go on for a while, like a Triad politician who repeats the same gospel about his innocence, the causes of gang violence, the problems in Chinatown. In a way, he'd learned the politician's first media lesson: keep to your old tracks.

"This is for you," I said, handing over the 75-page report.

He read the title aloud, then discourteously dismissed it as useless to him. "I already got it. This the one with the list?" He flipped to the back. "Okay, yeah, I'll show you the bullshit. See, they call this guy an 'Unk' Triad?" He pointed to the listing for Macau's billionaire gambling king, Stanley Ho. "Unk means 'Unknown.' So I seen police reports where they say, like, 'He is a member of the Unk Triad,' hee, hee, hee, hee. Unk! Stupid assholes."

"Unk, unk. Sounds like a pig Triad."

"Right. A pig gang."

Fanning the embers of our old fellowship, I hauled from my briefcase the outline of my script, still in paragraph form, and showed him where Park Lo was described as the big bad gang guy of Vancouver, and where Steve was merely described as a rival gang leader. "See, you don't have to worry—that's it for you. It's all to do with the Lotus."

"Your Lotus friends know that?" he inquired, nearsightedly reading down the page, and then turning it.

"They know I'm working on it, Steve. It's not a crime exposé. I don't know if you know it, but Moieni was trained by a Buddhist ninjitsu master—his best friend says he was a Buddhist himself."

"He was mouthy to the wrong ones in the Lotus, that's what I know about him," Steve said, continuing to flip pages. "Then he ratted—fuck, everybody knows that. If you got that in here, then that's it."

"So who killed him?" I asked, holding his eyes.

"You want me to get sued?" he asked, holding mine. "That's what you guys do, not me."

I then decided to totally confuse the meeting, and launched into the airiest three-minute lecture he'd probably ever heard. I said that the theme of the script was not that crime didn't pay, but that the most important thing in life was to understand why we did things and what we were after when we did them. I said that almost every culture assigned seven levels to our actions, from the lowest to the highest. The Hindus called them the seven spinal chakras; the Elizabethans had seven links in their Great Chain of Being; and the psychologist Abraham Maslow had written about a

Hierarchy of Needs with seven plateaus. "You're a Buddhist, Steve," I said. "So was Kwan Kung. So what did Buddha say? Right thought, right action, right speech—"

My lecture was interrupted by his phone chirping. Steve took the call without apology, broke into Cantonese and turned his back on me. It was Kim Tam, back in jail for a violation of his bail on the old assault charge. When Steve got off, he removed his sneakers and pulled on his cowboy boots to head over to Fraser Billiards. As if he hadn't heard a word I said, he repeated his line that the cops were wasting their time running after the little guys battling on the streets, instead of the big guys, who were using street violence to distract them. His eyes were completely empty as he spoke, almost as if he was now in the habit of telling this to other reporters as well. Then, going out the door to our respective cars, he surprised me.

"What's your religion?" he asked.

"Me? I'm Jewish."

"Yeah, someone was saying that. My lawyers was Jewish," he said, apparently referring to the Rankins. "They was sucking me dry so I got new ones now. So the Jewish control all the money over here. What does that tell you?"

"It tells me I should be a Jewish lawyer with you as my client," I replied, which seemed to me as valid a non sequitur as his own.

"It tells you, the Jewish in Brooklyn now, they're the ones causing all the gang trouble. There's some Jewish up in the British Properties now. So why aren't you writing about them?"

"Give me time," I said, strolling beside him in the yard.

"Yeah, but you'd do it different, eh? They'd fucking slit your throat in a second you do what you did to me. Me, I rolled with it. I didn't lose any face. We expect that from you guys. That's why you don't bother us. You know what they call you?"

"Ghost people."

"Fuck no." He got in his car. "That's when they don't mean nothing." He turned the key. "What they call you behind your backs is *jing mao ho.*"

Hairy monkey.

By Labor Day everything seemed to be going according to plan, chancy as that plan was. I'd distributed preview copies of the *Vancouver* magazine article to all the cops in my life and then spent my days working on my script, nervously awaiting the call I knew would come. At 3 P.M. on the day "Leader of the Pack" hit the newsstands I answered the phone on its first ding. "Yeah, yeah—"

"If you were Chinese and you wrote this article, you'd be gone," Steve said, and giggled. He was calling on his staticky cell phone, and through my receiver I could hear the clacking of pai gow dominoes in the Hoi Ming Gwok Social Club. "Even the cops are telling me how calm I'm taking this. Hee, hee, hee! They say, 'That Gould's a pain in our butts, Steve. He'd be safer leaving you alone instead of making us protect him.'"

"Steve, I write about you with respect," I said. "You got the article there?"

"My lawyer's got it now! Neil Sacks. The next call you get's from him."

"Okay, but listen," I said, actually relieved that his lawyer was in on this. "Look on page 134. 'Wong is a likable chap,'" I read from the article, "'with a winning smile, a sharp wit and a very ingenuous manner—'"

"Yeah, well twice is too much," he cut me off. "How many times I let you come visit my house? How many times I introduce you around? And how many times you fuckin' *burn* me?"

"Steve—"

"You're a joke around here, you know that? You screwed yourself, Terry. You think the Lotus is gonna like you writin' about the Cache? Who the fuck is gonna talk to you now? Even the cops are gonna start patting you down. They tell you what they think of you? 'He's a sneaky slime bucket. He turns *everyone* in.' That's what the cops say. Buddhist this, Gwang Gong that— Terry, I'll tell you true. I'm the only friend you got left."

"That's nice of you to say that, Steve, after the trouble I keep causing."

"Well, sure," he squeaked. "Because I told you, I don't hold a grudge, hee, hee, hee. I don't stay enemies. Ask anyone. I'll make a deal with you. You don't write about me anymore. That's the deal. Why don't we go to the game tonight and shake on it?"

When I suggested that the cheering that attends a home-team touchdown might camouflage a gunshot, Steve joked that maybe I'd get lucky and the B.C. Lions wouldn't score. "I ain't threatening you—fuck no!" he said, apparently for the record. "What am I gonna do, take you out in front of ten thousand people?"

"I know you wouldn't do that, Steve. You've actually never threatened me."

"I never threaten anybody—fuck, I'm a pussycat. . . . But there's a lot of guys besides me that hate your guts. And I can't control them. Some's sixteen, you know. You think they give a shit about doing time in juvie detention? Hee, hee, hee!"

"Okay, Steve," I said. "You got a deal. I mean that. I really do. But it goes both ways, hombre."

"Hee, hee, hee," he said, and hung up. An hour later his lawyer Neil Sacks phoned to instruct me that it was unfair to imply his client was engaged in the heroin trade when his last trial had been stayed for lack of evidence.

"I'll put a man on it and get back to you," I said.

When I played the tape of Steve the next day for my CBC boss, Helen Slinger, and my script editor, Linda Coffey, Slinger remarked, "He sounds like a little *boy!*"

"Oh he is," I said. "They all are. Hurt little boys. Even when they're sixty."

Always pressing for the source of my fascination with gangsters, Coffey observed thoughtfully, "You know, it's almost like you two like each other."

Not long after my crime-stopper tip to CLEU about the No. 4 heroin deal, an officer chanced upon the Paper Fan in a meeting with a Dai Huen Jai operator named Tommy Ho, a large-scale heroin importer then under investigation. The meeting took place at the Vancouver docks, and the suspicion of the cops was that the topic of discussion had no relation to Steve's airport shuttle service.

Meanwhile, closer to Chinatown, Constable Littlejohn capitalized on the offer of Kim Tam's street dealer to sell him kilograms of junk. Littlejohn told Douglas Scott that he had proven himself a bumbler and that he wanted to negotiate directly with a *dai lo*. Scott gladly set up a meeting for June 21, in a hotel suite in Richmond. Hoping to meet Wong, Littlejohn showed up with a corporal from the heroin squad named Wayne Schauer, also posing as a biker. Instead of Steve, however, a low-level Gum Wah member named Daniel Lee answered the door. Testing the two bikers, Lee at first played footsie around the subject of drugs, then, apparently satisfied he was dealing with legitimate criminals, he began to talk business. He said his unnamed *dai lo* had just left for "the Orient" to arrange a shipment to Vancouver, and could sell them heroin at $110,000 a pound.* The underfunded Mounties said they would like to start at half that, and agreed to seven ounces for $70,000. Lee said he would be in touch, but a week later Scott met with Littlejohn and told him Lee actually had nothing to do with the sale, he was just a messenger sent to check them out—an investigation that was still under way. The bikers should please be patient.

---

*Traffickers frequently mix metric and imperial measurements in their dealings. To complicate matters, they also have their own measurement standard for heroin, called a "unit." A unit of pure Asian heroin weighs 700 grams, or 1.543 pounds. Strange to say, even teenage street dealers have no problem managing these conversions in their heads.

In the steep terrain of drug transactions, this switchbacking routine was the norm—and the reason Unit One stings often progressed at inch-worm speed. Generally, heroin strike forces were like mountain-climbing expeditions, in that they were extremely dangerous, took a long time, and were failures if they didn't reach the top. At this point, in fact, failure seemed an option for Project Bugs: the inspectors at the Drug Section became concerned about the Gum Wah's suspicion of their two undercover officers, and ordered them to call off the buy. Luckily, the canceled deal threw Scott into a panic, and he maintained contact with Littlejohn, by and by telling him that the officers' credentials had been approved by his bosses, who would shortly be returning from the Orient.

On July 6, a heroin squad cop named Mike Hiller applied to tap the phones of Scott, Tam, and Lee, based on the probable grounds that they were low-level members of a heroin importing and distribution organization, "controlled and directed" by others higher up in the group. As yet, the Mounties had no direct evidence that Steve was controlling and directing his flunkies, but, in the Unit One planning room, Steve was still the declared target.

Ironically, the operation to sting Steve ran into a hitch with the publication of "Leader of the Pack." A couple of days after Steve phoned me that last time, Scott informed Littlejohn that his people "were all heated up"—that is, the subject of unwanted police attention—and that they had "all left town." And so another month went by, with much foot-tapping over at RCMP headquarters, until Scott phoned Littlejohn with "good news." Littlejohn and Scott met the next day, and on October 4, Mike Hiller, who was now heading the operation, swore out an affidavit stipulating that the police strategy was to have "Littlejohn arrange a purchase of five pounds of heroin from Scott and establish contact with someone higher up in the organization than Tam."

Monitoring the heavily coded October phone taps between Tam, Lee, and Scott, the Mounties were delighted to hear the conspiracy expanding to include a Dai Huen Jai businessman named Yak Wah Cheung, whose gangland wedding Steve had attended as a guest of honor. Unit One broadened the wiretap net to include four other Dai Huen Jai, and began monitoring a blurring number of heroin imports that involved Tam, hoping that if Steve got involved a dangerous series of buys might not be necessary. Then, gloriously, Steve was in the picture, appearing to take charge of a conspiracy that now included 15 people. Under Steve's direction, Tam was receiving frequent small deliveries of Asian heroin from Yak Wah Cheung's contacts in Guangzhou and injecting them into the Gum Wah's distribution network.

Because big busts make the headlines, it's generally assumed by the public that heroin arrives in North America by the billion-dollar ton-load, concealed in anything that has a large hollow cavity. That's certainly one way of doing it. The short-term profits are astronomical, but so is the amount of manpower and international organization required, and so are the all-or-nothing risks. Another way to run a heroin business is to establish a steady stream of small loads that are worth about $100,000 when sold by the ounce, or five times that if "stepped on" (diluted) and marketed by the gram. The profits of each shipment are proportionally smaller, but so are the difficulties in getting the smack over from Asia. In 1990, half a pound a week arriving in Vancouver by mule brought in about $25 million a year when sold by the ounce. At this phase in his career—the phase monitored by Project Bugs—the incremental way appeared to be Steve's way.

In early November, planning a month ahead, Tam set up what should have been a routine mule run. On November 28, a young Philippine woman named Josette Copon flew out of Vancouver for Guangzhou. On December 2, the Mounties secured taps on 15 suspects, topped by Steve, who by now was importing "T-shirts," with Yak as his middleman. The Mounties knew Copon was returning to Vancouver via Shanghai on December 9, and, after eight arduous, expensive months, they decided they had enough on Steve to make their move. At 11:30 A.M. they grabbed Copon at customs and came up with a small bust—11.2 ounces of No. 4 pure heroin, later announced to be worth about half a million "on the street." It made no headlines, and hardly anybody noticed but me. The cops knew the big picture, however, and told the handcuffed and weeping Copon that, although she might be the lowest rung on a tall ladder, she was still looking at eight to ten years.

With Copon in custody, the Mounties decided to wait and see what would transpire over the telephone in the wake of the seizure. The next 24 hours were very entertaining, at least regarding the coded repartee between the Big Circle Boys and the Gum Wah. It turned out that Yak trusted Steve as far as he could throw him, and was in the habit of sending undercover gangsters to the airport with pictures of the mules to verify their arrival. On December 9, Yak's goons compared their picture of Copon with another young Filipina who arrived on the same flight from Shanghai and then got into a taxi on the breezeway. Unaware the real Ms. Copon had been waylaid by the Mounties, they phoned Yak and told him of the mule's safe arrival.

By 1 P.M., Tam was beginning to get edgy. The flight had arrived, but Copon hadn't phoned, and he used the redial on his phone every few minutes. Yak was beginning to wonder what had happened as well. At 3:40 he phoned Tam with the good news. "Well," Yak said in Cantonese, "my friend went to have a look. She arrived at 11:30."

"Huh?" Tam said.

"My friend went to have a look," Yak repeated.

"Is that right?"

"Yeah," Yak said. "He came back and told me the arrival was at 11:30."

Tam said he'd get back to him as soon as Copon phoned. As the hours wore on, however, Yak began to get even more impatient. Where the hell was Copon? "Still waiting," Tam truthfully replied.

The next day, a hysterically crying Copon was released on $25,000 bail and finally phoned a panicky Tam to inform him of her arrest and bond. "Eight to ten years!" she wept. "Do you wanna get together at all or anything, 'cause I really wanna talk to you!"

Tam stalled her, awaiting instructions from Steve, who returned a coded page four minutes later. Steve took the news of Copon's arrest neutrally. "You'd better go straighten it out, eh?" was all he said.

As soon as Tam hung up, Yak phoned again. "How's it going?" Yak asked Tam.

"Hasn't called yet," Tam lied.

"Well, what's actually going on?" Yak asked.

"Can I talk to you later?"

"Nothing happened, right?" Yak asked. "Anything happened?"

"Yes," Tam admitted. "Something happened now."

"How come something happened?"

"I'll talk to you later, okay?"

"Fuck his mother's cunt!" Yak cursed, referring to Steve.

Yak was now certain he'd been ripped off by the scumbag Paper Fan, and phoned a mean gangster buddy named Dai Gwai for backup. Now, a rule of the North American underworld is that you don't mess with an outraged Big Circle Boy. They skin people alive. Eavesdropping on a 5 P.M. phone conversation, the Unit One translators could only marvel at Steve's courage as the two Cantonese grizzlies reared and roared at each other.

"Once I say it," Yak declared, "fuck it, I will do it."

"Do you know what my group of people think?" said Steve, turning the tables on Yak. "My group of people think that the two of you are conspiring to play tricks."

That was too much for Yak. He jumped in a car with a gun. The Mounties jumped in their cars and, sirens wailing, arrested him before he got to Steve's house. They then proceeded to Clarendon Drive and grabbed the Paper Fan and Tam. Strung out on his own product, Tam was visibly upset. Steve shrugged the arrest off and called his lawyer. He'd been through this before.

Honoring my agreement with Steve, I stayed away from the August 1991 preliminary hearing. Copon pled guilty and, because of her help in another case, was sentenced to two years less a day. Fearing for her life, though, she refused to testify in the Project Bugs case, but the wiretap evidence still made things look bad for Wong, Tam, and Yak. The trial of the three men was set for September 1, 1992.

Steve never made it for the opening day. Before the trial began, he went though a radical life-change. He missed the months of arguments over the admissibility of the wiretaps. He missed the Crown's day-by-day recounting of Project Bugs—from Douglas Scott's four-ounce sale on Hastings Street to the meeting with Daniel Lee in Richmond to Copon's arrest at the Vancouver Airport. He missed the testimony of the Mounties Schauer, Littlejohn, and Hiller. He never faced his accusers and the nation's justice system. For 18 months the trial went on without Steve until finally, on April 7, 1994, he missed the verdict on Yak and Tam. I didn't.

Supreme Court Justice G. Peter Fraser pronounced Yak Wah Cheung guilty of conspiring to import heroin. As number two man in the conspiracy, Yak was sentenced to 14 years and two months. Kim Tam was also pronounced guilty, and sentenced to seven and a half years. Both prison terms, I thought, were extraordinary for such a small bust. Steve, had he been found guilty as the head of the conspiracy, would probably have been looking at 18 to 20.

Mike Hiller was in the gallery for the verdict. I went up to the Mountie and congratulated him on his two-out-of-three win, then handed him a copy of my latest article, "The Search for Steven Wong"—coincidentally published that very day in *Saturday Night* magazine. I had been working on it for close to a year, traveling 12,000 miles in my personal search for Steven Wong. I swear, though, I'd honored our agreement until the day I learned he was dead.

PART II

CHAPTER 10

EXTENSIVE TRANSFORMATION AND UNITING WITH HEAVEN

———

*It's amazing, this should be a Hollywood movie. Nothing
I've ever seen of suspected fraud cases comes close.*
—JAMES GALLAGHER, VICE PRESIDENT, PRUDENTIAL INSURANCE

The private eye wore a blue trench coat and was driving a van with the windows darkened in the back. That amused me. From my own car I watched Mike Richards standing in the parking lot and looking around for me. Three things crossed my mind as I waited for him to guess I was the person he'd phoned yesterday. He might not be who he said he was. His reason for meeting me might be a total lie. And he might shoot me as I extended my hand in greeting. Stupid thoughts, but that was my state of mind when I got out of the car and walked towards the man who'd stunned me with the news that Steve had been killed.

It was early spring 1993. Since July I'd been traveling quite a bit, working on articles about health food scams in the States and illegal logging in Sarawak, plus others on heroin-addicted schizophrenics, organized crime lawyers, and a fund-raising ruse in the British Properties. But while on these projects I'd missed something. On August 14, 1992, a cop had left a warning message on my answering machine saying I should stay away from Steve's latest caper. He hadn't mentioned a funeral and I remember thinking it was probably another shoot-out or another bust, not worth breaking my deal with Steve over—at least not until he'd been jailed for a long, long time. By the time I returned the cop's call he was on vacation and I let it go. Meanwhile, the cops had told no one about the funeral or that Steve had missed his trial, and the story never made the press.

Richards was in his late 20s, with gelled hair atop a frat-boy face, sharply creased slacks, and shiny black shoes—too corny by half, in my opinion. "Mr. Richards," I said. "Your boss give you the budget to buy me a beer?"

"Of course," he replied, and we crossed the lot to my neighborhood pub, the Queens Cross. He held the brass handle to the door.

"You first," I smiled, squeezing the record button on my pocket tape machine, fully expecting that he had done the same.

Over Richards's shoulder I lifted my brows to a good-looking waitress named Vicki. I often brought bad guys here for interviews and Vicki was adept at guiding me into a booth that put my face and Bad Guy's back in her direction—just in case. As Vicki reached towards Richards to wipe the table, he pointedly averted his eyes from her loose V neck.

"I think I gave you a little bit of background regarding our interest in Steven Wong," he said.

"Too little."

He took out his private-eye card from Major Investigations—the number two firm in town—and flicked it down like an ace in front of me. Then he slipped a steno pad from his trench coat pocket and laid it on the table. I took out my own steno and touched my spirals to his. Richards looked at our fencing pads. "I'm afraid I can't add much to what I told you over the phone," he said, raising his eyes. "Mr. Wong appears to have been killed in an overseas road accident and burnt beyond recognition. That's the extent—"

"There's no way to ID the body? No teeth?"

"I won't be able to go into that," Richards said. "Basically, we've been retained by a large company back East that has some interest in what has happened to him. Our job is to get a picture of Mr. Wong before all that happened. The reason I've made you my first stop—well, it became apparent to me from your *Vancouver* magazine article that you had obviously developed an insight into the workings of his mind."

He was referring to "Leader of the Pack," now two and a half years old. "Who brought the article up to you?"

"I'm sorry, that has to stay confidential too."

It was irritating being on this end of a one-way interview with an ingenue dick who looked like Ricky Nelson. Strange to say, though, I *wanted* to talk. So this is what it feels like, I thought. The urge comes up from between your stomach and heart and upsets your better judgment. This is why crooks, dyspeptic with screaming self-importance, talk to *you*. Everybody wants to be a somebody, and when you're interviewed you're a somebody. How interesting.

"I'm in a tough spot now, Richards," I said. "Perhaps it's necessary for you to keep me in the dark about what's going on, but Steve was a murderer, a drug dealer, an official in the 14K. He was connected at significant levels with significant swordsmen in Hong Kong. Oh, he was a likable guy, I really liked him, but he could turn around and put one in your head. Maybe you heard I was under police protection from him for six months?" Richards was writing all this down, with me thinking, Jeez, listen to you, here you are, babbling away. I hit the brakes. "So at the very minimum, I need to know which company back East has hired you. It could be the Cosa Nostra, for all the fuck I know."

Not a glimmer of a smile spoiled his gumshoe mien. Actually, I kind of liked the wooden technique. I'll try it sometime, I thought. "I can't tell you anything about our client either," he said, "except to say our client is perfectly legitimate."

"Okay, just tell me when Steve was killed; where was he killed."

"I can tell you when, I don't know if I can tell you specifically where. He was killed, allegedly, on July 19, 1992. In Asia. So I don't mind telling you he is allegedly dead in Asia."

"He was supposed to go on trial September 1st. So he turns up dead in Asia. Hmmmm. It concerns me you're saying allegedly dead."

"How so?" he asked, getting ready with his pen again.

I took out a Nicorette. Since my goodbye to the Paper Fan in September 1990, I'd quit smoking. Having avoided a quick death, I didn't want to invite a slow one, but every now and then I liked a dose of the harmless chemical to juice my normal New York belligerence.

"All right, look, if you start going from rock to rock to get to some destination on behalf of some mystery client and my name comes up as one of your sources, it could be very dangerous for me."

"I can understand that, and that won't happen."

"Good, but that's just the first part. The second part is that if you want me to help you with your involvement, without helping me in mine, forget it. That kind of discussion's not the way I work. You can tell that to your client. Or I'll tell him. As soon as you and I say goodbye, I'll find out who he is."

I took some satisfaction in having rearranged the bottom and top rails on this fence. "Mr. Gould," Richards said finally, "this is my job, I'm under instructions. I was just interested in talking to you so I know how to proceed on this. I'd like to get a better understanding of Mr. Wong's life—his underground associates, perhaps his friends, certainly his family."

"His family? Is his family collecting insurance on this? Is that what's going on?"

His eyes tracked rapidly to the left. "Uh, I don't know the details too much on that."

There it is, I thought. That's what this is all about.

"So you're working for an insurance company. Steve's been killed or murdered overseas and been incinerated, so you're not sure if it's Steve. So knowing Steve from my article, a scam seems consistent with his career. So you're investigating an insurance scam. Am I right or wrong?"

His only answer was another inadvertent glance away from me, which caused me to feel a surprising cascade of relief. I hadn't exactly cried when Richards gave me the news yesterday, but I'd felt awful enough. I'd leapt to the conclusion that Steve had been murdered by his own people, burned to a crisp as a lesson to all who would transgress, and his death, I was sure, would be written below my name in the karmic minus column. Now that grief was turning into excitement. He was "dead" and our deal was off. God, did I miss Steve.

I shook Richards's hand. "Okay, Richards, your ends are my ends," I said. "Lemme call a Mountie and I'll get back to you."

Acting Corporal Rick Aselton was a drug cop who'd been called off another case to help arrest Steve in the Project Bugs sting. I phoned and gave him the news that a life insurance company's private eye was looking into a claim by the relatives of Steve. "Who supposedly disappeared off the face of the earth," Aselton said.

"I think the guy's still alive, Rick."

"Oh, I'd have to agree with you on that one."

"It sounds like he took out a ton in a life insurance policy."

"He sure did. It was quite a bit of money, a substantial amount. We found that out after, of course. The big joke is about Steven Lik Man Wong going missing over in the Philippines, killed in a car accident."

"The Philippines, yeah. A car accident—burnt to a fucking crisp is what I heard."

"I don't know if it was actually *in* the car accident. What I heard, he went over to the Philippines and supposedly was killed in the jungle, on some remote island called Negros. Then his body was cremated, burned locally, and everything else—no proper identification was ever made. A real crock of shit. I would suspect he's in Hong Kong, waiting for the insurance money to come through. Yeah, that's the standing joke in the drug office, Terry. It's a joke because, first of all, the judge should never have let him travel, I don't know why the judge ever gave him his passport back—"

"*The judge gave him his passport back!?*" I shouted.

"You didn't know that? Well, welcome to British Columbia's world of justice. Unit One has quite a bit of information on all of that. Mike Hiller's the investigator who's in charge, he'd probably be the best to talk to—but I should talk to him first and see where the investigation is at this point. You can nose around on your own, of course, but in your situation—you know—you still wanna live to tell it."

"Ah life's too long anyway, Rick," I cracked. When he didn't laugh I mentioned my theory. "The insurance company doesn't wanna pay the money. Steve made it out to his family—or was it Laura?"

"I'm not sure if it was his girlfriend or his mother, it was one'a the two anyways," Rick said. "But I wouldn't wanna pay it either. Suffice it to say there's a lot of people now would love to see him come to justice. Everybody's worked on Steve at one time or another and we're all frustrated. Why don't we deal with it like this: I'll call Unit One and speak to Mike Hiller directly. He'll talk to the staff sergeant and then take it from there. I think everybody pretty well read that drug-war article you wrote. Everybody was talking about it when it came out."

The drug-war article Aselton was referring to was published as a cover story in *Vancouver* magazine's May 1992 edition. A month later, that is, four weeks before Steve had taken off for Asia, the RCMP's Drug Intelligence Unit had republished "Drug War? What Drug War?" in the June issue of their eyes-only bulletin, distributed to drug agents across North America. The bulletin's editor, Corporal Roy Bergerman, had added my home phone number to the article's end, inviting readers to call me with "comments you may have on the article." Within days of its appearance, my Rolodex doubled. The calls came from U.S. DEA agents and INS officials, from Asian squad city cops and Mounties like Aselton. "Drug War" hadn't mentioned Steve once, since I was still living under a death sentence if I broke our "deal," but its thesis explained why the Paper Fan would shortly find it so easy to get out of jail free, pass Go, and then try to collect $200 after his miraculous rebirth.

Contrary to popular belief, there *was* no war on drugs being waged in Vancouver. The cops were certainly arresting traffickers, but the courts were nullifying those arrests. At the time I wrote the article, only 7 percent of the people convicted of dealing hard drugs went to jail for more than three months and a third of the trafficking charges filed that year had been stayed. I tracked down David Lim, the drug dealer whose record Steve had unscrolled for me. Now supposedly an ex-trafficker, Lim was a veteran of 16 arrests, 27 charges, and 12 guilty verdicts, which had cost him only $1,400 in fines and three 10-day jail sentences; until he was finally handed a 10-month sentence, he hadn't even factored jail into his multimillion-dollar business plans. Neither did his gangster buddies. The upshot was that Vancouver had become a magnet for thousands of junkies shooting up in the streets, and out-of-town traffickers who considered it a safe haven. It was a frustrating state of affairs for drug cops like Aselton, Bergerman, and Staff Sergeant Jerry Moloci, who headed Unit One.

A couple of weeks after my call to Aselton, Moloci gave me the okay to visit Hiller at the RCMP's concrete and glass HQ at 33rd and Heather. By then the investigation into the disappearing Paper Fan had long since been terminated. Steve's ashes had arrived in Vancouver from the Philippines on August 7, 1992, a death certificate had been issued on August 13, and his funeral had been held the next day. Two weeks later, on September 1, the judge at the opening of his conspiracy trial found Steve "not compellable." Although he let the charges stand, he did not issue a warrant for the dead man and later severed Steve's case from Yak and Tam's. On September 8, Steve's lawyers, Neil Sacks and Jim Hogan, applied to Mike Richards's mystery client for Steve's benefits, backing up the claim with a thick stack of documents from the Philippines, including numerous eyewitness affidavits and police reports. No funds, no time, no manpower, no cooperation from the Department of External Affairs, and, most particularly, no warrant from the judge, were the reasons Unit One had found it necessary to put Steve's file on ice.

Nevertheless, neither Moloci nor Hiller had given up. Hiller was a six-foot-four-inch, 13-year veteran, as soft-spoken and clean-cut as Gary Cooper, to whom I thought he bore a vague physical resemblance. As we rode the elevator from the headquarters lobby to Unit One's floor, Hiller said Steve's lawyers were now pressuring the Crown "to abate the charges," that is, wipe them from the books, on the grounds that the Paper Fan had died before trial. Hogan and Sacks reasoned that since a man was innocent until proven guilty, and a dead Steve could never be proven guilty, it was only fair to nullify the slight against his good name. Meanwhile, as word of Steve's caper began to make its way through the gangster underworld, Chinese drug dealers were watching to see whether the Paper Fan could pull this off.

"How you dealing with the lawyers?" I asked.

"I'm quite adamant, this is a scam," Hiller said, leading me down the fluorescent-lit corridor to the unit. "If we abated the charges we could never reinstate them. I'm standing my ground."

Hiller introduced me to his boss, Moloci, a barrel-chested mustachioed fellow whose voice boomed through the office in good fellowship. We shot the breeze about other bad guys I'd been writing about for *Saturday Night*, the national magazine I was now working for as a contributing editor, and then Hiller took me down a passageway to a small interview room near the planning office where Project Bugs had been developed. The walls of the interview room were done up in white and yellow tiles that swirled in patterns vaguely reminiscent of an Aztec relief, which for me lent an air of magical importance to the moment.

"The insurance companies handling this are Prudential and Voyageur," Hiller said, looking at his notes. "At this point they're being sued by Steven's parents and I think they'll give you any information that we can't—just based on the fact that a lot of what we have is sourced or privileged." He said the insurance companies were on the hook for $1,080,000 to Yue Kim Wong, and he thought I could expect them to be very cooperative. He asked if I wouldn't mind keeping the Mounties informed of anything I found out on my own.

That was okay by me, and I started right in informing him of some inquiries I'd already made. "You ever meet David Lim?" I asked.

"Yeah, I worked on him," Hiller said.

"He knows his way around, and more important he hates Steve. He says Steve's two white buddies know what's going on." I took out my notebook. "Charles Gough and Sonny Newson. He calls Gough 'the Chink.'"

"We're familiar with those two," Hiller replied. "You'll see Newson's name coming up repeatedly in documents from the Philippines."

"Okay, here's something else. There's an old Triad guy at the Hoi Ming Gwok named Ming, eyebrows like a sheepdog. He used to be Steve's mentor."

"Shows up there at two every afternoon," Hiller said.

"That's him. Lim says Ming's aware of what went on, although to get it you'll need a Cantonese speaker in plainclothes on him."

Hiller made a note. "Mmmhmm—"

"So what I'm planning—I'll follow up on all these leads, put it all together here. Then I'll go over there, I'll get the proof, and I'll find him for you. Then I'll tell you where he is, you get the warrant, and arrest him. All I want in exchange is to be sitting behind him on the plane when he comes back in chains."

"Sounds like you got it all worked out," Hiller nodded soberly. Then he cracked a smile—the first of the interview—and handed me a sheet. I looked down at half a dozen insurance company contacts. "Apparently Prudential's got an ex-CIA guy on it who's talking with the Philippine National Bureau of Investigation," he said. "It's their version of the FBI. The NBI's a small force. There's another police force, though—the Philippine National Police. That's the big one."

"You mean big in Steve's scam, or just big physically?"

"Both. Put it this way: I don't think you want to contact the PNP directly about Steven before you go over. Overall, I think you're going to have to be pretty careful on this."

"Have you talked to anybody in the NBI?"

"Nope. That's country to country. We can't do that unless DOJ okays it. We don't have a warrant so we haven't gotten an okay. So, no, we haven't phoned the Philippines once on this." Hiller turned a page. "The trial's set to start up again in September. Obviously we've got an interest in getting a warrant; the insurance companies have their own interest—they don't want to pay the money. See, we're coming at this from two directions." He placed his elbows on the table and put the tips of his fingers together. "And it's checking out. It does make sense. I don't think you'll be on a wild-goose chase over there."

The vice president and associate general counsel of Prudential didn't think I'd be on a wild-goose chase in the Philippines either. After James Gallagher got the results of his own investigation, he flew to Vancouver to meet me at the company's downtown law offices on the 27th floor of 700 West Georgia Street. A secretary showed me into a conference room, from whose windows I beheld a spectacular view of the mountains and Burrard Inlet. While I waited for Gallagher, I eyed the parade of Asian cargo ships floating under the Lions Gate Bridge. One of the vessels was almost certainly carrying a shipment no bigger than a shoe box that would make the town's addicts happy. Hidden among thousands of other shoe boxes in a container stacked on a ship with hundreds of other containers—each of which cost $1,000 to inspect—the smack would be almost impossible to detect. I looked east to where that smack would end up. Chinatown's alleys and the blocks bordering them had been taken over by users and sellers, and as their numbers grew, they were advancing into other lower-middle-class areas. The residents felt their neighborhoods had been sacrificed to the open drug market, and their sense of hopelessness was becoming extreme. I had witnessed this same downward progression in New York, and I didn't want to see it here. The network of people who brought the drugs in and who marketed them had to be stopped. People like Steve.

On entering the conference room, Gallagher plopped a large brown envelope on the table. He was a stout man, quite staid in dress and expression, but he was as excited as I was by this criminal melodrama. "It's amazing, this should be a Hollywood movie," he said, opening the envelope and pulling out sheaves of stapled reports. "Nothing I've ever seen of suspected fraud cases comes close, at least not on the scale of all the people involved, and all the countries!"

We browsed the reports one by one, and what Hiller had not been able to give me, Gallagher now offered up. When we were done reviewing the files, he turned on the speakerphone and put us through to his undercover agent in the Philippines, Danilo Mendez, who seemed to know someone of importance on each of the archipelago's 7,000 islands. Danilo then gave the phone to his cousin—an NBI cop, Supervisory Agent Virgilio Mendez. As part of an investigation into corruption in the Philippine military and the national police, Mendez had been looking at the doings on Negros after Steve's suspicious death. He explained that his information pointed to a powerful international drug syndicate at work on the island: lawyers, government officials, top police officers, and the military appeared to be involved with Steve's 14K Triad. Certain Steve's death was faked, Mendez wanted to implicate and prosecute the kingpins involved in the Steven Wong affair, since the NBI was finding it impossible to catch them at drug trafficking and money laundering.

Unfortunately, Mendez had a problem: the NBI needed the Canadian government to make an official representation to the Philippines before they could launch a full-scale investigation into the death of a foreign national. "So far we have not heard a word from your embassy," he said. "Is there perhaps a reason for that?"

I took a stab at addressing what he was hinting at. I told him I didn't *think* there was any funny business; there was just no warrant for Steve's arrest. "The Canadian government believes your police reports," I said. "They think he's dead."

"I see," Mendez answered softly. There was a long silence, during which I could hear the chaos of a Philippine street in the background. "All right," he said finally, "shall we approach the situation perhaps in the following manner: if a Canadian journalist were to come over here on a reputable assignment, then I and some of my men could accompany him in his investigations to see that certain procedures were followed. So as to make his reports legally sound for your authorities to be persuaded of the fraudulent death. Shall we say it like that? Does that perhaps sound feasible?"

"Certainly Virgilio," I replied, "let's say it like that. That sounds perfectly feasible."

After the crackly conference call, Gallagher stacked all his reports, re-inserted them in the envelope, and handed the package to me. As I took the envelope, he said, "Just to inform you, we've been told that there are very few people we can trust on Negros. I mean by that, our own people, for their own safety, have tried to go in and get out without anyone knowing they were there. But obviously, as a journalist, you're going to be opening this up."

"More than that, Jim," I said. "I obviously want to find the guy."

"And that is certainly congruent with our ends," he said. "You're the expert on Mr. Wong. But at a very basic level there are personal-security issues if you walk into that rat's nest and start asking questions. So we've decided to have our agent arrange protection for you in the Philippines; as well, we'll offer you the services of a security firm in Hong Kong if that's necessary. We're going to be as helpful as we can—but I have to say this: we can't guarantee your safety. I just wanted you to know that."

To warm the sudden coldness in my butt and lighten the mood of this clearly decent man, I replied in wiseass mode: "Ah, Jimmy, I can take care'a these characters. All I want from Prudential is a break on a million-dollar life insurance policy and a ten percent bounty when I come back with Steve's head."

I had to tell Gallagher three times I was just kidding.

I went home with my pile of material and began collating it with what the Mounties had been able to give me and with what I'd learned on my own time. To my mind there were still some gaping holes I would have to fill in before I took the leap and traveled to Asia. But I now had enough to begin drawing a wall-length schema of the events leading up to July 19, 1992.

When I had known him, at the height of his dangerous days battling the Lotus and Los Diablos, Steve had held a Prudential life insurance policy of a mere $80,000. On January 25, 1992, the day before his 28th birthday, he changed his policy. He'd been busted and his war-torn nights had actually calmed down by then, but he nevertheless drove to Chinatown and applied for another three-quarters of a million from an insurance agent named Stanley Leung.

In March, after the policy was approved, Steve went to his lawyers' office on Alexander Street and instructed Neil Sacks to draw up an affidavit applying for a loosening of the terms of his bail. It was an 11-point deposition that ranks as one of the more audacious documents submitted to the court that year, and deserves to be quoted in full.

I, Steven Lik Man Wong, of 5018 Clarendon Drive, Vancouver, British Columbia, MAKE OATH AND SAY AS FOLLOWS:

1. THAT I was charged on December 12, 1990, with conspiring to traffic and import heroin.

2. THAT on December 14, 1990, in Courtroom 102, Vancouver Provincial Court, His Honour Judge K. Smith ordered that I be released on a recognizance in the amount of $100,000.00 with one or more

sureties and that I surrender any passport in my possession and not apply for a passport.

3. THAT it was my understanding that I would be permitted to request the return of my passport if I required it for travel so long as I submitted an itinerary to the R.C.M.P. regarding such travel. I took this understanding from submissions made by my lawyer at the bail hearing referred to in paragraph 2 above as well as submissions made by the Crown prosecutor at that hearing.

4. THAT I have maintained contact with my lawyer, James W. Hogan, throughout this proceeding.

5. THAT my trial in this matter is set for September 1 through October 2, 1992, in the Supreme Court of British Columbia.

6. THAT I have lived in Vancouver for twenty-four years, and have resided at 5018 Clarendon Drive in Vancouver with my mother and father for approximately four years. I have many other relatives in the Vancouver area and all of my personal roots are in Vancouver. I am a Canadian citizen.

7. THAT I have made one trip outside of Canada since I was charged in this matter and that was to New York for two weeks with my nephews. I took this trip without incident and returned as planned.

8. THAT my girlfriend, Patsy Chan, who I have known for over one year, resides in Hong Kong with her family. We have intentions to marry in the future and it is traditional that I meet her family which we both desire me to do as soon as possible. I require my passport in order to travel to Hong Kong for this purpose.

9. THAT if this Honourable Court sees fit to increase the amount of my surety recognizance I would be in a position to comply with such an order. My parents, Yue Kim Wong and Cheung Ing Wong, own the property located at 5018 Clarendon Drive in Vancouver. This property has an approximate equity value of $500,000.00. Both of my parents are willing to act as surety to an increased amount.

10. THAT if this Honourable Court sees fit to order that I report to the R.C.M.P. in Hong Kong, I would comply with such an Order.

11. THAT I swear this Affidavit in support of a Petition for variance of my bail.

Beneath Point 11 Hogan's partner, Neil Sacks, notarized the sworn affidavit at the bottom and, to the right, the Paper Fan signed a cramped and stubby "Steve Wong."

On March 17, 1992, the affidavit was quietly registered at the Supreme Court of British Columbia, where it was examined by the Honorable Mr.

Justice Cohen three days later. Typically, the schedule of prosecutors in the underfunded DOJ was overloaded on the day Steve's application came up, and the prosecutor of the moment neglected to inform the Mounties of what was taking place. He did argue that the charges were serious enough to keep Steve's passport in the custody of the government, but, with no witnesses called, Judge Cohen had to consider whether in fact those charges would tempt the accused to jump bail overseas. One other factor was the criminal record of the "auto sales manager" before him. Steve did not have a criminal record. Had the Mounties known what Steve was up to, they could have testified to his past—but they didn't know.

On March 20, Judge Cohen amended the Paper Fan's bail as follows:

> 1) Mr. Wong's (the accused's) passport is to be returned to him forthwith.
> 2) The accused, Mr. Wong, is to report within twenty four (24) hours of his arrival to the R.C.M.P. in Hong Kong and is to inform the R.C.M.P. of the date of his departure.
> 3) The accused, Mr. Wong, is to surrender his passport on or before July 20, 1992.

In accordance with a literal reading of Point 2, Steve did not inform the Vancouver Mounties that he would be departing Canada; he only felt inclined to tell the Mounties *in Hong Kong* (when he was already there) that he was leaving the Crown Colony—for the Philippines.

As soon as he got his passport back, Steve did three things. Tax time was rolling around and in order to camoflage his considerable proceeds of crime, he declared personal bankruptcy. He then broke up with Laura, his girlfriend of several years—for reasons that would not become clear to me until I spoke with her. Next he phoned his girlfriend in Calgary, Lily Lee, and invited her to accompany him on his trip to Hong Kong, all expenses paid. He told Lily he wasn't sure of his departure date—he had to make certain arrangements—but would let her know. According to what Lily later told the Mounties, Steve mentioned absolutely nothing about going over to meet the family of his supposed fiancée, Patsy Chan.

May was a busy month for Steve, much of it spent making plans with the two white men in his life. Sonny Newson had a kite tail of convictions for drug trafficking and violent crimes that was as long as he was tall, and he was then engaged to marry a Filipino woman on the island of Negros. He had been traveling to the Philippines regularly since 1989. The other white guy, Chuck the Chink, had accompanied Steve to Hong Kong on most of his trips in the years before the Project Bugs bust. The trio met in a penthouse pad that Steve had been sharing for a year with a Gum Wah gangster named Edison Yee (contradicting the claim in his affidavit that he resided with his parents). The penthouse, at 711 Broughton, just off Robson, sat four stories above a flat that the Chink rented. Possibly figuring that the timing of the climax of his trip too neatly preceded by a day the July 20 date he was supposed to surrender his passport in Vancouver, on May 27 Steve applied to Judge Cohen for an extension. He immediately received it: "The accused, Mr. Wong, is to surrender his passport on or before August 1st, 1992."

A few days later he phoned Lily Lee and solidified their departure plans for the first week of July. Steve then went down to his travel agent in Chinatown and purchased the tickets, plus a $250,000 life insurance policy from Voyageur. He was now carrying $1,080,000 in life insurance, with his mother, Yue Kim, the beneficiary.

Lily flew in from Calgary and flew out with Wong for Hong Kong the next day on Canadian Airlines. The couple arrived late Saturday afternoon, July 4, and checked into a new hotel, the name of which Lily couldn't remember. On Sunday they took a taxi to a market and "did a lot of shopping," all on Steve's tab. For his mother Steve bought a ring encrusted with emeralds and diamonds, a jade pendant, and an ivory mah-jongg set. The next morning Steve kept his promised engagement with the RCMP, taking the elevator up to their 14th floor liaison office at One Exchange Square, where he startled an officer named George Gibbs with the announcement that he was just checking in, and that he would be leaving for a week's vacation to the Philippines the following Saturday, July 11, to attend his friend's wedding. Gibbs hadn't a clue who Steve was; and the Mounties at Unit One only learned Steve was out of the country when Gibbs phoned Vancouver and asked: "Who's this character Steven Wong who says he's supposed to report to me?" By then Steve was out the door.

According to what Lily later told the Mounties, the couple spent their week touring, shopping, and enjoying the Hong Kong high life. During one of their outings, Steve met with someone Lily identified as Patsy Chan, but according to Lily, Patsy was "just a friend. I don't think there was any love involvement. Not that he told me." And there was no meeting between Steve and Patsy's family. On Friday, July 10, Lily and Steve took the 40-minute jetfoil ferry to Macau, where they were met at the terminal by a limo containing some important-looking colleagues who proceeded to give the couple the red-carpet treatment in the Las Vegas of Asia—whose underworld was dominated by the 14K Triad.

On July 11, his last day in Hong Kong as a living man, Steve, on the way to Kai Tak Airport, handed the jewelry and mah-jongg set to Lily, instructing her to give the gifts to his mother in Vancouver. ("Did you not find it strange that Steven asked you to give the ring to his mother—wouldn't he want to give it to her himself?" the Mountie asked her after Steve's death. "No," Lily replied, "I don't find it strange. He's disorganized. He would probably lose it.") An hour after she boarded her flight home to Canada, Steve flew on to Manila, where he was met at Ninoy Aquino International Airport by Sonny Newson, who had flown in from Canada that day.

The movements of the two gangsters over the next week are lost in the mists of desperado lore, but at 11:30 A.M. on July 19, they surfaced, walking out of the Royal Palm Hotel into the solar furnace of Bacolod, the capital city of the Hawaii-size island of Negros, 310 miles south of Manila in the Visayan Sea. The pair must have looked like what cops call a Mutt-and-Jeff deuce. The low-altitude Paper Fan, his eyes and backside now a bit baggier than they were at his arrest 19 months ago, strode alongside the tall lanky Newson through the killing heat of this poverty-stricken town, with its potholed streets lined by open sewers and a beggar on every corner.

Steve could not have asked for better environs to arrange his next few hours—desperate places offering unique opportunities to desperate men. Aside from Goldenfield, a 10-square-block area of Bacolod next to the airport—which was devoted to gambling casinos and nightclubs filled with teenage hookers who catered to Chinese gangsters and other Asian tourists—the island of Negros was destitute, a paradigm of all that was wrong in the Third World. Much of the mountainous interior was in a state of armed insurrection against the lowland's oligarchic abuses, official corruption, and rapacious mismanagement. Excluding drugs, gambling, prostitution, and a couple of beach resorts that catered to the rich, "Sugarland," as the island was known in the Republic, had a one-industry economy: the cultivation and processing of sugarcane on huge plantations lorded over by a few wealthy families living in palatial haciendas amidst the squalor of their landless workers. In 1985 the bottom had fallen out of international sugar prices and 250,000 plantation workers had been thrown out of work. Because the *hacienderos* refused to make even a tiny fraction of their one million acres available for growing food crops, many starving peasants went to the mountains to join the Communist New People's Army in a guerrilla war against the government. The lawless, denuded mountains, now covered in secondary jungle, were a virtual national reserve for criminals who had the right credentials: according to Virgilio Mendez, some of the guerrillas had recently replaced their dried-up cold war funding by growing poppies, refining heroin, and running methamphetamine laboratories for members of Steve's 14K syndicate.

About noon, Wong and Newson arrived at the dilapidated Hernaez Street bus station, just a few blocks from the air-conditioned office of Sonny's soon-to-be father-in-law, Alex Abastillas. The wealthiest and most influential lawyer on Negros, Abastillas represented the *hacienderos* in their dealings with the government, and his business card sported the slogan "In God We Trust." As Sonny was a frequent visitor to Negros, he had made all the arrangements for an expedition Steve wanted to take to a town called Santol, high up in the NPA-dominated mountains.

Waiting at the bus station for the two Vancouver big shots was Sonny's Filipino friend, a peasant's son with high ambition named Stephen "Bindo" Granada. Sonny introduced Steve to Granada, who respectfully took the suitcase in which the mobster kept his ample undershorts and his bullet-proof vest. Steve held on to his cell phone, whose scramble-codes were now so complicated that he'd recently boasted to his friend Chuck the Chink, "Even the FBI in Quantico can't break them."

At 12:45 Steve said goodbye to Newson, then boarded the air-conditioned Ceres Line bus with Granada for the first leg of his journey south along a road bordered on the west by the powder-blue Panay Gulf and on the east by sago palms and the omnipresent sugarcane fields. An hour and 15 minutes later, Steve and Granada arrived in a ramshackle town named Binalbagan, Granada's home ground.

Beside the bus stop was a line of gaily colored "tricycles"—taxi-licensed motorbikes whose frames were welded to sidecars that could, in a pinch, seat two people. One of these lightweight vehicles was owned by Granada's friend, Ronald "Kulas" Gamboa, who agreed to take Steve to Santol, "as it would be a matter of sight-seeing," he would later swear in a statement to the Philippine National Police.

If the PNP reports are to be believed, at about 2:30 Steve squeezed in beside Granada in Gamboa's sidecar, and the trio headed inland, passing, 20 miles later, through Isabela—a heavily fortified police-and-army barracks town, the last outpost before the rebel-held mountains. It was the height of the rainy season, and as the jungle closed in and the road narrowed to little more than a rocky buffalo track, the cumulus clouds, which had been building all day, suddenly let loose a torrential downpour, turning the trail into a running stream. According to their affidavits, Granada and Gamboa told Steve that it would be best to turn back, but Steve told Granada "he will answer for everything in case the tricycle shall be damaged."

At 5 P.M., just a couple of miles shy of Steve's destination, with Gamboa gunning the tiny engine to pull the combined 400-pound weight of the three passengers up a steep incline through rushing water and over two-foot rocks, the tricycle bumped "a stone," tipped over, and Steve was hurled violently from his seat, smashing his skull against "another stone." "The injury on the head was so severe that he died on the spot," Granada attested later. The two men unceremoniously left Wong dead in the ditch and, "in panic . . . we went to report the incident to [the] PNP."

In their panic, however, Granada and Gamboa raced right by the Isabela police station, reporting instead to the Binalbagan station. The cop they spoke to was the highest-ranking PNP officer south of Bacolod, Senior Inspector Celestino Guara, a longtime acquaintance of the lawyer Abastillas, Sonny Newson's future father-in-law. Guara told Granada and Gamboa that they should travel the 50 miles back to the capital and inform Sonny and Abastillas of the mishap. Then, without telling his subordinates, Guara strapped on his guns and went alone where other lawmen dared not tread to view the body. It was still pouring rain and completely dark, but Guara found the corpse and all of Steve's identifying papers, and noted Steve's "severe head injuries," "several tattoos," and "Oriental features." Without reporting the accident in either Santol or Isabela, Guara returned to Binalbagan with the body and stashed Steve in an undisclosed location separate from the two modern morgues east of town. Here he went through Steve's pockets and scrupulously listed the "personal effects of the deceased," including: "ONE (1) passport Canada CN 144816, one (1) male wallet containing one card BCAA CAA, one (1) British Columbia driver's license," plus all Steve's credit cards and roughly $1,000 in Canadian, Hong Kong, Macau, and Philippine currency.

All these effects, plus the body, Guara turned over to Sonny and Abastillas when they arrived the next afternoon. Apparently shocked at the rapid decomposition of Steve and also ignoring the two available morgues, the lawyer and the drug dealer ordered that Steve be shipped immediately to Bacolod for cremation.

Over the next couple of days, Guara, Abastillas, and Sonny collected a stack of affidavits and certificates, which included a death certificate signed by a local doctor; a certificate from a 78-year-old Santol police captain (a rare official the rebels had not yet killed), who in Binalbagan gave a detailed description of Steve's tattoos and attested that Steve had died exactly as reported; a municipal permit to transfer the cadaver to the capital; a Bacolod Health Department certificate granting permission to cremate the body; and a certificate from a "licensed cremator" named Aaron Menace, who stated that on July 22, he burned Steve's remains in the crematorium of the Bacolod City Cemetery. Guara then filed his report, which declared Steve's end "purely accidental in nature," and recommended "that this case be dropped and closed." Abastillas placed the report atop all the other paperwork and shipped the package to the Canadian embassy in Manila.

While all this was going on, Steve's penthouse roommate, Edison Yee, received a call from Sonny Newson on Negros telling him of the tragedy. Yee phoned Steve's parents, then phoned Lily Lee. From the hysterical reaction of the women in Steve's life, they almost certainly believed the news that Steve's days of gangs, dope, and shoot-outs had come to an untimely end.

In the Philippines, however, Virgilio Mendez and a Negros NBI boss named Philip Pecadre were not so sanguine. According to what Mendez had told me in that conference call at Prudential's law office, the NBI knew there was no crematorium in Bacolod, nor was Aaron Menace a licensed cremator, nor could a tricycle make it up to Santol without someone pushing it most of the way.

CHAPTER 11

THE CHINK

———

I'm on my nineteenth arrest. I got nothin' to hide.
—CHUCK GOUGH

I was standing in the first-floor apartment of the middle-aged managers of 711 Broughton, just a few blocks from Tsunami Sushi in the downtown's swankiest rental neighborhood. "I guess Mr. Wong and Mr. Newson didn't want nobody to know they were here," said Carol Smith, one hand touching at her hair and the other jangling the big ring of keys in her housedress pocket. "We only knew their names after the RCMP showed us their photographs."

"We never even got the rent from anyone in penthouse 2002," said her lanky husband, Al, leaning against the fridge in dusty work clothes, a pipe wrench hung like a gun from his belt. "It was Chuck Gough always paid the rent. He's the one we dealt with on it."

"See, Mr. Yee was supposed to be the tenant there," Carol explained, pointing 200 feet skyward. "But Mr. Gough was on the rental contract for 2002 *and* his apartment 1605. That's why he paid the rent for both units. The Mounties were sayin', 'We don't like the looks of it, be careful.' I told 'em, 'Well, if I half act like I don't know nothin'—'"

All this was very helpful, I thought. Over the phone Carol and Al had agreed to buzz me in but seemed too suspicious to offer anything else. Now that I'd talked myself from the building's art deco lobby into their humble quarters, however, they were gushing geysers of gossip, as if the pressure had been building inside them for a year.

"Were all three living together at once then?" I asked.

"Well, Mr. Wong and Mr. Yee, they moved in together," Carol said, "but only Mr. Yee was full-time. Mr. Wong, he'd be here a month and then not. Mr. Newson, he'd just be on some weekends. Then, when Mr. Wong was supposed to have died, Mr. Yee stayed a couple months, then he moved across the street to the Sheraton-Landmark. Mr. Newson, we don't know when he moved in, except that when Mr. Gough give us the notice for the penthouse in March, I went to show it and there was Mr. Newson living there. And I'm thinking, Okay, Mr. Gough pays cash—never by check—so at least it's covered—"

"Hey listen, that man, he doesn't use a bank for anything," growled Al. "I seen stacks of bills this high all over his apartment, I just can't believe this man, stacks with paper straps, you wouldn't *believe* the amount of money! He says, 'That's why I don't want anybody in my suite.' I said, 'Well, why don't you put that stuff in the bank?' He says, 'I don't need one.' I guess he doesn't need mail either, because he doesn't get mail here. No mailbox, no bank account—"

"Anybody tell you he was arrested nineteen times on thirty charges?" I asked.

"Well, I kinda knew he didn't get that dough from no janitor business," Al replied, referring to the Chink's official occupation. "Strange thing is, he *admits* he's friends with all of them that's involved in Chinese gangs. He's pretty damn well open about all this, talks about it all the time to me. He's even got a fairly well-known tattoo from the gangs he showed me. See, we have Asians like that here, they usually shy away from whites—I guess the language—but Charles, he's an exception, he was raised in Hong Kong, speaks the language fluently—he's a very likable guy so I guess they take him as their own. Kind've a remarkable fellow, actually—"

"Al, wasn't he saying something about going over to Hong Kong to marry Mr. Wong's sister?" Carol asked her husband.

"Ed Yee's sister," Al informed me. "Says he's headed over August 15 and bringing her back to start a family, but I don't believe it. He's likable but not respectable—girls in, girls out—all the time. Everything with him is pretty heavy-duty gang stuff. Certainly they own a big casino over there and everything else."

This took me by surprise. "They? Where? In Macau?"

"Outside of Hong Kong somewhere. His people. You oughta talk to him yourself. You'll probably get more information outta him than from anyone. Just maybe you wanna take this," Al cracked, reaching for his pipe wrench. "Man, the people I seen around him all the time—one's charged with murder and he's out on bail and poking around his apartment all the time. Newson's there off and on, too. Him I wouldn't—"

The phone rang and Al grabbed a call from a tenant. When the conversation turned to a dispute over a damage deposit, Carol discreetly offered to walk me to the door. "I guess it's pretty important you find out what's goin' on from Mr. Gough," she said to my card, then looked up with a shrug of mild concern.

"Well the guy's been tied up with Wong for ten years. Even if he doesn't know where Wong is, he knows Newson, and Newson knows where Wong is."

"Okay just—like Al says, he's very friendly—but you can see it in his eyes—" Carol looked up and down the hall, then whispered "—him goin' psycho on a person."

Maybe it was stage fright, but the elevator seemed awfully slow rising the 16 stories. As the doors grumbled back I inhaled the floor's sweet disinfectant several times, then walked the quiet corridor until I got to 1605, where it was quiet no more. Through the paneled apartment door I could hear what sounded like a whorehouse party going on, complete with loud rock music, a man's hearty laughter, and two women squealing as if they were being thrown into a hot tub against their will.

I knocked. Waited. I knocked again, more loudly. Still no answer. Finally I BAM-BAM-BAMMED the door with my fist. Still nothing.

It occurred to me that if I were a heroin dealer living in a secure tower I wouldn't be answering my door either—unless I was expecting company. I would, however, answer the buzzer downstairs. So I took the elevator down and waited in the landscaped breezeway, chewing Nicorettes by the flower bed that encircled the splashing fountain, giving Chuck enough time to finish his engagement. After half an hour I found his code on the buzzer panel, and pressed. A grouchy voice answered my ring with a "Yup."

There you go, I thought.

"Chuckie, ay, Chuck the Chink!!" I called into the polished metal receiver, as if I'd known him for a million years. "I'm a friend'a Steve's! It's Terry, for Christ's sake!"

Silence. Then. "Who are ya?" he asked.

"Terry Gould! You must've heard'a me from years back. Ay! I was just up at your fucking door but you were fucking, so I'm comin' back up!"

Again there was a silence, followed by: "How did you know to find me?"

"Chuck, everybody's talkin' about ya since Steve went over to visit Sonny."

Another moment of silence. I could picture him staring at the rug, wondering whether it was better to ignore me or find out what was going on. "I'll come down," he said.

Fifteen minutes later a big-gutted guy in baggy sweatpants and a mustard T-shirt pushed through the glass doors. He was maybe six foot one, with gray hair that was fashionably buzz-cut on top and shaved on the sides. Al and Carol were right: Chuck had a friendly face—almost avuncular, with a sweet porpoise grin—at odds with his black little pupils set in icy pale irises. Those killer eyes cased me hard, head to toe, as we closed on each other. "Hey! Great to see ya, Chuck," I greeted him. "Ya remember me?"

He grasped my extended hand, said, "No. I don't know ya at all."

It took an awkward second of silence for me to realize that he was inappropriately holding on, and another second to realize his huge palm was tightening. He darted a look over my shoulder, and I swiveled to see a cobalt Carrera double-parked. At the wheel was a T-shirted young Chinese, staring at us, hand in the console. Now where did he come from? I thought. I told myself: be cool, this has nothing to do with you, Chuck's just being on the safe side, standard procedure given the threat to him of surprise visits. "Hey, I'm Terry *Gould*, Chuck," I beamed. "The writer. About 1990 I hung with Steve for a while and I wrote quite a bit about the guy?" I held my left hand up like a Hollywood Indian, then moved it slowly into my breast pocket and pinched a card, showed it like a ticket.

Chuck lowered his semipsycho eyes to nearsightedly inspect my credentials. "Oh, *you're* the one that did the writings?" he said, not unkindly, letting go of my hand. He threw another look over my shoulder and hitched his head towards Alberni Street.

"And of course Steve's gone now from that accident in the Philippines," I went on, pretending to ignore the tires screeching behind me with heart-stopping panache. "I mean, I don't know if he's alive or not alive, but what I'm doing now, Chuck, I'm writing a history of Steve and the Gum Wah. And since Steve left, they've become a pretty dispersed gang. So Ed Yee and James Newson—everybody's saying you still hang with them."

"Who's everybody?" Chuck asked.

"Oh, you know," I began, and then broke into my usual strategic story, peppering it with the names of the gangsters with whom the Chink had committed his crimes, the cops who'd arrested him, the judges who'd convicted him, the judge who was listening to his current case, and the lawyers who were now defending him, Hogan and Sacks—getting traction on him by pouring his secret biography over his head, letting him know I could be a good friend or a poor enemy. I concluded this threatening shower with a bowl of cream: "Because I gotta tell ya, Chuck, you're a legend for where you are." I shook my head in wonder. "Nobody, but *nobody*, gets there who's white. I mean, couple'a years ago Bill Chu told me you talked the language and everything, but to get that kind of respect—you're kind of a giant to anybody that knows what's what, who cares what's what."

I actually meant that last part, and Chuck seemed to respond well to my sincerity.

———

"Ah, from what I hear they're all chasin' ghosts," the Chink said, 15 minutes later, sitting on the hood of a rattletrap Camaro at the curb and smoking a cigarette. He took a puff and flicked the butt in the general direction of CLEU headquarters. "Somebody put the bug in their ear somewhere that he's not dead, but as far as I'm concerned, they're chasin' ghosts. I mean, I was at the house, his mom and dad's, and at the funeral. And I stood—like from where we are, the mother was where that bus is—and I could hear her just going through pain and agony. You know, you can't do that to your mother. I don't believe he could."

"Well, you know what they're saying, a million-dollar life insurance policy," I reminded Chuck. "Steve's looking at a tough trial, so Sonny helps him out on Negros—and now the jungle's got a story to tell."

"Ah, if you believe that you probably think Elvis Presley's alive," Chuck retorted. "Christ! There's nothin' to hide. It's all in black and white. He goes for a holiday with Sonny and it just happens to end in tragedy. 'Chuck, I was kicking an $800-a-day habit,' Sonny told me, 'but I still know what I was looking at. I still know Steve. He was all rotted and the top of his head may have been crashed in, but you still recognize the face of your best friend, and the tattoos!' You seen these on him yourself." The Chink compressed his fleshy chin to indicate the heads of several signature Triad dragons I could see writhing beneath his wiry gray chest hairs. "Is there any mistaking them?"

"Of course not." I brought my face so close to inspect his red and blue monsters that I could whiff his girlfriends' lavender perfume.

"See, Steve never had to worry about money," Chuck went on. "It's not money with the Orientals, it's face. You got your face, the money comes anyway. You lose your face, you lose everything. Steve was a man of face. I know that personally. I was there when the Buddhist priest blessed him and put that chain and dragon around his neck. And the guy that's the head of the Triad in Hong Kong, the 14K, him and his three sons, they treated him like a king."

I nodded along, as if I knew what he was talking about—Steve must have received that trinket and blessing after we'd said goodbye. "So did you go through the whole initiation yourself?" I asked. "With the chickens and walking over the burning stones and all that Triad Society Lodge stuff?"

"Years ago," he shrugged. "When he got promoted for his deal over here, he put it in for me. Fact is, I've always been well respected in the Triads. Them that knows me knows me, but I've always kept a low profile. Steve, though, he was number one here and he never hid nothin'. That's why the cops just hated him. They tried to put him away, and he told 'em, 'You'll never get me.' Did they get him? No. They had everybody on him. They had Strike Force on him, Mounties, CLEU, Asian Gang Squad. They had him constantly under surveillance. They even tried to get him through his phone in the Philippines. Couldn't get the phone back for ages [after the accident]. They sent it to the FBI and they still couldn't break the codes. That phone was important! Man, it had everything. Only other thing the family couldn't get back was the watch. Sonny figures somebody in the Philippines snaffued it because it wasn't on him when he unzipped the bag. He says he almost threw up. 'Bad enough Steven was dead, but this is like three days later—only thing to do was cremate him.'"

"Well, if he's gone, he's gone—just—" Letting him know I was getting a little tired of the propaganda, I asked if there was an outside chance Sonny would talk to me about the ultimate event—maybe we could trade some information on other matters of concern. Chuck thought my chances were slim. "Sonny don't talk to nobody. Anyway, he's checking in. He took the rap on that passport job. He had his wife over here—"

"Yeah, Ajile Abastillas, the lawyer's girl from Negros," I said. "She got deported yesterday."

Chuck looked at me, a smile finally reaching his cruel eyes. "Not fucking much you don't know, is there?"

"Well it's a sad story," I told him. "It breaks your heart to love a girl and then she's outta the country—"

Sad, but entertainingly congruent with everything else I'd heard about the Sonny-Steve saga. Four months before the Paper Fan had skipped town Sonny decided that his criminal record would probably demolish his fiancée's chances of immigrating to Canada, at least if she applied as Mrs. James Newson. So Steve had offered his assistance, persuading his own girl-friend, Laura, to sponsor Ajile as an immigrant. With no employment prospects, however, Ajile had only managed to get herself on a waiting list. Sonny, who lived by the credo "Ask once nice and then take," had then forged a Canadian passport for Ajile after the wedding, and brought her over as Brenda Yargo. Unfortunately, on June 5 the couple had been driving away from the Broughton Tower when they were stopped by the Vancouver city police. For ID Ajile produced her ersatz passport, showing she was born in Vancouver, but when the cops asked her the location of Stanley Park (just six blocks away and visible from the corner) she said in a thick Tagalog accent that the famous park was near the airport, 12 miles south. After checking with the Department of Immigration, the city cops handed Ajile over to the feds. "She was from a very substantial family, by my judgment," one officer had told me, recalling his interview with the hysterically crying Ajile, who wouldn't admit she knew anything about Steve. "Very well dressed, very sophisticated, and very good-looking. So we said to Newson, 'Look at the mess you got your wife into.'" Newson wasn't interested in cutting any deals for Ajile in return for information on Steve, but he definitely didn't want his wife to go down for the passport, so he pled guilty to uttering forged documents, and, despite an attempt at a delay by his lawyer, Phil Rankin, Ajile had been shipped back to Bacolod.

When I told Chuck that I would be showing up for Sonny's sentencing next week—whether he wanted to talk to me or not—the Chink cautioned me, "Well, buddy, just don't make him jittery. Even the Asians are scared to death of him. They're the ones who gave him his nickname, Son of Sam. The guy's got a paranoia that counts."

"Oh, I'm sure he doesn't do anything casually," I acknowledged.

"I would say so. And you never know who he is. He must have a couple thousand pieces of identification. To this day, I don't know where he lives. When he wants me, he'll call me from a booth and he'll tell me to meet him somewhere. I don't know if he lives in Vancouver or Richmond or Burnaby. The guy wants privacy, he wants privacy. He's a good guy, really, but—" Chuck frosted me with his pale irises. "I mean, for your own safety, I'm sayin' just don't cross him. That's my advice. You're better off speaking to the ladies."

"Well jeez, Chuck—" I punched his arm "—there's a fucking lot to talk to!" I boosted myself onto the car hood beside him. "And between you and me, I'll let you in on something. *That's* what sticks in the craw of the cops, you know, is that Steven got his bail because he was going to marry Patsy over there, but he went over with another girlfriend, Lily Lee, eh?"

"Ex-girlfriend," Chuck reminded me. "Just because you break up with a girl, does that mean you gotta be bad friends for the rest of your life? There's such a thing as friendship, and Lily was really close to the mother and father. It just didn't work out with Steven and her, that's all."

Chuck was disappointingly mum on how to get hold of Lily, who'd disconnected her phone and moved since her interview with the Mounties. So I went at the subject from another angle. From Lily's interview with the cops I knew she hadn't had time to deliver Steve's gifts to his mother, and so she had given the ring, pendant, and mah-jongg set to her sister, Lisa Lee, who'd dropped them off at the Clarendon big house. Lisa, I'd recently learned, was a Vancouver auxiliary policewoman.

"You ever meet Lily's sister?" I asked the Chink.

"Oh yeah, Lily, Lisa—they're good friends of ours and the family. We all threw a party for Lisa upstairs when she made the force, she's a Vancouver cop now, you know. I told her, 'Congratulations—but now stay away from me. You're one'a them now!'"

I made a mental note of that little nugget. What's a cop doing being partied up in the penthouse by the likes of Chuck and Steve? "I always knew Steve had his connections," I said. "Because he went into his bedroom once and he came out with a stack of police reports. He implied it's coming from the Royal Hong Kong Police, Vancouver's sending it out, and it's coming back to him, eh?"

"Well, the Royal Hong Kong Police Department is so corrupt it's unreal," Chuck volunteered. "I remember, I was in a room in Hong Kong, and I heard BAM BAM BAM. I look through the peephole, and there's the cops out there. When I opened the door, all I saw was the uniforms. I was panic struck. But one'a them's *Steve*—dressed up in a uniform! He took his dark glasses off, took his hat off, and there he was. What he did, he went around for two or three days on patrol. He never made any arrests, just wanted to go and trip around with the Royal cops, tour the slum areas and scare the shit outta his friends. He's mysterious. That's what I used to tell him. 'Steve, you're a mysterious guy.' He always told Sonny—"

The front door of the tower swung open and out strode a woman who would stop any gangster conversation. She had silky ash-blond hair, was sunburned the color of an orange and attired in high-heeled sneakers and a terry-cloth two-piece number that held her buttocks and breasts like tightly wrapped packages. She winked with full meaning at Chuck, and then headed for a bike locked to a rack. Chuck must have seen me swallow.

"My gal," Chuck said.

"Get outta here," I whispered. "She looks like a movie star." I meant porn star, but under the circumstances—

"No, her and her sister—both students here. Just a casual thing with us. Actually, I like the women in Hong Kong. They're loyal, faithful, keep their mouths shut."

As she pedaled away towards the park I confided something that had been on my mind for years. "Chuck, you I could see it. But with Steve— maybe it's prejudice—but I always found it nuts that Steve was boyfriend to so many chicks who looked like—" I nodded in the direction of his babe, whose rear was in the air as she rounded Alberni. "Because he wasn't a phys- ically impressive guy, like you. He wasn't tall, he wasn't handsome at all. But he had all these gals—it used to blow me away."

"Another face thing," Chuck said. "You see, they know who he is. We're in our world over here, they're in their world over there. Like I say, every- thing's face in their world. Steve had face. He had money, yeah, but some of 'em, money was just a toy. The girl that met Steve in Hong Kong? Her family owns the Lisboa Hotel in Macau."

Abruptly, I remembered Al and Carol's gossip. A spiderweb of chills spread inward from my shoulders to my spine and then traveled up my neck to freeze my scalp

"The Lisboa. That's Stanley Ho," I said, using Herculean restraint to keep my voice casual. The man owned the monopoly license on gambling in the Portuguese colony, and was the dapper multibillionaire whose name Steve had pointed out to me in the U.S. Justice Department's report. The 72-year-old Ho had three wives and over a dozen children and was now planning a five-story mansion on the corner opposite Stanley Park because the park bore his first name.

"They have an Oriental restaurant up the street here," Chuck went on, pointing down Alberni. "Her husband does," he added, referring, I assumed, to the husband of the woman Steve had met in Hong Kong. "It's beside the Red Robin. Tomakazu. You go into Red Robin, look to the right. It's just a plaything with her husband. Ray. He's the one with the family connection. She was heavy involved with Steve. Just an extra-marriage thing was all it was."

"Patsy is her name. The one he went to meet. It's her you're talking about?"

"Yeah," he said, and I thought, My God, he's giving me the peg the scam hung from.

"Her husband's family owns the Lisboa with Stanley Ho?" I asked. "He's like the third-richest man in Asia. After Li Ka-shing and Cheng Yu-tung, then comes Stanley Ho."

"Oh, he's big all right," Chuck said.

"Look, there's no charges on Ho, but there's been a lot written about him in police reports." I was thinking of an Asian Organized Crime Roster put together by the Mounties in 1990, which listed Ho as a suspected "leader/member" of the Kung Lok Triad—the group senior Mounties believed to be the Toronto extension of the 14K. The roster was secret, but it was wide-open news that the Triads thrived side by side with Ho's legitimate empire: one gangster was a partner in his Jumbo floating restaurant; others ran loan-shark operations on the eighth floor of the Lisboa, in Macau, held leases on his VIP gambling rooms, and headed his casino security. Wouldn't it be just like Steve to use Patsy or Ray to insinuate himself into the Lisboa's Triad paradise? "Ho just about owns Macau," I said, "and you know what they say about Macau, Chuck—it's even looser than Hong Kong. It's one big safe house." (See source notes.)

"Oh, yeah, I love Macau," Chuck mused. "Go upstairs to geisha row. Eat what you want, relax, gamble. Gambling's my big thing. What really floors everybody over there is that I got no accent when I talk Chinese. Steve, he couldn't write in Chinese, couldn't read it or write. Whenever we'd go into a restaurant—I was with him seven days a week in Macau—he'd sit there and ask me, 'What's this, what's this?' He'd tell me what he wants to eat, and then I'd order it. It used to blow the waitresses away. His family too. I'm sitting with about fifteen or twenty Chinese people, and they're looking—'Who's that talking?' I'm used to that, because for years and years . . ."

But by then I was barely listening.

CHAPTER 12

THE SPOOK

———

The Lisboa turns over millions a day!
That's how come Ray can afford to lose so much.
—RUDY DIAZ

The Tomakazu restaurant was exactly where the Chink had described it—
on the second floor of a glass and marble building that took up half the 700
block of Thurlow. Location, location, I thought, strolling the chichi strip in
Vancouver's Asian tourist heart. The 10,000 square feet of retail space
beneath the Tomakazu housed a line of astronomically pricey boutiques,
packed with platoons of shop-happy Japanese wearing tour-company
badges. Within blocks were all the big-name hotels—the Four Seasons, the
Vancouver, the Meridien—the latter owned by Stanley Ho.

I had a coffee across the street and plotted my next move. I needed to
find out more about Ray Chau. There were some cops who might tell me.
They basically moved through town like spooks, collecting information on
likely targets for an investigation. I made a call, then another. A couple of
days later a meeting was arranged for me in the Wong Kee restaurant on
Broadway, where I shared a bowl of sweet and sour MSG with a spook I
would wind up working with on stories about everything from Asians and
Russian Jews to retired senior cops who worked for both. This was my first
meeting with him, however, and I'd been warned he'd probably cover his ass
by writing me up as an informant. That meant the usual criminal-cop info
exchange rate would apply—a ton for him, an ounce for me—with me feeling like a snitch the whole way.

Over lunch, I took him through the entire Steve epic—Goldstone 1989
to the Tomakazu—but he pretended only passing interest, wordlessly sipping
his soup and barely glancing at the paperwork I'd worked so long and hard
to put together. After it occurred to me that he just might be up to speed on
all this, I told him something that he didn't know. If he did know it, Ray Chau

wouldn't still be in Canada. Back in February 1990, Steve had offhandedly mentioned that Ray had an old heroin conviction he'd neglected to declare when he immigrated to Canada. "That's from Wong himself," I said.

He finally graced me with a monosyllable—"Sure."

"I'll bet it's still undisclosed," I added.

"It might be productive," he said. Sip. Sip. Sip.

"So can you tell me something about Ray?"

My spook smirked. "Oh right—*that's* why you're here." He licked his finger and opened his pad.

Ray's full Chinese name was Ray Kam Wing Chau, born August 10, 1949, in Hong Kong. The same immigrant registered as the owner of Kouzins Security, the bodyguard firm that had employed Steve to protect visiting Triad bosses. Ray had moved to Canada in 1988, the same year he'd married a woman whose full maiden name was Patsy Cheuk Ying Chan.

"All right, I'm positive that's the Patsy Chan Steve went to meet," I said. "Could be."

"So where does the family connection to Stanley Ho come in?" I asked.

My spook smiled. "Stanley who." No question mark. He closed his pad. "You're the first journalist I've ever talked to."

"Obviously, but you still kissed me on the first date," I jived him. "When can I see you again?"

Mr. Personality gave me his pager number. "See what else you can get me."

"Tonight we connect the dots, baby!" I told Leslie on Saturday night, in a Thurlow Street parking lot. I holstered my minirecorder, we walked up the stairs to Red Robin, and turned right into the Tomakazu.

The restaurant was L-shaped, with a dozen tables covered by silky gold cloth, bamboo light fixtures above each, Japanese prints on the walls, and a karaoke stage at the apex of the L. As we stood at the cashier waiting to be seated, Leslie almost jumped into my arms when someone shouted, "*Mr. Gould!*" I spun around to see a pretty Japanese hostess of about 20. "Jesus—Wendy!" I yelled in delight.

"Are you digging up dirt here for an article?" Wendy whispered, conspiratorially.

"Only if they serve dirt," I cracked.

I introduced Leslie to Wendy Akune, a student of mine when I had taught high school in the British Properties—one of the brightest kids in any of my classes, and a big fan of my gang articles. I wasn't surprised when she told me she was now a criminology major at Simon Fraser University.

"Wendy, do you know Ray, the owner?"

"Actually I just met him last Saturday," she said, still *sotto voce.* She picked up a couple of menus and held them to her chest. "I only started two weeks ago, so I didn't know who he was. He came in and bought drinks for everybody. He doesn't come in that often. He came in at two-thirty in the morning and stayed till four o'clock."

"That sounds about right—he's a midnight man," I said. I inclined my head towards an empty table beside the karaoke stage. "We're gonna sit over there. Don't make a big deal about it, but if Ray comes in, just gimme the high sign."

"Sure, but you might be able to tell," she said, as she walked us to the table. "He's a very important-looking guy. I could tell he was the owner just from the way he carries himself. He's not a tall guy, though; he's kinda short in fact—"

"Gangsters are generally short, Wendy," I instructed her. "Like movie actors. You'll learn that in criminology."

Wendy pulled back our chairs. I opened the menu and said to it: "How about his wife, Patsy? Ever meet her?"

"No, I haven't met Patsy but—"

Her eyes moved to the left and she shut up.

An Asian fellow of about 50, his long hair tied back in a ponytail, was watching us from the east wall of the L. He was bent over a table, his hands affably on the shoulders of a seated Chinese couple. The way he laughed and moved on to the next table, not at all shy about putting his paws on customers, told me he was some kind of saurian maître d'. He was definitely glancing at us with fixed interest all the while he beamingly jabbered.

"Who's he?" I smiled to Wendy, as if I were asking about the teriyaki.

Wendy smiled back and said she'd get our waitress, then whispered, "Entertainment director."

"She looked really nervous just then," Leslie said, eyes above the menu, holding it high like a book. "I hope you're not getting her into trouble."

"For what, talking to customers? She's a hostess, it's her job."

"I don't mean her job," Leslie replied. "She trusts you. You shouldn't use a coincidence to put her in jeopardy."

"God forbid," I said, and I meant it.

I drank some water, chewed a Nicorette. The subject of jeopardy, I knew, was on Leslie's mind. Increasingly, in the last year, I'd been roping her into my research on various stories. My face was becoming fairly well known and she was terrific cover in public places: she had a great body that drew men to her, a sweet bunny face that brought out the tender side of killers and cons—made them jabber when they should shut up—and a PR exec's ability to flatter and manipulate. And then there was that cabby side to Leslie that allowed her to gossip with gang tarts in the ladies' room, my tape recorder in her purse. I don't want to imply I *forced* my wife into being my accomplice. I was winning awards, making money—she figured maybe I'd soon be earning enough for her to quit her job and devote herself to painting nudes at a bohemian studio on the east side of Chinatown. A night out with me now and then for research purposes seemed worth it to her.

There was something else, too. As long as she didn't have to deal with panic buttons and cops camping downstairs, Leslie, at 43, *liked* the frisson of visiting the gangster milieu with me. She may have despised the foul-mouthed tacky bad guys, but she got a thrill playing Nora to my Nick.

"I know that guy from somewhere," I said, staring at the entertainment director.

Leslie glanced at him. "He does look familiar."

His black shirt was open three buttons, showing heavy gold chains. I sized up the rest of him: black jacket and pants, gold on both wrists and five of his fingers. In other words, the Chinese underworld costume, although as I tried to recall where we'd met I didn't feel any constriction in my stomach. It couldn't have been a bad encounter. Then I remembered—another nice break. "I should buy a lottery ticket tonight," I said to Leslie.

I raised my chin at him and he shouted across the room, "I'm looking and I'm looking and I know that guy, but who is he?!" not meaning anything threatening by it, because Rudy Diaz was, at all times, loud and hyperactively friendly. I swung my arm for him to come on over and, when he got to us, shook his hand, introduced Leslie, and reminded him where we'd all met—an Asian-run nightclub, three years ago. He was the lounge singer, and I'd interviewed him. At the time, I'd been looking into the Lotus gang's control of the entertainment industry, but Rudy hadn't known that. He had sincerely thought I was impressed by his version of "Climb Every Mountain."

"Right, right!" Rudy said. "You know, after that I was looking through *Vancouver* but I'm not in it."

"Sometimes it's hard for Terry to convince the editor to fit everybody in," Leslie told him, and I thought, That's it, kid. What a team.

"Because right after I was trying to buy that place. I figured, man, I could use the publicity!"

"Didn't happen?" Leslie asked.

"Well, the owner wanted $300,000, just for the lease!" Rudy told her.

"There was some trouble there I heard, good thing you didn't," I said, not faking it, because I was truly glad he hadn't bought in. Rudy, I believed, was just a hapless straight Joe trying to get by in the middle of guys who played by the wiggliest of rules.

I asked him why he didn't buy *this* place, and he said it was even more money. "So get Ray and Patsy to help out," I advised. "Except they're not getting along, I heard." I said it just like that, because with Rudy you could.

"No, they're not," he said.

"Are they still living together?"

"Yeah, they're still living together. But I don't know what the arrangements are. I'm not gonna *ask!* Sometimes, you should see Ray when he gets drunk—you know how he is when he gets drunk."

"Yeah, yeah." I waved my hand in despair, as if I'd endured that experience once too often.

"Poor Patsy," Leslie said.

"One time he got so drunk, I thought he was gonna tear the place down. You know, Ray's the black sheep'a the family. He's got one bad habit: he *loves* to gamble."

"Well, in Macau, what else is there?" I said. "And if he's tied in with the Lisboa—"

"Up to date, last year, he lost eight million. Eight *million!*"

"In Macau?"

"Not in Macau. *Here!* Hockey, baseball, football. One time he walks in, he's very depressed. I say, 'What'd you do, you lost again?' He says, 'Yeah.' I said, 'There's ten games today, which one did you play?' He says, 'All of 'em.'"

"You know who his bookie is, don't you—André Ouellette," I guessed. "The guy who used to own the Three Greenhorns?"

"Yeah, yeah, yeah! It's the same guy!"

With that kind of action, I knew it had to be. A French Canadian, André Ouellette was not a made Mafia guy, but he had the Montreal mob's license to run their bet-and-loan operation out on the West Coast. I happened to have been introduced to André by his braggart lawyer, Richard Israels, the top organized crime counsel in town, who'd scored 11 murder acquittals in a row, including one for André. In fact, Israels used to represent the Chink before the Chink had decided he could get good service from Hogan and Sacks, for one-quarter the price.

"Gambling's not my thing, I know it," Rudy was saying. "I went four times to the race track in Hong Kong—I lost. The odds are always with the house, not with you. I go to the racetrack, I bet one horse, I lose, that's enough. Ray says, 'Come on, come on, there's still four more races.' I say, 'Enough—why give it to them? Give it to me!'"

"Patsy doesn't gamble though," I supposed.

"No, she doesn't."

"I mean," I guessed again, "she's always mad at him for that, but—"

"Yeah, they were in love at one time. But something happened to Ray. I don't know. You know, I met Ray in '67, when I started out over there. Then I left in '73. And I didn't see him. Then, about five or seven years ago, I saw him. I said, 'Ray, what're you up to?' He said, 'My mother kicked me out.' I said, 'Why?' He said, 'I lost money in the casino.' I said, 'How much ya lose?' He says, 'One point five.' I said, 'In a year? That's not bad.' He said, 'No, one day.' I said, 'Ah shit!! That would kill ya!' One point five million in *one day!*"

So his mother's the connection, I thought. "Well, Stanley Ho's the third-richest man in Asia," I remarked, thinking, If Ray's mother is in Ho's family, one point five wouldn't kill him.

"If you ask me, he's the richest," Rudy said.

"Ahead of Li and Cheng Yu-tung?"

"Apparently he's even looking at Vegas. Ray plays down in the Mirage. I went down there and saw where they got that volcano show. I was impressed! How long that show runs? Twenty minutes? You know how much it costs? Even for Vegas?"

I was wondering when Vegas would come into the picture.

"And those guys that run those tigers there! Those guys get seventeen million a year!" He was talking about Siegfried and Roy.

"Chicken feed compared to the Lisboa," I told him, bringing the subject back to where I wanted it.

"Well, the Lisboa turns over millions *a day!*" Rudy said. "That's how come Ray can afford to lose so much. One time, when George was still working here, I went looking for Ray. I said, 'Where's Ray?' George says, 'Don't bother him.' I say, 'Why?' He says, 'His mother's in town.' I say, 'So?' He says, 'He's begging! Ten, fifteen days is a good time to come back.'"

I tried to telepathically communicate a question I wanted Leslie to ask: *Ray Chau's mother—what's the connection?* Out loud I said: "You should get Ray to introduce you to Stanley Ho."

"He asked me, but I'll tell ya something—" Rudy raised his eyebrows with an exhausted, out-of-my league expression "—Ray's mother and Stanley Ho are partners in another casino in Macau, bigger than the Lisboa. But the thing is, they went public. So George invested two hundred grand. In less than a year, he got back eighty in dividends. But I didn't have two hundred grand—if I did, you think I'd think twice about it? When it comes to gambling and you own it, you can't lose."

"So is Ray's mother Stanley Ho's sister?" Leslie asked.

"No, see, Ray's mother is Stanley Ho's right arm. In business. Not through blood. Because when Stanley Ho is behind you, you can't lose. Because when people find out who your connection is—" He began peeling imaginary millions off his palm. "'How much you want? Whatever you like, whatever you like!' It's sad but that's how it works."

"Yeah, it is sad," I agreed. "You know—*guanxi*." The Chinese word for *good connections*. "So is Ray coming in tonight?"

"I don't think tonight. He's at a party upstairs by the beach watching the fireworks."

"Can you get us invited?" Leslie asked.

"Naa, this one's private," Rudy said.

"Well, if he's drinking I hope he stays away from the balcony," Leslie joked.

"Ha ha ha ha!" Rudy slapped her back. "Hey, come on, come on you guys." He pulled us up by the arms, dragged us to the stage. "Whaddaya wanna sing?"

"How about 'Climb Every Mountain'?" Leslie asked me.

I had another meal at the Wong Kee—and this time I told the waiter to hold the radioactive MSG. Over tame wonton, my spook seemed to like Ray's connection to André Ouellette. "You can confirm that with Rudy," I said. "If Ray's a slow pay on the millions that Rudy says he lost, he's in trouble."

"Did you talk to André?"

"His lawyer. Israels was bullshitting with him about it and André says he doesn't think Ray's mother will ever cover it. I wouldn't be surprised if Ray's got some investments out there."

My spook gave me one of his disinterested shrugs. "That's old news."

Jeez, I thought, is this ever frustrating!

"Okay, I'll break a confidence and give you something else," I said, although I'd already broken the confidence and given the information to Unit One, as well as to Dan Foley, the head of San Francisco's Gang Task Force. "When I was standing there with Chuck, Ray Sam's wife walked out." The woman had left the building about a half hour after Chuck's girlfriend, carrying herself like an aristocrat and getting into a chauffered car. "You know who Ray Sam is?"

I guessed he didn't because I was able to hold his eyes.

"Ray Sam is Vincent Jew's second-in-command. Of the Wah Ching gang. Chuck told me Vincent Jew and Ray Sam were up here that morning, swimming with Chuck in the pool. Then they went fishing out on Pender Island, stayed in Pender Harbor."

"You shoulda told me that before."

"I have to be very careful with informant information," I said evenly.

My spook licked his finger, opened his pad, and started to write.

I waited. He looked up.

"So—we were talking about Ray's mother," I said. "Stanley's right arm—in business, not through blood."

He turned back a few pages—finally.

Fong Ngo Lam was her name, and she lived at Road House #5, Ocean Court, Clearwater Bay, Kowloon, Hong Kong. Administrator of Shun Tak Enterprises, Stanley Ho's Hong Kong–based corporation, and partner in Ho's Sociedade de Turismo e Diversões de Macau, STDM for short. STDM owned the casinos in Macau, a substantial share of its real estate, and the jetfoil ferry service between Hong Kong and Macau; Shun Tak's portfolio included international shipping, real estate, television, and the aviation industry.

Would Ho or Ray's censorious mother be aware of Steve's existence? I wondered. It didn't seem likely to my spook: a guy like Steve would have been operating several tiers down, serving the kinds of Triad characters who ran the rackets alongside Ho's legitimate empire. One of the rackets was heroin, and the "old news" was that Ray was a suspected big league heroin trafficker. "Take Wong and times him a few times."

"You got Ray's address for me?" I asked.

My spook gave me a thin smile, meaning, I presumed, he wanted something for it.

"All right, well, it's Patsy I'm interested in anyway. I know people that know her."

"That's a good way to work it. Let me know what you come up with."

He looked at the bill but I took it. "You get the next one," I said.

CHAPTER 13

STEVE & PATSY & LAURA & LISA

———

But excitement: Shall we not worship excitement?
And after all, what is life for, except for opportunities of excitement?
—STEPHEN CRANE

Laura could have been sauntering down a runway rather than a hallway in a real estate office. Her tight tube dress revealed a model-lean body, and her cheekbones were dramatically high—even for a Chinese. When she reached the reception desk I asked if she remembered me from the pool hall. She ran her eyes from my trench-coat cop costume to my face and said no, but the gang-girl smirk said yes. I was with *Saturday Night* now, I informed her, writing about Steven's life and death.

Laura surprised me with a burst of warm laughter. "Don't you have anything better to do? Can't you let the guy rest in peace?" Then she turned on her toes and walked back down the hallway. "Sorry, I don't have anything to tell you," she announced, with a contemptuous lilt and a good-bye wave.

"Laura," I called after her. She stopped, swiveled her head sideways to look at my reflection in the glass wall of the boardroom. "I don't have to use your full name or where you work," I said, "*if* we talk. Otherwise you're in there all the way—number one girlfriend of heroin boss Steven Wong until he dumped you for Patsy and Lily."

"*Dumped* me?" She spun around to confront my flesh-and-blood self, her uncertain expression transformed into wide-eyed outrage, and I thought, *Jeez, classing her with the other girlfriends was even more persuasive than mentioning exposure.*

"Patsy was *obsessed* with Steven!" Laura explained an hour later, hissing at me from across the boardroom table. "God, she's like forty? She's married?"

"Sounds pretty tacky," I said, taking her side.

"Exactly! Edison Yee told me Patsy had a crush on Steve, he couldn't get her off his back. So you know what she did? She told Steve, 'Oh, Stevie, Laura's at all the clubs, drinking and cheating.' Which was a total lie—I was at some clubs, but I *never* cheated! She didn't care what was true. For her it was only what she wanted: Oooh, there's Steven Wong—everybody follows him around. . . ."

Not that Laura hadn't been impressed with the Paper Fan's status as well—at least at the beginning. She'd admitted as much at the very start of our interview, stressing that the fascination had been completely age appropriate. She was 15 and Steve 20 when he'd picked her out of a crowd in the school yard at John Oliver. A middle-class girl with high marks and a fast streak, Laura had been dating a Lotus gang member named Barney, a low ranker whose purview was street enforcement. Steve, on the other hand, was then the royal co-chief of the Red Eagles. "Everybody knew Steve and what he was, so I talked to him," she said. "I was curious. Then he told me all these terrible things that Barney did in the Lotus, and that guys like Barney were trying to take over by killing everybody. That really upset me so I told Barney about it. Instead of denying it, Barney said, 'He's trying to pick you up? Well, I can't see you anymore.' See, John Oliver was Red Eagle territory, so the next day Barney saw me with Steve and he ran away."

"Wise man," I observed. "But I gotta tell you, Laura, Steve used to play that good-gangster-bad-gangster routine with school-yard recruits. He used the same technique on you."

"Well, I wasn't *stu*pid." She fluffed her hair and narrowed her street-smart eyes at me. "I knew he was a smooth-talking guy. In fact, I told him, 'If you think you're gonna get back at the Lotus by breaking up me and Barney—' Because I liked Barney, he was actually a nice guy, really cute and shy."

"As opposed to loudmouth fatso Steve," I said. "Laura, if I'd'a been a teacher at J.O. I would never have pictured you two together—because you could've probably been a teen movie star, right?"

"I know it's hard to believe from looking at him," she laughed, "but he did have a lot of girlfriends. Like you mentioned Lily Lee, she was his age, and a few others, so I guess the impression everyone had was: 'He's glamorous.' Also he could be very romantic. See, when I wouldn't go out with him at first, he sent me chocolate and flowers. And then he went away to Asia, he wrote me very romantic letters every day, he said, 'I may not make it back, it's really dangerous and everything, but I really want you to know I'm thinking about you way more than Lily.'"

Lily got so jealous she ended up bopping Laura over the head with a baseball bat at a party. "Can you believe it!?" Laura exclaimed. "I would never do that to someone! She was frustrated that Steve liked *me* so much and not her. But it was really hard for me because he still kept seeing her. Finally, a year later, she gave up and took a job in Calgary and we began going steady. That was actually a thrilling time for me. Steve's a very generous person. He bought me jewelry and rings he had specially designed, he took me to Hong Kong, I once mentioned to him I wanted a better car, but I didn't want to spend a lot—so what does he do? He goes out and spends like $30,000 cash on a new car for me."

"You knew where the money came from, of course," I said.

"No, not really," she hedged, looking at her watch—an end-of-interview threat she'd been flashing whenever I'd pushed the conversation towards her knowledge of Steve's business dealings. "I just didn't understand that stuff. I just thought he was mysterious. He'd say he had to do his own things, 'There's some things that you don't have to know, Laura.' So I just stopped asking and I didn't know."

I let it slide. "How long did that honeymoon period last?"

"I'd say three years." That is, until Laura turned 19 and could go into bars with her girlfriends after work. "I haven't told this to anybody, so don't make it sound too weird. He was very insecure about his looks—I didn't find him ugly but he was always saying he was ugly and that he was gaining weight and that I was looking at this person or that person. Just looking was a threat to him. Finally he wouldn't take me anywhere but his hangouts. He would say, 'I won't go to those karaoke places anymore, the older guys from Hong Kong want to pick you up, you could get drunk there and cause me problems.' Things like that. I said, 'Steve, I'm with you.' But Steven wouldn't go to those places with me anymore. He decided to keep me really sheltered. So it came to a point I wasn't allowed to go anywhere—just to where he went."

"How charming," I commented, remembering the dingy gambling clubs and the crushingly depressing Fraser Billiards.

"I got *so* sick of those people," she went on, referring to fun folks like Phu and Kim. "They were very crude and ignorant. In fact, that's why I didn't go to the funeral, I just didn't want to see them again. And I have to say, for the last year that we were together, we argued every day, we argued every night, we argued every morning—we always argued. By then we didn't have a lot of trust going either way, to tell you the truth. He would go through my things and I would go through his, looking for whether there was cheating—which I wasn't doing. We were always breaking up and getting back together. Finally he told me he was losing his mind, he had so much else to worry about besides losing me."

"Wasn't that about the time he was also worried about his trial?"

"Really worried. In fact, he would say, 'I'm going crazy, Laura. If I don't get out of this, I swear—' I think he got something from his lawyer about his case and he said he was thinking about suicide. He couldn't face jail, not for ten years."

"Twenty with bad behavior."

"I guess I should've been more understanding of the pressures he was under. Because he was also worried what would happen to his mother and father if something happened to him. You know, a couple of times he was shot at and he was afraid for them if he wasn't there to support them. So I actually went with him and we increased his life insurance like ten times, just so he'd feel a little better, at least about that. I'm in the real estate business so I'm a big believer in being insured. What are you writing?"

I was writing: *She thinks it was her idea.* "Was that when Patsy entered the picture?" I asked.

"All I know is what Edison Yee told me later. Because I actually didn't know anything was going on with Patsy then. Apparently, though, she did get him a birthday present."

"Laura, to me it sounds like he was scheming behind your back even then," I said, "running around with this Wicked Witch of the East he's supposedly marrying. Because you're aware how he got his passport back two months later? He had to have been cooking it up with her."

"I don't think he thought of marrying her for a second," she said. "He was just using her. I know who the husband is—they own that Japanese restaurant next to Red Robin—Ray didn't say anything about a divorce, and he's the type who would. See, he actually tried to pick me up. I met him at a karaoke club, he gave me his card and told me to come eat at the restaurant. So I had it in my purse, Steve was going through my purse one time and he says, 'Who's *this!?*' Really shocked. 'How do you know Ray?' So right away he drags me to the restaurant. Ray didn't show up but we had a fight anyway. He says, 'He's trying to take advantage of the situation.' Meaning he's so rich and Steve and I are breaking up—"

"Or meaning that he's having an affair with Ray's wife," I pointed out. "His *boss's* wife."

"Oh, that I don't know," Laura replied, again looking at her watch. "He never told me he worked for Ray."

"Okay, I won't take up much more of your supper hour," I backtracked for the umpteenth time. "So then what happened?"

"We broke up again and this time I gave him back the rings he gave me." She placed both hands on the table and pointedly leaned forward. "You say 'dumped me,' but I'll tell you how much he loved me then. He started to cry and said, 'People that know me, Laura, would never believe you would get me down like this. Like the police can't get me; they call Revenue Canada, get the tax people after me, they can't get me. The Lotus can't get me. Everybody's trying to get me down—but who does it? You do.' And he begged me to go back with him but I wouldn't. Are you writing that now?"

I was writing, *He begs her to go back so she could sign for Sonny's girl-friend.* "Right, about his love for you," I said.

"In fact, he went to my parents and asked what they could do to get me to go back with him. So my mother said, 'You want us to make her go back with you when we didn't want her to go with you in the first place?' It was really sad—he even went to my brother—my brother never liked him either. Anyway, finally he called me for my birthday in February, he told me he had a present for me, and then we saw one another and it started up again."

"Was that also about the time you sponsored Newson's girlfriend?"

"Let's see—yeah, about then, maybe a little later—but I don't think that's why Steve got back with me, if that's what you mean. He would never use me like that."

"Laura," I said. I leveled with her. "He begs you to get back with him and then asks you to do something that's equivalent to cosigning a loan for his partner in crime? Come on!"

She leaned forward again, this time pointing at my pad and shaking her head as she ordered: "Don't write anything funny like that, because he wouldn't! Steven asked, so I did it for Norm—"

"Norm? Oh, you mean Sonny!" I had to laugh at that. "Tall skinny white guy?"

"Well, his friend—I knew him as Norm, I guess that was his name that week," she said, reciprocating my smile. "But Steven would not get me to do something that would get me into trouble. All she was coming over for was to be Norm's wife anyway—I don't think she was involved in anything else. Steven felt it wouldn't do any harm. I'm sure if anything happened he would back me up anyway, he wouldn't desert me, so I did it for him. But then she never came over anyway. Steve told me she doesn't want to come over because her dad's a big-time lawyer over there and she was happier living in the Philippines."

"But not living happily ever after," I pointed out. "Because she did come over and just got deported, with your name popping up on her file. And Steven's not around to deal with the fallout."

"Oh, really? I haven't heard anything about that."

"Well maybe you're just lucky on it."

She restlessly teased her hair and looked at her watch.

"Anyway, you say he didn't dump you. So how'd he wind up going over with Lily?"

"Okay, see no one knows this, but he asked *me* to go. *I* was the one who was supposed to go over with him, not Lily. *Not Lily!*" she repeated, once again indicating the correct words she wanted on my pad. "He said he had to get away before the trial and wanted to go maybe in July, visit Hong Kong and his friend Norm in the Philippines. But—" She took a deep breath and fell silent.

"But?" I asked.

"But when he got his passport and started talking about buying tickets, there was so much between us, I said no. See, that was the time when we broke up in March for a lot of reasons, but I was also getting fed up with Patsy, that's when I found out from Edison Yee that she was telling him I was going to bars and cheating. And he believed her and started with her."

"You didn't know about Patsy before then?"

"No, that was the first."

"So it was one of Steve's best friends who told you?"

"It was Edison, yeah. He was the only one of Steve's friends I liked. So I guess Edison wanted me to know the truth finally."

Or else Steve asked him to tell you, I thought.

"So what does he do the day after we broke up?" she asked rhetorically. "He calls Lily Lee! And one girl I didn't want him speaking to at all was Lily! I only found out because after our breakup I went by to see how he was doing, and he wasn't there, so I went into his room and I found all her letters! She was writing to him all those years. And I found a piece of paper in with them that he'd just written, it had her name and a new number on it, and I knew that he was talking to her."

"What a low blow," I said. "First Patsy, then Lily—"

"When he came home he admitted he'd phoned Lily, but he said he just really needed someone to take with him over there, he didn't want to go alone. Then Lily right away called me at home and tried to explain it wasn't true she was going, she told me that she's married. I told her, 'Don't lie—I seen the letters, the last name's still Lee!' So that lie didn't work with me. Because he did make the decision to go with her. Later I found out he sent Lily money to buy an Audi—"

Laura's eyes were closed. She tightened her lips, sniffled and squeezed out two makeup-stained tears.

"He wrote me a letter after that." She reached over to a black plastic box and sat back with a tissue, patted her eyes. "He said, 'I'm sorry about the way things have turned out between us.' He said, 'I know you're going out with

Mike'—which wasn't *true,* Mike was just a guy who was calling me. But Steve probably thought it to make himself feel better. He said, 'If you guys are ever together and we bump into each other, don't cry, because I'll respect you till the end of time.'" She covered her eyes with the tissue and began blubbering mightily into it. "'Till the end of time,'" she wept.

"Laura," I said, reaching over and holding her hand. "I'd take all that with a grain of salt."

"That was the last I ever heard from him. And in July I found out he passed away."

"So when did you find out he actually met Patsy over there?" I asked.

She instantly stopped crying, and snatched her hand from mine. "Who told you that, did Lily tell you that?! I don't want you to write he was serious about Patsy!"

I raised my hand and swore scout's honor that she had me 100 percent wrong on that. I flipped back a dozen pages in my notes, scanned what she'd been telling me. "Believe me, I'm on your side, Laura. Listen to this— because this guy's a virtuoso of deceit. He didn't dump you for *any*body. This is what *I* think happened." I then began enumerating for her what I thought of as the deep structure of Steve's actions, literally placing numbers beside paragraphs as I narrated the events between February and July.

"One: he begs you to go back with him on your birthday and then asks you to sponsor Sonny's fiancée; that's so he can swing a tit-for-tat with Sonny and his father-in-law in the Philippines. Two: he asks you to go to Asia with him, but that's *before* he firms things up with Patsy. Three: he sets up this marriage bullshit with Patsy. Four: we're talking March now, he draws up the affidavit and realizes the last person he wants in Hong Kong with him is you. Why? Because it'll interfere with what he has going on with Patsy—"

"Don't say it like that!" she protested, but I hushed her.

"*Not* because he feels anything *for* Patsy but because she's tied into Macau, where he's looking for a haven. Five: he gets Edison Yee to tell you about Patsy so you'll break up with him. Six: okay, this is the one time in all those years he *doesn't* beg you to get back with him. Seven: that leaves him free to go to Hong Kong with Lily. Lily's not gonna complain when he meets Patsy—Lily's just an ex who's getting a free trip and a car and who'll wash his underwear and bring back his gifts to his mom. So eight: he goes over to Hong Kong, meets with Patsy, then goes to Macau—for reasons I'm pretty sure of—then flies off to the Philippines and stages his death with the help of Sonny and the crooked lawyer—whose daughter he's just helped out, thanks to you sponsoring her. That," I said, looking up from my pad, "makes perfect sense to me, Laura."

Laura lowered her eyes to a spot on the hardwood tabletop between us, soundlessly drumming her lean fingers on the wood. She remained quiet for so many seconds in a row that I could hear my wristwatch ticking. She seemed to be applying her businesswoman's mind to my logic. "You want to know what I think?" she finally asked.

"Please," I said.

"Some of that may be true, but not all of it, because, from my point of view, I personally don't believe he's alive," she said. "Because I would have heard from him by now."

"Not likely," I retorted. "He doesn't need you anymore. You'd only hear from him if he needed something he couldn't get from Patsy. He didn't die in any jungle accident, Laura. Nobody believes that: not the police, not the insurance companies, not his friends, at least if you listen to them carefully. I think he set up a haven for himself in the Lisboa. The Lisboa's where Triad guys like Steve hide; *that's* why he's involved with the daughter-in-law of Fong Ngo Lam."

"*Who?*" she asked.

"The lady that administers the corporation for the guy who owns the goddamn place." I told her that Steve's Triad ran the Macau underworld, and that Macau was one of those rare countries that didn't include the offense of drug trafficking in its extradition treaties with other countries. "Whether he's there now or not, I don't know. It's a year later."

I left it at that, went back to waiting, because her fingers were drumming again and her beautiful almond eyes were contemplating something on the table.

"Okay, Terry," she said, using my name for the first time in two hours. "Actually, everybody's gonna have different things to tell you about that," she said. "I mean, I do hear things about Steven. Myself, I don't know what to believe about them. But my father does have a friend who called him from Hong Kong a few months ago and said he saw Steve Wong alive—just saw. I don't know the circumstances. Whether it was in a crowd or what—" She leaned over. "Is that what you're writing now?"

I looked up just as she put her finger on the corner of my pad and rudely twirled it her way on the smooth tabletop. "I have to talk to your father," I said, twirling it back. "Can you tell him I'll be phoning him?"

"Oh no, I don't want to get him involved in any way, that's not why I said I'd talk." To make the point, she stood up, grabbed my pen and drew a line through the top of my page, dotted it vociferously. "His friend's not even here and anyway I'm sure he doesn't speak a word of English and neither does my father. My parents have been here for twenty-something years, but my dad works in a kitchen, he's always with Chinese people, he never learned English. Even I don't want to be involved in any way. The police are trying to get me to show up at his court case. I don't want to go. Even if he was alive I wouldn't go." She shoved her sleeve up and looked at her watch again. "It's really late."

"Okay, okay. How about this, Laura—" I circled her negative exclamation point on my page, fattened the period "—I'll stay away from your family. But I *have* to talk to Patsy, I need to find out what's what. Where's a good place to catch up with her?"

"I don't know if I should tell you that," she said. "What are you gonna ask her?"

"Not about you. And whatever I find out, you'll be the first to know. I promise."

She relented. "Well, everyone says she hangs around the Bauhinia now—I only saw her once myself, and it was there."

"Yeah, I know it. High-tone Thai place on Broadway. It's a pretty young crowd in there. Like your age."

"Right. Just look for a pudgy older lady trying to look sexy."

Not long after this interview I was sitting in a friend's pad on Oak Street, just a few blocks from the Bauhinia. Gary Bush was a documentary film director, and we were drawing up a list of investors for an avant-garde film we wanted to make. (My Moieni script was still sitting unmade over at the CBC, but the experience of writing it had given me the film bug.) Gary happened to have a black belt in kung fu—an accomplishment that meant more to me than his Academy Award nomination when I decided I wanted his company at the Bauhinia. When Leslie said she was hungry, I suggested Thai food.

Twenty minutes later, we strolled into the second level Bauhinia. There were a hundred or so young Chinese at the tables. Gary said, "I'm not getting into any gang brawl here."

I led us around to the bar and ordered three beers. I put down three 10s, fanned like cards. "Tell Patsy I need to pass on a message from Steve. Tell her it can't wait."

The bartender shouted something to a fellow standing at the other end of the counter, who went up to a middle-aged woman playing Rock, Paper, Scissors with some kids at a crowded table. He pointed us out and she stood up and headed our way. "Queenly" was the word that came to my mind, if the queen were a true shorty. No more than five feet, a little chunky, but quite pretty actually, with boy-cut hair and dripping white gold and diamonds over her formal black dress. "What do you want?" she asked, with a barely detectable accent.

I started out as if we'd just broken off an argument two minutes ago. "Where's your head, Patsy? Where is your head!?" She backed up a step, poor kid. "I just got back from Steve. You know what he gave up for you, and now that he needs friends, where are they?"

Patsy looked left at Gary and right at Leslie, and then said, "Come here," leading me to a table that overlooked Broadway. "Where is he now? Is he all right?"

"The guy's on the balls of his ass," I said, as I sat down, mean as a two-bit drifter in a gas station heist. "He gave up Laura for you, Patsy. Eight years he threw down the drain for you!"

Patsy theatrically covered her diamond-draped ears with her diamond-ringed hands. "I'm sick of hearing that," she said, shaking her head, as if we'd been arguing this subject every day for the last year. Talk about instant intimacy. "You know I'm sick of hearing that?!"

"You want me to tell him that? Is that your message? You're sick of hearing that?"

"Why doesn't he call?!" she begged. "He's disappeared from me, he said he would phone, where *is* he now!?"

"Did you even *try* and find out!? You're the one with the connections there! You can't pick up the phone?"

"But I'm not supposed to—"

Oh yeah, of course. *Idiot!* To recover I jabbed air her way with a forefinger. "He's on the run, Patsy. You think that doesn't cost money?"

"But I sent him fifty thousand!"

"How long did you think that would cover him? How long, Patsy!?"

"But he said he was all right. How much does he need now?"

"Bottom line another fifty," I said. "I don't know where he is myself. He's gonna be in touch with me over there. Where'd that money catch up with him anyway?"

Unfortunately, you only have so much line to play on this kind of con, and I reached the end of it as soon as those words were out of my mouth.

"Listen, please, I don't even know who you are."

"You don't have to! They're on his tail, Patsy, he needs help, *that's all you have to know!*"

"Gimme your pen." She ripped a strip off the bottom of the drink menu and wrote her cell phone number—351–6133—saying, "If he lost it I'll send him whatever he needs when he calls. Tell him to call! I know they're on his tail, but just tell him to call!"

She stood up, and in three steps was swallowed by the crowd. I sat there for a minute, so tense I knew it would take me an hour to come down.

"Ah, she doesn't know where he is now," I said to my compadres at the bar. "But at least she knew where he *was,* enough to send him fifty grand. I'm thinking Macau or Hong Kong."

If Patsy was of minimal help in locating Steve, the most I could expect to accomplish with Sonny was to spark some international pages that might develop into a call to Patsy's cell. On the day of Sonny's sentencing for the passport caper, I went through the metal detector at the provincial court-house, thinking, At least I won't have to worry about getting chopped in these corridors. I considered Chuck's admonition that Sonny had "a para-noia that counts," but the sheriffs would be leading him away in chains after the gavel came down.

Not surprisingly, Sonny was late for his appearance. His counsel of the moment was a wild-haired, middle-aged hipster named Alex Murray, who was filling in for Sonny's vacationing lawyer, Phil Rankin. I recognized Alex right away; he'd been written up in the *Province* newspaper as a noted racehorse owner who'd made a midlife career change. That gave me material to gossip about while we strolled the corridor waiting for his client to show. Eventually I was able to broach the subject of Newson and learned the reason for his delayed appearance: Son-of-Sam had been arrested last night on a cocaine charge. "I suspect he's probably in and out on it under one of a dozen names or other," Alex Murray said dryly, "so he'll be here. Then he's got a surprise."

"What's that?"

Murray chuckled at the vagaries of the justice system. "Well, the judge who's supposed to sentence him isn't here. He's over at 190 Alexander"—that is, traffic court.

"So he won't be going to jail today?"

"I suspect it'll get held over till the fall."

I didn't like that.

"Did you ever meet his wife, Ajile? I heard she's some beauty."

"He thinks so."

"Done in by a femme fatale?"

"Actually, he's a very intelligent guy. There's a possibility that Newson is smarter than any of us."

Murray pushed into the bathroom, leaving me to ponder that intrigu-ing assessment while I took a seat in the court gallery.

Sonny finally arrived, two and a half hours late. I was struck by his looks. Despite the millions of dollars' worth of drugs he'd pumped into his body in his 38 years, he was a handsome dead ringer for the late actor Tony Perkins. I wrote: "The picture of health. At least 6'1", lean, with a strong chin, brilliant blue eyes. Dressed for Bacolod: a thin Hawaiian shirt, light blue jeans and loafers with no socks." Murray brought up the business about the judge being in the wrong place; the judge on the bench politely asked Sonny if he could come back September 1 at 9:30; and Sonny consulted with his lawyer. I leaned forward. "A clear, articulate voice that is remarkably intelligent-sounding," I wrote. Sonny didn't share his sensitive side with the judge. "Sure, I'll be here," was all he said. He turned and his azure eyes passed neutrally over me as he walked out.

I followed him outside the courtroom. "Sonny!" I called and when he turned, I extended my hand. He looked at it coming towards him. Reluctantly, he raised his own hand 10 degrees. I reached for it—reached *down* for it—and held it, limp as a fish in my own. I thought of the evolutionary origin of the handshake: it shows you don't have a weapon. Sonny's high-IQ eyes told me he thought mine were filled with menace. I dropped his cold palm and played Ping-Pong with that perception.

"Hey I'm Terry Gould! I was interviewing Laura for a few hours, and I'm doing an article on Steven now! Did Chuck get in touch with you—did he let you know? Because I was talking to him for hours, too. Guy really has a high opinion of you. Maybe Chuck let ya know that basically what I'm after is Steve's spiritual side. When I knew him, back in '90, we discussed Buddhism, and with his Triad initiation, he believed really deeply in Buddhist stuff. And I'm just wondering if you ever saw him practice it?"

Sonny's head moved slowly right and left.

"No, huh? You're not giving me a line of BS because it's Triad stuff? Do you know who I am? Do you know what I had to do with Steven?"

This time Sonny's head didn't move. But something definitely registered inside it, which was reflected in his eyes.

"Well, if you ask me he was a dozen cuts above Kim and Phu and those guys. Like when we were driving around town once, he showed off his photographic memory for me. He rattled off license plates we just passed, then came around the corner, and there they were. So he had an enormous degree of intelligence."

Sonny seemed to be coiling back into himself, occasionally blinking—this must be his reptilian version of the gangster "look." Very effective. No there there.

"Anyway, what people are talking about was that you did a wonderful thing for Ajile, if you want the feedback from Chuck, Laura—although

Patsy, I can tell ya, probably doesn't give a fuck about Ajilc. That's not her movie. But, hey, I'm just putting together some pieces in Steve's life. Like I say, he had a high degree of intelligence, he had a heart. Yeah, he was into things, but if he had a genius, it was his personality. You knew him as one of the closest, aside from Eddie Yee, so I thought you wouldn't mind telling me where Celestino Guara kept him until you identified him over there in Binalbagan."

At that his eyes went completely dead. I took that as a challenge and tried something else. Fuck him. What's he gonna do to me here?

"You know, I'm asking because Chuck's saying, there's Steven dead, and there's you IDing him. So we're talking about over a million dollars in insurance. Your name's on all those documents."

"So?" It was his first word.

"So, since I'm writing about all this, I was wondering about the rumors that you maybe know he's alive and where he is."

A couple of sheriff's deputies were standing to our right and left, and Sonny's lawyer was watching us uncomfortably from about 30 feet away. Sonny looked at all four points on the compass. I loved the thought of him losing his composure and not being able to strike.

"Sonny?" Alex Murray called. "Sonny?"

"I thought Steve told you never to write about him again," Sonny enunciated in a clear whisper, with maximum subtext, then turned away, trying for that calm, uncoiling slither.

"Yeah, but he's dead."

"Hisss, arrr," I said to my spook over the phone, in answer to his question about what Sonny had told me. I gave him Patsy's cell phone number and brought up the 50 grand. "If there's overseas calls to it, maybe somebody should be tracing where they came from."

Two weeks later I headed down to Las Vegas with Leslie and Gary Bush. I knew that Ray Chau liked to gamble at the Mirage and that his bookie André Ouellette was tied into its underside. Coincidentally, the avant-garde documentary for which Gary and I were trying to raise funds had a Vegas connection: the film was to be about a fast-growing subculture that at the time the mainstream media was ignoring—middle-class married swingers. That week, 3,000 of them were holding a "Lifestyles Convention" at the Riviera Hotel. Given Steve's connection to Ray and Patsy, and Ray's connections to the Mirage, I thought it might be possible to attend the swing convention and also discover some rounder at the Mirage who had knowledge of my disappeared desperado.

The first thing I unpacked in our Riviera hotel room was a package containing copies of the Paper Fan's four-color mug shot. Steve had a strangely celestial look to his hooded eyes, staring to the right of the camera as if communing with a divine birdie. Otherwise, he looked like he'd had a bad day. Concentric creases of flesh circled his neck beneath his Adam's apple. His complexion was greasy and mottled. His wormlike lips were redder than usual. Studying him, I had to wonder again why so many impressive women threw themselves at his feet.

I set to stapling my *Saturday Night* card to a corner above his messy hair, since I was planning on handing Steve's photo out to swinging police officers. From talking to swinging cops in Vancouver, I knew there would be lots here.

At the opening dance in the skytop ballroom, Dr. Robert McGinley, the California-based impresario of the three-day extravaganza, introduced us to an Orange County detective who was on the organizing committee of the convention. At the Erotic Art Exhibition the next afternoon, the detective introduced us to a patrolman from Detroit. That evening, at the Black-and-White costume ball, the Detroit patrolman introduced us to a Vegas-based drug agent he'd met at a seminar. I'll call him Edwin. I showed him Steve's photo and a copy of my article in the RCMP bulletin, and we spent almost an hour in that crazy environment talking about the Mexican cartels and the frustrations of drug enforcement.

On the last day of the convention, Edwin drove me to the Mirage to meet an André Ouellette–type who he said might be able to help out in the Steve search. The fellow said he'd hold on to Steve's picture, but he seemed more interested in finding out what the escort services in Vancouver were charging these days. Then he unwittingly insulted Edwin. "I heard the girls in the bar last night complaining there's no work on the north end. That pervert swinger convention's killing 'em! Ha ha ha!"

As we drove back to the Riviera, Edwin was furious. He said that bad guys were sexually square—in a twisted way. "Someone's always gotta lose on the deal or they get nothing out of it. Big bad dudes with their big-mouth bimbos. You should see them around this guy."

I told him that Steve had crowds of girls around him, too. Maybe the dangerous-guy thing turned them on.

Edwin thought that might hold true in the nonswinging world, but not in his lifestyle. "Guy thinks he's big and bad here, women go the other way. You never find guys tryin' to brag it up when they meet a lady. It's just strictly friendly."

After the grand-finale masquerade ball I sat at my laptop and began typing, occasionally looking up at Steve while 1,500 mainstream couples cavorted in their rooms. I was convinced there was a reason I was on these two stories at once.

It took me some time to work it all through, and one day I would set to writing a whole book about it (that is, after three years of "fund-raising" left Gary and me 30 grand in the hole). But even in 1993, running with subcultures on opposite ends of the human rainbow, I beheld the first glimmerings of a golden insight. The world that occupied most of the bell curve considered both subcultures extreme, but I believed they informed each other and everything else. All these gang tarts ran to Steve and his gang guys because of their gangster "face," which was accrued through violence; on the other side of the law were the men who fought the good fight against them—but for not entirely different reasons. At some level, every male (including me) understood that one of the rewards of living dangerously was being considered attractive by women. The equation was one of the biological mysteries of life. Lawmen, lawyers, gangsters, and journalists were particularly well placed to demonstrate to women that they were hunters able to provide resources and excitement. Yet at swinger parties even undercover cops didn't need to posture as dangerous risk takers in order to make themselves more attractive to women. Their swinging women didn't need them to do so. The exhibition of strength and assets was not necessary to the acquisition of partners in their world, whereas it was a *prime motive* for criminality in the underworld. I had the feeling I was perceiving something profound, and was only slightly tempted to deface this perception with a crude punch line.

CHAPTER 14

PROJECT LAZARUS

———

*I'm one of those guys that believes no one has the right to walk
the face of the earth with impunity. Every criminal
has to have somebody on his case.*
—TOM SPAN, VANCOUVER POLICE

By the end of August my chart on Steve showed his connections reaching from Macau to Hong Kong and from the Philippines to Canada and the U.S. Forty circled names were linked by vectored arrows that went straight between bubbles or swooped around the margins like end runs in a complicated football play. That was exactly what Steven's life had become since his death. Opposing him—trying to keep the Paper Fan from playing his drug game from the other side of the Pacific—was Unit One. There was still no warrant for Steve's arrest, and before the Mounties could move—here or overseas—they needed that warrant. On August 31, Staff Sergeant Jerry Moloci invited me into his office at RCMP headquarters to see what I had come up with to help get that warrant.

Moloci was beginning to remind me of Detective Andy Sipowicz in *NYPD Blue*. Gruff and energetic, a veteran of the Steve chase, if Moloci ran the world he'd be over in Asia hunting Steve right now. In the early '80s he'd made a dozen trips there, but budget cutbacks had kept him home for the past decade, basically seething in frustration while the visiting team of bad guys buzzed in and out.

Moloci called Mike Hiller into the office and I unfolded my schematic map against the wall for the two cops. Moloci drew his chair close. "I know him," he said, pointing to André Ouellette and tapping the name twice. He traced the connections sideways to Ray Chau, and upward to Fong Ngo Lam, Stanley Ho, and the Lisboa. "Ho owns that big development in Hong Kong, too, right on the waterfront there, it's got those big shopping malls." He was referring to the Shun Tak Centre, from where the STDM jetfoil ferry left for Macau.

"Ho owns a lot," I said, adding that Triad mobsters hovered around a lot of what Ho owned. "The Lisboa is notorious as a safe house for gangsters on the run. That's where I think Steven is—or was."

I pointed to Sonny Newson. I thought it likely the Son of Sam had helped procure Steve a new identity in the Philippines. Then, with the help of Alex Abastillas's friends in the police and military, the Paper Fan had been hustled across the South China Sea to Macau, whose extradition treaty with Commonwealth countries had not been updated since 1892. "Back then the narcotics trade was Commonwealth-sponsored," I said, "so naturally it wasn't included as an extraditable offense. Ergo, Macau's popularity with fugitive drug dealers since World War II. Almost every other extradition treaty with Canada has drug offenses in it, except Macau's."

"I can't believe he's gonna live in that little place all his life," Hiller said.

"Knowing Steve Wong—not a chance," Moloci agreed. "That'd be home base for him, but he's gonna be back and forth to Hong Kong."

I concurred. It was my conjecture that, safe from arrest in the Las Vegas of Asia, Steve had waited as his 1992 trial date came and went. When no arrest warrant had been issued for his failure to appear in court, he would have felt like a free man—at least free enough to travel from Macau's six square miles to Hong Kong. Which wouldn't have been that difficult, I said, because Steve had influence with the Royal Hong Kong Police. In Hong Kong, Wong's local Triad boss would not have had a problem finding the young outlaw some interesting work. And, in Hong Kong, in the event that a warrant were to be issued in Canada—making Wong liable to arrest on his drug charges in most places *except* Macau—he would have been just a subway ride from the ferry-departure ramp, and a one-hour trip back to asylum at the Lisboa.

"Like everyone else he'd believe there's no extradition treaty with Macau that covered drugs," I said. "He'd be correct—but he'd be wrong that he was out of reach in Macau. I've been doing some research." I opened my brief-case and took out a fax from Prudential. "Prudential had to really dig to find a footnote to that extradition treaty for me. And what they found you can apply to Steven Wong. Not for drug trafficking, but for things that relate to stuff that went on in 1892, like piracy, train robbery—and *fraud*. It's for 'the mutual surrender of fugitive criminals . . . charged with obtaining dollars or services for false pretenses.'" I handed over the fax to Moloci. "I'm going over to Hong Kong in a couple of weeks, and I'm going to be in the Philippines a few days later," I said. "The NBI is going to meet me in Manila and take me to Negros to prove the fraud end." I'd gather affidavits from the so-called cremator at the Bacolod cemetery; the doctor in Binalbagan who signed Steve's death certificate; the chief of traffic for the area; and the head of the police garrison in Isabela, located at the start of the trail to Santol. Then the NBI and I would head up into the mountains and I'd take pictures of the spot on the trail where Steve had supposedly died, proving the event was a near impossibility. "So the fraud that Steven has perpetrated is covered by the treaty. If that body of evidence were given to the fraud squad, they could make the case that a fraud charge is justified. And that could be used in extraditing Steve from Macau."

Moloci reminded me that whatever I did would have to be repeated as part of an official Mountie investigation. Which didn't bother me, I said, because that's what the NBI wanted. The Canadians just had to initiate things. I handed over a copy of Prudential's most recent report from the Philippines, and Hiller said he would get an original and ship it over to the office of Peter Eccles, the prosecutor of Wong's case. Wong's endlessly held-over trial was set to resume September 13, and with all this new data, Eccles would finally have enough to request a warrant for Steve's failure to appear in court for his drug charges.

That got me thinking. By then I'd learned from an officer with sources close to Sonny that Sonny himself was keeping Steve abreast of events at the drug conspiracy trial through a complicated system of coded pager-and-phone relays that took at least a few hours to complete. "Newson's gonna be sentenced tomorrow at nine-thirty," I said. "You think he'll get jail time?"

"Well he should, considering everything else," Hiller said. That is, considering the fact that Sonny had forged the passport while out on bail for heroin-trafficking charges, and considering the fact that he'd been picked up on a cocaine charge while awaiting sentencing for the passport fraud. But then, this was B.C. "To tell you the truth, I don't think he'll be held in custody."

"Okay, supposing he doesn't get jail time," I asked, "how long before the warrant kicks in in Hong Kong?"

Moloci said that depended on how quickly the judge acted on it after the request. It would certainly take at least 48 hours to get to the desk of Garry Clement, the staff sergeant at the RCMP Liaison Office in Hong Kong, and Clement couldn't ask the Hong Kong cops to arrest Steve until he had that warrant.

I took out my calendar and started figuring out the time zone difference, then began playing chess with the crooks. If Sonny were not in jail, he would try to let Steve know about that warrant before it reached Clement's desk. If the judge agreed to the warrant on the 13th, and the back and forth between the coded pagers took a few hours, that meant Steve would learn of the warrant with a margin of about one and a half days in which to flee to sanctuary in Macau. Eighth-grade dropout he might have been, but Steve had a lawyer's knowledge of the workings of international arrest warrants. Hong Kong was a day later than Vancouver, and it was my guess that Steve would know it would not reach the Crown Colony until, at the earliest, 2 A.M. on September 16. The quickest way for him to get over to Macau was by STDM's jetfoil ferry. Having no suspicion that people were theorizing he would be headed to Macau, he would feel he had all the evening of the 14th to pack. He would probably head out from wherever he was living on September 15, Hong Kong time. Here was a narrow enough margin to feasibly pin Steve down to a place and time.

I made the decision to attend court on the morning of the 13th, and fly out right after I confirmed the request for the warrant had gone down. There was a Cathay flight leaving for Hong Kong that day at 3:30 P.M. I'd arrive well ahead of the warrant.

"So you'd have to surveil him," Hiller said. "That's the way you'd have to do it. You know," he laughed, "if Jerry would lighten up his wallet and send me over, I would surveil him."

"It's difficult for us to travel these days with the government cuts," Moloci moaned. "They're not letting us go anywhere. It's hard to do the job staying at home."

"The thing is," Hiller said to me, "Steven knows you."

"Still, Macau'd be the place Steven Wong would run to," Moloci said. "If you make a sighting that goes a long way to help us."

Hiller clicked his tongue. "The only thing I'm concerned about is that he put a threat out on your life. As soon as you get tied in with spotting and squealing on Steven, your life would be in danger."

"Yeah, it's like six seconds and who draws first, ha ha ha."

The laugh was pretty lame, because I was not feeling cavalier about what could actually take place over there.

After I'd returned from Vegas I'd gone for a walk up Mosquito Creek Canyon in North Vancouver, the hillside suburb where Leslie and I had bought a house the previous year. Near the top of the creek, surrounded by the giant trunks of old-growth cedar, a log bridge spanned the canyon. I stopped in the middle of the bridge and gazed north up the boulder-strewn creek towards the peaks that formed a dark green wall behind the lighter green stand of rain forest. I turned around and gazed south to where the canyon fell steeply away through forest to the city and the sea. What a glorious place to live, I thought: a veritable national park in my backyard and a lovely city in my front. Why would I leave it all behind and risk my ass for a $5,000 story?

I reasoned that I had made it through six years of gang reporting without being kidnapped and tortured to death. In order to experience a few exhilarating moments and make it out with a good story, I'd always hedged my bets, watched my back, planned carefully, assessed the odds, made allies, outflanked enemies, and sometimes strategically retreated when necessary. But all of that had taken place in surroundings never more than a few feet from Canadian civilization, where up was up and down was down, and where even sociopathic criminals held the suspicion that gravity couldn't be defied indefinitely.

Macau and the Philippines were something else again. In Macau the police were famously in the back pockets of the Triads, and you were out of luck if you called them because one of their gangster bosses was on your tail. (As *Lonely Planet* advised travelers to Macau, "The only advice on what to do if you get on the wrong side of the Triads is, don't.") The Philippines was even worse, and not just in the field of Chinese organized crime. In that volcanic archipelago there had been nine coup attempts since Ferdinand Marcos had been overthrown in 1986; from Luzon in the north to Mindanao in the south, kidnapping was a police-sponsored growth industry; on Negros and three other islands the back roads belonged to cutthroat brigands and battalions of gangster-guerrillas; and in the poverty-stricken towns and smog-choked cities everything was for sale, including the murder of nosey journalists, who were being knocked off at the rate of three a year, with none of the murderers coming to justice. In short, I was headed off to where chaos reigned. God knows what Steve or his friends would do to me if they got me alone in a room with no threat of consequences.

For several days, that 3 A.M. terror sat naked on my shoulder like a clawed and drooling gargoyle, keeping me figuratively stuck in the middle of my bridge. What made the overseas trek worth taking? If I was going to risk Triad torture for something, shouldn't that "something" be more than a terrific story, which I might never live to write?

Then, a week after I came down from my bridge, the Mounties told me a U.S. liaison intelligence officer named Omar Longoria had pasted Steve's mug shot above his desk in Richmond, near the Vancouver airport. I called Longoria and asked him why—of all the bad guys he had to worry about—he had chosen Steve's puss to greet U.S. and Canadian cops coming through his door. "Because if what the Mounties are saying about him is true, Wong personifies the wave of the future in Asian crime," Longoria told me. "Here's a very flamboyant individual, almost to the point of arrogance, very proud of his connections all over the world, and very sophisticated in what he's pulled off in several countries. He thinks he can break the law with impunity."

That was a word I'd heard cops use over and over when they talked about Steve. As Tom Span, an officer who'd been on Steve's ass for years, had told me: "I'm one of those guys that believes no one has the right to walk the face of the earth with impunity. Every criminal has to have somebody on his case." The fact was, *nothing* violated the rule of law more than criminals who did not have to pay the consequences for breaking the law. Without consequences, criminals could do anything, and that struck at the heart of civilization. In societies where impunity reigned, ordinary people eventually joined the lawbreakers. Even the cops became criminals. I had seen it myself in Brooklyn.

And so I'd shown up here at RCMP headquarters telling myself the risk was worth taking. Finessing my way into Steve's house that snowy day in February three and a half years ago had been part journalism and part game. Now the game part was over. I wanted to get the evidence, hand it over to the Mounties, get a fraud charge rolling, and have Steve nabbed.

Moloci stood up, jammed his hands in his pockets and then pointed to my chart. "This is really something the police shoulda been doing a long time ago! We've been fighting this battle now for how long?! The fact is, what our management did to us was say, 'Hey, it's a fraud, that's not your mandate, blah blah blah.' And so here we are, we can't go either way." Meaning Unit One hadn't been able to expend resources on an investigation without a warrant, and hadn't been able to justify a warrant for fraud because they weren't a fraud squad.

Moloci turned to Hiller. "His unofficial sighting will go a long way to help us sell the fact that this is for real. I mean, *he is alive!*" he insisted. "As much as you speculate and say anything you want, the fact is if somebody spotted him, nobody can deny that."

"So we'll get the Commercial Crime Squad involved and get an investigation going in the Philippines when he gets back with his affidavits," Hiller said.

"Well that's something we can maybe help ourselves on here now," Moloci said, impatiently going around to his side of the desk. "We'll talk to Garry Clement once we get things rolling here with the charges; we might get lucky and even spot Steven coming out of those spots, coming in or out of Macau."

"Would Garry meet with me?" I asked.

"Sure he would," Moloci said. "He's a good guy. Problem is, he's under the same restraints as we are, and being the L.O., he can't really get involved in an investigation until it's official. We'll phone him ahead of time and tell him you're coming, and we'll make sure he's there." He turned to Hiller. "We can fill Garry in on what's going on, and when Terry goes over there—"

He stopped, thought a moment, then slapped the desk.

"Okay! that's the way we're gonna do this. If we can keep Garry juiced up on that end, and you do your thing, Terry, and if you get lucky seeing him that's a bonus, and then we'll lay the charges, play out the string, and when we figure the time is right, we'll get the lawyers in the situation and then we'll do it!"

Moloci burst into laughter, thrilled by the closing trap. "My superintendent was saying to me—when we said we got Steven Wong this last time—he said, 'You got Steven Wong?!' I said, 'Yeah, we got him!' And of course, all he's hearing is the history—how hard this guy is to catch, because they been trying for years. Then we catch him, he asks me, 'Did you *actually* get a case against him?' I said, 'Yeah! Mike got a case against him!' He couldn't believe it. But then, he *skips out!* Just ano*th*er way to thumb his nose!"

"Well," I said, "we'll have to put a stop to that."

The next morning at 9:30, I showed up at provincial courtroom 306 for Sonny Newson's sentencing. I sat on the opposite side of the courtroom from Hiller, over by the wall and neighbor to a talky court watcher, a retired gent who enjoyed a daily peek at the shaven-headed mean types, the insouciant street sellers, and the bewildered middle-class people getting ready to stand their first time before a judge.

At ten o'clock I looked over at Hiller, ready to smile at Sonny's repeat tardiness, when I noticed the cop's eyes pass over mine and rest beyond my shoulder. I turned around and there was Sonny, directly behind me—a maneuver that must have taken him some distance out of his way.

Sonny's name was called, he joined his lawyer up front, and my courtroom friend muttered cryptically, "Bad man Jose"—probably because of Sonny's tropical attire. Alex Murray made a case for leniency, "given the facts of this case and my client's attempts to better his circumstances." Newson was now working full-time at Green Auto Body, he said, plus taking an evening first-aid course on Tuesdays, Wednesdays, and Thursdays. Sonny was saving his money so that he could rejoin his wife in the Philippines. Therefore, if a sentence were to be imposed, Sonny requested that he be allowed to serve it on weekends.

The judge reviewed the facts of the case, assessing that Sonny obviously had not engineered the passport forgery to further his own criminal ends. "Indeed, it would seem that Mr. Newson has not been involved in crime since then and has made efforts to improve his life," she said, and I could see

Hiller shift in his seat. In B.C., being arrested and charged with cocaine trafficking did not mean being "involved in crime"—at least until conviction.
The judge went on to note that Sonny had completed high school, and that
he was a member of the Longshoreman's Union. There was every chance he
could become a productive taxpayer. "Given your recent efforts to change
your lifestyle," she said, "and also your cooperation with a guilty plea, I will
sentence you to ninety days, served on weekends, beginning Friday,
September 3 at 6 P.M., and ending Monday at 11 A.M."

I reached into my shoulder pack and looked at my Day-timer.
September 13, the day the warrant for Steve's arrest would be requested, was
a Monday. Court started at 10 A.M. Sonny would be on the street at 11.

The full cast was in attendance at Supreme Court on September 13.
Representing dead Steve was Neil Sacks, a balding, short, bespectacled fellow
in a dapper-looking suit. I watched as Sacks had a few pleasant words with
Crown Prosecutor Peter Eccles, a boyish-looking blond man in horn-
rimmed glasses. Representing Prudential's interests was Jo Anne Carmichael,
whom I'd been dealing with since Jim Gallagher had flown back to Toronto.
Voyageur's lawyer, Alison Murray, was talking with Hiller, done up sharply
in a green suit—the first time I'd seen him out of jeans—looking taller and
slimmer than usual.

Yak Wah Cheung, out on bail, took his seat in the dock, wearing the
usual zoot-suit jacket, mauve pants, and a baggy shirt. Kim Tam, doing jail
time on another offense, was led in from the back in government clothes. He
was a broadly built, strong-looking fellow, with long black hair cut into
bangs like Galahad's. He sat beside Yak, then turned around and our eyes
met. Beat, beat, beat. I smiled. Judge G. Peter Fraser entered, and Regina *vs*
Kim Tam, Yak Wah Cheung, and Steven Wong was called to order.

Sacks stood up and told the judge he had a matter to discuss. Wong's
parents had put up their house as guarantee for their son's $100,000 bail.
That surety still hung over their heads. Fourteen months had come and gone
since their son's passing. They were therefore applying to the court to have
their son's charges withdrawn and the surety lifted.

Judge Fraser looked at Eccles for the Crown's position.

Eccles stood up and began reviewing the facts of Steve's supposed death.
He cleared his throat: "The Crown has some concerns about the circumstances and the nature of the identification of the body. And the entire circumstances of the alleged demise of Mr. Wong have rapidly changed us to
the conclusion that the rumors of his death were somewhat exaggerated. As
a result, the Crown takes the position that Mr. Wong is not dead, that he is

somewhere. Accordingly, we have not withdrawn the charges, and are not willing to withdraw charges. I advise my friend that the Crown will be seeking a bench warrant forthwith for Steven Wong."

I saw Kim Tam lean over and whisper something to Yak Wah Cheung. Then Tam turned around and looked at me.

The judge announced he would issue an "order of committal for Mr. Wong" and stood up. "Order in court," the clerk pronounced. The judge stepped down. Yak strolled by and into the hall; Tam was taken back to a holding cell until trial resumed after lunch. I looked at my watch: 11 A.M. Sonny was just then getting out of jail.

Outside the courtroom Jo Anne Carmichael said to me: "I'll let Jim Gallagher know you're on your way. Good luck, eh? Take care of yourself."

I waved goodbye to Hiller and caught a cab to the airport. Flight CX839 left exactly on time.

CHAPTER 15

HO! HO! HO!

Macau is in essence a Triad city.
—MARTIN BOOTH, *THE DRAGON SYNDICATES*

At sunset we made our approach to Hong Kong, passing over the multibillion-dollar Chap Lok Kok Airport being constructed north of Lantau Island, then banked steeply right and began the breathtaking descent over Kowloon to Kai Tak, the single-runway airport that was the world's busiest in terms of cargo and third-busiest for international passengers. The green mountains—Kowloon Peak out one window, Victoria Peak out the other—were spectacular, but the apartment high-rises were so close to the wingtips that you felt as if you were about to land on the street. I laughed out loud as we bounced down with a thump, the brakes squealing and the reversers roaring to keep us from running into the drink.

It was then the height of the Asian boom years and the top-end Royal Pacific on the Kowloon side was the only hotel with a room available, so I endured the riot and heat of a double-decker that took me through the crumbling tenement blocks to the northwest end of Tsim Sha Tsui. There, for 150 bucks a night, the desk people put me into a coffin on the 23rd floor with a view into a rat-warren office across the way. Before retiring I sat on the lumpy bed and, as arranged, phoned Prudential's Jim Gallagher in Toronto, who gave me the name of a detective agency–cum–bodyguard outfit I should call if I got into a jam. "Martin Lister, our lawyer in Hong Kong, has recommended to me that Guard Force is the best, and he urges you to contact him if you have the slightest concern about your safety. He will take care of the rest."

"How about stop two?" I asked, referring to Manila.

"You will be met at stop two and taken under guard to a nearby hotel. At the moment, I'm actually less concerned about that than I am about your excursion before you arrive there." He meant the side trip that I was planning on taking to Macau when the warrant came down.

"I'll let you know how that turns out," I said. "I plan on winning big there."

The next morning I awoke four hours ahead of my ten o'clock appointment with Garry Clement and donned a John Deere baseball cap, a pair of mirrored shades, and an olive monkey suit over my business shirt and slacks. It worked—I looked like a diesel mechanic from Moline, Illinois—but the heavy coveralls from my farm up north were a burden. Out on Canton Road the temperature was already in the high 70s, the air humid and gritty from pollution, and I was soaked in sweat by the time I got off the MTR at Sheung Wan, on the Hong Kong Island side. I strode up the stairs into the fluorescent-lit mall of the Shun Tak Centre, followed the cute little steamboats that illustrated the way to Ferry Hall and, just past a collection of tony brand stores, came to a clattering food mart opposite the gangway entrance to the jetfoil.

Now, where to wait so I could face the hordes of souls who enjoyed risking the condo on a day's fun at Ho's tables? I decided on a position a few steps west of the wide departure gate, in a cozy nook the other side of the emergency-exit doors. By then I was so sweaty my socks were drenched, but a hunt was a hunt, my disguise was my camouflage, and here was my blind. The nook was in shadow, and the departing passengers walked straight into the white glare of the glassed-in ramp that took them down to the choppy waters of Victoria Harbor. I shoved my hands in my pockets, leaned casually against the jamb of the exit doors, and began surveying each of the 300 holiday gamblers who surged by every 15 minutes. By 9:45 I had surveyed perhaps 3,000 faces.

An effort in futility, I told myself, feeling as I must have looked: a *gwailo* on a break hoping to catch his Chinese lover on an illicit jaunt. Still, I knew my lover boy was a late riser. He'd risk extradition before setting his alarm. I'd try again about the time Steve would be shaking off sleep.

Up on the 14th floor of One Exchange Square, at the RCMP Hong Kong Liaison Office, Garry Clement was getting ready to sting a guy thought to be responsible for the death of 68 Vancouverites. Kim Kong was the bad guy's wonderfully allusive name, a tall, bespectacled, smartly dressed 36-year-old who lived in Quarry Bay and cruised around Hong Kong Island in a big new Mercedes. A Dai Huen Jai dragon head, Kim controlled much of the heroin shipped to Vancouver, and thus a fair proportion of the heroin shipped onward to the States. He was also a clever marketer. In early spring he'd ordered his street dealers to treble the smack in their single-dose caps from 7 to 20 percent, and cut prices. In May alone more than 40 Vancouver addicts had overdosed on Kim's cheap and potent product. Despite the collateral damage, however, the marketing strategy worked. Those who survived liked the richer mix. They upped their addictive consumption, stepped on the high-grade doses, and dealt one-for-three to new kids on the train. As usual, supply increased demand, and Kim's net profit increased.

While the addicts were dying on the Downtown Eastside, Clement had been coordinating Vancouver's Unit One, the Hong Kong Narcotics Bureau, and the Triad Bureau to stop Kim Kong. On March 30, a shipment of paintings from Bangkok had been inspected by Canada Customs at Vancouver International Airport and the hollowed-out frames were found to contain 6.9 kilos of 97 percent pure heroin (an irony of supreme proportions, considering the fact that "picture frames" were the hypothetical means of concealment that Steve and I had joked about in our CBC interview). Unit One was called in and the drugs were removed and replaced with smack-look-alike and a bug. Officers then moved into an Eastside hotel room beside the one listed on the shipment forms and let the deal go down. The bugged exchange that followed gave them a Hong Kong phone number, which they traced to an apartment building just north of Kai Tak Airport. A fellow by the name of King Shing Chu was arrested by the RHKP two weeks later and he agreed to cooperate in an investigation that nailed the picture frames to Kim Kong.

Now Clement was arranging a whole slew of crucially timed events: the cops at the Narcotics Bureau had to arrest Kim at a 3 P.M. sting; the Triad Bureau had to be lined up to testify at Kim's extradition hearing the next morning; and a Unit One officer named Rico Wong had to be on a plane to Hong Kong to whisk the informant King Chu to Vancouver, where he was scheduled to plead guilty and then testify against Kim.* Clement didn't reveal his target's name to me until the sting went down, but as I listened to him on the phone making last-minute preps for his arrest and extradition, I thought: here's the man who'll get Steve to Canada for me.

Clement was a 21-year veteran, with striking blue eyes, a fit torso, and the ever-present Mountie mustache. He'd started his drug-cop career working Jewish groups in Toronto in the late '70s, then Asian groups in Vancouver for much of the '80s, which had helped to land him in Hong Kong as an authority on Triads. During his time in plainclothes, he'd worked in some extremely dangerous undercover projects, and had come

---

*Kim Kong was extradited to Canada on November 29, 1993.

to know firsthand his prey's opinion of the B.C. courts. He was therefore a fan of my jail-time prescription for bad guys: put them away for years, and if they hit the street and were convicted again, don't let them out until they were old men.

After we went through my schematic diagram and the pile of paperwork I'd brought him from home, he picked up the phone, punched in some numbers, then held his palm over the receiver: "Gonna put you in touch with the Superintendent of the RHKP Organized Crime and Triad Bureau—Bob Youill.

"How ya doing, buddy!" he said into the phone. "Would you be willing to sit down with a journalist by the name of Terry Gould? He's assisting on a guy by the name of Steven Wong, he's 14K, did a disappearing act in the Philippines—basically, he's wanted on drug charges in Canada and he fabricated his own death, he's connected to the infamous Macau. So Terry's over in Hong Kong and he's going to Macau and the Philippines and his focus now is to get a sighting on this guy, 'cause what Wong did was. . . ."

I sat back and listened to a three-minute recapitulation of the epic, right up to my last meeting with Moloci. "Terry's done a hell of an investigation proving it and supplied it all to the RCMP and we're looking at laying fraud charges," he concluded, giving me a thumbs-up. "He's in my office right now. I'll give him your number and he'll give you a call."

When he got off, he handed me a sheaf of press clippings from his file on Macau. Then he warned me that I'd have to keep a very low profile over there. "Any appearance of publicity to anybody who doesn't want it could lead you into serious trouble."

"I'll be staying in the Lisboa for four days," I said. Yuk Yuk Yuk.

That almost brought him out of his chair. "Really?! I'd be really careful asking around—I really would."

"I'm basically gonna put on this pair of sunglasses and hat and act like a goof," I told him, putting on my mirrors and John Deere cap. "The Macau tourist people think I'm writing an article on the Lisboa and are putting me up when I get back from the Philippines. Tomorrow they're paying for me to go over for the day for a 'familiarization tour.' But I've been really careful about who knows what I'm about. I'm not gonna ask a single question. But—I don't know. I'm hoping to see him."

Garry took a deep breath and let it out with an audible sigh. He was up to his ass in alligators with this Big Circle Boy thing, and now here I was, telling him I'd be wrestling the alligators in their nest.

"Okay," he said finally, "if you see that he's over here, and I get something officially from Vancouver, then I will use it to contact this guy and confirm." He meant that he had somebody in Macau he totally trusted, an assistant commissioner of police whose name I would later learn was Tony Salvado. "Probably I can go through him and maybe have Wong arrested on a provisional warrant, if that's the thrust of what the Department of Justice asks for. But it's—" He sighed and rubbed his face with his hands. "I mean, I don't know. . . . Macau is very much the domain of the 14K.

"And Steve is 14K."

"That's right. It's just recently other factions have been allowed in. Like the Kung Lok Triad from Toronto, but I believe they're just an extension of the 14K. I've been saying that all along, everybody tries to differentiate between the two of them, but they're one and the same. The Kung Lok *is* the 14K. So Wong ran the 14K's bodyguard service in Vancouver. So whatever he wants—you name it, it can be done. I'd be really careful asking around— you'll end up as fish bait."

"I'm aware of how dangerous this is, Garry, and I'm *not* suicidal," I protested. "It's just I've spent months making all these connections. Ray's married to Patsy and Patsy's smooching Steven—and the hipbone's connected to the thigh bone—"

"Right, it all falls into place, this group is the most incestuous group of people I've ever been around in my life. What you're telling me makes perfect sense—that's the way things operate here. He'll probably feel safe enough just being in Macau, nothing's gonna happen to him in terms of inquiries, formal or otherwise, because they can't get the inside information on him."

"Not yet," I said.

I wrote out my schedule of travel to Macau and the Philippines, and he gave me his home number, told me to phone him in the middle of the night if I got in a jam.

I tucked the info into my wallet next to the numbers of Unit One, Martin Lister, Guard Force, and Gallagher. "Most of Macau's in Stanley Ho's pocket, isn't it?" I asked, because even though Ho had probably never even heard of the Paper Fan, he all but ruled the territory.

"Anybody will tell you," Clement said, indicating the stack of press clippings in my hands, "Macau *is* Stanley Ho."

At noon I was back in my nook at Shun Tak, killing time thinking about old Stanley as I watched the parade to the ferry. Most journalists who'd written about Ho stated that while his corporate empire was legitimate, Macau—the city synonymous with Ho—was a Triad town. Macau was in that fix because its main business was gambling, which drew gangsters like flies to scat. In that regard Macau was no different than Vegas in the '50s and '60s. But whereas Las Vegas had been more or less cleaned up by 1993, Macau was still overwhelmingly dirty.

In their off-the-record conversations with journalists, the police alleged Stanley Ho was in some way complicit in maintaining the dirt, even if only by looking the other way at what went down on his premises (see source notes). For his part, Ho vigorously denied any connection to Triad criminality. He pointed out that the Triads had attempted to kidnap and extort him a couple of times and that he'd fought against them ever since he'd won Macau's casino monopoly license. To try to break that monopoly and share the wealth, the Triads in the early '60s had threatened to close his hotels, attack his boats, flood his casinos with beggars, buy off his dealers, launch grenade attacks at his offices, torment the Portuguese government until they withdrew his franchise, and kill him slowly. In fact, beyond pointing to Ho's business associates and hirelings, the police could not substantiate any rumors that would sully his civic reputation. He held an honorary doctorate from the University of East Asia, had received service decorations from various governments, including Malaysia, the Philippines, and the United States, and was an Officer of the Most Excellent Order of the British Empire as well as a Portuguese Commander of the Order of Benefaction. In addition, he was a noted philanthropist, generously supporting and sitting on the boards of the University of East Asia, the University of Hong Kong, the Community Chest of Hong Kong, the Lions Club, the Hong Kong Ballet Group, and various amateur sports associations.

And yet, for all his good works, power and wealth, he couldn't get rid of the notorious Triads who worked within his enterprises—the cause of all the rumors and speculation in the first place. In this he reminded me less of a gambling pioneer like Bugsy Siegel—who had embraced his criminal colleagues and paraded his gangsterism in Vegas—than of a respectable version of Jay Gatsby, novelist F. Scott Fitzgerald's elegant, charming, and self-made icon of a glittering demimonde.

When authors quote Fitzgerald on the rich they limit themselves to the famous platitude "They are different from you and me," forgetting Fitzgerald's more profound observation that the rich "are cynical where we are trustful." When it came to Stanley Ho, the cops who listed him on their secret rosters would probably agree he had a cynical side.

Dr. Stanley Ho Hung-sun was born rich—on November 25, 1921—into one of the wealthiest families in Hong Kong. His grandfather, the Honorable Ho-fok, and grand-uncle, Sir Robert Ho-tung, were chief compradores for

Jardine Matheson, and his father Ho Sai-kwong was a director of the Hong Kong trading company Sassoons, which, like Jardine, had made millions dealing in Chinese opium in the 19th century. As Stanley Ho told British reporter Jill McGivering for her book *Macao Remembers,* a collection of interviews with Macau hotshots, in the 1930s Ho Sai-kwong "speculated heavily in Jardine's shares" and "lost heavily. He was on the verge of bankruptcy, and he ran away to Saigon." In fact, Stanley Ho put the best face on a bad past: his father had not just had a streak of hard luck, but had participated in a flagrant insider-trading scheme, causing a scandal even in Hong Kong—the capital of insider schemes—which led to the suicide of Ho Sai-kwong's partners before his own flight to Indochina.

Left penniless with his mother and sisters, Ho renounced his pool-playing rich boy's youth, buckled down, and in 1939 won a couple of scholarships to the University of Hong Kong. Two and a half years later, when the Japanese conquered Hong Kong, the 20-year-old Ho threw away the British army uniform he had briefly worn, fled to neutral Macau, and joined a firm that was one-third owned by the Japanese army. That was how he made his first fortune—trading with the brutal conquerors of his birthplace, in the process building up a network of valuable contacts in the Axis-leaning Portuguese administration. Throughout the war, while the Hong Kong Chinese cringed under repression, and POWs of all nationalities rotted and died by the thousands in hellish camps, Ho smoked the best cigarettes in Macau, drove motorcars and motorbikes, and hosted parties almost every night, serving the Japanese officers delicacies out of reach of ordinary citizens.

Ho never felt guilty about getting his start this way, or even tried to conceal his past. On the contrary, he bragged about it. "Macau was paradise during the war," he congenially told McGivering. "In Hong Kong, many people, even some of my relatives, suffered considerably because of shortage of food, bombings, and harassment from the Japanese gendarmes." But not Ho in Macau. "In those days, if you had the money, you could enjoy the best kind of cigarettes, American, British, right up to the end of the war. If you had the money, you could carry on using motorcars and motorbikes all through the war—gasoline was available. And you could have excellent food—if you had the money. I had big parties almost every night. Bird's nests, roast pork.

"Agreed, there was a lot of killing," Ho went on, but "I became the teacher of the most important Japanese man in Macau during the war. There was a Japanese Special Branch in Macau, which was even more important than the Japanese consul general. The head of it, a man called Colonel Sawa, went to see the governor one day and told him he wanted to learn English—but he needed a reliable person who mustn't murder him."

Colonel Sawa had good reason to fear for his life. The Special Branch worked in league with the Kempeitai—the Japanese equivalent of the Nazi SS. The Special Branch had had the Japanese consul general shot in the stomach and then ordered his body mutilated as a lesson to others who might make the mistake of being too friendly with the British consul. Sawa was understandably hated and feared in Japanese-occupied China—as well as in Japanese-surrounded Macau. In fact, Ho's own boss, the Macau businessman Roger Lobo, was under some threat from Sawa's Special Branch. Lobo worked undercover as a British intelligence agent, risking his life picking up downed British and American pilots and sending them on an underground railway into China, where they could meet up with the Nationalists and be sent back into battle. It was Lobo who witnessed the sadistic mutilation of the Japanese consul general.

The governor of Macau was therefore on the spot as to whom to recommend to Sawa to be his instructor. As Ho tells it: "The governor thought about it and said [to Sawa]: 'What do you think of the grand-nephew of Sir Robert Ho-tung? You were such good friends with Sir Robert—would you trust a member of his family?'

"Colonel Sawa accepted immediately," Ho went on proudly. "From then on, he sent his car—with no number plate, just one Japanese star—to my house to pick me up, every morning at six, and drove me to Zhongshan, across the border in China. There, the two of us would climb together to the top of a small hill. Then he started singing in Japanese and taught me how to sing with him—and in return I taught him English. I was his teacher for one year, and in that time all the Japanese soldiers in the Special Branch would kneel down to him—and to me, as his teacher. What a great difference! While my relatives, my mother, were suffering in Hong Kong, the Japanese gave me excellent treatment."

Ho thus found himself in a unique position—a trusted liaison between the conquerors of East Asia and the quasi-fascist Portuguese government. He was promoted to the rank of superintendent of supplies and began trading with the Japanese, profitably exchanging Macau's stash of war materiel, which the Japanese army so desperately needed, for Chinese rice to be sold to Macau's starving half-million people. "I started a small trading company myself," Ho said. "By the end of the war, I'd earned over a million dollars—having started with just ten."

As soon as the war was over, Ho bought a boat and established the first regular ferry run across the Pearl River Estuary between the British and Portuguese colonies. Then he started buying and selling Hong Kong real estate. His fortune grew, until by 1960 he was one of the wealthiest men in the colony. And then came the venture that would make him one of the wealthiest men in the world.

Gambling had been legal in Macau since the middle of the 19th century, but there were never more than a handful of casinos, unairconditioned and mixed in among the red light and opium districts in the backstreets by the harbor, offering only Chinese games like fan-tan and pai gow. Ho saw the potential for high-class gambling hotels that catered to Hong Kong's ultrawealthy, who would be served by high-speed ferries that could get them to Macau in an hour, and that would offer them sophisticated games like baccarat and roulette. In 1961 he bid on the monopoly rights to gambling in the territory, and thanks to his contacts in the Portuguese administration, got the franchise. His company would eventually build nine glitzy casinos and attendant hotels, the first and most famous of which was the Lisboa, a corncob-like hotel tower topped by a ring of spikes cradling a bizarre object that looks like a cross between a Sputnik and a lotus. From its breezeway to its batty mast, the Lisboa is arguably the ugliest building in Asia.

There was also some ugly work that went along with Ho's contract to build high-speed ferries and high-class hotels. "I also promised to clear the resettlements along the Praia Grande and outer harbor," he told McGivering. "In those days, the early 1960s, all these Nationalist farmers, who'd run away from Guangzhou and the Pearl River Delta to settle in Macau, occupied the outer harbor. There were over a thousand families in little squatter huts. One of my obligations was to clear all that away."

After clearing "all that away," Ho expanded into other parts of Asia, which included, in the 1970s, cutting a deal with the Philippine dictator Ferdinand Marcos to run nine casinos in the poverty-stricken archipelago, most of the revenue going into the pocket of Marcos himself. At the same time Ho was working with the brutal Marcos, his director of security at the Lisboa was a 14K Triad boss, Lau Wing-kui, who would soon become a part owner in Ho's Jumbo floating restaurant in Aberdeen, on the south shore of Hong Kong Island. In 1974, Lau immigrated to Canada and formed the Kung Lok Triad in Toronto, taken over by Danny Mo after Lau was deported in 1980. That same year, the San Francisco Asian Gang Squad alleged that Ho's business partner, Yip Hon, was a heroin trafficker and a Triad member. Ho had a falling-out with Yip Hon, bought out his interest in the company, and was free of that taint until, in 1987, a 14K dragon head by the name of Kai Sze Wai moved to Macau after a stint at running gambling casinos in the Philippines. Before the year was out, Ho's personal secretary and the chief manager of STDM, Thomas Chung, was chopped to death—

an unsolved murder that the Hong Kong police thought was related to an unnamed Triad group's attempt to muscle in on Ho's business. Along with a 14K up-and-comer by the name of "Broken Tooth" Wan Kwok-koi, Wai eventually negotiated a lease on several VIP gambling rooms in the Lisboa, allegedly laundering Triad drug money through them, and set up a loan-shark operation on the eighth floor of the hotel, which was still running when I showed up in town.

Given all this, it was no surprise that when the subject of Stanley Ho came up in law enforcement circles, his relationship with the Triads was, as they say, "of interest." Did he serve them, or was he coerced into doing business with them? Did he fight them, as he claimed, or did he legally capitalize on them in a society seamed by gangsterism, in the same way he had legally capitalized on the Japanese during the war and Marcos in the '70s? Whatever the answer, something was wrong in Macau, and, as Ho was the most powerful man in the territory, the cops felt they had every justification for surmising that he was at least partly responsible for establishing a climate in which the Triads thrived. He leased his premises to their front companies, partnered with alleged Triad members in business, and perhaps played one off against the other.

This last speculation was being privately talked about in cop shops throughout Hong Kong the very week I arrived, and it highlighted how the Triads had tainted the reputation of Macau. A couple of months previously, two ruling council members in the Sun Yee On Triad, Ki Ming Po and Ben Chan, had opened two floating casinos in international waters, beyond the jurisdiction of the Portuguese governor. The police received intelligence that the Hung brothers, dragon heads of the Sun Yee On, viewed the operations of Po and Chan as competing with their own plans to establish a stake in the Kingsway Casino, located between the jetfoil pier and the Lisboa. In the first two weeks of September, both ships had burned to the waterline.

By 3:30 P.M., I had surveyed some 4,000 Macau-bound faces and was bored to tears. Hold on till five, I told myself, and then the hell with it.

Long before then, at 3:50 (I did look at my watch just afterward) my heart went for a loop and my breath turned to panting gusts. No, it couldn't be. *That's him!* my brain screamed, as I watched a low-altitude head bobbing among hundreds of others crowding from the mall hallway, then turning hard right at the food mart in a race to catch the four o'clock sailing. He was carrying a black case—too small for a suitcase. The white silk shirt was his style; and the man was the same height. He's lost a lot of weight, I thought, which would fit, considering the anxiety he'd been living under; aviator glasses, hair cut short on the side and long on the top; waddling walk; the *same* walk. In my mind I saw his face sneering at me as we sat on his couch on Clarendon Drive three years ago, but now he seemed childlike, bewildered, very worried, and suffering.

That's him!

No side glance—he hadn't noticed me, I realized, thanking God—as he hustled past the jetfoil marquee and the "No Smoking" sign and the block glass partition—then stepped onto the knobby rubber of the gangway.

Gone.

What should I do, what should I do? If I chased after him down the ramp, they couldn't hold him at customs on my say-so. Then again, he might lose it and shoot me dead. On the other hand, by blowing my cover I could screw up an arrest when the warrant came through. I knew where he was going, and if he knew I knew, he might not stay there.

And while all these thoughts were boiling between my ears, I was feeling, in my heart, Why can't we just call time-out, you and me, and sit down in the food mart, you tell me what's been going on with you? Because I felt *bad* for Steve—the trouble I was causing. Making him run here, run there— the Philippines, Macau, Hong Kong, back to Macau. You lovable fuck, just stay in one spot so I can get you!

I ran to a pay phone opposite Rainbow Leathers, called Clement—but he was out on the Kim Kong thing. "Tell him to call me at my hotel as soon as he can," I told his secretary. "It's about Steven Wong." Then I phoned his home and told his wife, Lee, the same thing. Then I phoned Bob Youill and gave him the scoop. Then I went back to the hotel and waited. Waited. Waited. Because the goddamn Liaison Office had the budget for only one cell phone, and Garry's boss had it.

"You're kidding!" Garry said when he finally got home from the arrest of Kim Kong and called me. I stayed calm, although I'd gone through a whole blister pack of Nicorettes by then.

"I was watching every face in the crowd as they were coming through, and at 3:50, at the entrance to the STDM jetfoil, the arcade entrance to where you walk through there— Listen, what can I say? I am ninety-five percent sure I saw the guy. Now, there's a possibility that you could get the passenger manifest for the four o'clock sailing for the jetfoil. There'd be at least a list of names."

"They don't keep a manifest on the jetfoil," he said. "You just go and buy tickets."

"Aw shit!"

"Except he would've had to have used an immigration document. What I will do tomorrow, I will get hold of Bob Youill and I'll see if we can check that time frame. He still gets checked going out, he still has to clear immigration. I think I can get that checked tomorrow. But I'm a hundred percent sure he's gonna be on a false passport."

"Yeah, he would have something all set up, in another name and another identity," I agreed. "*Shit,* I couldn't chase after him, I couldn't very well shout 'Steven'—so I don't know what to say. I'm virtually certain that I saw him—I looked through hundreds and hundreds of faces before I locked onto that face."

"Okay, what I'm gonna do is this: I'm gonna be talking to Vancouver on that other matter," he said, referring to Kim Kong. "I'll just see what the chances of Canada asking for Wong's extradition are. Because if they ask for extradition, then I can start doing some inquiries through the contact I have in Macau. I would think it's in our vested interest to go for extradition on him. That's my own view. . . . It's unfortunate that he wasn't coming *in* to Hong Kong. If we could've put him in a hotel, we could've really had some fun tomorrow. I could have arranged with Bob Youill, we could have just paid a visit on him, with you in our presence. I'll work on it tonight just so I can see what I can come up with. You're going over to Macau tomorrow?"

"That's right," I said. "I'm going over on the ten o'clock jetfoil. I'm scheduled to come back on the 10 P.M. I phoned Bob Youill today and I have to phone him Friday afternoon to confirm a meeting for Friday evening."

"Okay, take care of yourself. I'll give you the cellular-phone number, I'm gonna be packing it tomorrow—I'll be in and out on this extradition proceeding, but as far as I'm concerned, the urgency is over on that because the arrest has gone down and he's in custody."

Oh, Garry, I thought, if those words were only for Steven Wong.

The bench warrant for Steve's arrest had still not arrived by the next morning, Thursday, September 16. I was scheduled to leave for the Philippines at 10 Saturday morning. About all I could hope for on this trip, then, was to make Steve in Macau so that when Clement received the telex, he could get on the phone to his guy and— Who knows? There he is, Officer—arrest that man!

I decided against the sweaty diesel-mechanic disguise and mixed and matched with shades, green shorts, black socks, sandals, Hawaiian shirt, and a big Calvin Klein shopping bag. Mr. Goof from Biloxi, here for a few bargains, a rush at the tables, and maybe a little Chinese fanny if I won.

Down at Shun Tak I discovered it was a good thing I had a VIP reservation from the Hong Kong office of Macau Tourism; otherwise I would have had to wait a whole 15 minutes for the next sailing. Nobody on my trip could have borne that. On the other side of Customs, at the glass doors to the departures lounge, I walked into a loud argument between two uniformed hostesses and a couple who were apparently getting bumped. Losing a quarter-hour at gambling was a big deal to the passengers on this flying boat. Weekday morning or not, the jetfoil's airplane seats were filled with well-dressed, grim-faced Chinese men and women who looked about as much in the holiday mood as people in line at the methadone clinic. This was serious business. The engines whined like a DC-8, the safety instructions were given in English, Cantonese, and Portuguese, and we took off—literally. Within minutes we were skimming the blue-green surface on winglike foils at 60 miles an hour. Not a second to waste.

I looked out the window at the Chinese silk screen of green islands in white mist and russet junks riding the waves, but most people were ignoring the view. They had their heads down, scratching the lottery cards the stewardesses sold. The instant cards were illegal in Hong Kong. Here they were hors d'oeuvres to the main menu of high-stakes roulette and poker, pai gow and craps. At last! The freedom to gamble! My seatmates hungrily ripped through one $10 package of cards after another, and another, preparing for a day's spree at tables that, all told, would contribute about a billion dollars to Stanley Ho's coffers that year.

There were two old Chinese gents in sports jackets on the other side of Macau Customs holding up a sign that said: "Mister Jery Gold." One was beaming and bald and the other silver-haired and sweet-looking. I assumed they were from the tourist office, here to accompany me on my "familiarization" tour. I shook their hands and discovered they spoke as much English as I spoke Chinese. They had a waiting car for me.

"Where we going?" I asked.

The bald one looked at me without comprehension.

"Are you from the Macau Tourist Office?"

He didn't understand, but heard the question in my voice and ecstatically beckoned me to the back seat. I was suddenly as tempted to get in that car as I was to walk down Avenida da Amizade with sandwich boards that read, "Steve—I'm here," I gave the old duffers a US fin each and refused their ride, or tour, or one-way trip to the woods. They looked devastated, talking to each other in loud singsong as I strolled west away from them, towards the Lisboa. Feeling awfully naked at my back, I heard the car door slam, the engine gun, and looked right to see them creeping beside me. They both called out in Cantonese, shrugged helplessly to each other at my friendly but dismissive wave, and then were gone. Or maybe not gone. They knew who I was. Jery Gold.

Just down the street from the Kingsway, I saw that Stanley Ho and the government of Macau were adding another 10 percent to the size of the tiny domain, constructing a 50-square-block jetty into the Outer Harbor where the squatter huts used to be. It was a massive project, a forest of derricks, pile drivers, and D-8 Cats building roads into the ocean. In addition, a half-completed bridge arched up over the bay on its way to Taipa Island to the south. To the north, condo towers and hotels were going up everywhere I looked. Why not? Prospects were bright. Revenue projections for Ho's casinos in 1997, when the jetty and bridge were to be completed, were over $2 billion, almost a third of it to be paid in taxes to the Macau government, which relied on the casinos for half its total revenue.

At the end of Amizade I saw the 200-foot Lisboa. Even in Vegas I hadn't come across a structure as overwhelmingly disharmonious. The neighborhood around it was terrific, of course—a backdrop of European boulevards and cafés running along the glittering Praia Grande Bay, but you had to look past the Lisboa's eye-crossing kitsch to see it. The white-and-orange tower brought to mind a garish condo in Miami; the three-story sphere on top was out of an Ed Woods sci-fi film; and the casino roof, rafters exposed, looked like a whitewashed elephant cage. Chinese doormen dressed as Portuguese matadors ushered me into a lobby that had millions of dollars' worth of vases behind glass, a first-century A.D. seismograph, an ancient warlord's gold-lamé uniform, a porcelain Kwan Kung, life-size cloisonné lions, and naval junks in full sail, miraculously carved from solid ivory. There were no chairs or couches where I could sit and admire these precious works or watch for Steve, though. Not one. Sitting was not the point of being here—unless I took my seat beyond the metal detectors, at the end of a corridor down which it seemed the whole world was headed, heedless of the museum in the lobby.

I checked my empty Calvin Klein bag and entered a stadium-size casino suffused in gold gloom, where thousands of people were packed around scores of tables that ran 24 hours a day, seven days a week—even in the midst of typhoons that shut down Hong Kong. Several stories above the heads of the gamblers was a domed roof—an upside-down thousand-petaled lotus. Botticelli-like reliefs gazed down upon the masses from within the immense flower. Roman columns encircled them. The crazy decor and sheer size of the place seemed to have an effect on the decorum of the players. The chain-smoking gamblers behaved as frenetically as traders at the Chicago futures exchange—shouting, reaching, jostling one another as they stood several tiers deep around each table, throwing money down, picking money up, racing to other venues and starting all over again.

To think that I would spot Steve in here was wishful thinking, but I went at it for two hours anyway, surveilling every table and corner until, my third time around, I noticed some goons on their cell phones obviously relaying information about me—the only *gwailo* in here. I kept a dingbat's smile on my face as I left the Astrodome of casinos and climbed the flight of plush-carpeted stairs to loftier realms.

In those days you had free access to VIP rooms with names like the Royal and the Golden Palace, each level progressively higher in stakes, each more quiet than the one beneath. But despite the high-class hush, it was still a low smoky world. The ever-present security guards suspiciously eyed Mr. Goof as he made his tour. I kept smiling with a rube's wonder as I watched the bigshots lay down their $10,000 bets. Softly they offered prayers to Kwan Kung's statue, then, millimeter by millimeter, peeled back a jack or a king that put them over the top. A groan, a shrug, and then another prayer—without, I was sure, promising to make the effort to be good afterward. It was all a lie told to God—and they knew it. Which was why so many criminals gambled, I surmised. Please, Kwan Kung, let this dope deal go down without a problem.

That night, after a wander around the entire town, inspecting every pedestrian I passed, I had a meal at an outdoor restaurant on Praia Grande. Then it was over to the Lisboa again. This time I took the elevator to the eighth floor of the hotel and emerged into an utterly quiet and quite civilized corridor. I don't know what else I expected up here. Perhaps to hear the bloodcurdling wails of men who'd crossed the Triads and were dying slowly from a thousand cuts.

Oh God! Don't even think about that.

The next day, on my way to visit Clement, I stopped into the Macau Government Tourist Office and asked a rep if he'd set up two guys to meet me at the ferry yesterday. He found the correspondence on my trip from their Tourist Information Bureau in Richmond and said that somebody from the B.C. office must have arranged for the two chaperons. But it wasn't his office. That information sparked a flurry of international calls from Clement to Prudential's James Gallagher and Gallagher to Martin Lister and Lister to the detective agency Guard Force; and finally from Gallagher to me at 2 A.M. Saturday, with dire warnings like, "Do not, repeat, DO NOT go to Macau when you return from stop two unless accompanied by Guard Force security! Richmond Bureau did not arrange chaperons! We think your cover has been blown! Meet with Lister and Guard Force immediately upon your return!"

I said I definitely would, and then tried to get back to sleep. I was still wide awake when I had to get ready for stop two.

CHAPTER 16

SUGARLAND

———

You will get there quickly if you go slowly,
but if you go quickly it will take a long time.
—PHILIPPINE SAYING

We were sitting by a window that overlooked a squatter shanty town. Between us and the shacks was a weedy runway with a derelict Constellation and several DC-3s parked by a hangar that bore the name Philippine Fish and Agricultural Corporation. On an adjoining runway I counted 15 Huey choppers and half a dozen C-37 military transports. The electricity had been out for a couple of hours and the air conditioner was only beginning to dilute the astounding heat. "I suggest you will have to wear a disguise on Negros," Danilo Mendez advised me, raising his voice above breathtaking torrents of rain. Danilo was the cousin of NBI agent Virgilio Mendez. He was also Prudential's man on the ground in the Philippines, reporting directly to the ex-CIA agent in charge of Steve's file in the States. "Minimum: your hat and sunglasses," he said. "Of course, we will have a guard contingent for you, similar as here today."

Danny was referring to the three NBI agents, each sporting automatic weapons, who'd met my flight at Manila's Ninoy Aquino Airport, named after the liberal reformer who'd been assassinated on the tarmac 10 years earlier. In a three-car convoy my guards had melodramatically whisked me around the runway perimeter to this hotel, the Philippine Village, a four-star edifice with hundreds of rooms, several restaurants, a ballroom, and a view onto Third World squalor and Vietnam-era hardware. I rode in Danny's luxury car, between the two government vehicles, and on the way he'd told me he was the Philippine director of the World Association of Detectives, a lawyer, an accountant, president of the Rotary Club, and the leader of a Catholic marriage-counseling service. He hinted that his résumé also included liaisons with the CIA station in Manila.

Danny turned to my chart, which I'd spread on the table. "If Wong is found alive, these two men will surely be brought to justice," he said, pointing to Guara and Abastillas. A bolt of lightning struck the Quonset hangar and a huge clap of thunder shook up the room—and me. Danilo didn't even blink. He was almost albino, with pink-white skin that didn't fit his Filipino features. But he was absolutely sure of himself, and advertised his wealth and position with a gold Rolex and a powder-blue *barong*—the gossamer shirt worn outside the pants that is the national dress for businessmen and politicians in the Philippines. According to what he'd been telling me, a lot of the barong-set seemed to be in Danny's network. Guests at his recent 25th wedding anniversary included the county's secretaries of defense and state, the former director of the NBI, several top judges, and the mayor of Manila. "The important thing is that we keep this out of the hands of the Philippine National Police," he said. "We have some contacts in there, but very few. We cannot trust them."

"Jeez Danny," I laughed, "that sounds serious. A hundred thousand policemen watching the country and you can only trust a few? How many NBI agents?"

"Sadly, only two hundred," he said, lifting a hand and shaking his head at the absurdity. "It is a very serious situation in our country. The Chinese Triad element from Hong Kong are coming here and are not finding it difficult for themselves."

He stood up and straightened his barong over his hips. "Wong is the key to this web of corruption," Danny stated, with the theatrical conviction of a politician. "If he is found alive, the whole networks of their evil deeds on Negros will be brought to justice." He turned and walked over to the hardwood bedstead, made his hand into a fist and startled me by pounding hard three times on the wall. "Yah!" someone called. "S'okay," Danny answered, adding a few words in Tagalog.

"So now your private guard is in position in the next room," he said to me. "You will bang on this wall as such if there is trouble. Please. Do for practice."

I walked over to the bedstead and banged thrice. "Yah!" came the voice. "S'okay," I said.

Danny extended his hand to me. "Therefore—thank you for your helping us on this matter. Tomorrow I will pick you up at ten. I suggest you do not go out by yourself at night. I say that merely because of the danger of foreigners being kidnapped, a terrible problem. So I suggest you eat in the hotel this evening with your protector."

I took his advice, dining with Tomas a few hours later in the deserted Copa Restaurant. My squat bodyguard ordered us stewed chicken deliciously marinated in vinegar and garlic, pumpkin cooked in coconut milk, and pork on a stick lathered in lemon juice. Unfortunately, for the entire meal I had to contend with two dozen famished cats of every shape and color that fought for space beneath the table, hissing at each other, meowing plaintively, and rubbing against my legs. Tomas explained that the squatter town beyond the airport fence was overrun with rats, so the management put up with the cats. There was talk of clearing the squatters, but Tomas didn't think that was a good idea. Over 30 percent of the nation lived below the official poverty line. Here in Metro Manila, up to a quarter of the population couldn't afford to pay rent. They had to live somewhere, so a couple of million of them had built shacks along highways and shorelines, in cemeteries and garbage dumps—wherever there was unoccupied space.

"What a mess," I said.

"*Bahala na,*" Tomas shrugged. *That's the way it is*—the national philosophy of the Philippines. He kicked a cat away and ordered dessert.

With the shaved ice and sweet beans came another plague. Three professional girls arose from a table by the karaoke stage and tried to get me to sing with them. I was the only paying customer tonight, so, like the cats, they wouldn't take no for an answer. None of the girls looked more than 18, and they accentuated their adolescent panache by wearing very short, Sunday-school party dresses of pink taffeta and peach ruffles—their stick legs, white socks, and patent-leather shoes marking, I assumed, the erotic ideal of many of the Western businessmen who ate here. They giggled, squealed and uttered obsequious coos of admiration as they stroked and fluffed my curly hair. Each time I pushed at their hands they pouted petulantly, stepped away, and then came back. Finally I picked up two cats by the scruff of their necks and threatened to throw them on the girls' dresses. That did the trick, but a disapproving Tomas shook his head at my strange stodginess. "They are from the town," he said, pointing across Airport Avenue to the squatter dwellings. "It is just their job, they are the GRG."

"GRG?"

"Group Responsibility Girls."

Bahala na, I thought.

There were three other common sayings—"the three Bakas," according to Tomas—that summed up Filipinos' fatalistic attitude towards life in the last decade of the 20th century. *Baka bukas*—"perhaps tomorrow." *Baka maagawan*—expect to be extorted by the authorities or heavily leaned on for a bribe. And *baka makalusot*—essentially, "Everybody does it, nobody gets caught, so I'll do it too." Coupled with the many common terms used to describe the evil spirits of the sea, earth, and air, and the passionate veneration of the Virgin Mary as a protection against malevolence, the general Filipino state of mind reminded me of the attitude that dominated the Ukrainian *shtetl* where my grandmother had grown up, surrounded by evil eyes, *dybbuks,* Cossacks, and daily prayers for the Messiah.

As I dug into the history of the Philippines, I found this perception was more or less accurate. In 1896, Dr. Jose Rizal, one of the fathers of Philippine nationalism, stood before a Spanish firing squad in Manila, convicted of promoting a broad program of social reform, including universal education, land distribution, constitutional democracy and, most culpably, a gradual end to three and a half centuries of Spanish colonial rule. Rizal was a Renaissance man—a medical doctor who was fluent in several languages, an accomplished sculptor, poet, and novelist, and a naturalist who had cataloged the flora and fauna of the tropical paradise that was then the Philippines. However, in his writings, Rizal had stressed that before Filipinos could assume responsibility for their own fate, they had to move beyond a Spanish-colonial heritage that had kept them frozen where the Spanish wanted them—in a state of tribalism, feudalism, corruption, and animist and Catholic superstition. Just before leaving his prison cell, Rizal penned his last words to his people: "I am most anxious for liberties for our country, but I place as a prior condition the education of the people so that our country may have an individuality of its own and make itself worthy of liberation."

In 1949, after 40 years of the American colonial rule that had replaced the Spanish, four years of torment under Japanese occupation, and four years of independence, a Philippine political cartoonist named E. Z. Izon drew a caricature of the state of the nation. A woman, "Filippinas," was shown shackled to the wall of a dungeon, her two chains named "Lawlessness" and "Graft." Her feet were chained to iron balls named "Superstition" and "Corruption." Izon had drawn in the figure of Rizal, looking at the woman in disbelief, and crying, "Still here!"

Forty-four years later, at the time of my arrival in the Philippines, the very same Izon published his latest caricature of the nation. This time President Fidel Ramos, smiling and smoking a cigar, held up his millennial slogan, "On to Philippines 2000," while at his feet a Filipino everyman sat bound in a straitjacket, driven out of his mind by criminals in the police, military, and government, with the detritus of violent street crime and corruption strewn all around him.

In other words, nothing had changed since 1949, or, for that matter, since 1896, when Rizal had been shot. "In the face of all the rhetoric about tiger economies and rapid progress," the British writer James Hamilton-Paterson wrote in an introduction to his social-realist novel *Ghosts of Manila,* "unchangingness" was the watchword of the Philippines. Indeed, things had gotten worse since 1949, and "the Worst as I describe it is nothing like as bad as the great underclass knows it to be."

Corruption beyond belief was the order of the day in the Philippines. Between his election in 1965 and his overthrow in 1986, President Ferdinand Marcos had stolen an estimated $12 billion from government coffers and hidden the money in Swiss banks. By 1993, none of this loot had been recovered, and, with the courts packed with Marcos's cronies, and the legislature filled with Marcos's beneficiaries, the prospects of getting the money back seemed slim.

These legislators were descended from the ranks of rich landowners who, under American rule, had passed bills in the colonial congress that had benefited their enormous holdings (and American companies) to the detriment of the vast majority of Filipinos, who owned almost no land at all. The modern legislators, now business entrepreneurs as well as landowners, continued the tradition by passing bills that benefited their land holdings *and* their companies—still to the detriment of the vast majority of Filipinos. In "House of the Elite," an exposé article published in the *Manila Times* the month before I arrived, journalist Eric Guttierez pointed out that only 16 of the 180 legislators in the House of Representatives were not millionaires; more than two-thirds came from families that had held political office for at least one generation, and one-third came from families that had been in power for several generations, their reign spanning numerous changes in government. According to another exposé by journalist Stella Tirol, published in the *Philippine Daily Inquirer,* over the course of the past 10 years the venerable House speaker, Jose de Venecia, had chalked up as much as $100 million in favorable business loans and loan guarantees from government banks—loans that his company had never paid back and that were apparently "used for purposes other than that for which they were supposedly intended." De Venecia was investigated by a government commission and never charged with wrongdoing, but Tirol argued that the commission's findings were "false" and "anomalous."

The Philippines had a wildly free press, but the corruption that dominated the headlines was immune to exposés. Readers laughed or cried and then said, "*Bahala na,*" partly because those very same readers were regularly bought off by the people who stole their taxes. Every year the House of Representatives and the Senate voted themselves an annual "pork" allowance, euphemistically called a development fund. Representatives were each allotted about $1 million to disperse, and senators about $4 million. The Philippine Center for Investigative Journalism, and even some irate senators and cabinet officials, revealed what happened to the money. In most projects, between a quarter and a half of the pork fund disappeared into the pockets of the politicians connected to the projects, from the federal level down to the local level; another 10 percent went into the pockets of their cronies in the government agencies that contracted out the supposed development work. The politicians who received the kickbacks then paid off journalists to write glowing articles about the projects, or, failing that, to expose the corruption of their rivals. They also used the money to flagrantly buy votes at special fiestas, during which thick wads of 50-peso notes (worth about a dollar apiece) were thrown in the air for indigent locals to grab as they fluttered down. The total estimate of pork-related graft varied somewhat, depending on the project and the exposé, but usually only between 40 and 65 percent of the development funds went to the purpose for which the money was intended, which often left roads, airport runways, bridges, and schools unfinished for years, or unsafe when they were completed.

The courts, right up to the Supreme Court, provided no redress for these shenanigans because the justices set a very poor example. Another Stella Tirol article, "Fake Ruling," published in the *Inquirer* in early 1993, documented a landmark case that preserved the monopoly (and high rates) of the Philippine Long Distance Telephone Company: all the evidence pointed to the fact that Supreme Court Justice Hugo Gutierrez had allowed the lawyers for the phone company to write his decision. (Guttierez resigned after the article appeared.) Still another 1993 *Inquirer* exposé of the Supreme Court, by journalist Sheila S. Coronel, documented how a Supreme Court justice, a senior justice of the Court of Appeals, and a brother-in-law of the chief justice of the Supreme Court had handpicked a sympathetic judge to try a case involving a large real estate transaction, to the eventual benefit of the chief justice's brother-in-law when the case was won. Other exposés on the Supreme Court by Coronel uncovered a network of well-connected brokers who fixed cases for a price, influence-peddling by lawyers and litigants, and, of course, the return of political favors in the form of favorable decisions.

Considering the behavior of the Republic's exalted judges and highest elected officials, it came as no surprise to me that the situation of policing in the Philippines was bleak. Earning on average less than $1,000 a year, a PNP patrolman or corporal virtually *had* to steal to make ends meet for his family. Five years before I arrived in the Philippines, a study by Yolanda Lira of the National Defense College revealed that almost *all* cops were crooked. "In the police, you are deviant if you are not corrupt," Lira wrote. "The upper levels of corruption become the role models of the street-level cop. If the higher-ups are doing it, why can't he do it too?" (*Baka makalu-sot.*) Aside from the ubiquitous graft and shakedowns, brutality and sadism were accepted as normal procedures in police stations. "The police operate with virtual impunity," wrote investigative journalist Gemma Luz Corotan in *Brother Hood.* "A person can be taken right off the street or be killed like a dog for no reason. His rights are not sacred." As might be expected, the courts were not trusted by those policemen who actually cared about justice. Judges of the criminal courts were bought off regularly by rapists, murderers, drug dealers, and kidnappers. The solution arrived at by some cops was to kill the worst criminals upon arrest. The murder of suspects even had a name: "salvaging," which was perceived as one of the only ways to curtail the plague of violent crime that made the Philippines nearly unlivable.

How did the Philippines become one of the most corrupt societies on earth, ranked right up there with such countries as Chad by watchdog groups like the Political and Economic Risk Consultancy Group and Transparency International? According to the small band of souls who ran the Philippine Center for Investigative Journalism, the nation's "metastatic" corruption, its "total systemic affliction," had a history that made it explicable, if not forgivable. In a book called *Pork and Other Perks: Corruption and Governance in the Philippines,* the PCIJ traced how corruption had originated in a tribal method of governance called "*personalism,* which sets the cultural base of corrupt behavior." Before the arrival of the Spanish explorer Magellan in 1521, Philippine tribal leaders had attained their power in small communities, called *barangays,* based on face-to-face contact. Aspiring chiefs promised favors in order to gain power and returned favors in order to stay in power. Thus, barangay chiefs did not represent their constituents, they represented themselves, their immediate family, and their small circle of allies, although on the village level the needs of the group and the chief were often congruent. When the Spanish encountered this form of personal rule they took full advantage of it, buying off chiefs and converting them to Christianity. Rulers and priests then ordered that the chiefs run their barangays for the profit of Spain through the administration of her civil servants. All levels of government became, perforce, "an instrument for extracting money and labor from the people without providing public services commensurate to the level of extraction." The "highly personalized leadership of these barangays," and the Spanish tradition of "public officials behaving as if government were their private preserve," fit neatly together to produce a machinery of governance that "established patterns of political relations, some of which continue to this day."

As in government, so in land ownership. Blessed by a thuggish clergy, the Spanish seized most of the arable land, deeded it to a few colonial land-lords, and set the population to work upon it as sharecroppers, with their barangay chiefs acting as overseers for the *hacienderos*. A small number of extended families, mainly of old Spanish ancestry, still controlled most of the land in the Philippines.

Oddly enough, nationalism—which should have been the rallying point against corrupt governance—further ingrained corruption as a way of life in the psyches of ordinary Filipinos. Because Spanish officials ruled by overwhelming force, nationalism sparked passive resistance: "cheating the government was regarded as patriotic." Stealing property, protecting thieves, and not paying taxes came to be viewed as revolutionary goods.

In 1898 there was a brief moment when it seemed as if the cycle might be broken. A dispute over control of sugar in faraway Cuba led to the Spanish-American War, which soon spread to the Philippines, where the United States allied itself with the nationalist *insurrectos* against Spain. U.S. Commodore George Dewey destroyed the Spanish fleet in Manila Bay and, on June 12, the insurrecto general, Emilio Aguinaldo, raised the Philippine flag for the first time. Unfortunately, the victorious Americans then turned on their former nationalist allies and waged a brutal, three-year jungle war that ended in the death of thousands and the defeat of the first Philippine Republic. After that, corruption picked up where it had left off under the Spanish, but with a twist.

By the mid-1930s the U.S. colonial administrators had helped Filipinos to draw up a federal constitution that provided for an American-style, nationally elected president, a bicameral federal legislature, and provinces with governors. It was to prove but a veneer of democracy over a centuries-old tradition of personalism. Filipino politicians took the American system and used it as a means to legalize their theft, based on their time-honored notion that government existed to enrich those who governed. Indeed, after the U.S. granted final independence to the country in 1945, politicians who had served U.S. mining and sugar interests entrenched themselves in power by harvesting vast amounts of govern-ment money to finance their election campaigns. The 1961 election that brought to power Diosdado Macapagal (father of the future president Gloria Macapagal-Arroyo) used up 13 percent of the national budget; by the time of the Marcos election in 1965, it was up to about 20 percent, and Marcos's reelection in 1969 harnessed 25 percent. The practice continued even after Marcos's overthrow by the nonviolent "People Power Revolution," which installed the supposedly reformist Cory Aquino in 1986. The revered wife of Ninoy Aquino managed to sidestep her own reform legislation, earning her administration the derisive name "Relatives Incorporated" because of its rampant patronage and simony. In 1992, her successor, Fidel Ramos, Marcos's former chief of the army, siphoned millions from the passport office to elect himself and his chosen candidates.

Marcos and his wife, Imelda, were human vacuum cleaners when it came to theft of the Philippine treasury, and one would think any president would look good by comparison—except in the Philippines, ruled by "unchangingness." In his first years in office, Ramos's mistress, Rose Marie "Baby" Arenas, openly wielded extraordinary power in the governance of the nation, using her access to the presidential palace to benefit her own business interests and place her friends in power. Midway through his term, Ramos became embroiled in what the PCIJ called "the Grandmother of All Scams," the sale of $600 million-worth of public land in Manila Bay at a 95 percent reduced price in order that Ramos cronies—government brokers, politicians, and bureaucrats—could collect payoffs of millions from the Thai-owned Amari Coastal Bay Resource Corporation, which claimed it wanted to develop the land into a minicity. In the end, greed trumped value, nothing was developed, and the government was defrauded of several hundred million dollars by its own public servants (not one of whom was ever criminally charged for the scam). All of this larceny would, in turn, be surpassed by the corruption of Ramos's vice president and eventual successor, Joseph Estrada.

"You see, it wasn't Marcos," Danny insisted as we flew over the Visayan Sea to Negros the next afternoon. "It was Imelda. Himself, Marcos, he was good, but Imelda did him in. She was the power behind the throne, for good or bad."

I held my tongue, staring down at the coral reefs that gave an electric glow to the powder-blue shallows around Panay Island. However, the country's physical beauty couldn't distract me from the political ugliness that overlaid it. Marcos had jailed, tortured, killed or driven into exile at least 50,000 of his own citizens. "Filipinos in Vancouver tell me life under Marcos was almost as bad as under the Japanese," I said. "Imelda was a witch, but Ferdinand was a fascist."

Danny agreed that Marcos had taken advantage of his absolute power "towards the end," but disagreed with those leftists who maintained that a declaration of martial law had not been necessary in 1972. The country had been in chaos; the Communists wanted to overthrow the government. There had been mass demonstrations in front of the presidential palace, national strikes, and frequent bombings. From their mountain bases, the New People's Army had launched daily guerrilla attacks against civilians, the military and the police. On Mindanao, the Muslims were in open revolt. "So after the declaration, stability was restored. But then Imelda got her way."

I let it go, admitting to him that Canada had had its own experience of martial law two years before Marcos's declaration, and that while Native Canadians drank themselves to death on tiny reservations, our prime minister's wife had indulged her love of discos and rock stars the same way Imelda had indulged her love of shoes.

The fact was, I had faith in Danny's personal honesty and his sincere desire for "stability," even as I was aware he was a member of the ruling class. That morning he'd invited me to his house in Las Pinas, south of the airport. He lived in a stone hacienda with a swimming pool and servants. The floors were tiled with blue marble, and lining the walls were magnificent lacquered cabinets and all the accoutrements of the good life—48-inch TV, VCR, and high-end Catholic icons. Was I going to get testy about his power and influence when they were supplying me the assistance I needed to prove Steve's death a fraud?

On the other hand, as we passed over hundreds of green islets haloed by white beaches, the sea dotted with fishing boats and cargo ships, I reflected that with its booming tourism and trade, natural resources, and First World electronics industry, the Philippines could have been another Japan—an Asian Tiger in its own right. Unfortunately, the wealth at the top seemed to trickle down only during vote-buying fiestas.

"There was terrible disorder under Cory, too," Danilo piped up as we began our descent into Bacolod. "Her own fault—she did not know how to govern. So a group tried to overthrow her."

"Nine times," I said. "Hundreds of people killed."

"Yes, nine times," he grimaced. "I did not support them—very destabilizing. But they were all from the army and wanted order. What can I say? The people now have much faith in General Ramos—President Fidel Ramos. The army respects him and he has a definite program: 'On to Philippines 2000.' He is taking steps which will help the situation, socially, politically and economically. We are to be an Asian Tiger soon, for this I have the greatest hope that everyone will be benefiting."

As we stepped out of the plane onto the gangway of the Bacolod City Airport, Danilo pointed out three men waiting on the tarmac, one a young and sensitive-looking fellow with a drawn Uzi, another a large middle-aged man carrying a 9mm pistol. The two armed men were set at a 45-degree stance to the plane's gangway, covering the points of the compass, with the distant chain of volcanic mountains where Steve had died at their shoulders. The third man, who was facing us, held out his hand to Danilo and greeted him in Tagalog, then broke into English for my benefit. His name was Philip Pecadre, chief of the NBI office in Bacolod—a thin fellow about my age, wearing a striped polo shirt and, above his lip, a dashing Errol Flynn mustache.

"Where's Virgilio?" I asked him as we walked through the searing sun towards the mildewed terminal.

"Too frightened to come," Philip replied.

"Yes, he is holed up in his office in fear," said the man with the Uzi.

"You are?" I asked.

"Rommel," he replied. "Like the Desert Fox. Rommel Ramirez. I will tell you that we are all very disappointed in the cowardice of our colleague Virgilio."

"Maybe he is merely afraid to talk to reporters," said the big fellow with the pistol.

"Joking time over," Danny pronounced. He pointed to the big fellow. "This is Virgilio."

I slapped Virgilio's arm and shook his logger's-size hand, delighted at meeting the fed I'd talked to across the sea. He was a bear of a guy, with the wide face, black curly hair, and giant gut of a Polynesian chief. As it turned out, he also had the sense of humor of a late-night talk-show host.

"After you, Mr. Ambassador," he said, opening the door to a four-by-four pickup in the breezeway. "I am to protect your right side. Your left side is your responsibility."

I jumped in the front seat, with Virgilio at my right and Philip behind the wheel. Danilo and Rommel climbed in the back, Rommel holding his Uzi in the air to discourage assassins. We drove past sugarcane fields half a mile north, entered the south edge of town and pulled in to the white porte cochere of a new luxury hotel called the Sugarland. Two uniformed doormen pulling luggage racks on wheels approached either side of our truck, whipped open our doors and saluted Philip and Virgilio. All of this royal ambience contrasted with the rude Third World out on Araneta Street, where rattletrap jeepneys, buses, and trucks overloaded with cane brayed without mufflers, sending great black clouds of oily exhaust over us. To the left and right of the hotel was a lineup of sidewalk vendors selling gasoline in Coke bottles, beer, cigarettes, towels, candles, fruit—in short, anything that would make them a few pesos.

"Your evil man like to gamble," Virigilio said to me.

"That's right, Chinese-style."

"So that is where your evil man gambled." He pointed across Araneta to what looked like a shopping center in Fort Lauderdale, the new Goldenfield Commercial Complex. "We talked to the assistant manager, asked him if he has seen Steven Wong. He is very familiar with the ugly face of Wong. We showed him the picture, and he said he saw him before he went to heaven. We will take you there for some fun after our briefing."

The "briefing" took place in Danilo's suite. I stood at the front of the room, my chart on a tripod supplied by the hotel. Five NBI agents, plus Danilo and my new bodyguard, a quiet man named Toto, lounged on the beds and chairs. "Okay, this is something I spent months researching," I said, launching into my shtick, all the way from Steve's heroin bust to my sighting four days ago. "Eventually I'm going to write an article on all of it. The important thing now is to convince the Canadian Department of Justice and External Affairs to have the Mounties come over here and fully cooperate with you."

"Yes," Philip said. "That is the thing that must be accomplished. That is where you can help us."

I explained that the day before I flew to the Philippines, Friday September 17, the Canadian warrant for Steve's arrest had been issued in Vancouver, and by now had probably been telexed to Garry Clement in Hong Kong. "Clement's raring to come over here to pursue this investigation. Vancouver is eager, too. What they require is overwhelming evidence that all this has been a ruse."

"We will get that for you tomorrow," Philip said. "However, our goal is to arrest all these people," he added, presenting his chief's operational perspective on the names on my chart. "We can have a very strong case if the Canadian government only will cooperate in the investigation of its citizens who have done the deed. We need them to come to us and say, 'This man is not dead.' Then we can proceed with the arrests."

"They are anticipating official word so they can stop these Triads," Danny emphasized. "Because, don't forget, we are dealing with a big lawyer, a chief of police, probably the military involved with them. So you can imagine what it will be like here if they win."

"They just arrested another Triad member in Bacolod," Virgilio informed me, "the same tattoos as your man, but this one, he's Taiwanese. They caught him in possession of drugs and also firearms. So now we are seeing more and more of these lovely types."

"All I can say is that the Mounties in Hong Kong *want* to come over here," I declared, playing the part of honorary consul. "They would be on a plane tomorrow, but they can't without the government approving. If it was the Americans—"

At that the whole room burst into laughter, each agent familiar with the split-second reaction time of the DEA. "Over here in middle of the night.... They travel with big suitcases. . . . One, two, three—criminal is back home."

"But Canadians are very polite," I said, naming the nation's most salient characteristic. "They don't want to break any rules. Me, I'm a pushy New Yorker," I added, handing Philip a sheet with all my Mountie contacts. "You arrest Newson when he gets back here and starts his dope business, and that'll be an excuse to phone Garry Clement in Hong Kong. He's not gonna hang up on you. Meantime, I'll have snooped around Abastillas at his office and Guara at his new posting—"

But Philip Pecadre, somber foil to my civilian exuberance, leaned forward, pointed to the bull's-eye of the chart and said it was very important that I stay away from Abastillas and Guara. With the Canadians sitting on this case for a year, there was no telling how long before Wong would finally be arrested in Macau. The last thing they wanted was for the conspirators to fly the coop before then. "For you in the Canadian media to be a bridge between governments is the way to proceed until something official can take place," Philip concluded. "We know the way these two think. 'Nothing will happen.' But if you frighten them too soon—"

"Either your police come over here or he is apprehended—that is the way," Rommel Ramirez said. "His arrest would be the best. No need to prove anything."

I agreed on that, and said that when I was done here on Negros I would be going over to Macau. "I'll have protection from a bodyguard service Prudential is giving me. I'll be there for four days and I hope to have him in chains by the time I go home. If not, and the Canadian government starts dragging its feet with you guys, in my article I will make sure that the Canadian public is aware of it. I'll push for public pressure because I believe that it's time for Steven Wong and all his cronies on Negros to be in jail."

"I like this man," Virgilio said to Danny.

Danny slapped his hands on his thighs, happy at the progress here. "So—everything we need we will get on the expedition tomorrow—the affidavits from the different people, which you will bring back to Hong Kong. Then the affidavits will be passed to the people that make the decisions. And we will get some action."

"Plus photographs of the exact spot where Wong bumped his head, I'll need that," I reminded him.

An explosion of hearty coughing, moans and mysterious Tagalog jokes greeted that remark. Everybody spoke at once. "Not possible to go to *exact* spot . . . Very nice people up there . . . Serve you head for supper . . . A lot of people with bazookas . . . New People's Army take you hostage . . . Hostage at the least."

"So none of you have ever been up there?" I asked.

"We tried," Virgilio said. "But we were advised by the chief in Isabela not to proceed to the exact area because we would come down in coffins. So we'll make some arrangements with the military, we'll find out how to breach the area, and get soldiers to escort you. A whole company. We will get transport trucks and cover the whole area."

"And tanks," said Rommel. "And helicopters. The air force will fly us cover."

"Probably even the captain will not even land in the place," Philip remarked glumly. "You can take a look from the air, I don't think the pilot will go down. Unless the place is invaded and secured and surrounded."

"Is it worth your life?" Rommel asked me.

"I'll tell you why it would be worth it," I said, and, even now, listening to my words, I have to wonder at the *mishegoss* that made me so unfazed. "I've got to convince a lot of people back in Canada he could not have died in that spot. So far there's no legitimate witnesses to say he could not have died there. So if it's possible—"

"They will send your wife back your ears," Virgilio said. "We can take you so far so that you can establish your point. You can take some photographs and you can personally see: no motorized tricycles can get in the area, it's highly impossible for him to travel to that faraway place."

"We will only have the pickup truck," Rommel pointed out. "No tanks."

"Maybe it's not such a good idea," I allowed, figuring there was no point in arguing it now, I'd wait till I got up there. "I know you're being very gracious to me, you're risking your lives—"

"S'okay!" Danny pronounced, ending the debate. "So put your materials away, we are going down to dinner!"

After a delicious supper at Prudential's expense we crossed Araneta to the Goldenfield Complex "for some fun." Every face turned to look at us through eye burning cigarette smoke as we entered Casino Filipino. It was a Sunday night but it may as well have been Saturday, since it seemed half the males in the town were here, puffing and losing their money to the beat of Michael Jackson's "Thriller." There were older men in business suits and younger men in shorts, T-shirts, and flip-flops. There were men dressed like pimps in tight polyester shirts with flared collars and working men in baggy cotton pants and grease-stained denim jackets. And there was a group of four smartly dressed Chinese at the card table. All the others gambled in groups of similar ages, but the Chinese at the card table were strangely arrayed in what looked like 20-year intervals, almost in hierarchy, from a white-haired gent who seemed in his 70s down to a greased post-adolescent wearing a black sports coat over a tank top that showed the dragons on his chest. Each had a fortress of chips stacked in front of him. As we walked behind the group, Philip took his left hand and placed it on the neck of the Crisco kid, forcing him forward. The fellow didn't resist, his forehead going almost to the felt on the card table. Philip ran his hands smoothly down either side of the fellow's jacket, into his pockets. He handed a wallet to Virgilio, then continued frisking the boy along his ribs and chest. Philip pushed the boy's jacket open and examined the dragon. His Chinese companions, meanwhile, examined their cards, paying no attention to the little drama, although action had come to a halt in the rest of the casino. The casino's deejay cranked the volume on the pounding disco, just to let everybody know it was okay to go back to losing. Virgilio read the identity card, put it back in the wallet and dropped it into the boy's pocket. He questioned him in Tagalog and the boy pointed north, explaining, I presumed, where he was from and why he was here. The NBI agents talked among themselves for a moment, then walked along to the other side of the casino, stopping to buy some chips before moving on to the craps table.

"Who're they?" I asked.

Philip shrugged. "I have talked to the old one before. The young fellow I've never seen. Probably the same kind as Steven Wong almost certainly."

"From Manila," said Virgilio, "if I can believe his identification and story. They come here to stay at the Mambucal Resort, in the mountains from here 40 kilometers. Grandfather, father, and two brothers. Anyway, they have lots of money to gamble."

"More and more like them are here all the time," said Philip.

"So that is the current problem," Virgilio said. "They have their feetholds on Negros. They are forming this network, you see, and using it as a station. They have the friends of the NPA movement and your nice friends from home. We think they make and process the *shabu* and heroin. So: are the NPA now a whole army of drug dealers working for the Chinese criminals? It's possible they are funding their terrorism now this way."

"*Shabu?* What's *shabu?*"

"It is what we call methamphetamine. Anyway, you first," he said, handing me the dice. "You have the luck tonight."

Hardly. Fifteen minutes later I was $50 poorer. It wasn't even a good investment, since the NBI agents discovered that the manager who had recognized Steve's picture was now down in Damaguete, on the southern end of the island, looking into setting up another government-owned casino at the Santa Monica Beach Resort. To salve my losses they took me across the Goldenfield Complex's parking lot to the Abuji Laser Disk Karaoke Club, a dark bamboo den crowded with Group Responsibility Girls. Several of them immediately chose a favorite and took a seat beside him. As the only Westerner I was the choice of the girl at the top of the bar's pecking order— at least she said she was the best girl in the town, and her friends laughingly backed her up. Imelda H. Lagarito was her name. She unabashedly sat in my lap, took a pen from my pocket and laboriously spelled her name out, along with her address and telephone number. "I want you take me America, Joe," she said in my ear. "I cook and clean for you there, okay Joe?"

Despite the sign above the karaoke stage—"Are you ready to Fanta*size*—Enjoy five new Fanta flavors!"—the feel of her starched crinoline and her baby-powder smell were the opposite of flavorful to me. Philip looked as uncomfortable as I was with the company, but Rommel and Virgilio had a laugh over the repartee and got up to sing with the girls. To occupy myself with Imelda I took out a Xerox of Steve and asked if she'd ever seen him. "Ooo, Joe, he look mean!" she said. "Look very cold. Not like you, I like *you*, Joe! You want to sing with me karaoke, Joe?"

I turned to Philip. "Is this like Hong Kong, where they tell you you owe them by the minute afterwards?"

"This part is free," he said. "If you have a drink, though, that will cost you for service. Please do not turn around."

"What?" I said.

I noticed his eyes focused beyond my shoulder and then his hand go to his waist, over the spot where I'd seen him stick his gun. I ignored his request and turned to see the four Chinese men from the casino at the door. When I looked back at Philip, the girl beside him was off her chair. Imelda, whiffing danger, leapt from my lap and hurried to the other side of the room. I looked back at the door again. The Chinese men casually turned and walked on. Philip waited, his eyes still on the door, keeping his hand at his belt. He gave Virgilio on the stage a quick look.

"You think there's a problem?" I asked.

Philip shrugged. "Maybe they were mad at me. Maybe nothing."

Virgilio and Rommel came back from the stage, leaned over and huddled with the NBI chief and two other agents. Then Virgilio said something to Rommel, who high-signed the other two. Rommel and the two he'd signaled walked quickly through the beads at the back of the bar. Philip must have seen something on my face. "It's nothing," he smiled at me. "Just to be sure. Danilo and Toto, please stay with our guest."

Philip and Virgilio moved towards the front door in echelon, Virgilio three steps behind and to the side of Philip. They waited until, I presumed, the other three agents had had time to go out the back and come around the other side of the shopping center. Philip and Virgilio then walked through the door and went to the right. A moment later I saw Rommel and the others running into the lot from the street, hands at their belts. "Now you see, they are trained," Danilo told me quietly. "So if there is a problem they are surrounding the problem." I sat there, dreading an eruption of gun fire from the parking lot. But there was none. Ten minutes passed and then they all came back in, laughing, and sat down as if nothing had happened. The girls stayed at the bar.

"So there's no problem?" I asked.

"I would not say no problem," Virgilio replied. "But no problem now."

"So therefore you see what we are saying that you cannot afford playing games on this island," Danny said to me, with a paternal air. "You will see yet more what I mean. Tomorrow, when the really serious business starts, you will see."

"Government Admits Negros Reds Still a Force," was the headline of the *Visayan Daily Star* that was left outside my door the next morning. The article stated the Philippine National Police estimated that the rebels controlled four of the island's barangays and had infiltrated another 51; meanwhile, the PNP and the army were "continuing reduction of [the rebels'] political cadres, armed red fighters, mass-based supporters and controlled barangays." Despite claiming to have the situation under control, however, the PNP issued a warning in its report: "The rebels will continue to pursue their terroristic activities by destroying farm machineries of sugar planters who refuse to pay revolutionary taxes, [by] extortion, threats, robbery . . . and kidnapping."

As I walked down the corridor for my 7 A.M. meeting in the lobby with the NBI, I read an accompanying article called "Remembering Escalante Massacre." It pointed out that today was a particularly salient date in the history of the NPA's armed struggle. Eight years ago, September 20, 1985,

27 protesters had been massacred and 30 seriously wounded at a roadblock north of Bacolod. It was the middle of the sugar depression, there was hunger on the island, and the protesters had blockaded the highway to demand the right to grow food on some of the one million acres of plantation land held by the gentry. President Ronald Reagan, President Marcos, and several Negros politicians were burned in effigy. The police tried to disperse the demonstrators with water cannon. When they ran out of water they dispersed them with rifle fire, mowing down the tiers of demonstrators.

"You see this?" I asked Virgilio, showing him "Remembering Escalante Massacre."

"Yes, yes, maybe we will encounter a fiesta in the mountains, in honor of its memory."

"It was the doing of the previous administration," Philip told me outside the hotel. "I think [Marcos] encouraged the landlords to not give land to the peasants to grow food. Just in order to encourage the reinforcement of the NPA, so that he would have an excuse to ask Reagan for more military support."

"Your disguise," Danilo reminded me, and I popped on my cap and shades.

We drove up Araneta towards the center of town and turned right onto San Sebastian Street, "Bacolod's Fifth Avenue," according to Virgilio. At the corner of Lacson and San Sebastian we parked opposite a modern clothing boutique called Ivy's. The second floor of the white office building bore a blue sign. "Alex Abastillas: Attorney-at-Law; Notary Public."

"You take your picture here through the window," Philip told me, "but do not come back here on your own."

"He doesn't want to investigate another disappeared Canadian to do with Abastillas," Virgilio cracked.

We doubled back towards the square and pulled up at a mildewed concrete annex to the relatively new provincial building, in sight of the San Sebastian Cathedral. "You want to go in and say your prayers before we pick up reinforcements for the mountains?" Virgilio asked me.

"I prayed before I left the room," I said.

"As did I—that they take you and let me go collect the ransom."

Danny, Toto, and Rommel jumped out of the back of the pickup, and Philip invited us in for morning coffee. The NBI station was nothing more than a narrow, stifling, battleship-gray room with two wooden desks, one huge, WWII-vintage typewriter, no photocopier, no fax, and no computer. For air-conditioning the cops had overhead fans, black as pitch from years of grime. For light they had dirty louvered windows and the open front door, which let in the racket of the square, around which all the traffic of this town of 300,000 circulated. A heavy black phone whose age matched the typewriter's sat on Philip's desk by a wooden doorway to a water closet. Between the constantly bleating horns of jeepneys, buses, and trucks, the scream of motor scooters, the barnyard smells from the outdoor stalls, and the vicious heat even at this early hour, it was a wonder any work got done here.

"I'll ask Prudential to make a contribution," I said. "Which would you rather have, an air conditioner or a computer?"

"First a toilet that flushes," Philip replied. "We have a very small budget to fix things."

Philip's phone rang and he excused himself, shouting a hello over the street racket and the poor connection. He sat down and began taking notes on tissue-thin foolscap, asking the caller to repeat himself again and again. I was introduced to a young agent named Christopher, who cracked jokes in Tagalog with Virgilio as he opened a locked cabinet. From it he withdrew Uzis, automatic pistols, two M-16s, and extra clips of ammunition.

"There are deer and pigs in the mountains for our supper tonight," Virgilio said. "You can make gloves from the hide for Canada. Or maybe the NPA will make gloves from your hide."

"I will not be able to accompany you," Philip said, when he got off the phone.

"We will be leaderless," Virgilio said to me. "Well, he can deliver the letters to our loved ones."

Intent on rescuing a felon from the hereafter, we peeled off for the Bacolod City Cemetery, fighting our way through the suicidal scooters and Wild West jeepney drivers on Rizal Street, until we turned left and headed up a pleasantly treed avenue. Lopez Jaena marked the east edge of town, made all the more obvious by the scratching chickens and rooting pigs in front of the shacks that lined the rural side of the road. The tumbledown stanchions to the cemetery wall were on the far side of the crossroads of Burgos and Lopez Jaena. "That's him," Virgilio said.

On the steps to a moldy plaster shack by the gate, watching the pickup full of lawmen rolling up to him, stood Aaron Minase, the cemetery's middle-aged and ponytailed caretaker. Led by Virgilio, the federal investigators got out and showed their badges. Virgilio then opened his briefcase and offered the nonplussed caretaker an affidavit, which bore Minase's signature. "Please read this," he said, "and tell me if it's true."

Minase's dark brows furrowed as he began to read the paper.

REPUBLIC OF THE PHILIPPINES
CITY HEALTH DEPARTMENT
Bacolod City
CERTIFICATION

TO WHOM THIS MAY CONCERN:

This is to certify that I, Aaron S. Menace, Bacolod City Cemetery Caretaker and a Licensed Cremator, have cremated the remains of one STEVEN LIK MAN WONG at the Bacolod City Cemetery on July 22, 1992, the said deceased appeared to have died on July 19, 1992 at Santol, Binalbagan, Negros Occidental, due to a Motor Vehicular Accident wherein he sustained severe head injuries.

Further, the descriptions of the subject who was cremated are as follows, to wit:

"The person has Oriental Features, about 5'4" in height, black hair, with several tatoos over his body, a tatoo of a dragon fully covering his back, two (2) heads of dragon on his front body and one (1) Tatoo of an eagle on the right upper arm."

This certification is issued upon the request of James Patrick Newson, also a Canadian Citizen and a friend of the deceased, for whatever purpose or purposes it may serve him best.

IN WITNESS WHEREOF, I have hereunto signed this document this 22nd day of July, 1992 at the City of Bacolod.

Aaron S. Menace
Bacolod City Cemetery
Caretaker and Licensed Cremator

When he got to the end of the document, the cemetery caretaker vehemently shook his head. "I know nothing about this," he said. "It is a forge. A fake. This is not my signature." He pointed to the red and blue sign beside his shack.

NOTICE

SEE MR. *AARON MINASE*, OFFICIAL CEMETERY IN CHARGE FOR ANY MATTER OR PROBLEM, FOR PROPER GUIDANCE OR INFORMATION

"My name spelled M-I-N-A-S-E! Whoever sign this spell my name M-E-N-A-C-E."

"Are you a licensed cremator?" Virgilio asked him.

"No. No place here to burn bodies. Nobody ever burned here! Never! I never see a Chinese man with tattoos!"

Virgilio looked at me and winked.

"No cremation, no nothing," Minase insisted. "This is a lie! I never know this Newson. I never know this Wong! Somebody makes a trick."

"Please come inside and swear to that," Virgilio said.

Half an hour later, exiting the shack with an affidavit refuting every last detail in the forged one, Virgilio chuckled to Danny, "They probably thought, 'Who in Canada would come six thousand miles to visit an old cemetery?'" He gave me my signed copy. "Maybe this and a few others will convince your government to help us out."

The distance between Bacolod and Binalbagan is roughly 60 miles. In 1993, almost every hectare of the flat fertile land that lay between the eastern mountain massif and the sea was owned by the *hacienderos,** and most of the central range south of Kanlaon Volcano was controlled by the NPA. Despite the rebel activity in the mountains, loggers had illegally denuded the entire chain; what little they had left standing in Kanlaon Volcano National Park the peasants had illegally cut down for charcoal. At Pontaverdra, the turnoff to the national park, stood a billboard. "On September 15, 1993, one million trees were planted in these deforested mountains, by order of his Excellency the President, giving work to the people and beauty to the Republic."

We stopped at a beer concession beside the sign.

"They planted one million trees five days ago?" I asked the bartender. "In one day?"

"It never happen. The TV camera and newspaper come here, they plant two dozen baby tree around the ranger station up there, then everybody go home."

"That is the way it is here," Virgilio said. "Only for the announcement, then forget all about it."

"'Here is the money to buy the trees,'" said the bartender, "'here is the money to pay the workers.' Then some people takes the money for the trees, some people takes the money for the workers. Only enough left for the sign."

I toasted him. "*Bahala na.*"

"Ah ha ha! He knows!" the bartender laughed.

An hour later we pulled into the outskirts of Binalbagan, where the two funeral homes I'd read about in the insurance reports were located. We stopped off at the quite modern Nalagon Memorial Homes, I took a photo, and then

---

*One of the largest landholders was the family of Mike Arroyo, the husband of the future president, Gloria Macapagal-Arroyo.

we proceeded along the street to the medical clinic of Dr. Jeanette Tronggo, the Binalbagan physician who had signed Wong's death certificate. Virgilio sent one of the agents to the PNP station up the block to fetch Captain Roberto Mediodia, the fellow in charge of "traffic" for the area and a former colleague of Inspector Guara, now the chief of police in Silay City, north of Bacolod.

"So you will not go up there after this to visit him," Danny said while we waited on the porch among sacks of food aid marked "USA," and a gathering crowd of barefoot children who began to squeal "Hey Joe! Hey Joe! Hey Joe!"

"I won't stop off, but I have to pass through it," I said. "I have this travel article to write. I'll be going to an island up north—Bantayan?"

"Yes, very beautiful—reefs, beaches, raise best cocks for fights in Visayas. But just for that you go through Silay, eh? I am responsible for your life."

"Just for that," I assured him.

Mediodia, a middle-aged cop wearing mirrored sunglasses under his cap, pulled up on a motorcycle and swung off. The NBI agents didn't shake his hand, merely pointed the way through the wooden door into the clinic. In the sweltering interior Dr. Tronggo stood up behind her desk, adjusted her whites nervously at the crowd of big men closing on her. Virgilio opened his portfolio and took out the death certificate she'd signed, which listed "cerebral hemorrhage" and "vehicular accident" as the "immediate" and "antecedent" causes of Wong's death. Virgilio began to talk to her in Tagalog. Tronggo patted her forehead with a hankie and sat down. Virgilio switched to English. "Explain the situation of that day, please," he said, directing her attention to me.

"They came in my office. They told me to sign this," she said, holding up the certificate to me.

"Who's they?" I asked, getting right into the cross-examination.

"Inspector Guara and Alex Abastillas. I told them, 'But I need to see the body.' They said, 'There will be no problem. There's other witnesses. We saw it. It's decomposed. We just need this as a formality.' So I signed. I thought it would be all right."

Beside the frightened woman, Mediodia shifted nervously and took off his mirrors as he too read the death certificate.

"Did Guara store a body in the police station?" I asked Mediodia.

"No, there was no body," he said, dropping his eyes to his lap. "There was no accident." He looked up. "I would have known about both. Abastillas came here with the fellow Newson. But there was no body."

"We need you to sign an affidavit saying you did not see the body," Virgilio said to Dr. Tronggo. "And we need you to sign as a witness," he said to Mediodia.

"What about Guara and Abastillas?" Dr. Tronggo asked, worried.

"We'll leave their names out of it for now." Then he turned to Mediodia. "In your well-run jurisdiction we will expect no problems."

"They both had a taste of this," I said, as we climbed back in the pickup. "Probably."

"What about this old cop Biches in Santol that the NPA hasn't killed?" I asked. "He examined the corpse up there, too."

"We can send for him to come down again, but maybe not necessary." As we bounced inland to Isabela, Virgilio took out photographs of the 78-year-old wizened captain placing his thumbprint on a sworn statement in the Isabela station. Then he gave me a copy of his statement. In it Agapito Biches stated that Guara had sent Sonny's friend, Stephen Granada, up to Santol on July 20, 1992, to summon the old man down to Binalbagan. Granada had used a motorcycle, not a tricycle, to make the trip. When Biches got down to the Binalbagan station, Guara and a lawyer, whose name Biches couldn't remember, gave Biches a prepared report, which made it seem as if Biches had examined Wong in every detail, had fully investigated the accident, and that "the cadaver was turned over to the friend of Steven Wong, also a Canadian citizen James Patrick Newson for transportation to Bacolod City." Biches's sworn statement to Virgilio explained: "At first I refused [to sign] for fear that I might be involved in any irregularity but the lawyer insisted that there is nothing wrong with it because he will take care of everything. . . . I just looked at the Certification but I did not understand the contents and allegations in the Certification. . . . The allegations in this Certification is not true and correct. When I was made to sign in this Certification, the lawyer claimed that the same will only be used in order that a deceased person will be buried. It is not true that a vehicular accident happened in Barangay Santol and I have not come across with a foreigner who met an accident in my Barangay." He then stated his education: "I am grade two, elementary."

"Poor old guy," I said. "No use putting him through it again."

Forty minutes from Binalbagan we passed a Huey helicopter base, then a barracks with soldiers sprawled in hammocks on the veranda, then a 155mm howitzer aimed at the mountain foothills to the east. Just beyond the hardware was a military parade ground and the flat-roofed Isabela Town Hall. Under its front eaves were the tile-embossed words "Sovereignty Resides in the People and All Government Authority Emanates from Them." We hauled up in front of the adjoining police station and were greeted by a crowd of officers who piled out to greet us as if they hadn't had company in a while—a reception that added to the besieged feel of the lonely place.

Inside the station Virgilio introduced me to a trimly built police chief in a T shirt named Bautista Esteva. After he explained to Esteva in Tagalog what was up, the chief took a pointer and went to a chalkboard map. "It is physically impossible for tricycle drive to Santol," he said to me, putting the tip of the pointer on the town at the map's edge. "A four-wheel-drive truck, yes. Maybe motorcycle. Anyway, I should have been informed of this accident, and I have no knowledge of it."

Virgilio opened his briefcase and I took photos of Esteva signing and putting his thumbprint on an affidavit that stated these points. After another word with Virgilio, Esteva went back to the map. He pointed to the symbols for gun emplacements that ringed the town, as well as to the white lines that showed the NPA-controlled areas and a chalked arrow that indicated a recent firefight. "If Guara claims he went up himself, I don't believe him. Too dangerous without heavily armed guard—or unless he know the right people. Last two months, kidnappings here, here, and here," he tapped the map. "Rescue column fired on here."

"Did you prep him on that last bit about the kidnappings?" I cracked to Virgilio as we walked out of the station.

"If he say in his district people go up but do not come down, believe him."

We had lunch and opened some beers in the parade ground in front of the station. Horses and water buffalo were grazing in a cropped pasture on the other side of the grounds. Beyond that were a few thatch-roofed huts, a windbreak of palms, and then the lushly overgrown mountains, patch-worked in sun, with the sky growing darker behind them. Another after-noon storm was building.

Nobody said much as we ate—at least in English. I imagined Steve pic-nicking here—if he had even been here. Strange birds were making piercing calls in the trees around the station. Did Steven cut up the netting to his mandarin oranges so the birds wouldn't strangle? "Your theory is that Steven Wong never even went there," I stated, tilting my beer to a peak.

"Never went there!" Virgilio said, uncharacteristically grouchy. "Abastillas did not even go to here. He only stayed in Binalbagan. Because only these two guys, Gamboa and Granada, they were the only ones to go to Santol to pick up Biches, because somebody or the lawyer wanted him. So Biches signed this certificate as mentioned in the report, that somebody has to be buried, and the body could not be released until it was signed. And it was probably Abastillas that arranged and paid."

"So Granada and Gamboa made it up there without incident," I said.

"Yes, but on motorcycle only, just the two, and they are the types that have free passage into that area."

"I see," I said.

Danny said something in Tagalog to his cousin. Virgilio sighed heavily and shook his head, as if at a thought inside it. "Probably we could go towards Santol, but not too far so there is an incident." He looked at the darkening sky, then over his shoulder at the helicopter base. "Probably no one would be flying to there today."

Rommel didn't like that at all. "We cannot assure your safety beyond a certain point."

At that everybody began to talk at once in Tagalog; someone interjected a sentence in English: "What about *my* safety!"

Danny turned to me: "If you want to talk to Biches we can make some arrangements with the station commander and Biches will come down."

"It's more than Biches," I said. "I've got his pictures and the paperwork. I know Gallagher would like a photograph of the spot up there. My magazine would like one. The cops too."

They all began talking in Tagalog again.

I stood up. "Maybe we should go," I said, "before it starts to storm."

According to the military maps in Esteva's office there was no real danger for the first 10 kilometers, that is, roughly the reach of the artillery from Isabela. As we left that perimeter, about five kilometers from Santol, the agents in the back of the pickup began to knuckle the hood of the cab. Not wishing to alarm unfriendly residents by our noisy approach over the bone-jarring trail, Virgilio pulled the truck over and shut it off. Nobody moved for a while. We just sat there listening to the strange birds and the loud drone of insects. "It's quiet," I said.

An agent jumped out with his rifle and came around to the cab. "So, he can see right here," he whispered. "No tricycle can come up here. What we are doing, Virgilio, I don't know."

Two other agents came up either side of the cab, their Uzis covering the trail that went like a tunnel through the brush. Water was running down over the rocks. I heard the distant rumble of thunder. "Must be raining up there," I said.

Virgilio got out, opened an ammunition box in the back and silently distributed extra clips for the rifles. The banana clips with their big bullets spooked me. I didn't want to go any farther. "Well let's go," I said, and began walking steeply uphill, over the slippery rocks.

Nobody said a word after that. Our squishing footsteps sounded awfully loud in my ears as we proceeded up the switchbacking path, platoon style, me in the middle of my protectors' line. By now I was hoping Virgilio would announce enough was enough. The vegetation began to change, with hardwoods replacing the palms as we entered another climactic zone, around a thousand meters' elevation and climbing the range to Santol. A couple of kilometers from the spot of the supposed accident, I caught up to Virgilio. "So this is serious now."

"Very serious," he said under his breath. "They do not play here. Playing time over."

He halted the column on the path, which was now so rugged it would give a donkey pause. He looked up to the tops of the hardwoods, a few of which had escaped the saw. High above, gray smoke drifted into the sky from the jungle. It could have been from a peasant encampment; it could have been from a methamphetamine laboratory, or a heroin refinery, since the poppy plots were somewhere up there. Up ahead I suddenly noticed the glint of metal. "What's that?"

"Yes, I've seen," Virgilio said. It was a roof.

"Is this worth getting our heads blown off?" an agent hissed from behind, but I didn't look around. My eyes were glued on the shack up ahead. "We don't know where the exact spot is. We're not equipped for drug raid of encampments. The whole affair is a fraud. What's the use?"

Virgilio turned to me. He'd heard the trepidation in my voice, and now smiled. "You're our guest, you go first and draw their fire."

I snapped another picture of the impassable trail. "All right, it'll have to do."

CHAPTER 17

STEVE FOUND

———

He's exactly where you thought he was. . . . We'll move on him.
—STAFF SERGEANT GARRY CLEMENT, MAY 27, 1994

One thing that helps in a lot of these matters is time. The passage of time.
—TONY DOHM, CANADIAN DEPARTMENT OF JUSTICE, NOVEMBER 8, 1994

"These affidavits are conclusive," Garry Clement told me, after reading through the sworn statements of Minase, Tronggo, Esteva, and Biches. "You just saved the insurance companies a million and a quarter dollars."

He called in the burly boss of the mission, Inspector Garry Lagimodiere, and I beamed like a schoolboy as the big Quebecois gave me a congratulatory clap on the back and announced in a basso profundo voice: "He's been filling me in—good stuff, Terry! Steven Wong, what a piece'a work, eh?"

I opened my notebook eagerly. "So—tell me the state of the investigation now. What's the plan?"

The plan, Clement said, was to ship these affidavits to Vancouver for Jerry Moloci to give to the Department of Justice. Clement would then start the paperwork to get himself to the Philippines to officially duplicate my research with the NBI, after which the Mounties' Commercial Crime Squad would look into the possibility of laying a fraud charge against Steve. While that was taking place, Bob Youill of the Triad Unit and Steve Carruthers, an RHKP drug inspector who had a file on Steve, would put the word out to their informants in the Lisboa. Unfortunately, Clement added, all of this was likely to take some time: the meetings with the Macau informants had to take place under the radar of certain parties who might blow the whole operation; on top of that, the Mounties were working across numerous international boundaries—Canada to Hong Kong, Hong Kong to Macau, Macau to Portugal—and everyone had their rules.

"Well fuck, *I* don't have to pay attention to international protocol," I declared. "The Macau tourist bureau's got my bed made at the Lisboa right now." I told them I'd head over there tomorrow with Guard Force, spend two days taking pretty photos of old cannons with a reputable bureau guide, then spend the next two days looking for Steve in downscale Triad haunts. "If I find Steve, I'll phone you directly."

"You can disappear awful quick over there doing that," Lagimodiere warned.

An older and wiser hunter than I was, Clement thought a moment on the situation, then began to discuss Steve in a way that made it sound as if the Paper Fan really was a dead spirit, and if I tried too hard, he would dissolve before my eyes.

"He's been spooked, I'm convinced of that, so for now he's not going to be where you think he's going to be," Clement said. "If you go over there looking for him, if you *purposely* set out to find him, I'm convinced you're not going to succeed. But if you go over and do your story strictly on the tourist thing, I think you'll have a better chance of running into him."

Looking at Lagimodiere he drummed his fingers on his desk three times. "Now, is *that* a risk?" he asked himself. "My feeling is no; it's gonna look pretty funny—here you are under the auspices of the Macau tourist association and something happens to ya? Not likely. Wong doesn't want that kind of heat. If, however, you spent the extra couple of days there, then I think the questions are gonna start being asked by other people: what the fuck is he hanging around for . . . ? So, do your travel article like you intended, let them take you where they want to, and that's it. Two days, then you're back here."

"If you have to stay over here for the couple'a days, we'll make the reservation," Lagimodiere generously offered. "We get the corporate rate. We could pull some strings for you."

"Yeah, I can get you in the Hilton for $950," Garry cracked. "Actually, I know what I'd be doing—I'd be hitting Prudential for some of these expenses. Because you're not gonna get much protection from Guard Force, if you're going under the impression of that."

This was news to me, but Clement said he'd garnered the intentions of Guard Force at a stormy meeting yesterday with one of the agency's executives, Paul Taylor, as well as Prudential's lawyer in Hong Kong, Martin Lister. Lister had couriered to my new hotel a detailed affidavit they wanted me to sign before I went over. The affidavit had gone missing for a couple of hours. I told Clement and he went to their office. That was when he found out they wanted the affidavit because they had decided not to accompany me when they'd been unable to determine the identity of the two old duffers who'd met me at the ferry. "You better be prepared," Clement said now. "You probably won't have that other set of eyes behind you."

Lagimodiere whistled, laughed, clapped me on the back again, wished me luck, told me to stay out of trouble, and then went back to his office. Clement began scribbling in his Day-timer. One way or the other—whether the ID came from me or the informants—he was determined to have his ducks in a row when the Paper Fan appeared through the mist. "I wanna be prepared to move quickly when there's a need to move quickly." He would alert his impeccable source in Macau—the one who would arrest Steve for us—as soon as I left the office. Garry then mused on how he could speed up the extradition process. His opinion was that it would be best if the DOJ allowed him to handle it directly. "The question is," he said, "can they send the extradition request to me so I can personally hand it to the head of the Macau judiciary and say, 'We know this is the place; here he is; now can you go make the arrest?' It would have been *so* easy if we could've picked him up here in Hong Kong."

"Yeah—well," I said, packing up, "Canada's wheels of justice moved too slowly for that. I better get over to Lister's office and deal with this Guard Force thing. Wanna come?"

"I got ten reasons not to," he replied, not anxious for another row. "Meantime, I'll get a report out to Vancouver on this. If you get into trouble over there I will call my source and pull out all the stops; otherwise, when you get back from Macau gimme a shout and I'll get you the government rate at a hotel. And hey?"

I turned at the door. "What's'at—?"

"I can't thank you enough."

See, I thought, taking the elevator down to Exchange Square, a remark like that, coming from a guy like Garry, makes it all worth it.

I crossed Connaught Road to the Mandarin Hotel and passed the usual coffee-break crowd of Filipino maids at Statue Square, just across from the ornate Legislative Council building. There were over 150,000 such Pinoy guest workers in Hong Kong at the moment, a fraction of the millions around the world providing the Republic with precious foreign exchange. I'd heard it mused by ordinary Filipinos that overseas maids kept the country afloat—not Ramos and his windbag plans to make the country into an "Asian Tiger" by 2000. At the very least, the money sent home by the maids wasn't being heisted by bureaucrats in the Development Assistance programs.

I took the elevator up to the 38th floor of the Asia Pacific Finance Tower and was ushered into a plush-carpeted, wood-paneled office that looked like a London gentleman's club. Two men greeted me. Martin Lister was a fluffy-haired fellow who bore a distinct resemblance to actor Gene Wilder—quite a contrast to Paul Taylor beside him, a big, Cockney-accented ex-cop, with a voice even deeper than Lagimodiere's. After a half-hour briefing on my Negros adventures and my plan for the morrow, Lister came out with the expected news. "We're no longer offering you a bodyguard service there. That implies a certain level of danger, which means, at the level of danger we're talking about, Guard Force shouldn't be there in the first place."

I looked at Taylor. "So you and your crew will not be going with me?"

His reply made me realize I didn't want to be in a tight spot with this guy anyway: "Well, basically, as Martin said, Prudential and Martin are our clients, and obviously they are under instructions, provided it's in conjunction with the investigation, and unless it is, I don't see in any way, shape, or form for us to comply with anything but the instructions because otherwise we would not be instructed."

Lister smiled. "The best evidence is you—unless there's some good reason you can't testify—like you're going to get shot—"

"Which brings us to the affidavit," I said.

"Precisely."

I looked at the expensive bond envelope in my hand:

Terry Gould, Esq.,
c/o Windsor Hotel. . . .
FOR COLLECTION BY YOUR GUEST
TERRY GOULD ON 29TH SEPTEMBER
STRICTLY PRIVATE AND CONFIDENTIAL

I took out the heavy bond paper:

"I, TERRY GOULD, of the City of Vancouver in the Province of British Columbia, MAKE OATH AND SAY AS FOLLOWS. . . ."

"You got a couple'a dates wrong here," I said. "The 'two-part news feature' was in 1990, not 1992."

"By all means, make any alterations in the margin, and we'll have a fresh copy prepared before you leave."

"I'll put this in a safe place and see you when I get back," I said. "Meantime, I'm going to Macau."

———

Before heading to Macau the next morning, I decided to pray to the god who might be of some help to me even if Guard Force wasn't. Two gods in fact.

The Buddhist-Taoist Man Mo Temple stood at the top of Ladder Street, where it crossed Hollywood Road, about half a mile from Exchange Square and a hundred feet above it. Back when the film *The World of Suzie Wong* was made, Suzie's neighborhood had consisted of bamboo shacks and whorehouses, but now the 1847 temple at its heart was hemmed in by condos and office buildings. Despite the urban ambience, I felt transported to an ancient realm at the sight of the old white walls and green pagoda roof. Man Mo was the domain of both Kwan Kung (known locally as Mo or Kuanti) and Man Cheong—a third-century B.C. statesman who'd evolved into the Cantonese god of literature, office seekers, and civil servants. The place looked pretty deserted this morning, but I'd read in my *Lonely Planet* guide that parents still flocked here to pray to the twin deities in the hope that their children would be blessed with the wisdom of Man and the strength of Mo.

As I walked through the temple pillars two red-robed fortune-tellers beckoned to me by shaking bamboo cylinders filled with inscribed fortune sticks. I wasn't even tempted to see which stick matched my fate. If something bad was about to happen to me, and these old geezers could divine it, then it was unavoidable, and I'd rather not know about it. On the other hand, if something good was to happen to me, why spoil the surprise? In any case, right now I knew my fortune: you will travel to exotic places and meet interesting people.

Inside the temple, dozens of huge beehive-shaped incense coils hung from the rafters and from bamboo poles stretching the length of the walls. The overpowering sandalwood scent from the lit coils ascended through the open eaves to feed the souls of the dead and carry messages to the gods. Two gold pots, filled with cigar-size incense sticks, stood before the steps to the main altar, on either side of which were divans for carrying Kwan Kung and Man Cheong through the streets during their assigned days of worship. On the left, Kwan Kung held a sword; on the right, an equally fierce-looking Man Cheong held a pen. On a plank in front of a pillowed stool for kneeling I saw a few drops of red, which might very well have been dried blood. Old-timers (and Triads) still came here to settle disputes: they killed a chicken, soaked yellow paper in its blood, and then burned the paper to send the oaths of settlement up to the gods.

I pronammed deeply, lit a joss stick, knelt with my knees on the stool and prayed that Kwan Kung would send Steve my way and that Man Cheong would give me the smarts to write about him for the third time. I took a piece of yellow paper from the stack in front of the stool, wrote "Steven Lik Man Wong" on it, and burned the paper in one of the pots. As the paper smokily crinkled and shriveled, it suddenly occurred to me that Steve's middle name Man had very likely been derived from the god of literature whose help I was now seeking. Yue Kim Wong had possibly even prayed here for Steve to become a scholar or a high office holder—maybe even a Paper Fan.

It's quite likely that the gods canceled each other out, because my two-day trip to Macau proved boringly safe and journalistically fruitless. A middle-aged tourist agent in a red silk choker and scarlet miniskirt met me at the ferry, then taxied with me down to the Lisboa and efficiently checked me in. My room was in an older section and looked out on a yellow clay school yard and stacks of ugly office towers. The yard was gaily decorated with lanterns from last night's Full Moon Lantern Festival, so I took a picture of the view, and, for some reason I still can't figure out, the toilet with the lid up. (I've gone over that picture a dozen times with a magnifying glass. Was it the marble wall behind the tank that made me click it? Did I expect to include it in the article with a cutline: "Lisboa Hotel Room Toilet"?)

Twenty minutes later, Daisy (or Dai See—I never found out which) met me for lunch at the 4, 5, 6 Lisboa Restaurant. No amount of flirtation or out-right begging got me any more than qualified answers about the possibility of interviewing Stanley Ho. "Dr. Ho so very busy now—maybe you write letter and someone future can arrange." I told her about the old guys who'd met me at the ferry, and she seemed offended that I thought the Macau Tourist Office would send non-English-speakers. "Maybe hotel think you stay night, send courtesy car with driver and porter." That sounded plausi-ble, but when we stopped at the reservation desk and asked if they had a no-show for me on September 16, they found nothing. "So is your mistake," Daisy said, smiling, and I decided to drop trying to figure out if my cover—such as it was—had been blown.

Daisy then took me for "Unique Tour Day One—Little Visited North Sights." By horse and buggy we toured Barrier Gate up by the Chinese bor-der, the Cinidrome dog-racing track, the Kun Lam Temple, Sun Yat-sen's Memorial House, the Lou Lim Ioc Garden, the Old Protestant Cemetery, and the Cameo Gardens. We finished off day one at the Praia Grande Restaurant on the harbor esplanade. Over a romantic Mediterranean-Cantonese meal of tapas and duck, we went through Daisy's stack of glossy tourist brochures in her Gucci satchel.

"So much see in Macau," she sighed, "so sad when people just go casino then back."

"Can we visit an opium parlor tomorrow?" I asked, just to bug her. "I heard the Triads still run them."

"Opium?" she asked. "Oh, no no, ha ha, that old days, no more opium places, ha ha ha."

Maybe it was the rowdy question or the fact that she suspected I really liked her outfit, because the next day she met me in the lobby wearing a sober pants outfit and no choker. "Standard Tour Day Two" included the main churches, the Monte Fort (I got my cannon pictures), the ruins of St. Paul's Church, Senado Square, the Maritime Museum, and several of the big, new hotels—the Hyatt, the Mandarin Oriental, the Kingsway, the Holiday Inn, and, finally, of course, the Lisboa. This time an outright offer of a $50 tip couldn't convince her to let me in the casino with my camera. When we said goodbye I kissed her hand.

"You know," she wagged a finger at me, "you very bad boy."

Back in Canada, I wrote like a demon and then we delayed the article month to month—waiting for the good word that would send me over the moon. It took until February 1994 before all the paperwork went through permitting Clement to head to the Philippines and do the official investigation with the NBI. Unfortunately, when he got back, there was still no word from the informants in Macau. Meanwhile, the Canadian Department of Justice had decided to hold off on a fraud charge against Steve. While the case was overwhelming that he had staged his own death, the Mounties didn't have him in hand yet as *prima facie* evidence.

I took advantage of the extra time to call Lisa Lee and ask her about the bash Steve had thrown when she had made the force, but all she said was, "Um, well, I'd rather not talk about that, actually." Using their own sources, the Mounties looked into that party, as well as information from Chuck the Chink that, back in the summer of '92, Lisa had informed him she'd been questioned by the RCMP about Wong's disappearance. The Mounties complained to the Internal Investigations section of the Vancouver Police Department, and on February 15, a cop from Internal named Scott Driemel called me in and we sat down for an hour and discussed Lisa, Lily, Chuck, Steve, Edison Yee, Newson, the penthouse apartment, and what I knew of the party.

"You keep talking *over* her!" Driemel cried in frustration, as we listened to the tape of my conversation with Lisa.

"Sorry, I was nervous."

"You ask a question, then let *them* talk!" he instructed me testily, as if I were a new recruit.

By the middle of March, Garry Clement still had no news for me. He was set to be transferred back to Canada in June and so *Saturday Night* and I decided to go with the article in April. My guess was that Steve was still sitting pretty in Macau, and that "The Search for Steven Wong" might spark the Macau administration, or somebody who could profit from his surrender, into taking some action.

The guess proved correct.

Six weeks after the article came out, my spook contact informed me that Ray Chau had just been deported from Canada on the grounds that he hadn't declared his heroin conviction on his immigration form. Two weeks later, on May 27, 1994, Garry Clement phoned me from Hong Kong.

"I just wanted to let you know—and I will confirm it when I'm positive—but I may have located our man."

"Oh!" I breathed. "Fabulous!"

"And if all goes well, I would think he'll be in custody late next week. It's just right now fifty-fifty. But just to let you know, I'm still— This is the last thing I wanted to clean up before I left."

"What a last thing to clean up! Did you get the article, by the way?"

"Yes I did—thank you very much," he said.

"Now! Where is he?" I asked.

"He's exactly where you thought he was."

"You're makin' my day!" I squealed.

"It's not a hundred percent yet, but I promised I'd call you if I got anything on him, so I thought I'd let you know."

"I appreciate that. So it's not a hundred percent but what is leading you to believe—?"

"I'm fairly confident. I won't tell you right now how I'm doing it. I just don't want to burn anything on this."

"No, not at all, not at all," I said. "I'm not going to anybody with this, don't worry about that. But just let me ask you—you think he's gonna voluntarily give up, or you're gonna move on him?"

"Oh, no—we'll move on him, we'll move on him. I'm meeting with another person today. And if all goes well— you know, it's gonna take a little bit of luck—but hopefully we'll luck out."

"When are you leaving Hong Kong?" I asked, a little worriedly, because I'd had enough to do with police to know that when investigating officers were transferred, new guys were lost in space for a while.

"June 24," he said.

"Okay, so you got a little bit of time to stay on it. So, we're talking about one of the hotels I mentioned to you?"

"Yep, the first one."

"Jackpot!! What is he doing anyway? Is he working in that hotel?"

"Yeah. It's exactly—it's a hundred percent what you originally were told."

"Or, what I concluded from all my—"

"Your investigation. It's right on that."

As it turned out, the "other person" Clement had met with was Macau's Assistant Police Commissioner Tony Salvado. To make the arrest, Salvado needed an affidavit from the Canadian Department of Justice stating that, as soon as he nabbed Steve, Canada would press for extradition on a fraud or perjury charge (also an extraditable offense, based on Steve's false affidavit to Judge Cohen in March 1992). I found out later that Salvado's informants had identified a short, 30-ish 14K Triad on the lam from Canada who was working security at the Lisboa. The make was confirmed by none other than Ray Chau, the cuckolded husband of Patsy. From Macau, Ray offered a recently retired CLEU inspector $100,000 to broker a deal: in return for setting up a sting on Steve, Ray would be allowed back into Canada. Clement turned the deal down because it was totally unethical. It was also unnecessary, since Salvado had the pull to arrest Steve where he stood without an elaborate sting involving a gangster who, as my spook had told me, was "a few times" worse than Steven on the hierarchy of Triad criminality.

Clement telexed his report requesting the affidavit to Unit One, who handed it over to the Department of Justice on Friday, June 3. Everyone expected an immediate return telex ringing with the bugle call of a cavalry charge. But a week went by with no response. Then another week. By the third week I began to get worried.

Almost daily Clement pleaded by telex, fax, and phone with DOJ bureaucrats to fire off the document Salvado needed. With Clement's transfer to Ottawa only a few days away, I began to suspect *something* was wrong. They simply never got back to him except to say it was now out of the hands of the RCMP and in the hands of people who knew how to deal with these very complex matters. In other words, the request had dropped into a web of Canadian bureaucracy that would try the sanity of the most hardened cop—not to mention the equilibrium of a writer who'd spent over a year on the story.

I was assured it was useless to resist Canada's slow-motion functionaries, famous for staring at forms like Third World customs agents pondering a language they didn't understand. Arrest a gangster who had taken refuge in the Asian territory of a European nation? You want an affidavit saying we "will" extradite somebody "once" he's arrested? *For dat I must talk to someone else beside me. Because me, I have already asked myself, and he don't know.*

On June 24, Clement returned to Canada. And that brought us into vacation season, when bureaucrats were entitled to their month at the beach. Alone in Hong Kong all summer, awaiting Clement's replacement, Lagimodiere had no time to hector Vancouver and Ottawa. By the middle of July my eyes were welling with tears of frustration. By the end of August, I was crying blood. Then, the day before the Labor Day weekend, an affidavit was produced—only to be rejected in Ottawa a week later and returned to Vancouver with suggestions for changes. Its intended destination was suddenly not Tony Salvado via Garry Lagimodiere, but the Portuguese authorities in Lisbon via Sergeant Leon Letour, liaison officer for the RCMP in Madrid. That was apparently "the proper way" to get it to Salvado. But, I wondered, would the authorities in Lisbon really care about a Canadian in Macau on the run from a 12-ounce heroin-trafficking charge? Worse, once in the hands of Portuguese bureaucrats who had no knowledge of the sensitivities involved in the case, and no knowledge of Salvado's crucial involvement, what was to prevent them from sending an open letter to Macau asking some desk sergeant to see what he could do about Wong?

All of which worry was (for the moment) moot, because by October the affidavit—four *months* after Clement had requested it—had still not left Canada. The DOJ bureaucrats kept passing endless drafts from one side of the country to the other niggling about the wording. At my wits' end, I called my spook; I called Andy Nimmo, the head of the Asian Crime Squad; I called the San Francisco Gang Task Force and the DEA; I called *all* the contacts on my Rolodex and shared my grief and outrage. The Canadians said, in effect, What else is new? That's why we have early-retirement plans. The Americans just laughed: Four months? We'd have had the paperwork done in one day, and the bad guy home the day after.

The autumn rains began, Clement's replacement, Sergeant Dan Ouellette, arrived in Hong Kong; in Macau, Tony Salvado was transferred, replaced as assistant commissioner by an officer named Sebastio de Rosa. By the last week of October, the affidavit still had not left Canada, although translators were busy working on a Portuguese draft for Lisbon. On Halloween Eve, the translation of the affidavit, along with a provisional warrant for Steve's arrest, finally "went forward."

And then a fatal error occurred—although by then I was certain it hardly mattered. On November 1, Interpol took charge of the file, and without using the RCMP as liaison, they forwarded a file on Steven Wong to the diplomatic adviser of the governor of Macau. They might as well have given it to a clerk at the Lisboa.

A meeting was scheduled for November 4, and on that day Lagimodiere and Ouellette took the ferry across the Pearl River estuary and sat down with Sebastio de Rosa, a morose Tony Salvado, and the diplomatic adviser to the governor. The Mounties were informed that a search of the location where the suspect Steven Wong was supposed to have been employed had turned up nothing. From what they could gather, the suspect hadn't been seen in the Lisboa for some time.

Ten months later, August 1995, the ownership certificate for Steve's old Mercedes SL was transferred to Patsy Chan. When investigators learned of the transfer in September they jumped on customs records, cell phone records, and gangland sources, and became convinced that the laughing man had been back in town during the summer. Two weeks later I discovered the Mercedes parked in a carport at Patsy's new quarters on Oak Street. At the time, I was working on a column about last year's DOJ fizzle, so I watched the car for a whole Saturday, then, at eight in the evening, followed it to an Asian nightclub on Cambie Street called The Mirage. I thought about going in, but the truth is, I considered my column, entitled "A Letter to Steven Wong," the swan song to my hunt for the Paper Fan. *Go—live your crooked life—see if I care!* I told myself. Who needed the heartache? Maybe Steve *is* like a spirit, I thought. If I stopped pursuing him, he'd come to me when I was ready to receive him. "Do nothing and nothing will not be done," as Lao-tzu advised.

PART III

CHAPTER 18

SEX WITH STEVE

———

I know you, kid, you'll never be satisfied.
—AL GOULD

Cops talk in code when they're tailing someone. If they need to reverse direction they announce over the radio, "We're changing feet." After my last article on Steve was published, I changed feet to swingers. A little over three years later I broke the story of millions of club-going couples to a bug-eyed public. And yet, Steve was in my book—right there in Chapter One—an example of a promiscuous male who led the gangster life in order to impress women.

To celebrate *The Lifestyle: A Look at the Erotic Rites of Swingers,* I threw a theme party on the last Valentine's Eve of the century, at Vancouver's Club Millennium. Somewhere around midnight I found myself standing with a government spook—one of several I'd invited. We discussed the South Asian gangs that frequented this club; I mentioned my cameo portrait of Steve on page 20; and the spook told me his colleagues were sharing reliable information about Steve being in Cambodia.

I put my drink down, looked left and right at my 200 provocatively dressed guests. "Cambodia?" I pictured land mines, skulls in the monsoon mud, and no electricity. "Last I'd heard, Cambodia was a basket case and even the basket was coming apart. What's he doing there?"

"What he usually does I'd imagine," he replied. He turned and watched a bank manager leave the dance floor in a Frederick's of Hollywood getup.

"And—?" I rolled air with both hands.

"It's already a few months' old news, eh?"

"Is he still there?"

He shrugged. "If he is it'd be because there's no way to do anything about it." He turned back to the dance floor, smiling at the interesting costumes and some girl-girl dancing. In a booth across the floor sat Robert

McGinley, the Lifestyles Organization's CEO, who'd flown up from Anaheim for my do. Talking to him was a journalist friend of mine, Daniel Wood.

"That guy there knows a college teacher who knows Cambodia," I said. "Guy with the glasses talking to McGinley?"

His eyes took note of Wood.

"Steve likes glitz and rich chicks, he wouldn't stay long in Cambodia," I said, mostly because I didn't feel like flying off to Phnom Penh tomorrow morning. At least not based on old news and with so little chance of the Canadian government doing anything even if I did net him this time. Besides, I was having a lot of fun doing the swinger book shuffle. With the press coverage over the last two weeks, *The Lifestyle* had made it to the best-seller lists, I was getting calls from all over the world (*The New York Times* and Dan Rather's *48 Hours* included), and international speaking requests were pouring in. As for Leslie, she said she preferred the fallout from swingers to the fallout from gangsters. I was almost famous, and nobody wanted to kill me. On the contrary.

"Kind of an interesting place to set up shop, if you look on a map," he said.

"Yeah, it's a back door to the Golden Triangle. But I still would've thought Thailand's more Steve's style."

"Might've found some opportunities. Talk to the guy your friend knows."

On my way over to Daniel I was intercepted by an earringed character who looked like a cross between Sinbad the Sailor and a Venetian gondolier. "Is this a swinger party or what?" he demanded.

"Naa, naa," I said, "too many cops."

As it turned out, Cambodia was exactly the kind of place where Steve would set up shop, according to my friend's friend, Cam Sylvester, Vancouver's resident Cambodia expert. When I called Cam at Capilano College he told me the land of the killing fields was finally emerging from 30 years of chaos, which made it very attractive to criminals who wanted to do business fearing neither war nor arrest. In July 1997, a former Khmer Rouge colonel named Hun Sen had staged a murderous coup that had smashed his troublesome opposition, then won a multisided civil war that had also ended the terrorism of his former colleagues in the KR. Eight months ago he'd held a semilegitimate (most said fraudulent) election, and since then he'd given the country just enough stability to open it up to the outside world. Now all elements from that world were inspecting the new opportunities and, not surprisingly, Interpol had just announced that its hundred most-wanted fugitives were ensconced in Cambodia. Indeed, glitzy gangster nightclubs and gambling casinos were opening up in instant towns in the middle of the jungle.

"Gambling casinos?" I asked Cam.

"Yeah, the gamblers are coming in from Thailand, where it's illegal," Cam said.

If there were casinos, I thought, then Macau's gangsters couldn't be far behind. In fact, Macau's gangsters were probably leading the way.

Swingers may have been endlessly entertaining and instructive, but all the time I'd been researching and writing *The Lifestyle* I'd never really lost sight of what was going on in Macau. In 1996, the 14K, the Sun Yee On, and the Wo On Lok Triads had begun turning the pretty little place into a war zone, each gang jockeying with the others for control of Stanley Ho's VIP gambling lounges before the Chinese took charge at a second past midnight on December 20, 1999. The rumor was that the Communists were planning to open up Ho's gambling monopoly to competition, and who could resist killing in order to be in a better position to share in the expansion? Several dozen gangsters had been cut down and, on one day in May 1998, 14 car bombs had exploded in the streets. The man held chiefly responsible for the chaos was the new head of Macau's 14K, "Broken Tooth" Wan Kwok-koi. He legitimately leased a VIP lounge in Ho's Lisboa Hotel, but the government considered him to be getting out of hand, especially after three members of the Portuguese administration investigating Broken Tooth had been assassinated. Then, about 10 months ago, a bomb destroyed the car of Macau's chief of police, who was not in it at the time. In a move that I wished he'd made with Steve, the enraged chief had led a platoon across town and into the Lisboa itself, personally collaring Broken Tooth at a baccarat table. As for the ultimate proprietor of the Lisboa, after spending years denying there was a problem, Stanley Ho had finally admitted there was a problem. But Ho was sure all would be cleaned up before the Chinese took over Macau—or at least that the Chinese would clean it up shortly thereafter.

Not likely, I thought. Since I'd lost Steve, organized crime groups around the world had been forming alliances with political leaders in the governments that had emerged in the post-Communist world, as well as with leaders in those tenuous democracies that already had entrenched syndicates. The compliant states, from Eastern Europe to Southeast Asia, represented the new world order for a large segment of the globe's population. Free markets, democracy, the rule of law, and public accountability—these were the lofty promises of the day, but by the time the promises reached the

Steve's unmarked plot in the Garden of Reflection at the Forest Lawn Cemetery near Vancouver, B.C. There's an urn buried in Row 2–C, plot 582, but the ashes in it aren't Steve's.

19 November 2003

Interpol information

Terrorism

Fusion Task Force

Wanted

Search

Recent

National wanted
websites

Fugitive investigations

Guide to extradition
procedures

Children and Human
Trafficking

Works of Art

Drugs

Financial crime

Corruption

International crime
statistics

Forensic

Football hooliganism

Vehicle crime

Regional activities

Information
Technology Crime

Weapons/Explosives

Criminal Intelligence
Analysis

1996/35245 WONG (7806) LIK MAN (0500) (3046) STEVEN

WONG (7806), Lik Man (0500) (3046) Steven

Dead man running. Steve has been on Interpol's Red Alert Most Wanted list for most of his busy afterlife.

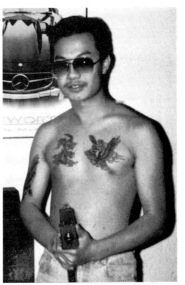

These photos of Steve, taken just after his initiation into the 14K Triad, were passed on to me by the police in Vancouver. Winged dragon Triad tattoos spread across his then-skinny pecs. He holds a machine pistol.

Steve at 28, the year he faked his own death, in front of the Brooklyn Bridge. He spent much of his childhood working in a bean-sprout factory owned by his brother-in-law in New York's Chinatown.

Pro-Erap People Power III demostrators at the shrine to the Virgin, EDSA Square, Manila—the epicenter of the Philippines' revolutions-by-means-of-holy-street-party. I had come all this way with a fair shot at finally getting Steve, and landed in the middle of a revolution.

May Day 2001. Soldiers at the square on Recto after driving the EDSA mob away from the Presidential Palace.

Jose Luis, my fixer to the Manila underworld. He believed Arroyo's regime to be far more corrupt than Estrada's, and was prepared to die for People Power III.

Mary "Rosebud" Ong spent a dozen years money-laundering and gun-running for the 14K and another seven as a Philippine National Police and Hong Kong Police undercover agent. When I showed her Steve's mug shot, she immediately said, "I know him. You better know who you're up against."

February 2003: Mary Ong with NBI Chief Reynaldo Wycoco and her lawyer, Leonard de Vera. She drew a line linking Steve and the 14K to a Filipino family with direct ties to Ping Lacson, the man I had hoped would help me catch the Paper Fan.

Senator Panfilo Lacson, a contender for the Philippines presidency in 2004, in his Senate office.

street they were only rumors. Too many politicians were making too much money from gangsters for anybody to quickly "clean it up," and Interpol was now issuing warnings to the press and national law enforcement agencies that the criminal underworld seemed to be entering a new phase, one that darkly mirrored the transnational corporations leading the way in the trend towards "globalization."

On October 25, my eye caught a front-page *Vancouver Sun* article about Cambodia, with the headline "Gangsters Flee Macau Before Handover." The article was completely congruent with the information I'd received back in February about Cambodia. By then my publisher and editor, Anne Collins, had been urging me to change feet back to Steve, and as my eyes moved down the page I got that sickening feeling that if I didn't write this book, somebody else would—maybe even coming up with Steve in the process:

> There are signs that Triad members operating in the Portuguese gambling enclave of Macau are moving into Southeast Asia ahead of the territory's handover to China. Three members of the Hong Kong-based 14K Triad were killed in a gangland-style assassination a week ago on the airport expressway in Bangkok. . . . Thai police say the killings are related to control of casinos in Phnom Penh, capitol of neighboring Cambodia. For over three years the 14K Triad had been involved in a street war with rival gangs in Macau over control of aspects of gambling in the territory. The spoils of war are sub-leases of so-called "VIP lounges" for high-roller gamblers in the nine casinos all operated by Stanley Ho. . . . The Triads may well be looking for new pastures ahead of Beijing's takeover of Macau. . . . In Cambodia in particular there are links between the drug traffickers, gambling and government. Gambling is illegal in Thailand, but it is big business in Cambodia where international law enforcement agencies have detected links to well-known drug traffickers.

I called Cam Sylvester again, and what he told me caused me to spray coffee over the *Sun*. "Speaking of Stanley Ho," Cam said, "I understand he's moving out of Macau to the Philippines, have you heard that?"

"No!"

"He's bringing a floating casino into Manila Bay. He's kind of tied into President Estrada. Ho's giving himself some options to diversify in anticipation of the Chinese."

"I think I mentioned to you the Philippines is where Steve staged his death," I said.

"That'd be a good place to do it."

"And the Lisboa, which Ho owns, is unofficial headquarters of the 14K Triad, to which Steven Wong belongs, and the members of which are headed to Cambodia. Cam, it seems to all tie in. When I heard that there was a good reason for my guy to be in Cambodia, then that the 14K was opening gambling casinos there, all the little pieces fell into place. Now, what you're telling me about the Philippines—I'm thinking, Could he be back there?"

I wrote down: *Pick up trail in Macau, follow to Cambodia, then to the Philippines?* "Have you heard anything lately from Cambodia?" I asked while scribbling.

"Actually, I've had a couple of students who've come back and things seem to have settled down, but that's for the tourists—for what you're trying to do I'm not quite sure things have settled down. I'm not sure what the parameters would be for your safety."

"What I'd be trying to do is get proof he was there and the alias he's traveling under. Then I could track his movements to wherever he is now. The alias he used in Cambodia would be the key."

"In that case you should try and get the help of the Canadian embassy in Phnom Penh. I mean if the Canadian government still wants this guy—"

"They do—there's a warrant, he's on Interpol's Most Wanted list. I know the cops are still pursuing it from this end. But they don't have the budget to go gallivanting."

"I'll tell you who to talk to here."

He gave me the name of the ex-Canadian ambassador to Cambodia, Gordon Longmuir, who'd just returned from a four-year posting in Phnom Penh. "He's a law-and-order-type," Cam said. "I think he's gonna be pretty sympathetic to you."

Longmuir had just moved into a condo in North Vancouver, right by the ferry, at the bottom of the mountainside on which I lived. He was a gray-goateed, seaworthy-looking man—the ruggedly handsome picture of everything he'd been in life: 30 years a navy man; four years high commissioner to India; another four as an ambassador in the heart of darkness. I'd sent him my *Saturday Night* article to read, and one of his first sentences to me when we sat down in the Cheshire Cheese Inn at the Lonsdale Quay was: "If your guy would want to go to ground in the region, Cambodia would be a very good place to do it."

I asked him if he knew any Cambodian gambling barons who were allegedly "well-known drug traffickers."

"Teng Boonma," he replied without hesitation. "Chiu Chau Chinese, used to run the chamber of commerce—still runs it behind the scenes." Teng, Longmuir said, was Hun Sen's longtime crony, the owner and builder of semirural Phnom Penh's only five-star Vegas-style tower, the InterContinental. A short-tempered entrepreneur, the 55-year-old Teng had shot out the tires of an Air Cambodge 737 jet after his luggage had been delayed upon returning from Hong Kong. In 1998, the DEA had listed Teng as an alleged drug trafficker and barred him from entering the United States. Thailand, Hong Kong, and Taiwan had then followed suit. The richest man in the country, the president of the Cambodia Mekong Bank, and the acknowledged leader of the large and dominant Chinese-Cambodian business community, Teng was also a major investor in the wave of Triad-affiliated casino developments in jungle towns all along the border with Thailand. Indeed, until last year Teng had run a high-stakes casino in the health club of the InterContinental itself—that is, until the World Bank had instructed Hun Sen that it was unseemly for such operations to be operated so flagrantly in the capital by shadowy friends of the prime minister.

"One casino you should definitely visit is over on the Thai border," Longmuir said. "It's on a bit of land called Koh Kong, cut off by jungle and water from the rest of Cambodia. Two weeks ago the casino's manager and assistant manager were gunned down there. It's owned by a Thai-Cambodian, Pat Supapa. Close adviser to Hun Sen—you can find him on the Internet."

I circled the remote nubbin of land in my *Lonely Planet* guide and later discovered that Mr. Pat was as "well known" as Mr. Teng, his name appearing under the *Bangkok Post* headline "Popular Way to Launder Money from Drugs and Illegal Deals." The article, about Koh Kong, stated that Pat and three of his Thai partners had been "black listed by Thai and Cambodian narcotics suppression units for their involvement in the drugs trade and other businesses, and for money laundering in Koh Kong." During that search I also read a *Post* article, "Invasion of the Triads," which reported that the Thai Crime Suppression Unit had discovered that the Bangkok airport murders last month were connected to a war between the 14K and another "Macau based Triad," the 4 Kings, over control of the casino in Koh Kong. The three dead men at the airport apparently weren't 14K, as first reported, but 4 Kings, and their assassins were almost certainly working for the 14K, which had moved into Cambodia's burgeoning gambling scene in 1998— that is, shortly after Hun Sen's coup and shortly before I'd been told that Steven Wong had been working there.

"I'll bet Koh Kong's one Wild West town," I said now. "Would I be safe to assume that smuggling is also big business there?"

"Goes without saying, some of the senior generals and the civilian officials in Cambodia are up to their necks in it," Longmuir said. "A civil servant in Cambodia below the rank of undersecretary makes about twenty or thirty dollars a month. You need a hundred and fifty to live any kind of life at all in Phnom Penh. So there's absolutely no alternative to it—you take the squeeze when you can. If I was a customs officer working on the Thai-Cambodia border, I probably paid a lot to get that job in the first place, so I want to amortize my investment pretty fast. I'm sure not going to be too surprised if somebody comes and tucks a few bucks in my pocket if I turned my back."

"What about heroin?"

"The Cambodia-Thai border is wide open, the Cambodia-Laos border is wide open. So think about it. If you take the path of least resistance from the Golden Triangle, you go up through Burma, through Laos, and back down through Cambodia . . . out to sea from Sihanoukville or Koh Kong. Another bad problem is child prostitution. The people you're interested in would probably be involved in that too."

Longmuir gave me a good contact at the Canadian embassy, Bunleng Men, a Canadian-Cambodian who would tell me who to see, who not to see, and who to see who might have seen my man. One high minister Longmuir had infinite respect for was named Sum Manit. A light amidst the darkness, Sum Manit, now secretary of state, had been the director of Cambodia's National Authority to Combat Drugs during the period when I'd heard Steve was there. Sum Manit had actually been making arrests, although, not surprisingly, Hun Sen had recently replaced him with one of his cronies.

"Hok Lundy is the chief of National Police—I would not recommend you talk to him," Longmuir said. "If you do, don't be frank with him. You don't mess around with the Cambodians. You look at their history and what they've been through in the last thirty years, these people who are still around are survivors. And they survived by being pretty ruthless. You can be frank with Bunleng Men. He's worked for us for six or seven years. Very trustworthy, very discreet. Sum Manit also is impeccable. Otherwise, you'll have to stay on your toes, no doubt about it."

"What I'm doing now is arranging plans to go over for December and January," I said over the phone to one of my knowledgeable spooks. "I'm going to the embassy in Cambodia and talk to the ambassador there, and maybe get some help from this guy Sum Manit on Steve's alias. Then I'll catch up with my people in the Philippines—"

"The Philippines?" he asked.

"Yeah, that's my plan. Hong Kong, Macau, Cambodia, and the Philippines. Because I just got word that Stanley Ho is expanding out of Macau to the Philippines. He's setting up a floating casino in Manila Bay. And he's negotiated it with the president, Joe Estrada. So the Philippines is starting to look good again for me. You know it's a big round world and I'm looking for one guy outta six billion, and I wanted to take a larger overview about where he's been, what he's been doing, how it all ties in. It's just that he's so much a part of that world, and it's so fascinating, I just got focused on it all over again. It all fits together."

"Yeah, the Philippines, that is a very interesting spot," he said, "and there's so much corruption there that that would be—" He hesitated. "Let me put it this way, okay? It would be of concern for you, if you were to follow up on anything over there at the moment. You know, the fact that there are lawyers and police and everything else that work with these guys, right? And now you got Stanley Ho going over there who's a very influential businessman. . . . It does all fit, it would be conceivable that these things are developing, since Macau's turning over. But there's a man with a lot of influence, Ho, and when you think of the chain of people that associate there and associate with each other, as you go down the links—"

"Well, there's Patsy Chan and Ray Chau," I said.

"Yeah, there's a direct link there, right?"

"I must tell you that I had amazing cooperation from the National Bureau of Investigation on the island of Negros," I said. "They met me at the airport with drawn Uzis, they bodyguarded me for days."

"Yes, the NBI was the reputable one," he said, and then fell silent.

I noted his use of the past tense, then said, "I suppose you never know, there could be a flip side to that. What do you think?" When he didn't reply, I said, "It sounds as if the Philippines might be a better place to go find him."

"I wouldn't make any travel plans to Cambodia based on finding Steven there," he replied. "A trip to Bangkok or Cambodia might prove interesting to that particular murder case you read in the paper, and the infiltration of the 14K wherever they are worldwide, probably being Cambodia and Thailand as well, that would fill in that gap of the story for you. But I'm not particularly confident that would fill in any gap about where Steven Wong is at this point."

"Well, it's good to know he's still alive. It's one of those stories, isn't it? It's like a string, and you pick up one end and you just keep following it."

"He'll be at the top end of it."

———

The ex-DEA/CIA agent leaned over his whiskey in the Mexican bar. "I'll do some quiet checking, but I can tell ya right now: most of the guys we ran in the Philippines played both sides of the fence."

Around us a hundred couples frolicked by the pool of the Qualton Resort, where a Lifestyles tour was in full throttle. It was mid-November '99, and I was down in Ixtapa producing a nightly Internet radio show for Eyada.com's "Love Bytes." Last night the Lifestyles host, an LAPD corporal named Tony Lanzaratta, had introduced me to ex-agent Richard at the Rio Ha! Ha! disco. Once I discoverd Richard was still connected to spooks in the Philippines, I tripped over myself running back to my room to get him the *Saturday Night* article on Steve.

"I'll be traveling on my American passport this time," I said now. "It's not Steve so much I'm worried about, it's his friends in high places who could tip him off if I ask the wrong person for help."

"Be so careful," his wife told me. "Richard says you never, *ever* go into an operation where you can't even make one mistake."

"They covering your expenses?" he asked.

"Why? You wanna come with me?"

"No way!" his wife said. "That's over with."

We glanced over at a burst of laughter coming from the pool. Half a dozen women stood in waist-deep water, turning slowly in a circle, body to body. They looked like middle-aged nymphs from a Pre-Raphaelite painting. I lowered the camera below their faces and took a photo to send "Love Bytes."

"Is that what you're going to do in Cambodia or the Philippines—take his picture?" Richard asked.

"It's a thought," I said. "Interpol has a red alert for him, and if I can get his alias—"

"That may not get you anywhere," Richard said. "When a guy pulls a stunt like this, and you say, 'How in the world did he walk away from all this?' a lot of times they work both sides of the fence. He's over here dealing drugs, but yet he gives some government just enough information to make him a hero and keep them off his back. If that's his game, you ain't gonna get him, he's too well protected. I'll just put some feelers out trying to find out, in a quiet way, if there's this possibility that the people you'll be talking to to get his name, if it's in their interest not to have you catch him."

One of my well-connected contacts and I had just come back from a hike to the Mosquito Creek waterfall above my house. It was late November and we were both soaked from the rain and the spray. We sat down at the kitchen table, where Leslie joined us with three bowls of hot soup. I briefed him on my discussions with swinging Richard and Longmuir. By then I'd spent a week in Richmond's Chinatown, now the main hangout for B.C.'s Big Circle Boys and a reconstituted Lotus gang. I told my contact that, from winking answers to direct questions, I was convinced Steve was somewhere in Manila. I said I was leaving December 13: I'd check out the Jumbo Floating Palace in Aberdeen—the one that Ho was going to send to Manila; then I'd catch the lead-up to the handover in Macau; then take off for Cambodia, where I hoped to get Steve's alias from Sum Manit. I'd continue on to the Philippines, snoop around Ho's floating casino when it arrived, and meet with the NBI. I was going to make the call to Danny Mendez tomorrow. I opened a folder and showed him the list of people I'd met in 1993 whom I was planning on getting in touch with when I was over there. With Steve's alias in hand, who knows but that the NBI might come up with him in the capital?

He seemed awfully restless listening to all this. He looked at Leslie, then down at the table.

"If you can just tell him something that would keep him from walking into a trap," Leslie pleaded.

"I can tell you who *not* to see," he said. "The police over there are corrupt, and he's got himself tied in in such a way that any inquiry with the police in Manila—"

"Well, you know," I said confidently, "there's the PNP and the NBI, and the NBI guys I worked with, if they weren't trustworthy, they could have arranged my disappearance no problem."

"They could have," he said—but that was six years ago, and things had changed. "Particularly in this case. Although they are the most trustworthy police force, it looks like that's the police force that Steven has aligned himself with."

"*The NBI?!*" I shouted.

"Oh my God," Leslie said. "Terry, you can't go."

"So you're not gonna find out what you wanna find out through them—unless you had somebody that you totally, totally trusted."

"And I do," I said. "Or—I did."

"If it backfired on ya, you'd be in trouble."

"That's what I was gonna tell you," Richard explained over the phone the day before I left. "The NBI over there got this agent system—call it CA—Confidential Agent. Five thousand of them. I can't see your guy's gonna be a main man—a full agent, because it's like the FBI—you gotta have a Ph.D.

or be an accountant or a lawyer, so they only got five hundred'a those. But these others, they're deputies, they're informants—they give them badges, they walk in and outta headquarters, but they're just quasi. So they let the CA's operate, protect them, and get their information. You go asking, they'll probably just tell 'im, 'Reporter's over here on your ass, Chico, move on.' He moves on, you lose 'im again. That's your *best*-case scenario. Worst-case is if he's one'a them all the way—highly unlikely but just say—then someone'll just take you out to the dump, avoid the scandal."

I heard his wife screaming in the background and Richard muffled the phone and yelled for her to pipe down. "Raisin' hell here—over *you*," he laughed.

"The guys you got," I asked, "will they work with me to get him outta there?"

"I did explain your situation," he said, "but the answer's no. There's very few people they can trust in the Philippines now. Say they hand you over to someone and you wind up dead? It's just not worth it to them gettin' involved."

I got off the phone assessing my prospects as far more dim than my last trip. Garry Lagimodiere was long gone from the Mountie Liaison Office, replaced by an inspector from Unit One named Paul Brown. He hated reporters, considered us nothing but trouble. His assistant in Garry Clement's old spot, Henry Chan, wouldn't make a move without Brown's say-so. Here in Vancouver, a monosyllabic inspector named Murray Dauk, cut from the same mold as Brown, ran Unit One. So my old freewheeling trips with charts and affidavits into Hong Kong's Mountie stables were over. I did have a number to call if I found ole Stevereno, but otherwise, I'd be on my own.

CHAPTER 19

GO BACK, JACK, DO IT AGAIN

———

Mishegoss: Literally, insanity, madness.
—LEO ROSTEN, *THE JOYS OF YIDDISH*

I'm squatting at the edge of a muddy creek, trying to peer below the surface. Jungle vines border the spot. I look closer at the water. I can make out little black forms. They begin heading for me. One leaps from the water onto my leg, another onto my arm, more onto my neck and face. I feel the sharp stabs of their mandibles. I'm being attacked by biting spiders!! "Help! Help!"

I lurched up, stared into the hot room—jungle hot—causing me a thousand pinpricks of blossoming sweat. I must have forgotten to lower the thermostat when I checked in last night. My Indiglo Timex told me it was five in the morning, Hong Kong time, and I threw the covers off, turned the thermostat from 30 °C to 15 and tried to get back to sleep. But the jet lag and the metaphorical terror of my nightmare turned my racing mind to the Triads.

As soon as I'd landed, I'd seen them on the garish movie posters. When I got off the Airport Express in Wanchai, the karaoke bars showed them shooting each other up on music videos. Every book stall I'd passed on Lockhart Road had up-front displays of the newly published *Dragon Syndicates: The Global Phenomenon of the Triads,* by British journalist Martin Booth. In short, the Triads were the talk of the town. And with good reason. Rumors that they had all fled Hong Kong after the arrival of the Chinese were false, Booth reported. Much as they always had, after 1997 thousands of Triads had figured out how to operate under (and with) their new overseers, giving double irony to the Communist phrase for Hong Kong: "One country, two systems." Most spookily (for me, anyway), they'd just crippled one journalist and hacked off the arm of another.

I raised my head and looked around at the room, barely big enough for a bed. I shuddered at what it would be like to be kidnapped and locked in a Kowloon hellhole, waiting for sadists to arrive with choppers and blowtorches—

Enough!

I got out of bed, popped a Nicorette, and got ready for a long day.

The captain of my sampan on the south side of Hong Kong Island shook her head when I jumped aboard and told her to take me to the Jumbo Palace, the floating restaurant Stanley Ho would be towing 700 miles to Manila.

"It close now," she said. "No more meal. Send away next week."

"That's okay. I'm a writing a story about it, I'll get someone to let me on."

"Will no let you!" she insisted. "I take you Jumbo Number One, right next Jumbo Palace. You get off there, okay?"

"Whatever you say." I put out my hand for a shake. She was a sturdy old gal in coveralls and gum boots. "I'm Terry," I said.

"Tin," she replied, offering me a sailor's grip and a wink. She pushed the throttle forward, sending me tumbling, and her into a fit of hearty laughter as she caught me with a hug.

We headed up a lane in Aberdeen Harbor's quaint suburb of junks, where a couple of hundred fisher families lived under rattan roofs on ramshackle decks. Before I'd left Canada I'd read that 6,000 people had once made this corner of the harbor into a floating city, but that fish stocks had plummeted and most of the seafaring families had moved into the town's tenements, hidden behind the 30-story condos rising in pink and white stacks around me. What I hadn't known was that these *Tan-ka,* or "people who live on the water," had been the inspiration for Ho's multimillion-dollar fleet of floating restaurants. This tidbit was contained in *The Jumbo Kingdom: Realization of a Legendary Fantasy,* a glossy booklet put out by Stanley Ho that I'd picked up at a kitsch shop across from Tin's sampan. It seems that the junks had first arrived in the 1700s to serve the needs of pirates; when the British drove the pirates away, the *Tan-ka* stayed, their numbers swelling with each successive upheaval in Mainland China. Eventually the fishermen converted several junks into temples and gradually the temples evolved into evening gathering spots for eating, drinking, and socializing.

"*Tan-ka* make first floating restaurants," Tin verified this info. "Then Mr. Ho come 1955, build first big one, call Tai Pak, mean god who love food and wine; then 1976, Jumbo; then 1991, Jumbo Palace."

We were now passing under the bridge to Ap Lei Chau Island, and Tin pointed ahead across the harbor to a line of immense floating structures that resembled four-story temples in Beijing's Forbidden City, complete with stacked rows of scarlet pillars and delicately tiered eaves of green tile. "Jumbo Number One—two thousand guests," Tin told me proudly. "Jumbo Palace—almost two thousand. Little cousin, Tai Pak, eight hundred. You know how much Jumbo Palace cost?"

"How much?"

"Almost fourteen million Hong Kong dolla'! Two year to make. Now sail Philippine, too bad."

To my eye the Palace looked about as seaworthy as a prop in a Monty Python film. It was 200 feet long, towered 60 feet above the waterline, and the walls to its decks were made entirely of glass. I looked towards the beige-colored breakers at the entrance to the harbor, then out past Brick Hill to the white-capped ocean. I told Tin this pile of wind-catching roofs would never make it across the typhoon-swept South China Sea.

"Mr. Ho, he do, it make money, no worry," she laughed, swinging the tiller around to bring us into a buoyed area on the shore side of the restaurants. I leaned over the gunwale, thinking that Grauman's Chinese Theater had nothing on the Jumbo Palace's grand entrance. A 20-foot gold-leaf dragon roared atop an arched marquee decorated with tile sculptures of whiskered bats. Squares of gold-leaf flora and twisting branches made a vignette frame around the gilded doors.

"Stop here," I said, as we came abreast of a scarlet dock roofed by kelly-green tiles. Tin threw the engine into idle, and a guard standing on the deck moved towards us. I put one foot onto the gangway, asked to see his boss, but he shouted something angrily to Tin and waved her away. She gave me an I-told-you-so scowl, throttled up and pulled up at the Palace's fraternal twin, the Jumbo. "Dim sum very good here," she said, shooing me off onto the steps. "You like, bye-bye, so long."

I looked around. On this megabarge *two* gold dragons blew their whiskers at me, while no fewer than nine dragon heads shot streams of water into the harbor. I walked up the marble steps and into a lobby more encrusted with crazy *tchotchkes* than the outside. Ahead, at the bottom of a gold balustrade that led to the upper levels, was a full-scale replica of the throne of His Imperial Majesty the Emperor, flanked by chairs for the emperor's wife and the chief of his concubines. Above, the ceiling was fitted with a thousand lightbulbs hung from a thousand mirrors framed in scarlet wood, suffusing the room in a lobster glow. Like the Lisboa, the Jumbo was beyond tacky.

I introduced myself to the service manager, a lean fellow of about 40 in a black jacket. He bowed and with two hands offered me his card. I told Chan Wing I was doing a story on the Jumbo Palace's last days in Aberdeen and first days in Manila—was there any chance I could go aboard? "Oh sorry, sorry, no chance. Working now," he said.

I took out my pad. Could I ask him a couple of questions? For instance: How long would it take to pull the Palace to Manila?

"Maybe four, five day," he said. "It will be ready for open New Year. Millennium Eve! Big celebration! You visit then?"

"Shoot! I'll be there a couple of days after New Year's," I said. "Will the whole boat be converted to a casino?"

This query seemed to change the tenor of our discussion. Chan smiled and I could tell that he no longer trusted me. "Oh, ha ha, I only know it will be a restaurant."

"Well, why is Dr. Ho sending it then?"

"Maybe business. Not enough business here for three restaurant anymore." At that he turned to an assistant and began talking with him in Cantonese about something that seemed to have nothing to do with me.

"Just one more thing. Can you tell me when it'll be sailing?"

"December 21," he said, without looking up.

"The day after Macau's handover?"

This time he did look up. "One thing nothing to do with other."

Two hours later I was on the jetfoil to Macau, reading the Sunday edition of the now PRC-friendly *South China Morning Post*. A full-page article, called "Gangsters Who Have Forgotten the Rules," was filled with terror tales about Macau, and how, in a few days, the Chinese would save the territory from those who had forgotten the rules—that is, the ones who shot it out in the streets Steve-style. The implication seemed to be that if gangsters remembered the rules—taking their cut in a businesslike way—they would be more acceptable.

To illustrate the thesis the *Post* featured photos of the fearsome 14K dragon head Broken Tooth and a smartly uniformed PRC army garrison with their fists in the air, with the cutline "Community leaders support the post-handover garrison in Macau, hoping it will stop Triads from creating as much havoc as 'Broken Tooth' Wan Kuok-koi did." That was Stanley Ho's line, too, one he'd been using to ingratiate himself with the new rulers, who knew perfectly well he'd leased VIP gambling rooms to Broken Tooth. Ironically, the appearance of the People's Army in the territory was completely illegal; they were supposed to have waited until the day of the handover, and thereafter be used only as a defense force against external threats. Their arrival as saviors was made all the *more* ironic because (as the *Post* pointed out) many of the recent gangland slayings "were carried out by hitmen hired by local Triads from the Mainland." Well then, I thought, who was saving whom?

When I got off the ferry a raven-haired hostess in a red silk cheongsam handed me a map and schedule of the handover events. Beside her a classical Chinese trio was playing some many-blossomed tune. Around us the newly built glass-and-polished steel terminal was done up with flowers, lanterns, and trilingual red and gold banners. I became suddenly giddy. I was stepping onto a chip of land where political history was being made, where gangster history had just been made, and where both past and present had come together to kick Steve down the road.

Looking my information package over, I plotted how I might accomplish my mission. I wanted to discover Steve's alias and find out when he had left Macau permanently. Had he gone straight to Cambodia, or first to the Philippines? Was Cambodia just a side trip from the Philippines or a main show? These were my questions, but how was I going to even begin getting answers to them? All Garry Clement's old contacts had retired and moved back to Portugal. Given the closed-door policy at the RCMP Liaison Office in Hong Kong, I was in a far more isolated position than six years before. I couldn't very well walk into the Lisboa, flip out a photo, and announce I wanted to find out the Paper Fan's name and activities. I might never walk out. I therefore decided on a safer, if less easy, method of operation. I would visit Broken Tooth where he was locked up on Coloane Island, offer him the flattering press I knew he craved, and ask *him* my questions.

There was a tourist information booth behind the hostess in the Suzie Wong dress. A rep in a red business jacket within the booth told me that for special interview requests I'd have to speak with somebody at the Handover Ceremony Coordination Office, where they were set up to accommodate the hundreds of international journalists in town for the celebrations. She put a pen to my map. The office was in a building just across from the new $100-million Cultural Center, at the south end of the vast landfill that had added a square mile to Macau since I'd been here in '93.

Outside the terminal I waved away the hack drivers and strolled down Avenida da Amizade, along the Outer Harbor, and turned south where it doglegged west towards the Lisboa. I stuck to the water, following the land-fill to the Cultural Center, where the "I Love China" and "Return to Motherland" events were to be held. Workmen were hammering wooden forms into place for the new sidewalks being poured. A crouching army of white-gloved landscapers were laying squares of turf. Security guards seemed to be stationed every 10 yards—probably outnumbering the Triads, for this week anyway.

When I got to the Handover Office building I sat down on a bench and block-printed a request to interview Broken Tooth in jail. Upstairs, a uniformed woman behind the main media desk read my letter and looked at me as if I'd just propositioned her. She told me to have a seat, and, holding my missive by the corner as if it smelled, went into the back, then came out and ignored me for an hour. When I asked her what was going on she curtly told me to come back in a month, this was a bad time for such a request.

"You could have told me that before this," I said.

She turned her back on me. Obviously, the Handover Office wasn't enthusiastic about too much being made of Broken Tooth during these joyous celebrations.

"Just tell me how to get there," I said.

"You want to go to prison?" she replied, an unsettling question under the circumstances.

"Just to see it. Is there a bus?"

I think she saw this as an opportunity to get rid of me, because she said, "You know Lisboa?"

"Vaguely."

"Bus in front. You take No. 21. Give driver this." She wrote some Chinese characters on a pad and handed it to me.

Bus 21 must have been one of the least-used in the fleet, because it took almost an hour for one to pull up. It was, of course, a beautiful spot to wait; I had the comings and goings of the Lisboa to ogle and the Avenida Da Praia Grande to admire. With the trees and glittering bay on one side and quaint cafés and Mediterranean hotels on the other, the Praia Grande was still the colony's showpiece, and it was because of what had taken place there two and a half years ago that the world had learned something was terribly wrong in Macau—and had been wrong for years.

On May 4, 1997, a couple of blocks west of where I was standing, amidst bumper-to-bumper traffic and strolling throngs of locals, two motorbikes with passengers on the back pulled up beside a stretch limo carrying three 14K officials away from the Lisboa. The motos' backriders yanked out Chinese military automatic pistols and opened up for 20 seconds, splattering blood and glass all over the car and street. When a gangland hit is well planned, as this one was, the *rat-a-tat-tat* comes and goes so swiftly that it sounds like happy-go-lucky fireworks, and most of the people on the boulevard merely turned to see where the lion dance was. Word soon spread, however, drawing crowds so dense that it took 15 minutes for the police to fight their way through to the limo. When the victims inside were identified as Shek Wing-cheung, Broken Tooth's right-hand man, and his two senior assistants, Fong Mou-hung and Lo Wing-hwa, investigators with the Public Security Police deduced the hit was the work of the 14K's chief rival, the Soi Fong, or "Water Room Gang," an offshoot of the Wo On Lok Triad.

The international press converged, reporting that since the New Year there had been 17 gangland assassinations, and dubbed Macau the "Chicago of the Orient." Reacting to this colorful characterization, Macau's Portuguese governor, General Vasco Rocha Vieira, reassured the world that the killers were professionals; that the gangsters were only killing each other; and that neither innocent bystanders nor police were being hurt. The governor forgot to mention that Lieutenant Colonel Manuel Apolinario, deputy director of the Gambling Inspectorate, had been shot six months before.

A multisided civil war had in fact been raging in Macau for over a year: within Steve's 14K Triad; between the 14K and the Wo On Lok; and between all the Triads and the police, who sometimes actively favored one of the gangster armies over the other. When I had last been to the territory, Macau was a smoothly running, mobster-seamed city-state: the Triads, Stanley Ho, the corrupt police, and the passive Portuguese administration had pretty much worked out an arrangement on how to best get along peaceably. Then several things happened in the mid-'90s that made Macau explode into gangland anarchy.

According to Stanley Ho's own China-friendly explanation, offered to the British reporter Jill McGivering, "In 1996 the Hong Kong police, in order to give a clean city back to China, launched a tough anti-Triad campaign and tried to drive them out of the territory. As usual, the Hong Kong police were very competent, and did clean up a lot. With such easy immigration laws in Macau, most of the Triads came to Macau for shelter, but Macau is a tiny place—it cannot accommodate so many Triads."

The local police were part of the problem, Ho said: "With the cost of living going up every day, and the police working on a very tight budget, it has been suggested that some of the police, in order to earn more money and knowing that 1999 was coming up, may have become involved with the Triads to earn more money. Since 1996, we've had this violence in Macau, and the government has found it very hard to rely totally on the police because part of the force is really involved with the Triads. . . . I'm also told . . . the police were too kind to some gangs and not so kind to other gangs and that again caused fights."

It became clear to the gangsters—this was a factor Ho didn't mention—that whoever ran the most action at the time of handover would be in the best position to negotiate with the PRC for the right to grab some of the new gambling opportunities when the aging Ho's monopoly expired in 2001, as well as to negotiate the right to work the lucrative chaperon market from China to Macau. The chaperon market—essentially a travel agency for booking gambling tours—generated two-thirds of all casino revenue.

Finally, the "Asian Flu" ended the boom of the past 15 years, squeezing the dizzy earnings that had yielded enough for everybody, which in turn caused a real estate crash that left 30,000 apartments vacant and houses selling at half what they were a few months before.

At the start of Macau's gang war, one in 25 men in the colony were Triad members, making for a total of about 10,000 hard-core criminals, giving the gangsters twice the manpower of the three branches of the police, of whom a considerable percentage were on the Triads' payroll anyway. As the opening shots were fired, the stakes were huge. Each of the Triad-leased VIP rooms in Ho's casinos was raking in millions a month. The Triads also controlled the city's 10,000 prostitutes who worked within or around the casinos. Selling consolation to the losers and dessert to the winners, the hookers brought in over $300 million a year. A not inconsiderable sideline of the Triads also worth fighting over was smuggling drugs, guns, and girls out of China—historically easier to accomplish through compliant Macau than through Hong Kong.

Just after the Avenida Da Praia Grande assassinations the Macau Government Tourist Office issued an optimistic press release that stated "eight million tourists shop with confidence in Macau," but the fact was that the very business over which the Wo On Lok and 14K had been fighting suddenly dropped off precipitously as tourists and gamblers stayed away from what seemed like a war zone. Soon after the killings, a torso was found in a factory, then a businessman approaching a bank died after his arm was nearly hacked off by Triads trying to separate him from the money handcuffed to his wrist. For the month of August 1997, tourist arrivals were down 36 percent compared with the same month the year before.

For Stanley Ho, enough was enough. At the time less forthcoming about the violence than he would be a couple of years later, and anticipating the public release of tourist statistics, Ho called his own news conference on July 24, 1997, and told the world not to worry. The 14K and Wo On Lok had nothing to do with his casinos, and, at any rate, they were holding peace negotiations. The government would see that civility would be restored to the quaint streets of Macau. In any case, "when Macau changes hands to China, all the Triads will run away."

Lest the government try to put Stanley Ho's words into action before Macau changed hands, the Triads exploded a bomb in front of the governor's palace, and continued to go at each other, setting off car bombs and hurling firebombs and hand grenades all over the city. By year's end the official body count in the tit-for-tat killing spree had risen to 29 (police suspected there were more bodies in concrete or watery graves), and the American State Department warned people not to visit the territory. Some hotels ran at 20 percent occupancy, taxicab use was down by two-thirds after dark, stores closed at sundown instead of the usual 10 P.M., and the busy restaurants along the city's main boulevards stood empty.

As is usually the case when the world looks like it is spinning out of control, the government and the police sought to put the blame on one bogeyman, and they found him in the Al Capone of the "Chicago of the Orient," whose arrest would put an end to the chaos in the colony. That man was the 41-year-old dragon head of the Macau 14K, Wan Kwok-koi, aka Broken Tooth.

Wan got his sobriquet cutting his teeth—that is, breaking them—in gang fights whilst growing up in Macau's back alleys. Like Steven Wong, he was a grade-school dropout, and like Wong he proved a master at recruiting young loyal followers and at underworld tactics aimed at outmaneuvering competitors in his own Triad. One of them was Macau's senior 14K member, Kai Sze "Market" Wai, who'd got his start (and his nickname) in Hong Kong, extorting money from businessmen in the Mong Kok market, then moved to the welcoming Philippines, where he amassed a fortune running gambling casinos under Marcos. Wai showed up in Macau in 1987 and formed an alliance with the then-rising Broken Tooth to overthrow the reigning head of the 14K, "Touch Hair" Peng. Wai then purchased from Ho's STDM company the legal franchise to several of the private gambling rooms. That put him next in line to be overthrown.

If Broken Tooth were a businesslike gangster who played by the rules, the ensuing gang wars of the second half of the '90s might have been slightly less violent, or at least more clear cut. But he was a sociopath with megalomaniac tendencies. As he gained in stature and power he began boisterously challenging Market Wai's control—and his dignity (in one case, posting signs all over the city alleging Market Wai was a narcotics trafficker). Market Wai reacted by attacking Broken Tooth's poster-pasting 49s. Broken Tooth retaliated, and the two factions went to war with hatchets, bombs, and machine guns. Wai got the worst. When Wai's New Century Hotel was raked by AK-47 fire, he stayed holed up in his suite instead of coming out and fighting like a man. This was a final loss of face for his followers, who took Broken Tooth's threats to heart and switched sides. Broken Tooth then took over Wai's franchises in the Lisboa and set up his own club, called the Wan Hau, which began raking in $6 million a month. He used his wealth to invest in several legitimate enterprises, buying a popular disco called the Heavy Club, promoted several Canto-pop concerts, bought real estate, became a licensed seller of gambling chips, and of course, a high-stakes gambler, particularly favoring the game of choice on the Macau Riviera, baccarat.

He then made the same fatal mistake as John Giotti and Al Capone—the same one that Steven Wong unwittingly made: he gave media interviews in which he openly bragged about being the top dog in Southeast Asia's underworld, with thousands of followers, at least a hundred of whom were ready to pour into the streets at a moment's notice. He drove around town in a purple Lamborghini (only one of a fleet of custom-built luxury cars he owned), wore a solid-gold, diamond-encrusted Rolex (prominently displayed in a five-by-seven glossy publicity photo showing him smiling into a cell phone), and paraded into discos and casinos with an ever-changing roster of beautiful women on his arm. Amazingly, he also financed a bio-pic about his exploits, called *Casino,* starring Hong Kong film star Simon Yam. *Casino* is in the same genre as dozens of other films that seduce young Chinese into the gangs and that feature murder and mayhem mixed in with glamorous images of ultra-well-dressed gangsters making their just way in an unjust world. Broken Tooth humbly left his name off the credits, but he took part in every aspect of production, from screenwriting to filming. Typically (and laughably), within hours of its release, the Wo On Lok Triad pirated the film and began selling thousands of cheaply priced copies.

As with Capone, Giotti, and Wong, the police took Wan's flagrant hoopla as a wildly waving red flag. After the May 4, 1997, massacre, the Macau Legislative Assembly drew up an anti-Triad bill modeled on the one Hong Kong had had for 30 years. The bill came into effect on August 15 and was drafted to stop the uncivilized Triads generally, but some of its provisions seemed specifically targeted against dragon heads such as Broken Tooth, who was among the first to be charged under the statute. It made being a member of a Triad a crime punishable by a three-year prison term for junior members and 12 years for senior members. It also offered amnesty and witness protection to Triad members who came forward to testify against their bosses. Broken Tooth took the legislation personally. On June 7, all eight Chinese newspapers in Macau and its local television station received a press release: "Warning, from today it is not allowed to mention Wan Kuok-koi alias Bang Nga-koi [Broken Tooth–koi], or the 14K, otherwise bullets will have no eyes and knives will have no feeling."

Arresting Broken Tooth in Macau in 1997 proved as difficult as arresting Steven Wong three years earlier. After the warrant was issued, Wan had no difficulty leaving Macau for an overseas holiday. Then, on July 28, a judge mysteriously declared the warrant invalid and dropped the charges. The judge then retired and moved back to Portugal, and Broken Tooth moved back to Macau. Another warrant for his arrest was issued in the PRC, and this too was suddenly dropped. According to Broken Tooth, there was no funny business involved in these legal cha-chas—at least none that was his fault. Both warrants were issued, he claimed, at the corrupt instigation of Market Wai.

To discourage police harassment (the police alleged) Broken Tooth tried to send law enforcement a message by less than subtle means. On March 24, 1998, senior gambling inspector Francisco Amaral was shot dead a few feet from security headquarters. On April 16, the chauffeur to the territory's undersecretary for security, Manuel Soares Monge, was shot in the head as he left home to pick up his boss. The next day, Dr. Rui Afonso, an adviser to the Chinese and Macau governments drawing up the new Basic Law, openly accused the Macau government of lacking the will to put a stop to the Triad chaos. Then, two weeks later, on May 1, the car of Macau's judicial police director, Dr. Antonio Marques Baptista, was bombed.

This rule-breaking behavior was too much for Baptista, who was jogging nearby at the time. He hastily organized a posse and, 12 hours after the explosion, marched into the Lisboa and personally arrested Broken Tooth as he gambled at a baccarat table. Dressed in a gaudy shirt decorated with a camel and rider striding through date palms, Broken Tooth was led handcuffed down the Lisboa's grand porte cochere before a crowd of onlookers and reporters and shoved into a police van. This time the police threw the book at him, charging him with organized crime membership, running illicit gambling businesses, blackmail, loan-sharking, dealing in contraband, and possession of firearms. The cops swept the city and arrested nine of Broken Tooth's lieutenants on the same charges. A week later, on May 8, presumably in sympathy with Broken Tooth, a coordinated series of explosions were detonated all over the city, which reinforced the belief that while the 14K leader could be jailed, those who displeased him could be reached. Fourteen cars were firebombed and a number of shops and motorcycles lit up the night sky with flames. By the end of the year, 27 men had been killed in gangster-related violence.

On November 10, 1998, while Broken Tooth stewed in the pretrial remand jail awaiting the beginning of his trial, set for March 17, 1999, the court froze $20 million of his assets. Threats of "disruptions" began to be received, and fearing a courthouse bombing, the trial was delayed. On April 22, 1999, Wan was additionally charged with the criminal intimidation of Lisboa casino workers, but in a separate trial, he was acquitted when witness after witness took the stand and said they had no idea what the prosecution was talking about—a bad sign for the main trial. On April 27, the main case was delayed again because witnesses (and witness statements) began to disappear. Over the summer, as the inter-gang violence continued (a remote-controlled nail bomb tore to shreds two Soi Fong Triad gangsters in August), the judge in Wan's case quit, and a brave replacement had to be brought in from Portugal. Finally, on Wednesday, October 6, 1999, with the death toll standing at 37, and Macau set to be handed over to China in 10 weeks, the trial began at the Court of the First Instance.

Just the fact that it was taking place at all sent shivers through the underworld. Shortly after the Mainland Chinese took over Hong Kong in 1997, PRC police had showily tracked down and arrested on their own soil a Triad boss from Hong Kong named Cheung Tze-keung, who was accused of masterminding sensational kidnappings. Minutes after he lost his appeal, the Chinese executed him. In addition, after concluding negotiations on the Basic Law with the Portuguese, the Chinese announced they would be stationing troops in the Macau Special Administrative Region even before the handover. Gangsters in the know feared that, despite promises that these soldiers were to be used strictly for military defense, they would instead be used to maintain law and order. All over Macau—all over Asia—the so-called underworld (it was often hard to tell under from over) was in a state of movement and flux. That very week, October 11, 1999, Stanley Ho made a trip to Manila and announced he was moving the Jumbo Palace to Manila as a floating casino. Also that very week, 14K hit men gunned down three of their 4 Kings rivals at Don Muang airport in Bangkok over control of the casinos in tormented Cambodia.

Broken Tooth's trial lasted five weeks and the prosecution called 50 witnesses. The civilians testified they had trouble remembering seeing Broken Tooth doing anything worse than losing his temper when he was losing at baccarat. Public Prosecutor Augusto Serafim Vasconcelos admitted to the three presiding judges that the memory lapses of his own witnesses were curious in the extreme, and so he entered into evidence Wan's own words, published in the numerous magazine interviews Wan had granted in the last few years, and in which Wan all but admitted to being the dragon head of the 14K. Vasconcelos showed the film *Casino*, asserting it was clearly Wan's self-produced autobiography. Then he called less amnesia-prone witnesses—cops such as Police Director Baptista—who testified to evidence, gleaned from anonymous informants, that showed Wan was responsible for the gangland assassinations and bombings. The defense objected strongly to the inclusion of this hearsay, the judge overruled the objection, and one of Wan's lawyers, Pedro Redinha, quit the case in protest.

On November 8, the last day of the trial, Wan stood up and addressed the court for seven minutes, accusing Baptista of uttering "nothing but lies." He said he'd made his fortune from legal gambling at reputable establishments (e.g., the Lisboa) and sound business activities like promoting pop concerts and trading in real estate. Of course, he said, like everyone else he'd heard of the 14K, but he had nothing to do with the gang. He admitted to only two vices: gambling and a bad temper. Otherwise, "I've always obeyed the authorities."

Presiding Judge Fernando Estrela said he would hand down the decision two weeks later, November 23. A week before the verdict, amid fears of commando-style rescue attempts, Wan and the nine co-accused were secretly moved from the remand jail to the new high-security unit of Macau's central prison on Coloane Island.

For the historic verdict, Zhu Entao, the head of Interpol China, paid a visit to the territory, announcing that he was pleased with the way public security had recently improved. At 3 P.M. the three judges filed into the Court of the First Instance. Wan stood up. Judge Estrela looked down at the charge sheet and read the counts, pronouncing Wan guilty on all. Broken Tooth was sentenced to 15 years, and led away to an armored car that took him in a caravan of police vehicles to Coloane Island.

I jumped on the No. 21 bus in front of the Lisboa and told the driver, "Coloane Prison." He looked at me without comprehension and I handed him my Chinese note from the Handover Office. He read it and looked at me again. I took my pen and knocked it against my tooth. "Where Broken Tooth is. Wan Kwok-koi."

"Yes, yes, Wan Kwok-koi," he said, shrugging. When I sat down, I noticed the entire busload of passengers staring at me.

"Are you America government?" asked a fellow in a worn suit beside me. I was pleased by the mistake. That morning in Hong Kong I'd donned a blue shirt, blue tie, a trim jacket and mirrored sunglasses, in mind to impress authorities, who always responded warmly to the outfit.

"I'm a reporter," I said. I noticed he had a packet of Marlboro sticking out of his jacket pocket and an unlit cigarette in one bony hand. I popped a

Nicorette and gave him one. "I'm here for the handover. Were you just gambling in there?"

"Yes, yes!" He smiled ecstatically, which probably meant—in that contradictory Chinese way—he'd lost. Or else he just liked the hit of the Nicorette.

"Do you know where Broken Tooth's VIP lounge used to be?" I asked. "Before he got arrested?"

"Oh high, very high, upstair." He held his hand a foot over his head, then pointed to the top floor of the casino receding behind us.

"Too high for you?"

"Yes, yes." Chewing loudly, he gave me that Buddha smile again. "Too high for me. On'y rich rich. He very bad man, Wan. Kill lots people. Now no more fun for him. Finished."

"How do you feel about the handover?"

He looked left and right, lowered his voice. "Nobody like. Want stay like it is. No good for young people. Chinese no free."

"I guess you're stuck with them though."

"Yes, stuck. No more Wan, but now Chinese. Stuck."

The bridge south from the Lisboa climbed over the Praia Grande Bay to Taipa Island, which looked like a pocket of Mediterranean quietude compared to the Vegas bustle on the peninsula behind. My neighbor got out at a beautiful old square, calling "Bye bye!" to me as we pulled away. We followed an avenue called Marques Esparteiro through leafy hills, and came down onto a causeway that was lined with sculptures replicating the signs of the Chinese zodiac. "Help me, Ox," I mumbled as we passed my sign.

If Taipa looked quiet, then Coloane Island, at the end of the causeway across the next muddy bay, looked positively somnolent. Good place for a prison, I thought, contemplating the treed hills interrupted by neither homes nor high-rises. We wound our way up switchbacks, until we reached the top of a low mountain. My driver pulled over to the side of the country road at a place where you could see the ocean. He looked back at me and pointed to a small white blockhouse with no buildings behind it. "Prison?" I asked, stepping hesitantly down.

"This, this! Prison," he said impatiently, and pulled away.

Where was it? In the middle of the blockhouse was a steel door set flush with the concrete, with no knob or keyhole, just a little glass window. A speaker with a button was set in the wall beside the door and above it hung a video camera, tilted down at me. It suddenly occurred to me that the Coloane Prison must be an underground institution, built right into the mountain. Inmates would have to tunnel through bedrock to escape. I pressed the buzzer, and a long couple of minutes later a voice answered in Chinese. I asked if someone there spoke English. Another couple of minutes went by. Finally a voice answered in Portuguese. *"Quem e ou, señor?"*

"Yo esta journalista, aqui para handover," I said, hoping Span-English resembled Portuguese. *"Quiero habla con chef."* I looked up at the camera watching me, held up my notebook. *"Journalista,"* I repeated. "I want to speak to the warden." There was some mumbling, and then silence for a couple more minutes. Finally a voice said, "No—no. Not possible. Go away."

Go away? Well, that was pretty direct.

Now what?

Across the road two matrons in cleaning uniforms wearing ID badges stood waiting for the bus back into town. I noticed a service road going downhill around the blockhouse, and I asked them where it led. "Escola Superior das Forças," one woman called.

"The what?"

"Police Academy," called the other.

Well, that's all right! Around the world police academies are reservoirs of well-connected cops. Maybe some officer would know someone who knew someone who could get me my interview? At the very least, I might bump into someone who might gossip about what was going on in the force vis-à-vis the 14K. "Can I just go in?" I asked the matron who seemed to speak English.

"I don't think. *Area proibido.*" A secure area.

I walked to the top of the road and looked down. Halfway to the bottom of a steep hill the road was blocked by a cross-arm gate, beside which a couple of uniformed guards lounged outside a shed. Okay, then, activate disguise. I fished out my cell phone and put it to my ear. I adjusted my shoulder bag so that I carried it by the handle, like a briefcase. Then I set off downhill in a confident gait, talking loudly on the phone about the stupidity of the home-office boys, their utter ignorance of what I had to deal with on the ground. As I closed on the guards I gave them the briefest of nods, angrily preoccupied with what I was saying on the phone. I raised the level of my argument to outright shouting as I ducked under the gate, and then just kept going. I should have been shot in the back for pulling that stunt, but it worked. As I would discover over the next couple of months, imitating a pissed-off DEA agent in a hurry to meet with the chief gets you in almost anywhere.

Okay: *now* what? I thought.

At the bottom of the hill was a modern concrete building, with a blue-and-white coat of arms on it. "ESFSM" was written across the top of the shield, with the letters spelled out below: *Escola Superior das Forças de Segurança de Macau.* Macau Security Forces College. I pushed through the doors. Opposite was a bank of glass-walled offices. To the right was a passageway into what looked like a canteen. To the left was a stairway, with a spray of WWI–era rifles and bayonets affixed to the wall. I heard someone's lonely whistling echoing up the stairs. I took out my note with the Chinese lettering on it and showed it to the uniformed whistler as he crested the landing and approached me.

"There's a prison around here."

"Not here," he said. "There," pointing to the hill.

"Yes, there."

"Okay," he said, and walked away.

I chewed another Nicorette, stood waiting for five minutes. Suddenly, through the glass doors I saw a parade of cadets dressed in blue knit sweaters and crisply pressed slacks marching by, in rows of four. I walked outside. The cadets passed in perfect step, eyes front and blind to me. When the last of them passed I fell into line behind them. It was kind of amusing: I felt like Roberto Benigni marching behind the camp guards in *Life Is Beautiful.*

They walked up the lane and, dressing their line into pairs, turned right through a narrow stone archway into an old section of the compound. They marched up a steep flight of well-worn stone steps between ochre walls, crossed a walled balcony, then mounted another flight.

We came out on a high veranda and I caught a stunning view of the green forested peaks of Alto de Coloane and Ponto Central, the shallow strait between the island and Mainland China, and the town of Coloane below, nestled in a cove. In the foreground were Moorish barbicans and an eight-sided turret with a flared pagoda roof, the architectures of the two cultures layered side by side in the academy, as they were in official buildings all over the territory.

I followed the cadet corps into a cafeteria, filled with about 200 men eating a late-afternoon Portuguese lunch. The young men halted at a room-length table, marching in place. Someone shouted an order and they left-faced smartly to the table. Another order, and they sat down. I was the only one left standing, now the center of attention of the entire room. Mercifully, I spotted a single empty seat by the plate glass window on the east side of the building, at which several middle aged Chinese men and a woman in uniform were dining.

"Hi, I'm a journalist here for the handover," I announced to the table. "I'm looking at the Police Academy today." An older fellow with his back to the window held out his hand to the chair beside him. "You from?" he asked.

"I'm from Canada," I beamed.

A collective chorus of approval went up from the table. "I am Cheong Kiang-chum," said my new host.

"Pleased to meet you," I enunciated. "And I am Terry Gould." I didn't have much time here and so made the decision to get straight to the point—vaguely risky, but I knew I couldn't ask for a safer time to be flaunting my mission in this Triad town. "I am writing a book about Chinese criminals," I said.

My companions either didn't understand or were concentrating on first things first. Cheong took an empty plate and placed it in front of me. The others passed down plates of fish, rice, soup, bread, fruit, and a bottle of wine. Digging in, I told them that in Canada our police force was called the Royal Canadian Mounted Police. "Mounties," I repeated, although it was obvious I wasn't getting the point across. Cheong announced something in Cantonese to the others, and they all smiled and looked at me perplexedly.

"Congratulations on Broken Tooth," I said.

They again looked at me without understanding. "Broken Tooth—the Triad boss," I repeated, and they began to talk among themselves in Cantonese, turning back to offer me polite smiles. I began riffling through my shoulder bag. "He's in jail now," I said. I took out the *Morning Post* article with his picture.

That got their attention. The whole table burst into laughter. "Ohhh, Wan Kwok-koi!!! Wan Kwok-koi!! He is here, here!" Cheong turned around and pointed through the glass, across a gully to the thickly forested hillside. At the bottom of the hill, barely peeping from the junglelike growth, was a long whitewashed building. "Under building," Cheong said.

"Under that building?"

"In hill, yes."

Someone shouted from the other end of the table, "Are you a fan?"

"No," I said. "I want to talk to him. I want to talk to the warden to get permission."

"Ohhhh, ohhhh," they said, and returned to talking among themselves. They passed down a bottle of olive oil for me to dip my bread. Cheong said: "You want talk Wan Kwok-koi? For book?"

"Yes, yes, that's right. I want to interview him about a Canadian criminal I know, a Triad man, who probably worked for him here in Macau. I think he knows him."

"Ohhhh, ohhhh." More discussion among themselves, then Cheong said: "I think no possible. He not allow visitor. Too dangerous."

Well, maybe. But I'm getting close. At least I can see the wall between Wan and me. I just have to get through it.

"Did you see his movie, *Casino?*" I asked Cheong.

"Casino—uh, I no go Wan's," he replied, and I realized he thought I'd asked whether he'd gambled in Wan's VIP room.

"No, no, he made a video, about himself. *Casino.*"

"Oh," he said, then looked away.

It turned out Cheong wasn't even a cop, but a fireman, teaching a course in emergency rescue. They were all teaching courses. At my table were a customs agent, a ballistics expert, a bomb squad officer, and a homicide investigator. His specialty naturally intrigued me, but carrying on a conversation about the two-score murders over the last few years was next to impossible. His accent was so heavy he had to repeat each word thrice, and I knew he would never be able to put them into a comprehensible sentence for me. My agony must have been apparent, because suddenly two young cops appeared beside me. "Maybe we can help you," one of them said.

"Oh, that's nice of you! You speak English!"

"A little."

As the older gentlemen excused themselves to go back to work, the younger ones sat down beside me.

Simon Wong was one fellow's name—a sweet-faced, clean-cut cadet in his late 20s. He said he used to be a bank clerk before he entered the academy last year. His companion was Lin Heng-chi, who was taller, leaner, and older but equally friendly-looking; he said he'd been a Macau policeman on street patrol for five years and, like many other officers, had been assigned to the academy to learn Mainland Chinese law, "because after Macau go back to China, Portugal law go back, so there will be more China law we in police department must learn."

I explained my book project about Chinese criminals, and Simon said, "You come at the right time. We are having a course about the Triads later, law against the Triads association. Would you like come to our canteen talk with us?"

Wild horses couldn't have kept me away.

"So it's happening today?" I asked Simon down in the cadets' canteen on the first level.

"Yes, this afternoon. It's about five. Concerns the new Triad law of 1997."

"Can I go?"

"I don't know, you have to contact our commander before you can come in."

The commander! Great! Maybe he would help me climb the ropes to Broken Tooth. Even if an interview couldn't be arranged for today I could catch the gangster when I got back from Cambodia, before I went to Manila.

Lin, the older one, said, "We can give you his name. Commissario Cheang Lek-sang." He looked at his watch. "Oh, now I think he is still in Macau. Because many things go on. Maybe about four you go to his office."

"Is your book on just Macau?" Simon asked me.

"Macau and all of Southeast Asia. I'm writing about the handover's effects on the criminals. The criminals are running all over Asia. They go to Cambodia, they go to the Philippines."

"Yes, most of them run away," Simon said. "They are scared that now the Chinese will catch them. We learn in class, the more the world develops, the criminal is going to develop as well. They will develop in a certain fashion, but the way they work will be probably fresh. I mean that people from China will go United States, people from United States will go China, they will join together. Because they have money, they can hire people of good skills. They can tell them to do some bad business. So more and more effort need to be done by policemen, by keeping noble, vigilant."

"You're an idealist," I said.

"Yes, yes," he laughed. "Just new. I hope I stay like this."

Some student cops playing cards at a table beside us shouted at their hands, then threw their cards down and stood up. One of them said something in Cantonese to Simon, who said to me, "Excuse me, they are in my class, go to swimming practice. I go. You will stay to talk Lin?"

"Maybe we'll speak again tonight," I said hopefully, "at your Triad class."

Over espressos a few minutes later, Lin said to me: "Information we learn is that years ago, before Hong Kong go to China, a head of the Hong Kong syndicates, he met with Chinese syndicates. Chinese boss say to him, 'You can invest in China but you can no come here.' Then Hong Kong boss, he come Macau instead, he make things very confused for Wan."

"What was his name?"

He hesitated, looking at my pad. "Doesn't matter. Because now Chinese come in, all calm down. Because Macau members of syndicates they run to Thailand, Cambodge, other places."

"Did you know Wan—as a policeman?" I asked.

"No," he smiled shyly, "because I'm a young member—just sidewalk. So I just see young Triads. Maybe there are thousands, but most of them are kids, temporary. They think there is no way to make money. Sometimes they go away and leave this syndicate. Temporary measure. Not like Wan. He is crazy killer. You stay for the handover?" he asked me.

"Just for the day," I said, "because from here I'm actually going to where the Triads went. See, I came here looking for someone. A Triad man I know from Canada used to work for the 14K here. So I'm going where he goes. Here, Cambodia, the Philippines."

"I think is very dangerous for you."

"Well, I was here in 1993 and nothing happened. Many Canadian-Chinese gangsters came here—to gamble, do business. So I was here looking for him. He's a 14K official." I reached into my briefcase and took out the photo of the Paper Fan in front of the Brooklyn Bridge, as well as the ones that showed his tattoos. "Maybe you saw him? His name is Steven Lik Man Wong, but I'm sure he changed it because he was on the run. He left but I don't know when."

Lin looked at the photo, pursed his lips, shook his head gravely. "You looked for this 14K official and you still live—?"

"Oh, I'm sure it *was* dangerous but—"

"Very dangerous for foreigner," he said. "You talk to someone they don't understand what you say, so you cannot make to communicate. Explain you are not police. Because you look like foreign police. Maybe they make mistake, want to kill you."

"Do the Triads target policemen?" I asked, probing a topic I'd initiated in the cafeteria. "Or do they work with them?"

"Some of them," he said. Then he lowered his voice. "Some of police have secret relationship with Triads, so Triad friends not hurt them. But then other side want to kill policeman because he is friend with enemy gang. But if someone in police is always *against* Triads, then they try and kill him too. So the situation is severe." He looked uncomfortable with what he'd just said. "But I think Macau in a few days become calm," he added, moving onto safer ground. "Because Chinese law is strict. Only thing—" He hesitated, then came out with it. "Sometimes they don't do straight law. They arrest person for political crime. That is what we are a little afraid. We will see. Now I go study. Farewell. I'm sure I will read something about you soon."

I hoped he meant something *by* me soon.

I had an hour or so to kill before looking up the commander, so I walked back up the stairs to the cafeteria veranda to take pictures of the splendid views. The academy occupied a series of terraces and I ascended another stone flight to the highest plateau. Here, facing a wide concrete courtyard, was a baroque administration building that wouldn't have been out of place in a square in Lisbon. It was several hundred feet long and two stories high, pastel ochre in color, with windows sealed by green wooden shutters and embellished above with white curving pediments. The central bay of the building had a pediment encrusted with the Portuguese coat of arms, and from its middle rose a white flagpole from which flew the red and green Portuguese flag, flapping south in the wind blowing from China.

As I photographed the flag, a stocky, middle-aged cop in a T-shirt and blue cap wandered out of one of the sleepy offices on the first floor and crossed the courtyard to me. "December 20—flag come down," he said. "No more. Five hundred year, then no more."

He stood a few feet from me, looking up at the flag with his hands on his hips. I didn't say anything at first, merely appreciated the quiet—a thoughtful, almost mournful interlude in the late-afternoon sun, with the birds chirping. He turned and looked at the Mainland and I contemplated his sad face.

"Do you think China will make the criminals afraid?" I asked. "Is China good for the police?"

He pursed his lips and shook his head. "China very very strict to all people. China not so good to all people, I think."

"Do you have children?" I asked.

"Yes, yes, I have children."

"Now they will grow up Chinese," I said. "Communist."

"Yes," he said, sadly. "Yes, Communist." He rested his foot on the old stone wall at the edge of the courtyard and looked out through the semi-tropical foliage, silhouetted green-black against the silvery-blue bay. A lone motorbike accelerated up the mountain road below, disappeared from view, then roared around the wall and pulled up beside us. The police-woman driving it holstered her radio and said a few words to him, looking at me. He joked softly with her. She looked at me without smiling and drove away.

I pointed to the prison. "Wan Kwok-koi is now far down underground," I said. "He's in the basement jail by himself, in solitary."

"Yes, killed many people—police, politician, killed many many people. It's special cell for him and his friends, special prisoners. You know the Nepal soldier? One hundred special Nepal soldiers guard him."

"You mean Gurkhas?"

"Yes, yes, special come to guard Koi. Because Koi Triad maybe kill Macau police. Macau governor call one hundred Nepal soldier look-see Koi."

"Wow!!" I held my hand as a phone to my face. "He can call to someone to say, 'Kill that man'?"

"I think not now. He cannot telephone another—I hope so," he chuckled.

There was a long pause while he surveyed the view, looking out to a forested finger of land across the bay. "You are here because—?" he said to the view.

"Well, today there is a special class to learn about Triads at five o'clock," I said. "I will go see your boss, the commissario, to see if I can go."

"I think he no let you. Maybe secret. Are you invite guest here?"

"Well, I just came by. I'm a journalist."

"Okay. You want something drink—go downstair here, senior officer canteen. I something to work now. Okay, bye-bye."

Ten minutes later, I was under arrest, standing in the officer canteen in front of the seated Commissario Cheang Lek-sang. Flanked by the two cops my friend up top had sicced on me, Cheang was going through my briefcase, trying to get to the bottom of what I was up to in his fortress academy.

I'd explained to him that I'd merely taken the public bus south from the Lisboa and wandered up a deserted delivery lane. Unfortunately, a minor investigation had shown him I'd ducked the gate without presenting credentials to the guards. So Cheang was aware I'd lied to him right off the bat. There was also the little matter of my having made a beeline to the cafeteria, where, he'd just learned, I'd interrogated idealistic cadets about Triad infiltration of Macau's police department. Now, with knitted brows, he was comparing two contrasting letters of introduction from my publisher, Anne Collins: One certified I was writing a book describing my travels through Southeast Asia; the other that I was writing a book about Asian organized crime.

Cheang rubbed his forehead and scratched his head. He was a round-faced, avuncular cop of late middle age, pleasant enough—a Chinese headmaster, really—and I got the feeling he just wished this hadn't happened. Apparently there had been a tour of journalists who were shown around the facilities for an hour early that morning, and they had departed without leaving any stragglers. Why hadn't I come and gone with them? Why was I prying and breaking the rules?

"Please, you must tell me the truth," he said, pulling papers from my briefcase. "It is a question of security for me." Cheang unfolded my tourist map of the island, on which I'd marked an X and written: "Wan Kwok-koi."

"That's the reason, Commissario. I was hoping you could talk to the warden for me and I could interview Broken Tooth."

"You came *here* because you want to talk to Wan Kwok-koi, *there?*"

"I wanted to tell my country about his bad deeds. He's very colorful."

"Yes, yes, colorful," he soberly agreed.

He pulled from my briefcase a white manila envelope and used two fingers to gingerly spread it open, as if it were evidence. He glanced through the 10 pages of my *Saturday Night* article. Then he pulled out the single-page column I wrote a year and a half later. His lips moved as he translated it. When he was done he raised his eyes. "This man—he is in the Lisboa? Now?"

"No, no," I said. "He's gone now. Ran away."

"Ah, I see." He thought on that a moment. "So this man, and Wan—"

"He was in Wan's Triad."

"I see. I see." I was beginning to make sense to him. Perhaps my methods were objectionable, but what I was saying sounded at least plausible. "Why do you tell me there were no guards then?" he asked, pointing up the road. "Why?" He said this with such aching sincerity that I was hoping I was past the worst. He just wants the right answer so he can throw me the hell out, I thought.

"I didn't want to get them in trouble. They saw I was on business and just let me in. I wasn't up to anything illegal. Just trying to find someone who could get me an interview with Wan."

I leaned over and took the articles, put them back in the envelope, took the letter about me being on assignment to write about organized crime, and left him with the other letter. "Okay, I'm going to let you guys get back to work now."

"Not permitted what you have done!" he announced, this with such cruel authority that he frightened the daylights out of me. "You can*not* do this!"

He stood up, barked something in Chinese to the two cops, who came around to me and took my arms. "Must deal with this, *must!*" he said, and I was praying this was only a face-saving gesture, that I wasn't going to be thrown into a dungeon guarded by stony-faced Gurkhas.

The cops hauled me out the door and held my arms as they pulled me down the road towards a back entrance to the compound. When we were out of the sight line of the commissario, however, they suddenly let me go. We proceeded to merely stroll to the gate, with them beside me, but well outside my personal space.

"How long you stay Macau?" the younger one on my right asked, not unkindly.

"I have an appointment with a Canadian official tonight," I lied, just to let them know someone important would be asking questions if I disappeared.

"You must be very careful. 14K fellows—" He tapped my briefcase. "Very bad. Very bad. We find people—*phttt.*" He sliced his hand down his middle, pulled open an imaginary coat. Then he pointed over his shoulder to the prison. "He have them killed. *Ile!*"

"Maybe it's not a good idea to interview him, then."

"No him, no anybody with him! Otherwise, that—" he pointed to my head "—there—" he pointed to the curb. "And the rest there"—indicating that my torso and legs would be on the other side of the street.

The official handover was still four evenings away, but my schedule showed that every one of them was clogged with events, including tonight's main feature, called the "Nam Van Lakes Lighting Exhibition," to be viewed at 10 P.M. from the esplanade southwest of the Lisboa. An hour before those festivities began, the Bank of China building opposite the casino was officially lit up. The crowd oohed and aahed at the neon Sputnik balls emanating sprays of light and lotus petals, reflecting the trademark oddity atop Ho's tower. A flying dove delivered another Sputnik lotus to the top of the facade of the famous Ruinas de Sao Paulo. Atop this, the Great Wall of China snaked to the roof, with more spiked balls tumbling down its central walkway. What is it with Ho and these stupid balls? I thought. Did his mother have a nightmare?

Some dignitary then delivered a speech on a bandstand, followed by a dress rehearsal of the takeover flag-raising, with blaring martial music that, to my ears, sounded like the theme for the 1936 Berlin Olympics, orientalized. Three guys in tuxes and white gloves slowly raised red star flags almost to the top of the poles, then lowered them.

After the applause I strolled with the crowd up the Praia Grande to the Nam Van Lakes, a new addition to the town since I'd been here, created by a landfill that encircled a section of the bay, with something called The Gate of Understanding in its middle. Fifteen minutes later, at exactly 10 P.M., the lakes were lit up. The still, black water became studded with dozens of floating lucky lotuses, red with yellow lights in their middle, and red leaping carp—glowing Sputniks in their mouths, of course. Against the skyline, two 30-foot-tall goddesses slowly twirled, the equivalent of giant music boxes playing orchestral tunes that reminded me of the strains Ronald Colman heard when he beheld Shangri-La. Strung along the water between them were red and gold lotus pads, each with black Chinese characters.

There was a China-TV crew filming the lights, and I introduced myself to the cameraman and asked, "What does that say?"

"This say, 'The People of Mainland China Say Welcome to the People of Macau.'" The cameraman moved his finger left. "Next one say, 'Macau Love China.'"

"You think they do?" I asked.

"Yes, because this start of new era for Macau. Come home. Peace, prosperity."

"No more gang violence."

"No more. Bad people no more. Only good people now."

Those who played by the rules, I thought. One country, two systems—or maybe four. I wished him luck and then caught the midnight ferry to Hong Kong. I regretted I would miss the official handover, regretted even more that I'd found out zilch about Steve. But it was time for me to move on to a country with about a hundred systems, one for every crook on Interpol's wanted list.

CHAPTER 20

BEWARE OF CRUEL DOGS

*Anywhere that a hundred of Interpol's most wanted fugitives can
safely call home is somewhere you wouldn't want to live.*
—ROBERT YOUNG PELTON, *THE WORLD'S MOST DANGEROUS PLACES*

School was out in the West, but there were no backpackers or couples wearing holiday smiles waiting to disembark my Dragonair flight in Phnom Penh, though I'd seen crowds of travelers making connections in Hong Kong for Bangkok. Cambodia was then attracting only 3 percent as many tourists as neighboring Thailand, and most of my fellow passengers were dour Europeans connected to the dozens of NGOs helping the Kingdom move beyond its decades of madness. After a quarter hour standing in the aisle, however, it became apparent that none of us were moving beyond the fuselage. "Seems they've managed to break the wheels on their gangway," the British captain explained with a sigh of resignation. "I'm assured new wheels will be found and installed. Sometime."

We took our seats again. The sun set. Night descended. The temperature rose. I flipped through my *Lonely Planet* guide, which cautiously predicted better tourist days ahead for Cambodia. Prime Minister Hun Sen's main opponent, Prince Norodom Ranariddh, had acquiesced to His Excellency's strongman rule, and Ranariddh's supporters were no longer being murdered in the streets of Phnom Penh. In the hinterland, you could now visit Angkor Wat without getting shot by the Khmer Rouge or stepping on one of the country's six million land mines. Nevertheless, *LP* warned, "Cambodia is something of a lawless society"; expect "rampant corruption"; and stay away from the capital's gangster-ridden north end, "the kind of place where drunk Khmers shoot each other over a karaoke microphone."

I dozed off to sanguinary images of karaoke mayhem and awoke an hour later to a stewardess's voice chirpily directing us to the back exit. From the top of the repaired gangway I tried hard to see and hear through Steve's gangster senses. Not that I could see or hear much. The terminal's flood-lights weren't working and the place was eerily quiet for an airport on the edge of a capital city of a million people. Soldiers holding Uzis and flash-lights led us through a ground fog of wood smoke to the dingy arrivals room, an unairconditioned blockhouse where the smell of smoke pervaded everything, giving the impression that the fires of war may have been out for a year but the country was still smoldering.

Under portraits of King Norodom Sihanouk and Queen Monineath, a green-uniformed immigration agent stood behind a counter collecting passports. When he had them all in a heap in front of him, he flipped rap-idly through each one, sending two down the line of form-signers and stampers. He looked up meaningfully and a couple of Chinese passengers in business suits moved out of our crowd and went to the far end of the counter to collect their documents. Only then did the immigration officer sit down, adjust his shoulders, and scrupulously inspect the first passport in the pile he'd tossed to the side.

I asked an NGO worker beside me if those suited fellows had special visas.

"The special visas are in the form of a ten-dollar bill," he said, slipping one hand between thumb and palm. "The rest of us have normal visas."

That was my first taste of why Steve had found Cambodia so conducive to doing business.

My second came as the car the Canadian embassy had hired to meet me entered what could be called Phnom Penh's downtown, although not in the sense of a modern Asian capital. It was eight o'clock in the evening, but Monivong Boulevard was deserted and dark. There were no office towers, Indeed no buildings over five stories, and the architecture seemed frozen in the 1950s. As in some abnormally still African town, I got the feeling you could pull off any deal you wanted around here.

A mile on we turned onto the capital's grand thoroughfare, Sihanouk Boulevard, and I saw the reddish-brown stupa of Independence Monument up ahead. This was the central square of the city, yet just before the monument we turned onto a rural side street, or a decayed former city street, scattering goats as the lane degenerated into a muddy track with angle iron and smashed concrete lying in heaps on either side. In a great splash of muck and gravel we finally hauled up in the driveway of the hotel the embassy had booked for me.

The Goldiana it was called, and it was indeed gold—the lap of bizarre-looking luxury in a shell-shocked neighborhood. The place seemed to have been destroyed and rebuilt three times by three different owners: it had a central section topped by an orange peak with a high golden eave that was classic Khmer, a left side that bore a black marble face that was classic Vegas, and a right side that showed plain white gypsum with moldy plaster awnings that was classic Sunset Strip. In a way it was as Dada as the Lisboa— a pastiche beyond tacky that the current managers probably thought catered perfectly to the exotic expectations of Western tourists and the four-star comforts required by Western diplomats.

The lobby staff leapt off couches when I entered, grabbing my bags and ushering me with whispered solicitations and graceful palm gestures to the wooden front desk. The six of them moved like svelte dancers but they were totally unpracticed at the check-in ritual, and very nervous, comparing their entries and paperwork with one another like interns in a school for hoteliers. With their sibilant apologies and obsequious promises of "one moment, one moment," I got the feeling they had seen people beaten for messing up, and then *chap teuv*—taken away.

A young porter rang the elevator for me and we waited a good two minutes until it decided to respond. Killing time, I looked above the doors and read the plaque: "In recognition of your contribution to the U.S. Embassy Consular Warden system in ensuring that American citizens were fully informed of Embassy warning notices during the difficult and dangerous period of 1997 to 1998."

"You like lady massage?" my porter asked in a subdued voice in my fourth-floor room.

I didn't reply at first, enthralled by the decor: pink satin window curtains and a matching art deco spray of pillowed Naugahyde above the bed, making for an ambience as Cambodian as Mae West's suite in *Going to Town*.

"Man massage?" my porter offered the alternative, this time so quietly that I could barely hear him. That might have been because of the delicate subject matter, but I was beginning to recognize a pattern in the way Cambodians spoke. My Khmer students at Britannia had talked that way, as had the immigration officers, my driver, and the staff downstairs. The tentative whisper, at least when talking English to foreigners, had earned Cambodians descriptions in the guidebooks as "a gentle people" and "remarkably courteous," yet I'd read enough about modern times to know that many of these gentle, courteous Cambodians considered it a sport to beat to death street kids caught in the act of petty thievery.

"That's fine—I'm all right," I said.

"Very clean no problem," he added.

"I just want something to eat." I took out my wallet and gave him a dollar. "Where's a cheap place?"

"No here, hotel I think not cheap. 'Cross street, more cheap—lots places."

"Is it safe?"

He pursed his lips, wobbled his palm. "I think better you leave wallet in safe."

Five steps out of the Goldiana I was glad I'd taken his advice. Picking my way through the mud and blasted concrete in the dark I was suddenly surrounded by young snipes softly touting restaurants, moto rides, and, of course, girls. I was still trying to see things through Steve's eyes, imagining what he would have done his first night in a dead town like Phnom Penh. Probably party it up at Teng Boonma's InterContinental Hotel across town, I concluded. I was vaguely considering grabbing a moto and heading over there for a look-see when, across the street, still drawing whispering youngsters like metal filings to a magnet, I stopped at the wrought-iron gate to a floodlit white mansion that was totally out of place in the wrecked neighborhood, although it wasn't the mansion that had caught my eye. It was the large metal sign affixed to the gate. There was a line of Khmer script that must've said "Beware of Dog," because below it a growling German shepherd was amateurishly painted in profile. But underneath the dog was an askew English translation, a remarkably evocative warning about life in general: "Be Careful With Cruel Dogs."

Over a dinner of unseasoned beef, watching a couple of street cops extorting money from a white guy on a motorbike, I thought, If I was being careful, would I be here?

Early the next morning, before leaving for my appointment at the Canadian embassy, I sat in the café of the Goldiana drinking sweet coffee, reading the front-page story of the *Bangkok Post* that the waitress had handed me. "Still reeling from a July sex scandal reportedly linking the murder of a star actress to the prime minister's wife," Agence France-Press reported, "Cambodia's government yesterday faced further accusations of sleaze as a beautiful karaoke star neared death after the jealous wife of another government official allegedly doused her with nitric acid."

The government official was an undersecretary of state and adviser to Hun Sen named Svay Sitha. Svay was having an affair with a nationally famous, 16-year-old karaoke performer named Tan Samarina. In front of dozens of witnesses, Svay's wife, Khoun Sophal, and two bodyguards had cornered the teenager in a market, wrestled her to the ground and then poured five liters of acid over her head and body. The attack, which burned off the star's face, ears, and fingers, had happened on December 5, but a week and a half later no arrests had been made. A police inspector said "intervention from the top level" had forced him to hand over the evidence he had gathered at the scene to the Council of Ministers.

In the case of the "July sex scandal," the article went on to explain, Cambodia's most famous actress, Piseth Pelika, was gunned down over the summer by two hit men in front of Phnom Penh's Old Market—again before a crowd of witnesses. Rumors had been abundant in Phnom Penh that Prime Minister Hun Sen had been having an affair with the beautiful actress, and so the French magazine *L'Express* sent a team to the capital and uncovered Pelika's diary, which detailed the affair, Pelika's fear that Hun Sen's wife, Bun Rany, was planning to kill her, and a meeting Pelika had had with the police chief, Hok Lundy, who told her to end the relationship because of the danger of incurring the wrath of Bun Rany. *L'Express* also published documented evidence that Hun Sen had given the actress a house and $200,000 cash. Hun Sen promptly blamed the *L'Express* story on Sam Rainsy, a political opponent whose rally alleged henchmen of the PM had interrupted with hand grenades two years before. Pelika's hit men were never found, although Hok Lundy said he was hard on the case.

"This is amazing," I said to the French NGO at the table next to mine who was reading the same article.

"What is amazing?" he replied. "Would it be amazing in America if Hillary Clinton hired the Mafia to shoot down Monica Lewinsky and then Madeleine Albright poured acid over her own husband's lover?"

"I'd say that would be treated as amazing."

"Ah," he said, "but then in America such things don't go on every day. In Cambodia, they are the least amazing things you will hear about."

Canada shared an embassy compound with the Australians on a street called Senei Vannavaut Oum, a well-swept, palm-lined lane just north of Independence Monument. Sliding off my moto taxi I saw that the Canadians did not run what you would call a major operation here. The Australian side looked like serious business—its large, multitiered building had an intelligence agency's air about it, with a tall red radio antenna on its roof and several parabolic dishes aimed at space. The Canuck side looked like a dentist's office on a suburban side street—just a cube of whitewashed walls and venetian blinds. Inside its glass door I found a tiny waiting room that could seat three and a Cambodian secretary named Planeth, who buzzed the door and ushered me into a small open-plan office with a couple of desks and a picture of Jean Chrétien crookedly smiling at me.

A round-faced, bespectacled man in his 30s rose from a desk and shyly shook my hand. He was Bunleng Men, the embassy's development and commercial officer whom Longmuir had put me in touch with via e-mail. Soft-spoken in the Cambodian way, Bunleng explained that he'd briefed his new boss on my project, and then went into a side office to call him. Ambassador Normand Mailhot was Bunleng's opposite—red-faced, with a full head of silver hair and a happy cannon of a voice. He definitely had ambassadorial "presence."

"Oh right, right! Very good, *very* good!" he said, his conversational tone several decibels higher than any I'd heard since I'd arrived. "You're writing a book on—?"

"Generally on Asian organized crime," I reminded him. I took out the articles and photos of Steve and placed them on the table. "Specifically on this Canadian Triad guy who staged his death in the Philippines and then holed up in Macau."

"That's right, yeah, yeah, *yeah-h-h!*" he said, looking closely at Steve's puss.

"I heard he was here last year," I went on, "so I'm looking at the effect of Macau's handover, how some of these 14K guys moved from there to here and into gambling casinos in Koh Kong and Poipet and Sihanoukville, various places in Cambodia."

"O'Smach?" he asked Bunleng.

"O'Smach," Bunleng quietly agreed.

"There's a big controversy over that casino now," Mailhot said, walking over to an American military map on the wall. He pointed to the far north of the country, on the border with Thailand. The map showed a dotted track leaving Siem Reap and heading up through what looked like jungle wilderness to O'Smach, connected on the other side of the Thai border to a modern highway. "They forcibly removed the people, drove them into the hills. Pretty brutal, according to the papers. They're down here protesting now, camped out in the park in front of the National Assembly."

"Who's building the casino up there?" I asked.

"It's a company," Mailhot said. He looked at Bunleng.

"Ly Yung," Bunleng offered, referring to a man whose full name, I would later discover, was Ly Yung Phat, from Koh Kong. "It's a Chinese with Thai connections," Bunleng added. "Same as the one in Poipet."

"Of course it would be," Mailhot said. "They come across from Thailand to gamble. You oughta look into O'Smach. You could trace who the powers are behind that casino. But the thing that you might find—" He looked at the map, smiled. "You might run into some *difficulty*. You might find that it's some highly placed government officials in this country that have an interest in the thing."

I said I knew all about that: Casino Koh Kong was the baby of Pat Supapa—Hun Sen's "adviser"; and then there was Teng Boonma. "So I don't think I'll be too frank about my purposes. See, I know where my man is now—he's got a job with the Philippine police, and I'm headed there next."

"Ha ha *haaa!* I would be a little on the dis*creet* side then!" Mailhot loudly advised me. He looked at Steve's pan again and broke into even louder laughter. "Not the kind of guy you want marrying your sister! *Who-o-a!!!* Ha ha ha!! You'll have a good time, I'll tell you that! I'll let Bunleng carry on here!! Here's my card, stay in touch."

As Gordon Longmuir had promised, Bunleng had done his homework for me. He returned to his desk and set down a pile of papers from his file cabinet. He explained that about a month ago the United Nations and Canada had participated in an international law enforcement conference in Phnom Penh on Cambodian drug trafficking. The report and accompanying documents noted that the situation had "deteriorated significantly over the last few years"; there were now "a number of major organised crime groups based in Cambodia," and the freedom of these groups to do business called into question "the integrity of parts of some enforcement agencies."

"Past year there has been lot of things going on," Bunleng said, looking over his list of contacts while I continued to flip through the papers. "Must be careful who you talk. There has been fighting between colleagues at Anti-Narcotics Commissariat."

"You mean gun fighting? Like in Colombia?"

"Yeah! Yeah!" he laughed. "General Heng Peo, former chief of anti-narcotics, a good man, I think he tried to stop what he see, so military police try arrest him, he run to U.S. embassy for protection. Also a good man is Colonel Skadavy, former with Interpol Police, he is suspended too. Lieutenant General Ngoun Soeur, he used to be deputy chief National Police, and I think he found something, so they suspended him too."

"So what happens, every time one of them does a good job they get suspended?"

He held up a hand. "I no say *that*. You phone and see. Only problem, maybe they change phone or leave city since I talk them." He ran his finger over his list. "Hok Lundy, he not guy you want to talk to," he said seriously. "He's chief of national police."

"Just for the fun of it I might want to," I ventured.

"Yes, but—" He shook his head vehemently.

"Hmmm, Bunleng, what I *don't* want to happen is for someone to say, 'No, sorry, I don't know Steve,' and then call him in Manila. Steve'll be waiting to stick a pound of heroin in my luggage when I go through customs."

"That's right! Because someone knows him and then—" With his hand, Bunleng suggested a man reaching for a phone.

"Gordon mentioned Sum Manit," I said.

"Sum Manit, yes! He is the one for you to speak! He know what's going on! If fellow here, maybe he know him."

Bunleng recited the minister's past and current positions, a long list that called into question the notion that not one honest man could survive in the Cambodian government. Sum Manit obviously could, although, judging by the switcheroos Bunleng had just related, the odds were slim he could be effective, and he was possibly kept in place as window dressing for foreign donor countries. He was currently the secretary of state in charge of the Council of Ministers, the secretary-general of the Administrative Reform Council, the chief of the newly formed Anti-Corruption Unit, as well as in charge of putting together the Millennial Celebrations at Angkor Wat. "He *used* to be secretary-general of the National Authority to Combat Drugs," Bunleng laughed, "but they give it to Em Sam Man. Em Sam Man very close to Hun Sen. All I know, Em Sam Man doesn't have to worry much."

I deduced that meant Mr. Em didn't have to worry about either the police or the Triads. "Gordon told me I should go to Koh Kong, too," I said.

"Oh yeah, yeah, yeah!! Koh Kong, that's the place!! Koh Kong you see the crime from Burma, China, Thailand, Macau. Must be careful there, though. Very remote. No help for you there on Cambodia side if trouble, because cut off." He thought a moment, contemplating the end of his list. "For Koh Kong, Sam Rainsy you could talk. He is the head of the opposition party, always fighting against casinos and Chinese mafia. Reporters like him because he say Hun Sen, Teng Boonma—all mafia. Also, good idea before you start, talk to *Phnom Penh Post,* English newspaper. Editor is Michael Hayes, he tell you the name of a reporter so you no make mistake."

I wasn't crazy about seeing a story appear in the *Phnom Penh Post* announcing that a reporter named Terry Gould was in town looking for a Triad official named Steven Wong, so I made the decision to be very general with Michael Hayes. Over the phone I told him I was here on a book about Chinese organized crime, and he gave me over to a Canadian reporter named Phelim Kyne, who'd covered the subject in Taiwan for 10 years and spoke fluent Mandarin. Kyne told me I'd have to watch my step around that beat and said I should meet him in a couple of hours over at the Foreign Correspondents Club, half a dozen blocks away on Sisowath Quay, on the banks of the Tonle Sap River and just across from the Royal Palace.

It sounded like a terrific locale so I moto'ed over right away, intending to read through Bunleng's reports while I waited, but I wound up sitting on a stool drinking Angkor beers and simply gawking over the banister towards the junction of the Tonle Sap and Mekong rivers. In the crux of the two vast rivers sat a long spit of green farmland grazed by Brahman cattle. Beyond that were rice paddies, palms, and village huts all the way to the horizon. It smelled like tropical heaven—of flowers, water, and turned earth—unadulterated by car pollution because, at the time, there were almost no cars in Phnom Penh. For all the causes of its arrested development, Phnom Penh was still one of the only capitals in the world where you could look from its quiet heart to countryside unblighted by modern suburbs, squatter slums, or highways—the only one that hadn't jumped the banks of the river it was founded on.

You could also smoke marijuana in public, which a couple of lazy-looking fellows in T-shirts and shorts were doing on the back veranda. I took my second beer and walked beneath the spinning fans towards them. The slackers' stoned view of the city was even more magical. Up the ochre alley, past wrought-iron colonial balconies, beyond the russet National Museum, King Sihanouk's Royal Palace spiked the air with a forest of golden pagoda needles and a flock of winglike orange roofs tipped by graceful *naga* serpents. With a cooling river breeze clacking the palm fronds, the setting reminded me of Clara's Oriental dream in *Nutcracker Suite*.

I sat down at a table and then noticed the long line of legless beggars on the National Museum lawn. I thought, It *is* only a dream. Cambodia was synonymous with the worst that could happen in life because it had all happened here: wars, revolution, mass evacuations, and mass murder; starvation, invasion, foreign occupation, and a train of dictatorships and coups; millions of land mines that left thousands of people limbless; terrorism, disease, poverty, two generations of children without education, and, in the last year, an influx of Asia's most wanted criminals. These crooks and killers now worked hand in hand with the country's corrupt and incompetent bureaucracy—who themselves pocketed 70 percent of all government revenue and sanctioned every crime under the sun save the petty thievery of the poor.

Before leaving home I'd read through volumes that tried to answer the Big Question: Why Cambodia? Most authors, such as the American scholar

David P. Chandler and the *New York Times* correspondent Henry Kamm, viewed Khmer history, ancient and modern, as dominated by a cult of personality similar to the Philippines. This helped explain the pervasiveness of patronage, corruption, and the willing subordination of the Khmer people to despots, from Jayavaram II who in A.D. 802 proclaimed himself a "God King," to King Sihanouk who in the mid-1960s said "I am Cambodia," to Hun Sen who in 1999 told a sympathetic biographer, "I am a nation. I cannot listen to anyone's advice." In addition to this monocratic heritage, the Khmer Kingdom was the luckless victim of forces beyond its control, the first of which was simple geography. Situated between two powerful, antagonistic neighbors—Thailand and Vietnam—Cambodia's leaders had always found it necessary to ally themselves with one country against the other, keeping the nation in a perpetual state of tension. The second (and literal) force was a century of French colonialism. Like the Spanish and Americans in the Philippines, the French had cultivated a tiny corrupt elite at the expense of Cambodia's increasingly impoverished masses. And third, colonialism's terrible consequence: the 20-year war in Vietnam, which had created a firestorm so powerful that Cambodia had been sucked into its vortex and spit out in charred embers.

That era of Cambodia's tragedy I was very familiar with, having begun to worry about being caught in the storm about the time I realized that if I didn't learn how to handle equations I'd be asked to learn how to handle Claymore mines. Indeed, in 10th grade I remember reading accounts in the *New York Times* of the tubby playboy Norodom Sihanouk, and the mischief he was causing America's Vietnam war planners. Back in 1965, Sihanouk, in power since 1941, had become convinced the American-backed South Vietnamese and Thais were plotting against him. And so, in time-honored Cambodian fashion, he'd tilted towards their enemy, North Vietnam. As it turned out, that policy not only ensured the battlefront would be extended to his country but it exacerbated the already extant rifts in Cambodian society. The right-wing Cambodian army and the urban elite were infuriated by his new alliance; at the same time the left-wing intelligentsia were not in the least placated, as Sihanouk allowed no public dissent and arrested and imprisoned those who now felt emboldened to speak against the rampant corruption that kept him in power and plagued the entire nation. Meanwhile, in the countryside, the impoverished peasants continued to view the rulers in Phnom Penh as decadent oppressors who danced the night away in discos while they struggled without health care, schools, or aid for their primitive methods of agriculture. It didn't help that Sihanouk had then decided to embark on a bizarre movie career, producing, directing, and starring in nine awful films that cemented his image as a self-aggrandizing dilettante, literally fiddling (he wrote the string-heavy musical scores to his films) while the country burned.

In 1967, about the time I entered college, a peasant uprising broke out, supported by Communists whom Sihanouk named Khmer Rouge, or Red Cambodians, and led by the Paris-educated Saloth Sar, later known to the world by his nom de guerre, Pol Pot. Perceiving the greatest threat to his power as now coming from the left, Sihanouk swung his ship of state to the right, giving the army a free hand to brutally suppress both the uprising in the countryside and dissent among intellectuals in the capital. In order to placate the North Vietnamese, however, he continued to allow Communist military aid to land in the port of Sihanoukville and be transported across Cambodia to their sanctuaries on the Vietnamese border. Corrupt army generals, while suppressing the peasants and Khmer Rouge, gladly hired out their trucks to carry the Communist equipment, which then made its way into the hands of the Khmer Rouge they were fighting.

On March 18, 1970, Sihanouk, on a trip to France, was overthrown by his pro-American prime minister, Lon Nol. The king fled to China, where, not surprisingly, he reversed himself again, forming a United Front with the Khmer Rouge and their allies, the North Vietnamese. Six weeks after the Lon Nol coup, American forces invaded Cambodia and wave after wave of B-52s began bombing the countryside, killing untold thousands of civilians, which sent American college campuses (mine among them) into an orgy of protests and student strikes. Rather than fight against overwhelming odds, the Khmer Rouge withdrew into the heart of Cambodia, in June conquering the town of Siem Reap in the north and its adjoining Angkor temples, the symbol of Cambodia's past greatness. Within months the KR controlled half the country and began massively recruiting young peasants to fight in the war against Lon Nol.

That was when another long-lasting figure of Cambodian history got his start. Hun Sen was then an 18-year-old peasant in the province of Kampong Cham, east of Phnom Penh. He joined a local front of the Khmer Rouge and, fighting along the Vietnamese border, rose rapidly through the ranks, eventually becoming the KR's chief of regimental staff for the area, with the rank of lieutenant colonel. In his official version of events, Hun Sen has painted himself as a royalist patriot who fought merely to restore Sihanouk to the throne, largely ignorant of the ultimate plans of his superiors. On April 17, 1975, entering Phnom Penh with the victorious Khmer Rouge, Hun Sen lost his left eye to a piece of shrapnel, and ever since has claimed that he was in the hospital recuperating when the Khmer Rouge's slaughter of civilians commenced, leaving him completely ignorant of what his side was up to. The happy coincidence enabled Hun Sen to serve the KR loyally for the next two years, his conscience clear.

It's hard to see how he missed the mass murder. The Khmer Rouge declared their day of victory "The Glorious Seventeenth of April," and celebrated by force-marching into the countryside two million Phnom Penhois, plus every civilian in every provincial capital and village with more than a few hundred people. Most white-collar professionals were murdered, hospitals and schools were closed, modern conveniences like refrigerators, telephones, radios, and televisions were swept into piles in the streets and sledge hammered. Money, postal services, private property, Western medicine, formal education, and religious practice were abolished. The country was completely closed to the outside world and 1975 was marked as "Year Zero" in a plan of radical Maoist social engineering whose professed end was to turn Cambodia into a self-sufficient country of huge agriculture communes where everyone lived and labored equally.

As all this was getting under way, Sihanouk accepted the invitation to return to Phnom Penh. The Khmer Rouge welcomed him as king, then imprisoned him in his Royal Palace, eventually killing three of his sons, several of his grandchildren, and most of his entourage. The leaders of the Khmer Rouge then moved into the villas of the former elite, from which they issued anonymous orders under the sinister name "The Angkar"—the organization. The entire country was turned into a slave labor camp, with most Cambodians laboring 12 to 15 hours a day digging irrigation canals and preparing fields. Those who offered any complaint were executed, even if their complaint was an inability to work because of sickness. The result was "the killing fields." In the four years of Khmer Rouge rule, two million people died out of a total population of eight million.

Like all psychotic dictatorships, as things began to go wrong the Angkar became suspicious that its own ranks were filled with traitors and counterrevolutionaries. In 1977 the Angkar sent military units into historically disputed border areas with Vietnam; Vietnam retaliated by a limited invasion of Cambodian soil; and to eliminate disloyalty in the face of a brewing war with a former ally, the Angkar carried out murderous purges of their Khmer Rouge followers. Some KR leaders at the border fled for their lives to Vietnam. Hun Sen, receiving word that he was to be executed, was among these defectors.

From the cadres of defectors the affronted Vietnamese chose leaders to head what they called the United Front for National Salvation. The 25-year-old Hun Sen was appointed head of a 20,000-strong force and joined the Vietnamese when they launched a full-scale invasion on Christmas Day

1978. Two weeks later they took Phnom Penh, and Hun Sen was appointed foreign minister of a Communist puppet regime, the newly named People's Republic of Kampuchea. Within two years, he was deputy prime minister, and in 1985 he became prime minister.

Meanwhile, the West crazily threw its support behind the Khmer Rouge, viewing Vietnam's invasion as somehow worse than the Pol Pot regime it toppled. Backed by the U.S., the Khmer Rouge established itself in enclaves along the border with Thailand, and kept its seat in the U.N. as the official government. In an astonishing marriage of opposites, Sihanouk, once again in exile in China, joined with his former Khmer Rouge jailers and an anti-Communist conservative politician named Son Sann in a war to topple Hun Sen. As usual, the losers in this new conflict were the Cambodian people: foreign observers noted massive corruption in Hun Sen's government, with most aid from donor countries winding up on the plates of the Communist elite.

In 1989, the collapse of Vietnam's main backer, the Soviet Union, altered the dynamic of this conflict, and Hanoi—cut off from its $1 billion-a-year in aid—withdrew its troops. Hun Sen, nothing if not sensitive to ways of keeping himself in power, came to an agreement with Sihanouk in 1991 to end the fighting under the auspices of the United Nations Transitional Authority of Cambodia (UNTAC). A year later, the Khmer Rouge reneged on the agreement, Hun Sen followed suit, and the war was back on. UNTAC soon realized that the best bet for peace was to organize elections in the midst of a ceasefire. The chief opposing political forces (exclusive of the crazed Khmer Rouge) were divided between Sihanouk's son, Prince Norodom Ranariddh—a man with professed liberal beliefs who headed the National Front for an Independent, Neutral, Peaceful and Cooperative Cambodia (the French acronym was Funcinpec)—and Hun Sen's Communist Cambodian People's Party, the CPP. Through his military control of most of Cambodia, Hun Sen was able to sabotage the creation of UNTAC's "neutral political atmosphere." He instigated widespread political violence against Ranariddh, murdering his campaign workers and ambushing his rallies. Despite these tactics, in May 1993 Ranariddh won a plurality of the National Assembly seats. Hun Sen refused to accept the result and staged a secession of the provinces along the Vietnamese border. In September, Sihanouk (now king again), dreading another plunge into civil war, awarded Hun Sen the position of second prime minister and Ranariddh the position of first prime minister.

Essentially, this left Cambodia with two governments. Sam Rainsy, a French-educated liberal economist, became the minister of finance under

Ranariddh, but Hun Sen, having established a system of corruption that ensured his support among the old-guard Communist generals, held control of the majority of the army—the real power in the country—enabling the second prime minister to torpedo Rainsy's Western-style reforms. Once again, the country teetered on the brink of chaos. Declaring that the first prime minister was not stalwart enough in his struggle against the second, Rainsy left Ranariddh's cabinet and formed his own political party, maintaining his vocal (some said reckless) opposition to Hun Sen—who seemed to have had enough of the ballsy economist. On March 30, 1997, assailants threw a cluster of hand grenades into an anti-CPP rally held in front of the National Assembly, killing 16 and severely wounding 150. Rainsy survived only because his own bodyguard, standing directly in front of him, took the full force of one of the grenades.*

The final showdown came on July 5, 1997, when, financed by a million dollars in gold and cash from the accused drug dealer Teng Boonma, Hun Sen staged a military coup against all opposition forces. Over the next two days the headquarters and homes of many opposition party members were ransacked and more than a hundred of Ranariddh's and Rainsy's aides were tortured and murdered, including Ranariddh's intelligence chief, whose tongue was torn out when he refused to reveal the whereabouts of one of Ranariddh's generals.

The prince and the economist fled into exile and the country was plunged back into civil war, with Ranariddh's forces fighting along the Thai border in the north. Two months after the coup, on September 8, the *Bangkok Post* ran the headline "Cambodia Emerges as First Narco-state," quoting a Western anti-narcotics agent as saying, "It is worse than Burma in many ways. In Rangoon, the government controls drug traffickers. But in Cambodia we think the drug traffickers control the government."

By then the *Post* had sent a team of investigative journalists to Phnom Penh to look into the links between drug traffickers and the CPP, as well

---

*An American citizen with the International Republican Institute was wounded in the attack, and so members of the U.S. Senate Foreign Relations Committee and the House International Relations Committee traveled to Cambodia to investigate the massacre. A final report on the investigation was drawn up on September 21, 1999, by James P. Doran, a staff member for East Asian Affairs. It concluded that "members of Hun Sen's Bodyguard Force participated in the planning and execution of the March 30, 1997 attack. Hun Sen, being only one of two people with authority over the Bodyguard Force, must have known and approved of the attack. . . . It is my opinion that sufficient evidence exists in order to yield *a very obvious conclusion: Hun Sen and his Bodyguard Forces were behind this crime*" (italics in original).

as between drug trafficking and the causes of the coup. The *Post* team discovered that "the two most powerful men accused of drug trafficking are close to Hun Sen and travel on diplomatic passports." The first was the aforementioned Teng Boonma; the second was an export magnate by the name of Mong Rethy, "an official adviser to Hun Sen himself," who had contributed $45 million "to various projects supported by Hun Sen." The *Post* reported that back in May 1997, Cambodian police had come across seven tons of marijuana in export containers belonging to the Mong Rethy Import-Export Company. Ranariddh's secretary of state for the Interior Ministry, Ho Sok, launched an investigation, but Hun Sen intervened, warning that anyone attempting to arrest Mong Rethy "better wear a steel helmet," and dispatched a platoon of CPP soldiers to protect the businessman. When Hun Sen launched his coup two months later he ordered Ho Sok arrested. Hun Sen's troops caught up with Ho as he was trying to seek asylum in the compound of the Australian/Canadian embassy. They dragged him to Hok Lundy's police headquarters, where he was tortured and murdered. "Hun Sen has since blocked all attempts to probe the killing or the drug shipments," the *Post* reported, and to this day neither have been investigated by the government.

After the coup, Hun Sen ordered Ranariddh tried in absentia on charges of rebellion, gun smuggling, and collaboration with the Khmer Rouge. Not surprisingly, Ranariddh was found guilty, and by March 1998, with his forces clinging to toeholds around O'Smach, it appeared that he had had enough. Through his father he sent peace feelers to Hun Sen, and, in return for a pardon, he agreed to return to mainstream Cambodian life. In April, Pol Pot died (or was murdered) and in July, triumphant on all fronts, Hun Sen allowed elections. Amidst widespread allegations of fraud and murder, the Cambodian People's Party won 64 seats, Funcinpec 43 seats, and Sam Rainsy's party 15 seats. Again, Hun Sen's allies in the election were the likes of Teng Boonma, who backed him with $7 million, plus other accused drug dealers, gambling-casino gangsters, and the thousands of civil servants, policemen, and soldiers who had been vastly profiting from his regime through everything from drug trafficking to the illegal logging of the now quickly disappearing rain forest.

Finally, on November 23, 1998, in what Sam Rainsy called "a self-interested and pusillanimous sellout," Ranariddh entered into a coalition government with Hun Sen, accepting the largely ceremonial post of president of the National Assembly and a minority position for several of his legislators in Hun Sen's cabinet. A month later, promised amnesty, the last of the ragtag Khmer Rouge surrendered to Hun Sen's forces. It was six weeks after that,

Valentine's Day 1999, that I found out Steve had been present in Cambodia during this historic year of reconciliation, when the Kingdom entered its new phase of stable gangsterism.

I didn't notice Phelim Kyne when he came into the Foreign Correspondents Club. I suppose I had been expecting a Chinese Canadian named Fei Lim Kine. The Gaelic-named Phelim, however, eventually noticed the stranger in town and came striding up—a square-jawed handsome Ontarian in a loose cotton shirt and jeans. He shoved a folded napkin under my table leg—"these wobbly tables here drive me crazy"—and ordered us something to eat, chatting in Khmer with the waitress, then turned and conversed in Mandarin with a Chinese reporter at the next table. Looking out to the view, I remarked that I almost wished the inevitable building boom that accompanied peace would hold off a while and the dreamlike rurality of the capital would last. Phelim said I wasn't alone. *GQ* had just published an article on the FCC, calling it one of the best bars in the world, and wistfully lamented that the dolorous ambience probably wouldn't endure the peace.

"When I got here a year ago I thought the same thing," Phelim said. "Two years and it's all over, Bangkok's just around the corner. But if you look at the last ten years, every time they've been building to a boom, something happens. So I got into the Khmer way of thinking: things might seem calm today, but something bad is gonna happen tomorrow."

"Always look on the dark side," I cracked.

"Yeah well, that's the attitude you get covering this place," he shrugged. "A mob catches a thief? They torture and kill him right on the street. The police stand there and watch. Why interrupt? It's Phnom Penh's public sport, the nicest people join in—middle-class ladies, art students. Nobody trusts the court system, it's thoroughly corrupt, so might as well have a party and kill the guy. Tourists won't put up with that. Also, you go just outside of town here, the road system disintegrates—there's no tourist transportation, nothing gets fixed because corruption's so ubiquitous, the money to fix it gets pocketed. They have some nice beaches in Sihanoukville, so what did they do? They dumped toxic waste from Taiwan right near them. I actually broke that story."

I liked him more every second, but I could tell right away he was an extremely smart journalist on a news beat, so I kept to my resolve to stay very general. "Now you got these Triad guys taking over towns like Sihanoukville and Koh Kong," I said.

"Right, because this is the place to come to do it. The new administration in Macau is saying, 'Hey guys, we're gonna bring the broom in here.'

Just like Hong Kong in '97. I was in Taiwan for ten years before here, the Triad there is the Bamboo Union. They declared the Triads persona non grata too. The Bamboo Union chief is a guy named Chen Chi-li. He's living here now with impunity."

"Did you get to interview him?"

"I would have but Michael Hayes is reluctant to do anything on him. Because those guys will just get somebody to come up on the street and kill you. Michael says, 'Hey, I gotta walk home from work every day.' Same with the Koh Kong murders. I expressed an interest to go down there when it happened. Even the dailies didn't touch it, they wrote it off as a dispute over prostitutes, a typical Koh Kong thing."

"It was more than that."

"It was way more than that, but no one's touched it. I said, 'Let's go down there'—it was like, 'Uhhh, that could be dangerous.' He's right. Depending how far you want to get into whatever you're writing about, you'll have to watch yourself. With the court system here, these guys have no restraints. See, we can write about Hun Sen, he'll just sue. There's no percentage for him in killing Western journalists. I pretty much write what I want about corruption. Back in June, I did this three-part series on corruption and its various aspects—"

"They let you get away with threatening their pocketbooks?" I asked.

"That's a whole other story in itself," Phelim said, because, surprisingly, the *Phnom Penh Post* was relatively unfettered in what it could print regarding politicians. There were two reasons for that: it was an English weekly, which not many Cambodians read; and Hun Sen, forced to beg on the streets of donor countries, recognized that a semifree English press, like a semilegitimate election, was an unavoidable evil that had to be allowed to appease Western donor countries. Thus, Hun Sen trumpeted the country's "press freedom" in every conference with donor countries. "The local Cambodian press is under a lot of pressure, though," Phelim went on. "They're periodically threatened, there've been bribery scandals regarding reporters. But so far, we've been able to print the truth about the government without too much interference—not that it's changed anything."

After lunch I went with Phelim back to the French colonial office building of the *Post*, a few blocks from the Canadian embassy. It was ringed by a high metal fence, and the windows were barred. Going through back issues, I saw that Phelim had been permitted to write amazing stories. He'd exposed it all: the laws of the country were ignored, the courts were compliant to political pressure and bribes, most officials were openly on the take, and influence almost always counted over merit. Still, exposure in the *Phnom Penh Post* was mere expression: it hadn't changed a thing.

To understand why Steve had chosen Cambodia after Macau, I knew that (as in the Philippines) I needed to understand Cambodia's special brand of corruption. And so I took a year's worth of *Phnom Penh Post* issues to my hotel, I got my balky air conditioner to lower the temperature to the mid-80s, and began reading Phelim's oeuvre.

Cambodian corruption, it became obvious to me by evening, was no ad hoc arrangement, but a formal system run along the principles of organized crime. At its most fundamental level, I knew, organized crime was a licensing system, a sure means of governance that kept track of who was doing what and where. A controlling don or dragon head, through his far-flung subordinates, awarded the rights to engage in illegal activities in particular spheres or territories, expecting tribute in return and providing protection from the law. Any freelancer who started up some activity—say, a gambling float or a cathouse—pretty quickly met the enforcer responsible for collecting from similar operations in his area. If the freelancer ignored the licensing system, his next visit would be from men who knew how to make him pay, teaching him the usual hard lesson of how "organized" organized crime can be.

Because the cooperation of corrupt officials was necessary for the smooth running of this licensing system, official corruption in the West was, of necessity, kept secret, and therefore hard to study. Not in Cambodia. Cambodian corruption was a hundred-power enlargement of what took place on a much less visible scale in most other countries. It followed the universal MO: *the rise to power is always accompanied by the return of favors,* the built-in corruption of all politics—even where politicians are not criminals themselves. It became blatant where criminals—or those who were tied to criminals—helped politicians achieve and maintain power. Cambodia operated on this open base of criminality.

In this it followed another global pattern: the poorer the country, the more likely official corruption is going to be run in the open, since constituents are powerless to do anything about it. To say the least, Cambodia was a very poor country—the poorest in Southeast Asia—with a 1999 budget of about $500 million to take care of 12 million people. (Seventy percent of the budget came from donor nations. Half of that budget went to the military.) In 1999, the cost of living was about $150 a month. The average government wage was $20 a month. Even the most senior generals and politicians officially earned only enough to cover the minimum monthly cost of living.

The ruling Cambodian People's Party appointed almost all the officials in customs, law enforcement, the military, the judiciary, as well as the bureaucracies in city, provincial, and federal affairs. Most government employees received their appointments either by outright purchase (bribing the men who made the appointment), or because of some act of service that had helped the CPP get elected. Thus, while all the appointees owed their jobs to the government, the government also owed its power base to the appointees.

Given that jobs were so poorly paid, people wanting to do business in Cambodia—legitimate or illegitimate—had to bribe officials from several fiefdoms who wanted to top up their salaries. Businessmen had to pay a politician to get a working visa, then pay a government bureaucrat to issue a business license, then pay a customs official to sign off on a shipment, then pay a policeman to guard the goods, then pay a soldier to see the goods across the border. The people who took the bribes then paid a portion to their bosses, who paid a portion to *their* bosses, and so on up the line. Eventually, a cut of all the bribes paid out by all the businessmen and criminals in Cambodia made its way into the coffers of the CPP, controlled at the top by Prime Minister Hun Sen, and just below the top by all the senior party bureaucracy. The party officials deducted a portion so they could live in comfort (Hun Sen owned one villa near Independence Monument, and a sprawling Corinthian-pillared palace in the suburbs), then wisely invested some of the remaining bribe money to build the odd school, canal, or road in areas necessary for the officials to "win" elections.

Corruption, of course, was also why the Triads were drawn to Cambodia's Wild West gambling industry. While there was a rigorously enforced law forbidding Cambodians from entering casinos (effectively making it a monopoly of the Chinese-Thai Triads), there was no law which set out the rules for the *running* of gambling casinos. Instead, casinos were run under the personal stewardship of CPP officials—all falling under the purview of the police chief, Hok Lundy. There were 11 luxury gambling casinos operating in the nation, and though the casinos earned hundreds of millions of dollars in revenue each year, they paid almost nothing in "normal" taxes. According to the opposition economist Sam Rainsy, all their taxes were paid out in bribes. (Bribes naturally figured heavily in the all-but-sanctioned Cambodian drug trade, although, at the upper reaches of power, these bribes were called political donations.)

Cambodia had had laws on the books prohibiting these shenanigans since 1993. Articles, 37, 38, and 54 of the Compendium of Cambodian Laws, drawn up with the help of UNTAC, provided stiff penalties for conviction of taking bribes or embezzling revenue. But in the seven years that these statutes had been in effect, no one had been charged. The practices of bribery and extortion were so ingrained that a survey of Cambodian attitudes in 1998 showed that 84 percent regarded corruption as a "normal" way of doing business. Fifty-nine percent thought vote-buying was perfectly acceptable.

I encountered the human victims of this open-air corruption the next morning. I rode a moto from my hotel up Sihanouk Boulevard, around the Independence Monument traffic circle fronting Hun Sen's white city villa, and up Sotheros towards the National Assembly building, a gorgeous Khmer structure with immense gilted eaves carved with the Kingdom's eloquent seal: an urn engulfed in flames. The O'Smach demonstrators were camped in the park across the street from the National Assembly, in the exact spot where Sam Rainsy's demonstration had been interrupted a couple of years before.

My moto driver, a Sam Rainsy supporter named Sophion, shouted "*Johm riab sua!*" and a weathered face shone at me from the crowd. He was a middle-aged man in a T-shirt and shorts named Kao Sophal, the leader of the peasant protesters. Sophion explained that Kao used to be a rice farmer in O'Smach. He once owned a thatch house, a couple of buffalo, and about $50 in savings. Now he had nothing but the torn letter he waved like a limp wing in the direction of the National Assembly. He'd been trying to get the letter recognized as an affidavit by one of the legislators inside, or even deliver it to Hun Sen himself if he happened to take a stroll from his nearby villa.

Unfortunately, proximity to power hadn't helped him much. The protesters had been in the park for weeks, ignored by all who made the rules in Cambodia, with no shelter, no water, no toilets, just the thin clothes on their backs and the checked cotton *kramas* on their heads to keep off the tropical sun.

Kao's story, Sophion explained in translation, was braided into a two-year slice of Cambodian history—typical of any in the last 30. After Hun Sen had deposed Prince Ranariddh in the 1997 coup, troops loyal to Funcinpec had retreated to their enclaves around O'Smach. When Hun Sen's troops moved up during the dry season in pursuit, the civilians of O'Smach crossed to the refugee camp on the Thai side to escape the fighting. A year later, when the civil war ended and the election was concluded, the O'Smach villagers returned home to rumors that the Phnom Penh government believed they had given up title to their land because they had favored Funcinpec against the CPP.

In the last week of August 1999, several Cambodian government officials and two representatives from an ethnic-Chinese-Thai development
company arrived in O'Smach. The company's representatives, Ly Yung Phat
and Lim Heng, summoned Kao and other village leaders to a meeting in the
town's square and explained that they would like to open negotiations to
purchase the town site. Their intention was to build a huge casino and five-
star hotel, and, in return for moving out of the way, each of the 500 families
in O'Smach would be paid the equivalent of a year's wages (roughly $300)
for their farms and houses, plus given a 15-by-40 meter plot of land in a new
location two kilometers away. When Kao made the point that most of the
residents of O'Smach farmed highly productive fields of several hectares
each, the local government officials replied that the vast development would
yield benefits far greater than rice farming—over a million dollars a day.
That was the end of the negotiations. The Cambodian army moved in,
burned the town and drove the villagers into a mine-infested, malarial
swamp that had been staked out for them. Within days, one of the villagers
stepped on a mine and was blown to bits, several others lost limbs, and
malaria was soon prevalent in the new "community."

By the beginning of October 1999, the amount offered by Ly and Lim
to the citizens of O'Smach had been reduced by two-thirds, and even this
hadn't been handed over. And so Kao Sophal decided to lead a hundred of
his townsmen on a 400-kilometer protest trek to Phnom Penh. When they
arrived and set up camp in the park, the vocal opposition party leader and
former minister of finance Sam Rainsy showed up and addressed their rally,
calling them "victims of the government's partnership with the mafia."

The peasants around me believed that in full. They all knew that a similar evacuation of villagers by Ly Yung Phat around Poipet had turned the
area into a muddy hell of squalor and misery, where drug addiction and
child prostitution were the norm and where multimillionaire Triad bosses
had most customs officials, cops, and soldiers on their payroll. Remote from
Phnom Penh and out of the reach of Thai law enforcement, much that was
illegal in the rest of the world could take place with impunity in these
instant border cities.

I took a picture of Kao Sophal holding up his letter in front of the
Assembly Building, and asked what he thought of the prime minister. I'd
expected that he would have expressed sentiments filled with revolutionary
resentments, but I heard quite the opposite. "He want stop the bad things,"
Sophion translated, "but bad people around him no let. Hun Sen good for
Cambodia—strong, end fighting. Now must stop the bad people. He can do,
so we here to say, 'Do.'"

When I eventually met Hun Sen face-to-face at a private dinner in Siem Reap, I saw how the man Kao Sophal considered "strong" had inspired a faith, perhaps misplaced, that he would "stop the bad people." His strength, spectacularly on display, was certainly impressive to Cambodians. Everywhere he went, Samdech ("My Lord Daddy") Hun Sen was accompanied fore and aft by a dozen motorcycles and a couple of pickups filled with his well-armed personal Bodyguard Force. But his panache came from more than firepower. At 47, Hun Sen was athletically trim, his face framed by an intellectual's gold-wire glasses, and he had an endearingly lopsided way of smiling, as if half his mouth had been frozen in the dentist's chair—the result of the shrapnel that had plucked out his eye and damaged some facial nerves. Entering the dinner party at which I was a guest, the raven-haired prime minister fixed me with his good eye, greeted me warmly in broken English, then smiled and pronammed. I returned the pronam, impressed by his undeniable magnetism. Then, as he moved up the line of well-wishers with his uniformed entourage, I reminded myself of his public explanation for the grenade attack on Sam Rainsy in the park where Kao Sophal protested: Rainsy had staged the slaughterous assault on himself to garner public support.

December 21, the day after Macau's handover to China, I packed my bag with pictures of the Paper Fan and visited Sum Manit in his office just beside Hun Sen's at the Council of Ministers building on Pochentong Road. Sum Manit's desk was piled high with stacks of press releases and brochures for the upcoming Millennial Celebration at Angkor Wat. Behind him were two windows with white silk curtains tied in the middle and, behind that, translucent lace. Thus haloed in white, the 70-year-old Sum Manit looked to me like a cross between the Dalai Lama and Nelson Mandela—an impression which increased with every word he uttered on government corruption.

That morning Hun Sen had held a televised forum on corruption in the grand ballroom of Teng Boonma's InterContinental Hotel. Flanked by his generals, ministers, and senior cops, Hun Sen had addressed an audience of mostly foreign businessmen—gambling casino magnates, lumber barons, and textile sweatshop owners—promising to promote accountability and root out official malfeasance in the Kingdom. "If someone wants to squeeze you for money, I can find them, just tell me," he declared. Unfortunately, Sum Manit, the head of the Anti-Corruption Unit—who more than any other of Hun Sen's shady officials should have been at that forum—had not been able to attend.

"Because I am very busy, busy on *this!*" he told me, waving impatiently at the Millennium brochures and a matching wall poster showing the stupas of the central wat at Angkor. "I'm having a lot of headaches because of this! The prime minister has appointed me to this in the midst of my anti-corruption duties. It is taking all my time now."

Perhaps not coincidentally, I thought.

I watched the small gray-haired man in shirtsleeves rub his face, as if washing it of the burdens of trying to organize an event for tens of thousands of citizens and VIPs at the end of a 300-kilometer road that was then being called the world's longest motocross track. I suspected that his tension was due in part to the well-known fact that much of the money he was sending to Angkor was draining into the bottomless pit of Cambodian People's Party corruption.

After spending about 40 minutes discussing his travails running the National Authority to Combat Drugs I asked how someone of his integrity and honesty had risen so high in a system that was so strange and confused.

"Well look, I cannot say that I have been a hundred percent clean in my life," he laughed. "In my youth—" He paused, smiled to himself. "But since my twenties I have been clean. You know, you *must* be clean when dealing in that field of drugs. Because at the time of my appointment as head of the NACD it would seem that there were some high-ranking people who were actually involved in the trafficking." He sighed in exhaustion. "It is very difficult to make change. In Cambodia we have an expression: 'Like throwing water on the head of the duck.' The water cannot go in the feathers, it just drops out."

At mention of the waterproof duck, I decided to bring the discussion around to Steve. "It's Gordon Longmuir's feeling that you're the one to talk to about this," I said, handing over a two-page letter from Anne Collins that contained Steve's CV in bullet form—from date of birth to date of death, from criminal charges to height, build, and tattoos. I watched Sum Manit as he read the pages carefully, with a cop's eye, jotting notes in the margins beside the brief description of Steve's scam on Negros. Finally he looked up at me.

"I believe my man was here in 1998 and that you might have run into him," I continued. "You were the head of the National Authority to Combat Drugs then. When China took over Hong Kong many Chinese Triads moved out. Similarly, yesterday, China took over Macau. I think you know that some Triads have moved to Cambodia. You're familiar with the Triad called the 14K?"

"Oh yes, yes."

"I want to show you a picture of Steven Lik Man Wong," I said. "He is thirty-five years old now, and this is him in 1992, in New York City. He would have been in Cambodia in 1998 and perhaps 1999, although he has since left. He would have changed his name, of course."

Sum Manit took the photo and studied it long and carefully. He looked over the letter again, running his finger down to the details on Steve's physical description.

"Yes, yes, I think I saw this man," he said.

I waited, breathless, as he went back to studying Steve. Then he looked up, almost apologetically.

"But I don't remember where."

I asked if perhaps he had an alias for Steve. He shook his head. "I have no information about him, but, yes, this photo looks familiar to me."

Well, there it was. *Almost* something to go on, which was as good as nothing.

As I was packing up I mentioned that Longmuir had advised me to head down to Koh Kong via Sihanoukville. "Because there might be some leads for me down there. What do you think?"

He looked down at his hands for a length of time without answering. I wondered what was up and stopped fussing with my shoulder pack. Finally he said, "We have information that this group you mention is down there. In Sihanoukville there is some business—passports, drugs—it is a port, you see. In Koh Kong, there is also business."

"So if a 14K Triad came to Cambodia from Macau, would it be likely he would have headed there?"

Again he looked at his hands without saying anything.

"To Koh Kong?" I broke the silence.

"It would be very likely," he said. "From here, when do you go?"

"Three, four days," I said.

"I think you know Sam Rainsy. He is not in a position to act, so that is why he is in a position to talk. He talks *a lot,* but sometimes he knows what he talks. It would be better for me— You see, I am in a most sensitive position with that area."

I didn't press him on it, recalling what he had said to me at the start of our conversation: "Don't get me killed."

The next day I met with Rainsy in a restaurant in the Riverside Hotel, on the banks of the Tonle Sap, a block north of the Foreign Correspondents Club. To say that Rainsy talked a lot didn't even come close to the mark. That morning the tall, wiry economist had held a news conference in a meeting room downstairs, during which he'd accused many of Hun Sen's senior people of working hand in hand with the Macau Triads to run the casinos, traffic drugs, and launder profits through "fifty phony banks in Phnom Penh." When I now mentioned that Sum Manit was sincerely working to change all that, Rainsy replied that he didn't stand a chance. "His officials are afraid to walk *into* the casinos!" he declared, his eyes burning into mine with radical righteousness. "They will get *killed.* The CPP policemen protect the casino owners and threaten the investigators! It is a ridiculous and astonishing situation. There is an Interpol report on Cambodia. Of the world's most wanted—"

"Yeah, I know about that one," I interrupted him. "That's why I'm here. I'm looking for someone on their list. I'm headed to where I think my guy was." I looked left and right at the restaurant crowded with Rainsy's supporters. He seemed to like the conspiratorial gesture and we turned away from the table, moved in close to each other. "I'm going to Sihanoukville and Koh Kong," I said quietly. "To try and get his alias."

"Mmm*hmmmm.*" He cogitated that fact for a moment. "So you want to know what? Sihanoukville, I can tell you in 24 hours you can get a Cambodian passport for $230. You can imagine how easy it is to escape justice and Interpol by spending $230 to have a new virginity in Cambodia. Sihanoukville is among the most corrupt in a corrupt land. Drugs, child prostitution, passports—"

"What about Koh Kong?"

"Ah, Koh Kong, Koh Kong—the mafia capital. There you can kill anyone if you are a friend of the government."

"What do you know about the casino murders?"

My question elicited a thin approving smile from him. "*This* should be exposed!"

He explained that last year the 4 Kings Triad from Macau had apparently wrested control of Koh Kong's underworld from the 14K. The 14K were now fighting to get it back. The murders, he said, had to do with the gangland struggle, although it was a "very dubious war," one whose chief combatants would surprise me. He covered my pad with his hand. "Come here to me, closer," he said, at which point he went off the record, which is saying something for Sam Rainsy.

CHAPTER 21

PORT OF PLENTY

———

Among strongmen I am strong. . . . I want to develop my country
like other Southeast Asian strongmen did.
—HUN SEN: STRONGMAN OF CAMBODIA

Almost all the vehicles traveling Route 4 to Sihanoukville displayed bunches of bananas on their dashboards. At first I thought the fruit was the budget lunch in these parts, but I discovered the bananas weren't for eating at the crest of Pich Nil Pass, in the Elephant Mountains, a hundred kilometers southwest of the capital. Below a shell-blasted bunker stood a bungalow-size temple surrounded by hundreds of gaily colored spirit houses, their little spires connected to the temple by a rope hung with bow-tied notes. My driver parked the car, took his bananas from the dash and handed me a couple, saying, "For Ya-mao."

I pretty much pray to whatever god is in front of me and so I pronammed and studied the deity. Ya-mao's effigy was made out of black stone, her lips were painted pink, she was wrapped in a gold silk robe and surrounded by a forest of phalluses. Not just hardwood erections carved with vaguely ridged glans, as you find in other Buddhist countries. On her right was a full-metal penis with big golden balls.

After leaving her some riels and the bananas, I got back in the car and read in my *Sihanoukville Visitors Guide* that Ya-mao was more than a fertility goddess: she seemed to be an ancient symbol of the Khmer worship of the strongman as God's representative on earth. She had lived during the late Funan period, around the sixth century, and was married to a powerful king who ruled the south from Ream, a seaside village across a bay from present-day Sihanoukville. The king left her to go to war in Koh Kong and, unable to live without him, Ya-mao followed on a fishing boat and was drowned in a storm. She awoke in the next world still longing for her husband and appeared to him in spirit, tormented by her inability to consummate her desire. He was so touched by her devotion that he appointed her goddess of the south, empowered to give blessings to travelers who worshiped him by offering her symbols of his manly strength.

The Ya-mao myth blended two traditions: the Khmer custom of offering tribute to the strongman, and India's ritual worship of the lingam—the phallic representation of the gods Vishnu and Shiva, the Hindu embodiment of the Strongman in His alternating roles as preserver and destroyer. Eventually, lingam worship spread across Cambodia, becoming incorporated into the Angkorian cult of the god king. Those who held the royal lingam collected the king's due, melding obedience to authority with the mystical belief that the authority figure *was* God—the Infallible Phallus.*

All of this went a long way to explain My Lord Daddy Hun Sen's oxymoronic rhetoric on corruption. On the one hand, the prime minister flaunted his efforts to democratize the state and end payoffs. On the other, in his just-published biography, he openly bragged that he was "Cambodia's strongman," that he embodied the nation, and that he wasn't required to "listen to anyone's advice." It certainly helped explain why in almost every town on Route 4 the most prominent building was not a Buddhist temple but the Cambodian People's Party headquarters, which served both as the district house of the ruling party and the bank in which offerings were openly received, then transferred upward to the capital. In exchange for kickbacks, lawlessness could take place within the law, and district-level subordinates routinely marketed the country as a dumping ground for Asia's most-wanted criminals and least-wanted substances.

I was about to see that not all of those substances were drugs.

Eight miles from Sihanoukville, just after the turnoff to fabled Ream, we passed an open field dappled with Brahman cattle grazing placidly among peasants using shovels and sticks to search for their next meal of beetles and lizards. Spoiling this pastoral vision, however, were scores of derelict shipping containers at the edge of the field. I touched my driver's shoulder and told him to stop.

---

*Lest this practice be written off as purely an Asian superstition, it should be pointed out that the United States and Canada have their own form of lingam worship. The symbol of authority in Congress and Parliament is the Mace, a long shaft topped by a silver orb. Without the Mace, proceedings cannot be opened, and under its power all taxes are collected—some of which taxes, as is often revealed, go into the pockets of those who derive their power from the federal lingam.

The field was the site of what environmentalists from the NGO Forum on Cambodia called "the worst act of toxic-waste dumping in recent times." Almost exactly one year ago, on December 4, 1998, a ship called the *Chang Sun* had docked in Sihanoukville and unloaded 2,900 tons of what was listed in official documentation as "cement cakes." The ship belonged to a Taiwanese manufacturer of polyvinyl chlorides, the Formosa Plastics Corporation. Within hours of the dumping, impoverished residents of the adjacent Bettrang Commune swarmed the site, thinking the cakey white substance was phosphate fertilizer. Farmers spread the powder on their crops and used the triple-lined bags to store rice or as bedsheets and window screens. Within a few days, over a third of the commune's people began complaining of exhaustion, a perpetual feeling of being thirsty, and a paradoxical inability to urinate no matter how much water they drank. Half of the port workers who had handled the substance also fell ill. Then, on December 16, a young Sihanoukville port worker who had swept out the *Chang Sun*'s hold died in agony. Three days later, in Koki village, adjacent to the site, a 23-year-old man who had slept for several nights on plastic sheeting he'd scavenged from the dump site died under similar circumstances. Tests were run on samples taken from the acres of white cakes and they were found to contain "concentrations of mercury more than 20,000 times above safety limits as well as dangerous levels of dioxin and PCBs."

The city of Sihanoukville panicked in a way that hadn't been seen since the Khmer Rouge evacuations in April 1975. Rumors swirled that Formosa Plastics had paid a multimillion-dollar bribe to government agents to facilitate the export of the ship's contents to this site. One man was killed when residents stormed the headquarters of Kamsab, one of the government agencies they blamed for importing the waste. Four died in car accidents as people fought their way out of the city over packed roads—in their confusion, actually fleeing in the direction of the dump site. On December 23, cargo containers were brought in to ring the rubble and contain the drifting poisonous dust. The army was then called in and, dressed head to toe in white contamination suits and breathing masks, began shoveling the cakes into barrels. On March 30, 1999, the waste was shipped out of Cambodia and 4,000 tons of topsoil were removed from the site, which was then declared safe by Cambodia's Department of Pollution Control at the Ministry of Environment. Cattle were set to grazing the reseeded wasteland and locals began digging for grubs. In the year since the dumping, 14 more commune residents—all healthy before the dumping—fell ill and died, and the grazing cows developed mysterious shiny bumps on their bodies.

Six months before I arrived, the government had tried to assuage local resentment by trying in absentia the Taiwanese officials behind the dumping, sentencing them to five years in prison if they should ever show up in Cambodia. No investigation of local officials was ever launched, and in covering the disaster, Phelim Kyne made the point that "the most poignant lessons of the Sihanoukville toxic dumping have been to underline the rot within the country."

We came over a rise and headed steeply down towards Sihanoukville and its dockside parking lot of Maersk containers. My driver hauled up at a slough clogged with lily pads near a dilapidated train station at the corner of a street called My Lord Daddy Hun Sen Beach Drive, which led to the Koh Kong ferry dock. "Koh Kong?" he asked, but I told him to head on into town. I'd decided to spend the night in Sihanoukville. The port town had three big casinos and four discos where the 14K hung out in between their runs up the coast to Koh Kong.

Sihanoukville (or Kompong Som, as it is called by most Khmer) had never really been a stranger to dark deals in smoky places, having been in the thick of international intrigue ever since construction of the town began at the dissolution of French Indochina in 1954. Prior to that, Cambodia had exported its goods down the Mekong River, but the independence of Vietnam had cut Phnom Penh off from the sea. And so the French, trying to keep a foothold in their former colony, and the Americans, wanting to stay on Sihanouk's good side in that era of guerrilla insurgencies, had formed a consortium to help the king develop his namesake city.

The port facilities were finished in 1960 and a 10-year building boom began, with luxury hotels sprouting on five beaches patronized by the jet-set families of the Cambodian elite, while the gravel streets of the town became peppered with the offices of shell companies secretly run by the KGB and the CIA. After the U.S. Air Force began bombing eastern Cambodia, the second phase of port construction was brought to a halt, and in 1975, the construction was reversed. The Khmer Rouge seized the *Mayaguez*, a U.S. container ship in port, and the U.S. Navy retaliated by bombing the Cambodian naval base at Ya-mao's home village, Ream, plus Sihanoukville's warehouses and train yard. Unwittingly, the U.S. Navy aided the Khmer Rouge's de-industrialization plans. At the time, as in Phnom Penh, the Maoists were tearing things apart to help hustle in the golden agrarian age. Sihanoukville's evacuated streets and deserted beaches were littered with the smashed refrigerators and televisions of the surf set.

Like the rest of Cambodia, the city stood as a ruin for the next 15 years, and only started peeping through the rubble towards the late '80s, when the Vietnamese left. With the arrival of the U.N. in 1991 and the elections in 1993, it began to look as if Sihanoukville's beaches might again serve as resort attractions; old hotels were restored and new ones built in the hopes the peninsula would evolve into a Cambodian version of Phuket. A year later, three tourists were kidnapped and murdered on Route 4 and development came to a halt. It started up again the following year, and stopped once more for a year after the '97 coup. Then, a few months after Hun Sen consolidated his hold on power in the 1998 elections, casinos and disco nightclubs started to go up. At that point the go-ahead was given for the dumping of the toxic waste, and fear of death by mercury poisoning drove the town into another tourist depression. Not that the gangsters minded. That was when they began to thrive.

I'd been warned by Rainsy about asking pointed questions in Sihanoukville, but it was a bit of advice I forgot almost as soon as we entered Ekareach Street, the downtown's pitted and potholed main drag. We got stuck behind a bullock cart that was trying to make a left and, while my driver was leaning on his horn, I noticed in the parking lot opposite us a dozen Cambodians arguing with a couple of Chinese guys in sharkskin business suits. The two Chinese stood above the crowd, under the gold marquee of the Long Beach Resort casino, and it almost looked as if they were dealing with some kind of union protest. I told my driver to turn in, but he sniffed trouble and stopped halfway up the incline to the lot. There wasn't a single tourist in sight, and as I walked to the edge of the Cambodian crowd every eye turned on me. I offered my usual introduction, "Hi, I'm writing about travel in Cambodia," then shook imaginary dice in a cupped hand, threw for a bet, and snapped my fingers. "Can I go in and play?" I asked.

The expressions of the Cambodians instantly changed from scowls to smiles—but the faces of the Chinese guys above them were immutably sour. "No open today," said one sternly, looking me right in the eye. "No business for you," said the other, pointing with his cigarette at my taxi.

The Cambodians seemed to recognize that I was a potential ally in whatever was going on, and one of them informed me, "Owner run away China yesterday!"

"No pay us!" said another. "Some men win here, say, 'Now broke, casino no more!'"

"New owners," said the first, pointing to the duo. "Say, 'Go away.' But open again tonight, *tonight!!* New workers, but no pay *us!*"

My mind wrapped itself around one thought. A casino will sometimes go broke in the face of a string of house losses, but usually not by chance. More often than not, organized crime figures holding a debt will engineer a takeover by seeding professional cheaters to break the bank. I looked back at my driver, who seemed the picture of misery parked in the lot. He turned the wheels on the Toyota, put the stick in reverse, and gave me the palm-down Asian-wave to join him.

I smiled at the no-nonsense Chinese men on the stairs. "Can I come back tonight when it's open?"

Neither replied. One stepped down from the stairs, forcefully shoved his way through the crowd, and went over to my driver. He said something to him in Khmer, which sounded none too compromising, and my driver rolled the car backward onto the street, then threw it into first and started to roll east. His palm-waving was now almost frantic. When I got in I asked him what the fellows had said to him.

"He say not your business, take you away quick. No come back. Otherwise trouble."

"You think they were Chinese mafia?"

He didn't reply for a moment, then finally said: "You want know, somebody else tell you."

I had intended to get a room in town, but now, thinking about pursuing this Long Beach thing, I reconsidered. Rainsy had described Sihanoukville as a tropical Marseilles where troublesome people disappeared as casually as boats over the horizon, so I decided I'd be safer staying at the most touristed beach—Ochheuteal, south of the city, and gave my driver the name of a hotel there. I'd forgotten Rainsy's other cautionary words: that down here I would find myself either in the hot pan of Chinese mafia crime or in the slithering pit of criminal Caucasian sex.

We swung away from the center of town and around one of the most curious traffic circles I'd ever seen, offering a light touch to this creepy place. Atop a 10-foot brick base squatted a two-story-high lioness, while her three-story roaring mate, apparently prepatory to mating, stood beside her. They were both painted bright gold and faced the rising sun. Underneath the lion's basketball-size testicles someone had placed a bunch of bananas.

We turned down Mithona Street, the beachside drive, passed a military-police base and pulled up at the hotel called the Crystal, a blue glass building that was undergoing expansion in anticipation of the tourist boom, although at high noon in this high season it looked like they still had a year or two to wait.

"I send girl your room?" the bellhop asked me at my door, on which was pasted a poster of a smiling condom walking into a room with a tart. Above it were written the English words: "No condom, no sex."

"No thank you," I said.

"You want boy?"

"No."

"You want lady-boy?"

"No!"

He obviously thought I was just being shy.

"You ask me when you want, okay, okay," he smiled. "Some girls no good you bring—make trouble."

I gave him a dollar bill and asked if he could set me up this evening, not with a girl but with a moto driver who knew his way around the Chinese casinos and nightclubs. As expected, he had "a cousin" who would fit the bill exactly—a fellow named Am who would pick me up after dinner.

Prescribing myself a short dose of non-Triad-related tourism, I left the hotel for Ochheuteal Beach, supposedly the nicest in Sihanoukville, the one that was about to draw the hordes of tourists. To get to it you had to cross a trash-strewn field, then a plank bridge that spanned a smelly ditch where pigs and cows rummaged in the heaps of garbage the locals dumped there daily. Beyond that was a windbreak of straggly Australian pines—not a coconut palm in sight—and then the beach itself, just a narrow hard strand lapped by cloudy water that looked oily from the city's effluent. Half a dozen tattered thatch umbrellas were planted in the sand at intervals, all taken by white-bellied, middle-aged men capitalizing on the sad menu my bellhop had offered me. Beyond them, the beach arced southeast a few miles to an inlet, across which you could see the naval base of Ream, which was just then adding a thick black cloud of smoke to the bluish haze. The land, the beach, the sea, the sky—everything seemed poisoned.

There were swarms of 13-year-old girls in loose smocks buzzing about the beach with thatch platters of pineapples on their heads. As soon as they saw me spreading out my towel, they converged. I'd only taken 1,000 riels with me the pineapples, they shouted, were 1,500—and so I shooed them away with my briefcase. They persisted, of course, bargaining down. I finally gave one of the girls all the money I had and she drew an eight-inch knife and began expertly skinning and slicing. "Why you buy hers?" one of her companions complained, waving her own knife around. "Why you no buy mine?!"

I told her I had no more money, but that when I came back from the hotel later I would buy hers. "I go hotel with you," she said, which caused her friends to giggle. "Okay, okay?" she asked, petting my neck.

"*I* go hotel with you! No, *I* go hotel with you!" her friends chanted.

It was hard to tell if these other kids really meant what they were saying, but I think the petulant one did. Her companion handed me my sliced pineapple on a stick and walked away with the others. The other girl remained. "*Why* you buy hers? *Why* you no buy mine?!" and burst into neurotic angry tears.

"*Sohm toh*—I have no more money with me," I apologized, and turned around and began reading some material I'd been given by Sari Nissi, the Finnish head of Phnom Penh's International Organization for Migration— the body that was investigating Cambodia's Triad-run, burgeoning child sex trade. Suddenly I felt a stinging slap on my shoulder and turned to see the little girl running away up the beach. There were splashes of red all over my thighs and the sand. I looked at my shoulder and saw a two-inch gash where the girl had hit me with her razor-sharp knife blade. Rivulets of blood ran down over my ribs. "I'm stabbed!" I shouted, but I really wasn't. Nevertheless, she *could* have put the knife in my back, or cut my throat. I ran back to the hotel, furious—not with the kid, but with these criminal johns. You go looking for a gangster and wind up cut by a sick child who's suffered God knows what abuse at the hands, perhaps, of one of these gross white men under the umbrellas.

My disgust with johns increased with my Christmas Eve dinner at the neighboring Sea Dragon restaurant. There were only four diners in the open-air lounge, all white guys my age with teen consorts—one of the fellows with two kids either side of him. I recognized the men from the beach—they were probably staying in the Crystal, or else at the luxury Seaside next door. At the red oilclothed table closest to me a middle-aged pedophile cleaned his ear with a Q-Tip while his date looked at her purple-painted, stubby fingernails as if she were on the verge of suicide. He was a square dude in starched jean shorts, black sandals with white socks, a leather vest, obscene-looking tits and no chin. She wore a flower in her hair, a floral party smock, and those ridiculously stacked clogs then in fashion among Asian teens. Sihanoukville, as Sum Manit mentioned, was a port town, and of course, prostitution was to be expected—maybe there was a case for it being legal—but these guys were getting away with what to my mind was the next worst thing to murder.

"Why don't you just give her the money without torturing her for the night?" I asked the guy beside me.

"*Comment?*" he asked.

"Are you French?"

"What do you want?"

"Back in France you'd get five years in jail for this shit."

He called something angrily in Khmer to the kitchen, where the guy who ran the place was cooking. Alerted by the fuss, the other gents turned my way.

A ponytailed fellow in a bathing suit and a muscle shirt called over, "What's your problem, mate?" Definitely Australian. So was his bald buddy, who pushed his plate away and said, "Do you *want* a problem?"

Here it goes, I thought. The French guy I could handle; not two Aussies. Motivated as I am sometimes when I see something I don't like, I'm not an effective barroom brawler. One time in college, on Saint Patrick's Day, I squared off against anti-Semitic frat jerks and wound up in the hospital. I didn't want to wind up in Sihanoukville's hospital. On the other hand, why should these guys be able to have their way with impunity? They were both cigarette smokers, and I'm pretty fast, so I chose the next best form of aggression. Boot and scoot.

"I'm a journalist covering the child sex trade in Cambodia," I said, standing up and moving off the hardwood floor to the sand parking lot, as if in disgust, not flight. "I've seen what it does and you guys are doing it."

In a second I was safely out of sight in the dark, probably spared a run by their fear of exposure. Which made me think: Next time I blow through a scene like this I'm gonna talk the assholes up, get their names and pictures, and deliver the goods to their embassies. So watch out, diablos, because I travel a *lot*.

Two hours later Am and I stepped past a lineup of two dozen taxi girls and entered the NASA Nightclub, just off the Golden Lion Traffic Circle. Save for the mirrored beams and disco ball it was a bare, square barn, black lit so the white tablecloths and plastic chairs glowed radioactively purple, as did the dance band's white elf hats as they sang Khmer Christmas pop—"Silent Night" with a deafening electronic reverb.

The floor was crowded with older Khmer men dancing with taxi girls, girls dancing with girls, and men dancing with men, which had no homosexual connotation in Cambodia. In this puritanical society, most women did not date. Since men never took their wives to clubs, and single men didn't go to clubs to meet marriageable women, dance halls like the NASA were strictly hooker strolls. Problem was, some men who attended couldn't afford a woman. So the guys who drew the short straws in life danced with other guys in similar circumstances.

While we watched the strange show on the dance floor, I speculated to Am that the Long Beach owner had probably fled because the Chinese mafia had run him out. Am laughed and replied that he didn't know a thing about the Chinese mafia, he was just a moto driver. He also seemed shocked when I told him Sam Rainsy alleged that Sihanoukville was a hotbed of passports for sale. "No, no, Mr. Terry—illegal, *il-legal!*" he said, seductively enough to let me know he knew about both topics. His shyness, I assumed, was due to the fact that I hadn't done anything to make him trust me—like ask him for drugs or pick a girl from the lineup outside the door, which was no doubt highly unusual and suspicious.

He was charging me five dollars for the night, only a little above average for a town tour, so I said, "Am, why don't I pay you now, in case I forget later."

"What you want, okay," he shrugged.

"Is fifteen enough?"

He took the money and recognized it for what it was. "You make story about bad things here, Mr. Terry?" he asked.

"Yeah. Bad things. You won't have to worry for yourself. Okay?"

He leaned forward and patted my shoulder—the wounded one, which hurt like hell and opened the cut. He left the table and was gone for 10 minutes, somewhere over by the coat check. Then he came back.

"I think maybe nobody here now know what you say," he shouted over the shrieking female lead's rendition of "Jingle-Bell Rock."

"Where then?" I asked.

"I take you by port—high, high, high. Peak Casino. Very expensive. Beautiful view."

The evening was comparatively cold all across Southeast Asia. The *Bangkok Post* the next day showed Japanese tourists in Chiang Mai wearing balaclavas on a subfreezing morning. In Sihanoukville the temperature never got below 65 but, with me in just shorts and a thin dress shirt, the wind climbing up to the Peak Casino made it feel a little like winter. "I think maybe you look for Bela-Russie girl," Am said, rubbing his hands in the parking lot that overlooked the glittering port. "Work gambling. Upstairs. High, high." He flipped his hand to the top floor of the floodlit Mandarin-roofed palace. "Name *Lar-i-sa.* She know what you ask."

The joint was bronze-banistered and lushly carpeted, mobbed with Chinese on every level, with magnificent picture-window views all around. The only white person in there was a pretty, pertly lipsticked blond lady in her 30s dealing baccarat on the third floor. I bought $50 worth of chips and sat down at Larissa's table. She did a double take at my pale face, then focused her almond eyes on my shoulder. I wasn't wearing a T-shirt and had bled right through, staining my shirt halfway down to the pocket. That in itself would not have been completely unusual—wounds being part and parcel of hanging around Sihanoukville on a holiday eve—but I think what struck Larissa as even more strange about me was that I fumbled stupidly when the bet was on me. People had wagered up into the hundreds while I sat there looking at my chips like a nearsighted grandmother trying to distinguish between two coins at the grocer's—sending the whole table into exasperated Cantonese mutterings.

As in the Philippines six years ago, in two hands I completely lost my stake. When you lose you learn to lose, but it's a bit of wisdom I've never absorbed, so I just sat there taking up space without going to the cage for more. "You from Eastern Europe?" I asked. "You have the accent."

"Minsk," she said, sliding face cards from the shoe to everyone but me. "And you?"

"Vancouver, Canada, by way of New York. Actually, I spent years in Little Odessa—Brighton Beach."

"Is suppose to be interesting place. I like visit New York after here."

"How long you been here?"

"Ha! Too long—year and a half—Poipet, Pailin—all over."

Hmm, I thought. What's a good-looking Belarus gal doing buzzing around Cambodia for a year and a half? Right time frame, anyway, I calculated, getting my mind back to Steve.

The floorman showed up at my side, flashing Larissa an angry look. "Please," he said to me. "You must play you want sit here."

"I can stand," I said, slipping off the stool.

The floorman's eyes rested on my colorful shoulder, then darted to a goon in the corner. He held up a warning finger to Larissa, turned back to me with a smile. "She no allow socialize with customers," he said, his smile instantly disappearing as he looked back at Larissa, who shook her long bleached hair off her shoulders in a leonine show of independence. The floorman wore a nameplate saying Marco, just right for a Vegas casino, but awfully strange for a Cambodian one. "Look, Marco, it's not like I'm not playing the house. My name's Bud Abbot and my girlfriend Lou Costello is just downstairs playing a fortune." I winked at Larissa, but I don't think she'd seen many reruns of '50s television in Minsk. I shook Marco's hand. "I'll have a drink downstairs and maybe she can join us there when she's off, okay? I'm asking permission."

"I am done at one," she told Marco, petulantly, then looked back at me and smiled, as if to spite him.

I went down to the parking lot and told Am I was fixed up, I'd find my way home all right. He smiled lasciviously and I shoved his arm. "You think because I write bad things I do bad things? I told you I was married."

"I no say that, Mr. Terry. I only tell you, friend to friend, she married too, dealer man, work another casino."

"Well why didn't you bring me to see him then?"

"Not know where find him now. He work Long Beach, ha ha ha!"

An hour later Larissa came up to me at the bar. "Where is Lou?" she asked.

"That was just a joke. Abbot and Costello—they're an American comedy team. I was humiliating Marco for you, Larissa."

"He is a rodent. Is new here, from Macau."

"*That's* where he got his name from!" I exclaimed, not bothering to conceal my excitement.

"And my name? How did you know?" She said this looking up coyly, over a cigarette she was lighting. She lounged back in her stool, crossed her legs, put one arm on the rest, the other back over her chair—wide-open body language which I appreciated less for the sexual opportunity than the ambience. The Asian casino, the Steve-pursuit, the Natasha-informant. She was still wearing her red dealer's jacket, her bosom pulling at the buttons of her white blouse and revealing black bra. Her tapered blue slacks ended above strap heels showing painted toes and a naked instep. You really couldn't beat it.

"You know my moto driver," I said. "Or he knows you. Am."

"I think my husband know him," she said.

"Yeah, he mentioned you were married to a guy worked at the Long Beach. What went on there anyway? I came into town, there was trouble out front."

She looked me straight in both eyes. "What are you doing here?" She leaned forward. "Are you a drugs agent?"

Cardsharp that she was, she had a highly developed personal lie detector behind her pupils. I knew if I shifted mine, I'd lose any chance of getting information out of her. I had no choice but to be up front—so unusual for me that I was afraid she'd mistake my effort at honesty for dissemblance. "Larissa, I'm not a cop. I'm a writer on a story about a gang guy who might have been here. I'm just curious what went on there yesterday. It could be the same gang he's in."

This information constricted her from neck to midriff. She took her arm off the chair and turned back to the bar. Then she looked sideways at my epaulet stain. "What happened that you are bleeding?"

I told her about the little girl on Ochheuteal Beach, how I hated what my white kind were doing to their brown children. "They are all like that here," she said. "Not all—the backpackers—they fuck each other. But the government ones who come to help, the United Nations, the businessmen—they fuck the kids. It is a sick joke. You should write about that."

"I intend to. I heard it's worse in Koh Kong. That's where I'm headed next."

"Koh Kong you will see it is slavery. They go from here to there. Then—no one knows where they end up."

That brought me around the corner to asking why she'd been hanging around the snake pits of Cambodia for a year and a half. She asked if I'd ever been to Belarus. I said no, but my grandparents had come from the Ukraine. "The same. They left. Everyone wants leave from there, except the oligarchs." She'd been a math teacher in Minsk, earning less than a Cambodian moto driver; her husband had made some money "at something," and they'd taken off across Siberia, then down through China and Laos to here, where, because they both had good heads for numbers, they'd become prized itinerants at the three casinos, plus the floating Naga Casino in Phnom Penh and the ghoulish dens of Poipet and Pailin. "Me more than Vlad," she said. "I am very popular with Chinese gamblers. They give me crazy tips. You wouldn't believe if I told you. *Before* they play. For luck. When I dye my hair, they give me double. Gold is good luck for them. Red too—so I dye my nails." She held up her crimson-lacquered nails and sighed. "For white women, Chinese men are very easy to manipulate. Is not just me. Ukraine girl at Holiday Palace casino, is just new, but she know already."

"I knew a Chinese Triad member I was able to manipulate," I said. "I destroyed his career."

"Why didn't he kill you?"

"He died first."

Her beer arrived and we clinked glasses. She asked if I had written anything that had been published in Eastern Europe. I told her about the swinger book, that there were now clubs in Minsk, Moscow, and Kiev, so a Russian translation was a possibility for the future. I asked what the Slavic slang word for swinger was. The thinnest of smiles stretched her red lips. "We say just swingers. There is not enough time to have our own word for it."

"You've heard of them then."

"Of course."

Of course.

"So what went on over at the Long Beach? I'm thinking gangster business."

"They are all over. Everything here is gangsters, as you say. Same as East Europe. Maybe is worse there. For the girls anyway."

"I'm thinking they broke the place with cheaters," I said, steering back to the Long Beach, "then closed on a deal, sent the owner running."

She looked behind her.

"They try in Koh Kong, too," she said quietly, reinforcing some prior knowledge I had on the subject.

"You mean with the manager and his assistant? The ones who were murdered?"

"It is not something to talk about here. Do you need a lift to town?"

Larissa had a putt-putt Vespa parked in the lot. She took out a pair of clogs from the hatch and replaced them with her heels and two bottles of beer I'd bought at the bar. "Where's Vladimir tonight?" I asked, getting on behind her.

"He is home."

We coasted down to the port, then up Ekareach and past the lions. "They are the biggest balls in the world, no?" she asked into the wind.

"I've seen bigger in swing clubs," I said. "Big fat guys—halfway to their knees."

"You must have good time research for that, ha ha ha! What do you do? Walk with a pad? Like a doctor? One fuck, two fucks?"

"Not quite, but something like that. I take notes after. You guys ever been to a swing party?"

"Why would I tell you? For your next book?"

Walking along the beach by the Crystal I pressed her on the Koh Kong thing again—the manager and his assistant.

"I think perhaps this mafia should be a part of it—if there is cheating to get the ownership. So maybe they cheating for the one which want to get it. Or else for themselves. Is confusing. I just hear. BJ dealer at casino name Chang maybe tell you what you want."

"Chang? What's his last name?"

"I don't know, I don't want to know. Just he come here when it happen. He know all this gangster business. My opinion? They can't succeed break Koh Kong. Too big. Long Beach is small. One night they can break it."

"Did you ever hear the name of the gang 14K mentioned?"

"Of course. They are the ones around here. From Macau. Marco, I don't know if he is one. But to work, everyone knows someone."

"Do you want to come upstairs?" I asked. "I want to show you something."

In my room I took from my suitcase a copy of *The Lifestyle*, signed it and gave it to her as a present. "There's no sex in it, per se. It's mostly about the behavior."

"Reubens," she said, smiling at the cover, a detail of lightly clothed dancing figures from *The Worship of Venus*. She was the first person I'd ever met who'd identified the artist. "It is a good choice. Are you the one who choose it?"

"Actually, my wife did," I said, digging down into my suitcase. "She's an artist."

This didn't seem to make any impression on her. She flipped the pages as I came out with a folder. "'The Inside Story,'" she said, reading the title of Chapter Seven. She slipped off her dealer's jacket and leaned sideways onto the bed on one elbow. "Who is Jodie?"

"A woman who showed us around the club. That chapter's about what goes on in their bodies when they're swinging."

She looked up and laughed, pulled her hair from her face. "Is it different than normal?"

"Very much different." I sat down beside her. The light from the bed lamp shadowed her high cheekbones. She really was a beautiful woman. "A man ejaculates three times as many sperm cells after he's seen his wife doing it with another guy," I said. "It's the way his body tries to deal with the competition inside her uterine track."

"My God, did you count?"

"Someone else did." I opened the folder. "Larissa, have you ever seen this guy?"

I placed Steve's puss on the pillow and she glanced casually sideways. She crinkled her forehead. "Is he the one you are looking for?"

"Yeah—the dead one. He's not dead, though."

"Thick glasses."

"Right. Very short, tubby. Maybe about a year ago or more."

"Aren't you afraid if I know him I will get rich to let him know you are looking?"

"I'm taking that chance."

She sat up and placed the photo in her lap, studied it seriously. Then she shrugged, quite girlishly, and leaned against me. "No, I have never seen him. I would tell you." She turned her head and brushed my ear, put her hand against my chest. "What's this?"

I didn't reply. What could I say?

She reached into my breast pocket and pulled out my tape recorder. "It is not on?" She held it to the light, saw the spindle turning, turned back at me with her mouth open. I took the Realistic from her. "Larissa—"

"What have you done—mentally rape me?!"

"If you knew him, I needed proof. Your name would never be used."

She jumped up, grabbed the recorder, clocked me sideways across the head with it—a metal roundhouse that sent me to the mattress, almost out cold. She threw the recorder on the linoleum and stomped it to pieces. By the time I could see straight she was out the door. Am I in trouble? I wondered, following her with my hand at my head. The desk boy hardly looked up as I staggered through the lobby in chase. He'd probably seen bodies on this tile floor, no comfort to my fear of the revenge she might beg from Vlad, Marco, or Chang. I caught up to her as she was kicking the Vespa to life.

"Larissa, I'm working with the police on this," I said. "There's a DEA cop in the next room to me. Don't try anything."

She spat a Slavic curse at me, from the bottom of the Pripet Marsh, I'm sure, then puttered off, up Mithona and around the corner, leaning into the turn. I turned around, checking for witnesses. There was a band of fluorescence glowing over Ream. Above the goddess's home the smoke was still rising. "Protect me, Ya-mao," I prayed.

She did. Five hours later I was safely on an express boat to Koh Kong—wondering if the next person I should see on Steve was the mysterious know-it-all Chang.

CHAPTER 22

THE BIGGEST LITTLE TOWN IN CAMBODIA

―――――

Located on the private beach, framed by calm unspoiled sea. . . .
418 kms. to Phnom Penh. . . . Meters to Thailand.
—KOH KONG INTERNATIONAL RESORT CLUB BROCHURE

Three and a half hours into my voyage to the mafia capital of Cambodia, sitting on the roof of the *Sea Naga,* I began to pick the brains of a flashy slots salesman with a four-inch pinkie nail. Twice a year Tha-nom and his two Bangkok partners donned their wraparound sunglasses and circled the Kingdom, hawking the latest slot machines in Poipet, Pailin, Sihanoukville, and Koh Kong—their last stop before heading home. We were just then closing on the jungly Koh Kong peninsula, but I didn't see any instant city dominating the shore. "No here, no here," Tha-nom said. He pointed to a spot on my French map and explained that all the development was on the other side of the green mountain, right on the border. With his nail he engraved an X at the southwest tip of the peninsula. West of the X a fast highway took off to Bangkok; east of the X was the mountain, a wide inlet of the Gulf of Siam, then a village called Krong Kaoh Kong, and then nothing but 200 kilometers of rolling rain forest until you hit Route 4 near Sihanoukville.

This, then, was the topographical gift to Pat Supapa that I'd heard about. Mr. Pat, the Thai-Cambodian "adviser" to Hun Sen, had been given the go-ahead on Koh Kong's huge development just after the July 1997 coup. Since then, beyond the reach of Thai laws and under the protection of handpicked officials, Koh Kong International Resort Company Ltd. had developed a megamillion-dollar seaside gambling extravaganza, although gambling was just a part of Pat Supapa's enterprises. In addition to the *Bangkok Post*'s allegations that Mr. Pat's involvement in the drug trade had caused him to be "black-listed by Thai narcotics units," he was a partner in 10 logging companies voraciously eating through the rain forest and in hundreds of shrimp farms that had destroyed the fish-spawning grounds along whole swaths of Cambodia's mangrove coast.

Not that Tha-nom, the slots-seller, viewed Pat in these dark terms. Pointing to the ramshackle document checkpoint we were approaching, he said the gambling magnate had just donated millions of dollars to build a bridge across the inlet and then a road to Route 4. "Make ocean port, golf course, big park like Disney for Phnom Penh people come." If there was a delay in getting started on the road, he said, it was because they'd only had one year of uninterrupted peace along the border. Tha-nom was referring, I assumed, to the final surrender of the Khmer Rouge last November, but I happened to know that right after peace was declared disgruntled troops from the Cambodian army itself had attacked Pat's resort with rocket-propelled grenades and heavy-caliber machine guns. "The attack," according to the *Bangkok Post,* had been "aimed at intimidating Pat Supapa," who had brought in elite troops from Phnom Penh to guard his casino, instead of using "the local troops from Koh Kong, depriving them of protection fees." (Mr. Pat had assured the *Post* that "the incident was a minor one and could be resolved quickly.")

"Thanks God no more fighting-fighting," Tha-nom smiled, standing up. "Very good you come now. Only nice people."

"I'm actually visiting a friend of mine," I smiled back. "His name is Mr. Chang. He's a blackjack dealer. He probably knows you."

Tha-nom pursed his lips, scratched his hairless chest beneath the numerous gold chains that adorned his sternum like a breastplate. "Mr. Chang," he said ruminatively, examining his stiletto pinkie nail, then spoke something in curt Thai to his thuggish partners getting to their feet beside us. One, in a purple silk shirt, shrugged. The other shook his head at his chunky rings. "Sorry, no know you friend," Tha-nom said, to my relief, since my blond babushka might have phoned ahead to tell Chang to expect me, and I was actually hoping I *wouldn't* be able to find him.

At the same time I knew I would go on asking. I figured: someone like Chang gets dropped in your lap, he might tell you Steve's alias.

We bumped the dock. Tha-nom and the other passengers—which included two Western backpackers and a couple dozen construction workers—jumped onto the pier with their bags. They presented their documents for examination, and then boarded a flotilla of perilously tippy outboard motorboats. As the *Sea Naga* backed away from the pier to take me across the inlet to Krong Kaoh Kong, I watched the outboards buzz north around a point towards a collection of shacks on the west side of the inlet. From there the passengers would hire motos or taxis to take them five kilometers over the hump to the Vegas in the jungle, or, if they were traveling on, to catch the express bus that departed every hour for Trat, Chanthaburi, and Bangkok.

I was the only passenger left on the *Sea Naga* as it tacked slowly through the busy cross-inlet traffic towards the iron warehouses and rusted roofs of Krong Kaoh Kong. Shacks on stilts lined the shore to the right, with the town's dirt streets and wooden houses visible through a line of seaside palms. It was a primitive place, looking every bit the haven for pirates working the Gulf of Siam and smugglers ferrying goods across the river—the main occupations of the village, according to my travel books. Given the uncertainty of this Chang business, however, I had decided to base myself here. I preferred to sleep among the town's smugglers and pirates rather than the casino's Triads.

As we came up alongside the dock, a kid in the waiting crowd of *krama*-covered peasants called out to me, "You need moto, mister?" He was no more than 18, and slick as a Tijuana tout—with hair greased straight back from his forehead, wearing a button-down pink dress shirt, shiny black trousers, and patent-leather shoes. He said his name was Sam and offered to be my tour guide.

He saw me looking around for other moto options, so he tried to reassure me. "I work for German man, own tourist company," he said. "Otto Weyer, at restaurant in town." He reached into his shirt pocket and with the pinched tips of his fingers delicately withdrew a tattered flyer. "Otto's Restaurant, Koh Kong: Food & Drinks Nice Athmosphere [sic], Now Open," said the flyer. It featured a computer-generated cartoon of a Beat Generation couple sitting at a checkered table over caffe lattes and reading the papers. Beside it was a photo of a tropical beach at sunset, and beside that was an art nouveau cartoon of piano keys cornily juxtaposed against a sax player and a champagne bottle filling a glass. Sam followed this flyer up with a hand-cut card for Otto's Restaurant.

"Does Otto really think he'll get Westerners here?" I asked.

"Just start now, because much here for tourist. Visit islands, go diving, go hiking. Very good for look at forest and birds."

All in all, the kid was probably authentic, I thought, and plunked my bag on his gas tank, got on behind, and told him to take me to the cheapest clean hotel he knew. We took off down a road alongside the inlet that ran away from town, passing a number of stone archways on the right, each guarded by soldiers holding automatic rifles. For all its reputation as an end-of-the-world sanctuary for smugglers of goods, drugs, and humans, Krong Kaoh Kong's outskirts were dominated by sprawling government bases—army, police, customs, immigration, and the Cambodian People's Party—which raised the inevitable question: how was all the illegal activity taking place under the noses of all these enforcers of the law? Even with his broken English, Sam had a sophisticated answer. "Cambodia law say 'No can do it.' But you need pay permission first, then you can do it."

We continued along the fenced perimeter of a National Police base until I saw a whitewashed two-story building in the middle of a parade ground, with the words "Koh Pich Hotel" written in gold along its eave. From the inside it appeared to be an old government building, perhaps once a French military barracks or colonial office. The walls had hardwood wainscoting, there was an old-style hardwood bench at the door with slats and curving arms, and the divide at the front desk was hardwood as well. The fellow behind the desk took down my passport number and asked if I wanted a girl. Before I could refuse, Sam interrupted to tell me he had to run, he'd be back at eight. "Tonight I can invite you to very important party with my friends. Militaire. Customs. I have friends because they are useful, for advantage."

Well, the kid's more up front than most, I thought.

Sam showed up an hour late, dressed in a white shirt and white slacks. By then I'd had a dinner at the hotel's restaurant, patronized by a crowd of shady-looking, late-middle-age Thai-Chinese, each with a teen Khmer girl at his side. "You like here so far?" he asked. "Very beautiful sunset. Much to do for tourists."

"Far as I can see the main thing for tourists here is prostitution," I said.

"Oh 'specially in red light—Walker Street!" he replied, probably thinking I was impressed with the opportunities. "You want 'nother girl there before we go to party?"

"No," I said. "But I'd like to have a talk with one."

We headed back up the main road, turned down a muddy block past the ferry pier, then swung into what Sam had called Walker Street. "It not so easy for lady get job here. So many young lady, they work for this. You see what you like, I wait."

As in Phnom Penh's north end, the prostitution district here consisted of consecutive blocks of shacks lit by neon black light, with waving, beckoning Vietnamese and Khmer girls in front of them. It was the lowest rung on the prostitution ladder, the purple light within each shack showing a sagging flophouse mattress on bamboo posts that stood on a bare dirt floor. Dozens of prostitutes lined the three blocks, clustering in groups of threes and fours around the shack entrances, dressed in cheap miniskirts, flounced childish blouses, and plastic sandals, with quite a few barefoot and almost all merely in their teens—if that.

"Who's their boss?" I asked Sam, figuring some local government satrap had to be giving the okay to run this strip.

"Maybe many *mamasans*," he said, skirting the question. "Very cheap for you. You want I stop?" he asked.

"Pull up anywhere."

I'm sure he didn't believe I just wanted to talk, but you'd have to be a very sick man indeed to want anything else from these kids. The just-released report of Sari Nissi's International Organization for Migration, *Paths of Exploitation*, featured a profile of the children, who were almost all from rural villages. "Some of the women were kidnapped and forced to work as prostitutes, some were tricked by false promises, some had agreed to be sold [by their parents], and some had come on their own initiative to look for work in the brothel." However they wound up in these huts, they were, as Larissa had told me, slaves now, at the disposal of the brothel 24 hours a day, seven days a week, except when menstruating. They received 1 to 6 percent of the money they generated, with the rest going to pay off the investment of the extortionate *mamasan* who controlled them. They had unprotected sex with anywhere from 4 to 15 clients a day and almost all of the kids had multiple STDs, including HIV, syphilis, and gonorrhea. While the brothels in the village were once freelance affairs, Sari Nissi had informed me that the girls were now being bought and trafficked by organized crime groups that transported them across the border to higher-paying locales along Route 3—particularly the Thai resort town of Klong Yai, a few miles north of the Koh Kong casino. IOM had found that "the brothels in Klong Yai are either controlled by Thai police officers or directly owned by relatives of police officers." Despite being underage, the Khmer sex workers of Klong Yai had all been supplied with work permits. Unlike Thailand, in Cambodia all prostitution was illegal, but the law against it was almost never enforced and to date nobody had been convicted of pimping kids.

I sat down at an entrance to a tent and, via Sam, talked with a couple of the children in exchange for a five-dollar bill. Their daily dose of clients ran the gamut of the town's male inhabitants—from senior officials to fishermen. One of them said that on a couple of occasions the *mamasan* had rented her to men who stayed at the Koh Kong Resort hotel, and she found that very exciting. Both of the girls said their ambition was to move to Klong Yai where they could work out of hotels permanently. Eventually, ultimately, they wanted to return to their villages, marry, and raise families. One of the girls giggled and said she was waiting.

"Waiting for what?" I asked.

She explained the situation to Sam, who laughed and said: "Wait for her first period so she get days off."

Sam pulled his Honda into a hotel parking lot that was crowded with dozens of other motos. Squealing Asian rock music sung in high-wire English poured through a blue archway that framed a wide atrium filled with young Khmer teens. They were bouncing to the music around a table piled high with gift boxes and a Christmas tree. Some wore conical party hats, others Santa hats, and there was a friendly intermingling of boys and girls off the dance floor. I was taken aback: these were the first bourgeois-looking and -acting kids I'd seen in Cambodia. They were dressed in neat school clothes that would not have been out of place in North America, and they were all smiling—but not neurotically. It reminded me of a Catholic high school party. I said that to Sam.

"Yes—it is our school party. We all go to English Language School."

"There's an English language school in town?"

"Yes." He pointed to a table of five male adults. "Our teachers."

The men were in their late 30s and 40s. They sat in dress shirts drinking beer from mugs, which a couple of fellows raised to me in greeting. Sam introduced me all around and I quickly learned that, indeed, three of the five had law enforcement jobs, and, aside from Sam, the students were the children of CPP men who worked the border. The teacher who spoke English most fluently was a captain of the immigration police named Khim Keo, and the strangest thing about him was that he openly admitted he was moonlighting as a teacher because he was both unwilling and unable to attain a position that would earn him any bribes.

Khim was Vietnamese, 43 years old, and he'd come to Cambodia as a soldier with the conquering Vietnamese army in 1981, then stayed on in Phnom Penh after his regiment left, getting a job in 1991 as an interpreter for UNTAC. He backed Prince Ranariddh in the 1993 election and then joined the Cambodian National Police, which, it will be remembered, had two competing factions within its ranks for four years. Since the north was Funcinpec territory, Khim was stationed in Siem Reap with other backers of Ranariddh. When Ranariddh was overthrown in the '97 coup, however, Khim's political affiliation turned into a liability. He was exiled to Koh Kong—a posting with a lot of potential except for the fact that he was barred from the lucrative customs branch and assigned a desk job in the town's immigration building. Even if he'd wanted to, he couldn't put the arm on people for bribes at the border.

"You know, I work hard, and I have more capability than the other people," he complained. "But I have no money. I have no sponsor, I have no supporters, no one of the high forces, therefore I am kept down. I can say I am an important officer, but it's no power, I have no power. The other policemen have smaller rank than me but they make more money than me. It's not only me. Everybody in Cambodia not in CPP cannot make money."

"How much money do they pay you?" I asked.

"They pay me almost a thousand baht, is equivalent to twenty dollars a month. How can I survive on that? I have my wife and I have my children. The other policemen, they want to get the houses and the high jobs. With their high jobs, they can make corruption. They don't care about how much they have to pay for the senior job."

"So they buy the job?"

"Yes, they want to get the higher job, they have to pay the money. After they get the job and the houses then they turn to corruption."

He had an older brother in Victoria, B.C., he said, who'd escaped Vietnam as a boat person in the late '70s. His name was Nguyen Chuong and he owned a landscape business. Six years ago Nguyen had sent Khim a thousand dollars, but that was the last he'd ever heard from him. He wrote his brother's name on my pad and asked if I could look him up when I got back to Canada.

"One thing I hear a lot about is trouble at the gambling casino," I said, figuring that, in Sam's words, if I was of advantage and use to Khim, he might tell me something about the murders. After all, he commanded the CPP men who worked right there at the border, which was actually the property line to the casino. "Chinese Triad gangsters go to the casinos in Koh Kong," I said. "Weren't there two murders there last month?"

"Sorry," he laughed. "I have never been there, I know nothing about it."

"Well, in Phnom Penh everybody talks," I said. "I was just wondering whether you knew if it was all just gossip."

"Sorry, I know nothing," he smiled.

I decided on a less dangerous question—about the trade in Cambodian passports. His response was that Sam Rainsy was making too much political hay out of criminals needing to buy fake passports in Sihanoukville. It was actually far more straightforward in Koh Kong. "Here, when want to pass the border of Cambodia, they have only to pay for the immigration. To take money from people that go through the border is no problem. That kind of corruption is not a problem for Cambodia. The problem is selling drugs, smuggling drugs, smuggling children—very, very bad. But taking money from people that cross the border, that is the price of the world, that is the way of Cambodia."

I asked him if he thought "the way of Cambodia" might have been different if Ranariddh had prevailed. He seemed to doubt it. He still supported Funcinpec, he said, but was deeply disappointed with the prince's rapprochement with Hun Sen. "They fighting one day and then they are good friends tomorrow. Now they make a deal. Ranariddh wait to be king. You see, Hun Sen, he has a very cunning way. He is a man with a lot of tricks."

"Oh, I'd agree with that," I said.

"But that's not my problem. I stay away now. Let them do what they want—I just stay away from them. The police, too. The policemen in the CPP, they can break the law, and they can break the law by themselves. It is very tough for me to work near that. So I try never think about what they do. I just pay attention to my teaching the children. Teaching is much purer. Teaching is hopeful."

At that, Sam pulled me into the middle of the dance floor to teach the students Christmas carols. My class of eager charges thought I was just being shy when I tried to explain I only knew one—"Jingle Bells." It was far too complicated to explain that I was a Brooklyn Jew who'd never sung a Christmas carol, so, in addition to "Jingle Bells," I taught them the first lines to "Frosty the Snowman" and "White Christmas" and led them in humming the rest.

"You have good voice," Khim Keo flattered me when I sat down. "You should be professional performer."

The next morning, before I went over to Koh Kong, Sam took me to meet his other useful friend, Otto Weyer, the only resident white guy between Trat and Sihanoukville. Otto was a middle-aged expat from Hamburg who in 1998 had invested in renovating a restaurant on a quiet, palm-lined street a block from the ferry. He was now building a five-bungalow guest house, banking on his bet that, with an end to the civil wars, adventure tourists would start to show up—either stopping off while using this route to Thailand, or headed for the (as yet) unspoiled tropical island of Kaoh Kong to the south.

Smugglers were not an issue for Otto; they imbued the place with a certain forbidden allure that he felt might ultimately attract bargain hunters, a point I actually agreed with, being in the market for a backup mini-recorder at the moment. "This whole town is a smuggler's cove—it's been this way for hundreds of years," he said. "It's a way of life—of course it is—the same as Koh Kut and Koh Chang Islands in this part of Thailand. This is the living they are making here. I mean what else they do? There is nothing here—there is no agriculture, no factories, there is nothing you have to live, except maybe fishing, and then there is nothing else."

"So they have boats and they use them."

"They have boats," he shrugged. "They smuggle things in and they smuggle things out. Everyone knows, everyone does it, nobody cares." His only problem in this romantically perfect location was the tacky publicity being generated by the casino monstrosity across the inlet and over the hill. Triad rub-outs and pitched battles between competing armies were not the kind of "wild-life" that ecotourists were interested in observing.

I truly felt for Otto. He was a gentle bohemian in a turtleneck living in a beautiful little cove, listening to Miles Davis on his CD player, inhabiting a post-and-beam house with a thatch roof, smoking a little grass that was all but legal here, and hoping to make a modest living off adventurous schoolteachers with binoculars. Except the gangsters were ruining the neighborhood.

"This mafia casino change everything," he sighed wearily. "There's tremendous money in this casino, so they kill each other. Two mafia guys just got shot—the manager and his assistant."

I told him I'd heard it was the 14K from Macau trying to break the bank and take back control of the tables from the 4 Kings, that the fellows who got shot were possibly 14K plants.

"Who knows these things?!" he said, echoing Larissa. "All I know is the owners are something very big. The ones who fight them must be very big. And one mafia did something, some kind of business with the other. They kill them when they steal—maybe that was it. Ultimately I believe it was Thai mafia hit men hired to come over the border and do this. It wasn't from here. Honestly. It's all Thai mafia, this whole business is mafia, it's not from here."

I tried to reassure him that "here" was still pristine, and that I was sure things would work out for him. Then I told him I was headed "there" today. I asked if he knew a fellow named Chang who worked the blackjack table.

"Are you kidding?! I know nobody there! I don't want to know anybody there. I never go there, and my advice to you—"

"Don't go there."

"That for sure. Let Sam show you Wat Toult'nian on hill here. Otherwise I hear next week you are caught in a fishing net."

The ride across the choppy inlet would have caused a North American customs agent to burst into laughter and tears. Stacked to the gunwales with boxes that had Thai and English script all over them, an echelon of three blue-bottomed motorboats were making the crossing from west to east, threading around the one I was in. After a smuggler got his goods this far he loaded them on the ferry to Sihanoukville and was home free.

Of course, if anyone was making a fortune it wasn't the motorboat drivers, at least judging from the dock they used. Hay Lat, as the landing on the other side was called, was a collection of corrugated-roofed huts with verandas held up by skinny crooked poles. The boats were chained three deep to a boom, so that I had to teeter-totter across each deck, then step up to the rotting wooden pier, where I was mobbed by drivers wanting to sell me a ride to the border. Otto had told me to take a car, since the motos were too dangerous on the back track, and after haggling a bit for a 50-baht fare I got in a Toyota with no windshield and whose back seat had been removed. "Drive slow," I told the driver. "I'm not in a rush."

"Slow, yes," he replied. "Very slow. No want hurt."

Five bone-jarring klicks on, we crested a hill and I beheld another world. Laid out against the glittering ocean below was a glaring white gambling town that made Pat Supapa seem Cambodia's equivalent of Stanley Ho. The palm-lined main street and emerald lawns stretched for a mile to the border, with hotels and hotels-in-progress the whole length. Backhoes and Caterpillars were digging into the hillsides and excavating the flats, sending up red and white clouds of dust to the tops of the aluminum streetlights. At the end of it all was the border-hugging flagship of the development, the five-star Grand Hotel and Koh Kong International Casino, a postmodern Xanadu that looked partly like a Chinese city hall and partly like a Fort Lauderdale condo, with a six-story pediment and a nine-story blue glass middle tower crowned by a Mandarin copper cupola. Beside its sweeping porte cochere stood a glass and concrete clock tower with a radio antenna and rooster on its fastigated top, circled by spot beams. I had to reflect that a few miles over my shoulder 90 percent of the homes were lit at night only by candles.

I got out of the Toyota and gave my driver a 10-baht tip. "Have you ever been inside the casino?"

"Me—no. Cambodia people no allow in. But much fun for tourist—if no lose everything, ha ha ha!"

The designers of the Koh Kong International Casino must have been well aware of the theory my father had held on gambling addicts: he said gamblers played not to win, or even to lose, but in order to cultivate a heroic sense of themselves. At the marble entrance to the casino, just beyond where you checked your guns and directly in front of the plush stairs to the high-stakes rooms, was a floodlit display case filled with hard evidence of the dire peril gamblers faced every time they crossed this threshold. Atop the case was a big sign that said, in Chinese, Thai, and English, "PAWN"— the embodiment of gambler risk. A smiling man in a crimson uniform and white gloves beckoned me to pause and review the contents. Looking in the case, my eyes were dazzled by coruscating gold, sparkling diamonds, and silvery pearls. Each piece of jewelry, hocked by some bottomed-out roller, had a price tag in Thai and U.S. currency. A Rolex was $9,000, a ring $18,000, a necklace $30,000. There was a woman's diamond tiara, with a price tag of $80,000. I looked up. A six-foot mirror behind the fellow gave me a gold-hued view of myself bent over the challenge, Chinese characters signifying "Good Fortune" over my scalp. To a compulsive player, this was the ultimate, inebriating dare, an announcement of the hazard that the brave faced squarely, and cowards ran from. No better than any hotshot gambling on a long shot, I turned and headed up to where the murders had taken place, not far from where Chang probably dealt.

At the top of the first landing was a mural of a Greek statue demurely posed by a fountain in a forest clearing, a cool image to comfort the sweaty sportsman before he rounded the landing to behold a six-foot statue of fiery Kwan Kung, the largest I'd ever seen indoors, roped off by a red velvet cord. At his feet were offerings of fruit and, of all things, an extra-large pizza. I stopped and pronammed, smelled the garlic and hot sauce, prayed for good fortune, and set down a 1,000-riel note in his dish. Me being white, my obeisance caught the attention of the floor manager at the pillar beside KK; I smiled at him and saw his glance go over my shoulder to a mountainous plainclothes guard. I put the wrestler and the overseer behind me, entered the low-ceilinged, smoky card room, done up in polished ochre wood. To my right was the refreshment bar—coffee, tea, drinks. Straight ahead were the card tables: poker, baccarat, and blackjack.

There was a young guy with thick spectacles dealing the blackjack table, not looking exactly like the archetype of an Inside Charlie. But of course you could never tell. I went over to the cage for 2,500 baht in chips and sat down between a middle-aged Thai woman at home base and a squinting overweight Chinese at first. I was figuring that if Larissa had phoned Chang, and this fellow *were* Chang, the info would be so fresh in his mind that there'd be some glow in his eyes as his gaze met the one belonging to the Jew from Little Odessa—showing up exactly on schedule. But his glance moved over mine, staying empty, on auto, on the job.

I was trying to decide when to make my move, but I was up $200 so suddenly that, spellbound and basking in the back pats of my neighbors, I became distracted from my mission, and didn't return to it until I crested and was on my way down. "Chang," I said, touching a 10,000-baht chip, ready to tell him I wanted change. But the dealer didn't give me that reactive glance we dogs and humans offer when we hear our name. He did look over, but not until he saw my proffered hand.

"You're Chang?" I asked, smiling.

"No, not Chang," he said, taking the chip and shoving me 10 from his rack. "Kai."

"Oh, hi Kai. Is Chang dealing today?"

"No."

"Because he was dealing the last time I was here. You look a little like him."

This aroused an askance look, and I cursed myself for not finding out from Larissa whether Chang was 20-something, like this guy, or an older gent. I'd automatically assumed that, because he was a big-mouth, Chang would be young. Being the only Americano this place had likely seen for months, I was already suspect. Now I was probably being assessed as a threat—Vegas bad guy, DEA, Interpol, or, most threatening of all to a casino covering up two murders, the press.

I had to stick it out, however—a forced gamble that bought me nothing but another 50-buck loss. At which point I got up and wandered into the roulette room. At the entrance, just this side, was an ornate lacquer wheel, a grand old antique with a gorgeous hardwood bowl, a four-foot lacquered black mast, ivory slots, and what looked like real diamonds set in the canoe eyes. To the left of the entrance the air-conditioning system throbbed like a Morlock engine, spoiling the effect of the museum piece. I was actually jotting those words, "Morlock engine," when the plus-size security guard—not a bad candidate for the part of a Morlock—came up behind me and asked if he could be of assistance.

"Do you know how old that wheel is?" I asked.

"Yes old," he said. "Come from United Stay, I think. Where do you come from?"

"Near there," I replied vaguely, "I'm traveling."

"You write travels?" he pointed to my pad, smiling.

"Yeah, this is for my diary. The minister of tourism in Phnom Penh told me Chang would show me around, explain the expansion."

"Chang?" he asked.

"He deals blackjack."

He thought on that for a moment. "No Chang. Kai. Have no Chang work here."

"I guess I got the wrong information. Oh well—where's the restaurant?"

Friendly as a doorman, he told me to go downstairs, make a left at the pawnshop and go straight. "It by pool. You see. Nice for you. See ocean." I walked straight out of the casino, waved goodbye to the floor manager, and descended the stairs. At the landing I looked back up and saw the manager on his cell phone.

From that moment on I was kept track of by a relay of employees on cell phones: check-in desk, where I inquired about a room; pool, where I sat and drew a map of the place; and restaurant, where I ordered a soup lunch of tum yum goong, and asked a truly innocuous-looking young waiter if he knew a fellow named Chang who dealt cards upstairs.

"Deal cards upstair?" he repeated.

"That's right."

"He no here today. Think go home Bangkok."

"Oh shoot," I said. "You know when he'll be back?"

"Think Tu-day. Off Sunday Monday."

Well, there it was. I had to get back to Phnom Penh to catch the boat up the Tonle Sap to Siem Reap on Tuesday. It had been a bitch getting tickets on that ferry, and if I missed it I'd never make the millennial celebrations. Might as well put down my last hundred baht and see if I could lose it all. "Here's my cell phone number. When Chang comes back on Monday, give it to him and tell him to call me collect."

Slightly nonplussed, the fellow took the note and service fee and pocketed both. I glanced over my shoulder, away from the sea and towards the stairs. "Those guys that were killed—"

But that ended the conversation. "Sorry, sorry," he smiled, holding his hand up and backing away.

I was back outside on the pool patio, chatting up the bar waitress about all the hubbub in the casino after the killings, when here came the wrestler, this time not smiling. He sent the waitress running, then asked straight out. "What you want here?"

I told him, "Writing a *travel* article"—all squealy innocence.

"Never mind, never mind," he said. "You check bag? I need to see!" He put his hand on the strap and tugged.

"No, *you* never mind," I came right back at him. "Here." I fished in my case that was now stretched between us and gave him Ambassador Norm Mailhot's card, Sum Manit's card, Sam Rainsy's card. He looked at them confusedly, like a bull going cross-eyed at a blur of sword points, then let the case go. I took the cards back. "I was *told* I would get a friendly reception here, so I could write that tourists should come here. I'm sorry, but I'm disappointed." I turned, feeling awfully naked at my back, and headed straight for the entrance, where the floor manager was waiting to see me out. As I huffed past I said snootily: "I'm gonna let the prime minister know about this when I see him in Siem Reap."

I just about did, too.

CHAPTER 23

DAWN OF A NEW MILLENNIUM

———

Those who violate the law will never prevail.
—BILLBOARD OUTSIDE SIEM REAP POLICE HEADQUARTERS

"I think if you can understand these men you will know why your man comes here." Senator Khieu San, vice chairman of the Cambodian Senate Legislative Committee, said this to me *sotto voce,* his eyes on the long table to our left. There sat Hun Sen, flanked by his generals, ministers, and senior policemen.

"You know what I am saying?" asked Khieu, whom I'd known a bare 12 hours.

"Yes, of course."

"In CPP, most of them are corrupt," he whispered. "Murder, corruption. But we will change. By the law, we will change the regime of Hun Sen."

It was millennial eve and Hun Sen was hosting a private dinner for his regime in Siem Reap's Kulen Restaurant, across the street from King Sihanouk's mansion and down the road from Angkor Wat. The Kulen fit the elite occasion. It was an open-air palace, with magnificently engraved pillars holding up golden roofs topped by *naga* serpents. At the east end of the restaurant was a brick courtyard and then a stage made to look like a classic Khmer temple. Five female *apsaras,* costumed in sequined lamé and stupa-like headgear, were dancing barefoot to an ancient Angkorian tune played by musicians on three-stringed fiddle, wooden xylophone, and leather drum. The heavenly nymphs moved to the eerie music with their supplicating palms bent backward, their eyes dreamily focused on the stars, turning and arching their bodies in angles that replicated the bas-reliefs on the hundreds of wats that graced the Kingdom.

I was observing this gorgeous performance from a table reserved for senior Funcinpec party members, headed by Khieu, who'd audaciously invited me to the dinner in the face of an understanding that no Western journalists were to be allowed in. In an hour we were all to leave in a motorcade to attend the New Year's celebrations, organized on the temple grounds by Sum Manit.

"Oh my God, why don't you eat your fish?!" Khieu shouted, less to get me to chow down than to mask any sign we were colluding in antigovernment sedition. He was an energetic short man of 60, with a high, crackly voice that could be heard for blocks when he raised it. "Have more fish, fresh from Tonle Sap Lake, what'sa'matta wit you?" he asked, sounding exactly like my grandmother. Then he leaned forward and resumed his conspiratorial tone. "You take the photograph of him and Bun Rany?" he asked, referring to Hun Sen and his wife, whose chalked and polished face reminded me of Michael Jackson's.

"Yes."

"Good. Hok Lundy?" he asked, meaning the meaty Cambodian director of police, whom I'd photographed before the dinner.

"Yes."

He patted my hand, and nodded with satisfaction. "This is what I am saying. Okay? Your man come here do business—no problem. Army, police—all corruption, all time. Sam Rainsy, he can run with his mouth, but he can't run with the ball. He think he the savior, but his mouth eats his brain. He brave but he change nothing. *We* will change, by the law!"

I'd met the delightful Khieu that blasting hot morning on the west portico to Angkor's main temple. It was 7 A.M., an hour before Cambodia's chief monks were scheduled to give a millennial blessing of peace to Sihanouk, Ranariddh, Hun Sen, and Senate President Chea Sim, a former committee secretary for the Khmer Rouge who was now chairman of the CPP. The ceremony was to be held up ahead at the Western Gopura, the pillared entrance to the passage that leads to the Vishnu Shrine under the 20-story main tower, symbol of Mount Meru, abode of the gods. I'd dearly wanted to be there for the historic occasion, but I had a problem, as I explained to the soldiers at the portico checkpoint. Someone at the Phnom Penh press office must have taken my money and pocketed it, because my press identity card hadn't arrived at the Siem Reap press office, as promised. "Let me just go in and find Sum Manit," I said, pointing to the three famous stupas standing against the morning sun a kilometer east. "He'll give you something official for me."

I edged forward, smiling, but the guard, not smiling, gave me a shove backward. I landed against Senator Khieu, who happened to be standing behind me.

"You want to go in, come with me," he announced, then turned to the guards. "This man my guest!" he commanded in English, at which point the guards lowered the rope and stood to attention as we passed.

Serious man, I thought. *Stay with him.*

"I hear you problem," Khieu said, striding the causeway across the moat and introducing me to his wife, Neang Chhayana, a pharmacist. "You a reporter, so you know already the problem with our country: everybody take, take, take—then no give what you pay for. Corruption everywhere."

"Well, I've actually been here long enough to find a couple'a bright spots—"

"Ay baby, where you from, man?" he boomed incongruously, in a pseudo African-American accent. When I looked at him totally bewildered and said "Brooklyn," he shouted, "I *t'ought* so!! I hear way you talk, man—sound like old time to me."

It turned out the senator had lived a year in my hometown as Ranariddh's foreign emissary and, as we strolled towards the stupas, he began reflecting on the old days, reciting all the high-crime stops on the Brooklyn IRT, mentioning names I hadn't heard in years, such as Utica Avenue and Nevins Street. He knew the black gangs who lurked aboveground, too. And he was thoroughly familiar with the Asian organized crime situation—tongs, Triads, and the psychotic Vietnamese groups. All in all he thought New York was far more dangerous than Phnom Penh—at least if you discounted the last quarter century.

"How the hell did you get from Cambodia to commuting for Ranariddh on the subway?" I asked, liking him more each moment.

"Crazy, man! K-A-*ray-zy!*" he exclaimed, and in the 20 minutes it took us to dawdle the kilometer to the Cruciform Terrace, the extremely loquacious politician gave me a précis of his life during the traumatic years. A graduate of both medical school and law school, he was arrested by the Khmer Rouge on the Glorious Seventeenth of April and put in a concentration camp called Bétail Mountain, surviving the first mass executions because he'd convinced his peasant jailers he was a barber. For four years he worked 18 hours a day cutting hair, digging irrigation trenches, and planting rice, until the Vietnamese conquered the country and drafted him as a translator. Because he was one of the few surviving professionals in Cambodia, the Communists made him the general secretary of the medical and pharmacy schools. In 1982, hating the "liberators" and their brutal puppet Hun Sen, he joined Funcinpec and went to the Thai border to fight with Ranariddh, returning 10 years later to run for office in the 1993 elections. He won a seat in the split government, then fled for his life during the 1997 coup, whereupon Ranariddh assigned him to tour the world to enlist support against the CPP. Basing himself in New York, he addressed the United Nations and founded fund-raising centers for the liberation of his homeland across the U.S. and Canada, then returned to Cambodia for the 1998 election and won a seat in the Senate and appointment as vice chairman of the legislative committee. Today, he said, each piece of legislation had to pass under his eyes before it could be voted on. At the moment he was trying to stop passage of a bill awarding lucrative pensions for 8,000 CPP veteran soldiers, not because he was a fiscal skinflint but because he'd discovered the soldiers were all dead. "It is a ghost army. The CPP will distribute the money to themselves," he told me. "Eight t'ousand dead soldiers will have good retirements."

As we mounted the steps to the Cruciform Gate he declared, "Come come, I will get you close to Hun Sen and Ranariddh, stand right beside them, look into Hun Sen's one eye and take the picture."

"How about the king?" I asked.

"No come today, too sick, many things wrong with him, you know this." He was referring to the fact that the 77-year-old king had had two strokes, suffered from diabetes, and on this day (I learned) was receiving a chemo treatment for his colon cancer.

Thanks to Khieu's pushy manipulations—"Out of way, this man wit me! Teddy, what you wait for? Go, *go!*"—by the time the ceremonies started I stood directly behind the four head monks in their ochre robes, taking pictures over their shaven heads of the chiefs they'd come to bless. The party leaders faced me on cheap-looking folding chairs: the round, bullet-headed Chea Sim in a military shirt and khaki pants; Hun Sen in a silver-gray sharkskin jacket and open-collared white shirt; and the middle-aged but still collegiately handsome prince, wearing a high-fashion navy blue shirt and matching slacks. Up close like this, Ranariddh appeared too refined and gentle to have led troops in jungle warfare. Indeed, his body language spoke volumes about his present vanquished state, and I felt a surge of sympathy for him. The thuggish leaders of the CPP leaned his way, chatting in pushy but friendly tones, while Ranariddh, perhaps with the thorny memories of his information minister's tongue torn out and his interior minister tortured and shot, leaned away from Hun Sen as if he had dragon breath. Both hands clasping his knees, the 56-year-old prince looked like a frightened bankruptcy case being railroaded into a sale by loutish businessmen.

To be sure, I had no way of knowing what kind of a leader Ranariddh would have made had he won the war. Khieu San notwithstanding, there were certainly enough instances of corruption in Ranariddh's own ranks to make Funcinpec run a close second to the CPP in scandals. Sam Rainsy's call for a plague on both their houses might be a feckless one, but it didn't seem over the top in this Marquezian land. Hun Sen had won, Ranariddh had lost, Rainsy was nowhere. Someday the law *might* prevail, but for the next decade the best Cambodia could hope for was that with unchallenged power the ever more secure strongman, his one good eye on history, would begin to take his own liberal pronouncements to heart. Fat chance, but in Cambodia one could argue that a corrupt peace was better than what had gone on before.

The priests intoned their throaty blessings over the three leaders, who now bowed their heads in prayer. In the cavernous minute of silence that followed I too tried to pray—but I couldn't concentrate for trying to guess what the big shots in front of me were asking of Vishnu. Hun Sen had claimed he couldn't have had an affair with the murdered Piseth Pelika; he was "incapable of such actions" because he'd had an appendix operation a month before Pelika's diary said they'd first had sex. (This was some admission coming from the Strongman of a Kingdom where previous god kings had claimed the power of eternal erections.) Now that he was back in vigorous health, was he fantasizing spending New Year's with some other starlet? And Chea Sim, the Khmer Rouge brute: at Hun Sen's forum on corruption, Chea's alleged personal bagman, Customs Director Pen Siman, had been singled out show-trial style by the prime minister as an official whose avaricious days were numbered. Was Chea now scheming a replacement that would keep his pipeline to the riches of the nation open? As for Ranariddh—all he seemed to want these days was for Hun Sen to anoint him king upon the death of his ailing father. Unfortunately, according to Phelim Kyne, the prime minister was not anxious to have his old enemy placed in a position where he could nix senior CPP appointments. Instead, he was said to be planning to install Ranariddh's half-Italian mother, Queen Monineath, as a temporary "symbol" of the crown, gradually doing away with the monarchy entirely. Was the prince praying for guidance on how to handle Mom if the Hun tapped her?

Ranariddh lifted his hangdog face first, pronammed to the priests, then to Hun Sen and Chea Sim. They returned the honor. The men shook hands all around, looking as if each were taking turns at wishing the other goodwill. I asked one of the PM's bodyguards beside me what they were saying. "Forgive past, make promise work for future," he summed up their millennial conversation. Then he clamped my elbow with a tight claw. "No go closer!"

The triumvirate stood and moved to the south side of the Cruciform. Thousands of Cambodians on the lawn below us—a lot of whom were legless and most of whom didn't have two riels to rub together—let up a cheer. Under a gold silk tent, Ranariddh and Hun Sen joined their wives. They lit joss sticks and raised them above their heads in another silent prayer. As they did so, the minister of culture and fine arts gave a short speech thanking the gods that the ancient heritage of the nation had been revived in peace after years of repression in war. When he was done, a quartet of musicians began to play on the other side of the terrace. That was the cue for the first of 1,500 orange-robed monks to begin filing out of the Gopura. Helped by their wives, Ranariddh and Hun Sen began ladling rice and offering gold-wrapped care packages to the monks. When the monks were all fed, Chea Sim (unaccompanied by any wife that I could see), the PM and Bun Rany, and the prince and his wife Marie, were handed doves. The politicians released the birds above their heads and the crowd gave another cheer. And then, the millennial peace pact blessed and sealed, prosperity for the future sworn, the leaders paraded away.

"Meet me tonight, six-thirty at Kulen Restaurant," Khieu told me as he hurried to a Funcinpec meeting. "Make like you are friend from New York. I have lots to tell you."

I grabbed a moto and returned to my hotel to catch up on typing two days' worth of notes. The Ta Som Guest House was actually a flophouse for Cambodian laborers—all I could get on this hectic weekend when 10,000 visitors were fighting over 1,000 hotel rooms. Uncollected bags of food garbage littered the halls, which crawled with giant roaches and geckos hunting them. My "room" was the kind you stood in the middle of with your arms folded for fear of touching anything. It was broiling hot; the fan didn't work, there was no soap, no toilet paper, no toilet seat, no hot water, and the blanket on the straw mattress was a threadbare towel that stank of mold. Later that night, when Khieu San returned me to the Ta Som, he remarked: "My God! How you stay here? When the Khmer Rouge retreat they destroy everything except this place—leave for example how people should live."

The Ta Som matched my apocalyptic mood as I hunched over my laptop on the straw bed. I'd arrived from Phnom Penh after passing through yet another travesty of Cambodian corruption, this one revealed to me on the five-hour ferry that made its way up the Tonle Sap River and then the length of the 2,000-square-mile Tonle Sap Lake. The lake and the river were the historic and ecological heart of Cambodia, owing to a natural phenomenon that was a near miracle. For eight months of the year the lake flowed into the river and the river flowed into the Mekong just south of the Foreign

Correspondents Club. But in June something magical happened. With the coming of the monsoon rains the Mekong overflowed and flooded north, reversing the direction of the Tonle Sap for four months, almost doubling the size of the source lake and filling it with tons of nutrients picked up along the Mekong's 2,200-mile run from its headwaters in Tibet. The result: Tonle Sap Lake was the richest freshwater fishing ground in Asia, and the annually replenished mud-bed around it among Asia's best rice-growing regions. Twelve hundred years ago this abundance had led to the founding of Angkor on high ground 10 miles north of the lake, which became the capital of the greatest empire of Southeast Asia—the Angkor Kingdom—whose wealth produced the grandiose temples that were the backdrop for the Millennial Celebration.

Now, however, the CPP regime's greed and corruption were destroying the fishery in the cradle of Cambodian civilization. A British NGO worker on the roof of the fast ferry had explained the situation as we entered the freshwater sea—so large that the shore receded out of sight as we traveled down the lake's middle. The Brit's name was Matt Wheeler, an official with Wetlands International, whose office in Phnom Penh was then fighting ecological disaster in the nation.

Cambodia's lakes and rivers were divided into fishery sectors, Matt had told me. In theory, about two-thirds of the sectors were held by Cambodia's two million fishermen, and a third by a few private companies that bid in public auction for the exclusive right to fish for two years in designated lots. In reality, the bidding process was anything but open: corrupt fisheries officials took up to 10 times the bid price in tea money for the fishing lots, then accepted regular payoffs for ignoring the practices of the lot owners. To reap the massive harvests necessary to recover their investment and turn handsome profits, the lot owners used illegal fishing technology condemned around the world, including dynamite fishing, electrocution, the use of "catch-all" mosquito netting rather than legal gill nets, and the dyking and draining of segregated ponds—all of which effectively swept fish clean from the private lots, as well as from public lots for miles around.

Having fished out their own areas, the private leaseholders then turned to the public areas: with the help of fisheries officials, they terrorized locals who tried to fish these lots, confiscating their equipment, booby-trapping their nets with hand grenades, regularly beating up fishermen and arresting them on trumped-up charges of illegal fishing. Even if the corruption were to be cleaned up tomorrow, Wheeler told me, the Tonle Sap faced another impending disaster. China had plans to build 15 dams along the Mekong, and Laos and Cambodia had plans for another 11, which would vastly decrease, or perhaps even eliminate, the reversal of the river during the rainy season. Combine all of this with the increasing pollution of the shallow lake, and, Wheeler said, the most productive freshwater fishery in Southeast Asia—supplying more than 60 percent of Cambodia's protein intake—was on its way to being destroyed.*

Sum Manit was now at a podium that had been rolled into the Kulen Restaurant's courtyard. There, in a barely audible monotone, he welcomed the men at the head table, then read a speech recounting the genesis and planning behind the celebrations we were to witness tonight at Angkor Wat.

Khieu San leaned around me, his crinkly eyes squished together as he tapped a colleague of his named Chhanrith Sok Cham, Ranriddh's personal assistant, who was representing the prince at the dinner. "Mr. Chhanrith, tell him what you find out 'bout Sum Manit trouble!"

Chhanrith, a handsome fellow in his 30s with a modern brush cut and a thoroughly Westernized mien, leaned nonchalantly sideways and spoke to his dessert. "Sum Manit ran out of money even for portable toilets," he said. "Now we are proving why. Hun Sen's men took the money to buy buildings that will go to the CPP after the celebration."

"That is why they have only forty toilets for t'irty t'ousand people," Khieu cracked, laughing so hard it seemed like he was not even trying to hide the joke. "Have to hire two hundred people clean up. So watch where you step tonight! Like minefield—we walk in single row!"

Sum Manit finished his speech with an expression of gratitude to the good company and a confident wish that the new century would hold great hope for the Kingdom. And then it was Hun Sen's turn.

"Quick, quick, go up, take anudder picture, take the picture," Khieu said to me. "Use it in your book."

"But I want you to translate what he says," I told him.

"It will be bullshit, take your picture and come back."

---

*The rape of Tonle Sap Lake would not be addressed by Hun Sen until almost a year later, when it had reached a point past all denial. Hun Sen publicly declared he would end the graft and greed of fisheries officers and fishing-lot owners. "Fisheries officers are leeches that suck the people's blood and they are the dogs that guard the fishing concessions," he announced in a televised speech in Siem Reap. He dismissed his Fisheries Department director, but, as usual, the old ways continued. A month later, fisheries officials went on a vengeful rampage, arresting fishermen and confiscating their equipment. When the *Phnom Penh Post* contacted the newly installed Fisheries Department director, Nao Thouk, he told them he knew almost nothing about Cambodia's fisheries sector, and hadn't heard about the urgent calls for reform.

But I moved too quickly, and got too close. There'd been a couple of attempts on the PM's life in the last year and so Hun Sen's phalanx of guards were understandably hair-triggered for action. They were pretty subtle, though. As I was moving forward to the podium, my eye in the viewfinder, a palm went into my belly and another gripped my shoulder, spinning me around like a top, my momentum smoothly conserved and, with a shove, redirected back from whence I came.

"Never mind, never mind," Khieu said, "take from here, take from here."

Over the mike Hun Sen's twisted, frozen mouth gave the consonantal clacking of Khmer an even harsher edge to my Western ears. He picked up where Sum Manit left off, referring, Khieu whispered to me, to the future, the bright future, "the end of the past, the beginning of the new." Reconciliation. Human Rights. Democracy. The Rule of Law.

"He talk bullshit," Khieu mumbled. "Mean not'ing."

Probably that was true, I thought, looking over at Hun Sen's round smiling wife. There wasn't a person in the room who didn't know the scandal surrounding the murdered movie star, Piseth Pelika. There wasn't a person who didn't know the sad fate of the 18-year-old karaoke star Tan Samarina, now lying in a hospital without a face—a case of acid mutilation that Hok Lundy's police had still made no progress in solving.

"You know story 'bout Hok Lundy and Ho Sok?" Khieu asked me. "Ninety-seven coup, Ho Sok run to Australians, Canadians, no sanctuary?"

"Yeah, I know that story. And you?" I asked. "Aren't you afraid for yourself?"

"Wait, I show you."

As we left the Kulen Restaurant, Khieu San introduced me to his bodyguard, So Peap, a captain in the national army who was still loyal to Funcinpec. He was armed to the teeth, with bayonet, sidearm, and an auto mini-rifle in a holster by his seat, clips of extra ammo at his feet. If Captain So survived the first salvo, I thought, he could stand off a platoon.

We drove through the throngs of civilians marching from the town to the temples, with Khieu reflecting how silly it was for a Buddhist country to be celebrating the turn of a millennium based upon the birth of a Christian god. I told him the explanation was easy: I'd passed a sign on Pochentong Road hanging outside an English language school that said, "English Never Dies."

"So you're just joining globalization—"

He interrupted, "No, no, no, country-wester' never dies!" He leaned forward from the back seat, took out a tape from the console beside me and told Captain Peap to put it on. It was a recording of a two-day-old broadcast by a Florida country-western radio station. Was I surprised to discover that Khieu was a fanatical country-music fan and that his friends in the States sent him radio tapes every week via FedEx? No, I wasn't. "The time now is four twenty-nine and here's LeAnn Rimes but don't quote me on the rhyme, mama! Eeeee-HAAAAA!! Love this gal when she's blue lemme tell ya—mmmmm-HMMMM!"

The government had constructed a VIP grandstand near the temple's East Gate, and the misappropriation of the country's resources hit home when we took our life in our hands and mounted the platform, built with what little money had trickled down through the grasping hands of CPP officials. The rough wooden steps were so narrow and sagging the silken-gowned women in their heels could hardly get a footing. The floor of the grandstand, with inch spaces between slats, was even more dangerous for heels. However, at least the lines of light from below gave a clue where to set your feet, for the grandstand itself sat on thin crooked poles and was completely open underneath and lit by bare bulbs, which, for safety's sake, was both reassuring and terrifying. On the one hand, it looked like it could collapse 30 feet to the ground, taking the crowd with it; on the other, it could be easily surveilled for bombs.

About 500 hard Formica seats were arrayed on several sloping levels conveniently sectioned by thousand-year-old stone walls. We walked down to the Funcinpec section and sat six rows back from the stage and just across the aisle from the CPP, as if this were a session of the National Assembly. On the floodlit stage was an armless statue of Suryavaram II; in the distance, illuminated green against the black sky, were the awesome spires of Angkor Wat, which the god king had built. General Hok Lundy came down the aisle with his retinue of officers and took a seat just across the aisle from us. "Take the picture," Khieu ordered.

While we waited for the grand entrance of Hun Sen and Ranariddh, Khieu San took my notebook and drew four overlapping circles of Cambodian power. Watching the diagram develop, I thought that if there was a break to be had, Hun Sen and his backers wouldn't get it from Khieu, whose friends had been tortured and shot in the 1997 coup. He wrote "H.S." in the center of the innermost circle. In the second circle, which he numbered "1," he block printed "EDUCATED MAFIA." In the next circle, which he labeled "2," he printed "GENERAL/ARMY/POLICE: NO MUCH EDUCATED—FROM K.R., MURDER." In the next circle, he wrote "3.–V.N. UNDERCOVER, MILITARY ATTACHÉ."

"Okay, I explain you what go on," Khieu said. "Hun Sen center. He's uneducated, no completed more than high school, a farmer from Kompong

Cham, but Khmer *Rouge!* Then, number one circle, Hun Sen's entourage, who are making corruption. Everything in corruption, they do."

"Drugs?" I asked.

"Everything—you know that. Number two circle: all the generals who commit murder, all taught by the Khmer Rouge, you know that. All the generals they pay to Hun Sen, that's why he millionaire."

"Do they pay Hun Sen directly?"

"No, pay their own party, and own party pay. No pay, no favors. And number three, V.N.—the Vietnamese—all undercover military attachés, all three-star generals. They the ones put him in power, they the ones still here, all undercover, hiding. During coup, it was fifty-fifty did it, V.N. and CPP."

"Teng Boonma funded it too."

"Yes, he's a big mafia, but he just a poor guy before. They have monopoly now. Timber, cut everything. Fish, take everything. The human rights groups, NGOs, they know everything. What they know: Hun Sen he need them all. Number one, all educated doctors, engineers, architects, businessmen. Mostly corrupt. No one clean."

"Do you really think you can you stop it?" I asked. "I mean, really, do you think there's a chance?"

He let his breath out heavily, handed me back my pad. "By the law! We fight by the law! By the law we will win! Audit! The government must be audited!! But oy, I'm telling you!" he lamented, again sounding like my Gramma Rose.

Over the PA a voice intoned in Khmer: "Victory to Cambodia, Victory to the King!"

The arrival of the guests of honor—Hun Sen and Ranariddh—was timed five minutes apart, each coming down the main aisle to applause and pronams, with Khieu pushing me into the aisle (and their faces) for more pictures. They took seats up front, silhouetted against the stage in rattan chairs. We all stood for the playing of the national anthem. The governor of Siem Reap Province gave a welcoming speech, and then the performance commenced.

According to my program it was to be a two-hour spectacle, a play and three ballets involving 750 artists in all, the first three segments performed by troupes from the provinces, the last by the King's Royal Dance Troupe. For all his pessimism, Khieu San said that more than almost anything else, the resurrection of dance and acting across Cambodia gave him hope. It had been at the center of Khmer culture for 1,200 years, celebrating the Angkorian glory and the founding religions of Hinduism and Buddhism that had merged about the time of the building of the temples before us. Then, in four years, the Khmer Rouge had attempted to eradicate the past, and had almost succeeded in murdering every dancer and actor in the land—with only one old woman who knew how to make the elaborate costumes of the *apsara* surviving. The KR's goal was to annihilate all memory of the *apsara*, who danced in the temples in worship of Vishnu and Shiva, and their embodiment on earth, the god king.

"Now you see," Khieu said, "they come back, thanks God! Okay, watch, watch."

The first act was a colorful comedy of manners about an old guru and his two warrior disciples. Despite its intended lightheartedness, it was a particularly appropriate morality tale, for it centered around the conflict of the two disciples over an *apsara,* dressed in glittering red and gold satin, who appealed to the guru in a heartrending falsetto voice to prevent her two suitors from killing each other. The guru lectured the two disciples on their foolishness, then called down from the heavens another *apsara* in green and gold. Now both men had brides. The play concluded with the guru's admonishment that there should always be peace between men, for the heavens provided enough for all. (I did note that during the applause Ranariddh and Hun Sen leaned their heads towards each other and seemed to converse amiably.)

This was followed by a pastoral dance in celebration of the bounty of the land, with about 50 farmers and their wives partnering in lively gambado with the gorgeously personified winds and rain. The number of performers on stage doubled for the third act, a reverent ballet in honor of the spirits who dwelled along the southern coast, which included, to my delight, a cameo appearance by Ya-mao, borne across the stage on a divan held aloft by red phalluses. And then, close to 11:00, came the finale, the performance of the Hindu epic *Churning of the Ocean Milk* by several hundred from the Royal Dance Troupe. If the Royal Troupe ever manages to get the funding to go on the road with this piece, and they show up in your town, drop everything and go see it.

It is an enactment of one of the most prominent bas-reliefs on the East Gallery of Angkor Wat, the most famous of all Khmer myths, inherited from the ancient Indian traders who called at the southern ports. For almost an hour on stage, in an explosion of blinding primary colors and gleaming flashes of silver and gold, 88 *asura,* or devils, battle with 92 *devas,* or gods, churning up the metal-blue sea to extract the white elixir of immortality, coveted by the lords of heaven and the lords of hell. It is a vast tug-of-war, a psychic, and psychedelic, battle that explodes in frenetic drumbeats, screaming strings, and impassioned jujitsu dance—with no letup from the moment the lights go up. It is, in fact, a parable of humanity's catharsis at the beginning of time, when consciousness first emerged and death was understood and anticipated—the dreaded knowledge imparted by a *naga* serpent in the ocean, who tantalized humanity with his jealously guarded antidote to death—a milk that must be released from within a watery solution. In a literal and symbolic life-or-death battle, the scarlet *asura* demons hold on to the head of the *naga*; the yellow *deva* gods hold on to its tail. Reluctant to yield to either, the serpent coils itself around a fire-spewing volcano, Mount Mandala, in the center of the blue roiling sea. Vishnu joins the battle on the side of the *devas*. He is incarnated as a huge turtle and settles his shell atop Mount Mandala as a fulcrum for the *devas*. Losing his balance, Vishnu calls out for help, and Brahma, Shiva, the monkey god Hanuman, and Lakshmi, the goddess of beauty, join the fray. In the heavens above— that is, in a kaleidoscopic gallery above the stage—a chorus of rainbow *apsara* shout, sing, and dance encouragement to the *devas*. In the course of battle the desperate tug-of-war churns the water, until the pure foamy milk of eternal life rises to the surface. In a final titanic clash the devils are defeated, and in Wagnerian triumph heaven celebrates. The milk of immortality is now heaven's gift to offer man.

Churning of the Ocean Milk ended a few minutes over schedule—five to midnight. Ranariddh, in a white Nehru jacket with gold buttons, mounted the stage, joined behind by 200 robed monks. Glancing at his watch he hurried through a speech, emphatic in English that there must be "peace, progress, prosperity for our future, born from our reconciliation." The crowd, on its feet, applauded as he gestured to Hun Sen, who didn't quite make it to the stage before the cannon blast signaled the changeover to the new millennium.

While the fireworks rent the night (somewhat unsettling in this land) I hugged Khieu San, kissed his wife on the cheek, shook hands with Chhann ith Sok Cham, and took another picture of them all. "Happy New Year! Good luck to you!" I said. "And good luck to Cambodia!" For now, the smell of ocean milk in my nostrils, I was off to raise up Steve and bless him with mortal life. As in Macau, I'd found no new leads on his identity here, but I was certain I would have better luck on my next stop. I was off to the Philippines—whose devils would shortly make Cambodia seem like a paragon of honesty and rectitude.

CHAPTER 24

THE GHOST OF MANILA

Ysabella couldn't decide if all this was a sign of an extremely backward society . . . or whether it was actually a preview of a sophisticated futuristic state likely to hold sway everywhere sometime soon.
—JAMES HAMILTON-PATERSON, GHOSTS OF MANILA

Waiting on line before the customs desk at Ninoy Aquino Airport I was a very nervous man. On the bottom of my declaration form were the scarlet words: "DEATH TO DRUG TRAFFICKERS UNDER PHILIPPINE LAW." If I were detained and set up, my only hope for rescue would come from the white-haired missionary woman who stood behind me. The woman, an evangelical Christian from Atlanta, had listened intently on the plane as I explained that the gangster-cop I was investigating might have flagged my name in the computer system. She'd written down my publisher's home phone number and promised to call if she saw me pulled aside. "Ephesians 6:17," she now whispered to my back as I stepped forward.

The Bureau of Immigration agent looked at my passport, looked at my face, and punched in my numbers. He studied the screen for a nerve-racking half minute. Finally he turned from his computer to flip through my visa stamps. "You were in Cambodia for which purpose?"

"To see the New Year's celebration at Angkor Wat."

"Hong Kong and Macau?"

"I went on a boat cruise."

He stamped me in and leaned sideways. In vast relief I turned and waved to my Christian lifeline. She smiled sweetly and pointed skyward.

Keep praying for me, I thought, because I don't have a single safe contact here, and no plan for coming up with one. On the taxi ride into Manila I considered how Steve's law enforcement status was making my mission in the Philippines infinitely more complicated than it had been six and a half years ago. Given that he was affiliated with the NBI as a Confidential Agent or even as a full-fledged one, what should I do first? Start looking for Steve and then find an honest cop to arrest him? Or find an honest cop and then start looking for Steve? The order seemed important, and I needed a sign. If I made a mistake and talked to the wrong cop, or to any cop who was not exactly the *right* cop, I'd be in deep trouble. "They'd set it up so you'd die a scandalous death," I recalled one officer telling me in Starbucks just before I'd left Vancouver. "And we'd all say, 'Oh, I didn't know Terry was into *that!*'"

Suddenly my driver pointed out the window towards Manila Bay and shouted, "You can see, look! look!" I rolled down the filthy window and beheld—beyond the palms of Roxas Boulevard, surrounded by tugboats— the magically transposed Jumbo Palace.

Well, here was my sign. The Ephesians were giving me a place to start.

Glancing through the newspapers in my cheapo hotel I saw that the Jumbo was at the center of the first Philippine scandal of the millennium. Pictures of the floating casino dominated the front pages, and filling the text below were stories of Macau gangsters, strange stock deals, drugs, and corrupt politicians. With all that I knew about the upheaval in Steve's world, I had a reporter's sense that this Jumbo story would plague the Republic for years.

According to the papers, Ho's many-layered dreamboat had arrived in Manila Bay at sunset on Millennial Eve—a week late but still mostly intact after surviving a typhoon in the South China Sea. For the next few days it had bobbed passively a kilometer from shore while customs agents and stevedores inspected its contents and prepared its decks for docking. Today it was being pulled and pushed towards a pier jutting from the most valuable piece of real estate in the capital—a 300-acre jetty on which stood the Senate Building, the International Convention Center, the Philippine Cultural Center, and the Folk Arts Theater.

I walked over to the bayside Roxas Boulevard and joined a crowd following the final transit of the wacky barge, reflecting that the papers were leading their stories with the Church's condemnations of the Jumbo in this overwhelmingly Catholic country. "With gambling, the other vices come marching in—drugs, prostitution, sex crimes and many more," Archbishop Jaime Cardinal Sin proclaimed in a press release. "There will be more families to be destroyed and more homes going bankrupt because of the arrival of the floating casino-restaurant." Cardinal Sin's colleague, Archbishop Oscar Cruz, even accused the government of committing an outright "crime" by inviting Ho and his Jumbo into town: "We already have enough gambling lords, drug lords and other vice lords. We are now importing more of them?"

For the press it was a quote worth repeating, because Cruz had actually offered that damning assessment 10 weeks previously, when Ho had flown to Manila on his private jet to announce he was taking over the chairmanship of a Philippine gambling corporation called BW Resources and bringing in the casino-restaurant. "Macau is returning to China very shortly but, of course, I will have one more place to operate in," the tall, fit, and still handsome Ho had declared at the Philippine Stock Exchange in Makati, the ritziest section of that otherwise destitute city.

Pointedly, on the day Ho made his announcement, the chairman of the nation's Securities and Exchange Commission, Perfecto Yasay, called a parallel news conference, declaring that he'd ordered the SEC's prosecution and enforcement branch to determine if appropriate disclosures had been made by BW to justify its 5,000 percent rise in price in the months before Ho's official announcement. BW had almost no assets, Yasay told reporters, yet it had attained a market value four times the country's number two food and drink manufacturer.

Not that Yasay's ominous news conference affected Ho's reception at his next stop in Manila, just across the Pasig River at the Malacañang presidential palace, where the gambling magnate was treated as if he were a visiting head of state by the 63-year-old president. Joseph "Erap" Estrada, elected in May 1998 with the largest margin of votes in the country's history, was a hard-drinking and high-living former movie star, whose flamboyant nickname was derived from the reverse spelling of *pare*, Filipino slang for buddy. A profiteer in shares of BW Resources himself (as the president had privately bragged to his finance secretary Edgardo Espiritu just the other week), Erap embraced Ho and his Filipino partner, Dante Tan, the controlling stockholder of BW and a heavyweight contributor to the president's election campaign, as well as Estrada's closest *pare*.

"They'll be long-term investors here in the country, that's why I welcome them," said the pompadored and piratically mustached Erap. "I also encouraged [Ho] to invest in socialized housing, which he agreed," he added, conscious as ever that he owed his political popularity to his film persona as a blue-collar defender of the *masa*—the masses—against the crooked elite. "Is that true, Mr. Ho?"

"That's correct, that's correct," Ho replied, stating that he had a long-term relationship with the Philippines and cared about the country's welfare. "I think some of the older people here would remember that a quarter century ago I started to operate the first casino in Manila Bay and thereafter another eight casinos for your late president—" Ho stopped himself, apparently weighing whether he should be alluding to that monstrous thief Marcos. "I don't have to mention names," Ho cracked.

The Church wasn't persuaded by this glib ole boys' fellowship. Egged on by the angry archbishops, faithful Catholics declared they would stage a mass protest at the rescheduled opening of the Jumbo. On the day it docked, however, I saw only excited picture-takers following the barge's final progress across the cloudy blue Manila Bay. At the breezy intersection where the palm-lined boulevard met the jetty, the curious citizens climbed the steps to the Cultural Center plaza and made their way around back to the cozy Folk Arts Theater, beside which the garish pagoda was nestling up to a floating gangway then undergoing some deafening jackhammering.

Security was tight at the gangway's entrance. Guards in ink-blue uniforms toting sawn-off Super Magnum shotguns patrolled a concrete barrier, itself protected by a steel gate. The spectators, not trusting the itchy fingers of the nervous men behind their elephant guns, stood safely back of a monument to Julian Felipe, composer of the Philippine national anthem. I scanned the scene for Steve, then walked up to a fellow in a suit holding a clipboard who was overseeing a small army of workers constructing a temple-like portico before the gangway. I told him I was a journalist writing about Manila's tourist attractions. I took a couple of pictures of the Jumbo through the gleaming white pillars and asked if it would be opening on January 11, like the papers said.

Even in their most stressed moments Filipinos never forget how to laugh, and this fellow hitched his clipboard helplessly around at the chaos of the half-finished dock and said, "Does it look it to you, my friend? Ha ha ha! Not to me! Maybe two weeks, three weeks after, then you come back for the opening."

"Will Stanley Ho and Erap be here?"

"An arrangement certainly made already," the overseer said, and then pointedly winked. "I think if it is a party then Erap will surely come to it."

As it turned out, neither Stanley Ho nor Erap showed up for the Jumbo's gala opening, nor was it ever refitted as a casino, nor did it serve dim sum more than once before pulling up its red ramps and boarding up its gold doors. I should have put down money on my reporter's prediction, because the day the Jumbo docked, BW Resources, President Estrada's administration, indeed the entire country began to come apart at the scams.

Alleging there was a "culture of corruption" in the president's administration, Finance Secretary Edgardo Espiritu resigned, a headline act that took place in the fresh wake of a press conference held by Senator Loren Legarda, chair of the Citizen's Drug Watch Foundation, at which she docu mented complicity between Chinese Triad drug runners, the Philippine National Police, and the Bureau of Immigration. A few days later the Philippine House of Representatives called for government hearings into Stanley Ho, based upon leaked RCMP and U.S. Justice Department intelli gence reports alleging that Ho was a suspected "leader/member" of a Triad. The chair of the Philippine House Committee on Order and Security, Representative Roilo Golez, was quoted in the *Daily Inquirer* as saying that the police reports pointed to Ho allegedly being "one of the world's biggest drug lords." If the police reports were true, Golez ruminated, "then the Ho floating restaurant would be like a Trojan horse that would disgorge tons of drugs and hundreds of traffickers while we sleep." These flaming comments were followed by more brimstone denunciations from the Catholic Bishops' Conference, which called the casino-restaurant an "evil form of vice con cocted by the organized crime Triads from Hong Kong."

After consulting with his Philippine National Police chief, General Panfilo Lacson, Estrada dismissed the foreign police reports as decade-old speculations "based on rumors," and the vocal reaction to them as hysteri cal hype. Meanwhile, an outraged Stanley Ho—who in his long career had never been charged with a crime—purchased full-page advertisements in two Manila papers declaring "the allegations are unsupported by any evi dence and are groundless," going on to aver that for 30 years he had helped the Macau government fight the Triad gangs. "These [police] reports only say that I know some Triad members," Ho told reporters in Hong Kong. "Well, maybe you have come across some. To be associated with or to know someone is completely different." He heaped praise on President Estrada as a "farsighted" leader whose election had changed the investment climate for foreigners like himself, and sympathized with Dante Tan, whom he called a "victim. . . . He is going up too fast so people are trying to bring him down again, taking me with him."

Within a week another political bomb dropped, provoking 150 demon strators to burn a poster of Ho and Estrada in front of the Jumbo. The head of the SEC, Perfecto Yasay, revealed that back in November 1999, shortly after Estrada had given Ho the red-carpet treatment at Malacañang, the president had phoned Yasay five times, illegally ordering the SEC to halt its insider-trading investigation of BW Resources and clear Dante Tan of any wrongdoing. In fact, Yasay claimed, Ho's partner, Tan, had nearly caused "the total collapse" of the Philippine securities market through his machinations of BW's stratospherically soaring and then plummeting shares—a pump-and-dump scheme for which Tan was eventually criminally charged and, looking at a sentence of 21 years, decided it was best to flee to Australia. Yasay himself fled to the United States, claiming he was receiving death threats from gangster goons working for Estrada.

The Philippine Daily Inquirer and the Philippine Center for Investigative Journalism pursued the reek of scandal like hound dogs, publishing a series of exposés on the president which included charges that Estrada had pressured the Philippine Gaming and Amusement Board to approve an application for an on-line gambling franchise by Dante Tan, despite the absence of any bidding or notice to the public; that Estrada had purchased palatial mansions for his numerous girlfriends with millions in government funds; that he frequently invited his Chinese gangster cronies to Malacañang to indulge in marathon mah-jongg sessions in which as much as $1 million was at stake in one night; and that he'd knowingly hired as his Latin-American affairs consultant a fugitive from U.S. justice, Mark Jimenez—a 30 percent shareholder in BW Resources and a major contributor to Estrada's election campaign—who was wanted by the FBI for $3.5 million in tax evasion, mail fraud, and illegal contributions to the Democratic Party. Almost all the exposés of Estrada and his cronies used the BW Resources scandal as the tipping point for a descent into a state of national corruption so abysmal that it rivaled the worst malfeasance of the Marcos years—an era ended only by revolution. The country's sense of betrayal was summed up by a Daily Inquirer columnist named Jerry Barican: "Some people call Malacañang a snake pit. That is an insult to the snake."

The cascade of revelations and apocalyptic denunciations went on all around me as I set to work in Manila during the first phase of the Estrada government's collapse. It was only to be expected in Steve's adopted homeland in the wake of Macau's handover, but one worrying fact did cross my mind repeatedly as I schemed for a way to get at the Paper Fan. The number of journalists murdered with impunity in the Philippines was now up to 36.

The headquarters of the National Bureau of Investigation occupied a nine-story building in the grimy heart of Manila's Ermita section, a dozen blocks north of the Jumbo. Being the nexus and repository of the Philippines' crime-fighting efforts, the building was shielded from busy Taft Avenue by a high concrete wall, with tight security at the two entrances to its seven-acre compound and its dilapidated outbuildings. Civilians who had business with the NBI had to pass single file through a narrow tunnel in the fortresslike west wall, upon which hung a sign that said, "No ID, No

Entrance." On the other side of the wall, guards recorded names, inspected shoulder bags, and patted down suspicious types. A little farther up the wall, flanked by two guardhouses, a steel cross-armed gate blocked a driveway used by official vehicles and agents on foot. Sporting ID badges that dangled from their necks, the agents ducked under the bar and then proceeded through the compound to the canopied entrance of the main building. Here, beyond an "Authorized Personnel Only" sign, two officers with radios sat at a desk in the building's foyer, raising a hand to greet each plainclothes officer as he walked in.

I was meticulously acquainted with all this because for the last several days, at 4:30 in the afternoon, I'd climbed a flight of stairs to an elevated Metrorail platform above the braying buses and jeepneys on Taft Avenue and studied the NBI compound, a block away, through binoculars. Steve was the type to leave work at exactly five and that was why I was back again today at this hour, trying to make out the face of every person pouring out of the building and into the compound, although I knew I was missing at least a third of them. I'd already shot two rolls of film for study back at my hotel, but these had turned out to be hopelessly obscure, just a distant mob of agents and federal employees fanning out in all directions, half of them facing the wrong way. I'd tried to look into the unmarked vans and cars lining up at the driveway, but almost all of the vehicles had darkened windows.

I decided this was an effort in futility; I'd have to get inside the compound and then into the headquarters building and conduct a search of its offices. Getting in wouldn't be a problem, I knew: the NBI was very open to press interviews if the proper procedures were followed. The difficulty for me was that, given my mission and Steve's status, I couldn't reveal my identity. I'd have to enter the place incognito and in disguise. That kind of hanky panky would take some planning.

By six o'clock the thousands of fuming vehicles below the Metrorail station made me feel as if I'd smoked two packs of cigarettes, and the killing heat and tension had turned every pore of my body into an oily spigot. I packed my binoculars in my shoulder bag and went down the stairs to Taft Avenue, turned west at United Nations Avenue, and strolled in front of the Ermita headquarters of the Philippine National Police, whose back doors opened into the rear lot of the NBI compound. I knew I'd never get through there unless I was under arrest, so I took a picture of the compound through the station's windows for study later, then walked a couple of blocks farther west, past the Holiday Inn, which contained a luxury casino where the city's Triad bosses liked to lose their money. I'd actually won 1,000 pesos in roulette there the evening before, and I thought about stopping in again, giving one more shot at searching the bruisers in sunglasses for a short guy. But I didn't want to check my camera at the security desk and risk having the film developed and plopped on the desk of God knows which agent of doom. In the Philippines, security-desk thefts were as common as security-guard holdups.

Beyond the Holiday Inn I turned up a narrow street called Del Pilar. It stank sweetly from rotten fruit swept into heaps along the curb and sourly from overturned garbage cans whose contents had been spread all over the sidewalk by skeletal dogs, one of which trailed a red prolapsed uterus. Earning not a glance from the pedestrians stepping around the disgusting mess, three nearly naked children, passed out from glue sniffing, lined the wall. Ermita, the so-called "tourist" section of Manila, was full of these glued-out kids. My first day in town I'd taken the pulse of one eight-year-old and when I couldn't feel any, I tried to call an ambulance. When I told the ER receptionist why I needed help, she said, "There is no help for them."

Two blocks and a dozen children later, on the corner of Padre Faura, I came abreast of my hotel, the Iseya, which I had chosen because of its affordable proximity to the Jumbo, the headquarters of the NBI, and the Chinese crime bosses at the Holiday Inn.

The Iseya meant "a simple place," an oxymoron to say the least. It was a six-story, water-stained blockhouse that was built in the 1950s by a Japanese entrepreneur, and it stood opposite a line of crooked plywood shacks—crooked in every sense. They had tin roofs that held cheap open-air restaurants where you could buy *shabu*, cambio booths that served as links in the drug dealers' chain of money laundering, and a "music lounge" that featured a coop where the block's barely conscious hookers turned their tricks.

Twenty-five years ago the Iseya had been bought by a 30-something Englishman who'd told me he had moved to the Philippines to escape problems back home. Now he was late-middle-aged and last night he told me he was still dealing with the things that had exiled him from England in 1975. His guests were mostly heavy-drinking Australians in their 50s and 60s, plus the teenage hookers they'd arranged to keep them company while they vacationed in Manila.

The thatch-walled, narrow lobby was always stifling hot, the big-bellied Australian men walking in and out always loud and vulgar, and their young companions usually maniacally laughing, as if they were flying on *shabu*, which must have made their time with these gross fellows slightly more endurable. "Fuck if it ain't the Canuck jorno?! Ha ha ha!" a sickly pale, sandy-haired creep bawled in my face as I passed him at the front desk. "If I was you, only thing I'd wanna expose is juicy pussy, ha ha ha!"

"Any messages?" I asked the large matron at the desk as she absently handed me the foot-long wooden block to which was attached the key to my fifth-floor room.

"No," she replied, without interrupting her phone conversation.

"Nothing?" I asked again, because that was the routine in the Iseya. Unless you asked twice, you never got your messages. I think that was because the men who stayed at the Iseya did not want to receive messages.

The matron looked at me petulantly, blew her bangs up from her forehead and invested some effort in searching through a layer of papers under a blue Formica shelf. She took out an envelope and wearily threw it on the counter.

"Thanks," I said.

The envelope contained a fax whose cover page bore the seal of the Senate of the Philippines beside the words "Office of Senator Loren Legarda," and the hand-written message: "To Hotel Staff: Pls. forward to Mr. Gould immediately."

"Thanks," I said again. "This is important to me. I'm gonna tell Senator Legarda about this."

Legarda, as mentioned, was then in all the papers because of her Drug Watch Foundation's report. A former TV news reporter, and a very photogenic woman, she'd polled the most votes of any senator in the same election that had installed Erap as president. Because she had gained a reputation as an "anti-corruption crusader," Legarda seemed to have replaced Cory Aquino in the hearts of her countrymen. It was my impression that if Estrada were to fall, Legarda could one day be president herself, and that even now she could be of use to my crusade. Perhaps she could introduce me to a cop I could trust? That was why for several days in a row I'd strolled south past the Jumbo and across the jetty to her Senate office, only to find her solidly tied up in meetings with Church officials right up until she had to fly overseas this morning. Last night her sympathetic press aide had advised me to dictate a list of questions for the senator and she would try to get Legarda's responses before she flew out of Manila. Here they were:

SENATOR LOREN LEGARDA'S ANSWERS TO QUESTIONS
FOR MR. TERRY GOULD'S BOOK:

... Local operators of the Chinese Triads enjoy the protection of some law enforcers at various levels. As we've pointed out these law enforcers have hampered drug arrests and prosecutions. They've helped some drug traffickers bolt jail. They've tampered documents and vital evidence to derail the prosecution of drug cases. They've tipped off members of the Triads to prevent their capture during raids and drug buy-bust operations. Over the years, dozens of junior police and military officers have also been caught actually trafficking drugs. . . . Most of the foreigners getting arrested in the country for trafficking large quantities of drugs are from China. There is strong evidence that Triad members have actually established clandestine laboratories for the processing of amphetamines in remote areas of the country. . . .

Good stuff, but I knew all this. What disappointed me greatly was that Legarda had left unanswered my question about a policeman I could trust. Or maybe that *was* my answer.

Even if I found a cop I could trust, would the NBI ever admit it had been duped into hiring a Triad gangster they'd once investigated for staging his own death on Negros? Would the government ever extradite a Confidential Agent to Canada?

I realized the prospects of this happening were slim when I opened the *Daily Inquirer* and read that the Supreme Court of the Philippines had just outraged the international community by delaying indefinitely the extradition to the U.S. of Mark Jimenez, who was facing a hundred years in jail if convicted on all 47 counts against him. To my mind, this threw into doubt Steve's being returned to Canada even if he were found, fingerprinted, and shown to be the living dead man who, as of January 1, 2000, was emblazoned on Interpol's new website.

Protection against extradition, I soon discovered, was literally just the half of the benefit package the Philippines offered to bad guys. Even if Steve were arraigned as a fugitive from Canada and forbidden from leaving the country until deported, it was very likely he'd be able to slip his chains with corrupt government assistance. That was because the agency charged with nabbing criminals and terrorists if they attempted to flee the country, or turning back criminals and terrorists when they landed on the Philippines' shores, was the Bureau of Immigration, "a subterranean world of hoods and tough guys . . . one of the most notoriously corrupt agencies in the Philippines government," in the words of the agency's director from 1988 to 1990, Miriam Defensor-Santiago.

Not that Defensor-Santiago's revelations had changed anything. In a published letter of resignation dated September 1996, a disgusted intelligence consultant for the BI named Colonel Salvador Rodolfo offered the nation a similar message about the BI's criminal behavior at the country's 34 seaports and three international airports: "The Bureau of Immigration is the worst agency in the Philippine Republic enmeshed in graft and corruption, and the only language spoken from commissioners down to clerks and janitors is money, money, dirty money."

Appointment to the BI was considered a dream perk—a promotion given to those who had served politicians well, a favor offered to relatives of other BI agents, or a commodity purchased from senior commissioners. The quite public understanding in the Philippines was that BI agents were *allowed* (in practice if not in law) to take bribes from criminals and terrorists and extort money from hapless aliens. Despite numerous exposés throughout the 1990s, there was no reforming the BI because there was almost no one who worked within the bureau who was not openly on the take. "Corruption at the Bureau of Immigration is from top to bottom, permeating every rung in the bureau's hierarchy," journalists Yvonne T. Chua and Luz Rimban wrote in a 1998 article published by the Philippine Center for Investigative Journalism. "Because it is so easy to buy their way into the country, and just as easy to get out when they are in a bind, international terrorists and drug lords have conveniently set up base in the Philippines."

Chua and Rimban pointed out that in late 1994, Ramzi Yousef, one of the 10 most wanted men in the world for his part in the 1993 bombing of the World Trade Center in New York, had slipped into the Philippines with impunity. He'd lived in a Manila apartment, liaised with Islamic terrorists on Mindanao, conspired to have Pope John Paul II assassinated when he visited the nation, helped set up the bombing of a Philippine Airlines plane in Cebu, dreamed up a plan for the simultaneous downing of a dozen intercontinental flights, and developed a theory for using jetliners to blow up buildings. Then he had flown out to Pakistan. All this, despite the fact that Yousef's photo and profile were on every BI airport computer in the Republic.

The next day I walked along the narrow crumbling sidewalk beside the outer wall of NBI headquarters, dressed as I had been on my sortie into the Police Academy in Macau, that is, in the manner favored by overseas American drug agents on official visits. As I passed the tunnel entrance for civilians and approached the driveway for agents I began talking into my cell phone with absorbed animation. The hundreds of smoking vehicles beside me made it difficult to breathe, or perhaps it was just the fear constricting my solar plexus. I turned left and came up to the steel crossbar between the guardhouses.

"He's not for real!" I laughed out loud. "How much did you say he wanted for that piece of shit?"

I ducked under the bar and came up the other side.

"Is he kidding? He told Eduardo he paid a hundred thousand pesos."

I kept walking, shaking my head in laughter, waiting for the shout or the hand on my shoulder, but I felt nothing and heard only my own voice.

I headed straight across the compound for the canopied entrance, still negotiating for the boat or car or whatever I was trying to buy. I looked into the eyes of the guards at their desk without focus, the way someone with sanctioned authority would. Absently smiling, waving at one guard, returning the wave of the other, I took the first right into a doorway, pushed it open, heard it close, and then stopped in the quiet corridor.

The building's walls were made of dirty yellow stone, set with a dozen brown doors on either side. I did some quick calculation: nine floors, perhaps a hundred offices. This was insane. I didn't know if Steve was even in this building. He might be on the street now, or working out of the NBI's Muntinlupa office, an hour south of the airport. Maybe, if he was just a paid informant, he only met with his handler once a month? Then again, suppose he now strode out a door and . . .

I pushed open a door and stuck my head inside. Four motherly women looked up from their computers.

"Do you know where the Office of Media Relations is?" I asked, figuring that every federal police headquarters in the world had one, and it was a logical question I could repeat again and again, office to office, until I'd checked out the entire building.

"Down the hall, just across," two of the ladies said at once.

"Thanks," I said, and walked right past the door with a sign that said in red, "*Sangay Kabutirang Panjmaldla,*" and under it in blue translation, "Public Information Division."

The ruse worked for a floor, until an agent in the hall stopped me, directed me downstairs, and then bumped into me 10 minutes later as I was walking up to the third story.

Five minutes into our interview, the NBI's public information officer asked me the question I had been trying to avoid. "Do you have a calling card, sir?"

"Of course," I replied, "I have a—uh—" My voice trailed off as I dug into my shoulder bag, purposely looking through the wrong pocket. "You know what, sir—?"

I smiled sideways across his teacher's desk, upon which was a 1920s-era wooden name block that said, "Alexander C. Carbonel." Agent Carbonel was about 40, the kind of trimly photogenic and patient cop that police departments put in charge of public information bureaus. Like all the NBI agents

I'd seen, he was in casual civilian dress—blue jeans, a checked shirt, with a photo ID on a chain around his neck. He'd had a few quiet, serious words with the agent who'd brought me here, but then had sat down with a neutral smile, apparently pleasant and collegial.

"I'm actually flying out this afternoon," I told Carbonel now. "I must have packed all my cards away."

"I see, I see," Carbonel replied, steepling his fingers in front of his face. I had presented myself as a disorganized travel writer who had read about a spectacular murder trial in the Manila papers and spontaneously decided to come down to headquarters and get a little background on the investigating agency. The story was plausible enough but, as in Macau, questions remained. How had I slipped by the streetside barricade on Taft Avenue without presenting ID? How had I breezed by the guards to enter the building without a visitor's permit? And why did I then begin to cruise around the building's upper stories, opening and closing doors to various offices until I was stopped by the agent who delivered me here?

"You are writing a feature, and it should come out when? What is it? Is it a magazine article or what that you are writing?"

"Well, I'm probably writing a book."

"I see."

"A travel book on Asia. But when I got to Manila, uh, a few days ago, the headlines were about this trial." I held up the *Philippine Daily Inquirer,* which bore the emblazoned words: "Life for Hubert et al." Below the fold was a backgrounder that led with a reproduction of the *Inquirer*'s 1995 front page: "NBI to file raps for slay of Vizcondes." I had kept the paper handy for just this eventuality.

"You are based out of where?" Carbonel asked.

"I'm based out of Vancouver and I write for Random House. It's a big book publisher in North America."

Worst comes to worst I'll try and make a run for it, I thought.

"From Canada you come to Asia and the Philippines."

"Yes, Canada. And the U.S."

"And you've been to other countries already."

"Yes, that's right. Hong Kong and—" I stopped myself before mentioning Macau and Cambodia. "All around Southeast Asia. And I'm looking at the current big stories in all these different places—news stories. And I got to Manila and the one big story was this. I really have to get going," I said. "What you gave me is good enough." I held up the little blue pamphlet Carbonel had handed me when he'd finished talking with the officer who'd brought me here. On the brochure's cover was a shield that featured a blindfolded goddess holding a sword above the NBI's motto: NOBILITY INTEGRITY BRAVERY.

"How come the NBI interested you again?" Carbonel asked, and I admitted to myself that we'd switched over to an interrogation. I was in a jam—no doubt about it.

"Because Americans don't know anything about the National Bureau of Investigation," I said, "and so I just wanted some basic facts, where it was founded and then where the offices are." I flipped through the pamphlet. "Um, does this give the total number of agents, how many agents in each regional office?"

"No, the exact number of agents in regional offices, as a matter of policy, we don't disclose," Carbonel said, appearing to be thinking of something else. "Obviously for purposes of security. The NBI is a sensitive agency."

"Oh, of course. I concur with that policy."

"You said that you're departing this afternoon?"

"Yeah, I'm late now." I glanced at my watch. "Jeez, look at the time!"

"Would I suggest, if you could, just please proceed with me to the office of the director, to the chief of staff, and we could ask if you could be quickly provided with some literature and reading material regarding the NBI. Other than this one."

He pointed to the pamphlet I was curling nervously in my hands. I opened it flat on my knee.

"Then you could introduce yourself and identify your project," Carbonel said. "You could study the material the director gives you at your leisure."

"Uh, what office is he in?" I stalled.

"Office of the director. That would be where you were, on the third floor. Director Frederico Opinion. He is in charge here. He is the chief."

I wrote that down. Then I pursed my lips and knitted my eyebrows, as if I were seriously debating whether I had the time. I tapped my pen once against the pad. "Say, all those civilians lined up outside, what are they doing?"

"The civilians? They are applying for an NBI clearance. An NBI clearance is a document which states whether you have a record or not. You cannot possibly leave the country if you have a derogatory or a criminal record. Because of course if you have a derogatory or criminal record, the Bureau of Immigration won't allow you to leave the country. So it's a way of seeing whether the person has a record or not."

"That's pretty thorough," I said, writing it all down. "By the way, are there any famous novels about the NBI? Like in the States, *The FBI Story*."

"It is a great misfortune that the NBI doesn't have any novels," Carbonel said. "In any case, so that you won't be losing any more time, I would suggest that we can please proceed upstairs."

He stood up. "Please," he said, "follow me."

As I got to the door he turned right, and I turned left, said, "Ah shit, I don't have the time, I gotta catch this flight," and bolted. In two steps I was in the main hall, then past the guards under the canopy, then under the cross-arm gate and in the middle of the *masa* on Taft Avenue.

At midnight I sat in my room with a dresser stacked against my door and a chopper I'd bought at a market on my night table. It must have reached a hundred degrees in the room since I'd shut the rattling air conditioner off to make sense of some sudden shouting I'd heard five flights below. I thought it might have been two cops yelling at the night clerk, whom I'd bribed not to let anybody by to see me. But then I'd heard the men had Australian accents, not Tagalog, and there were two young female voices rising in the midst of their shouts. I'd figured it was a late-night party or a fight, but they weren't coming to arrest me, or kill me, or arrest me and *then* kill me.

I hadn't turned the air conditioner back on because, once it was off, I kept hearing *things* in the hallway—rustlings, scratchings, hingey-type squealings. Rats, probably, but my mind raced to assassins and agents of medieval torture. Blowtorches. Things chopped off.

I carried the chopper with me for the next three days, until I finally tossed it in the garbage at the airport. God, I thought, after I got through customs without being arrested, there has *got* to be a better way to nab Steve.

CHAPTER 25

"PING"

---

*Immorality, bribery, graft and corruption, betrayal of trust and culpable
violation of the Constitution do not bother Filipinos. Many of them are
guilty of these charges, too. Or wish they were—and lived to enjoy it.*
—RENE Q. BAS, "ENTHUSIASMS," *MANILA TIMES*, DEC. 5, 2000

There was a better way. It showed itself in the autumn of 2000 in the person
of General Panfilo "Ping" Lacson, chief of the Philippine National Police
and the Presidential Anti-Organized Crime Task Force (PAOCTF). Like his
boss Erap, Ping was under considerable duress. One of his antagonists was
an ex-14K "Big Sister" named Mary "Rosebud" Ong, a strikingly beautiful
woman who'd served as an underworld agent for the PAOCTF and the Hong
Kong police. In November, 10 months after the docking of the Jumbo and
the attendant BW Resources scandal, Rosebud exploded on the tube, accusing Lacson of working hand in glove with the 14K for his own benefit. She
proclaimed that the police chief was a major international drug trafficker
though his 14K allies in Macau, Hong Kong, and Manila, that he was a
habitual kidnapper-for-ransom, a big-time money launderer, and a mass
murderer. She was supported in these allegations by an ex-PNP colonel
named Reynaldo Berroya, who had worked under Lacson as an anti-
narcotics officer in the late 1990s.

I was back in Vancouver and had no way of knowing if any (or all) of
the charges against Lacson were true. I did know that the Philippines was
a perpetual madhouse of warring accusations, and that bellicose politicians and feuding cops often hired "demolition teams" to plant the most
outrageous charges in the media. True or not, however, the charges made
me ponder the possibilities. I conjectured that the embattled Lacson might
perceive an opportunity for some positive international press by employing
his knowledge of the 14K to find Steve and hand him over to me in Manila.
I shared my thoughts with my wife, Leslie, and my publisher, Anne, who

both assessed them as reckless. If even one of the charges against Lacson were true, they said, I could very well wind up as the 37th journalist murdered in the Philippines.

Promising I would go slow, I leaned on Leslie to talk to her company's 24-year-old Chinese-Filipina secretary, Janise, who had recently returned from Manila. "In a roundabout way get her opinion on this Lacson business," I requested.

Ninety seconds after her hour-long conversation with Janise, Leslie called me with the spectacular news that Lacson was Janise's godfather, and that Janise's dad was a Manila businessman named Jerome Tang, who owned a medical-supply company and a couple of Jolibee restaurants. Back in 1995—grateful for Lacson's help in combating the hundreds of annual kidnappings plaguing the Chinese community—Jerome had hired a high-priced lawyer to defend the general on charges of mass murder. The case involved 11 members of the savage Kuratong Baleleng gang: after the gang's arrest, Lacson had allegedly ordered his men to "salvage" the prisoners in a paddy wagon, although Lacson claimed there had been "a shoot-out." The charges—dismissed, reinstated, raised to a higher court, and returned to a lower court—were still kicking around the byzantine Filipino justice system.

Over lunch with Janise and Leslie at the decorous Lazy Gourmet, I learned some more details about Janise's controversial godfather. Charges of murder and malfeasance had been dogging the 52-year-old general ever since he had graduated the Philippine Military Academy in 1971 and joined Ferdinand Marcos's feared Metrocom Intelligence and Security Group. Nevertheless, since Estrada had appointed him top cop, Lacson had ended the PNP's tradition of *kotung*, the God-given right of Philippine police to supplement their starvation-level salaries by preying on the population. Cabdrivers and small businessmen throughout the land felt as if a lifelong plague had been suddenly lifted from their shoulders. The police chief had also set records for arrests—over 37,000 the previous year, 75 of whom were Triad members—and rescued literally hundreds of kidnap victims. "He's a very tough policeman, but the Philippines isn't Canada or the U.S.," Janise said, alluding to the fact that Lacson's sobriquet "Ping" derived from his association with gunfire whenever he chased criminals. "When a criminal is caught here, he goes to jail. In the Philippines, a judge is bribed and he's back in business." Indeed, Lacson's reputation as a "tough policeman," coupled with his magnetic attractiveness to women and an affair he'd had with a sultry actress named Tina Monasterio, were the twin hot themes of a blockbuster movie just released about his exploits: *Ping Lacson—Supercop*. At the moment, despite all that was said about his supposed criminality, Lacson was still enormously popular among the million ethnic Chinese, the working class, and the poor—that is, 80 percent of the population. The powerful Chinese community even wanted him to enter politics.

I liked the sound of Lacson, but a couple of weeks later I learned that the accusations against him were in part the reason many North American cops were so hesitant to share information about fugitive criminals with Lacson's international liaison officer, Aris Gana. Indeed, Lacson and the black reputation of the PNP he headed were the reasons no action had been taken on Steve after he had returned to the Philippines and become connected to the NBI. That he was still there, hard at work in Manila's fetid swamps, was the chatter of Richmond's upscale Chinatown. Kim Tam was now out of the pen and cruising the casinos in Richmond, where there were some talky dragon heads who suddenly knew Steve's alias: Joe Co.

Getting wind of the Paper Fan's nom de guerre boosted my testosterone into the red zone. After a couple of months of debate with my wife and Anne, I decided to ignore everyone's advice and begin pulling strings to arrange a meeting with Ping in Manila, which by then was in such turmoil that anything was possible—even throwing Steve "Joe Co" Wong in a steamer trunk and having him mailed home.

It was the beginning of 2001, and the unceasing revelations about the Estrada administration had pushed the Philippines to the edge of its second revolution in 15 years. Around the time of Mary Ong's bombshell, a provincial governor named Luis "Chavit" Singson—feeling cheated out of an illegal gambling racket by Estrada, and with a claimed death threat from the president's men hanging over his head—stepped forward and announced that he had delivered almost $8 million in bribes from illegal gambling syndicates to Estrada, plus another $2.6 million from taxes collected from tobacco farmers. Panfilo Lacson was completely aware of the payoffs, Singson charged.

The accumulating landslide of charges and mountains of evidence behind them were too grave to ignore, even in a nation where governments routinely looked the other way in the face of gross official corruption that, according to the World Bank, had cost the country $48 billion since 1980. Three days after Singson's allegations, Vice President Gloria Macapagal-Arroyo, the constitutional successor to Estrada with support among the elite and the Catholic Church, resigned from her post as secretary of social welfare, citing a loss of confidence in Erap's leadership. In the House of Representatives, opposition legislators filed an impeachment motion against the president. Two weeks later, Macapagal-Arroyo formed a united opposition with Church factions and legislators, which was called the People's Power Coalition, taking its name from the People Power revolution that had overthrown Marcos in 1986.

Estrada's defense—accepted by the poor who had elected him—was that he had received only $4 million in intended bribes, and had actually deposited the money into the account of a presidential lottery for slum kids. "The poor have always been close to me, as they surely know, for I am from them," he said in a radio interview from Malacañang, alluding to his birthplace in Tondo, the poorest slum in Manila.

The House of Representatives was having none of it. Its members voted to impeach Erap and have him tried on charges of graft, bribery, and betrayal of public trust for attempting to shield BW Resources from the SEC. The case was passed for trial to the Senate, where Estrada entered a not-guilty plea, claiming he was the victim of a conspiracy between the upper class and the Church, both of which factions had always held him—and the poor—in contempt.

What seemed clear was that the country was facing a hiatus in government it could ill afford. Over a third of Filipinos were living on less than 70 cents a day, the peso was crashing, foreign investment and tourism were drying up, NPA-led revolutions raged on half a dozen islands, Islamic terrorists struck at will on Mindanao, and street crime was so rampant that Lacson had called out the marines to patrol Metro Manila.

The televised proceedings opened on December 7, 2000, and the entire nation watched riveted as numerous witnesses with knowledge of the president's under-the-table income testfied that Estrada had a secret account in the Equitable PCI Bank with a total of $66 million in deposits. The prosecutors demanded to have an envelope containing information on the Equitable account opened. In most nations, that would have been the next logical step in the trial. Not in the Philippines. On January 16, 2001, the 21 senators acting as judges decided in an 11-to-10 vote not to pry into Estrada's private finances.

With that vote it became apparent to the House prosecutors that the Senate would never convict Estrada, no matter what the evidence. The next day, they stormed out in mid-session and announced they were quitting. Jaime Cardinal Sin called upon the citizens of Manila to gather at EDSA square, on the east side of the city, to protest the Senate vote. "Go to EDSA, it is a holy place," Sin announced, referring to the treasured fact that hundreds of thousands had gathered there to overthrow Marcos in the first People Power revolution and that the site had since been made into a shrine, with a 50-foot gold statue of the Virgin out front.

Text messages were mass mailed by Church officials to the cell phones of the middle and upper classes. By the evening of the next day, January 18, some 500,000 of Manila's "elite" had assembled at EDSA. One after another, cabinet ministers deserted the president and showed up at the shrine to stand beneath the Virgin and beside Macapagal-Arroyo, Jaime Cardinal Sin, Cory Aquino, and former president Fidel Ramos. Estrada remained holed up in Malacañang with army generals and a still-loyal Lacson, trying to keep them onside, but after a couple of days of hectic meetings and cell phone negotiation, the military told the commander in chief the jig was up; their top generals then left the palace and joined the demonstrators at the shrine. At that point Lacson informed his boss that while his overthrow might not be legal, the only alternative would be violent resistance—something he was not prepared to contemplate. He left for PNP headquarters at Camp Crame, near the EDSA Shrine, and after consulting with his men, phoned the president in tears and said he was withdrawing his support. Left alone in Malacañang, the former movie star declared he would never resign.

"Glory Gloria! Glory Gloria!" the half-million demonstrators chanted in unison, demanding that Macapagal-Arroyo be made president. In a theatrical display of solidarity with the sea of well-scrubbed faces, the chief justice of the Supreme Court showed up at EDSA and announced that, based on the precedent set by the last People Power revolution, the presidency was now vacant.

Foreign observers on the scene scratched their heads. How could a 500,000-person demonstration, in the capital of a country with 78 million people, be viewed as an authoritative vote of no-confidence in a leader who had received almost 11 million votes just two and a half years earlier? Estrada was probably utterly corrupt, but surely the overthrow of a sitting president by such means had to sow the seeds for further so-called People Power revolutions. "People Power has become an acceptable term for a troubling phenomenon," editorialized Time.com, "one that used to be known as mob rule."

But the emotions of the well-behaved mob carried the day. January 20 was marked as People Power II, and the chief justice swore in the four-foot-ten, 53-year-old Macapagal-Arroyo as the new president. A couple of hours later, still refusing to acknowledge his presidency was at an end, Estrada and his family, facing forced eviction, left the palace by the rear Pasig River Gate and went home to their mansion in a gated community called North Greenhills, its back wall nestled against Camp Crame.

With his boss dethroned and now ensconced on the other side of Camp Crame's razor wire, Lacson offered his resignation to Macapagal-Arroyo.

She accepted it, but countered with an offer to appoint him to the number two spot in the PNP, under a suddenly anti-Erap general (and old enemy of Lacson's) named Leandro Mendoza. Lacson refused the offer, and, perhaps to keep him out of her hair, Arroyo offered him an ambassadorship in a European capital of his choosing. Ping refused again; then, weighing the sources of the new president's support and opposition, announced he would be running for the Senate in the upcoming May 14 national elections as a candidate with a pro-Erap coalition, ominously called Puwersa Ng Masa—Power of the Masses.

By the end of March 2001, polls showed Lacson was among the most popular politicians in the country, particularly among the ethnic Chinese and poor Filipinos. Ignored, excluded, or exploited, the poor still believed in Estrada's movie star myth, and were left boiling with feelings of disenfranchisement when their votes had been thrown to the winds and Estrada ejected. As Estadra's man, Lacson seemed to have a good shot at the presidency in the 2004 election—if he won his Senate seat.

At precisely that moment, polls in hand, the newly appointed leaders of the PNP and the NBI reviewed their "intelligence reports" and then declared to the press they would be investigating Lacson for acts of mass murder, kidnapping for ransom, $350 million in drug dealing, ordering the illegal wiretapping of senators, working hand in hand with the Chinese Triads, and embezzling funds from his task force to invest in a Jolibee franchise—a not-so-subtle swipe at his now-prominent supporter, Jerome Tang.

"I read your paper, the documents, but if you come in May it's going to be too late," Ping Lacson told me over the phone from Manila on April 5. "So if you want to—uh—collect something, I think it should be earlier."

"Are you still connected with some high-level honest people that can arrange it?" I asked. "I'll just tell you very broadly, he's with the NBI."

"Oh!" Lacson replied, sounding as startled as I was when I had first got the news. "He's with the NBI—at what level?"

"I'm not sure what level he's at, but it's going to be very difficult and very delicate."

"Do you have a name?" he asked, because in the letter and documents I'd sent him I'd been careful to leave out or redact specific details. I'd promised Leslie and Anne I would not trust Lacson until I met him.

"Yes we do, but I don't want to give you that over the phone," I said. "I've been on this fellow's case for eleven years, the police have been on him for eleven years, without success. Because obviously he's connected to some very sensitive people. I can tell you he's a 14K Triad official. And I'm going through you because I think if you can work this, it will do you a lot of good. But the object is to *get* him!"

"Bring him down," he said.

"Yes! Because he's not just a gangster. He's a gangster with power. I'm not going to go beyond what I said, but when I come over there I'll give you photographs of him, a full description, I have his regular name, I have an alias that he's operating under, an Interpol Red Alert warrant for his arrest, a Canadian national warrant, and an international warrant. I'll let them know in Hong Kong first," I added since, on this trip, regardless of Paul Brown's aversion to journalists, I was going to make sure the RCMP Liaison Office in Hong Kong knew I was on the ground and dealing with Lacson. "Are you still on good relations with some people in the NBI?" I asked again.

"Definitely," he affirmed. "My former officers with the task force, they're now back with the NBI. Their place was on detail with my task force, and now they're there."

"But would they protect one of their own?"

"I don't think so," he replied. "I chose these people, led them in the highest level of operations."

"Okay, I will be in Manila on April 24," I said, counting ahead on my calendar for a cheap flight. "I would say that it's important that you don't do anything until then, because this fellow will hear that somebody has contacted you looking for somebody in the NBI, and as soon as he hears that, several things could happen. One is he could take off; another is that he could have me killed when I show up; another is he could take care of somebody over there who he thought—"

"No, no, I won't do anything," Lacson assured me.

"Okay, I will come with all the documents," I said. Then, figuring I was not going to gain any points with Ping by leaving out a little detail he might go ballistic over in person, I added, "But I must tell you, Panfilo, you'll see that he has been very heavily involved with the PNP."

"Oh oh oh oh oh oh oh oh," Lacson said, and my heart sank and shriveled with each of his descending vowels. "Ahh, the PNP," he sighed.

"From years ago, Ping. I know that from years ago. With senior inspectors at the PNP."

"And now he's with the NBI," he said flatly.

"Yes," I said. "And let's face it, I'm putting my life in your hands, okay?"

"Yeah, I know, I know, I realize that."

I waited, but he didn't add, "Don't worry."

"Okay, now, the Canadian police will be aware I'm there," I declared, implying that men in serge would be monitoring my every move. "But they can't really do anything for me in the Philippines—" thinking, *Shit,* I phrased that exactly wrong! I'd meant to say Canadian cops couldn't help me arrest Steve, but would get *Lacson* arrested if he harmed a hair on my curly head. He seemed to take it the right way though.

"We have some good contacts with the Canadian embassy here and the police attaché," Ping said, "because when I was with the task force we used to network with these people and we've established some very good relationships with them."

Comforting as this news was, it disturbed me. It didn't exactly jibe with what I'd been told about the Canadian embassy's opinion of the PNP. I ignored my misgivings, however, and gave Ping the benefit of the doubt. I figured no one would have said anything to his face. In 1994, when Garry Clement was on Steve's ass and visiting Manila as the police attaché, Lacson, as chief of the president's anti-drug task force, would have been part and parcel of the "good relations" which had then prevailed. Either he thought the amity had never ended or didn't want to admit it had. "I can make the arrangements when you arrive," he said.

"How'd it go?" Leslie asked when I got off the phone.

"It went and I'm going."

Over the next few days I broke into my usual pre-hunt prep—arranging e-mail codes with Anne and Leslie, cell phone codes, letters of intro—all the while hanging on the Internet. The Philippines ombudsman had just indicted Estrada for plunder and seven other related charges of graft amounting to more than $80 million, which meant Estrada was looking at the death penalty; which meant, once arrested, he would not be granted bail. He maneuvered desperately to avoid being hauled into Camp Crame by launching an appeal on the grounds that he had presidential immunity. On April 10, the Supreme Court threw out his appeals, stating he was no longer president, and on April 16 an arrest warrant was handed down. The country held its breath, wondering if the warrant would really be carried out, and what the reaction of Estrada's millions of supporters in the poor *barrios* would be. With the country still wondering, I boarded a Cathay Pacific flight for Hong Kong and Manila.

Stepping off the plane in Ninoy Aquino Airport on April 24, my third time in my search for Steve, I literally walked into Jerome Tang, a short man who stood in the middle of the ramp holding my name high on a sign as 300 passengers parted around him. So much for my fantasy of keeping a low profile.

Jerome was 60, but his hair and eyebrows were dyed so shinily black, his handsome features were so smooth, that at first glance he seemed too young to be the father of Janise. We shook hands and as we walked double-time through the airport corridor Jerome informed me that thousands of Erap loyalists were now encamped at the gates of North Greenhills. They were pledging their lives to keep Erap from being taken to jail.

"Will Lacson be getting involved?" I asked, worried that this Erap business would distract Ping from the reason I had traveled 6,000 miles.

"It is an issue for the people, his constituency," Jerome said, then made it sound as if we were going to meet Batman. "The general has special powers. If he say he will do for you, he will do."

Jerome seemed to have his own special powers, at least at the airport. He wore a security badge around his neck and had a smiling acquaintanceship with all the right officials. When I picked up my suitcase and turned my luggage cart towards the end of the long line of passengers waiting to be inspected by Bureau of Immigration agents, Jerome said, "Not necessary." He pulled my cart out of line and ushered it and me past the immigration desk, right by a guard. He then asked for my passport and immigration card, went back to the desk and slipped them under an agent's arm. The agent absently looked around, smiled at him and glanced at me, then took the card. As we exited into the blast furnace that was Manila in this hottest month of the year, I thought: This man has the pull to protect me. I'll be okay.

Jerome's chauffeur drove us north up Roxas Boulevard, aggressively plunging into the gridlocked traffic around the Philippine Cultural Center. Just beyond the jetty's plaza I could see Stanley Ho's shuttered Jumbo floating forlornly in the harbor, about a hundred yards from where it had been docked at its opening. I asked Jerome if he knew what Ho would be doing with the barge. "If no casino, nothing." He shook his head and laughed wearily. "You know, Ho thinks government close it, but Cardinal Sin *really* close it. Because back then, Estrada was not giving gambling money to the Church."

"Well, no, he was keeping it all to himself!"

"I mean legal money, not *jueteng*," he replied, referring to the illegal numbers racket Erap had been scooping. "Now, though, with new government, Sin is getting gambling money from the government. I think Jumbo be opening again sometime."

"You mean Cardinal Sin's in favor of gambling now?" I asked, astonished.

"Maybe he look the other way, because the new government say, 'Here's some money to you from gambling.'"

I turned around and faced Jerome squarely in the back seat. "Do you mean to say the new government is giving him gambling money personally, or to the Church?"

"Same thing. He live in big villa in Mandaluyong City. So where does he get the money to live like that? From the Church."

He told me he'd give me an article in *Time* that proved the cardinal was a hypocrite. It seemed "Glorious Gloria" had scandalously agreed to become the godmother to the son of a notorious *jueteng* gangster named Bong Pineda, who masterminded a $100-million-a-year illegal operation. It was an unholy union that Sin had approved. I later read Gloria's lame explanation for becoming godmother to the criminal godfather's son: "Cardinal Sin said, as a Christian, if I am asked to be a godmother, it is my Christian duty."

Jerome looked ahead at the jeepneys and taxis pointing every which way on the road. "That the problem with this country. Everybody make up the rules as they go."

Jerome took me to a hotel he'd booked called the Palm Plaza, which was only six blocks south of the Iseya but a world away in class and comfort, with a banquet hall, piano bar, marble floors, and glittering lighting in the huge white lobby. When I asked Jerome how much this joint was going to cost me, he told me not to worry, "It's in the family."

I couldn't accept his money but let it go for now: we had to race right off to the dinner he'd arranged with Lacson, a man who'd probably made up a few rules in his life, but none, I hoped, that allowed him to commit the travesty that was making the very latest headlines.

I tried to take it with a few grains of salt, but the PNP and NBI had just accused Lacson of engineering the kidnapping, strangulation, and incineration of a political publicist named Salvador "Bubby" Dacer. The published police accounts did not lean in the direction of Lacson's innocence. The gruesome killing had occurred on November 24, 2000, two days after a meeting between Dacer and the president at Malacañang in the midst of Erap's mounting agony. According to Dacer's daughter, Ampy, who was a witness to the meeting, Estrada had accused Dacer of leading "a demolition squad" to ruin his reputation. In addition, an adviser to Fidel Ramos had just produced a letter in which Dacer wrote that he feared he was being monitored by Estrada and Lacson because Estrada believed the publicist was "the point man" in the conspiracy to oust him. Dacer certainly had somebody to fear. At a busy Manila intersection on the city's South Superhighway, Dacer and his driver, Emmanuel Corbito, were abducted from their car at gunpoint by eight men. Witnesses fingered two suspects, both junior cops. During interrogation the junior cops claimed that members of the Presidential Anti-Organized Crime Task Force, headed by Lacson, strangled Dacer and Corbito with electric cords before setting fire to the corpses in a town called Cavite. By the time I'd left for the Philippines, eight members of the PAOCTF had been arrested as the culprits, based on confessions and sworn statements of four of them. The confessed killers claimed they'd taken their orders from "people higher up," although none of the PAOCTF cops had specifically fingered Lacson or Estrada.

Jerome had an explanation for all of it. I could read it in the papers, he said. The letter to Ramos's adviser was never confirmed as Dacer's, and the police had taken it upon themselves to speak for Ampy. Indeed, Lacson's campaign manager, Angelito Banayo—also at the Dacer-Estrada meeting—said there had never been an argument. Quite the opposite. Dacer had told Banayo, "Let's work together to help your boss." Banayo claimed it was Fidel Ramos who'd had the motive to get rid of Dacer. Ramos had hired Dacer to destabilize the Estrada administration because, in the 1998 election, Estrada had soundly trounced Ramos's chosen successor, House Speaker Jose de Venecia—the point man in the House impeachment vote. Ramos admitted to a meeting with Dacer just before his abduction, and Banayo speculated that Ramos had taken his revenge for Dacer's betrayal.

Of the two versions, the police interpretation sounded more plausible to the *Philippine Daily Inquirer*. Still, in the Philippines, you could never be sure of any version of a murder. I knew that the PNP would not be averse to torturing confessions out of the accused cops. "You think Lacson will actually be charged for this?" I asked Jerome. "I mean, any or *all* of this—kidnapping, murder, wiretapping, drug dealing—"

Jerome laughed and waved his hand, as if he were relaxed about the whole thing. "No, no, no ooo, they just want to throw all the trouble to him, because the administration party don't want him to be elected, so want to give him the trouble, destroy his reputation. Because he's one of most popular politicians. Because if he elected senator, then in 2004 he will also become the president. It is all—how you say it—television play—"

"A soap opera?"

"Yes, yes—soap opera!! Look the police who make the most accusations! Look!"

The instigator of the accusations against Lacson was Reynaldo Berroya, Lacson's co-accuser in the Mary Ong affair. Last week, Macapagal-Arroyo had reinstated Berroya in the PNP, promoting him to senior superintendent and appointing him intelligence chief. The history of Berroya and Lacson went back eight years, Jerome said, and, in fact, as he related it, I remembered reading the headlines when I was on my first hunt for Steve on Negros. In September 1993, Lacson, the anti-kidnap crusader, had arrested Berroya for snatching a wealthy Taiwanese businessman named Jack Chow. The evidence Lacson had gathered resulted in Berroya's conviction three years later and the colonel was sentenced to life in prison. Berroya only served a year, however. On December 12, 1997, the Supreme Court reversed the lower court's decision, finding on appeal that there was not enough evidence for a conviction, although the justices went out of their way to state that their decision was not an exoneration of the colonel. Berroya was reinstated to the PNP in 1999 and Lacson assigned him to the anti-narcotics unit, only to dismiss him from the force when he found Berroya had gone absent without leave.

"You see, all connected," Jerome said, as we crossed the Manila line into Quezon City. "Berroya do so much—why make him intelligence chief now? Answer: because he the one hate Lacson, do the demolition work for Gloria."

I thought the charge that "Berroya do so much" could be equally applied to Lacson, who'd been appointed PNP chief in the midst of the Kuratong Baleleng case, but decided to leave it alone.

"What about this Ong business?" I asked.

"Mary Ong—she is already accused with drug trafficking, money laundering, many things."

"But never convicted?"

"No, because everybody is afraid of her, or else they owe her the favors. Beginning of that—she has many many lovers—but one was John Campos, senior superintendent PNP anti-narcotics under Lacson. Campos threw her away, so she decide to get back at PNP. She tell another boyfriend in the TV media, 'I have secret information, I am agent for PNP.' He calls Berroya, get two them together, they charge everybody—murder, kidnapping, drug trafficking. It is all lies. If Lacson do all this, wouldn't he be rich man? If he's rich man, why does he have to come to me pay for lawyer? He live in a normal house, one car, one watch. They want to stop him because, without demolition job, he the next president."

At seven we pulled up in front of the Golden Pearl Seafood Restaurant, located in a supposedly middle-class area of Quezon City called the West Triangle—totally indistinguishable in terms of strewn trash, shack buildings, and noxious traffic from any of the other urban messes we'd just crawled through for two hours. We were met by two smiling valets who ushered us under the plastic awning and then through the freezing dining room to a wall-length accordion door. Jerome slid the louvers back to reveal a large rotating table, seated all round with middle-aged Chinese men and women. Opposite the door, back to the wall as I'd expected, sat the trim general, casually dressed in a blue-and-green plaid shirt, his thick raven hair styled to flop youthfully down to frame a good-looking face accented by light wire glasses. You could sort of see how, before the media had turned on him, they'd sold him as a sexy supercop.

Everyone stood up and greeted the Western journalist warmly—or hopefully, since Jerome told me he'd passed the word that I was "a friend," and Lacson had very few left in the media. Lacson stayed seated, looking as if he was too exhausted to beamingly play the role of politician after two months of constant campaigning, much of which had been spent refuting the astonishing cataract of allegations.

"When did you arrive?" he asked, looking shyly at a point on the red tablecloth between lobster and mango slices.

I pulled my chair in beside his and glanced at my watch. "Just."

"You are in a sleep-deprived state then," he smiled.

"Actually I paid my respects at the Mountie Liaison Office in Hong Kong first," I stated truthfully, again letting him know there were people (powerless as they were to help me) aware of my being here. "I recuperated there for a day."

"Good, well, let's eat and then we can talk about your subject afterwards."

Because we were in the midst of this crucial senatorial election—in effect, a referendum on Estrada's overthrow—the ensuing discussion was exclusively about politics. Lacson, however, sat curiously silent as my table-mates complained that in the six months since Singson's allegations, the country had been in ceaseless and needless crisis. In their eyes, the president was merely a macho blue-collar guy who'd made it to the top and done what any Tondo boy would have done: have lots of women, father illegitimate children, drink, and party with underworld figures. The rich did it, too. They were more corrupt than Estrada at his worst—they just got away with it. Look at Ramos's involvement in the Amari scandal—several hundred million dollars lost to the government. Look at Aquino's handing out jobs to all her relatives. Look at Cardinal Sin, prelate of the poor in his giant villa. Look at Macapagal-Arroyo, tied in with *jueteng* gangsters like Bong Pineda. Look at her husband, Mike—a rich *haciendero* who was caught up in a bribery scandal now. "You think the poor do not see through this and that?" said Mark Tan, the owner of the restaurant. Everybody agreed the Ramos-Aquino-Sin-Gloria clique was behind the impeachment, because, with the exception of Estrada, the elite had uninterruptedly ruled the Philippines since Independence, and they couldn't stand that someone not in their class had taken the reins from them.

"Granted, they despise Estrada," I said, "but Erap still stole millions of dollars. I mean, you guys wouldn't excuse that, right?"

That prompted everybody to speak at once, shouting over each other, breaking into Chinese for sidebars, bursting into laughter or argument, switching to Tagalog and then going back to English. This is essentially what they said:

The *jueteng* racket Estrada had been skimming was so much a part of Filipino life that every president since Independence had profited from it. The government could have legalized the lottery at any time, just the way it had casino gambling, but it was far more profitable for officials to leave *jueteng* in the hands of the syndicates, who then had to pay those officials protection money. Since the vast majority of Filipinos played *jueteng* for a few pesos a day it was considered a victimless crime, as much a part of the national character as cockfighting. It was an open secret that people ran for office to get in on the *jueteng* bonanza, and no one had paid the price until Estrada. He had been impeached only because he was the first to flaunt his affection for the poor and the Chinese, both of which were openly disparaged in the most blatantly bigoted terms by the ruling Filipino classes and the press. Indeed, they said, that was why when Estrada was exposed as a *jueteng* profiteer, most poor people laughed and said, in effect, "Good on ya!" Erap was merely a tough guy with a golden heart (everyone had seen his movies) who had stolen his fortune from gangsters, distributing at least some of it to the *barrios*. To the *masa,* his late-night boozing and shmoozing came off as roguish and appealing—a lifestyle the poor knew they would lead if they ever made it to the top.

"And General Lacson?" I asked, not addressing this to Ping but to his supporters. At that, though, they all suddenly fell silent.

"I have never taken a centavo from *jueteng,* I had a no-take policy for all my men," Lacson said, sounding almost puritanical compared to those around him. "My salary was thirty thousand pesos a month, six hundred U.S. dollars. As director of PNP I am sure to get five million pesos each month from *jueteng,* plus other extras. We discover a schedule of payment based on rank. A regional director of the PNP—three million pesos a month. This is according to our intelligence reports. So the immorality of the *jueteng,* I don't speak about this. Just to the police officers, to spare them corruption by *jueteng* lords."

"When Ping elected he will expose what he know in the Senate—you will see," Jerome said. "Privileged speech in Senate. Then everybody know who get what. That is why they afraid of him."

"Ping from the poor *barrio* too," Mark Tan informed me. "In Cavite City. Nine brothers and sisters. Pull himself up because he is smart. So the people know this and elect him senator."

"I sent you our campaign slogan," Jerome added. "'What is right must be kept right; what is wrong must be set right.'"

None of it made the least bit of sense, of course. Lacson had been the top cop to a crooked guy who'd been into a lot more than *jueteng*. If he was a supercop, why didn't he bust his boss back then? And why not condemn him now? Was it because he was loyal to the man who had promoted him to the summit, or because of his outrage at the illegality of the People Power II revolution? I could sympathize with both motivations, yet, given the magnitude of Estrada's graft, Lacson was either a man with a monumentally misplaced sense of integrity, or a man with a lot to hide. However, it wasn't my business to make him feel uncomfortable now. I just wanted him to get Steve for me.

"It's amazing what they say about you in the press," I commented. "Thirteen murders, three hundred million in drug dealing—"

"The press will say anything that will sell papers," Lacson sighed.

"In the Philippines they either murder you or accuse you of murder," said the fellow sitting beside Mark Tan.

"Tell him why reporters hate you so much," Jerome leaned over and advised Ping.

"Oh it's probably quite simple," Lacson said. "When I became head of the PNP, I discovered a list. We were paying two million pesos a month in bribes to media on the list. I ordered that the list be torn up and the payments stopped."

"Worst mistake you ever made," I said, more than half believing his explanation, since the Philippine Center for Investigative Journalism had done a survey of reporters during the 1998 presidential election and found that a third *openly admitted* to taking money from their sources: how many more took bribes and simply denied it could only be guessed. The sad fact was, the PCIJ report pointed out, many in the Philippine media essentially worked as prostitutes—taking money to publish glowing press releases as hard news and suppressing bad news that their patrons were unhappy with. Or worse. There were some who acted as paid character assassins; others who investigated public figures in order to blackmail them; still others who actively extorted protection money to keep an embarrassing story off the air or the front pages. The corrupt practice, officially considered a firing offense but unofficially tolerated in Filipino journalism, was called "ATM Journalism," or "Envelopmental Journalism." The particular brand of bribery Lacson had "discovered" in 1999 was called "Inteligensia," defined by the PCIJ as "the regular payments that they [reporters] get from law enforcers." It was the reason, in fact, that I had not yet met with another journalist in the Philippines—not even one in the PCIJ. I didn't doubt the PCIJ's integrity, but, given the mixed reputation of their colleagues, a loose lip could sink my ship.

After dinner the 10 guests in the room obligingly left Jerome, Lacson, and me in private to discuss business. I took out my thick file and got down to work. I talked for 20 minutes, starting with my first article on Steve, then my second, then my third. I handed these over to the general, plus Steve's 10- and 15-year-old pictures and his detailed tattoo descriptions. These provided no short cut to journalistic heaven, however. Lacson said he didn't recognize Steve—or else the photos were so old that Steve no longer looked as he had in front of the Brooklyn Bridge. I handed over the Interpol wanted poster and concluded with the latest information, his alias, which I wrote in the corner of the poster. I added that nothing had been done on Steve in the Philippines in the last year and a half because of the "controversies" surrounding Estrada and the PNP.

Lacson seemed to take this last bit neutrally, but I couldn't really be sure if he was offended. In the three hours I'd sat beside him he had betrayed almost no emotions. He wasn't icy—wooden would be a better term, an anomalous characteristic for a Filipino. I remembered reading in the press that, aside from his classmates from the military academy, he had almost no friends.

"I don't know how you want to go about doing this," I said, "but I'll do whatever you say."

"It's too bad they didn't work with Aris Gana when I was still director. You would have this man now."

I held my tongue and a silence descended on the table. I didn't break it because I could tell his cop mind was turning. He was staring not at Steve's pictures or my articles but at the oilcloth. After a long minute he said: "This will involve a lot of planning. You want him captured and held."

"Can you put me in touch with your men in the NBI?" I asked.

"All of that will have to be done in a roundabout way. Since we spoke on the phone, as you know, new developments."

"The general needs to get the credit for this," Jerome said. "Not NBI."

"Of course, that's the whole point," I told Jerome. "But it'll be some credit! My experience is that when a foreign country praises a local boy, his stock goes way up among the locals." I turned back to Ping. "When can we begin?"

"How long will you be staying?"

"As long as I can afford—two, three weeks. Jerome's kindly offered to pay my hotel, but I can't let him."

"I will try and have a meeting tomorrow afternoon. In the morning I'll be busy on other developments."

I surmised he meant busy on Estrada. "So when will I hear from you?" I asked.

"I am always in touch with Jerome. I should have some word for you back tomorrow night."

"Great! And the embassy?"

"If I am lucky on the first, of course, then the embassy. They will be embarrassed they didn't inform me of this."

The guests were then invited back in and we all began taking pictures of each other, a noisy ritual that lasted half an hour. At the end of the photofest I told Lacson that I hoped Steve would catapult him into the Senate. We shook on it and I thought we were on our way out, but Jerome took Ping aside and huddled with him in a corner of the private dining room for 10 minutes. I could see Jerome pointing to the envelope containing all my material. *Good man, Jerome!* I said to myself. I guessed he now felt his own face was on the line with me, and was arguing for action.

"Keep cell phone on," Jerome told me as we got into the back of his car. "The general will work for you, he promise, then he will call me."

"Where will you be?"

"My office, Jolibee. Await developments." Again Estrada, I figured. Jerome closed his eyes a moment. It was now past 11 and the guy had been up for 20 hours. "Maybe you go Estrada's house. The general just say maybe arrest will be tomorrow. Very interesting for you to see situation."

"You think it'll be safe?" I asked. "I'd hate to have my head batoned by a cop before I get my man."

"What you say, maybe your man the one with baton."

CHAPTER 26

AMOK

———

What is madness?
To have erroneous perceptions and to reason correctly from them.
—VOLTAIRE

The next morning, crawling east over the fecal suds of the San Juan River, my taxi driver leaned over his furry steering wheel and pointed through the purple smog to three army helicopters hovering a couple of miles away. On his radio I could hear the ominous throb of the Hueys as an out-of-breath reporter shouted Tagalog commentary above a shrieking crowd. "Is Erap being arrested now?" I asked, craning forward to the scratchy radio. My driver listened another moment and then burst into laughter, saying, "No yet, people chasing reporters because on TV they say protesters smell bad. So they yelling at him, '*Mabuhay ang mababantot.*' Means, 'Long live the stinky,' ha ha ha!"

If the protesters came from around here then the reporters had their stories right, I thought. We were now rocking through a warren of narrow streets and dank alleys reeking with sulfurous sewage and sunbaked garbage. From the edges of ditches naked children waved at me and called their ubiquitous tourist greeting, "Hey Joe!" then went back to playing with splintered wood blocks in the brown runoff. This was San Juan, the municipality Erap had served as mayor from the time he'd retired as an actor in the late '60s until he'd been elected to the Senate in 1987. Judging by the *barrio*'s poverty, Erap's tenure hadn't done his constituents much good. Nevertheless, the clotheslines across the alleys were hung with posters showing their beefy hero haloed in front of the seal of the Philippines, one hand on a text called *Agrikultura* as if swearing his solidarity with poor peasants. Other, more mundane posters fluttered in support of several candidates in the pro-Erap senatorial coalition, including former Bureau of Immigration chief Miriam Defensor-Santiago, Ping Lacson, and Lacson's colleague from the Philippine Military Academy, Gregorio "Gringo" Honasan, a general who had led many of the nine coups against Cory Aquino. It stretched the bounds of sanity, but there were also posters for the megawealthy fugitive Mark Jimenez, now running for the House of Representatives. Smiling brightly, he offered voters a thumbs-up.

Ten minutes later we were close enough to Erap's North Greenhills subdivision to have overtaken crowds of threadbare people in flip-flops heading up the street towards the rally. My driver honked his way through them, crossed a wide avenue called Ortigas, and turned into the huge Greenhills Shopping Center—a middle-class landscape that was startling after the medieval blocks behind us. We hauled up at the mall entrance, my driver saying it was too dangerous to bring his cab any closer to the thousands of people gathered across the parking lot. The crowd stretched for about half a mile between some condo towers on the right and a mall blockhouse on the left, with the greatest concentration at a gate in a high concrete wall to the subdivision. Rabble-rousers stood atop jeepneys that had been stalled and engulfed by the *masa*, leading a rhythmic cheer: "*Ay-y-y-rap! Ay-y-y-rap! Ay-y-y-rap!*"

"Where does Erap live?" I asked.

"Go straight through crowd, Buchanan Street Gate." My driver pointed to the space in the wall. Then—" he angled his hand to the right "—end of Polk Street, number one. But you cannot go in now unless by them," he cracked, pointing to the helicopters hovering overhead. As I got out he added, "Wait—I give you protection." He leaned over to his glove compartment, took out a pint water bottle and a cloth hankie. "If throw gas, you make wet and hold over you face. Good luck, my friend!"

I wandered through the stunning heat towards the colorful crowd, which seemed, at least coming up to the back of them, more festive than fearsome. Not being a "foreign correspondent" craving a news hit off an angry mob, I was relieved at the street-party atmosphere. The feeling lasted only a minute. Hundreds of shouting people were soon pressing at my back from the *barrio* and I could feel the humidity rising and the oxygen diminishing. Worse, the pavement was coated with slimy plastic bags and other assorted squishy garbage. If there was a charge, from one direction or the other, the last thing I wanted was to slip underfoot.

I squeezed through the hot bodies and climbed atop the hood of a jeepney. Looking over the sea of black hair I saw the tightest knot of the demonstrators faced off against a phalanx of a hundred riot police on the other side of the latticed Buchanan Gate. "Are the police taking him out through there?" I asked a bare-chested kid beside me who was waving his tattered T-shirt over his head.

"We no let!" he shouted. "No can take him by! Because we protect! *Ay-rap! Ay-rap! Ay-rap!*"

How bizarre, I thought: on the other side of that gate Erap lived in another world from these people. I could see a tropically lush street with smooth pavement, intact curbs, and a newly painted white centerline—all rarities in Manila. The spanking road was lined on both sides by monster mansions—a mix of Spanish haciendas, Egyptian mausoleums, Greek temples, and English manor houses, each surrounded by palms, hedges, and yards elaborately decorated with fountains and statues. Jerome had told me that North Greenhills was almost exclusively populated by Manila's rich Chinese merchants, while the richer "Spanish"-Filipinos, who controlled the financial center, lived in a gated community called Forbes Park, down in Makati. For 19 months, San Juan's North Greenhills had usurped Makati's Forbes Park as the social center of the capital, and, according to Jerome, that was another reason the elite had been so irked by the election of Erap.

To the right of the gate and looming over it was a meeting hall called Club Filipino, a large colonial building with a red tile roof and two floors of wraparound balconies. On the lower balcony I noticed some media folks doing stand-ups and filming the crowd. It looked like a safer vantage point than down here, so I jumped from the jeepney, pried my way back out of the crowd and walked the long way around to the condos on Eisenhower Avenue and back along the inside margin of the demonstration to the steps of the building. Upstairs, from behind the shoulders of a cameraman, I looked down upon a scene of pure hysteria at the gate—the first time I'd ever seen hate in Filipino faces. Hundreds had their fists up at the cops; the men roared catcalls and the women wailed piercing screams about Jesus loving Erap and Cardinal Sin being in league with Satan. The young cops behind their Plexiglas shields looked terrified as they jabbed red batons at the protesters rhythmically rocking the gate. One rowdy got it in the eye and stumbled back screaming, blood running through his fingers. Things looked as if they were about to boil over. I asked the cameraman if he thought the cops would open fire if the mob broke through. "They are ordered not to shoot," he said. "But it just take a scared one, eh? Then lose control of situation. So let us pray."

I was happy to do my praying up here, but several officials and security guards from the club soon came out on the veranda and announced that the media would have to vacate the premises to avoid giving cause for an attack up the steps. Apparently the crowd had been threatening this sanctuary all morning because of the press's announced disdain for the supposedly unwashed and smelly multitude. Sure enough, as soon as we stepped onto the slimy pavement a couple of dancing teens jocularly emptied water bottles over the head of one ingenue female reporter and then upended her colleague's Betacam. At that I decided to separate myself from the perceived bad guys. "I'm a friend of Lacson! From Canada! Covering his campaign! I want to know the real story!" I said, pen on my pad. That did the trick. "Canada, Canada!" they shouted, introducing me around, pouring their hearts out about the injustices to Erap, the corruption of Ramos, the evil of Cardinal Sin, the strings attached to Gloria's head, and the handle in her back. Most of the half-dressed men around me said they had been keeping a vigil on this scorching street for days. I asked a kid where he'd slept, but never got an answer, because just then word circulated that the new chief of the PNP, General Leandro Mendoza, was on his way to serve the warrant.

That galvanized the mob. With ululations that made my ears ring they attacked the steel gate, gaining leverage by leaping up and pulling at its top and leaning down and pushing at its bottom, twisting it on its hinges while the cops beat at their hands and heads. I flinched at three sudden explosions and watched black canisters come sailing slow motion over the fence and land in the crowd, fizzing in circles and blowing holes in the press of people. I poured my water over the hankie, but barely caught the chloro-burn vapor because a few brave kids, bandannas around their faces, threw the canisters back over the fence, to loud cheers. Pulling and pushing to the commands of a couple of ringleaders the *masa* finally snapped one of the hinges and twisted the gate open a few feet on its heavy chain lock. With waves and screams of victory the crowd began pouring through the space into the exclusive condominium.

The cops, most of them probably from neighborhoods not far in poverty from where these folks were from, held their fire and randomly beat at human targets as they raced through their ranks. I hung back until I saw some journalists squeeze through the gate in pursuit of the story. As I took off after them I questioned what the hell I was doing. This had *nothing* to do with Steve. And yet I kept going.

Just as my driver had said, Estrada's mansion was off to the right of Buchanan, at the end of a leafy cul-de-sac on Polk Street. The strategic intersection of Polk and Buchanan was blocked by hundreds of police and soldiers carrying mini–machine guns, rifles, tear-gas bazookas, and drawn pistols—a murderous match for the perhaps 300 scraggly rioters who'd gotten through and were now faced off against their line. On the flat roofs of the gargantuan mansions I could see the running silhouettes of snipers. Above us the choppers seemed to grow larger, lowering their olive-drab bodies as if they were going to land on our heads. The thunder of their straining engines was deafening—which was the intended effect, I supposed.

I looked back at the Buchanan Gate. The cops had reformed a tight line and with swinging batons, shots in the air, and tear gas they beat the crowd back, plugging the dike. There must have been some military strategists in the *masa's* ranks, however, for suddenly, looking actually more frightening than the military blockade, thousands of reinforcements of the poor came running at us from the north—a flanking stampede that would have caused me to open fire right into their midriffs.

"Where are *they* coming from?" I asked a cameraman who was on his cell phone.

"Broke through Madison Gate, farther north!"

The two mobs merged and began celebrating, socializing, and exchanging intelligence. Then everyone began pointing to the Polk Street cul-de-sac, where soldiers were scaling Estrada's brown steel gate. The gate opened and word circulated that Mendoza was entering the premises. Wild kids in the front row began taking blind flying leaps at the shields, grabbing at the lashing truncheons and creating opportunities for breaching the line. Dozens squeezed through and ran in their flip-flops to save Estrada. Those too timid to risk gun butts turned on the press, furious that they had obstinately portrayed Estrada as a gross criminal and Gloria Arroyo as a virginal saint. I took shelter amidst a gaggle of journalists, as the *masa* began showering us with clods of turf, poured water over our heads, and upended some more cameras. Some of the rioting women kept their Filipino sense of humor, however. Into the mikes they sang bawdy songs about Arroyo's close relations with one of her allegedly corrupt ministers, Justice Secretary Nani Perez, then washed their underarms and asses for the cameras to show they weren't dirty.

All this time a senior officer on a bullhorn, surrounded by soldiers with raised pistols, had been lecturing the mob in Tagalog. Whatever he was now saying sparked half a dozen male demonstrators, masked like bandits with red bandannas, to come forward. They turned their backs on the cops and held their hands up to the protesters. The decibel level went down a 10th. The officer with the bullhorn slipped in front of his men and he and the mob marshals seemed to hold a powwow, while everyone else leapt and danced and otherwise went berserk behind them. I supposed the officer was negotiating for Erap's passage but after five minutes of fruitless argument he shook his head and walked back behind his ranks.

I knew what was coming next. There was a massive brown house to my right, and I boosted myself onto its outer wall and crawled through the bushes planted there. I was surprised to discover, crouched on the other side and peering through the bushes, the entire Chinese family from the house—middle-aged father, mother, and several teenage sons and daughters, plus hand-wringing maids in white uniform. "Okay?" I asked the old man of the house. "I'm a journalist from Canada." "Yes, yes, okay," he told me. "Keep head down."

Then came the explosions of tear-gas canisters, and the cops charged, swinging their long red sticks in front of their shields, beating the backs of the slower demonstrators as they fled and the heads of the obstinate ones who tried to fight them. A few women who'd been pushed off to the side wept hysterically on the ground, arms raised to Jesus; others crawled over lawns with bleeding heads and noses. One shirtless fellow in green shorts who'd gone down wasn't moving at all; I watched him trampled by peasants' thongs and soldiers' boots until a cop threw him over his shoulder and carried him off down Buchanan. Meanwhile, up the block to my right, a white bus came out of Estrada's gate. One of the weeping woman stood up and tried to get her claws under the face shield of a soldier; another grabbed a running garden hose from a rich man's lawn and, surrounded by cameramen, comically soaked the cops. I thought Estrada was inside the bus and leaned over the hedge to have a look at him, but the teenage boy beside me, listening to Tagalog commentary on a boom box, told me that the bus was carrying Estrada's son, Jose "Jinggoy" Estrada, the current mayor of San Juan, arrested for graft as well. Led by a phalanx of riot cops dispersing the regrouped rioters, the bus pushed past the corner and began inching north up Polk Street.

Five minutes later came Estrada's black Ford van. A human bulldozer of anti-riot policemen were in the vanguard, flanked sides and back by hundreds of soldiers with rifles and machine guns. They plowed through the wall of *masa* with a flying wedge of shields and flailing sticks, leaving the demonstrators sloughed off upon the streets and lawns as they passed. When the hubbub had crawled past I jumped down from the wall and joined the mob as it impotently followed the trailing convoy of army trucks loaded with soldiers. Wailing and weeping as if on the road to Calvary behind Christ, the *masa* moved north up Polk and west on Madison (all of the Greenhills streets were named after American presidents) back out to Ortigas, and then north to Santolan Road, where the parade snaked at five miles an hour along the outside walls of the subdivision until, an hour or so later, it came to a whitewashed side entrance to Camp Crame, several blocks west of Edsa Avenue. The steel gates were thrown open and Erap's van turned inside, followed by the convoy of military trucks.

The president was in custody.

Back in my hotel that night I saw that the TV cameras had been allowed to follow Estrada into the booking room of the Presidential Anti-Organized Crime Task Force—Lacson's former lair—a grand irony that the commentators made much hay out of. They filmed the old actor standing miserably in profile before the police camera, then turning face front, then turning the other way in profile—like a common thief. They showed him being fingerprinted, and, finally, led into a small cell with a thin prison cot. Erap looked around and gave a little laugh as if to say, "Ah shit." He threw his trademark windbreaker on the cot, opened his suitcase, took off his socks, laid them in the suitcase, then stretched out in his bare feet with his hands behind his head. Like a gorilla in the zoo he remained on display to the nation for over an hour, the footage endlessly repeated all night long.

"That's going to drive the *masa* wild," I told Jerome over the phone early the next morning.

"Yes, take away his dignity, humiliate him, that is the plan," he said, adding that the plan was backfiring. All the people who'd been demonstrating at North Greenhills had moved down the road to the EDSA Shrine after I'd left. They'd spent the night there and were now being joined by thousands more from San Juan, Tondo, and other poor neighborhoods.

I asked what Lacson had been up to yesterday afternoon. Jerome said the general had been meeting with his advisers and giving interviews on "the developments." There was a pregnant pause, after which I said, "Because I kept my cell phone on last night. I suppose he didn't have time for the meeting on my man."

Jerome laughed and said he didn't think so, it looked like this was turning into another People Power event. People Power Three, he called it. EDSA Tres.

"So when can I meet with him again?" I asked.

Jerome said he and the general were just leaving to catch a flight south; "the situation" had forced Ping to "rearrange" his schedule. He was needed immediately at a location Jerome couldn't reveal.

"So I guess I'll just wait," I said.

"Yes, wait. Meantime, go to EDSA—you will see what is going on. The general, everybody is telling people to go to EDSA."

I felt like saying, "Jerome, I don't give a shit about EDSA," but instead promised I would hang tight.

When I got off the phone I began to slip into a blue funk. This was all on the other side of the world from my Steve-mission. To solace myself I went down to the hotel's Internet café and sent Leslie and Anne complaining updates. Back upstairs I chewed Nicorettes and watched television. Oddly, there was no coverage of what was taking place at EDSA on mainstream TV stations like ABS-CBN—just wall-to-wall coverage of a supine Estrada staring at his bare feet over his big belly, some breaking news about where he was to be taken for a medical exam, and some reassuring statements by Gloria Macapagal-Arroyo that the country had turned a corner in its history. I found a grainy and amateurishly produced station called Net 25, which showed 100,000 people at the shrine, assembled before a 50-foot banner hanging beneath the Virgin that said "POOR IS POWER." I turned back to the mainstream channels and caught a brief clip of a circumscribed view of the EDSA demonstrators, followed by a spokesman from the Catholic Bishops' Conference, who decried the "desecration" of the shrine by "paid hooligans bused in from Tondo." Cardinal Sin, the spokesman said, had urged the authorities to "take appropriate action in the face of any discovered vandalism upon our holy shrine, which is the private property of the Catholic Church." He read a statement from Cardinal Sin: "They have profaned a house of prayer . . . offending our Catholic sensibilities. . . . We are grieving for the EDSA Shrine." I watched for another half hour, but that was the end of the EDSA coverage on the main channels. I switched back to Net 25 and noticed, in the lower right-hand corner, the logo of Iglesia ni Cristo, an evangelical sect with millions of followers that had backed Estrada against the Catholic Church. (I later found out that INC, as it was called, owned the station.) Coverage of what was going on at EDSA was constant on the INC channel. In her senator's office, incumbent candidate Miriam Defensor-Santiago was being interviewed. "Sooner or later, military support will come," she said. "Especially from those holding lower positions. This is just a numbers game. The Supreme Court ruling on Arroyo's legitimacy will have to apply. What is sauce for the goose is sauce for the gander." She called for Filipinos to rally at EDSA, predicting that a million people would be assembled there by the next day, given that the numbers were doubling as she spoke. "The rally will grow and grow until Mrs. Arroyo steps down and the president resumes office. They may try, but they ignore EDSA Tres at their peril."

Lacson was next. "The Arroyo administration has done nothing to uplift the lives of the masses," he told reporters as he hurried through a crowd. "We are calling on all our countrymen to go to EDSA to condemn this administration which is preoccupied with politicking, demolishing the reputations of the opposition, and making their candidates win the election."

I shut the TV off and sat there marveling at Steve's luck. Time and again over the past nine years the cards had fallen his way. First the judge had given him his passport back, then another judge hadn't issued a warrant. Then, when I'd found him, the DOJ took six months to issue its extradition request to Macau. Then the hunt for him had all but fizzled out. Then he'd turned up again. And now this. I'd come all this way with a fair shot at getting him this time, and had landed in the middle of a revolution. EDSA fucking Tres.

With each day over the next week I would come to feel that EDSA embodied, not the hope of the Philippines, but a fundamental anarchy that made it a cozy home for sociopaths like the Paper Fan. The word itself was actually an acronym for Epifanio de los Santos Avenue—Avenue of the Epiphany of the Saints. In mundane lowercase, Edsa was just a traffic-choked, black-fuming ring road that began at Manila Bay, half a mile south of the Jumbo. It snaked east through the shacks and shops of Pasay City and turned northeast as it entered the financial district of Makati. It then headed due north past Cardinal Sin's villa and the mental hospital in Mandaluyong, passed into the Greenhills section of San Juan and through Quezon City's West Triangle, where it swung back west to Manila Bay. At its most cosmopolitan point, between the Wack Wack Golf Course and Robinson's Galleria in Mandaluyong, Edsa rose up as a cloverleaf overpass, crossing high above Ortigas Avenue about half a mile south of Erap's house. It was here, on ground level, that you ran into the capitalized EDSA, a fiberglass-roofed church topped by the giant gold Virgin with her hands extended. In uppercase, then, EDSA designated the shrine, the square before it, and the revolutions-by-means-of-holy-street-party that had taken place there. Indeed, after the overthrow of Marcos, the building, the plaza, and its spirit had been declared hallowed by the Vatican. EDSA, a Filipino Trinity, had become, as Cardinal Sin said, "a Holy place."

But I just couldn't accept this sanctifying with a straight face. If EDSA I and II were holy People Power events, then what gave the Church the right to condemn the poor for "defiling" the shrine with their own EDSA? Then again, wasn't the *masa* version of EDSA equally paradoxical? The poor meant to take back what they perceived had been stolen from them in the last two EDSAS, but their savior was a megalarcenist. Didn't the repeated "people power" orgasms of EDSA signify, not power, but helplessness?

To be sure, when I got down there that afternoon, there *was* a feel about EDSA that reflected power—though I wasn't sure whether it radiated from the towering Virgin, weirdly draped with half-naked humans like a hellish statue in a Hieronymus Bosch painting, or from the police and military bases I passed walking in from the north.

Camp Aguinaldo was the name of the military base, just across Edsa Avenue from Camp Crame. It was the headquarters of the AFP—the Armed Forces of the Philippines—with a sign out front that read: "Freedom. Your right. Our responsibility." Aguinaldo had a lot of tanks, armored personnel carriers, and cannon on hand, and during the last two EDSAS the satraps in Aguinaldo had tipped the scales by ordering their hardware to support "people power." In this EDSA, it was fairly well accepted that the AFP would stay loyal to the barons in the government who richly rewarded their fidelity. Or would some contingents march out and join a revolt? "Especially from those holding lower positions," Defensor-Santiago had said, referring to the young officer corps, and Jerome had told me this morning that she would know. Her staunchly pro-Erap brother, General Benjamin Defensor, was the chief of the air force.

The square in front of the Virgin could hold perhaps 50,000, but the real power of EDSA drew its strength from the thousands and thousands on the overpasses above and the thousands and thousands that packed Edsa Avenue north and south, and Ortigas east and west. Masses of poor people, several stadiums' worth, were waving flags, singing, weeping, dangling dangerously off the cloverleaf circles 60 feet overhead, throwing confetti, and draping spray-painted sheets that said "Free Erap Arrest Ramos—Amari thief U Owe Us 1 billion," "In Jesus Our Love, In Erap Our Hearts," and "He Suffers for Your Sin, Cardinal."

In the shaded heat beneath the overpass entrepreneurial folks had established a circuslike village with eggs stalls, meat stalls, fruit stalls, and water stalls—supplying the multitude. I'd heard on the mainstream TV channels just before I'd left my room that the crowd had fallen off and only 10,000 were gathered here—a figure grossly, and (it was later admitted) purposely underestimated by the pro-Arroyo, anti-Erap media. Indeed, the mainstream media were nowhere to be seen at this massive demonstration, lending some weight to the contention of the participants that the controlling powers of the Philippines were trying to kill the rally with silence or, in their scant commentary referring to EDSA Tres as "pathetic," contempt. Net 25, on the other hand, had assigned all its reporters and cameramen to the square, giving it 24-hour coverage. Doing stand-ups they claimed there were close to half a million people here, and that miles-long lines of others were converging from all over Metro Manila, as if following ant trails. It did not seem possible that these masses had been "bused in from Tondo" by pro-Erap candidates. No, they had walked here on their own, with their heads wrapped in T-shirts they'd hastily grabbed off a hammock, sandal-footed and wearing ragged cutoffs, all they had in the world in their pockets. Unlike the first EDSA, which had been stimulated by mainstream TV stations and newspapers, and the second EDSA, which had been drawn by a million text messages mailed by Cardinal Sin, *this* EDSA, EDSA III, was word-of-mouth generated. The *masa* truly believed that if Erap came back he would wave his movie hand and miraculously fix their lives. They believed it so much that they sang "Erap's Truth Is Marching Home," to the tune of "Battle Hymn of the Republic."

At the moment they were leaderless, but I could see the first signs of organization. Towering floodlights and a powerful sound system had been installed on a bandstand beneath the Virgin. After "Erap's Truth Is Marching Home," a rock group began playing Filipino pop tunes and the square turned into a disco. Then, around 2 P.M., an Iglesia ni Cristo bishop named Roger Alliento began addressing the crowd in firebrand Tagalog slogans—all that could be reasonably communicated across the vast distances. Each slogan was followed by riotous cheers. "They have stolen the power of the poor!" "They are the thieves and plunderers!" "Seventy million poor Filipinos!! We want our country back! We want Erap back! Instead of Erap in jail, put in Ramos!!" That blew the roof off, it being the absolute conviction of the *masa* that the exposed deeds of Ramos had gone unpunished, while Erap had paid the full humiliating price. An emcee then came to the mike and led the *masa* in a mocking Tagalog song about Arroyo doing the wash of her justice secretary, Nani Perez. It was a pun on the urban myth of Gloria's relationship with Perez: Gloria was laundering Perez's money at the same time as she enjoyed his love. It was a tune everybody seemed to know by heart.

I had a handle on what was being sung and bellowed because a young fellow beside me had volunteered to translate. He was a born commentator, with an accent that was definitely not Tagalog. I would have mistaken him for a Spanish reporter except his skin was richly brown, there was an Incan hook to his nose, and he was dressed poorly in runners, baggy black track pants, and a red T-shirt, without the *de rigueur* safari vest of Continental journalists. My translator's name was Jose Luis, and he did indeed have Incan blood. He told me he was Peruvian, that he'd come to the Philippines five years ago, when he was 23, on a merchant ship, and had married a Filipina. He now lived in the Visayan Islands, but traveled frequently to Manila "for my affairs here," and had taken the ferry to Manila last week to participate in the North Greenhills demonstrations.

Jose seemed as informed about "the developments" as anybody I'd met. When I told him I was here interviewing Lacson he gave me a five-minute exegesis on the politics of law enforcement in the Philippines that reflected everything Jerome Tang had said. Lacson, Jose said, was utterly incorruptible and had refused to be appointed number two man under General Leandro Mendoza because of Mendoza's questionable affiliations and his ties to Cardinal Sin, whom Jose despised. He drew a map to show me Sin's vacation hacienda—on the highway opposite the main airport on Panay Island, near the town of New Washington. He urged me to go down there and see it for myself—it would explain why Sin disdained the poor whose welfare and salvation he supposedly looked out for.

He said the new government was feckless and utterly corrupt, and kidnappings had taken a big jump since Lacson's resignation. Why should anybody be surprised with that convicted kidnapper Berroya now the intelligence chief? he wondered. With Lacson gone, he went on, "the syndicates" were flourishing again in Tondo, Chinatown, and the Muslim quarter of Quiapo. Without fear of arrest you could once again buy a passport, a birth certificate, a kilo of *shabu*, and guns of any kind and caliber— if you knew whom to approach. Girls, they were everywhere, he said, but the best ones could be found in the nightclubs in Chinatown run by the syndicates, who paid off the PNP and Gloria's new officials.

When I asked where he got his inside information, he merely shrugged and said he followed politics closely.

"Are you NPA?" I asked him.

"No Communist," he said. "I am against the oligarchs, I am a social democrat."

I asked what he did for a living, to which he replied, "Whatever is possible." Then he added smiling: "If you are a serious journalist, perhaps you should have a guide."

War correspondents have a term for their guides. They call them "fixers." Fixers, usually intelligent men with checkered backgrounds, have a ground-level knowledge of everything that goes on in a cratered landscape. Where bullets fly and society has run amok (a good Malay/Filipino word), they can keep a journalist from getting shot or kidnapped as they arrange interviews with warlords or rebel chiefs you could never safely reach without an intermediary. Every seasoned correspondent knows that when he lands in the middle of a war, he is nowhere until he finds a good fixer. Thus, following the law of supply and demand, fixers sprout up at airports and around the breezeways of InterContinental Hotels wherever chaos draws the world's press. Quite simply, they are the Tenzing Norgays to the Edmund Hillarys of the cable news channels, the uncredited senior researchers of much of what you see on the tube about Chechnya and Afghanistan, Somalia and the West Bank.

Unfortunately, in the craziness of the criminal underworld, there are almost no fixers. Gangsters are sometimes warlords, but only in rare cases do they have a story they want to tell reporters who need some hot footage in a hurry. The lifespan of a professional fixer in the underworld would be very short indeed if word got around that he was leading snoopy foreigners into nightclub caves, making introductions where none were wanted. A fixer in the crime world is almost an oxymoron, since he's probably not in the business of fixing anything but your own kidnapping or murder.

It was a measure of how desperate I was feeling that I asked Jose if he could meet me near the American embassy on Roxas Boulevard at three the next day. I might want to hire him on a story I was on that could do some good for his cause, I said.

As I e-mailed Leslie and Anne that night, I just couldn't get rid of the gnawing feeling that I was wasting my time and money on Lacson. I was locked into the ex-chief, and he was where? And doing what? I was in the Philippines to the tune of over a thousand dollars in airfare and $150 a day in expenses and if Lacson didn't come across for me soon, I would *have* to expand this operation.

Over a lonely late supper of Bacolod chicken near my hotel I plotted a three-step Plan B. The first step would be Jose—he would supply me with the inside story of the Manila underworld. The next step would be the Philppine Center for Investigative Journalism—I would swear its executive director Sheila Coronel to secrecy, share some of what I had found out, and get the name of an NBI cop she absolutely, 100 percent trusted. The third step would be another trip to the NBI—this time up front and on the record. I would come bearing the classified gifts that Jose delivered to me, and then say, "Oh, by the way, here's something *you* can help *me* on." Then, when I brought out the Interpol posters— What?

I knew I was hoping for some metaphysical event. *Yes, I recognize him. He is in our next office here. Ask Agent Joe Co to come in here, please. We will see if he has these tattoos.* And suddenly, there would be Steve, presented to me for packing home. Like the split second after a lottery win, my life would be transformed.

I knew that the chances of winning a lottery were 14 million to one, so the next morning I took another shot at getting in touch with the general via Jerome. The Jolibee owner told me he and Ping were back in town but that Lacson would be very busy throughout the day. "There will be developments today. I will call you. Meetings are taking place. Very secret. We cannot talk about it on the phone." Three hours later I turned on the TV and saw live coverage of Lacson walking out of Camp Crame with Jerome, having just had lunch with Estrada. Very fucking secret, I thought. I waited till the TV screen showed Ping getting in a car and then phoned him on his secure cell phone, whose number I'd just pried out of Jerome. If Ping wasn't helping me get Steve, I figured, then the least he could have done was to help me to get a scoop on his *pare*. No journalist had yet interviewed Erap after his arrest.

"Why didn't Jerome tell me?" I said, sounding irate and silly, even to myself. "I would have liked to interview Erap."

"I am afraid that would have been impossible—no press allowed," Ping replied.

I dropped it. "How are you doing?" I asked.

"As you know, the situation grows complicated. I am quite busy now. Can we speak later?"

"Just tell me—any developments on my project?"

I heard some voices in the car, then Lacson said, "Nothing, except it is still in my thoughts, Terry. Excuse me." The phone was muffled for a minute, then Jerome came on.

"Teddy?"

"Yes."

"You must be patient. We are negotiating with the army and PNP to keep EDSA from dispersal. To preserve the *masa* democratic rights. You know how many there now?"

"Half a million?"

"More, maybe three-quarter. You hear what the cardinal say about them? They desecrate shrine, so police should chase them. So government getting worried. They know when will be a million what will be the result already."

"What's that, a coup?"

"Shh, shhh!!" he hissed. "I call you later. Keep cell phone open."

As soon as we greeted one another on the trash-strewn lawn of the Roxas esplanade Jose said to me: "Here is my wife name and telephone number. I trust you. If I die, tell her I was brave."

"Die when—today?" I asked, feeling my abdominals tighten.

"No today," Jose reassured me. He looked at a pump boat picking up three young prostitutes to take them out to a freighter in Manila Bay; then at the dozens of naked kids swimming in the putrid water; then at the children in Jockey shorts sprawled against the seawall, sniffing water bottles with an orange pasty substance at the bottom. "No more millions to live like this," he stated. "I willing to die to change. To die at EDSA Tres! We want to bring down government of oligarchs, we want—"

"Do me a favor," I said, glancing towards the uniformed figures guarding the embassy lawn, "keep your political beliefs to yourself today. At least don't let yourself be overheard. *I* don't want to die."

"No problem," he smiled. "I know, Mr. Gould, we are on the same side."

I punched his arm. "Call me Joe."

We sat down on the seawall and I explained what I needed accomplished today. I wanted to find out how to buy a new, fully-lived-in life—including a birth certificate and a passport. I wanted to see how you went about selling and distributing large shipments of *shabu* to the streets, and the mechanics of buying quantities of illegal weapons. Then I wanted to go where the really big bosses went to relax with their Chinese girls. I faced Jose squarely. "You know I'm good friends with Ping Lacson."

"That is why you are my friend," he offered.

"Okay, *hombre*, Ping knows what I'm doing today. He's on my side—and he'll be on your side if this works out."

I let the implied threat and the reward sink in, although both just seemed to raise a broader smile on Jose's mahogany face. I made the decision to trust him, and then made the decision to be specific. I told him that if by the evening he had earned my trust, I would give him $1,000 if he could lead me to a gangster.

Jose was right off the mark at that, heading to the other side of the line of seaside palms to wave down one of the hundred jeepneys crawling at 10 miles an hour north down Roxas. I eyed the sardined humans in the jeepneys and told him we were taking a cab. As usual it took some time getting across Roxas to flag one going the right way. The mile-long line of traffic lights that didn't work was something I never got used to on this perpetually clogged thoroughfare. In Cambodia they didn't have any lights, so that gave them some kind of excuse for their new traffic anarchy, but the Philippines had no excuse. All the accoutrements of a modern civilization were in place but nothing worked here. They'd let their infrastructure go to shit—were actually going in the opposite direction of Cambodia. So much for People Power.

Half an hour later, as we crossed Quezon Bridge into Quiapo, I saw a three-story-high poster of Ping Lacson, his bespectacled eyes squinting at the city like Doctor T. J. Eckleburg's and his lips proclaiming, "End Kotung."* A few blocks north, on the corner of Claro M. Recto Street, there was a big air-conditioned mall called Isetan Shopping Center. Jose told me to put my camera and pad away—this is where we got out. We walked west down Recto on the opposite side of the street from the mall, passing a number of fly-blown shops and restaurants until we entered a dirt-encrusted market arcade covered by a concrete ceiling held up by cracked pylons. I couldn't believe my eyes. The booths had sandwich boards on the arcade walkway, openly advertising college degrees, birth certificates, professional certificates for doctors, pharmacists, and engineers. "Man name Mr. Recto,"

---

*In *The Great Gatsby*, T. J. Eckleburg's eyes gaze from a billboard over a wasteland. Fitzgerald writes: "But above the gray land and the spasms of bleak dust which drift endlessly over it, you perceive, after a moment, the eyes of Doctor T. J. Eckleburg.... Blue and gigantic—their retinas are one yard high. They look out ... from a pair of enormous yellow spectacles."

Jose whispered. "Real name, no from street." The whole block, he said, was protected by the 14K—Recto's syndicate—which took care of the police, so there were no worries for Recto or anyone else here.

Jose stopped at one of the little shops and introduced me to a plump, round-faced, middle-aged Chinese with a soft, casual handshake, and a thin pink shirt opened four buttons down his hairless chest. The shirt was smudged with finger tracks of ink. Recto looked like a typesetter in a print shop, and there might have been a printing machine in the back since the office was stacked with bundles of posters for pro-Erap senatorial candidates. A fan turned slowly overhead, though I couldn't imagine it offered the least bit of cooling to the cooking alcove. Jose talked to Recto in Tagalog, indicating me with his head. Recto nodded and on the back of a campaign poster he wrote out a list of information I needed to give him: photos, name, DOB, place of birth, father's and mother's names.

"This will be a new name, not my own," I said to Jose.

"Yes, new name," Recto said. He switched to Tagalog and Jose translated.

"For Philippine passport with a U.S. visa," Jose said, "take three days and cost eighty thousand pesos. With no visa, only ten thousand pesos, next morning."

"Official?" I asked Recto.

"Malacañang," Recto nodded.

"You mean the official paperwork is from there? No trouble for me after?"

Recto spoke to Jose, who translated: "Yes, all official. No mistake."

"What about a birth certificate?"

"Same, same," Recto said. "Same for visa." He switched to Tagalog and Jose smiled.

"He say for eighty thousand more, can get birth certificate register in hospital, then Manila records. So no problem for you if you in trouble and they check. You just have story. I born here, U.S. Army father, then move to United Stay when little boy."

"Good plan," I said, and shook Recto's soft hand, adding I would be back with the money in cash tomorrow.

"The guy's not even afraid I'm a journalist," I told Jose as we crossed Recto Street to the mall. "None of them are—they fucking advertise."

"Is new regime. I tell you, it better than old for syndicates."

We walked back through the Isetan Shopping Center and down Quezon Street, then through the crowded Camedo Street Market until we came to a square in front of the white stone Quiapo Muslim Center. I hung back amidst the strolling crowds of women in black chadors as Jose went up to two dark-eyed and poorly dressed men on the corner and began negotiations for a .38 and a 9mm. Just like that.

Beside me old men sat on boxes, smoking cigarettes pinched between their fingers with their palms up. All their eyes were on the white man and his briefcase, staring at me without inhibition. I offered them a smile but got none in return. Jose held up his hand for his contacts to wait a moment. He came over to me. "The .38 is sixteen thousand pesos, the nine millimeter is fully automatic for twenty thousand, twenty-two with police permit."

"I get a *permit* with it?" I laughed. "Ask them about assault rifles and submachine guns."

"I no think you can get permit for tha-a-*A-T*," Jose cracked and walked back to the pair. He came back a moment later. "AK-47 want U.S. dollars five hundred—much cheaper than in United Stay. Uzi sub is one thousand U.S. You want to leave now or just—"

I asked him to find out if I could get the AKs in bulk—about 10. "Say I'm having a lot of trouble with pirates and need protection for my crew." He took another trip to the corner and came back with the news that 10 AKs would be $400 apiece, then said he was getting really nervous—if they found out I was a journalist they would kill us.

"Now you tell me," I said. "Are they just local criminals or are they with one of the Muslim groups on Mindanao?"

"I think the groups, too," he said. "Very dangerous men."

"And *shabu*?"

"Yes, they sell *shabu*, gun, everything."

I took out 2,000 pesos and told him to give it to them as a deposit, to say we'd be back tomorrow. "Then let's get out of here," I said.

While I waited for Jose, I speculated that Quiapo was probably where Steve had got his bona fides and outfitted himself for a new career when he returned here from points west. A new set of parents, citizenship, a new education, a line on *shabu*, and guns for a new crew. In the Philippines you could do it in a day.

The Ongpin Street Moongate to Chinatown was just a few blocks away, opposite the Santa Cruz Church. Just the other side of the red-and-green-tiled arch we were hit by a stink of hot car exhaust, boiling grease, and rotting fruit. I had a burst of longing for the minty air of my Mosquito Creek bridge. Manila was starting to get to me.

"What go on always upstair," Jose said. He lifted his chin to the wooden second stories above the shops, where the gambling, drugs, and prostitution were, he said. Not that street level was quiet. A block from the moongate we walked right into an armed holdup: a frenzied fellow in jeans, runners, and guinea T-shirt ran out of a jewelry store clutching a paper bag in one hand and a special in the other. He raced to the corner and disappeared, followed a moment later by the shouting store owner. The pomelo fruit sellers hardly seemed to notice. "Maybe don't want to see," Jose shrugged.

We turned onto an old littered lane called Ling Street and Jose led me into a modern restaurant that smelled from cigarettes and cooking meat.

"You want supper?" I asked him.

"If you want, thank you, I am very hungry." He leaned his head back without turning around. "Next door, you see sign?"

I looked up past his head at a large pink marquee sticking out from a second story into the street. The lettering was in Chinese and English: "*Top Royal:* KTV Music Lounge & Health Centre."

"A karaoke lounge *and* a health center," I said, thinking the Coin Cache guys had missed half the action.

"Health centre because Chinese women make you healthy," Jose explained dryly. "Very expensive. Manila nice clean girl all night fifteen hundred pesos. Top Royal, Chinese girl same for one drink just sit with you. Every drink, another thousand. Then, in health room, massage ten thousand. Take to room, twenty thousand."

"That's four hundred bucks—for fucking?"

"You want special girl take home to hotel, maybe six hundred U.S. dollar."

I asked him what the story was: did he bring Chinese guys here? "Only when my situation is critical," he said.

"Do you know the big ones—the Triad guys?"

"No for friends, like Recto, just to see. I never go upstair here." He waved at his shirt and pants. "No dressed right. Buy me suit I can go with you." He laughed sheepishly at that. He really was a straight-ahead guy.

"Are they open now?"

"Close now but open nine. Ten, eleven o'clock we go in, you see."

I glanced at my watch. It was just past six.

"You know there's one guy I'm looking for," I said. "Ping and me are looking for him."

"Yes, you tell me," he said, leaning forward eagerly.

I took out Steve's photos. "These are old—at least ten years. He's very short. About up to here on me. Have you ever seen him?"

Jose studied the pictures, shuffling them like cards. There was no gleam of recognition in his eyes. "I am sorry," he said, impressing me by his honesty.

Maybe I was lonely, but I felt a surge of affection for him. "We find him here tonight, you pay me thousand?"

"Absolutely. It'll give you a reason not to die at EDSA. Only—" I made a snap decision that it was too dangerous to suit Jose up and go into the Top Royal with him. I could just picture him walking from booth to booth trying to get his reward and getting me rubbed out, even if Steve had never been inside the place in his life. "I'll give you another fifty for new clothes anyway." This in addition to the $50 I told him I'd give him for the day. I had money to burn. "Meantime, you ask around about a short Chinese guy in the 14K. Let's get together Sunday morning on Roxas, whatever happens."

I cabbed back to Roxas with him and paid the driver to take him on to EDSA. Three hours later I was in the Top Royal, flying my baseball cap and dark glasses like an asshole sex tourist from Mobile. The joint was done up Vegas-modern—low light, lots of gold mirrors, a bar by the door, karaoke stage by the bar, and plush booths that took up most of the floor. The "health center" rooms were behind buttoned Naugahyde doors that faced the stage. I was the only white guy in there, the only male not in a jacket, but nobody seemed to pay me any mind as I sat in the company of one of the Group Responsibility Girls—a stylish gal in a burgundy leather cat suit who spoke no more than 10 words of English and flitted her hand around my crotch as she tried to get me to order another beer for 20 bucks. Every now and then a door opened and showed a fluorescent-lit health room. Bright promise and then darkness, like all my leads on Steve. Every day I was sinking deeper and deeper in mood. "Want real fucky-fucky?" the gal asked me. "Two girl suck you cock?"

"Not tonight," I sighed. I was getting set for something crazy, but not that.

"I tell you truth, they are no good," Jerome said, referring to the Center for Investigative Journalism. It was the next morning and I was sitting in his office across from his Jolibee restaurant in Quezon City. The office, a huge dingy loft, doubled as a storeroom, and the back of it was piled with a depressing collection of Disney characters, fat Buddhas, owl clocks, old tinsel Christmas trees, teddy bears, and porcelain eagles. Along with this dust-covered kitsch were police memorabilia in museum cases: a PNP patrol boat, a riot helmet, a sword, and an elaborate Sam Browne belt. These last belonged to Lacson's Camp Crame office, hastily evacuated when Estrada was overthrown and given to Jerome to look after until the general's return to power. One case, beside the riot helmet, had caught my eye when I walked in. It contained the most beautiful statue of Kwan Kung I had ever seen— polished bronze and three feet tall. Beside it was a picture taken the day the statue had been given to Lacson by the Chinese Filipino Business Club. Lacson was in full Third World police regalia—gold epaulets, big hat with gold olive leaves on the brim and gold martial shield on the crown. Jerome stood beside him, his arm around Lacson.

"They will tell you one side—side of Cory and Sin and Ramos," Jerome went on about the PCIJ. "You cannot trust them. They find out you friends with Ping, they cause you trouble."

The TV was on, tuned to Net 25. Jerome's assistant, Carmela, translated a Tagalog stand-up as Jerome took a call on his cell phone. The police were moving Estrada to a veterans' hospital in Quezon City. This was less for medical reasons, Carmela said, than to get Erap out of the orbit of the demonstrating hordes down at EDSA. "They afraid they attack Crame, to free Erap. What will they attack with, water bottles?"

Half an hour later word came over the TV that government forces were blocking access to EDSA; then that tanks from Camp Aguinaldo were outside the Net 25 station.

"It's like martial law!" Carmela complained. "First a news blackout, then they are blocking access to the poor people, then they surround the TV station. Ramos is behind it. Ramos, Cory, and Sin."

"I have been in this country for sixty years," Jerome said, punching off his phone for the fourth time. "Lacson is only one takes no money. They know this, so they want bring him down, accusing him things he want stop. Setting right that which is wrong. Lacson no take bribes and no give bribes. This is what cause him trouble."

"It's all a plot," Carmela said. "By the people who hate the Chinese. The Makati Business Club, they call us *Chekwa,* means like you say for black people. We just a million Chinese, so we are like the Jews here. The Makati Spanish hate the people that help us."

"You see," Jerome went on quietly, "since he take over chief of PNP, a lot of top police lose jobs. He transfer them, get rid of them, make lots of enemies. But rank and file, they loyal to him. Gloria know this, so she is an enemy, very afraid of him, try to bring him down. She know Lacson going to arrest the gambling king Bong Pineda—I tell you already, Gloria is godmother to his son. He run the *jueteng* in her province, Pampanga. Pineda ran away to California because Lacson was going to arrest him. Then, Ping out, so now Pineda back. Very bad man—not just *jueteng.* If Lacson come to power, no more *kotung,* no more kidnapping, try to arrest Gloria's *jueteng* friend. So they don't want him."

"You've got a wild media here," I said. "How come this stuff isn't blown up in the press if it's in *Time* magazine—"

"Because I *tell* you!" he replied, exasperated. "Don't report on these stories because they get bribe by the politicians. Because Lacson no pay bribes, try to stop bribes, so the media is against him. Oh, oh—look!"

There was Cardinal Sin on the screen, again somberly declaring that the poor were "desecrating" the shrine, bringing shame and disgrace on EDSA.

"Any chance I can meet with Lacson on my project today?" I asked.

"Schedule very busy now. Tonight he go to EDSA, address poor." Jerome leaned closer. "Be patient. Something happen, then he can help you again."

"What do you mean 'happen'?"

"Shhhh!"

The PCIJ was located in a modern, three-story office building on a tree-lined street in Quezon City, not far from Jerome's restaurant. When I got there the office was crowded with people on the phones and working at computers. I'd heard the center was run mostly on grants from UNESCO and the Ford and Asia Foundations, and that, until quite recently, it had employed only one full-time journalist. That was amazing considering the fact that it was the PCIJ which, in the last decade, had exposed the Amari land deal scandal, justice for sale in the Supreme Court, corruption in every aspect of Philippine society from journalism to law enforcement, and, most recently, Estrada's weird world up to but not including Singson's charges—although their previous exposés had given Singson the momentum to come forward and offered his allegations the weight of logic in the public arena. Sheila Coronel, the co-founder and executive director, whom I had come to meet, had an international reputation for writing, editing, and assigning stories that would have won her and her organization a few Pulitzer Prizes if she had been doing the same work in the States.

I entered her private office and found a diminutive, soft-voiced woman with huge glasses and boy-cut hair who seemed so absolutely sure of herself that I could see right off the bat how she'd had the courage to take on every crook in the country—this despite the fact that many of those crooks were, as a matter of course, killing the journalists who exposed them. I began by reiterating the very general e-mail I'd written her by way of introduction: I was looking for a Triad guy from Canada, probably connected to the police. I laid out what I had found out in Quiapo and that I needed an NBI cop I could trust to share all this with—someone the Mounties could trust, as well.

"I know the head of the NBI, General Reynaldo Wycoco," she said. "He can be trusted, he is one of the most decent police officers. Talk to him and maybe he will find someone to work with you."

"That's what I'm worried about," I said.

"Well, it ought to be somebody that *he* trusts," she said, without smiling. "There's another guy, but he is tied in with Ping Lacson, and his son was said to be involved in a kidnapping gang."

I almost didn't want to hear the answer, but I asked the question anyway. "What do you think of Ping Lacson?"

"He's frightening," she replied, without hesitation. "He has a past as a torturer—he was a torturer during the Marcos years."

"That's proven?" I asked.

She went over to her bookshelf and took down a weighty volume. "It's all in this book. It was recently published in the Philippines. Have you heard of it?"

"No, I haven't," I admitted, my heart sinking. It was called *Closer Than Brothers: Manhood at the Philippine Military Academy,* by Alfred W. McCoy, originally published in 1999 by Yale University Press. I'd done a search on Lacson but hadn't turned up McCoy. He happened to be one of the journalists I respected most in the world, the author of the seminal 1972 work, *The Politics of Heroin in Southeast Asia*—the volume that had blown the lid off the CIA's involvement in the Golden Triangle drug trade and the Agency's use of Air America during the Vietnam War.

"Lacson's a member of the class with Gringo Honasan," she said. "Gringo was behind the coups to overthrow Cory."

"That part I know," I said. "Ping came up through the ranks—but because of that he's been tarred with the reputation of all the—"

"There've been several charges against Lacson," she interrupted me. "It's been documented by Amnesty International—it's in Al McCoy's book. There's also been several cases of kidnappings, and those were clearly upon his orders, there are people now ready to testify he did those things—the Bubby Dacer killings."

"I hear that Ramos was behind it," I said. "They say he would do that to implicate Ping."

She dismissed this as nonsense. "No no! It's all Lacson's people, it's the task force people, how could Ramos be behind it? Lacson's men have confessed that they did it because they were told that Dacer was a criminal. It's that sort of people in the task force who feel that if you're a criminal it's okay to bump you off. He's not a nice fellow. There are a lot of other stories that are coming up. Certainly there's things emerging from the testimony of this woman Mary Ong. Then there is Estrada himself, he was involved in smuggling, illegal gambling, and they say drugs were number one, that Ping would be behind it too, because he and Estrada were really close. On the other hand, the thing is, Lacson has a lot of enemies, and the charges may be exaggerated, for example the ones from Berroya. However, it seems to be there's enough reason to believe he's involved in drugs."

Sheila had to take a call and I looked in the index of *Closer Than Brothers*. In 400 pages there were only five citations for Lacson, but McCoy's statements about Ping were unforgiving. The Metrocom Intelligence and Security Group (MISG), which Lacson had joined in 1971, was "a closed, tight-knit, psychotic club of martial law enforcers." Lacson was the aide to the MISG's commander, Colonel Rolando Abadilla. "At the MSIG, Rolando Abadilla and two close comrades, Roberto Ortega and Panfilo Lacson, tortured together for over a decade, forming a tightly bonded faction that would . . . rise together within the police after Marcos's downfall." Lacson and Abadilla were eventually sued in civil court by the Free Legal Assistance Group "for the brutal torture of nine victims." Lacson testified that he had never taken part in acts of torture, maintaining that his accusers had mistaken him for another officer. In 1993, a Quezon City judge found Abadilla and Lacson liable for about $10,000 in damages. "But the defendants appealed, insuring delays that could continue for another decade or more. . . ."

> Freed from judicial review [McCoy went on] the torturers of the Marcos era have continued to rise within the police and intelligence bureaucracies, allowing martial law's legacy of military abuse and corruption to persist, unaddressed and largely uncorrected. . . . After his inauguration in July 1998, President Joseph Estrada appointed PNP Chief Superintendent Panfilo Lacson to head the powerful Presidential Task Force on Organized Crime. Because Lacson was still facing charges for the 1995 mass murder of eleven members of the Kuratong Baleleng gang, the appointment sparked protest by human rights groups and the Catholic bishops. Nonetheless, with the president's backing and unlimited operational funds, Lacson soon emerged as the country's most powerful police officer. Within weeks, witnesses recanted and the murder case collapsed. Parallel promotion of two class-mates . . . to key PNP regional commands made their PMA batch the most powerful cohort in the national police. Significantly, each was notorious for brutal killings that marked the different stages in Class '71's troubled career. Then in December, President Estrada, apparently unaware of the macabre irony, marked the fiftieth anniversary of the U.N. human rights declaration with a palace ceremony honoring his "trusted aide" Lacson, formerly leader of the notorious torture unit and currently facing mass murder charges, for his "exemplary service to our country." A few weeks later, Lacson and two classmates . . . were promoted to two star generals in the police hierarchy.

I put the book down. Oh God, I thought, Am I using Heinrich Himmler to get Bugsy Siegel? When Coronel got off the phone, I said: "He has a dark, dark past. I didn't know about the torture part."

"Talk to Wycoco about it."

"I will, but I must tell you, Sheila," I went on sheepishly, "I've been talking to the opposition, and they're claiming that there's a secret triumvirate of Ramos, Aquino, and Cardinal Sin, that Sin has this mansion down on Panay Island, that you could take it as a given this faction would be plotting against all Estrada's backers, making accusations—that they're so entrenched and trying to preserve—"

"Sin is seventy years old," she laughed, "he undergoes dialysis, he doesn't have the capacity to plot, he's very sick. Cory's a grandmother, she's not capable of plotting anything that could affect government. And Ramos is seventy-something years old too, none of the younger officers would follow him. Those three people have influence, but I can't imagine they go around plotting—these two doddering old men and this grandmother, that's the most fantastic allegations!"

I began packing up. I apologized for the silliness of the rumors. I confided that I'd spun off into all these "side issues" simply because I was dealing with people connected with law enforcement who were now outside government and, it seemed, fighting a life-or-death battle. My real goal in coming to her was to find one good cop. I would have to judge Wycoco on my own, of course, but at some point I'd have to make the decision whether I would hand over the whole file to him. "Because if it turns out I can't trust him, I won't last long here," I said.

Sheila thought on that a moment, staring at her desk through her big round glasses. She looked up at me. In her eyes and brows was a statement: *You want me to tell you the obvious, I'll tell you.* Then she said: "Wycoco, you can trust him up to a point but who knows really?"

CHAPTER 27

CITY OF THE LIVING DEAD

———

It is better to be a dead Chinese than a living Filipino.
—FILIPINO SAYING

Call it a hunch, but Sunday, April 29, seemed like the kind of day Manila would go completely insane. Last night's crowd at EDSA had grown to a million and the Church of INC promised a few hundred thousand more by nightfall. Then there was the weather: 100 degrees at 10 A.M., with the humidity drenching me just crossing the street for a copy of the *Daily Inquirer,* whose banner headlines reinforced my premonition: "Lacson to EDSA III: 'Victory Is Nearly Ours,'" read one; "Miriam Linked to Junta Plot," read another.

As I threw down my 15 pesos for the paper, Jerome tweeted my cell. "The cows are gathering," he said, demonstrating a talent for haiku I hadn't heard before. "Be ready to go to EDSA." I had a good idea what was up but never got to ask. He became sidetracked in an agitated conversation and then signed off with the usual, "Keep cell phone open."

Back across Pedro Gil Street I felt the ground rumble, like the prelude to an earthquake, but worse. For the first time since I'd landed, the honking jeepneys fell silent as an armored military vehicle rolled by, 10 feet tall and wide as the street. Then came two camouflaged trucks loaded with soldiers wearing *Wehrmacht* helmets, tight fists high on their Armalites. I looked at the pedestrians on the corners. Even the watch sellers had lost their smiles as they gazed at the scary parade. These folks knew the signs, I thought, they'd lived through martial law. "There is now trouble," the Palm Plaza's old doorman sighed, looking after the roaring vehicles.

The coffee shop's manager, Florian Noceda, was unsettled, too. "This frightens me," she mumbled to the television in the piano bar. On the tube, Cardinal Sin was urging Catholics to assemble in front of the palace to defend the president against a march from EDSA. "It is immoral to grab power!" Sin warned the restless *masa.* Meanwhile, in the Mount Carmel Church in

Quezon City, the woman the cardinal had helped to grab power led a rosary prayer for her presidency. "Thank you for not forgetting that praying was what made People Power successful," Gloria Arroyo told the congregation. She might have added that having the armed forces on her side had helped, for force was now on her mind. At noon, when she received word that Lacson and a delegation of "coup plotters" were gathering at Estrada's mansion, she went on TV and told the nation she was ordering her attack helicopter on red alert at Camp Aguinaldo, seconds away from the hordes at EDSA.

The most militant attendees at that North Greenhills meeting were Senators Miriam Defensor-Santiago, Gringo Honasan, and Ponce Enrile— three of the 11 who had voted against opening the envelope at Erap's impeachment trial. According to an "intelligence report" leaked to the media days later, Lacson and the senators supported a million-man march on Malacañang at 2 A.M., with the goal being to force Arroyo to step down, return Erap to power, and resume the impeachment trial. Another group at the meeting, led by one of Estrada's sons, J. V. Ejercito, objected, saying the march should focus on the hospital where Erap was in detention, thus avoiding a confrontation with Arroyo's troops. Still another group, led by Estrada's former executive secretary Edgardo Angara, opposed a march alto-gether, arguing that the militants' demands would never be met and the affair would end in a slaughter of the demonstrators.

The meeting broke up at two in the afternoon without agreement, but five hours later the march appeared to be on, at least according to Jose Luis's sources at EDSA. "We march at two in morning!" he declared above the cacophony by the food stalls after I'd picked him up at Roxas. "Only to make government listen! I am nonviolent man for *masa*, but if government shoot me I am ready to die! You tell Vicki," he said, referring to his wife.

"You're not gonna die over this," I dismissed his fantasy. "You're gonna come through it and find my man."

Unfortunately, he was as unpreoccupied with the Paper Fan as Lacson, whose spirit now leapt into our midst with a Zen tweet. "The pasture is full," Jerome told me over the phone. "He will be there at midnight. Go to stage. Say he want you up there."

I decided to keep this encrypted intelligence from Jose, but discretion wasn't necessary. When I turned around, my fixer was gone. It would be a week before I saw him again.

The only way to get to the EDSA stage was via a narrow stairway. It began to the left of the Virgin's feet, but when I made my way over there at 11:30 I encountered thousands of the *masa* with the same idea. A forest of limbs reached skyward, as if ascension to the Virgin was step one on their climb to prosperity—or maybe to heaven. Beyond hoping for the impossible or the metaphysical, I don't think a single one of them had a logical reason for enduring the struggle to get to those steps.

The wet heat at ground level was probably up around 130 degrees, and the carbon dioxide level was high. Yet people must have been reaching their goal because the mob was moving slowly forward, pulling me deeper into it even as I had second thoughts about this adventure. Then progress stopped, and the human current began backing up, squeezing me. An impatient force pushed from behind and suddenly the goal of everybody around me switched from getting to the Virgin to getting free of the crush. Women were shrieking that they couldn't breathe and I felt panic in the air, as vivid as the smell of thousands of hot, packed bodies. Then came another tectonic surge from behind, my feet lifted off the ground, and I was carried sideways by a river of struggling humanity. Now *I* couldn't breathe. I tried to get a handle on my fear, but this looked as bad as those mass tramplings at Mecca.

Luckily, the EDSA demonstration around the shrine, if not tightly directed, had some sturdy organization. Up ahead I saw a dozen burly gendarmes in yellow and red vests keeping control around the area where the crowd funneled to the steps. "Help me, I'm a journalist!" I screamed, waving my white pad and camera. "I'm here to meet Ping Lacson! We're being crushed!"

They looked my way. Maybe they realized that as the only foreign reporter here I was the one to get their cause out to the world. Maybe they just recognized that they had a truly dangerous situation on their hands that had to be reversed. Whatever their motivation, they plunged in, grabbing collars and manhandling people, smartly turning bodies to face away from the stage, pushing at them and sparking a trend that redirected the flow of the crowd from the steps. Three of the men in vests then ushered me through the mob, fit me into the line of *masa* still ascending the steps, and finally escorted me to a segregated VIP section on the stage.

Roped off from the *masa*, I found myself suddenly cooled by large fans blowing upon seated dignitaries waiting their turn to speak. I thanked my saviors, then turned west and beheld a purgatorial view that caused my jaw to drop. Hundreds of thousands were draped over the cloverleafs like noodles, cheering on the crushed million below. "They *hate* the poor!!!" a former senator named Eva Kalaw screamed at them. The equivalent of a whole city responded in unison, launching a shock wave of sound that tickled my skin. "But eighty percent are poor!!!" Again the wave rolled over the stage, and I saw the "POOR IS POWER" banner sway like a sheet on a clothesline. "This means they hate their own country!"

The man translating Kalaw's speech for me was Joel Naga, the former minister of Muslim affairs under Erap, now running for Congress. I shared a fear with him: given what I'd just gone through, if these folks ever marched and were fired on, thousands would die in the retreating stampede.

"Why is there no media here so they do not have to march to be heard?" he shouted in rhetorical reply. "Look around. A million people. How can they ignore this? Media *must* be paid to look away."

"Well Net 25's here," I said.

"Net 25!" He waved an angry finger in the direction of Malacañang. "The National Communication Commission has cut their feed to Mindanao this morning. As of 11 A.M. they have phoned me this information. So it is censorship, blackout, martial law, which nobody dares to speak its name!"

Eva Kalaw concluded her speech with a ringing coda: "Gloria, Erap is your commander in chief, your loyalty is on the constitution, not yourself! *Bumaba ka na! Bumaba ka na!*" she set up a chant. Resign! Resign!

A female vocalist in spiked heels and tight jeans then took the mike and, backed by a rock band, led the crowd in what sounded like a patriotic song. With their palms waving in the air, the million below looked like enraptured evangelicals at a holy-roller stadium service. I asked Naga what the song was. "Faded Picture," he told me, a pop tune that had nothing whatsoever to do with the politics at stake. Another reason the middle classes had contempt for EDSA Tres, I thought. To them this was a free concert for the publicly defecating *masa* rather than a sanctification of righteous revolution—as their own two EDSAs had been.

When he found out I was here to meet Lacson, Naga accompanied me to the front row of VIP seats, where he sat me down next to a woman named Bihing Octaviano. She was not a heavyweight politico, but a massage therapist who'd been invited to the inner circle as a first-aid attendant. She took my hand in greeting, detected anxiety, and gave my fingers a very effective two-minute decracking. Then she mopped my dripping brow with a striped hankie from her purse, and told me to keep it. I loved the way Filipinos sized me up and concluded what I really needed was a good hankie.

The crowd broke into another song, this time a politically appropriate one, "Philippines, My Love." Streamers of toilet paper fell from the overpass into the bright white haze of klieg floodlights. Bihing dabbed her eyes with another hankie, weeping for her homeland and its jailed crook of a president. Someone launched a starburst rocket from the overpass, delighting the crowd but scaring the shit out of me. "Look there, speak with him!" Bihing said, pointing out a distinguished man with fine chiseled features who was giving an interview with Net 25. She told me his name was Vincent "Tito"

Sotto III, one of the 11 senators who had voted "no" on opening Erap's bank account. Pad in hand I approached him, but the Net 25 camera swung on me, and the reporter, finished with her last question, stepped between me and Tito and put a microphone in my face. "Can you tell us you name, where you from and why you are on stage now?" she asked.

"Is this live?"

"Yes, you are talking to the Philippine people."

Oh shit, I thought. "Uh, well, I'm writing a book, in part on the Philippines, so naturally I'm very interested in the political events here. Excuse me," I smiled, "I've got to do my own interview."

I sidestepped her, but now Sotto was making his way to the other end of the stage. I followed after him and then gave it up as he disappeared into a clutch of important-looking men in barongs. The camera was still on me, however; indeed, I was the focus of two cameras, the reporter's and one down below aiming up at me. The crowd cheered mightily. I looked out at them and understood why. I was standing all by myself in the middle of the stage by the empty mike, with a million sets of eyes on me, waiting for me to harangue them. If you can believe this, I felt a surge of anarchic power. All I had to do was grab that mike and shout, *I am from Canada! We support you! We urge you to march on Malacañang! Right now, let's go, onward to the palace!*

A crew-cut tubby guy in a red golf shirt came up beside me and took the mike. The crowd went wild. I stepped back and sat down with the dignitaries again. "Who's he?" I asked Bihing, as he launched into a passionate tirade in favor of freeing Erap and following the constitution.

"Erap's son, J. V. Ejercito."

Ah, yes, J. V.—"the moderate." As J. V. ranted slogans, I became more and more irritated with the camera resting on me. I could just picture Steve watching TV in the back of a limo. "Fuck! I think I know that fucking guy!" I put my face behind my own camera, took some pictures of the crowd and J. V., and then hunched down writing notes. I looked at my watch. It was now getting on to 12:30. Where was Lacson? Dignitaries were blocking the breeze from the fans and the heat was overpowering. Out in the sea of humanity people were fainting. Every few minutes, hand over hand, the crowd passed up swooning women to the stage, where they were laid out and soaked with water bottles, restored to consciousness by Bihing's neck-cracking technique, and led away. One never regained consciousness, however, and Bihing helped carry the near-dead woman offstage. Darn Jerome! I thought. I'm lucky I got up here alive. I tried phoning his cell and, by my phone's screen, it looked like he answered; I shouted I was on the stage waiting for him and Ping, but I couldn't hear a thing in reply.

To my left, just the other side of where Bihing had been, sat a refined-looking woman in rimless glasses named Santanina "Nina" Rasul, who was running for senator. Nina was just getting off her own cell phone and I moved into Bihing's seat beside her. By then I'd become convinced that when it came to cell phones, there was something about Filipinos that made them uniquely adapted to handling a conversation in a deafening crowd. I wondered if I could trust her to call Jerome for me.

"They're being worked to a frenzy," I said. "I don't know how they'll channel all this energy and emotion. It seems to be building to a climax."

"Yes, they are very excited now. They want justice. Because it has been taken from them."

A middle-aged matron in a flowered dress and a red Erap cap suddenly leaned between us. "That is correct—we want justice for *masa* and for Erap!" she enunciated. She leaned back up, mopped her brow with a tissue and fanned her face with a pad.

I decided to tell Nina what was up. "I'm waiting here for Ping Lacson," I said. "He was supposed to show up—" I looked at my watch "—an hour ago. Do you know if he's coming?"

"Do you have a phone number to reach him?" she asked.

Go for it, I decided. I gave her my cell, and hit redial. As Nina listened, the woman in the red cap leaned down again: "I think Ping Lacson will be the next president. Your opinion is that too?"

"He's a good man," I said. "I'm on his side. I was supposed to meet him here tonight."

This seemed to excite her. "Oh! I wanted also to interview him! How do you know him?"

"He's a friend of a friend."

I looked over at Nina. "One moment," she said, hitting redial again.

The woman in the Erap hat said she was a journalist, too, for a Puwersa Ng Masa newspaper. She wrote her phone number and first name on my pad. "Gloria—like the president, but I am not a server for *her!*" she said. Then she asked if I had a card. While Nina talked to Jerome, I fumbled through the cards in my wallet. "The Palm Plaza!" Gloria exclaimed, looking at the hotel card I showed to cabdrivers. "My sister used work there. Do you like it?"

"Jerome say not happen tonight," Nina interrupted, handing me back the phone. "He say to tell you he will call you in the morning. No more reason for you to stay. Tomorrow you speak with him."

"Jerome?" Gloria asked, walking to the edge of the stage with me. "With PNP? What last name? Because I think I know him also. Does he say PNP will be with us tonight?"

I looked at the cell phone she had cocked in her hand. "I don't know anything about that," I said.

I tried not to think about it on the cab ride home, but something told me this Gloria gal was no pro-Erap journalist.

Manila did not go insane that night. Two hours after I left EDSA a few thousand people did make their way to Camp Crame, where they rallied and chanted: "*Lusob* Malacañang! *Lusob* Malacañang!" Attack Malacañang. But Erap's son J. V. caught up with them there, climbed atop a car and declared through a bullhorn that an attack would be senseless. The checkpoint before the palace, known as the Mendiola Gate, was barricaded, and troops were in place waiting for them. The crowd milled around, sang the Philippine national anthem, and then dispersed back to the shrine.

The next morning, April 30, I awoke to see Arroyo at a news conference telling the nation she had thwarted last night's coup plotters. "I wish they had tried it so I could crush them," she said. This was followed by an announcement from NBI Chief Reynaldo Wycoco: Lacson, Defensor-Santiago, Honasan, and Enrile—all suspected of advocating the violent overthrow of the government—were being put under round-the-clock surveillance. The mainstream TV stations then reported that the Arroyo administration had summoned the executives of the Iglesia ni Cristo Church for a meeting. The INC execs left the meeting publicly vowing not to support a coup attempt against the president, and the head of INC, Minister Erano Manalo, went on to declare he was ordering his flock to pull out from the shrine. This was followed by an announcement by Net 25 that it was ending its 24-hour coverage of the demonstration. ("Net 25 returns to its well-deserved obscurity," the *Inquirer* stated on its next front page.)

By the late afternoon, as I sat with Jerome in his office watching myself in replays of last night's demonstration, we heard that the crowd at EDSA was shrinking by the hour. Malacañang reporters averred in stand-ups that last night had been the high-water mark of EDSA Tres. "Max-i-mum people, max-i-mum momentum," said one, speculating that had they marched on the palace it might very well have been theirs, although at a terrible price. Now the *masa* were flooding home in disappointment and the security around Malacañang was being relaxed. "WHY POWER GRAB FAILED" ran the banner head of the *Inquirer*'s next edition.

To my mind, this meant it was back to business for me. Lacson, weighing his troubles with the "surveillance," would see the benefits of returning his attention to my man. But when I broached this to Jerome, he disappointed me: "We wait yet. Things maybe not over. Keep cell phone open."

You wait, I thought. I can't afford it. At the Palm Plaza I wrote in my Day-timer: "Visit Wycoco at NBI." Then I went for a jog up Roxas to the Jumbo and back, had a late supper of *pecho* chicken wings, took a sleeping pill at midnight, and set my alarm for seven.

The sleeping pill was a mistake.

"Turn on the TV!! Look at the TV!! It has started!!"

It was 4 A.M., May Day, and Jerome was on my cell. Armed with sticks and a few homemade shotguns, 30,000 young men had left EDSA at 1:30 on the six-mile march to Malacañang. They were now rocking the chains of the palace gates, having overrun three roadblocks with commandeered dump trucks and suffering only one dead in their ranks. My first thought was, If there's only one dead, then the troops are letting them through. They might very well bring this off and plop Erap back in the president's chair, with Lacson at his right hand, in charge of all the cops in the realm again.

"Take nothing with you," Jerome advised. "Only cell phone for emergency."

I dressed, grabbed a liter of water and my trusty hankies and went outside into the ungodly morning heat. "Malacañang!" I told the cabdriver in front of the hotel. He waved me away and tried to close his door. I jumped in anyway. "Just get me nearby. I don't care if I have to walk a mile." We were stopped on the Ermita side of the Ayala Bridge by a platoon of soldiers in battle dress who pointed Armalites at us. In the distance I could hear the sharp crackling of rifle fire and the more sonorous thumps of tear-gas launchers. Waves of cheers floated on the air, as if from a sporting event. Curiously, as soon as I held up my pad and said I was a reporter the soldiers waved us by, but my driver refused the invitation. "You want to die, that your business. I have family."

Across the bridge, about a mile ahead in the smoky dawn, I came to a square at the corner of Legarda and Recto, massed with a crowd facing south towards the palace, half a mile away. When I got to their milling outskirts I saw the tree-lined Mendiola Boulevard solidly packed with leaping, dancing boys and young men. Several media vans were parked around the square, their windows smashed and their doors wide open. I wasn't happy that there were no film crews around, nor that I was the only non-rioter in sight. A hundred maniacally laughing youngsters turned my way, calling "Hey Joe! Hey Joe!" Mustering a teacher's air of authority, I pointed my cell phone at the oldest and told him I was a friend of Ping Lacson and that I was here to report back on the developments. The boy shook my hand with both of his, pointed south and said his comrades had some TV people and Cardinal Sin's followers holed up in a building down Mendiola.

"What's happening at the palace?"

"Somebody say we break through Gate Seven!" he screamed. "We are inside, everybody fucking her!" He meant the mob had broken through the main gate of Malacañang and were gang-raping Arroyo, but it was obvious he didn't know what was going on at the front. Like his *pares*, the kid was shirtless, I could smell booze on his breath, and his eyes were jaundiced and bloodshot at the same time. From the way these *masa* were now jumping and howling for no reason, I knew they were all seriously messed up on *shabu*. They were the dregs of EDSA Tres, the last holdouts, the ones with nothing to lose but their lives, the least predictable and most dangerous.

As if I needed privacy to call Lacson, I got away from them by walking to the north side of a backhoe parked in the middle of the square. The city was constructing a Metrorail line up Recto and the backhoe was surrounded by tons of rubble. I figured that if the fighting moved back this way there would be a lot of rock throwing. I heard the crackle of rifle fire from the palace again and picked out a spot in an arcade farther north to take shelter. But, in fact, the momentum of the mob seemed to be going the other way: Tagalog screams for reinforcements sent the whole mass of kids running south, as if indeed their front ranks had broken through, and within minutes the square was nearly empty.

Stay here, I told myself. You're not a news reporter. You're on another story, and this isn't it. Still, if Lacson, Miriam, and Gringo had allies among the palace defenders, and the *masa were* breaking through—would I really want to miss that?

I walked slowly down Mendiola until I could see the white palace up ahead. The closer I got to it, the more I realized I was entering a zone where the peril was immediate. The air was filled with acid fumes from the tear gas, the street underfoot littered with lost sandals and stones, and the *masa* in this sphere even crazier and more energized. As if marking the boundary, a boy lay flat on his back before an overturned barricade, his hands flung to his sides in a crucifixion pose, a pooled halo of bright blood around his head, running in rivulets over the dirt. I looked at the roofs but couldn't see the snipers who had picked him off. I heard more rifle fire, and a few seconds later the mob in the middle of the street behind me became hysterical. Holding a fellow by all fours they carried out his limp, skinny body, blood spewing from the side of his neck and splashing on the cement as they raced him north to the square. I shouted for them to put pressure on the wound, and ran a few steps after them, then heard something that sounded like a spike hitting the pavement in front of me. I realized that if soldiers were firing live ammo in the air, those bullets were going up and coming down. That's probably how the two kids had got it.

There was an arcade bordering the boulevard and I leapt for cover, stood alone behind a stanchion watching thousands of young men running this way and that on the street, waving Philippine flags, holding posters of Erap aloft, giving Malacañang the V sign and the fuck-you sign. Nobody was in charge, everybody was in charge, yelling adamant Tagalog orders with nobody listening. *This way,* they seemed to bellow in bloodcurdling shouts, *get rocks, keep going, don't stop, we'll win.* A few had sticks, some had stones, most were bare-handed, some barefoot. If the troops at Malacañang were standing firm, none of these guys had a chance.

I looked away from the palace, back to the relative quiet of the square. The sun was up and hot now. Atop a plinth stood a silhouetted statue of a kneeling anti-Marcos activist named Chino Roces, holding up a cross. I looked around at the dead boy and saw some kids lift his arms and begin dragging him in the direction of the square. His blood-soaked brains were visible through his hair. I gagged and brought up a mouthful of bile. My heart started to thump in a strange way and I leaned back against the cool of the concrete stanchion and drank half my water. I've never fainted in my life, but I was on the verge of it now.

The rifle fire stopped and the mob started forward again. "Go back to the square, idiot," I said, right out loud. But the writer inside me protested that I should be there if Lacson descended from the sky in a chopper and this ended in victory for the *masa*. Maybe I would get invited into Malacañang to witness Erap's restoration? I soaked my hankie, put it to my face, and left the safety of the overhang, following the tide of kids as they crossed over the flattened barricades of the Mendiola Gate. On the palace side I cut quickly to the right, away from the *masa* and against a wall, with the branches of the trees providing cover—I hoped. I wouldn't know if the shelter failed me, would I?

Halted half a block before the wrought-iron gate to Malacañang, the front line of *masa* were pelting hundreds of uniformed police with stones. The cops sheltered beneath a black-and-blue carapace of shields, the stones thudding down on the stenciled word "PULIS" with the sound of softballs against a roof. The no-man's-land between the two sides was drenched, probably from water cannon earlier that morning, plus strewn with more torn sandals and ricocheted stones. Behind the gates were thousands of milling soldiers in combat dress. There were also dozens of media guys on the south side of the action facing the crowd, or on the flanks of the cops, or on the palace side of the gates, or atop army vehicles. If this comes down to a bloodbath, I told myself, you're on the wrong side of the faucet.

Nevertheless, the riot seemed to have reached a standoff, with a lot of dancing and obscene posturing on the half-naked mob side, and a general air of stoicism on the uniformed palace side. I was amazed at the restraint of the government forces. Then, on the other side of the gates, senior officers began blowing shrill whistles and barking orders. The soldiers ranked up, positioned arms, the gates opened inward and the Armed Forces of the Philippines began to crowd out, the police moving off to the flanks. A couple of APCs revved their engines, blowing gray smoke from their exhaust, and moved forward into no-man's-land. In tight attack mode behind the armor, the troops were announcing that they meant business. I thought: If pro-Erap helicopters had been lined up to rescue this coup, they would have been here already. It wasn't going to happen.

I ran north, back to my refuge under the arcade. I got there just as a fusillade of tear gas and rifle fire sent the crowd back up Mendiola after me. Suddenly there were as many people moving up the arcade as on the street. I began to get tossed around as the unreasonably happy mob ran by me, and I joined the general retreat until we got to a small PNP station, just this side of the Roces statue. Shouting "Fuck Gloria! Fuck Ramos!", the kids smashed the locks with rocks, broke in and began mindlessly ransacking the place, throwing into the street chairs, notebooks, and a portrait of Arroyo, whom they pulverized with stones and sandals and then pretended to piss and shit on. Aware they could very likely turn on me next, I crossed to the north side of the square into the empty arcade I'd picked out, where I sheltered behind a pillar and got down on one knee and began writing notes. "Billboard above mayhem says, 'HUMAN: Alternative Clothing & Lifestyle.' Include for ironic contrast."

On the other side of the square the mob was taking its celebratory wrath out on the parked vehicles, the object being, it seemed, to destroy as much as possible before the government forces arrived. A couple of kids beat open the gas cap to a media van, then organized a dozen of their friends to rock the van until it overturned with a crunch. They put a match to the draining fuel. There was an explosion that sent a shock wave of heat all the way to where I was crouched. A mushroom of red-and-black flame went higher than the top of the lifestyle billboard. With rubbish and wood the kids built a fire under the engine of another van. Then they turned on the backhoe and built a fire in the cab.

They were getting closer to me, a couple of kids yelling from 20 feet away, with debatable good cheer, "Hey Joe! Hey Joe!" I held my fists up to them in people power solidarity and offered a bright smile, clapping my hands above my head to urge them on. Still applauding their revolution like a strolling flamenco dancer, I crossed the edge of the square and retreated northeast up Legarda, where I took cover in a drugstore arcade, from which I had a tunnel scope of the action a block away.

The day's most sustained explosion of gunfire and tear gas—which sounded like the opening of the Battle of the Somme down at the Mendiola Gate—came around an hour later. It lasted for several minutes, and in the relative quiet that followed the soldiers seemed to advance; at least, the *masa* now began arriving in the square by the thousands. They regrouped around the kneeling Roces and his crucifix, arming themselves with rocks and turning to face the army of the oligarchs, still out of my line of sight. For 10 minutes the mob held the square and the soldiers held their fire. Again I was amazed at the patience of the government. Then came a battallion's worth of rifle shots, followed by the machine gun–sputtering of tear-gas explosions from the APCs. I heard the soldiers send up a disciplined roar of attack and the packed square of *masa* turned as one and began madly running from the assault. This time they kept running, up Recto, in the direction of Quiapo, leaving the square almost empty and at least three (that I could see) flat on the ground behind. The last of the fleeing rioters were replaced by the rolling armor and a streetwide phalanx of soldiers, who kept on their tail at a double-time trot, followed by the police carrying yellow steel barricades.

The cops sealed the square and Mendiola from all sides, carried away the dead and wounded, began spraying the vehicles with fire extinguishers. An old gent came out of the drugstore with a machete in one hand and a revolver in the other. He surveyed the smoking chaos up the street. "There is no hope for this country," he said.

Maybe, I thought, but if this had been Cambodia or China, there would have been 700 dead, not, as it turned out, only seven.

At noon Arroyo declared Manila to be in a "State of Rebellion," a neologism for a quasi state of martial law that allowed for warrantless arrests and indefinite detention without trial. The cops arrested Ponce Enrile in his Makati mansion, and Reynaldo Berroya was sent to hunt down 11 others, including Lacson. I phoned Jerome, who told me Lacson was on the run, "go to hiding, Berroya if catch could murder him." Later that afternoon Miriam Defensor-Santiago appeared on television, posing with a gun at her Senate office desk, daring the authorities to try and arrest her. While all this was going on, the opposition coalition announced it was appealing the State of Rebellion decree to the Supreme Court, since there was no provision for one in the constitution. "This is an abnormality, a mask for an undeclared martial law," said Edgardo Angara. Either declare martial law, he demanded (something unthinkable since the bad old Marcos era), or allow the opposition candidates to return to campaigning without fear of arrest.

At five in the afternoon I was awakened from a nap by a very forceful knock on the door. Four knocks, in fact, repeated twice, the second set vibrating my water bottle on my nightstand. I leapt up, knowing I had the "Do Not Disturb" flag out. Since this was a high-class place where the help obeyed the rules, I figured it was not the maid. It could have been Jerome, but even if he showed up here without warning he would have called from the lobby. "Mr. Terry Gould!" I heard, and there was no request in that announcement.

I went to the peephole. Two guys in barongs were looking at the floor, one tall with salt-and-pepper hair, the other short and balding. I was scared, but then again, as with Steve so long ago, if they wanted to do me they wouldn't be knocking first. I cleared my throat. Out came the shield case, held up to the peephole. "Philippine Bureau of Immigration. Official business."

"Just a minute, I'm on the phone with the U.S. ambassador now. 'Uh, sir?'" I said, quite loudly. "'There's two guys from the BI at the door. Yeah, right, I don't know, I was interviewing Ping Lacson, maybe that's what it's about. Okay, I'll phone you back.'" I grabbed my money belt, took out my U.S. passport. Then I cursed myself for even thinking about letting them in. "I'll meet you guys in the coffee shop."

"We can tell you," the tall one explained to me at a table downstairs in the lobby, handing me back my passport, "you are permitted to visit our country as a tourist—"

"A journalist," I said.

"In whichever legal capacity you wish. Journalists are welcome. We are a free society. But you are not permitted to engage in activities with such people who are seditious or rebellious to good order, during this particular time."

"It is already publicized," said the short one, who seemed far less civilized than his partner. "The person you are associated with, Ping Lacson—he is engaged in activities which are suspected of coup plotting."

"I was interviewing him for a book," I said.

"That would be no problem, but our intelligence sources believe you are sympathetic, so to say, in a way to perhaps lend him assistance."

I thought, Should I risk a bribe to get out of this? Against all odds, if they were straight cops they might throw me in jail on an attempt charge.

On the other hand, I had things to do before being tossed out of the country, I definitely wanted to get back in, and a deportation order on my passport would be a major problem for me. "I've done nothing wrong," I said, trying to figure a way out. "There's gonna be big trouble with the U.S. embassy if you cause me trouble."

The tall guy flipped his pad open on Anne Collins's one-graph letter, the one about me being a travel writer. "Have you spoken with Ping since today by phone or otherwise?"

There it was. They weren't here to deport me: giving me the squeeze to get Ping's whereabouts was their mission, which didn't rule out being taken to the dump in the trunk of their car and tortured to make me give up what I didn't know. I said, "No contact with him today but—" I leaned forward. "I can get fired for giving you this information." I hesitated. Then I told them in a whisper about my ultimate mission in the Philippines. I took out a copy of *The Lifestyle* and explained the lesbian group sex at swing clubs and that it was a big draw for cops who liked to watch. "If Ping's a member of this orgiastic subculture, I'm gonna expose him for it in my book. That's why I'm on his good side. You know he had that thing with Tina Monasterio? It's my suspicion there was way more to that than made the movies. You can check out a club I'm investigating. The Lifestyle Swing Club Manila, Makati chapter."

"What is the address of this place?" the short one asked.

"I calmed them down," I told Jerome over the lobby phone, but he thought I was in bad trouble. At the very least, he said, they would toss my room when I was out. He said I should change hotels, that he was sending someone over in a car immediately. I thought of my strewn clothes upstairs. I was starved for sleep and farther off center from Steve than ever. The last thing I felt like doing was packing up and going underground. I told him I would carry everything of importance with me whenever I went out. I was going back to bed.

When he walked in the door the next morning, Jerome had forgotten all about moving me to another hotel. He went straight to the TV and turned the volume up. He explained Lacson might need to escape to Canada. He gave me the name of a Vancouver immigration lawyer, Peter Chapman, whom he would be hiring to represent Lacson. He wanted me to phone Chapman and fill him in on the situation, then testify on Lacson's behalf in front of a refugee board. I agreed I would testify, knowing I could deflect the request by informing Chapman I would have to state the allegations about Lacson's past as a torturer. But I didn't tell

Jerome that now. I still thought Ping would be of use to my mission if he wound up as president—the likelihood of which was very real in this crazy nation—and I wanted him to feel grateful to me.

Jerome punched his cell phone and handed it over. Lacson was on the other end, holed up in a safe house. He told me he hadn't participated in any plot to violently overthrow the government. He was merely a politician whom they now wanted to arrest for exercising his legal right to oppose a government that had a questionable right to be in power. He asked me about the Canada option and, to save his life, I explained the grounds he should base his refugee claim on, which I promised I would convey to Chapman: he was an opposition politician charged with rebellion in order to keep him from winning a Senate seat; he couldn't get a fair trial; the hunt for him was politically motivated and illegal; Berroya might shoot him if he tried to turn himself in. Ping thanked me profusely but then added, as I was hoping he would, that maybe flight would not be necessary. Arroyo's proclamation was totally illegal, and if he made it through the next few days he would probably make it through the next few years.

The next day, in fact, the Supreme Court ordered Ponce Enrile released, and three days after that Arroyo rescinded her unconstitutional State of Rebellion decree. This was followed by an announcement from Malacañang that the hunt for Lacson was being called off, and that he could resume his senatorial campaign. In Manila he and Gringo Honasan were treated like returning heroes by their fans, and on May 14 they won their Senate seats.

The final tally gave the pro-Erap coalition six seats, the People's Power Coalition seven. Overall, the PPC now had a tenuous one-seat majority in the 26-person Senate. None of which would be relevant to me until Lacson regained his influence with those in charge of Philippine law enforcement. Too long for me to wait now. Just after his arrest order was rescinded, the PNP and NBI announced they were still intent on pursuing their charges against him for mass murder, drug dealing, illegal detention, and wiretapping.

"You often don't get good gossip so I'll give you some," I said to General Reynaldo Wycoco in his office at NBI headquarters. "I had a meeting with Sheila Coronel and I asked her who among Philippine law enforcement I could completely trust. And she said you."

"Well, thank you very much!" he replied, shaking my hand with a firm, friendly grip.

He was a pleasant-faced, avuncular guy about my age, in a white barong, and he looked me straight in the eye, with no dark baggage behind his gaze. Which is what I expected. Sheila had told me he'd once headed the press office at the PNP, and so I would be spared the usual snarly suspicion of a top cop trying to figure out how I was going to sting him in the ass. In any case, his secretary had told him I had some important information for the NBI about organized crime. I'd got *her* attention by flashing the pictures taken of me arm in arm with Ping Lacson at the Golden Pearl restaurant.

Wycoco told me to have a seat at a conference table and introduced Moises B. Tamayo, the executive officer of the NBI's Organized Crime Division. Opposite Moises sat a weaselly looking fellow whom nobody bothered to introduce by name. He had entered the anteroom while Moises and I sat waiting for the meeting to begin. At the time, I thought he was a janitor with a vending sideline; he had casually wandered in with a big box and then tried to sell Wycoco's secretaries bottles of Chinese medicine that he said cured high blood pressure. Now that he was in the room with us, I figured he was a Confidential Agent—one of the 5,000 employed by the NBI, of which Steve, in all likelihood, was one. This did not thrill me.

"I'm an author with Random House and a contributing editor of a Canadian national magazine, and I specialize in Asian organized crime," I began. "Particularly the 14K Triad." I turned to Moises. "You're familiar with them?"

"Of course, continue," he said.

"So I'm here on a certain matter, but while exploring that certain matter I came across two things that I think you should pursue, in my opinion. You know the Isetan mall on Recto and Quezon?"

"Which area is that?" Moisies asked.

I presumed he didn't understand my accent so I opened my street map.

Fifteen minutes later I'd filled them in on the flagrant deals going down on Recto and in the Muslim quarter, which seemed to be news to them. They asked me the name of my fixer, and were very understanding that I couldn't give him up. (In fact, I'd run into Jose on Roxas five days after the May Day riot and put him on a ferry back to the Visayas. He'd lost a friend in the attack on Malacañang, but he himself had come through without a scratch.)

"So those are things that I discovered while I'm in town here," I said. "The *reason* I'm in town— Now this is very sensitive. Please don't link my name—"

"Oh yeah, yeah," Wycoco and Moises said, dismissing the possibility as absurd. The weaselly one said nothing.

"Okay, one of the most long-standing wanted men in Canada is a 14K Triad official by the name of Steven Lik Man Wong." I dug into my briefcase and took out my thick file folder, began dealing out the material. "Here are photos of him: this one was taken in 1992, in New York; these ones are of him when he was a kid, in 1985. You can see his tattoos—very intricate and distinctive. Here's his Interpol sheet, with all his essentials."

I waited as the three of them leaned forward over the pictures and wanted posters, shifting the sheets around. I studied their eyes. I didn't detect any widening lids.

"Yes, please, go on," Wycoco urged.

"Now, let me tell you his story," I said. "Because it's very interesting."

I gave another long lecture, starting with my walking into his house on Clarendon Drive, progressing to his heroin bust, to his Negros caper with Abastillas, Sonny, and Guara, to his flight to Macau, his escape from there, his sojourn in Cambodia, and finally his return to Manila. "Now," I concluded, "I must tell you something about him. Wherever he is, he affiliates himself with the police. In Hong Kong he would actually wear a Royal Hong Kong Police uniform, and go out on patrol with them. So I am fairly certain that he is affiliated in some manner with the police here, either as an informant or, under his assumed name, maybe even an officer."

I stopped there, just short of crossing the Rubicon by bringing up the NBI.

"Okay!" Wycoco said, slapping his palm on the tabletop resolutely. "What we will do, we will talk to our own Interpol here, we will make some calls and reports, and then perhaps we will issue an alert report to the police if they have seen a guy like this. This will go out to our police forces."

"I must say," I cautioned, "he's probably connected to corrupt officers."

"So—we can also remove the corrupt officers!" Wycoco countered with a chuckle, probably thinking I was referring to the PNP.

I was insistent though. "General, the important thing is that they don't tip him off. Because every time that he's almost been caught, this procedure that you're talking about has been followed. And somebody who is not trustworthy has told him—"

"We will definitely deal only with the commanders," Wycoco said, trying to reassure me.

But he didn't.

After all my fantasizing I desperately wanted to give up Steve's alias—but that would be a wilder leap of faith than mentioning the NBI. Frankly, the nameless guy at the table, his eyes narrowed at me the whole time, scared the shit out of me. I was beginning to feel all this was a mistake. Would they really turn over one of their CAs? Or would they tell Steve, as Richard the swinger had warned, that Terry Gould's on your tail, move on. And then I'd lose him again. Or worse: "Take care of him, you're a valuable guy, we'll understand." Not that Wycoco or Moises would do such a thing—I sincerely trusted them—but this other guy might. He and I didn't like each other. Or, rather, he didn't like me.

Then again: *"Wycoco, you can trust him up to a point—but who knows really?"*

The fact was, I felt like I had one foot in the boat and one foot on the shore and I was just too unsure of the current to step in with both feet and hope for the best. So I remained where I was, off balance and half-assed. I didn't know if I was making the right decision or the wrong decision. If I managed to get out of Manila alive, and Steve stayed here, maybe it would be the right decision. I still had Lacson in reserve, I told myself.

Wycoco, a busy man, said he had an appointment at Malacañang, posed for a picture for my scrapbook, and left in a hurry, leaving me alone with Moises and the silent one. Moises asked me where I was staying, but I demurred, saying I was leaving tomorrow—which was the truth. I gave him Inspector Paul Brown's telephone number in Hong Kong and told him if he came across anything to let Brown know. "Please, my safety is at stake until I get out of here, so keep this confidential." I looked at the weasel, who returned my gaze with blank rubbery eyes. Since hawking his blood pressure potions, the guy had not said one single word.

"Yes, yes, of course," Moises said. "I will be reporting this matter to Interpol."

Interpol, I thought. What good will Interpol do? They're the ones who helped screw up the Macau arrest. You're back where you started from.

I had one more place I wanted to visit before getting out of Dodge. On my map the huge, green trapezoid in the pink grid of streets was seven stops north of the NBI on the Metrorail. I got off at the Abad Santos station, just east of Tondo. It looked like a straight shot from the station to the green area, but down on street level I was soon lost in the worst squatter slum I'd seen in Manila. I followed a mud path between shanties, a sitting duck for the groups of shirtless teen boys seated on oil drums outside the cardboard lean-tos that served as their homes. They smiled lasciviously and called softly after me, "Hey Joe! Where you go?"

I could see a high whitewashed wall on a hill at the edge of the slum, but I kept entering alleys that ended in chicken-wire pens for pigs and goats, or else in tangles of salvaged trash—bald tires, balled-up electric wire, broken angle iron—impossible to climb over. By the time I found a path that led to the wall I had a covey of 20 naked giggling children on my tail, keeping up a refrain of "Hey Joe! Hey Joe!" I walked through litter-strewn tall grass along the base of the wall until I came to a pile of broken-up gypsum and stinking garbage from which fat rats with naked tails ran in every direction. I climbed the dump pile, jumped a ditch on its downward side, and emerged onto a normal-looking street with normal-looking people and jeepneys. I looked back. The kids stood on the top of the pile, waving goodbye, as if from behind an invisible barrier they dared not cross.

"Welcome to the City of the Living Dead," an old Filipino gent greeted me at the red moongate that interrupted the white wall at the top of the street. "We also call it the Living City of the Dead, because the dead here have all the conveniences of life, ha ha ha!" His opening joke to every tourist, I guessed.

He was poorly dressed in a T-shirt with a faded Chinese logo, red shorts, and sandals. There was a bulge on his hip under his T-shirt and I wondered if I could trust him on the immaculate but deserted lanes ahead. With its mansions and palms the place looked very much like North Greenhills, but you never knew in Manila. "How much do you charge?" I asked.

"Three hundred pesos only, for the tour."

"I didn't catch your name."

"Jun Salvadore. I am approved by the Chinese Cemetery Association. The guard will tell you." He held his hand out to a uniformed man in a kiosk. The man, sporting a sidearm, waved. "They have their own police force here. Because of the saying," he chuckled.

"Which is that?"

"It is better to be a dead Chinese than a living Filipino, ha ha ha."

As we walked up a street called Millionaire Row, lined on either side with two- and three-story concrete mausoleums, Jun launched into a formal lecture. The Chinese Cemetery, or City of the Living Dead, as Jun persisted in calling it, occupied 54 hectares, and held hundreds of mansion-sized tombs built since the mid 1950s. "These are all for Chinese capitalists," he said. "Only Chinese, and very rich. This one here is for Don Gregario Lim, cost three million pesos." He pointed to a gold-gated marble palace with a big dome and cupola atop the roof. With its arches, columns, and pediments the dead man's resting place looked like a scaled-down Capitol building. "Inside, ceiling is gold-plated leaf from China, walls special marble from Italy, floor tiger white marble from Philippines. Every Sunday, early in the morning, the wife comes and brings flowers, food and drinks for his spirit. Because the dead give your business luck, your business boom."

"What business was Don Gregario in?" I asked.

"Car accessories—luxury—for rich car."

I asked if there were any Chinese gangsters buried here.

"Oh yes, a few famous," he replied. "Lim Sing, the famous gambling lord, one. But the reputation— So they transfer him. He is now in China. Let us proceed."

Some of the mansions, Jun said, were air-conditioned, most had toilets, showers, liquor bars, mah-jongg rooms, TVs, VCRs stocked with karaoke videos, bedrooms with alarm clocks, kitchens with refrigerators, dining rooms with silver service, and offices with Internet access. All of this was for the dead to use when they became bored with the entertainments of the underworld and were inclined to wander their mausoleum monuments for distraction.

Each street had a name, each mansion an address on the high security gates, and the lawns that bordered the white-painted curbs were kept mown to a putting-green polish by private caretakers. The Chinese Cemetery even had its own K-9 unit. The cruel-looking guard dogs wandered around the yards of the biggest mansions, staring at me through the gates with killer eyes.

"Where do poor Chinese get buried?" I asked.

"The poor are buried here, too, but in a wall, just ashes and bones from the crematorium, in a little hole they make."

"How about the middle class?"

"They are in graves on the terrace below." He pointed to where the land sloped down to the white wall that separated the City of the Living Dead from the squatter slum. "But only the rich in the mausoleums," he said, as we strolled on. "You buy land for fifteen thousand per square meter for a twenty-five-year lease. To renew the lease you pay another fourteen hundred per square meter for twenty-five years. If you don't have enough money to renew, they move the bones and sell mausoleum; somebody else move in."

We stopped at a tall building with a Moorish facade, a black wrought-iron gate with gold-tipped points across its entrance. "This Tommy C. Pasqual Mausoleum, two million. Tommy C. Pasqual a movie producer, same for the Philippines as MGM, Warner Brothers. Inside you find expensive paintings from Europe. You can see inside, all decorations red. That is because red is a symbol of long life. But now is too late, ha ha ha! Let us proceed."

We came to a kiln in an open central square. Jun said it was called the *Sho Kim*, a fireplace for burning money, to honor the spirit of the dead.

"They burn money here?" I asked, looking back at the squatter slum.

"Every Sunday, a ritual, for the spirit to have on the other side," Jun replied. "And here is the *Toti Kung* altar, to burn the incense. So it fills the spirit world with sweet smells and riches."

"While they watch Tommy C. Pasqual's videos, I suppose," I commented.

"With the mistresses," he said, deadpan. "They also have them here with them, or wait for them to join."

We stopped at the mausoleum to the onetime owner of the eponymous Ma Mon Luk restaurant, the most expensive in Quiapo. Along a wall at the back of the mausoleum's courtyard hung a regally framed photo of old man Ma. On his right was a photo of his legal wife. On his left a photo of his mistress. "Chinese can have many wives if they are wealthy," Jun said, "but Filipino have only wife, except only Joseph Estrada, he has many mistresses, ha ha.

"Here," he went on. "This big tomb for a Chinese developer. His wife is the secretary of the Chinese Cemetery Association, employed at the cemetery. Her husband and his mistress is buried here, photo to the left of him. Mistress dead, but legal wife is alive."

"I doubt she's crazy about that arrangement," I said.

Jun reserved comment.

After tours of the palatial resting places of Ching Ling, a former textile magnate, Cheng Tsui-jun, a cigarette and cigar king, and Dr. Don Vincente Dison, among the richest men in Manila until he'd been kidnapped and murdered when his wife wouldn't pay a $100,000 ransom, I asked Jun if the cemetery secretary had some master list of everybody buried here.

"I think yes, she or owner, James Dy. President of both City of Living Dead and Chinese Hospital next door, it is just outside gate."

"That's smart," I said. "He owns the hospital and the cemetery. Out the hospital gate and in the moongate."

"First must stop at crematorium," he cracked.

It was past five by then, and all the cemetery officials had gone home. I asked Jun if he'd ever run across a grave or mausoleum or hole in the wall for one Steven Lik Man Wong. He pursed his lips, thought a moment, asked me to repeat the name, then said, "This one I have never seen."

"How about Joe Co?"

"Joe Co, Joe Co," he said. "Buried here?"

"I don't even know if he's dead—but if this is where all the Chinese get buried, I just thought I'd check."

He shrugged, smiled. "I do not know *all* the dead. But I think they know me, ha ha ha!"

I said goodbye to my Filipino Virgil, found the Metrorail without having to traverse the slum again, and got aboard the next train. Trundling over and through the hellish town, staring into the exhausted empty eyes of the rush-hour crowd in the cooking car, looking out over the putrid Pasig River to the smog that shrouded the once-beautiful bay, I almost began to cry. I didn't know if it was because of the hopelessness of the Philippines or the hopelessness of ever catching Steve. It was both, I decided, because one went with the other. A career's worth of leads had come to nothing because this side of the world was made to order for staying underground. Wasted years, wasted money, as if I'd burnt them up at the *Sho Kim* in the City of the Living Dead. Didn't those rubber eyes in the NBI office communicate the score? To catch a dead man, I'd have to become one. I just didn't have enough *mishegoss* for that.

Early the next morning, passing the Jumbo on the way to the airport, I spoke with James Dy's assistant in charge of names at the cemetery. No Steven Lik Man Wong, no Joe Co buried on the premises, sorry, sorry. Moises Tamayo at the NBI had no news either. He'd just got in, but he'd be on it. "Through the proper channels" he would let Paul Brown in Hong Kong know if anything turned up.

My driver heard me use the words "Chinese gangster" and began to express his worldview. He was anti-syndicate and pro-Erap because Erap only stole from the syndicates, not the *masa*. They could keep Estrada in jail while they were in power, but Lacson would win the presidency in 2004, and then Erap would be out. Then there would be no more *kotung*, no more kidnapping. "Because I have faith, I believe in future. I do not believe in anything they say, this Mary Ong, or anybody who they get make lies."

Mary Ong! I thought. The 14K chick! I forgot all about her!

As we swung off Roxas and onto Airport Avenue, I looked back over my shoulder at Manila.

CHAPTER 28

CAN WE START AGAIN, PLEASE?

———

One must imagine Sisyphus happy.
—ALBERT CAMUS

Mary Ong and I sit in her safe house in the compound of the Intelligence Service of the Armed Forces of the Philippines. Surrounding the compound is a 10-foot wall, and surrounding the wall is Camp Aguinaldo, separated from Manila by another wall. The government feels it needs concentric ramparts, an elite force, and an entire army to protect Ong. "Not from the Triads," Victor Corpus, chief of Army Intelligence, informed me when he okayed my visit. "From the police."

At the moment, the 47-year-old Ong is showing me the evidence she's presented to three Senate committees investigating Ping Lacson's running of the PNP. Ong's catalog of criminality, combined with the testimony of corroborating witnesses, led the committees to table a 100-page report in June 2002. "Kidnapping-for-ransom [and] drug trafficking have been prima facie established," was the report's conclusion, followed by a recommendation to refer the evidence to the Department of Justice "for filing of appropriate criminal charges against the persons named below . . . :" That is, against Lacson and 10 of his senior officers.

Today, February 3, 2003, the named officers are still enforcing the law from Camp Crame, and Ping Lacson is an esteemed member of the Senate's Public Order and Illegal Drugs Committee, having used his senatorial influence to get *Committee Report No. 66* shelved. This typically Filipino development, coupled with Lacson's announcement that he will be running for president, has sent Chief Corpus's fears for his government's star witness into the red zone. Just recently, an assassin trying to get at Ong penetrated the inner compound—allegedly on behalf of cops across the street at Crame. Corpus has therefore ordered that Ong be guarded round the clock by commandos who specialize in liquidating terrorists.

Two of these grim killers are on duty in the safe house with Mary and me, and, needless to say, I move very slowly under their gaze as I stand up, reach across the kitchen table for my briefcase and take out some photos. I've told Ong over the phone that I wanted to hear about her dozen years as a 14K *Tai Ka Tse*—a "Big Sister"—and her seven years as a PNP and Hong Kong police agent. Now I reveal that my broad interest in her career has a bull's-eye. "Have you ever run across this fellow?" I ask, feeling a weariness that has more to do with the passing years than jet lag. After all, Steven has just turned 39 and I, God help me, am 53. "I'm asking because the Canadian police—"

"I know him."

"You know him?"

Ong presses her hand against the yellow buttons of her black silk cheongsam as she leans forward, her almond eyes narrowing at Steve's 1992 photo. "You want to know his connection? This Steven is the *mat'sai* of Chong Yuk-sui, he is a 14K boss in Hong Kong."

"You're sure?"

"Yes. This Steven is supplying—" She looks up at me from the photos. "You better know who you are up against."

I sit down—as slowly as I stood up. "How do you know him?"

"I investigated him from late 1994 to the middle of 1996. The investigation was called Viking. He was the subject. Steven Wong was our subject."

Late 1994. That would have been after the DOJ screwed up Steve's arrest and he fled Macau. So he fled back here. "We heard in Canada he had an alias," I say. "Joe Co—"

"Joe Co?" she asks, looking startled, then points to herself. "I entrapped Joey Co for Ping Lacson. The PNP shot him July 1994." She thinks on that a minute, then smiles in apparent memory of the scamming Steve. "You know what, I think probably when Steven comes here he would hear that name and use it for outside. But Chong Yuk-sui calls him Steven Wong, everybody in the 14K know him as Steven Wong." She looks down again, moves her teardrop face back and forth between pictures. "This is the same Canadian. Fat, short, I saw these tattoos on him."

I can feel the upward flight of birds in my belly that occurs whenever I think I'm getting close. "Did you see him recently?" I ask. "Like, within a month?"

"No, no, sometime 1997 the last time," she says, and my birds stop climbing. "It was after Viking, because there were no arrests and I went to other cases. My assignment was to entrap Steven, so I introduce him 1994 to a wealthy smuggler in Makati, Consolacion Figueroa Coo, I used to work with her when I laundered money. Steven became her main supplier of drugs to the U.S.A. and Canada." Ong takes my pad and block prints the Makati smuggler's lyrical name. "Figueroa Coo worked with a big political family in Cavite. Now she is old and sick—I don't know, maybe she still talk with Steven. But the family you should be very afraid because Cavite is the killing fields of the Philippines."

I lean across the table into her personal space and tap the pad. "Mary, can you get in touch with Coo and find out if she knows where he is now?"

"Not possible, because this family is very close to Ping Lacson also," Mary replies flatly, looking me in the eye so I will appreciate the significance of the connection. "Ping is from Cavite. And Ping was in charge of Viking. So no arrests, even when Steven was at the house of Coo with drugs when I went to visit." She draws back, traces an arrow down from Figueroa Coo's name and writes in three others, then hands my pad back. "The PNP seize my computer files; I will see what I have in my old notes for you."

She crosses the room and drags a couple of cartons out from under a table and across the linoleum. While she digs through the strata of her investigations, I look at my pad's newly inscribed names and arrows, which indicate only two degrees of separation between Steve and Ping:

Steven Wong ➔ Figueroa Coo ➔ three Cavite bigwigs ➔ Ping Lacson

I should be flabbergasted, but I accept the connection with barely a shrug. A month after my visit to Steve's unmarked grave in the Garden of Reflection I watched the Senate hearings over the Internet, and since then I've doubted whether it was ever Ping's intention to hand the Paper Fan over to me—at least alive. During the hearings, Army Intelligence Chief Corpus produced phone records that showed Ping had for years been using the cell phone of a man Corpus said was Manila's 14K dragon head, a multi-millionaire restaurant owner named Kamsin "Kim" Wong. That forced Senator Lacson, who refused to testify at the inquiry, to nonchalantly tell the press that "a legitimate businessman named Kim Wong" had loaned him a cell phone, but it was "not the same Kim Wong" that Corpus claimed. Subpoenaed to testify, Kamsin "Kim" Wong contradicted Lacson, admitting that he had loaned his wife's cell phone to Ping when Ping became PNP chief and that he was still paying the monthly bills, although, he said, he had no Triad involvements. Weighing the testimony of Corpus and others on Kim Wong's affiliations, *Report No. 66* recommended a criminal investigation of Lacson "for using a cell phone whose bills were paid for by Mr. Wong and/or his wife, as admitted by Mr. Wong."

I look over at Mary Ong, now girlishly animated as, crouched on her knees, she tosses file folders every which way. Done up in her usual inter-view attire, she's a hard lady not to watch. Ong is a celebrity in the Philippines, partly because during her testimony the beautiful police agent wore high-slit cheongsam dresses, crimson lipstick, and geisha-girl face powder that whitened her lineless complexion. Indeed, after the press observed her first performance in the staid chambers, they dispatched sto-ries that read like movie star columns: "Mary Ong, a.k.a. Agent Rosebud, is everything one imagines a spy to be—sexy, glamorous, smart and foxy. And of course, fashionable."

Her glamour aside, the big question in my mind is whether I can trust her. Mary Ong, BA, MBA, spent the years 1979 to 1991 laundering billions in Chinese underworld cash, as well as running guns to 14K gangsters in Macau's Lisboa Hotel. A courier working for her was murdered and she wound up in jail for a year on drug-trafficking charges—although the charges were later dismissed after the city cops who arrested her were killed in a shoot-out with the PNP's Reynaldo Berroya. ("The policemen who arrested me were drug traffickers themselves," she told me. "They tried to set me up for the wrong racket. I was a money launderer, not a drug trafficker.") In 1993, while the drug charges were still hanging over her head, the crime fighter Ping Lacson personally recruited her as "a PNP asset," eventually assigning her the code name Rosebud. For the rest of the '90s Mary "Rosebud" Ong worked undercover for the various anti-crime units Ping headed, stinging 14K drug lords for up to $40,000 a pop. Her stratospheric fees (she later revealed) came from the PNP's partnerships with the biggest Triad members, who wanted to get rid of the competition, as well as from seized and resold *shabu*, criminals tortured to disclose the whereabouts of their drugs, and criminals kidnapped and held for ransom in a vacant town house that Rosebud owned on Roxas Boulevard.

In other words, Ong has a frighteningly unsavory past, but I consider it somewhat reassuring that, without any threat of prosecution, she stepped forward and tried to put a stop to all of it—an act for which she's paid a life-altering price. Rosebud's safe house (in which she could very likely spend the rest of her days) is a far cry from the marble-and-mirror mansion she once inhabited two blocks from Erap's home in North Greenhills. It's little more than a barracks coop, meant for four soldiers but now housing nine people. Lit by unshaded fluorescent tubes that highlight rusted venetian blinds and water-stained walls, it's furnished with army bunk beds, a junkyard couch, and plastic boxes for Rosebud's wardrobe. At night, Ong, her two teenage sons, her brother, her mother, her bodyguards, and a female caretaker/body-guard sleep on the couch, the floor and in the bunks, all of them sharing a three-foot-by-three-foot bathroom with no shower. The safe house is made even more cramped by a hospital bed in the middle of the room on which her skeletal father lies wheezing and dying of cancer.

"Steven Wong had very good connections to Japan," Mary says, now sitting sidesaddle on the floor and glancing over an old sheet she's discovered. "He was traveling there all the time. I know he had a business of his own in Japan."

"That matches what we know," I tell her, getting excited all over again. "I found that out after my last trip. We heard it was a pachinko franchise," I add, referring to the multibillion-dollar gambling game dominated by Yakuza, the crime group that has colluded with every Japanese administration since the war. During the Senate hearings, Intelligence Chief Corpus claimed there was a "tie-up" between Yakuza and Kamsin Wong's 14K, and so I routed myself through Tokyo on this trip. Unfortunately, as with all my visits to Asia save one, I inhaled a lot of cigarette smoke in crowded environs but ran across no five-foot-four-inch Chinese-Canadian with bad vision.

"I remember Steven was a big gambler himself, here, Hong Kong, Macau—probably everywhere he went," Mary says, "so pachinko, I can see it. Also *shabu* is very big in Japan, and Yakuza controls that. So that is another reason for him to go back and forth. But Manila was his home, here he had his own gang of Chinese boys."

Exactly the same MO, then: a Triad who was chieftain of his own juvenile army, liked to travel, and had his hand in a few pies. By 1997, nothing had changed. I look at my notes. "I never heard of this boss Chong Yuk-sui. I thought his boss's name was Eddy Wong."

"Maybe he's another, too, because Steven was only in the middle of the Triad. There were many people above him. I know Chong is still in Hong Kong, he trained Steven in the beginning, 1988, then he made him his *mat'-sai*—it means horse." She turns a page. "Steven had another partner in Hong Kong named Lau, he was known as 'Sai Wah.' He travels to Canada all the time on a British passport, not a Hong Kong passport." She reads off three of Steve's other partners in the drug trade—Lai Tak-sang, Sy Ching-po, and Cheng Chi-man, adding, "They use Coo's connection to the Cavite family that is close to Ping. But Ping stayed back to protect himself. The one who was dealing directly with everyone was Campos."

That is, the PNP's main informant-handler, Senior Superintendent John Campos—a handsome drug cop a decade Ong's junior with whom she lived for five years. As Jerome Tang explained to me on my last trip, the affiliation gave Lacson's men a hook on which to hang an attack on Ong's credibility. Police Director Reynaldo Acop, the number two man in the PNP and one of those Ong accused of kidnapping and drug trafficking, alleged in the Senate that Rosebud was "a woman scorned," out to "take her vengeance." Mary Ong angrily countered that it was she who had initiated the breakup with Campos, and that what made her go public was not vengeance but the sight of Campos torturing kidnap victims in her town house on Roxas. In the end, weighing Ong's motives against the documentary evidence she presented, the Senate ruled in favor of her credibility.*

Currently, Ong is claiming that her righteous motives for blowing the whistle on the PNP have been cruelly proven by events. Phone records at the Intelligence Service show that late on the night of December 4, 2002, there was a flurry of calls between Campos and Ong. Ong says Campos told her that Lacson had ordered her murdered and that he wanted to turn on his boss. She instructed Campos to come right over to the intelligence compound and put himself under the protection of Victor Corpus. But Campos never made it to the compound. At 12:45 A.M. he was shot dead while having a bite in an open-air eatery in Paranque, a town between Manila and Cavite. Witnesses said the shooters pulled up in a car, waited until the cop's back was turned, then pumped bullets into his midriff and head. A month after that, on January 7, 2003, PNP Senior Superintendent Teofila Vina, a main suspect in the Bubby Dacer killing, was shot dead in Cavite. During the investigation the NBI revealed they had discovered a list of nine people who were in line to be liquidated: Vina, who reported directly to Lacson at the time of Dacer's murder, was on the list. So was Mary Ong.

"Was Steven connected with the NBI?" I ask Mary as she returns to the table with an armload of files. "He was supposed to be a Confidential Agent."

Rosebud waves her scarlet fingernails contemptuously. "It is nothing for you to be a CA. Many Triads like Steven become a CA. It's not so official, you can buy an ID card that says you are a CA. If you are known by the NBI, they would only demand cooperation not to ruin your game. Then you are their asset. You should speak to General Wycoco," she advises me. "He will tell you what the CAs have done to the reputation of the NBI."

A couple of hours later Rosebud invites me to stay for a steak dinner, and, after a dessert of M&Ms, decides to take advantage of my visit. She gets

---

*"Rosebud's narration [is] full of details which by their nature could not have been the result of deliberate after-thought," *Committee Report No. 66* stated. "Though it may be said to have come from a polluted source, such testimony is acceptable as proof especially where it is supported and corroborated by other evidence, as is the case with Rosebud's declarations. And while there are discrepancies in her narration, a number of which have been noted in the footnotes, they are inconsistencies in minor details which do not impair her credibility."

permission from Corpus to leave the base for the evening—something she has not done for weeks. She dolls up in a pink cheongsam and, at nine, protected by six armed guards, we drive in a bulletproof van across town to the glitzy Heritage Hotel and Casino, on the corner of Roxas and Edsa, not far from where the floating Jumbo is slowly falling to pieces. She has some people she wants me to meet who can help with my hunt—a hunt she sees as serving a larger goal. For if Steve can be found and arrested, he might be persuaded to corroborate her allegation that Figueroa Coo, the prominent family in Cavite Province, and Panfilo Lacson all worked together during Project Viking, profiting from the multimillion-dollar drug deals she helped arrange.

"That is what she'll say and then for a change she'll point to me," Lacson tells me the next day in his Senate office, as soon as I mention that Mary Ong has identified Steve. He gazes down at Steve's wanted poster that I just printed off Interpol's website, then looks up and shares a laugh with his executive assistant, Jerome Tang. Ping turns back to me, still chuckling. "When I inquired about him I found out he was really killed. Of course, you won't believe it."

"No, because it was all fraudulent," I say, thinking, *Why are you suddenly telling me this now and not at any time in the last twenty months?* "The PNP investigation was part of the scam," I remind him. "Any inquiry made with them will show he's dead."

Ping shrugs, reaches for his cell phone, punches in a code and begins talking in Tagalog, staring vacantly at his uniformed portrait to the right of his senator's desk. I hear him say the words "Steven Wong," and then "Lik Man." While Ping turns to write notes on the Interpol sheet, I size up his silver suit and silver watch. He looks far more spiffy and confident than the last time I saw him, projecting a polished air that's congruent with his presidential ambitions. On November 15, he became the first candidate to announce he was in the running. Six weeks later, Gloria Macapagal-Arroyo declared she would not be seeking re-election, ostensibly because she was "told by God" to govern the remainder of her term "freed of politics"— although Lacson views her announcement as a cynical ploy to get him off her case until she finds the right moment to reenter the race.

Since walking through the Senate doors in July 2001, he's been hammering Arroyo as one scandal after another has blotted out the yellow glow of her EDSA II days, sending her poll figures into a nosedive. The two most serious scandals have involved the now-deported Mark Jimenez: the first one ensnared Justice Secretary Nani Perez, whom Arroyo fired after evidence surfaced suggesting that he had allegedly extorted $2 million in bribes from Jimenez; the second concerned Arroyo's husband, Mike, who is the subject of a Senate investigation (initiated by Lacson's party) for accepting millions of dollars from Jimenez when Gloria was vice president.*

On most other fronts under her watch the Philippines gives every sign (once again) of being on the verge of collapse—a state of affairs from which Lacson has also been making considerable political hay. Eighty-seven people were killed in the weeks that led up to last summer's barangay elections. In the jungles of the archipelago, pitched battles rage between an alphabet soup of rebel armies and government forces, but the government does not appear to be winning its newly named War on Terrorism, even with the help of a battalion of American advisers and their hardware. Since my last visit, scores of Philippine soldiers have fallen in combat and almost every day sees headlines like "MILF counterattacks; 16 gov't soldiers dead," and "NPA hit squads target gov't officials." In Mindanao's cities, 10 terrorist blasts set by Islamic rebels have killed 70 civilians and wounded over 400. In Manila, the embassies of Canada, Australia, and the European Union were recently closed for a week after a terrorist bus bomb killed or severely wounded two dozen civilians and information surfaced that the embassies would be next. Travel warnings from foreign capitals come and go with frightening frequency, the national debt has ballooned to a historic high, the peso is near its historic low, and organized crime now accounts for between 10 and 20 percent of the country's gross domestic product. On top of all this, the Philippines is the regular recipient of bad marks from overseas watchdog organizations. Amnesty International has just released a report stating that torture by the police is rampant, and the U.S. Bureau for International Narcotics and Law Enforcement Affairs has released another report stating that the country is a drug smugglers' paradise. Of particular concern to me, three more journalists have been murdered in the last eight months, allegedly on the orders of the politicians they had exposed. To date, naturally, no one has been charged, leading the Philippine Center for Investigative Journalism to banner on its website the judgment of the U.S.-based Committee to Protect Journalists: "Despite its free and lively press, or perhaps because of it, the Philippines is one of the most dangerous places in the world for journalists."

Meanwhile, Lacson has promised to end the chaos. He's just told the *Far Eastern Economic Review* that if elected president he will "take on the criminals

---

*On August 1, 2003, Mark Jimenez pled guilty in the United States to three of the 47 counts against him. For two counts of tax evasion and one count of illegally contributing funds to the Democratic Party he was sentenced to 27 months in a federal penitentiary and fined $1.2 million.

and terrorists who are tainting the Philippines' image overseas and hurting its economy." Aside from declaring that he "would rather be feared than loved," he didn't say exactly how he would restore order, although so many influential Filipinos believe he is the strongman for the job that the People's Power Coalition is scrambling for a candidate who can beat him.* It's frequently mentioned in the free and lively press that some of the current leaders of the PPC are worried for their safety if he is the next president.

Ping now signs off, pushes the Interpol sheet aside and contemplates a Senate memo on his desk. I wait, but he doesn't tell me what he's found out about Steve. He looks as if he's lost interest in the subject.

"She recognized his tattoos," I tell him. "She said right away, he's short, he's fat."

"And she was exactly right," he mumbles without inflection, writing on a pad. "Anyway, go ahead. I must write the opening prayer of the Senate. Because every day, three times a week, before we open session, there's a prayer, alternated of course by different senators."

"She said Steve was active in the Philippines right up to 1997," I explain. "And she said he was the main supplier to Figueroa Coo here in Manila. She says you would know Figueroa."

That detaches his interest from the prayer. "Figueroa? She's a dealer of commissary goods. In Makati. She was a known smuggler way way back."

"That's right, in Makati, very well connected to some other people she says you know." I bring up Ong's allegation that Coo was connected to the three figures in the Cavite family—but Ping says that's ridiculous, they are all upstanding figures in politics, and have never been accused of a crime—except by political enemies.

"You waste your time talking Mary Ong," Jerome snorts beside me. "She take him to Heritage Casino," he tells Ping. "Introduce him to her friends there."

Lacson bursts into laughter, adding that they must have offered me some very "colorful" stories about him—which I don't deny. The glum group of ex–undercover agents and businessmen filled the casino's coffee shop with dark vignettes. An East Indian named Danny Devnani told me he used to be Estrada's bagman, collecting ransom from the families of men kidnapped by Ping's PNP. He looked at Steve's face and said: "If you get this guy, he will maybe point to Ping for a lot of things. I will put the word around."

---

*On October 4, 2003, after receiving another message of "divine guidance," Macapagal-Arroyo declared that she was in the running.

Ping dismisses them as kooks and criminals. "Terry, these people will broadcast any lie, and then when someone repeats the lie to them, they say, 'Oh, see, he knows it too, so I was correct.'"

"What about the Senate report?" I ask. "They quote it like the Bible."

Ping explains that his colleagues decided to shelve *Report No. 66* until a parliamentary question he raised could be debated: the report was endorsed by two of the investigating committees, but the third committee's vote was tied. I'm aware, though, that the report's seemingly infinite shelving has another dimension. The powerful senator who arranges the Senate's calendar of debate, and who handed down the ruling in favor of shelving *Report 66,* is none other than Loren Legarda—who has shocked the nation by approaching Ping with a request to be his vice presidential running mate in the 2004 election.

"Who else will you be seeing?" Jerome asks me.

"Wycoco's one," I reply.

"I have just received a text message on him," Lacson says. "They are supposed to be sending him to be an ambassador to Libya. The administration thinks he has failed in his mission."

"What's his mission?"

"To put me in jail."

With her platoon of bodyguards in tow, Mary Ong and her lawyer meet me at NBI headquarters to swear a 15-point affidavit (see Appendix) that details her dealings with Steven Wong. Her lawyer, Leonard de Vera, a former spokesman of the Philippine Bar Association and the first to launch a private prosecution against Erap for corruption, could have certified Ong's affidavit in his office. But Mary suggested to me this morning that the NBI's notarization of the public document would send a dramatic message to Steve. Since our meeting she has made some calls and received information there was a Chinese-Canadian behind a large *shabu* operation that was busted two and a half years ago. Her sources were vague about the description of the Canadian but, in a month, she says, she will meet Sandra Lim, a woman convicted in the *shabu* bust, and find out more for me and the NBI. March 11 is the woman's sentencing. "If your informers say he is here sometime 2000, then maybe that was him."

We head for the office of Superintendent Auralyn L. Pascual, the chief of the NBI Academy and an attorney who has a notarization seal at the ready. After Mary swears her oath, presses her thumbprint on five copies of the affidavit and signs each, a dozen agents and secretaries watching from the door crowd in to meet the witness the *Inquirer* has dubbed "the thorn in Lacson's side." The women ask her where she buys her gorgeous cheongsams and the men ask how her movie deal is going. (Steven Spielberg's Dreamworks gave her a call over Christmas, and Ong now has a Hollywood agent working out the details—a flashy development in her saga that has made front-page news in the Philippines.) We take half a dozen group photos for as many cameras and then Ong pulls me upstairs to Wycoco's office for a conference on Steve, Ping, Figueroa Coo, and the Cavite family.

"You're sure he's not in a meeting?" I ask as we breeze by two sets of secretaries.

"For such a matter the director's door is open," she says.

Her lawyer, de Vera, a cherubic fellow my age with a very kind face, holds his hands up helplessly. "We follow the boss."

This is my second encounter with the director on this trip. In the first, yesterday, I showed up alone and presented Wycoco with the rumor that he was on his way to Libya.

"We were able to trace the source of the intrigue," he told me. "Somebody out there is trying to destabilize us. Actually, it has something to do with a senator who is planning to become president of this country."

"The senator who is planning to become president also says you told the DEA that all the charges against him are politically motivated."

"He says that to a reporter?" Wycoco inhaled deeply and let the air out slowly, regaining his rarely lost composure. "Terry, do you think I would be that careless to say something like that?"

"Not really."

"That man can look you in the eye and he can lie and you will not know that he is lying. I have known him from the Philippine Military Academy, I was three classes above him. If I knew Lacson to be a good guy I would not say anything against him. But I know different. We are expecting any day that the Supreme Court will decide on the Kuratong Baleleng case. If they rule in favor of the law it will finally be sent to trial, he will be arrested for nonbailable multiple murder and for stealing two million dollars from the gang."

"He says he's confident they'll rule in his favor."

"Of course he will say so. Ping Lacson has a criminal mind. He believes judges share his mind-set."

"Speaking of criminals," I said, and related Mary's information that Lacson was a friend of the big political family in Cavite.

"Yes, that's true. I know the family, they are crooks. Have you heard of Kim Wong?"

"His picture's on my wall."

Warmed up on the subject of Ping, I reminded Wycoco why I'd returned to Manila. "We met with Moises Tamayo and some other guy—I think he was Moises's CA. We discussed this fellow."

Wycoco opened the folder I handed him, studied Steve's Interpol sheet, then gazed pensively across the table to a portrait of Arroyo superimposed over a cheering crowd at EDSA II. "If I can remember, Moises made an inquiry with his asset and gave the information to our Interpol chief, Ricardo Diaz. But—" he tapped the pages of my nine-year-old *Saturday Night* article "—I don't believe anything came of the inquiry."

Knowing what I did about the NBI's "assets," I hadn't expected any exhilarating leads to have proceeded from the inquiry. "Maybe something will come of some new information I have for you," I told him, adding that I was on the last chapter of my book, trying to get some wheels in motion so the Paper Fan would be bagged on the last page, so to speak. "Mary Ong tells me she investigated Steven for Ping between 1994 and 1996. She could have entrapped him but there were no arrests because she said Ping had connections to a woman named Figueroa Coo through his contacts in Cavite. So when I mentioned Mary Ong to Ping and that she had investigated Steve, Ping immediately said, 'When I inquired about him I found out he was really killed.' But he's changed his tune from 2001. He knows very well the PNP were active in helping Steven stage his death, he knows that all the reports are fraudulent."

All of this seemed to sharply focus Wycoco on the reason I was here. He opened a pad and began rapidly writing notes on what I'd just said. "This makes me *most* interested in finding out what are this Steven Wong's affiliates," he said. "Please continue."

And so, with no mean-eyed CA looking on this time, I told him Steve's Joe Co alias and that he was supposed to have been a CA himself. Far from being defensive, Wycoco delighted me by calling in his secretary and asking her to run a search on all Confidential Agents in the computer. While she was gone, as Mary predicted, Wycoco wearily admitted that the official roster of 5,000 CAs was ridden with Chinese criminals and that these CAs had tainted the once-stellar reputation of the NBI. The subagent system had been instituted long before his watch, he said, referring to the tenure of an NBI director named Alfredo Lim, who'd retired from the NBI just before my 1993 trip to the Philippines.

The secretary came back with three names, one Co, one Koh, and one Wong, but in two cases the CAs weren't sworn until 2001, and, in the third case, Wycoco knew the CA personally, and he was clean. But, Wycoco shrugged helplessly, the information was not definitive, since so many Triad members had for years been parading around the city as CAs, having been unofficially appointed to the fold. "It is possible this Steven Wong befriended one of our agents, maybe treated him to a nice car, maybe gave him something, and then he became an asset to the NBI."

In any case, Steven "Joe Co" Wong, or whatever alias he'd used, would now be long gone from any affiliation with the NBI, in Manila at least. On July 31, Wycoco said, he had fired the capital's 500 CAs—although he admitted that still left thousands of others around the country, without whom the cash-strapped NBI couldn't operate, since they could afford so few full agents in the provinces.

Wycoco looked down at the tabletop miserably; out of courtesy I didn't bring up the news that the CAs were causing him endless grief. On December 13, on the resort island of Cebu, an estimated 15 CAs had put 73 bullets into a car filled with innocent civilians. "How could something like this happen?" the *Daily Inquirer* asked in an editorial. "Instead of enlightening or reassuring the public, Wycoco's explanation is both disturbing and frightening." From Wycoco's explanation, the *Inquirer* concluded that the NBI had criminal cowboys running around the provinces, out of the control of their chief and "with murder in their minds." Only five of the CAs had been identified by the NBI, "leading to the suspicion that the NBI is trying to spare some sacred cows among its confidential agents who had a hand in the near-massacre."

Ong's lawyer, however, doubted the NBI chief was trying to spare anyone; rather, Leonard de Vera told me, Wycoco was in charge of a polluted organization fully capable of resisting his efforts to clean it up. "That he has corrupt people around him, I have no doubt about it."

Mary, de Vera, and I now enter Wycoco's office and take our seats at his conference table. Soon we're sharing colorful tales of Figueroa Coo, the Cavite family, Steve, and Lacson. Wycoco hands me a *Daily Inquirer* column by a journalist named Ramon Tulfo, a long-time foe of Lacson who alleges that Ping threw two innocent women out of a helicopter to punish their gangster relative, and ordered the execution of a seven-year-old witness to a PNP murder. While I'm reading this column with my mouth open, the chief scans Rosebud's affidavit. He fixes his eyes on Point 12, which mentions the "prominent political family in Cavite." He's disappointed the Cavite figures are not in there by name.

De Vera explains that Ong is already being sued by Lacson for accusing the senator of killing John Campos in an emotional radio interview hours after the assassination, and she doesn't need another lawsuit filed by Cavite millionaires. Catch Wong, de Vera says, and let him be the one to name names. He says he's working pro bono for Mary, and more and more of his practice is being monopolized by her private prosecutions of Lacson and his many subordinates. In the criminal courts, the cases are predictably stalled by the legal maneuvers of their chief counsel, a former solicitor general who also represents Kamsin Wong and Joseph Estrada. Other cases are wending their way through the Internal Affairs hearings of the PNP, with Ong the star witness in all. In fact, de Vera's own life is under threat because of the private prosecutions, and he too must travel with bodyguards.

"I think you should stay away from Cavite yourself," Wycoco advises me. "Too dangerous for you to go there to question them about this guy." Instead, he says, I'd be better off to safely invest my time getting the Canadian embassy to cooperate with the NBI, perhaps helping him to procure the RCMP file on the Paper Fan. It seems the problems afflicting the PNP's liaison with the embassy afflict the NBI, too. The embassy won't cooperate with Wycoco, even on his investigation of Ping Lacson for allegedly transferring a large sum of undeclared money to a Vancouver bank. "I have no one in the embassy who will talk to me," he says.

"I'll get you an intelligence agent," I promise him.

Before heading over to the embassy, I decide to fill my notebook with some ammunition that will get me through the door for a discussion with the promised intelligence agent. I stop off on Recto Street opposite the Isetan mall to see what has become of the false-identity trade since I informed the NBI of it in May 2001. The new Metrorail has been extended from Mendiola through the neighborhood, and half of Recto Street is now replaced by 60-foot stanchions and an elevated line. But the other half is still doing a brisk business—with one difference. The crowded arcade booths are now peppered with male and female Muslim customers from Quiapo, most wearing distinctive head scarves. As before, there is no attempt to conceal what is going on, and I am offered business cards from booth owners openly offering deals on Canadian, Australian, and New Zealand passports. The icy question in my mind is: Why hasn't the NBI done anything about this since the last time I was here? Don't they know there's a war on terrorism going on?

"They probably get their cut," Martin Tremblay tells me in his office, just down the hall from his boss, Ambassador Robert Collette. Tremblay looks and acts the part of a spook. He's trim, handsome, and in shirtsleeves, with an arch Quebecois manner that I presume helps him keep his wits operating on the Philippine side of the looking glass. He says he is thoroughly familiar with Recto Street, as is every cabdriver and street cop in town. So what, he wonders sarcastically, was the NBI doing pretending that Recto Street was news to them in 2001?

"They [the Recto Street criminals] even advertise in the papers here," he says. "I've done an investigation." He gets up and opens a folder. "Buy-and-sell advertisement," he says. "Just one day in the paper. March 19, 2002. Open, leading newspaper, you just call the number, they provide you with a bank certificate for three hundred thousand pesos. Here—" He takes down a stack of false documents procured by prospective immigrants on Recto Street and plops them on his desk with a clap. "Documents all fake, we seized them at the window. Income tax, passbooks, letters of employment, business registration, ID cards, birth certificates. Openly done and with total impunity. We're well aware of what's going on."

"I was actually hoping I wouldn't be telling you anything new," I say. "It would be pretty scary if you guys were in the dark."

"We try not to be," he replies patiently.

Moving right along, I unzip my briefcase. "Let me tell you about another matter I'm dealing with the NBI on. I don't think you know about this guy, he's a 14K Triad from Vancouver. . . ." I give him the pictures and the latest Interpol sheet, then unfold the tale, right up to Mary Ong's affidavit, which I give him a copy of as well. "Now. General Wycoco would like a contact here at the embassy, so that he can deal directly with someone on this. He says he's not been able to get a lot of cooperation from the embassy. I realize there's probably a lot of reasons for that—"

I pause. He smiles.

"Go on," he says.

"According to Mary Ong, there's a good chance Steve is continuing to do his bad deeds out of the Philippines. That matches our information in Vancouver."

"Mmmhmm," he says, writing this down.

"Unfortunately, I have to be honest and tell you that at one time Steve was supposed to be connected to the NBI. They have this auxiliary Confidential Agent system?"

Again the patient face. "Yeah, go ahead."

"They have about five thousand of them. But Wycoco says he's gotten rid of the ones in Manila, so Steve's probably cut loose, I don't think he can call on any NBI guys anymore."

"Maybe," he smiles.

"Look Martin, Wycoco would like this guy, but for twelve years he's—"

"Been well protected. Naturally."

"So can Wycoco phone you? Can you take a call?"

"Yeah, yeah," he says, begrudgingly. "I'll take a call, I'll take a call."

"He's a nice guy."

"I never met him personally."

"I think he's about the best there is here."

He pulls that face again. "I'm sure."

I wait, but he leaves it there. "Go ahead, you better tell me."

"No no no, I cannot tell you anything about our relations with the NBI."

"But it leads you to have some—questions? Can you just tell me that?"

"No, I cannot."

"Because I'm putting my life in their hands at this point."

"Here it's hard to know who to trust and who not to trust," Tremblay says. "In any organization, at *any* level."

We're quiet for a moment, looking each other in the eye.

"You know that," he says.

"I know that."

"So good luck on your investigation."

Downstairs, beyond the three cordons of security, I make a note to question de Vera again about corrupt agents, but then scratch it out. I have no time to chase down a dozen more allegations on this trip. Like mud in March, there's no bottom to them in this country.

Back in my hotel room, shoving chairs against the door for the night, I tell myself that if I wanted to find a soul with no allegations against him I would have spent the last decade looking for snow leopards. This is Steve's world, after all, and in the nations where he's found refuge, almost every name worth mentioning has at least some taint to it. The worst kill or torture, steal or extort megamillions, throw women out of helicopters or douse them with acid. Just open a paper, on any given day, and read the headlines.

In Cambodia, King Norodom Sihanouk has just postponed a trip to China "because the political situation in our country has intensified." He's referring to a day of rioting and looting in the capital; to journalists arrested; to the murder of a prominent Funcinpec adviser; to threats of criminal prosecution against one of Funcinpec's leaders; and to a war with Thailand that was only narrowly avoided. The international press is laying this latest Khmer anguish at the feet of Prime Minister Hun Sen. There's a national election coming up this summer, always a harbinger of dangerous doings in Cambodia. Twenty people were killed in last year's provincial elections, yet Funcinpec and Sam Rainsy's party managed to make gains, causing a flowering of hope in the international community: Cambodia seemed to be proceeding on its incremental transition to democracy. Then, on January 29, 2003, the day before I left for the Philippines, all hell broke loose. Hun Sen's political opponents are now accusing the PM of engineering the chaos and the attendant repression to ensure he wins the national ballot. All of it bears witness to what journalist Phelim Kyne presciently told me in 1999: "If you look at the last ten years, every time they've been building to a boom, something happens."

The immediate cause of the intensified "political situation" is deftly phrased by the CanWest news organization's Asia hand, Jonathan Manthorpe. "Hun Sen is sexually over-engined like many powerful political men and has a special taste for actresses," he writes from Phnom Penh. "A few months ago, according to sources at the highest levels of Cambodia's establishment, Hun Sen met and was smitten by popular Thai soap opera actress Suvanant Kongying." The one-eyed PM invited Suvanant to visit the Kingdom, but, possibly aware of the fate of the last star Hun Sen had reportedly had an affair with, Suvanant rejected the PM's invitation, and was then misquoted in a Khmer tabloid as saying she'd never visit the country until Angkor Wat became part of Thailand. Angered, Hun Sen gave credence to the falsely reported insult by declaring that Suvanant was "not worth the grass that grows at Angkor."

Egged on by his implication that the country's honor had been defaced, several hundred protesters gathered outside the Thai embassy. The protesters were well behaved until they were joined by a gang of CPP-backed militia called the Pagoda Boys. Led by these paramilitary goons, the mob broke into the embassy, ransacked and then torched the place, forcing 10 Thai diplomats to flee for their lives over the back wall. The Thai ambassador phoned the Cambodian authorities for help, but they would not act against the Pagoda Boys except on the orders of Hun Sen, who was out of touch "playing golf." The Pagoda Boys then led the mob in an overnight rampage through the capital, burning three Thai-owned hotels and a score of businesses, one of which, a cell phone company, belonged to the Thai prime minister Thaksin Shinawatra. Thaksin mobilized the Thai army and prepared to invade to protect his country's interests. Finally, on the morning of January 30, the police were called out, although they merely watched as more Thai hotels were looted. The damage to Thai property from the riots was eventually estimated at $46.5 million, including $6.9 million at the gutted Thai embassy.

Hun Sen's reaction to the violence was typical of the strongman. He ordered the arrest of a radio-station owner and a Khmer-language newspaper editor, both of whom he accused of inciting the riots by airing rumors that revenge attacks against Cambodians were taking place in Bangkok. Human Rights Watch and Amnesty International condemned the arrests: "Attempts to silence free speech and opinion do not bode well for free and fair elections later this year," they stated in a joint declaration, published in the *Washington Post*. One of the leaders of the Funcinpec Party, the king's half-sister Princess

Norodom Vacheara, also took the arrests as a bad sign. She accused Hun Sen of trying to intimidate the press in advance of the summer's election, and demanded that the radio-station owner and the editor be immediately freed. Hun Sen allegedly called her "just a common girl," she threatened to sue him for slander, and Hun Sen charged her with criminal defamation. A few days later a message was sent to Funcinpec in the typical Cambodian manner: Om Radasay, senior political adviser to both the princess and Prince Norodom Ranariddh, was murdered in broad daylight as he left a Phnom Penh restaurant with two Funcinpec members. CPP officials said it was nothing more than a cell phone robbery, but witnesses to the killing said the "thief" interrogated the three diners until he had determined the identity of Om, then sadistically shot him through the groin. The shooter hopped on a waiting moto to make his getaway and, only then, the witnesses said, did the driver order the assassin to go back and grab the writhing Om's phone.

At Om's funeral Ranariddh declared that the killing was a political assassination designed to intimidate Funcinpec at the start of campaigning. "He had no enemies and was not involved in any affairs. He was a poor man and as gentle as a monk, so the only thing is a political crime." Hun Sen denied any political link. "I do not think this had a political motive," he told reporters. "We must find and arrest the criminals. We must not jump to any premature conclusions."

The riots (and their cause) shook confidence in Hun Sen, and it was rumored that an alternative to the PM was being considered by honchos in the CPP. The CPP politico most favored was Phnom Penh's popular governor, Chea Sophara, who bears the credit for preserving the capital's lovely ambience as it has modernized in the last couple of years and become a tourist destination. Hun Sen appears to have gotten wind of the threat to his reign, because he ordered Chea transferred to Burma as ambassador, where, as Manthorpe dryly notes, "The military regime can be trusted to thwart Chea's penchant for publicity."*

Not long after the burning and looting in Phnom Penh, Manila catches fire too—literally. The fires rage in the squatter slums of Tondo, Quezon City,

---

*On July 27, 2003, the CPP fell short of the two-thirds majority it needed to govern without a coalition. Ranariddh and Sam Rainsy declared they would not help the CPP form a government unless Hun Sen resigned. Motorcycle death squads were then unleashed on the streets of Phnom Penh. In one week in October, half a dozen public figures opposed to Hun Sen were shot dead. On November 5, Ranariddh and Rainsy agreed to discuss joining a coalition government, with Hun Sen as prime minister. By July 2004 the talks were still in progress.

and Paranque. From Roxas Boulevard I watch black cumulus clouds boiling up like nuclear mushrooms, then spreading out to obscure the bay and choke citizens in places as far away as Corregidor and Bataan. Thousands of shanty homes are destroyed and blocks of warehouses and factories collapse into cinders as the fires move about the town, dying down in one area and flaring up in another. The *Daily Inquirer* discovers why it is so difficult to put the fires out. "Metro Manila Has Only Half of Fire Trucks It Needs"—this despite the pork development funds awarded every year to buy the trucks.

"I liken the Philippines to a boat with many holes," Leonard de Vera tells me in his Makati office while Manila burns. "This boat is sinking with eighty million people aboard, and we are far from shore. The holes are terrorists, crime, drugs, overpopulation, poverty, pollution, and the depletion of our natural resources. But the worst hole is the culture of corruption that allows these holes to widen and go unfilled."

"Why don't you run for president and fix the holes?" I ask him.

De Vera, who I've noticed wears a perpetually bemused smile even when battling the PNP's lawyers in court, now bursts into open laughter. "My own friends want me to join the government. I have said: 'Why should I join the government when I have a lucrative practice and I would earn not even one thousand dollars a month?' You know what they say, my honest friends? 'The salary is low but the income is high.'"

Kicking the smoldering ashes in Tondo, talking to some of the suddenly homeless *masa* who owned nothing to begin with and now, sitting in their underwear, own less than nothing, I contemplate the universal *ipso facto* of Steve's world. For officials in every place where he has found refuge, the salary is low but the income is high, and therefore, no official is completely trustworthy, in any organization, at *any* level.

Down by the garbage-choked shore of Manila Bay I look northwest as a plane climbs through the smoke and smog. Who knows but that Steve might be winging his way to Macau on some *mat'sai* mission right now, or maybe he's just going there to meet with new cohorts? Networker that he is, I'm sure he's found out who's on top in the Vegas of Asia. For Stanley Ho is not, having had his monopoly officially terminated by the Chinese on March 31, 2002. They've invited in the former owner of the Mirage, Steve Wynn, who is decorating the peninsula with his own weird tastes, leaving the 81-year-old Ho to shoot for double happiness on-line with DrH0888.com, an electronic casino that features the good doctor thumbs-up on the webpage beside a voluptuous, half-naked croupier, saying "Check this out." In the Palm Plaza's Internet café, I wind up giving his virtual sexpot-dealer a night's rent.

Everybody who counts now has all the latest on Steve. I've sent thick packages to the RCMP Hong Kong Liaison Office and to Unit One, given them the phone numbers of Mary Ong, Martin Tremblay, Victor Corpus, and Reynaldo Wycoco. Out of cash, all I can do is go home and see if a fifth trip is worth another loan.

On the evening of March 11, I get an e-mail from Rosebud. She's attended the sentencing of Sandra Lim. "Sandra Lim turned hysterical after she heard the verdict. Lucky for her because the judge was compassionate. With 247 kilos, death penalty must have been implemented. Instead, life imprisonment was what she got."

What about Steve? I think, scrolling down the screen.

"She mentioned to me that her husband, a foreign Chinese national, was the one guilty with some cohorts. She mentioned her husband's associates are Canadian Chinese. Another case, in a Valenzuela laboratory raid, also leads to a Canadian Chinese. A Mayor [named] Mitra was arrested with 503 kilos sometime Oct 2001 and another 350 kilos in Pangasinan weeks after. A Canadian Chinese name always popped out, nicknamed *A-Tong* (Chinese character 'North'). Am just curious if this can be related in S Wong's group. Without the Chinese characters and pictures, it is very very difficult to identify."

"Dear Mary," I write back. "Thank you for all this information. It's possible Steven Wong brought some friends over and is now in the middle of these Canadian-Chinese associates. It would be great if you could ask Sandra Lim (or anyone else in the underworld) if they've come across a short, fat, 39-year-old Chinese who speaks English without an accent, and who could be Canadian.... Let me know if you come up with anything else."

INBOX 3/12/03: "Dear Terry, I will try. I verified information with NBI agents Lasala and Rey Esmeralda. They confirmed that several laboratory raids led to a Chinese Canadian. NBI arrested Sandra Lim, wife of Michael Lim, but to my surprise, NBI do not even have a picture of Michael Lim! My source in the jail said Sandra is still being supported by Michael Lim, the [one] Sandra said is into drug trade with some other Chinese including a Canadian Chinese.... I will still try to get additional information for you. From, Mary Rosebud."

I go downstairs and ask my wife if I should fly to the Philippines again and push at this latest lead.

"It would be cheaper if we just moved there," she replies.

OUTBOX 3/12/03: "Mary, Thank you for your detailed updates. I wonder if NBI Agents Lasala and Esmeralda would know if the Chinese

Canadian matched the description of Steven Wong: 5 foot four inches, 39 years old, etc. Terry."

INBOX: 3/13/03: "Dear Terry, I am not sure if Lasala and Esmeralda know about S Wong. I asked them if they had reported to NBI Director Wycoco regarding the findings that several laboratory raids led and pinpointed to a Canadian Chinese. They said 'No.' I did not share info of S. Wong because Lasala and Narcotics Director Reynor Gonzales (Lacson appointed) are friends, good friends. Gonzales is a very close ally of Lacson. Anyway, I will tell Wycoco."

OUTBOX 3/13/03: "Dear Mary, Yes, please tell Wycoco about any Chinese Canadians you hear of. I trust Wycoco, but the problem you phrase regarding the others is exactly the problem faced by the Canadian police, the Canadian Embassy, and myself. We are never sure who to trust when dealing with Philippine law enforcement. We never know who'll betray us or make some money by tipping off the target. . . . Try and keep safe. Terry."

INBOX 3/17/03: "Dear Terry, I will do my best to gather more informations regarding the Canadian Chinese partners that Sandra Lim mentioned. Definitely, I will not get the information from the NBI. I think Lasala and Esmeralda know more than just confirming that the several raids link and point to Canadian Chinese. They confirmed Canadian-Chinese links in two or three big drug laboratories but I don't know why they stop pursuing. A relative of Sandra Lim said that he even brought money to Ping's Presidential Anti-Organized Crime Task Force office when Sandra's condominium was raided in year 2000. It is so difficult for me to investigate at this point, not knowing who to trust. From, Mary Rosebud."

Her last sentence drops me into a slough. Two weeks go by. I stare at the date. April Fools.

OUTBOX 4/1/03: "Dear Mary, I'm *most* interested in finding out if any of those Chinese Canadians are Steven Wong. If the police can arrest him, and get him to talk, that would open up an international story that Ping and his bunch might have to answer to directly. It's my belief that international attention is one of the only hopes for justice in the Philippines. Thank you for all the time you spend on your e-mails. I really do appreciate them, as does my editor."

My editor.

"Anne, I'm always almost there. Always almost."

INBOX 4/1/03: "Dear Terry, You are right. Only international attention can bring hope for justice in the Philippines. Today, finally the Supreme Court has decided on Ping's Kuratong Baleleng Case. And the decision is really 'shock and awe' to Ping! Please read Phil Inquirer, Mary."

SUPREME COURT REVIVES MURDER RAP VS LACSON

SAYING the "state is entitled to justice," the Supreme Court ordered Tuesday the reopening of cases of the alleged murder of suspected members of the Kuratong Baleleng kidnapping-for-ransom gang in 1995, including a multiple-murder case against Senator Panfilo Lacson, who was a police task force head at the time.

Voting 10 to four with one abstention, the high court directed Quezon City Regional Trial Court Branch 81 under Judge Theresa Yadao to "forthwith proceed with Criminal Cases Nos. 01–101102 to 01–101112 with deliberate dispatch."

Lacson, who declared his intention to run for president next year, has 15 days to file a motion for reconsideration.

Leonard de Vera, one of the private lawyers working for the reopening of the cases, said the ruling allowed Yadao to issue a warrant for the senator's arrest.

Multiple-murder carries the penalty of death, and is thus non-bailable.

Lacson said his lawyers would seek the tribunal's reconsideration. "But as things stand now, there's a very slim chance that our motion will be granted," he said in a statement. Lacson described the tribunal's ruling as "most lamentable. . . ."

He added: "The decision of the high tribunal bodes ill for the rule of law in this country."*

INBOX 4/1/03: "Dear Terry, I just had dinner with Prosecutor Solis, the prosecutor on Sandra Lim's case involving 247 kilos of *shabu*. Fiscal Solis volunteered some information; he said that the drug lab cases and Sandra's case lead to one pipeline that involved Canadian-Chinese connection. But he does not understand why investigators opted to stop pursuing the upper level of the case. I need to check this out. From, Mary Rosebud."

Yes, check it out! By all means, check it out! Because it fits. It has always fit. With Steve, the pieces will *always* fall into place for me, except the one big piece. The Paper Fan himself. And I know why! The investigators always opt to stop pursuing the upper level of the case. Their salary is low but their income is high and *you can't trust anyone!*

---

*Lacson wasn't arrested, and on November 12, 2003, Quezon City judge Theresa Yadao dismissed the case against him, finding "a lack of probable cause for arrest." Government prosecutors appealed the decision. On May 10, 2004, Lacson lost the presidential election to Gloria Arroyo.

I do not hear from Mary for another two weeks, and then her e-mails come three-a-day, mostly about Lacson and other cases with more immediate rewards or threats to her. During this period, every morning, I do the homework she's assigned me and read the *Philippine Daily Inquirer,* then click "Favorites," go to Steve's Interpol poster—there to just stare and mope.

On this morning, quite by accident, I click on the "Interpol and Fugitives" main page, and discover nothing less than my motive for flying in pursuit of him 10 years ago. I could have written it myself the day I reasoned that impunity for Steve was something I just couldn't accept.

Fugitives in Context

One of the most important fields of activity of the global law enforcement community today is the apprehension of fugitives.

Fugitives, as a result of their criminal activity, pose a pervasive threat to public safety worldwide. Fugitives are mobile and opportunistic. They frequently finance their continued flight from the law by further criminal activities, which respect no traditional political or geographical boundaries.

Fugitives undermine the world's criminal justice systems. They may have been charged with a violation of the law but not been arrested; *they may have been released on bail and then fled to avoid prosecution* [italics mine] or perhaps they have escaped from prison. When fugitives flee from their charges, cases are not adjudicated, convicted criminals fail to meet their obligations, and crime victims are denied justice. If fugitives are not pursued by means of an aggressive investigation to locate them, it sends a subtle message to others that fleeing from the law or failing to comply with the law is somehow acceptable.

It's *not* acceptable, and with such a call to arms just a mouse click from his face, I know I'll never admit I can't find Steven Wong. I swivel in my chair, get up and approach Kwan Kung, pronam, and light a candle. Theatrically shadowed, my red god looks back at me with loving outrage. His scholar's left eye is wisdom. His general's right eye is determination. "Every criminal has to have somebody on his case," I whisper the good cop's mantra. "For Steve, I'm that somebody. I may be closing this book, Kwan Kung, but not before I've let everyone know about the Paper Fan. I'm taking him with me into my unfunded retirement. I'll die before I give Steve up for dead."

IMPUNITY

————

The perfect Way is without difficulty.
—ZEN POEM

You never know how a hunt will end until you've caught your prey or lost him forever. As this book goes to press, I've discovered a third way my hunt for Steven Wong could end. Canada now considers heroin trafficking to be a "victimless crime." After an accused heroin trafficker has been on the run for 10 or more years, the Canadian Department of Justice asks itself whether it is worth the time and expense to keep the charges active. Never mind Interpol's advice to its 181 member countries—in Canada, trafficking cases against successful fugitives are sometimes stayed after a decade. The criminal wins and the justice system admits defeat. The gangster gets his impunity.

On December 4, 2003, Steve won: his charges were stayed. At some time in the future, then, he could go on-line and find his mug missing from Interpol's website. In the midst of a drug deal he could place a call from Manila or Tokyo and learn that Canada's unofficial statute of limitations has kicked in for him. He could decide to announce he's had amnesia for a dozen years, come home, and start life again as a respectable citizen. In which case I could catch him without catching him. Then he and I could sit down in his house and start all over again.

SOURCES

———

This book is based on my interviews and reporting from the beginning of 1987 to the latter half of 2003. Many of my sources are cited in the text; where they are not cited or where there are additional sources, I have cited them below. Source notes are matched to page numbers and often include information that proved too lengthy to include as footnotes in the text.

The dialogue in this book comes from hundreds of hours of taped interviews and thousands of pages of notes. I have, in some cases, corrected grammar and made cuts to keep the dialogue readable or to protect a source.

Most of the people I have interviewed are identified by their full names. In a few instances, a first name or nickname is used in the text: either I did not learn the person's last name, or I've used a first name or pseudonym to protect the person's life or reputation. I have also not named specific law enforcement sources to protect their identities and their work. In the case of my former students, pseudonyms are the law: it is illegal in Canada to publish the name of a juvenile who is connected to a crime, and it is a violation of the teacher code of conduct to publish prejudicial details about students one has taught who are identified by name.

There are numerous government documents and sworn affidavits mentioned in this book that relate to the arrest, bail, and disappearance of Steven Wong. All are in my files. A number of the articles on the Philippines and Cambodia cited in these sources can be found by searching the online archives of the *Philippine Daily Inquirer* (www.inq7.net) the *Phnom Penh Post* (www.phnompenhpost.com), and the Philippine Center for Investigative Journalism (www.pcij.org).

CHAPTER 1 | The Garden of Reflection

[2]: Epigraph: Cerdeña's note accompanied the urn supposedly full of Steven Wong's ashes to Ninoy Aquino International Airport on August 7, 1992, along with

the forged affidavit of the so-called cremator "Aaron S. Menace," from Bacolod. A copy of Cerdeña's note, which was processed at Philippines Customs, was shown to me by NBI supervisory agent Virgilio Mendez on September 20, 1993.

[2]: Steven Wong's grave can be found at Forest Lawn Cemetery, 3789 Royal Oak Boulevard, in Burnaby, B.C., just east of the Vancouver city line at Boundary Road. Maps of the cemetery are given out free of charge at the reception building. My description of Steve's funeral is based on funeral documents and my interviews with Steve's friend Chuck Gough, the police, and Steven Wong's girlfriend Laura, who did not attend but received a firsthand account from Steve's family and Steve's friend Edison Yee.

CHAPTER 2 | The Goldstone

[8]: Information on Yip Sang: *Vancouver Sun,* April 7, 2001, p. H7. Rail workers: *The Canadian Encyclopedia* (Edmonton: Hurtig Publishers 1988), p. 416.

[8–9]: Statistics on Vancouver's Chinatown and early Chinatown days: Harry Con, Ronald J. Con, Graham Johnson, Edgar Wickberg, William E. Willmott, edited by Edgar Wickberg, *From China to Canada: A History of the Chinese Community in Canada* (Toronto: McClelland and Stewart, 1982), pp. 60–86.

[9–10]: Chinese Immigration Act: Con et al., *From China to Canada,* pp. 141–145; Martin Booth, *The Dragon Syndicates: The Global Phenomenon of the Triads* (London, England: Bantam, 1999), p. 509; and *Vancouver Sun,* January 9, 2002, p. B5. Home Districts: Harry Con et al., *From China to Canada,* pp. 7–8. The overwhelming majority of Chinese immigrants came from the eight contiguous counties in the Sze-yap and Sam-yap regions, in particular the four counties in the Sze-yap region.

[10]: "Armies protect the emperor, secret societies protect the people," from Gerald Posner, *Warlords of Crime: Chinese Secret Societies—The New Mafia* (New York: McGraw Hill, 1988), p. 31. "The officials draw their power from the Law, the people from the secret societies," from Fenton Bresler, *The Chinese Mafia: The Most Frightening New Organization in International Crime* (New York: Stein and Day, 1980), p. 29. Statistics on Chinese societies: Con et al., *From China to Canada,* pp. 315–318. "Hung Shan Tang, first founded by Chinese gold miners in the northern town of Barkerville in 1863," from Booth, *Dragon Syndicates,* p. 509; and Con et al., *From China to Canada,* p. 30. "Others, like the Chun Wah Commercial Association,

were run quite openly as legally constituted organizations," Con et al., *From China to Canada*, p. 317. Tong—"town hall": Bresler, *Chinese Mafia*, p. 172.

[11]: Early Triads similar to early Mafia: Bresler, *Chinese Mafia*, p. 27. Early Chinese community leaders as criminals: Booth, *Dragon Syndicates*, p. 510. Early police investigation discovering payoffs: Con et al., *From China to Canada*, p. 68. Chinatown viewed as "depraved": Con et al., *From China to Canada*, p. 67. "Hatchetmen" from Richard H. Dillon, *The Hatchet Men: The Story of the Tong Wars in San Francisco's Chinatown* (New York: Coward-McCann, Inc., 1962).

[12–13]: Goldstone incident, from interviews with Steven Wong, Vancouver City police officers such as Bill Chu, Lotus Gang members, CBC-TV *News Hour* files, and the *Vancouver Sun*. There are, naturally, a variety of versions of what happened that night. I have stayed pretty close to Steven Wong's version, confirming with a secondary source in the Lotus Gang that Steve was hit across the back with a chair.

[13]: "Shooting in Chinatown: Gang-fight charges expected," *Vancouver Sun*, December 29, 1989.

[13–14]: My interviews with the Wah Ching member Leo Ng took place in June 1989 at his Key Club Casino in Emeryville, a suburb of San Francisco. I was introduced to Ng by Sgt./Insp. Daniel Foley, head of the Gang Task Force of the San Francisco Police Department, Intelligence Division.

CHAPTER 3 | Britannia

[16]: In Vancouver, secondary schools start at the eighth grade.

[16–17]: My descriptions of gang activity from the mid-1980s to early 1987 are from my later interviews with members of the Vancouver City Police, gang members such as Steven Wong, gang lawyers such as Ian Donaldson, Richard Israels, and Harry and Phil Rankin, helpful discussions with crime reporters such as Paul Heeny (CBC TV News), Neal Hall (*The Vancouver Sun*), and Greg Middleton (*The Province*), court transcripts of trials, and from *Vancouver Sun* files and CBC-TV news reports.

[19]: Details of the lives of Arnold Rothstein, Meyer Lansky, and Ben "Bugsy" Siegel are drawn from conversations with my father, uncles, and their friends, as well as

from excellent portraits of their lives and times in Rich Cohen's *Tough Jews: Fathers, Sons and Gangster Dreams* (New York: Vintage, 1999) and Robert Lacey's *Little Man: Meyer Lansky and the Gangster Life* (New York: Little, Brown, 1991).

[21–22]: I lived at 35 Seacoast Towers, on the Brighton Beach boardwalk, from 1967 to 1971. Brighton Beach did not become notorious as the American capital of the *Organizatsiya*—or Russian-Jewish mob—until the mid-'70s, but Russian-Jewish jailbirds began settling in the neighborhood well before then. In 1968 I held a summer job at Brighton Beach Baths, which the earliest *gonifs* frequented. An excellent portrait of the later activities of the Russian-Jewish mob is given by Robert I. Friedman in "Brighton Beach Goodfellas," *Vanity Fair,* January 1993.

[26]: Details of the Golden Princess shooting are taken from my own reporting and trial transcripts contained in "Proceedings at Trial," April 21, 1988, the Crown's closing arguments, presented by Crown Counsel Jim McBride.

CHAPTER 4 | Gang Wars

[27–28]: Details of the massacre in the Wah Mee gambling club are taken from my June 1989 interviews with police officers in Seattle, particularly Det./Sgt. Don Yeowell, Intelligence Section; and Frank Chin's article "Our Life is War," *Seattle Weekly,* May 4–May 10, 1983. Details of New York's Golden Star bar massacre are taken from my interviews with New York and New Jersey police at the 1989 Asian Crime Conference in Vancouver, and Michael Daly's article "The War for Chinatown," *New York* magazine, February 14, 1983. Details of San Francisco's Golden Dragon Restaurant killings are taken from my 1989 interviews with Sgt./Insp. Daniel Foley of San Francisco's Gang Task Force, and interviews with other members of the Gang Task Force, particularly Richard Moses, Wayne S. Hom, Tom Perdue, and Felix Thieu, as well as Posner, *Warlords of Crime.* My description of Vancouver's gang situation in 1987 is taken from my own reporting; interviews with Vancouver police officers Tom Span, Bill Chu, Martin Turner, Peter Ditchfield, and Bobby Cooper, plus testimony of the Asian squad's Martin Turner at the trial of Allan Keung "Little White Dragon" Law, and *Vancouver Sun* files.

[31]: The gang-awareness instructional video is called "Where's Winston," produced in part by ESL teacher Hugh Hooper. "Where's Winston" is loosely based on the life of the Golden Princess shooter, William Yeung. Hugh Hooper also taught Bob Moieni before Moieni was murdered.

Ricky Tang was released from jail and deported to Hong Kong on April 9, 1987. See "Gang Member Deported," *Vancouver Sun,* April 10, 1987.

[32]: The version of the Ricky Tang–Steven Wong affair I've used is the one Steven Wong related to me in early March 1990. Steve admitted that he'd told a sanitized version to the police and in court. In those versions he claimed he was trying to break up a fight between Tang and a helpless victim on the Churchill school grounds. In fact, the helpless victim, he told me, was one of his own Red Eagles enforcers who'd accompanied him to the school yard from Fraser Billiards.

[34–39]: The overview of the gang scene in these pages is based on my interviews with the police mentioned above and in the text, as well as my interviews with gang members. Insightful information on Park Lo and Albert Kong also comes from my 1990 interviews with Tom Span of the Vancouver police. Before the founding of the Asian Crime Squad, Span investigated the Lotus and its leaders and also Steven Wong.

I also consulted: court transcripts of the testimony of Martin Turner during the sentencing phase of the trial of Allan Keung "Little White Dragon" Law, June 2, 1988; Philip Baridon's *Report on Asian Organized Crime: February 1988* (Washington, D.C.: U.S. Department of Justice, Criminal Division, Office of Policy and Management Analysis); *1988 Organized Crime Committee Report,* Canadian Association of Chiefs of Police; and *Vancouver Sun* and CBC-TV news files.

My description of the gang summit in the Miramar Hotel in Kowloon is based on my interview with San Francisco's Sgt. Insp. Daniel Foley, who referred me to Hong Kong police reports on the summit, plus Posner, *Warlords of Crime,* pp. 244–245. According to Posner, Tin Lung, Boston's Ping On gang dragon head, was scheduled to attend but never showed; representatives of New York's Hip Sing tong never showed because of a gang war going on with a rival tong, the Freemasons. The influential California businessmen in attendance were Pai Shing Ping and Peter Man. Also in attendance was Lee Yoo Ting, an alleged United Bamboo Triad affiliate from Taiwan.

Details of Vincent Jew come from my 1989 and 1993 interviews with San Francisco's Dan Foley, and interviews with other members of the Gang Task Force, particularly Richard Moses, Wayne S. Hom, Tom Perdue, and Felix Thieu, as well as Posner, *Warlords of Crime,* pp. 244–247, plus my 1989 interview with former Wah Ching gang member Leo Ng, my 1993 interview with Chuck Gough, and my 1990 interviews with Steven Wong.

Details of Lau Wing-kui as head of security at Stanley Ho's Lisboa (p. 36) come from Posner, *Warlords of Crime,* p. 175, and my 1993 interviews with RCMP (now Superintendent) Garry Clement in Hong Kong. Lau Wing-kui's legal name was Lau Wing-keung, and Posner refers to him that way. However, he went by the name Wing-kui and most police reports refer to him as Lau Wing-kui. In its *Report on*

Asian Organized Crime: February 1988, the U.S. Department of Justice listed Lau Wing-kui (then residing in Hong Kong) as a member of Toronto's Kung Lok Triad. Details of Lau as part owner of Ho's Jumbo restaurant in Aberdeen and the lease of VIP tables in the Lisboa come from interviews with police at the 1989 Asian Crime Conference and in Hong Kong, as well as James Dubro's *Dragons of Crime* (Markham, Ontario: Octopus Publishing, 1992), pp. 114–115, 162. Details of Lau's criminal history come from my interviews with Clement; Booth's *Dragon Syndicates,* pp. 511–513; and Posner's *Warlords of Crime,* p. 175.

Information on the 14K Triad as overseer of the Kung Lok Triad in Toronto comes from my interviews with RCMP (now Superintendent) Garry Clement; and police reports.

Steven Wong's appeal of his gun permit is based on my interview with him; Martin Turner, who testified at the appeal; Bill Chu; and the *Vancouver Sun,* November 23, 1988.

Information on the Big Circle Boys (Dai Huen Jai) comes from my interviews with Bill Chu, and later interviews with RCMP (now Sergeant) Mike Hiller, an authority on them. Information on the Vietnamese gangs comes from my 1989 and 1990 interviews with Vancouver gang leader Danny Win, head of Danny's Boys, at his hangout at the Lu Quan restaurant in Little Saigon; Bill Chu in Vancouver; Marcus Franks of the Westminster, California, Police Department; Randy Quan and Dan Parks of Organized Crime Intelligence, Los Angeles Police Department; and William Cassidy of Westminster, California, a private investigator and ex-CIA agent who served in Vietnam and who thought the problem of Vietnamese gangs in Southern California was overblown, and that the reaction of the police to them was excessive.

[39–41]: Information on Bob Moieni and his affiliation with the Lotus and Los Diablos comes from my interviews with Moieni's best friend, Daren Sherewood, who was also a friend of Kim Tam; Bob Moieni's mother, Robabeh; his father, Nosrat Moieni; his sisters Manijeh and Mattie; Moieni's girlfriend, Shannon Le Blanc; Los Diablos members such as Teo Gill; students of mine who were affiliates or members of the Lotus and Los Diablos; Steven Wong; Kim Tam; ESL teachers of Moieni such as Hugh Hooper; Moieni's karate teacher, Bill Hunter; Moieni's vice principal at David Thompson Secondary, Dave Cummings; Asian squad police officers Martin Turner, Bill Chu, and Peter Ditchfield, as well as Southside Gang Squad officers such as Brian Honeyburn.

[41–42]: Summary of gang battles between September 1987 and December 28, 1989, is based on my own reporting, interviews with police, interviews with Steven Wong, and *Vancouver Sun* files.

CHAPTER 5 | Laughing Man

[44–68]: My conversation with Steven Wong on February 15, 1990, lasted about two hours, of which 100 minutes were taped by John Collins and David Paperny in the CBC van. Each tape was 20 minutes long and Collins had one temporary tape failure of several minutes while changing tapes. Each subsequent change of tape took a minute or so before sound was running again. My editor and I have edited out rambling duplications in my discussion with Wong, as well as unsubstantiated allegations he made against certain parties. I've used only the first name of Steve's enforcer, Phu, as per our agreement for his appearance on CBC.

[49]: The full story of the Green Dragons and the White Tigers was told two years later by Fredric Dannen in "Revenge of the Green Dragons," *The New Yorker,* November 16, 1992.

CHAPTER 6 | Heaven, Earth, and Man

[70–75]: Frank Chin's "Our Life is War," *Seattle Weekly,* May 4–10, 1983, is one of the most sophisticated and sensitive portraits of Chinatown, Kwan Kung, and the roots of the martial Chinese psyche I have ever read. Stewart Culin's *Chinese Games with Dice and Dominoes* (Smithsonian Institute Report, 1893) also has a good section on the life and times of Kwan Kung, p. 523. I learned quite a bit about the inner workings of the Chinese-gangster mind-set from my 1989 interviews with Dr. Tsung-Yi Lin, a family psychiatrist in Vancouver who specialized in young gang members and the roots of gang-related antisocial behavior in the Chinese community, as well as Triad-related antisocial behavior in Taiwan.

[75–84]: W. P. Morgan's *Triad Societies in Hong Kong* (Hong Kong: Government Press, 1960) is *the* source for journalists who have written about the history, rituals, and culture of the Triads. Excellent summations of Morgan's scholarly work (and additions to it) are to be found in Booth's *Dragon Syndicates* and Posner's *Warlords of Crime.* I have relied heavily on all three works in relating the ancient and modern history of the Triads, as well as on my interviews with the numerous police officers mentioned above and, of course, Steven Wong. For the 14K's penetration of the U.S. heroin market in the 1970s and 1980s I have relied on my 1989 interviews with Drug Enforcement Administration agent Edward Madonna and Special Agent in Charge Gary D. Liming, both in Seattle. For the 14K's penetration of European heroin markets, I have relied on my 1989 interviews with Toon Schalks, an investigator with the Dutch National Criminal Intelligence Service, and Arie Bax, an investigator with the Dutch Regional Criminal Intelligence Service. I have learned much about the opium trade from Martin Booth's *Opium: A History* (London, England: Simon & Schuster, 1996). The counterintuitive theory I have put forth on the economics of the drug trade—increased supply leads to increased demand—is my own.

CHAPTER 7 | The Emperor of the North

[88–90]: Who actually invented pai gow—if any one person did—will probably never be known. Culin's Smithsonian Report lists several of the heroes in *The Romance of the Three Kingdoms,* with one version of the domino game, called O-Koan, deriving directly from Kwan Kung. Other possible inventors Culin mentions are: Hung Ming, who was an adviser to Kwan Kung's blood brother, Liu Pei (Frank Chin spells his name Low Bay in "Our Life is War"); Kiang Tsze-ya, who lived over a thousand years before Kwan Kung; and Fan Li, who predated Kwan Kung by 600 years. Obviously we are dealing in the realm of myth, but in myth, belief lends weight to an *attribution* of authorship. In the underworld, at least, belief seems to rest on the side of Kwan Kung. Leo Ng, the Wah Ching gangster who owned the Key Club Casino near San Francisco, told me he was certain Kwan Kung invented pai gow, and gave me a pai gow set to place beside my statue of Kwan Kung, where it has sat in its leather box ever since. Steven Wong, too, was certain the inventor of pai gow was Kwan Kung.

[94–95]: Sources for the tongs in New York's Chinatown are Steven Wong; Gwen Kinkaid's *Chinatown: Portrait of a Closed Society* (New York: HarperCollins, 1992); Daly's "War for Chinatown"; Booth's *Dragon Syndicates,* in which the FBI surveillance photo of the respectful tong mourners at Benny Ong's funeral was published; and my interviews with numerous East Coast police officers at the 1989 Asian Crime Conference.

CHAPTER 8 | Showtime

[102–103]: My on-camera interview with Chu lasted about 45 minutes, of which a couple of minutes made it to air. I am not restricted to sound bites in this book, however, and have included quotes from the interview that were cut for time.

[104–105]: Since 1990, when Steve explained to me how difficult it would be to assault the CBC building in Vancouver, the corporation has widened the main plaza a bit—but not much. The CBC Regional Broadcasting Centre was opened in 1975.

[106]: Phu's last colorful line never made it to air. Five "fucks" and one "mother cunt" in 14 words were too much for the supper-hour news.

CHAPTER 9 | Project Bugs

[112–113, 121–125]: The description of Project Bugs comes from interviews with police officers who were involved in the investigation, as well as Crown Prosecutor Peter Eccles and "Regina v. Cheung," in *Canadian Criminal Cases* (3d), pp. 507–529, the B.C. Court of Appeal's denial of Yak Wah Cheung's appeal.

CHAPTER 10 | Extensive Transformation and Uniting with Heaven

[132]: I was greatly helped in the research for my 1992 article "Drug War? What Drug War?" by Inspector Don Keith, head of Vancouver's Drug Squad.

[133]: The one-paragraph summary of the events between July 19 and September 8, 1992, is taken from court documents, such as the April 7, 1994 "Reasons for Judgement" by Justice Fraser; documents supplied to me by the insurance companies; and interviews with the police.

[134]: The ex–CIA agent was Jerry Gosnell, president of Gosnell & Associates, a private investigation agency headquartered in Shawnee Mission, Kansas.

[137–139]: The description of Steve's passport hearing comes from court documents and interviews with Peter Eccles and with the police.

[139–144]: The description of these events comes from court documents, documents supplied by Steve's lawyers to the insurance companies; Philippine National Police reports; my interviews with Crown Prosecutor Peter Eccles and his presentations in court; my interviews with the police in Canada, Hong Kong, and the Philippines; my interviews with Chuck Gough; and my on-the-ground research in the Philippines in September 1993. Description of the conditions on Negros in 1992 and 1993 comes from my interviews with the Philippine police, peasants, and resi-dents of Bacolod, Binalbagan, Isabela, and Bantayan, as well as Philippine newspa-per reports of the day, including the *Visayan Daily Star, Philippine Daily Inquirer,* and *Manila Times,* and *Philippines: A Travel Survival Kit* (Hawthorne, Australia: Lonely Planet Publications, 4th ed., May 1991), p. 301.

CHAPTER 11 | The Chink

[145–148]: Chuck Gough first moved into 711 Broughton in July 1991. Details of his criminal record and his career prior to my meeting him came from gangland sources; they were confirmed by Chuck in our interviews.

[150–151]: Details of Sonny's passport caper come from my attendance at his court cases, and interviews with the police and Chuck Gough.

[151]: Details of Lisa Lee as a Vancouver auxilliary police officer and her connec-tions to Steven Wong come from my interviews with Chuck Gough, the police, and Lisa Lee. (See Chapter 17, p. 235.)

[153]: Stanley Ho bought the lot opposite Stanley Park in 1973. An announcement that he was to construct a house on the lot had already been made when I had my discus-sion with Chuck, but Ho did not begin construction until February 1994. I wrote an article for the *South China Sunday Morning Post Magazine,* November 6, 1994, "Stanley Ho's House of Horror." Stanley Ho now has four wives and 17 children. See William Mellor's "Stanley Ho's Secret Weapon," *Asia-Inc.com,* October 2002.

The RCMP Asian organized crime roster was secret in 1993, but it has since been extensively publicized in the press in the wake of the Jumbo Palace's arrival in Manila Bay in January 2000. See Fabian Dawson, "The Ho Connection," *The Province,* March 9, 2000, p. A6: "The *Province* has obtained a secret RCMP Asian Organized Crime Roster—done in conjunction with three other police agencies in Eastern Canada—that lists Macau casino King Stanley Ho as a suspected 'leader/member' of the noto-rious Kung Lok Triad. . . . Ho has also been assigned an RCMP gang file number—89–1770—used for intelligence assessment by law enforcement agencies. Other information about Ho is contained in a secret Canadian police file numbered S84721 and in police intelligence reports on the Kung Lok Triad, which has strong connec-tions in Toronto." See also "Macau Casino King Faces House Probe," *Philippine Daily Inquirer,* January 14, 2000. Stanley Ho's career is covered extensively in Chapter 15, as well as Chapter 24. The issue of the Triads thriving side by side with Ho's legitimate empire in Macau has been extensively documented in Posner's *Warlords of Crime*, pp. 175–177; and Booth's *Dragon Syndicates*, pp. 380–385, 538–540, 542–547. The Triad gangster who was a partner in Ho's Jumbo floating restaurant and headed Ho's Lisboa security was Lau Wing-kui. (See sources for pp. 34–39). Information about the Triad gangsters who ran loan-shark operations on the eighth floor is based on my interviews with police in Hong Kong and Posner's *Warlords of Crime*, p. 176. Other known Triad members who have held leases on Ho's VIP rooms over the years were Kai Sze Wai aka "Market Wai," and Wan Kwok-koi aka "Broken Tooth" (Booth, *Dragon Syndicates*, pp. 540–545, and *Vancouver Sun*, October 25, 1999).

CHAPTER 12 | The Spook

[155]: The Meridien, at 845 Burrard, changed names to the Sutton Place in 1995. Stanley Ho retained ownership of the hotel under a holding company called the Vancouver Grande.

[162]: Summary of Ho's portfolio from Jill McGivering's *Macao Remembers* (Oxford: Oxford University Press, 1999), p. 105; Jonathon Karp, "The New Insiders," *Far Eastern Economic Review*, May 1993; and editorial staff at *Hong Kong Inc*, "The Ho Tong Dynasty," March 1990.

CHAPTER 14 | Project Lazarus

[178]: Epigraph: My interview with Tom Span took place on May 2, 1990. Span had investigated Steven Wong during the mid '80s. He retired from the force in 1987 and formed a private detective agency.

[182]: The *Lonely Planet* quote comes from *Hong Kong, Macau & Guangzhou*, 9th ed., p. 344 (Hawthorne, Australia: Lonely Planet Publications, January 1999). Figure of nine coup attempts in the Philippines since mid-'80s is based on my readings at the time and the number given later by Alfred W. McCoy in *Closer Than Brothers: Manhood at the Philippine Military Academy* (New Haven: Yale University Press, 1999), p. 2. Conditions in the Philippines in 1993 are based on my discussion with Danilo Mendez and my on-the-ground reporting. Number of journalists killed and the lack of prosecution of the culprits is based on my interviews with Mendez and later press reports published over the years. For instance, *Philippine Daily Inquirer*,

May 15, 2002: "The Philippine Press Institute (PPI) said Edgar Damalerio, 33, was the 38th journalist killed in the country since the mid-1980s. It said not one of these killings, including that of hard-hitting Pagadian broadcaster Olympio Jalapit Jr. in November 2000, had been solved." See also "Group says 3 media persons slain a year," *Philippine Daily Inquirer,* August 25, 2003, in which the National Union of Journalists gives the latest total as 41 (www.inq7.net/nat/2003/aug/25/text/nat_8–1-p.htm). Two weeks later the total was up to 43. See *Philippine Daily Inquirer:* September 9, 2003, "New Colombia." Yet another journalist was murdered on December 2, 2003.

CHAPTER 15 | Ho! Ho! Ho!

[187]: Epigraph from Booth, *Dragon Syndicates,* p. 538. Stats on Hong Kong airports and traffic at Kai Tak come from Lonely Planet's *Hong Kong, Macau & Guangzhou,* 9th ed., p. 139.

[188–189]: Description of Kim Kong case and heroin overdoses come from: my interviews with Garry Clement; Mark Hughes, "Police Hold 'Mr Big' over Canada Drug Trafficking," *South China Morning Post,* September 16, 1993, p. 3; and Neal Hall, "Hong Kong Hearing Set for Alleged Heroin Czar," *Vancouver Sun,* September 16, 1993, p. 1.

[191–192]: As mentioned in Chapters 9 and 12, the U.S. Justice Department's classified February 1988 *Report on Asian Organized Crime* includes Stanley Ho in its list of 58 notorious Triad members, although Ho's "primary affiliation" is listed as "Unk" (unknown). The classified 1990 Canadian Organized Crime Roster lists Ho as a suspected "leader/member" of the Kung Lok Triad. Posner, in *Warlords of Crime,* states (p. 176): "Members of Hong Kong intelligence and the Drug Enforcement Administration will talk about Ho, but only under the strictest assurance that they not be identified. The Hong Kong police say he is a Triad member." Booth, in *The Dragon Syndicates,* states (p. 385): "There has long been speculation over Ho's relationship with the Triads. Opinions vary. Some sources claim he is a very high-ranking official indeed: others emphatically maintain that he is not but has close ties with them. A third school of thought is that he has certainly had to come to more than one accommodation with them in order to stay in the gambling business." (See also source note for pp. 195–196.) Short summary of Ho's career, achievements, and awards comes from "The Ho Tong Dynasty," *Hong Kong Inc;* Karp, "New Insiders"; McGivering, *Macao Remembers;* Posner, *Warlords of Crime;* Booth, *Dragon Syndicates;* and my own interviews with police.

[192]: F. Scott Fitzgerald's quotes come from "The Rich Boy," *The Stories of F. Scott Fitzgerald* (New York: Scribners, 1951), p. 177.

[192–196]: Ho's biography comes mainly from his chapter-length monologue in McGivering's *Macao Remembers*, "Stanley Ho: King of Casinos," pp. 107–117. Details of Roger Lobo's life and his encounter with the murdered Japanese consul come from Lobo's monologue in McGivering's *Macao Remembers*, "Sir Roger Lobo: Wartime Resistance," pp. 71–78. Other sources for Ho's biography are: Booth, *Dragon Syndicates;* Posner, *Warlords of Crime; Hong Kong Inc; The Far Eastern Economic Review;* and my interviews with police in Hong Kong.

[195–196]: Details on Ho's 1970s venture in the Philippines come from his speech in Manila in October 1999 (see Chapter 24) and Booth's *Dragon Syndicates*, p. 383. Details on Ho's director of security at the Lisboa, Lau Wing-kui, who would soon become a part owner in Ho's Jumbo floating restaurant in Aberdeen, from Dubro, p. 114–115, and Posner, *Warlords of Crime*, p. 175. Details on Lau's Canadian career and deportation are from Booth, p. 512, and Dubro, pp. 145–149. Details of the San Francisco Asian Gang Squad's allegation that Ho's right-hand business partner, Yip Hon, was a heroin trafficker and a Triad member are from my interviews with San Francisco police in 1989 and Booth, p. 383. Details of Ho's falling-out with Yip Hon, the 1987 entrance of Kai Sze Wai on the scene, and the murder of Thomas Chung are from my interviews with police in Hong Kong and from Booth, p. 384. Details of "Broken Tooth" Wan Kwok-koi and Wai's lease on VIP gambling rooms in the Lisboa are from Booth, p. 545. Details of eighth floor loan-shark operations are from my 1993 interviews with police in Hong Kong, and Posner, p. 176.

[200]: The projections on Stanley Ho's casino earnings were for $2 billion; in fact they turned out to be $2.25 billion. McGivering, *Macao Remembers*, p. 105.

CHAPTER 16 | Sugarland

[203]: Epigraph: I first heard this saying in 1993; a version of it is in Lonely Planet's *Philippines*, 7th ed., p. 15. (Hawthorne, Australia: Lonely Planet Publications, October 2000).

[205]: The number of squatters in Metro Manila at the time of my 1993 visit is based on my interviews, observations, and a National Housing Authority report in the 1980s, quoted in Lonely Planet's *Philippines* (7th ed., p. 37), which "estimated that

25% of Metro Manila's residents were squatters," out of a total Metro Manila population then estimated at between eight and ten million. In the *Philippine Daily Inquirer,* May 4, 2001, the number of squatters offered was higher: "An estimated one-third of Metro Manila's 10.5 million people are believed to be living in poverty, most of them in squalid and stinking slums with no sewage or clean water facilities" (from a p. 3 article entitled "The More Things Change, the More They Stay Poor"). Statistics on Filipinos living below the poverty line vary, depending on the benchmark. The government's benchmark is 38 pesos a day—about a dollar in 1993 and about 70 cents at today's exchange rate. In 1993, Danilo Mendez told me the poverty figure was just over 30 percent, based on stats he'd seen in his community service work. The National Statistics Coordination Board (NSCB) gave the figure as 28.4 percent for 2000, published in the *Philippine Daily Inquirer,* January 16, 2003. On January 27, 2002, the *Inquirer* stated the figure was 40 percent. On March 27, 2002, the *Inquirer* quoted the social service IBON Foundation figure at an astounding 87.5 percent, based on the fact that 38 pesos a day was actually *dire* poverty, and that the peso benchmark should be higher. On July 25, 2002, in an article entitled "Angara: 'House of Cards'" the *Inquirer* reported: "Thirty-two million Filipinos live on less than 23 pesos a day." That is, 40 percent of the population lived on less than 40 cents a day, at the going exchange rate (http://www.inq7.net/ nat/2002/jul/25/text/nat_9–1-p.htm). Given the IBON Foundation's findings, Danilo Mendez's figure of "over thirty percent" is conservative for 1993.

[205]: *Bahala na* is the acknowledged national saying of the Philippines. *The Philippine Daily Inquirer,* February 25, 2003, defines it as "Leave to fate." Tomas D. Andres in the *Dictionary of Filipino Culture and Values* (Quezon City: Giraffe Books, 1994) writes: "The attitude is a fatalistic resignation or withdrawal from an engagement or crisis or a shirking of personal responsibility." Andres formally defines *Bahala na ang Diyos* as "God will take care of us." His examples of usage, and the pervasive context of the saying on the street, translates to the secular attitude, *That's the way it is*—which is how I have defined it.

[206–207, 210–211]: My summary of Philippine history comes from numerous sources I read while in the Philippines in 1993, including contemporary and archival newspaper articles that were later collected in *Pork and Other Perks: Corruption and Governance in the Philippines,* edited by Sheila S. Coronel (Manila: Philippine Center for Investigative Journalism, 1998), Howard Zinn's *A People's History of the United States* (New York: HarperPerennial, 1980), and Lonely Planet's *Philippines* (4th ed., 1991), plus interviews I had with numerous Filipinos, and later readings, including the National Historical Institute's *Filipinos in History* (Manila: National Historical Institute, 1996); various volumes published by the Philippines Center for Investigative

Journalism, including *Betrayals of the Public Trust: Investigative Reports on Corruption*, edited by Sheila S. Coronel (2000); McCoy's *Closer Than Brothers;* John T. Sidel's *Capital, Coercion and Crime: Bossism in the Philippines* (Palo Alto, Calif.: Stanford University Press, 1999); Teresita Ang See's *The Chinese in the Philippines: Problems and Perspectives* (Manila: Kaisa Para Sa Kaunlaran, Inc., 1997); Lonely Planet's *Philippines* (7th ed., 2000); Wong Kwok-Chu's *Chinese in the Philippine Economy: 1898–1941* (Manila: Ateneo De Manila University Press, 1999); Samuel K. Chan's *A History of the Philippines* (Manila: Manila Studies Association, Inc., 1997); and James Hamilton-Paterson's "Foreword to the Philippine Edition" of *Ghosts of Manila* (London, England: Jonathan Cape Ltd., 1994). Hamilton-Paterson enlightened me to the parallel between the two Izon cartoons, on p. iv of his foreword.

[207]: In a July 22, 2003, editorial, "Continuing Search," the *Philippine Daily Inquirer* reported that the total amount of money stolen by Ferdinand Marcos and hidden in Swiss banks could be as high as $13.2 billion. The Inquirer urged the government "to pursue the search for what has been called 'the mother lode' of the Marcos ill-gotten wealth." For over sixteen years the government and courts had known that $683 million of the money stolen by Marcos had been sitting in a Swiss account belonging to Marcos's daughter, Irene Marcos-Araneta. Finally, on November 18, 2003, the Philippine Supreme Court issued a ruling against the Marcos family and ordered that the money in the account be returned to the government. See: *Philippine Daily Inquirer,* November 19, 2003, "It's final: High court rules $683M belongs to gov't."

[207–209]: Except for *Brother Hood,* text by Gemma Luz Corotan (Manila: Philippine Center for Investigative Journalism, 1995), the Filipino articles cited in this section have been collected in the two above-mentioned volumes published by the Philippine Center for Investigative Journalism: *Pork and Other Perks* and *Betrayals of the Public Trust,* both edited by Sheila S. Coronel.

[208]: The latest irate senator to reveal what happened to the pork development fund was Panfilo Lacson. In May 2002, he announced that each senator was allocated 200 million pesos in pork funds and each representative of a district, 65 million pesos—of which up to three-fifths disappeared. "It's saddening because for every one million pesos [of the development fund] released for a farm-to-market road, only a high of 40 percent actually goes to the construction. The 60 percent is lost to corruption" (*Philippine Daily Inquirer,* May 19, 2002). The astounding corruption of the Philippine bureaucracy would be revealed in the summer of 2003, when the Macapagal-Arroyo government mandated "lifestyle checks" of all bureaucrats. The following article in the *Philippine Daily Inquirer,* August 21, 2003, tells the story:

80% of Revenue, Public Works Execs Are Multi-Millionaires
by Juliet Labog-Javellana

Despite public knowledge that certain departments and agencies of the
government are riddled with corruption, the top man of the Malacañang-
based Transparency Group said he was still amazed when he saw the numbers. More than 80 percent of officials in the Bureau of Internal Revenue
(BIR), Bureau of Customs (BoC), and Department of Public Works and
Highways (DPWH) are millionaires, said Nick Conti, head of the group
looking into the lifestyles of presidential appointees and public officials. To
cite some instances, he said, a customs collector in La Union province had
assets worth 96 million pesos [almost $2 million U.S.]; an assistant BIR
commissioner, 53.4 million pesos [$1 million U.S.]; and a DPWH regional
director, 43 million pesos. . . . He said some, if not most, of the officials
could have bigger undeclared assets.

[211]: In November 2003, the Supreme Court voided the multibillion-peso contract
between the Philippine government and Amari Coastal Bay Development Corp. for
being "unconstitutional and unconscionably undervalued." The judgment stated
that "based on the official appraisal of the Commission on Audit, the independent
constitutional body that safeguards government assets, the actual loss to the Filipino
people is a shocking 31.779 billion [pesos]," or roughly $600 million. The court
revealed that the Commission on Audit had valued the land at 21,333 pesos per
square meter, while the government had sold it to Amari for 1,200 pesos per square
meter—that is, at a 95 percent reduced price.

[219]: *Visayan Star,* September 20, 1993: "Government Admits Negros Reds Still a Force,"
no byline, pp. 1, 2; and "Remembering Escalante Massacre," by Primo Esleyer, p. 3.

[223]: Details of Mike Arroyo's family landholdings come from interviews I conducted on Negros in 1993. See also: "Farmers Ask DAR to Cover Arroyo Land,"
Philippine Daily Inquirer, on-line edition, June 14, 2002 (Nation section). As well as,
". . . Mike Arroyo comes from The Philippines' elite, a family of sugar plantation
owners," *Vancouver Sun,* October 17, 2003, p. A19.

CHAPTER 17 | Steve Found

[229]: I gave the originals of the affidavits I had collected in the Philippines to Garry Clement, and retained copies of them.

[231]: Statue Square is most famous for crowded Filipino get-togethers on Sundays, but they can be seen gathering there at other times. The number of Filipino guest workers in Hong Kong comes from my interviews with the NBI at the time of my 1993 trip. The NBI is responsible for checking to see that overseas foreign workers have no criminal records before they leave the country. Today, roughly 10 percent of the population of the Philippines, or eight million people, are guest workers around the world.

[236]: Ray Chau was deported on May 10, 1994. "The Search for Steven Wong" was published in *Saturday Night* in Toronto on April 1, 1994, and in Vancouver on April 7, as an enclosure in the *Vancouver Sun.*

CHAPTER 18 | Sex with Steve

[244]: Sources for the summary paragraph of Macau are listed below in notes for Chapter 19, which deals with these incidents in detail.

[245]: Jonathan Manthorpe, "Gangsters Flee Macau Before Handover," *Vancouver Sun,* October 25, 1999.

[247]: "Popular Way to Launder Money from Drugs and Illegal Deals," *Bangkok Post,* August 3, 1997. "Invasion of the Triads," *Bangkok Post,* November 11, 1999. Note: I have seen Pat Supapa's name spelled in various ways, including Pad Suphapha; I have chosen the simplest Anglicized spelling, used on a couple of occasions in the *Bangkok Post.*

CHAPTER 19 | Go Back, Jack, Do it Again

[253]: Information on attacks on journalists from Booth's *Dragon Syndicates,* pp. 325, 326.

[256]: Harold Bruning, "Gangsters Who Have Forgotten the Rules" *Sunday Morning Post*, December 12, 1999 (Sunday Focus Section, p. 10).

[258–265]: For events described in these pages I have relied on several sources: Booth's excellent reporting in *The Dragon Syndicates;* Bruning's "Gangsters Who Have Forgotten the Rules"; Stanley Ho's quotes in McGivering's *Macao Remembers* explaining the causes of the troubles, p.117; Ho's contention in 1997 that "when Macau changes hands to China all the Triads will run away," *Vancouver Sun*, October 25, 1999; *Bangkok Post* for accounts of the trial of Broken Tooth; interviews with cadets and officers at the Macau Police Academy on Coloane Island; Jonathan Manthorpe's reporting on Ho and Macau in the *Vancouver Sun*, October 25 and December 4, 1999; public relations press releases and tourist brochures issued by the Macau Government Tourist Office throughout the years described; CNN.com; Time.com; Lonely Planet's *Hong Kong, Macau & Guangzhou* (9th ed.); and *Macau Magazine*, December 1999.

CHAPTER 20 | Beware of Cruel Dogs

[278]: Epigraph: Robert Young Pelton's *The World's Most Dangerous Places* (New York: HarperResource, 2000), p. 411. Thai-Cambodian comparative 1999 tourism stats were given to me by *Phnom Penh Post* reporter Phelim Kyne. Total number of tourists visiting Thailand for 1999 was 10.5 million. The 3 percent figure for Cambodia is for tourists arriving by air, exclusive of day visitors arriving by land to pray for a few hours at a single temple on Cambodia's remote northern border with Thailand. In 1999, the Cambodian Ministry of Tourism published a booklet containing an estimate of the total number of tourists for that year, with 258,737 arriving by air and 440,662 arriving by land, three-quarters of the latter as day visitors to the temple. (The "328,424 land visitors to Preah Vihear temple . . . near the Thailand-Cambodia border . . . are only the same day visiting. They do not spend the night in this place visited.") By 2003 the figure for all tourist arrivals was up to 1 million, and the Cambodian Ministry of Tourism is predicting that the figure will be up to 2 million by 2006, according to www.circleofasia.com/News.asp?nlD=3. Other quotes and stats on Cambodia are from Lonely Planet's *South-East Asia*, 10th ed. (Hawthorne, Australia: Lonely Planet Publications, May, 1999); and Lonely Planet's *Cambodia*, 2nd and 3rd eds. (Hawthorne, Australia: Lonely Planet Publications, November 1996 and April 2000).

[281]: The Agence France-Press story on Tan Samarina and Piseth Pelika appeared in the *Bangkok Post* (and around the world) on December 14, 1999. I read the story on the morning of December 17.

[282]: Some background material on the Piseth Pelika story is from the *Phnom Penh Post*, October 29–November 11 and December 10–23, 1999, which printed Piseth Pelika's diary in full after *L'Express* printed sections of it. In October 1999, Hun Sen's wife, Bun Rany, threatened to sue *L'Express* over the diary, which stated that Pelika had received cash and a house from Hun Sen and that National Police Director Hok Lundy had warned Pelika that she might become the target of Bun Rany's wrath. A year later, the *Phnom Penh Post* reported in its October 27–November 9, 2000, edition that Bun Rany had taken no action on the suit.

[283]: For further information on Ly Yung Phat and the O'Smach story, see also "O'Smach vets battle mines and malaria," *Phnom Penh Post*, November 12–25, 1999, p. 1; and "Phnom Penh-Approved Development Prompts Turmoil," *Cambodia Daily*, November 13, 1999, p.14. See also this chapter, pp. 297–298.

[284]: "deteriorated significantly over the last few years" comes from page 1 of the "Phnom Penh Mini-Dublin Group Country Report, October 1999"; "a number of major organised crime groups based in Cambodia," comes from "Phnom Penh Mini-Dublin Group Second Meeting (5 October 1999)" p. 1. (The Dublin Group was founded in 1990 to help coordinate "counternarcotics efforts" internationally. It is composed of representatives from the United Nations Drug Control Programme (UNDCP), The United States, E.U. member states, Japan, Australia, Norway, and Canada. At the operational level, Mini-Dublin Groups meet periodically around the world to implement the goals of the organization.) "Called into question 'the integrity of parts of some enforcement agencies'" comes from the UNDCP October 4, 1999, draft report, "Strengthening the Secretariat of the National Authority for Combating Drugs and the National Drug Control Programme of Cambodia," p. 9.

[286]: The figure of 70 percent of government revenue disappearing into the pockets of corrupt politicians, and the later figures on Cambodian government corruption on pp. 295–297, come from Phelim Kyne's three-part series in the *Phnom Penh Post*: "Exploring Cambodia's evolution as the Kingdom of Corruption," "Cambodia's Kingdom of Corruption: The high cost of doing business," and "Cambodia's Kingdom of Corruption: Trying to find ways to turn the tide." The 70 percent figure was stated in the first article, June 11–24, 1999, p. 6, and was offered to Kyne by Sam Rainsy Party MP and veteran anti-corruption campaigner Son Chay: "From my point of view, Cambodia's [corruption] is the worst in Asia. In general, at least

70 percent of national revenue is lost to corruption." That figure was verified in my interviews with former finance minister Sam Rainsy, Senator Khieu San (vice chairman of the Senate Legislative Committee), as well as in off-the-record comments by a trustworthy Cambodian official and a trustworthy Canadian source working in Phnom Penh.

[287]: Henry Kamm, *Cambodia: Report from a Stricken Land* (New York: Arcade Publishing, 1998); David P. Chandler, *A History of Cambodia*, 2nd ed., (Boulder, Colo.: Westview Press, 1993).

[287–293]: My summary of modern Cambodian history is based on Kamm's *Cambodia*, Chandler's *History of Cambodia*, François Ponchaud's *Cambodia: Year Zero* (New York, Holt, Rinehart, Winston, 1977); Lonely Planet's *Cambodia* and *Southeast Asia*; my interviews with Cam Sylvester and Gordon Longmuir in Vancouver; the numerous people mentioned in the text whom I interviewed in Cambodia; as well as my own knowledge.

[293]: Patrick Symmes, "English Gin, Cambodian Tonic," *GQ*, October 1999, pp. 272, 273.

[293]: "A mob catches a thief? They torture and kill him right on the street." This is no exaggeration. A couple of days later, I witnessed and photographed a mob killing a thief just outside Sam Rainsy's headquarters, in front of half a dozen laughing policemen. According to the United Nations, at least 19 thieves were killed in this way in Phnom Penh in 1999, and 20 in 2000. See "Deadly mobs deal out justice in Cambodia," CNN.com, June 9, 2002.

[295]: Cambodian budget figures for 1999 come from Sarah Stephens, "Economic Data: A Familiar Story Emerges," *Phnom Penh Post*, November 12–25, 1999, and interviews with Senator Khieu San and Sam Rainsy.

[299]: The private dinner at which I met Hun Sen took place at the Kulen Restaurant in Siem Reap on the evening of December 31, 1999. See Chapter 23.

[299]: Hun Sen's televised forum was officially called "The Government-Private Sector Forum," but it dealt almost exclusively with the subject of corruption. See "PM Offers 'New Deal' to Private Sector," *Phnom Penh Post*, December 24, 1999–January 6, 2000, and "PM Slams Customs Corruption, Pledges Smuggling Crackdown," *Cambodia Daily*, December 22, 1999.

CHAPTER 21 | Port of Plenty

[303]: Epigraph from Harish C. Mehta and Julie B. Mehta, *Hun Sen: Strongman of Cambodia*, (Singapore: Graham Brash, 1999), p. 14.

[304]: Lonely Planet's *Cambodia* (3rd ed.) has a nice section on lingam worship and the blending of Indian and Khmer cultures, p. 13.

[304]: "I am a nation. I cannot listen to anyone's advice." Quoted in Mehta and Mehta's *Hun Sen: Strongman of Cambodia*, p. 79.

[305]: In Sihanoukville I confirmed the facts of the toxic dumping story; otherwise I have relied on Phelim Kyne's first-anniversary reporting of the event: "Sihanoukville Toxic Dumping: One Year On," *Phnom Penh Post*, November 26–December 9, 1999.

CHAPTER 22 | The Biggest Little Town in Cambodia

[319]: Pat Supapa is frequently mentioned as Hun Sen's adviser. See "New Routes to Link Trat with Cambodia," *Bangkok Post*, February 27, 2002: "The governor [of Koh Kong] said Hun Sen's advisor, Pat Supapa, who owns Casino Koh Kong International, donated US $7 million to the road project."

[319–320]: Allegations about Pat Supapa are contained in "Border Business/Gambling and Crime: Popular Way to Launder Money from Drugs and Illegal Deals," *Bangkok Post*, August 3, 1997, paragraphs 16, 17, 18 & 19: "Many Thai businessmen have been blacklisted by Thai and Cambodian narcotics suppression units for thier involvement in the drugs trade and other businesses, and for laundering money in Koh Kong.

"Among these business operators are ths so-called Four Tigers of Koh Kong: Praserty Siri, or Kamnan Jod, Pat Suphapha [sic], Siri Lertthasanakul and Nathee Anarmnart.

"The four have long played leading roles in cross-border trade and have close ties with Koh Kong authorities and the Cambodian government. They own a total of ten logging companies and up to 200 out of 500 shrimp farms in Koh Kong.

"Prasert, Pat and Siri are major shareholders of a one-billion baht Koh Kong International and Resort Project."

Information on the effects of the shrimp farms on Cambodia's mangrove fish-spawning grounds comes from Matt Wheeler, an official with the NGO Wetlands International.

[320]: Tha-nom's information about the road- and amusement-park development proved correct. Since I was in Koh Kong, Mr. Pat has completed his $7.2-million road from Phnom Penh, his bridge across the bay to Hay Lat, and the road over the hill to his casino megadevelopment on the Thai border. Most of the hotel-and-resort construction has also been completed, including a Seaworld-type amusement center that has outraged environmentalists. In May 2002, Mr. Pat purchased about a dozen endangered Irwaddy dolphins from local fishermen and hired a Russian trainer to teach them tricks. See "Dire Fate for Koh Kong's Dolphins," *Far Eastern Economic Review*, May 23, 2002. "Removing between 10 and 20 dolphins from Cambodian waters is a severe threat to an already endangered species," the *Review* quoted Isabel Beazley, of the New York–based Wildlife Conservation Society. The Ministry of Agriculture ordered Pat to release the rare mammals. "That's likely to cut little ice with Pat, who won friends in high places after recently funding a $7.2 million road and bridge link between Koh Kong and Thailand," the *Review* stated. "A grateful Cambodian Prime Minister Hun Sen designated him his personal advisor on the development of Koh Kong, according to one official." (The *Review* spells Pat's name Phat Supapa.)

[320]: The attack on Pat's resort: See "Gamblers wounded in grenade attack," *Bangkok Post*, November 17, 1998.

[323]: *Paths of Exploitation: Studies on the Trafficking of Women and Children between Cambodia, Thailand and Viet Nam*, International Organization for Migration, 1999, pp. 21–28.

For an additional portrait of the child sex trade around the time I was in Cambodia, see "Aid workers decry growing child-sex trade in Cambodia," CNN.com, September 18, 2000: "As governments in Southeast Asia crack down on the child sex trade, child protection experts say Cambodia is rapidly becoming the Asian destination of choice for pedophiles. 'It tends now to be a full-fledged destination,' said Sebastien Marot, a French aid worker who runs a Phnom Penh rehabilitation center for children. 'More and more tourists are coming to visit. More and more people are coming to be based here just for that,' he said. . . . Aid-workers say the police are little help; they say child-sex tourism is not only tolerated but protected by corrupt officials. 'There is corruption in the police,' said aid worker Pierre Legros. 'All these places are very well protected. It's very difficult to investigate and rescue people'" (www.cnn.com/2000/ASIANOW/southeast/09/18/cambodia.pedophile/index.html.

Stats on the lack of convictions for pimping children as of January 2000 are from Sari Nissi of IOM. Two years later, not much had changed. See "Sex offender jailed in Cambodia," CNN.com/WORLD, July 16, 2002: "In a rare prosecution for paedophilia, a Cambodian court has sentenced an Italian man to 10 years in prison for sexually abusing four homeless street boys between the ages 11 and 13. . . . Cambodia has a growing problem of paedophilia with thousands of tourists visiting the country each year from Japan, Europe and the United States for sex, often with children. . . . Cambodia has strict laws against commercial sex but they are infrequently enforced and convictions for paedophilia are rare."

CHAPTER 23 | Dawn of a New Millennium

[336]: Hun Sen acknowledged the existence of a ghost army on his payrolls a year and a half later. See "Cambodia: The Ruler's Rules," Hun Sen's interview with the *Far Eastern Economic Review*, May 10, 2001. The ghost army turned out to be even larger than Senator Khieu San had discovered. "I admit that there is corruption in Cambodia," said Hun Sen. "We have been cracking down on corruption in the army, in the police and in the administration because there has been what we call ghost soldiers, ghost police and ghost officials. We discovered that there were more than 15,000 ghost soldiers and more than 150,000 ghost dependents. Then we found more than 6,000 ghost officials and more than 4,000 ghost police. So this involves big sums of money. . . . We must solve these problems."

[337]: For Hun Sen's appendix operation and his ability to consummate the affair with Piseth Pelika, see "The Pelika Affair: 'We Have More,' Say French," *Phnom Penh Post*, October 15–28, 1999, p. 5: "Hun Sen's advisor Om Yentieng issued a statement denying the allegations of an affair and Bun Rany's involvement in the actress's death. . . . The statement went on to say . . . that there were inconsistencies in [Pelika's] diaries text, specifically that the relationship was supposedly consummated a month after Hun Sen had undergone surgery to remove his appendix. Yentieng said that Hun Sen still had stitches and an intravenous drip and was incapable of such actions. A western doctor spoken to by the *Post* said that generally stitches for such an operation would have been removed a week after surgery. He did not feel proficient to give a generic opinion on how soon a patient could resume marital relations."

[337]: For Hun Sen's singling out Customs Director Pen Siman at his televised forum, see "PM Slams Customs Corruption, Pledges Smuggling Crackdown," *Cambodia Daily*, December 22, 1999: "'Mr. Customs has to stop disturbing investors . . . customs is the king of corruption,' the prime minister said, singling out Customs Director Pen Siman in front of about 600 foreign investors at the Hotel Inter-Continental. 'Mr. Customs, you only have the right to practice the law . . . you are not allowed to change the price of goods imported to Cambodia at all.'

"Hun Sen pledged that customs officials who are found taking bribes will be fired. Though revelations of corruption have struck many government ministries and agencies, the prime minister chose Tuesday to single out the customs department, which is led by Pen Siman, a close associate of Chea Sim, the CPP president who is not part of Hun Sen's inner circle."

Two days after the forum, Phelim Kyne explained to me that Hun Sen perceived Chea Sim as a threat to his power, and "in order to sideline Chea Sim, he can cut his supply networks to cash, which [comes from] milking the customs branch."

[337]: "Life after Sihanouk," *Bangkok Post*, November 15, 2001, discusses Hun Sen's choice of Queen Monineath to replace the ailing king as a temporary symbol of the crown, and Hun Sen's ultimate motive: to end the monarchy in Cambodia.

[339–340]: Most of what Wheeler told me was backed up by an article on fisheries corruption, Bou Saroeun's "Fisheries Reform Seems All Talk, No Action," *Phnom Penh Post*, December 9, 2000, and a sidebar, "Anarchy and Violence: The Fishing Lot System." Hun Sen's quote in the footnote on page 340, and the comments of the new Fisheries Department director are from this article.

CHAPTER 24 | The Ghost of Manila

[347]: Newspapers: "Stanley Ho's P600-M Floating Resto Arrives," *Philippine Daily Inquirer*, January 3, 2000; "Sin Condemns Arrival of Floating Casino," *Philippine Daily Inquirer*, January 4, 2000; "Floating Casino Branded Vice Lure," *South China Morning Post*, January 4, 2000; "A Jumbo Headache Says Angry Cardinal," *Hong Kong Standard*, January 4, 2000.

[347–348]: Archbishop Oscar Cruz previously quoted: "It's a crime, bishops warn Erap on gambling," *Philippine Daily Inquirer*, October 14, 1999. See also "Sin, Two Solons [senators] Slam Culture of Gambling," *Philippine Daily Inquirer*, October 12, 1999.

[348]: Stanley Ho's trip to the Philippines to announce his chairmanship of BW Resources took place on October 11, 1999. Coverage of that trip, his announcements at the Stock Exchange and Malacañang, and Perfecto Yasay's news conference on BW comes in part from "Estrada Hails Investment of Macau Casino Tycoon" and "SEC Steps up Probe of BW Resources," both *Philippine Daily Inquirer*, October 12, 1999, as well as "Stock Market Nearly Crashed, Yasay Reveals," *Philippine Daily Inquirer*,

October 24, 1999. I also interviewed numerous sources in the Philippines about that trip, most of whom are mentioned in the text.

[349–351]: Edgardo Espiritu resigned on January 5, 2000; the undersecretary for communication, Josefina T. Lichauco, followed suit January 7. See "Lichauco Quits; Espiritu Hits Gov't Corruption," *Philippine Daily Inquirer,* January 8, 2000. The press conference of Senator Loren Legarda, chair of the Citizen's Drug Watch Foundation, took place on January 4. See "Solon [senator] Laments Corruption in Anti-drugs Drive," *Manila Times,* January 4, 2000.

The Philippines House of Representatives called for hearings into Ho and the Jumbo on January 14, 2000. See "Macau Casino King Faces House Probe," *Philippine Daily Inquirer,* January 15, 2000. The lead to the story reads: "Macau casino king Stanley Ho will be asked to answer allegations in Congress linking him to the notorious Chinese Triad gangs involved in drugs trafficking in Hong Kong."

Erap checking with National Police Chief Panfilo "Ping" Lacson on clearing Ho: "Erap, Ping Clear Ho," *Philippine Daily Inquirer,* February 1, 2000. Three days later the *Inquirer* reported that Lacson claimed to have been misquoted on clearing Ho. See "Stanley Ho Not Yet Cleared, says PNP," *Philippine Daily Inquirer,* February 3, 2000. Stanley Ho's reaction to allegations: "Stanley Ho Warns He'll Pull Out of RP [Republic of Philippines]," *Philippine Daily Inquirer,* January 24, 2000; "Ho Cancels RP Trip amid Public Uproar," *Philippine Daily Inquirer,* January 31, 2000; and "House Probe an Insult—Stanley Ho," *Philippine Daily Inquirer,* February 5, 2000.

Ho's ads in papers, Perfecto Yasay's claim that Estrada had pressured him to clear Tan, and demonstrations in front of the Jumbo with poster burning: "Ho Cancels RP Trip amid Public Uproar," *Philippine Daily Inquirer,* January 31, 2000. See also coverage in Vancouver: "The Ho Connection," *The Province,* March 9, 2000, and "Ho Buys an Ad to Deny Any Links with Organized Crime," *The Province,* March 10, 2000.

[351]: The daily exposés of the *Philippine Daily Inquirer* and the Philippine Center for Investigative Journalism are too numerous to catalog here, but are collected in the archives of both organizations, as well as in *Investigating Estrada: Millions, Mansions and Mistresses—A compilation of investigative reports,* edited by Sheila S. Coronel (Manila: Philippine Center for Investigative Journalism, 2000), and Dr. Dirk J. Barreveld, *Erap Ousted!* (Cebu, Philippines: Arcilla, Inc., 2001). The Philippine Gaming and Amusement Board granted BW the on-line rights to bingo gambling on January 5, 2000. See "Best-World Given Authority to Run Bingo-Jueteng Game," *Philippine Daily Inquirer,* January 5, 2000.

For first mention that the BW scandal was threatening Erap's presidency, see "Dante Tan: Bingo King Self-Made Man," *Philippine Daily Inquirer,* January 21, 2000:

"The self made man is in the center of a political storm that is now threatening the presidency of Joseph Estrada." Jerry Berican's quote comes from Timeasia.com, May 29, 2000. The number of journalists murdered since the mid-'80s (1986) comes from the *Philippine Daily Inquirer,* the Philippine Center for Investigative Journalism, and the Philippine Press Institute. The 37th journalist was murdered in November 2000. See, for instance, "Another Journalist Gunned down in Pagadian City," *Philippine Daily Inquirer,* May 15, 2002, which mentions the total to that point as 38, and "Group Says 3 Media Persons Slain a Year," *Philippine Daily Inquirer,* August 25, 2003, in which the National Union of Journalists gives the latest total as 43.

At this writing the number of journalists murdered is up to 44. However, the total number of all "media persons" murdered in the Philippines since 1986 has been estimated by the *Daily Inquirer* as being as high as 73. See www.inq.7.net, December 3, 2003, "Another Hard-hitting Broadcaster Shot Dead," in which the *Inquirer* reports that Nelson V. Nadura "was the 50th media person to be killed in the country since 1986, according to the National Union of Journalists of the Philippines (NUJP). *Inquirer* records, however, showed he was the 73rd fatality."

[355]: The Supreme Court ruled in Jimenez's favor on January 18, 2000. Under pressure from several foreign governments, including the United States, Canada, and the Hong Kong SAR—which all submitted briefs—the court reversed itself on October 17, 2000, and allowed extradition proceedings. However, Jimenez was not extradicted to the United States until over two years later, on December 26, 2002. For chronology of the Jimenez epic, see "Jimenez: 5 Years of Court Battles, Political Scandals," *Philippine Daily Inquirer,* August 3, 2003.

[356]: See Yvonne T. Chua and Luz Rimban, "Gatekeeper," in Coronel, ed., *Pork and Other Perks* pp. 150–185. Chua and Rimban wrote their article before the September 11, 2001, attacks on the World Trade Center. Ramzi Yousef's seized computer files revealed that Yousef plotted flying planes into buildings while he was in the Philippines. See John Miller and Michael Stone, with Chris Mitchell, *The Cell: Inside the 9/11 Plot, and Why the FBI and CIA Failed to Stop It* (New York: Hyperion, 2002), pp.122–124.

CHAPTER 25 | "Ping"

[361]: Mary Ong was interviewed over several nights by reporter Richard Rivera, on the Manila TV station Channel 9. The TV appearances of Mary Ong, her alliance with Reynaldo Berroya, and Berroya's history as an antagonist of Panfilo Lacson were extensively covered by the Philippine daily press. See, for instance, the summary

article "Berroya Is New PNP Intelligence Chief," by Christina Mendez, *Philippine Star*, April 18, 2001, pp. 1, 4. The article features a photo of Mary Ong with Berroya at his swearing-in as intelligence chief of the PNP. I interviewed numerous sources about these events, all of whom are mentioned in Chapters 25, 26, 27, and 28.

[362]: The Kuratong Baleleng killings, and Lacson's role in them, have been extensively covered by the Philippine daily media. I interviewed numerous sources about these events, all of whom are mentioned in Chapters 25, 26, 27, and 28.

[363–365]: The impeachment of President Joseph Estrada was extensively covered by the Philippine daily media. I interviewed numerous sources about these events, all of which are mentioned in Chapters 25, 26, 27, and 28.

On October 22, 2003, Hilario Davide, the chief justice of the Supreme Court who swore in Macapagal-Arroyo as president, was himself impeached by the House of Representatives over alleged misuse of millions of dollars of a judiciary development fund. On November 10, in a 13–1 ruling, the Supreme Court ruled the House impeachment complaint unconstitutional, stopping it from being sent to the Senate for trial. The House withdrew the impeachment complaint.

[370]: President Macapagal-Arroyo's quote can be found on: www.time.com/time/asia/magazine/2001/0129/arroyo.html

[370–371]: The Salvadore "Bubby" Dacer killings, and Lacson's role in them, were extensively covered by the Philippine daily media. The details related here, including Jerome's explanation, are to be found in the *Philippine Daily Inquirer*, April 1 and April 16, 2001.

[372]: 1993 arrest of Beroya: I still have the September 28, 1993, copy of *The Philippine Star*, whose headline reads: "Alqueza Surrenders; Berroya Set to Yield." The first paragraph reads: "Police Chief Superintendent Dictador Alqueza surrendered last Sunday to the military as the Presidential Anti-Crime Commission (PACC) readied five more kidnap-for-ransom charges against him and Senior Superintendent Reynaldo Berroya." Lacson, as the investigating officer, crops up on page 2 of the article: "Senior Superintendent Panfilo Lacson, chief of the PACC's Task Force Hagabat, told reporters at Camp Crame that they have started investigating the possible involvement of Alqueza and Berroya in five other kidnapping cases." A summary of the Berroya case can be found in Mendez, "Berroya Is New PNP Intelligence Chief."

[373]: The scandals of Mike Arroyo: *The Philippine Daily Inquirer* reported on the affair on July 21, 2001: "Ex-Malacañang-Aide Says Mike Arroyo Took Bribe."

Allegations of financial malfeasance against Mike Arroyo eventually led to the launching of a Senate investigation in February 2003 (see Chapter 28), and ballooned into a full-fledged national scandal in the summer of 2003, when Senator Panfilo Lacson uncovered evidence that Mike Arroyo had allegedly siphoned more than 200 million pesos (about $4 million) of campaign contributions into secret bank accounts. See "Lacson Accuses President's Husband of Pocketing P213M," *Philippine Daily Inquirer*, August 19, 2003.

[374]: "Jueteng Is Bleeding the Poor," editorial, *Philippine Daily Inquirer*, November 9, 2002: "It has been estimated that the gross yearly take of gambling lords from jueteng is 20 billion pesos." In 1995, the Philippine Center for Investigative Journalism ran an excellent series of articles on *jueteng*, which can be found in their on-line archives. For a discussion on the open disparagement of the poor and the Chinese in the Philippine media, see "Clash of Classes," *Philippine Daily Inquirer*, May 12, 2001.

[375–376]: Information on the Philippine media comes from Chay Florentino-Hofilena, *News for Sale: The Corruption of the Philippine Media* (Manila: Philippine Center for Investigative Journalism and the Center for Media Freedom and Responsibility, 1998) p. 91: "This is what our survey says. When offered money by their sources, one of every three beat reporters openly admitted to taking it." *News for Sale* is a remarkable book. Here is a passage from its introduction: "The organized way in which corruption takes place—through a network of journalists reporting to other journalists or to professional public relations or PR people—makes it seem almost like the operation of a criminal syndicate, a mafia of corrupt practictioners" (p. 7). Definitions of the corrupt practices such as "Inteligentsia" are to be found in the glossary, p. 16.

CHAPTER 26 | Amok

[386]: For a discussion on the great hope, and ultimate failure, of the EDSA Revolution, see "Real Change," an editorial in the *Philippine Daily Inquirer*, February 24, 2003 (www.inq7.net/opi/2003/feb/25/text/opi_editorial-1-p.htm).

[387]: For an article that highlights the rumors surrounding Air Force Chief Benjamin Defensor at the time of EDSA III, see the *Philippine Daily Inquirer*, April 29, 2001, "Armed Forces Top Brass Holds Closed-door Meeting": "Top officials of the Armed Forces of the Philippines (AFP) are now conducting a closed-door meeting at the AFP general headquarters at Camp Aguinaldo in Quezon City. Led by AFP Chief

of Staff Diomedio Villanueva, the top brass is holding the meeting amid speculations that some military groups are plotting a coup, according to a radio report.... Among those named as possible coup plotters is Lt. Gen. Benjamin Defensor, chief of the Philippine Air Force (PAF), the report said. The PAF chief is the brother of reelectionist Sen. Miriam Defensor-Santiago, a staunch ally of deposed President Joseph Estrada. Defensor has denied earlier reports linking him to a possible coup attempt."

[387]: The purposeful underestimation of the EDSA crowd:

In the weeks after the collapse of EDSA III, the mainstream Philippine media indulged in much self-reflection about the way they had purposely ignored the rally of the poor—that is, until it had exploded into an attack on the palace that almost overthrew the government. One of the first to do so was Conrado de Quiros, perhaps the most trenchant columnist in the the *Philippine Daily Inquirer*'s stable. On May 4, 2001, he offered the following analysis on the Opinion page: "I do have a problem with chest-beating [over the defeat of EDSA III], with pious exultation about the forces of good triumphing over the forces of evil. I do have a problem with reducing the two or three million people who massed at EDSA to 'Erap Loyalists' who would wither away, the way Marcos loyalists withered away. This is more than a 'loyalist' phenomenon, it will not go away by being ignored.

"We have to open our eyes to the size of that crowd, we have to open our ears to the cries of that crowd. Not all of what they were saying was mythical and emotional and superstitious. Some of what they were saying was perfectly rational. Chief of them, their call for past leaders who have been accused of corruption to be prosecuted as well—Cory Aquino and Fidel Ramos at the head of them. Why only Erap? The curious thing about 'EDSA III,' quite incidentally, was that it wasn't just directed against President Gloria Macapagal-Arroyo, it was directed against Jaime Cardinal Sin, Cory and Ramos. That perception isn't irrational either: it is based on the very real influence, if not control, of Sin, Cory and Ramos, over Ms Macapagal's administration, which is what gives it its elitist sheen. Which raises the more fundamental, and very rational, question of whom EDSA I and EDSA II were fought for. There is no doubt they were fought *by* the people: But whom were they fought *for*? For Cory? For Sin? For Ramos? For Ms. Macapagal? For the rich?

"But infinitely more than that, we must open our eyes and our ears to the throng that gathered at EDSA because of the non-mythical and ineluctable reality of their invisibility and muteness, an invisibility and muteness that, like volcanoes, produce catastrophic results when they blaze forth with fire and roar into visibility and audibleness."

[400]: Quotes and information on Lacson from McCoy's *Closer than Brothers*, pp. 206, 217, 267, 331, 335–336.

CHAPTER 27 | City of the Living Dead

[403]: Details about Gloria and Cory's attendance at church and helicopters being put on red alert are from TV reports that day, and the next day's coverage in the *Philippine Daily Inquirer*: "Gloria, Cory Summon 'Prayer Power,'" and "AFP Forms Anti-coup Task Force," April 30, 2001.

[413]: The number of dead from the attack at Malacañang was initially put at four, then raised to seven in accounts published a couple of weeks later.

[415]: Given the hysteria in the capital, Jerome Tang's concern for Lacson's safety was probably not unjustified. On May 4, 2001, the tabloid *People's Journal Tonight* proclaimed on its front page: "As government agents, armed with shoot-to-kill orders, intensified their hunt for Senator Gringo Honasan and former Philippine National Police Chief Panfilo Lacson, the Department of Justice yesterday revealed that the people who allegedly orchestrated the attempt to storm Malacañang had planned to kill President Gloria Macapagal-Arroyo and her predecessor, Joseph Estrada."

[416]: The opposition's appeal of the State of Rebellion can be found in "No Legal Basis for Rebellion Declaration," *Philippine Daily Inquirer*, May 3, 2001, p. 1.

[416]: I did in fact phone Jerome's lawyer, Peter Chapman, in Vancouver, and spent an hour explaining Lacson's plight.

CHAPTER 28 | Can We Start Again, Please?

[425]: Chong Yuk-sui is mentioned on p. 6 of Senate *Committee Report No. 66*, under the heading "The Rosebud Story": "One of the high-level Hong Kong Triad bosses whom she [Mary Ong] met was Mr. Lee Ming Yu, the head of the drug trafficking organization in Macau who, according to the Hong Kong police, uses three or four different aliases, one of them Ah Tau, and is the holder of Macau, Mainland China and Hong Kong passports. Another was Chong Yuk Sui, alias Ah Sui, a 14K Hong Kong North Point District Triad boss, who acted as the agent or representative of Lee."

[425]: The story of Joe Co, aka Jose Canino Co, is told on pp. 8 and 9 of Senate *Committee Report No. 66*.

[426–427]: The recommendation of a criminal investigation regarding Lacson's use of Kim Wong's cell phone is on p. 95 of Senate *Committee Report No. 66*. See also "Lacson Cell Phone Traced to Drug Lord," *Philippine Daily Inquirer*, August 12, 2001: "Sought for comment, Lacson said the phone did come from a Chinese-Filipino businessman and friend Kim Wong, but 'not the same Kim Wong' whom Corpus was accusing of being a drug lord."

The quote on Mary Ong's glamorous appearance comes from Monica Feria's article "China Chic," *Mirror* magazine, October 2001, p. 4.

[427]: The story of Mary Ong's life that she related to me is completely consistent with the one contained in Senate *Committee Report No. 66*, which was independently investigated. Her fees for services to the PNP are given in *Report No. 66*, p. 28.

[428]: Yakuza and the 14K: See "Lacson Cell Phone Traced to Drug Lord": "According to ISAFP [Intelligence Service of the Armed Forces of the Philippines] officers, the 14K crime group has a 'tie-up' with the Yakuza, the Japanese international crime ring." This "tie-up" was first reported by Japanese police in 1979. See David E. Kaplan and Alec Dubro of the Center for Investigative Reporting, San Francisco, *Yakuza: The Explosive Account of Japan's Criminal Underworld* (New York: MacMillan, 1986), pp. 217, 236.

[429]: The murders of John Campos and Teofila Vina have been thoroughly reported in the daily Philippine press. I confirmed the details I have related in the text with army intelligence chief Victor Corpus and NBI director Reynaldo Wycoco.

[430]: Arroyo's announcement that God had told her not to run in 2004 has been extensively quoted in the international press. See, for instance, "Philippine Mutineers Surrender," *National Post*, July 28, 2003, p. A9.

[430–431]: The Nani Perez case has been widely covered in the Philippine media. I was present in the Senate on Febrary 4, 2003, when the Senate voted to launch an investigative committee to look into Jimenez's allegations that Mike Arroyo had extorted $2 million from him. Arroyo's problems ballooned in the summer of 2003, when Senator Panfilo Lacson uncovered evidence that Mike Arroyo had allegedly siphoned more than 200 million pesos (about $4 million) of campaign contributions into secret bank accounts. See "Lacson Accuses President's Husband of Pocketing P213M," *Philippine Daily Inquirer*, August 19, 2003. For footnote on Jimenez, see "Mark Jimenez Pleads Guilty to Tax, Fraud Charges," *Philippine Daily Inquirer*, August 3, 2003 (www.inq7.net/nat/2003/aug/text/nat_9–1-p.htm).

[131–132]: Rundown of events in Philippines

—For 87 people killed in barangay elections, see "Election Violence Latest Count: 87 Dead, 45 Hurt," *Philippine Daily Inquirer,* July 17, 2002 (www.inq7.net/nat/2002 /jul/17/text/nat_3–1p.htm).

—"A battalion of American soldiers": see the *Philippine Daily Inquirer,* which a couple of months later, April 15, 2003, gave these figures for anti-terrorist exercises: "About 350 US Special Forces troops, mostly Green Berets, would be involved, backed by about 400 more US soldiers based in the adjacent key city of Zamboanga and about 1,000 Marines aboard US battleships off the coasts of Sulu" (www.inq7.net/opi/2003/apr/15/text/opi_editorial-1-p.htm).

—"MILF Counterattacks; 16 Gov't Soldiers Dead," *Philippine Daily Inquirer,* January 25, 2003, and "NPA Hit Squads Target Gov't Officials," *Philippine Daily Inquirer,* January 24, 2003.

—"In Mindanao's cities, 10 terrorist blasts set by Islamic rebels have killed 70 civilians and wounded over 400," see www.inq.net/nat/2003/mar/05/textnat_11–1-p.htm: "Chronology of Bomb Blasts in Mindanao over Last Year."

—"In Manila, the embassies of Canada, Australia, and the European Union were recently closed for a week after a terrorist bus bomb killed or severely wounded two dozen civilians and information surfaced that the embassies would be next." This story was widely covered in the international press. See, for instance, the *Vancouver Sun,* October 19, 2002.

—"Travel warnings from foreign capitals come and go with frightening frequency." These include warnings from Canada, Australia, all the nations in the EU, plus the United States and New Zealand, and continue to the present. See, for instance, "New Zealand, Canada Issue Travel Advisories against RP," *Philippine Daily Inquirer,* July 24, 2003 (www.inq7.net/brk/2003/jul/brkpol_18–1.htm).

—"The national debt has ballooned to a historic high": See, for instance, "S&P Downgrades Philippine Credit Rating," *Philippine Daily Inquirer,* April 24, 2003: "Rating firm Standard & Poor's said Thursday it has cut the Philippines sovereign credit rating because of the government's growing debt burden. . . . 'Servicing the growing debt burden is expected to consume about 38 percent of government revenues this year, considerably more than the 22 percent in 1999,' S&P said."

—"The peso is near its historic low": See, for instance, "Peso Falls to 2-Year Low," *Philippine Daily Inquirer,* February 20, 2003, "The peso closed at 54.199 per dollar . . . the lowest close since January 18, 2001," that is, at the height of the Estrada impeachment crisis. The peso continued to fall, and on October 27, 2003, surpassed the low of January 18, 2001.

—"Organized crime now accounts for between 10 and 20 percent of the country's gross domestic product." From the Philippine Center for Investigative

Journalism's *Public Eye* on-line magazine, January-March 2003, "Criminals, Inc.": "Organized crime is a multibillion-peso industry in the Philippines, its earnings, by conservative estimates, equivalent to 10 to 20 percent of the Philippine gross domestic product, or anywhere from P300 to P600 billion every year. (www.pcij.org/imag/PublicEye/criminals.html).

—"The Philippines is the regular recipient of bad marks from overseas watchdog organizations. Amnesty International has just released a report stating that torture by the police is rampant." See "Torture Still Rampant in RP: Amnesty International" (www.inq7.net/brk/2003/jan/24/text/brkpol_13–1-p.htm).

—"The U.S. Bureau for International Narcotics and Law Enforcement Affairs has released another report stating the country is a drug smugglers' paradise." See "RP drug smugglers' paradise, says US"(www.inq7.net/nat/2003/mar/17/text/nat_5–1-p.htm).

—"Of particular concern to me, three more journalists have been murdered in the last eight months, allegedly on the orders of the politicians they had exposed." See "Group Says 3 Media Persons Slain a Year."

—"Despite its free and lively press, or perhaps because of it, the Philippines is one of the most dangerous places in the world for journalists." See "A Dangerous Place to Be a Journalist," December 9, 2002, in the archives of the Philippine Center for Investigative Journalism.

—"Meanwhile, Lacson has promised to end the chaos." See "A Tough Line at the Top," *Far Eastern Economic Review,* February 20, 2003, p. 20.

—For other stats that show the Philippines on the brink of collapse around the time of my visit, see "Angara: 'House of Cards,'" *Philippine Daily Inquirer,* July 25, 2002 (http://www.inq7.net/nat/2002/jul/25/text/nat_9–1-p.htm).

—"Thirty-two million Filipinos live on less than 23 pesos a day." That is, 40 percent of the population of 80 million live on less than 40 cents a day.

—"More than one in three children are malnourished."

—"In April 2002, 500,000 more joined the unemployed of five million, bloating the unemployment rate from 13.3 to 14 percent."

—"At least 2,670 Filipinos leave the country each day to find work."

—"Four out of 10 students who enroll in first grade do not reach sixth grade."

—"Water rates have gone up by almost 150 percent after the privatization of the water system." (Despite the high rates, 20 million Filipinos don't have access to clean water, according to a later article in *The Philippine Daily Inquirer:* "20M Filipinois don't have access to clean water" (www.inq7.net/brk/2003/jun/02/text/brkpol_2–1-p.htm).

—"Since the passage of the power reform act, households are now paying up to eight percent of their 4,000 pesos monthly income to pay for the cost of Purchased Power Adjustment."

—"National government debt stock is at 2.6 trillion pesos. The total debt stock, however, including borrowing from other agencies, is now at 3.03 trillion pesos. This translates to a debt of 37,875 pesos for every Filipino."

—"Tax collection has reached an all-time low of 11.2 percent. The government has also been unable to collect receivables totaling over 336 billion pesos."

[433]: Legarda as Lacson's potential running mate: In my Februay 4, 2003, interview with Lacson, he confirmed that Senator Loren Legarda's representatives had approached him about being his running mate in the 2004 election. The link between Legarda's vice-presidential ambitions and the shelving of the Lacson report has been frequently made in the Philippine media. See Isagani Cruz, "When Will the Senate Decide Lacson case?" *Philippine Daily Inquirer,* editorial, April 5, 2003: "Last November, Senator Loren Legarda, Senate majority floor leader, assured me that the Lacson report would be calendared soon for deliberation by the Senate plenary. That was more than five months ago and the nation is still waiting. If the Senators did not intend to decide the Lacson case in the first place, why did they choose to investigate him at all? Maybe some of them now want to be his running mate?" (www.inq7.net/opi/2003/apr/05/text/opi_iacruz-1p.htm).

Later in the year, Belinda Olivares-Cunan was more specific in her charge, in the *Philippine Daily Inquirer* editorial "Let's Have that Report," June 25, 2003: "Current talk is that Legarda has not acted on it [*Report 66*] in order to protect Lacson, who has invited her to be his running mate" (www.inq7.net/2003/jun/26/text/opi_bocunanan-p.htm).

Lacson successfully blocked the report completely on August 6, 2003. See "Lacson Blocks Senate Inquiry Report about Him," *Philippine Daily Inquirer:* "Senator Panfilo Lacson on Tuesday succeeded in blocking the adoption of Senate Committee Report No. 66, which recommended that he be indicted for the capital crimes of kidnapping, drug trafficking, smuggling and summary executions" (www.inq7.net/nat/ 2003/aug/06/text/nat_7–1-p.htm).

[433]: "Thorn in Lacson's side," see: www.inq7.net/exclusive/2001/sep/27/rosebud_27–1-1.htm.

[436]: The *Philippine Daily Inquirer* editorial on Confidential Agents, see Inq7.net, December 20, 2002.

[436]: Ramon Tulfo, "More about Ping Lacson," *Philippine Daily Inquirer,* July 19, 2001. The column is addressed to Ping Lacson: "You personally kicked two women, Magdalena Apostol, 33, and her niece, Carmelita Intal, 25, out of a helicopter which was flying over Manila Bay. The women's only crime was that they were the sister and niece, respectively, of Alfredo 'Joey' de Leon, leader of a kidnap-for-ransom

syndicate. . . . You ordered the execution of two girls, 19 and seven years old, when you were still at the MISG because they were witness to the 'salvaging' by your men of a crime suspect."

[440]: Jonathan Manthorpe, "The Princess, the PM and Cambodian Politics," *Vancouver Sun,* p. A18, February 22, 2003. The incidents related were covered around the world.

[440]: The estimates of loss were given in "Cambodia Moves to Mollify Thailand," an Associated Press story published in the *Philippine Daily Inquirer,* p. A14, February 5, 2003.

[440–441]: Amnesty International quote in "Phnom Penh Governor Ousted After Anti-Thai Riots," Washingtonpost.com, February 11, 2003. Ranariddh's and Hun Sen's quotes are from "Cambodia King Delays China Trip as Crisis Deepens," Washingtonpost.com, February 20, 2003. "Motorcycle Death Squads Silence Those Who Oppose Prime Minister Hun Sen," *National Post,* October 23, 2003.

[442]: "Metro Manila Has Only Half the Fire Trucks It Needs," *Philippine Daily Inquirer,* February 22, 2003 (www.inq7.net/brk/2003/feb/22/text/brkoth_1–1-p.htm).

[442]: The expiration of Ho's monopoly: see Mellor's "Stanley Ho's Secret Weapon," Asia-Inc.com, October 2002, in which Mellor reports that Ho's 40-year casino monopoly in Macau "officially" ended on March 31, 2002.
    Steve Wynn: See Verna Yu's "Macau Gaming: Kingpins to square off," on-line edition of the *Las Vegas Review Journal,* June 25, 2002, in which Yu reports that on June 24, Steve Wynn signed a casino franchise with Macau's Tender Committee for Gaming Concession. The Tender Committee later awarded another gambling franchise to the owner of Vegas's Venetian Hotel and Casino, Sheldon Adelson.

EPILOGUE | Impunity

[447]: According to Staff Sergeant Karel Waversveld, the current head of Unit One, in the summer of 2003 there was some "paperwork" handled by the Department of Justice that dealt with the possibility of a stay of Steven Wong's charges. By December, the stay had gone through.

ACKNOWLEDGMENTS

———

For 12 of the 14 years I've been reporting on Steven Wong I've had a secret weapon—Anne Collins, the publisher and editor of this book. Mere words cannot express my gratitude to Anne for her genius as an editor, her vision as a journalist, and her egoless patience as a teacher. Anne edited my first story for *Saturday Night* magazine in 1992, back when Steve was still planning his death. Two years later, just after she worked her magic on "The Search for Steven Wong," she began urging me to write *Paper Fan*. When I took her up on that challenge in 1999, I knew that without her help there would be no book. For four years—through many drafts and trips overseas—Anne kept me going, then gave me the critical help I needed to cross the finish line. If I've had any success writing *Paper Fan*, I share it with Anne. If I've made any mistakes, they are my own.

If Anne Collins was my secret weapon, then my hidden collaborator was my wife, Leslie Hoffman Gould. Leslie's cameo appearances in these pages do not begin to reveal her ubiquitous presence in my research and writing. Since the age of 20 I have done nothing of value independent of Leslie; she was crucial to every plan I executed in my hunt for Steve and was behind every page I wrote. Leslie toured the underworld with me, read drafts of chapters, transcribed interview tapes, took long distance calls from me at 3 A.M. when I was in Asia, and sought out and met with cops who saved my skin—all while she worked a full-time job. My brave sidekick and constant helpmate has always seen the good side to my *mishegoss*.

Certain lawmen who have been of particular assistance to my research have requested that I not single them out from their colleagues in these acknowledgments. Others, because of the classified nature of their work, have asked not to be named at all. I thank all the men and women in law enforcement, both retired and active, who over the years both helped advance my knowledge of organized crime and protected my life. Some of them are listed below, followed by their assignments at the time they helped the reporting that has contributed to this book:

In the United States: Don Yeowell (Seattle Police, Intelligence Division);

John Scott (U.S. Department of Justice, Immigration and Naturalization Service, Investigations, Seattle); Robert Hughes (U.S. Department of Justice, Mediator, Seattle); Edward Madonna and Gary Liming (Drug Enforcement Administration, Seattle); Daniel Foley, Richard Moses, Wayne S. Hom, Tom Perdue, and Felix Thieu (San Francisco Police, Gang Task Force); John Lee and W. Earl Humphry (Immigration and Naturalization Service, Investigations, San Francisco); Geoffrey Anderson (U.S. Department of Justice, San Francisco Strike Force); Diane B. de Forest (U.S. Department of Justice, Organized Crime Strike Force, San Francisco); Michael Yamaguchi (U.S. Attorney, San Francisco); Louie Valdivia (U.S. Customs Service, Intelligence, Terminal Island, California); Samuel Blake (Immigration and Naturalization Service, Investigations, San Francisco); Barry Mawn (FBI, San Francisco); Jones Moy (Monterey Park Police, Asian Crime Intelligence); Randy Quan and Dan Parks (Los Angeles Police Department, Organized Crime Intelligence Division); Tony Lanzaratta (Los Angeles Police Department); Terry Cramer (Orange County Police); Marcus Franks (Westminster Police, Asian Task Force); Jack Willoughby (New Orleans Police, Asian Task Force); Omar Longoria (U.S. Department of Justice, Intelligence Liaison Officer); Phil Baridon (U.S. Department of Justice, Washington, D.C.); Charles Smith (New Jersey State Police, Intelligence, Asian Crime Group); Eric Kruss (FBI, New York).

In Canada, from the Vancouver City Police: Bill Marshall (Chief); Don Keith (Head of the Vancouver Drug and Vice Squad); Martin Turner, Bill Chu, Peter Ditchfield, Bobby Cooper, and Andy Nimmo (Asian Crime Squad); Scott Cooke and Viggo Elvevoll (Asian Based Organized Crime, Intelligence); Guy Pollock (Organized Crime, Intelligence); Scott Driemel (Internal Investigations); Brian Honeyburn and Tom Ritchie (Southside Crime Squad); Bob Law and Merne McClennan (Major Crime); Tom Span (patrol). From the Royal Canadian Mounted Police: Peter Eakins and Kirk Davies (Commercial Crime Squad); Jerry Moloci, Karel Waversveld, Murray Dauk, Mike Hiller, and Keith Hildebrandt (Unit One); Rick Aselton and Fred McCandie (Drug Section, Street Crew); Roy Bergerman and Serge Martell (Drug Intelligence); Glen Hooper (Immigration Squad); Garry Clement, Garry Lagimodiere, and Paul Brown (Hong Kong Liaison Officers); Mike Russell and Sharon McWilliams (patrol). From Revenue Canada: Bill McKissock (Chief, Enforcement Policy and Liaison, Interdiction Division, Ottawa). From Criminal Intelligence Service: Ernest Poupore (Ottawa). From the Department of Justice: Peter Eccles, Jim McBride, Harry Wruck, and Mark Levitz. And from the Canadian Embassy in the Philippines: Martin Tremblay (Intelligence Officer and Second Secretary).

In the Philippines, from the National Bureau of Investigations. Reynaldo Wycoco (Director); Philip Pecadre, Virgilio Mendez, and Rommel Ramirez (agents); Moises Tamayo (Organized Crime Intelligence); Ricardo Diaz (Chief of Interpol for the Philippines); Danilo Mendez (NBI liaison). From the Armed Forces of the Philippines: Victor Corpus (Chief of Intelligence). Mary Ong (former agent, Philippine National Police and Royal Hong Kong Police). As detailed in this book, my relationship with Senator Panfilo Lacson, former head of the Philippine National Police, has grown complex as it has evolved. I am very grateful for the time and help he offered me in 2001, and for his willingness to meet with me on numerous occasions since, both in Manila and Vancouver.

In Hong Kong, from the Royal Hong Kong Police: Stephen Vickers and Ken Taylor (Criminal Intelligence Bureau); Bob Youill (Organized Crime and Triad Bureau).

In Cambodia, from the Anti-Corruption Unit: Secretary of State Sum Manit (former head of the National Authority to Combat Drugs). Immigration: Captain Khim Keo. From Cambodian National Police: Colonel Chea Kimly (Deputy Chief).

In the Netherlands, Arie Bax and Toon Schalks from Criminal Intelligence Service.

Many academics, politicians, ambassadors, journalists, NGO workers, defense lawyers, businesspeople, and organizations have also been of great assistance to me.

I thank the Canada Council for the non-fiction grant that helped me pursue this project to its end. My colleague and friend Daniel Wood put me in touch with Cam Sylvester, who gave me invaluable background for my research in Cambodia. Gordon Longmuir, former Canadian ambassador to Cambodia, deepened my understanding of that nation and paved the way for my arrival in Phnom Penh. Without the support of the CBC, my first encounter with Steve in 1990 would not have come off as it did; I thank David Paperny, John Collins, Sue Rideout, and Graham Ritchie for their help in that unusual interview. My CBC colleague and friend Helen Slinger has been with me on my journalism ride ever since, always ready with words of encouragement. Without the cooperation of Prudential's vice president, Jim Gallagher, and Prudential's Vancouver lawyer, Jo Anne Carmichael, my very productive trip to the Philippines in 1993 would have been impossible. Defense lawyers Ian Donaldson and Richard Israels (now deceased) offered me unique perspectives into the minds of their organized crime clients over the years, and made invaluable introductions for me.

I thank the following people for their great assistance to me during my trip to Cambodia in 1999/2000: Canadian Ambassador Normand Mailhot; Embassy Development and Commercial Officer Bunleng Men; *Phnom Penh Post* Editor-in-Chief Michael Hayes; *Phnom Penh Post* reporters Phelim Kyne, Dan Woodley, and Yin Soeum; Wetlands International Officer Matt Wheeler; Sari Nissi, Program Officer, International Organization for Migration; Hunter Weiler, Cambodia Liaison, Fauna & Flora International; Noun Bunthul, cameraman and reporter of the National Television of Cambodia; Pierre-Yves Clais, a former French Foreign Legion officer who helped fill me in on the underside of Cambodian life; François Pelissier, Sampan Tour & Travel, who introduced me to Clais; Senator Khieu San, Vice-Chairman of the Senate Legislation Committee; Khieu San's wife, Neang Chhayana, Vice Chairman of Drugs Registration; Chhanrith Sok Cham, special assistant to Prince Norodom Ranariddh; Has Saren, Funcinpec Member of the National Assembly; Sam Rainsy, leader of the Sam Rainsy Party; Sam Kanitha, Funcinpec MNA and Secretary of the Commission on Human Rights; and Dr. Michel Tranet, Under Secretary of State in charge of restoring Angkor Wat.

Without Jerome Tang's assistance, guidance, and protection, my excursion to Manila during the tumultuous spring of 2001 would not have been as journalistically fruitful. He has worked hard ever since to keep me abreast of events and his point of view on them. Without the kind assistance of his daughter, Janise, I would never have met Jerome. Mary Ong's lawyer, Leonard de Vera, gave generously of his time during my 2003 trip to Manila. De Vera and Mary Ong allowed me the great honor of meeting Dante Jimenez, the founding chairman of Volunteers Against Crime and Corruption. Danny Devnani, former gambling partner to President Joseph Estrada, filled me in on what he personally knew of the dark side of the Estrada regime. I especially thank my Manila fixer during EDSA III, Jose Luis, without whose help I would never have found my way through the Manila underworld. Yvonne Chua, training director at the Philippines Center for Investigative Journalism, put me in touch with Army Intelligence Chief Corpus, and Fe Zamora, an Internet reporter for the *Philippine Daily Inquirer*, helped arrange my first meeting with Mary Ong.

I am also grateful to those tireless workers who helped take this book from manuscript to polished print: Liba Berry, copyeditor; Sarah Wight, proofreader; and Pamela Murray, managing editor at Random House Canada.

A final and special place in these acknowledgments goes to Sheila Coronel and her entire staff of reporters and researchers at the Philippine Center for Investigative Journalism. The PCIJ is an institution whose competence and bravery in the face of utmost danger are unsurpassed in any country in the world. At this writing, 44 journalists have been murdered in the Philippines since 1986, seven of them in 2003—a horrendous record equaled only by the narco-state of Colombia. Through the connivance of politicians, the courts, and the police, not one of the murderers has been brought to trial. Yet the band of heroes at the PCIJ keeps at their trade with a noble motto in their hearts: "You cannot have great Filipino journalism without a great Filipino audience." I've spent a decade studying the Philippines, and believe that the Filipino people—patient, kind, and optimistic in the face of endless betrayal—are truly great. Someday they will raise up leaders that will match their greatness.

AFFIDAVIT OF MARY "ROSEBUD" ONG

————

AFFIDAVIT

I, Mary Ong, of legal age, Filipino, with postal address at Camp Aguinaldo, Intelligence Service of the Armed Forces of the Philippines, Manila, having been duly sworn in accordance with law do hereby depose and state that:

1. Between 1993 and 2001 I served as an undercover agent for the Philippine National Police (PNP) and the Royal Hong Kong Police.

2. My duties as a police agent included penetrating Chinese Triad gangs such as the 14K, and to arrange sting operations targeted at the arrest of Triad drug lords.

3. Because of my undercover police work and testimony that I gave in 2001 before the Senate of the Philippines regarding corrupt senior police officers and politicians, I am currently living under a witness-protection program. I and my family are housed in special quarters at the headquarters of the Intelligence Service of the Armed Forces of the Philippines, at Camp Aguinaldo.

4. On February 3, 2003, Canadian journalist Terry Gould visited me at my Camp Aguinaldo protective quarters.

5. Terry Gould showed me a current (January 17, 2003) Interpol Red Alert Wanted Poster of a Canadian fugitive named Steven Lik Man Wong, wanted in Canada for drug trafficking.

6. Terry Gould also showed me other photos of Steven Wong which displayed Steven Wong's Triad tattoos on his left and right pectorals and on his right biceps.

7. I immediately recognized Steven Wong as the subject of an undercover PNP investigation I participated in between late 1994 and mid-1996. I recognized Mr. Wong's chest tattoos, his height (5-feet, 4 inches), and his overweight stature. I immediately recalled his affiliation with the 14K Triad in Manila and Hong Kong.

8. During the period I knew him, Steven Wong was using his real name among his inner circle of criminal confidants.

9. During the PNP undercover investigation, I learned that Steven Wong was highly mobile, with good connections in Japan, Hong Kong and Macau.

10. During the PNP undercover investigation I learned that Steven Wong's 14K Triad boss was one Chong Yuk Sui, of Hong Kong.

11. During the PNP undercover operation, I introduced Steven Wong to a prominent female drug smuggler in Makati, Metro Manila. Steven Wong then became the main supplier of large quantities of illegal drugs to the female smuggler.

12. The female smuggler worked in league with a politically prominent family in Cavite Province.

13. The PNP undercover operation was terminated in 1996 without any arrests being made.

14. The last I recall seeing Steven Wong was sometime in 1997, in Manila.

15. I am executing this affidavit to attest to the truth of all the foregoing as part of my decade-long efforts to bring Triad drug traffickers to justice.

IN WITNESS WHEREOF, I have hereunto affixed my signature this day of 7 February, 2003 at *NBI, MANILA PHIL.*

SUBSCRIBED AND SWORN TO before me this day of FEB 07 2003 at QUEZON CITY

Certificate No. issued on at

ATTY. AURALYN L. PASCUAL
NOTARY PUBLIC
UNTIL DECEMBER 31, 2004
PTR NO. 3890-8074
ISSUED AT QC 1-3-03 ON
TIN 152-636-858

DOC. NO. 09
PAGE NO. 02
BOOK NO. X4
SERIES OF 2003

Index